D0875797

The State at War in South Asia

The State
at War
in South
Asia

Pradeep P. Barua

University of Nebraska Press

Lincoln and London

© 2005 by the Board of Regents of the University
of Nebraska. All rights reserved. Manufactured
in the United States of America. Set in Quadraat
type by Tseng Information Systems, Inc. Design
by R. Eckersley. Printed by Thomson-Shore, Inc.
ⓧ
Library of Congress Cataloging-in-Publication Data
Barua, Pradeep.
The state at war in South Asia / Pradeep P. Barua.
p. cm. – (Studies in war, society, and the military)
Includes bibliographical references and index.
ISBN 0-8032-1344-1 (clothbound : alkaline paper)
1. South Asia – History, Military. 2. South Asia –
Politics and government. I. Title. II. Series.
DS340.B37 2005 355.02'0954–dc22 2004021050

CONTENTS

MAPS

ACKNOWLEDGMENTS

This book has evolved over a period of almost fifteen years, and the list of people I should thank for helping me along this journey is too long to include in this brief note. However, this project would never have come to fruition without the dedicated support of the following individuals.

I wish to begin by thanking my academic mentors, Gunther Rothenberg, Blair Kling, John Lynn, and Stephen Cohen. Their unstinting faith in me and their constant encouragement at various points in my graduate education have resulted in my being in a position to complete this book. Stephen Cohen and John Lynn were also instrumental in providing helpful suggestions at various stages of this project. To this list I must add the name of DeWitt Ellinwood, my "unofficial" mentor, whose suggestions and generous sharing of research materials have helped me refine parts of this manuscript. I would also like to thank all the librarians and archival staff on three different continents who provided me with assistance and help in researching this book.

I would like to thank my colleagues, both current and former, in the Department of History at the University of Nebraska at Kearney. They have provided me with constant encouragement and support. Our departmental scholarship seminars proved invaluable in perfecting various chapters of the book.

Finally, I would like to thank my family for their steadfast support. I am grateful to my wife, Dr. Mary Beth Ailes, and my sons, Christopher and Brian, for their understanding and help in allowing me to spend far too many hours working on this manuscript. My wife deserves a special thanks for her patience in reviewing and helping edit different incarnations of this manuscript. I also thank my parents, Ramola and Pannalal, and my brother, Sandip, for their lifelong support of me.

INTRODUCTION

Warfare and state building have been inextricably intertwined since prehistory. From the time of the great river valley civilizations wars have played a crucial role in determining the nature of a state. In recent times researchers such as William H. McNeill and Bruce D. Porter have studied warfare's contribution to state building in modern Europe.[1] What these works fail to address is how effectively these states have conducted military operations. Furthermore, these historians generally lump most of the Western European nation-states into one category. Their military success has more often than not been attributed to their abilities to harness the resources for war rather than to their armed forces' innate operational abilities. This is not to say that there are no studies of individual armed forces' military effectiveness. Case studies of the combat effectiveness of European states include Victor Davis Hanson's works on ancient Greek warfare, Geoffrey Parker's work on Spain's army in the Netherlands, and John Keegan's overview of the European armies from the medieval to the modern era. The main difference between these works and those by Porter and McNeill is that they concentrate on a particular time period and do not seek to offer a long-term evolutionary perspective on combat effectiveness.

What these works all share, however, is a generalized assumption about the nature of European warfare, specifically, that the "Western" way of war is inherently superior to the "non-Western" way. Hanson, in his book *The Western Way of War*, states that the fifth-century Greeks evolved a Western way of battle that called for a "decisive" confrontation between foot soldiers that sharply contrasted with the non-Western style of ambush, skirmish, ritual conflict, and single combat between heroes.[2] Parker, in his landmark work *The Military Revolution*, notes that Western invaders were distinct from the tribal societies of America, Africa, and Asia in that they "fought to kill."[3] State-organized military forces like those of Mughal India were inferior to the West because they "remained[,] essentially, aggregations of individual heroic warriors."[4] This idea is further developed in Keegan's *A History of Warfare*. In it Keegan articulates a clear distinction between "Oriental" and "Western" war cultures. He characterizes the former by evasion, delay, and indirectness with the central goal of restraint. In contrast, "Western" militaries celebrated the ruthless face-to-face battle. In the eighteenth century, when the gunpowder revolution added a technological edge to this style of warfare, the final element in the superior Western style of warfare was put in place.[5]

Perhaps the fullest expression of the Western military culture's superiority is found in Hanson's book *Carnage and Culture*. In it Hanson greatly expands his thesis on Western military superiority. He notes that in the 2,500 years since the Greeks introduced a decisive type of direct infantry confrontation, the West has continued to dominate the world with its military superiority. However, Hanson goes beyond a mere focus on the West's military superiority; instead, he develops a comprehensive, albeit unconvincing, argument that the West developed a congruent superiority in intellectual, political, and economic arenas.[6] A far more thought provoking and qualified study of military culture can be found in John Lynn's book *Battle*. Lynn offers a more modest but ultimately far more prescient thesis that argues for the importance of the cultural approach to military history. What sets Lynn's refreshing approach apart from the staid stereotypes of Hanson, Keegan, and Parker is his acknowledgment that each case study in his book is unique and does not fall into a neat Western or non-Western category.[7]

The notion of inherent Western military superiority has even spilled over into the study of South Asian militaries. In his book *Societies and Military Power* Stephen Peter Rosen embraces Keegan's and Hanson's notion that the Western military establishment's superiority comes from the societal structures that underpin it. However, Rosen's thesis is more focused because he chose to concentrate on India rather than the entire "Orient," and he based his case on a specific examination of the social structures generated from India's caste system. Rosen's central thesis is that Indian armies were always weaker than European armies because they maintained close links to Indian society. As a result, these armies reflected the caste and ethnic divisions that plagued Indian societies and could not match the European armies' battlefield discipline and organizational stability.[8] However, Rosen's thesis does not consider that factors other than cultural and societal may offer more plausible explanations for the Indian military system's weaknesses when compared to the West.

This book is an attempt to offer alternatives to the above-mentioned theses. Its focus is not on warfare's role in state building but on how the state from prehistory to modern times has managed to wage war. In other words, this is an exploration of the state's military effectiveness – another neglected aspect of the currently available studies of warfare and state building. Furthermore, the book examines South Asia as a case study. South Asia makes a compelling example for two main reasons. First, it has at different times since prehistory undergone long periods of isolation from external influences. Second, it has endured equally lengthy periods of foreign influence and domination. The central theme that runs through this book is an analysis of how the Indian state in its many guises has waged war. In order to accomplish this I have followed the relatively unorthodox step of combining detailed battle history with a general discussion of state building, politics, and strategy.

My attempt to construct battle history has several reasons behind it. First, a need exists to establish a clear picture of how a state's strategic plans translate into operational reality. Without a qualified examination of the battles (i.e., the "operational art") themselves, our understanding of military evolution in the subcontinent is essentially incomplete. Additionally, I want to regenerate interest in battle histories, seemingly a lost cause in the current historical trend. The few works that venture into South Asian military history focus exclusively on the region's social and cultural development. A case in point is Seema Alavi's *The Sepoys and the Company*. Alavi's work, which concentrates on British India from 1770 to 1830, rejects the notion that military capability had anything to do with the East India Company's dominance of North India. Alavi attempts to break away from "guts-and-glory" history by focusing exclusively on the East India Company Army's social and cultural aspects. According to Alavi, the company's ability to generate knowledge of "Indian customs and religious practices" through its recruitment of Indian soldiers enabled it to dominate North India.[9] The study ignores the fact that the East India Company managed to engage in an exhaustive study of its sepoys' customs and traditions only after its successful military domination of the North Indian powers.

Finally, Indian military history students have few scholarly studies of battle histories available to them. However, I want to point out that this book is only a small start in this massive undertaking. I readily acknowledge that many gaps exist in the battle reconstructions, especially in the prehistoric and medieval periods. There is a wealth of archaeological, epigraphical, and even archival material that remains untapped. My hope is that these battle studies will kindle an interest and desire in others to seize the baton in this quest. I also want to point out that this study's limited scope restricts me from engaging in the meticulous battle reconstruction, which focuses heavily on individual soldiers' experiences, that Keegan first introduced in his book *The Face of Battle*.[10] Finally, this is by no means a comprehensive review of all the "major" battles, campaigns, and wars fought on the subcontinent. Instead, it examines only those conflicts that offer us the most insight into the introduction of new tactics, organization, and technology. As a result, some famous wars such as the sepoy rebellion or mutiny of 1857 have not been discussed. On the other hand, I have examined in some detail engagements that have traditionally been considered "obscure." A case in point is the Maratha-Afghan campaign of 1763, which culminated in the pivotal battle at Panipat in North India and witnessed an Indian state entity's first large-scale use of European-style infantry armed with matchlocks.

To achieve its goals the book presents a considerable amount of historical data and analysis in thirteen chapters. These chapters have been categorized into six parts, which serve as the work's periodization. Part 1 begins with the Indus Valley civilization, progresses to the early and later Vedic periods, discusses the classical period, and culminates with the medieval period. Chapters 1 and 2 analyze the nature of state formation in addition to examining various Indian states' war-making abilities. The chapters show that state formation and warfare proceeded hand in hand, feeding and indeed relying upon each other throughout this period.

Parts 2 and 3 deal with the British conquest of and empire in India. In a sense they constitute the book's core because of the British bureaucracy's excellent records, which are now freely available to researchers. Part 2 examines the wars of colonial conquest and devotes considerable attention to state formation and the intense military competition this process generated among the mutually competing Indian states and the British East India Company. Central to this part's discussion is the introduction of Western professional infantry armies and civil bureaucracies to the subcontinent. Part 3 investigates the British-Indian Empire's military system. Here the focus is not so much on state formation but on state building and its subsequent impact on the military. By the early twentieth century the Indian state had evolved a system of "dyarchy," whereby the British controlled all aspects of the central government and the Indian nationalist politicians ran the regional governments. The maintenance, operational use, and indeed military effectiveness of the armed forces hinged on the often contentious debates between the British government in London, the British government in India, and the Indian nationalist politicians. Chapter 8 examines the evolution of the Indian army officer corps, which figured prominently in successive British-Indian governments' plans to create a modern Indian army that would be capable of helping to police the British Empire and even to assist the British army against its European rivals. Part 3 concludes by analyzing how this particular colonial military legacy provided independent India with a relatively modern and professional army free of domestic political ambitions.

Part 4 covers the period from independence in 1947 to 1971 and focuses upon a chronological analysis of India's major wars. I have restricted my examination to the various Indian Congress government's nation-building priorities from 1947 to 1971. This part examines the clash between the socialist economic policies of India's first prime minister, Jawaharlal Nehru, and the need for the rapid expansion and modernization of the armed forces in the face of multiple external threats. These chapters also discuss postcolonial civil military relations and their impact upon the military effectiveness of the armed forces.

Researching part 4 was challenging, although the hurdles were very different from those represented by part 1. Here the problem was not the lack of information but the censorship of available information. The Indian government has been loath to give independent researchers access to its military and politically sensitive civilian archives. To circumvent this roadblock I relied heavily on published material, including biographies, regimental histories, campaign histories, and investigative reports. Furthermore, the Internet now offers a relatively convenient venue for participants, observers, and researchers to publish their experiences and opinions. More importantly, this new publishing arena has proved to be difficult for the government to control and censor. Since a considerable portion of the battle histories in this part revolves around the three Indo-Pakistan wars, I have used comparative sources from each side to reconstruct the battles.

Part 5 includes a single chapter that examines internal insurgencies, regional interventions, and Himalayan border conflicts. These low intensity conflicts have engaged the Indian security forces since independence and represent the greatest threat to the Indian state system's continued existence. I have included the Sri Lankan intervention and the Himalayan boundary dispute with Pakistan because they have either a close connection to domestic insurgencies or the potential to do so. This chapter analyzes how the Indian state has evolved and implemented strategies to combat these threats as well as Indian security forces' operational conduct and counterinsurgency doctrines against an array of other threats from low intensity insurgencies to high intensity insurgencies to near conventional war. Research for chapter 12 was conducted in a manner similar to that for part 4. A welcome added source was the remarkable proliferation of media coverage of South Asian conflicts largely due to the communications revolution of the 1990s, which decisively outstripped most state entities' antiquated censorship abilities. Of particular interest is the news media's mobility and technological sophistication. During the recent conflict in the Kargil region of Kashmir, news crews from India, Pakistan, Europe, and the United States covered the battles from both sides of the border, often during engagements, resulting in real-time coverage. The impact of this unprecedented generation of audiovisual archives has yet to be gauged, but it is certainly changing the way researchers tackle the difficult issue of near term history.

Part 6 culminates this project. In chapter 13 I examine the structural and material evolution of the Indian armed forces' three branches – the army, navy, and air force – within the context of India's changing economic and defense priorities since the 1980s. Chapter 13 also concludes the book with a study of defense policy making in independent India, now a regional power, and the strategic and doctrinal evolution of its armed forces.

Although the book has a general focus on South Asia, it does not examine the peripheral regions that constitute Sri Lanka, Nepal, and Bhutan. Furthermore, in the postindependence period this book focuses exclusively on the Republic of India and not on Pakistan and Bangladesh.

The State at War in South Asia

Part One

CHAPTER I

Warfare in Prehistoric and Classical India

Our examination of ancient Indian military history begins with the series of excavations carried out around the ancient cities of Harappa and Mohenjo Daro in January 1921. During these excavations archaeologists uncovered the remains of a vast and flourishing civilization. Although the pictograms of this lost civilization have yet to be deciphered, researchers have created a remarkably detailed picture of these early inhabitants. However, we are far more limited in our understanding of their military institutions and practices.

The only evidence we have to deduce the military capabilities of the Indus valley peoples is the archaeological remains and the Rig-Veda.[1] One of the most visible indicators of the Indus peoples' military style is the remains of massive fortifications. Some 25 miles east of Mohenjo Daro we find the largest of them, the fortress of Kot Dijian, which Sir Mortimer Wheeler describes as "a strong walled citadel armed with rectangular towers of stone and mud-brick."[2] The cities of Mohenjo Daro and Harappa were also "dominated by a massively fortified citadel."[3] Wheeler describes Harappa's defenses as a parallelogram of about 460 yards by 215 yards, with ramparts made of baked mud bricks.[4] The western part of Mohenjo Daro has the same type of fortifications.[5] Similarly fortified structures have been unearthed in the surrounding regions, a noteworthy example being the one found by Sir Aurel Stein in Sutkagen-dor in Makran; it is an elaborate complex enclosing a considerable area.[6] Excavation at the Dholavira site in the 1980s led to the discovery of a similar citadel-type structure surrounded by huge gateways controlling access to it.[7]

Recently, scholars have expressed doubt as to whether city walls in the Indus valley were defensive in nature. Jonathan Mark Kenoyer notes that with regard to the walls in Harappa "it is impractical to have so many separate walled areas next to each other."[8] He thinks that none of the Harappa gateways were designed to repel frontal attacks and that the lack of any evidence of battle damage further proves his point.[9] Kenoyer believes that the scant evidence and lack of any depiction of warfare or captive taking are due to the Indus cities' evolution from local cultures that had roots extending back thousands of years to the earliest farming and pastoral communities. His implied conclusion is that the Indus peoples never engaged in warfare.[10] However, these conclusions are questionable, to say the least. A heritage of past pastoral lifestyles and local roots is hardly convincing evidence of a lack of warfare. Similarly, the lack of battle damage on the existing walls might simply mean that the city was abandoned during a time of peace or that the walls were rebuilt. A more plausible explanation is that the inner Indus cities' citadel structure is defensive in nature. Jane R. McIntosh notes that these raised citadels mirror Indo-Greek cities like Taxila and the cities of ancient Greece, where this citadel location served as the heart of the city's defenses. As for the existence of separate walled areas outside the citadel complex, McIntosh suggests that they were actually a separation between the public and private areas.

By themselves the fortifications offer no substantive evidence of the Indus peoples' military tactics. However, when examined along with weapons found in the sites, these fortifications show that the Indus inhabitants' military system was clearly defensive in nature and relied heavily upon the fortifications. The most common weapons found in the ruins were baked clay balls.[11] These missiles could not have been used for hunting; their sole purpose would have been to repel invaders attempting to scale the fortifications. Other weapons found in the sites include arrowheads made of thin copper pieces with long narrow barbs.[12] The many arrowheads suggest that the bow and arrow was also the weapon of choice at Harappa. Other weapons found in smaller numbers include spearheads, daggers, axes, and mace heads, all of poor quality. The spearheads, for example, were thin and flat without a strengthening rib.[13] Little evidence exists to suggest the use of swords, and this, combined with the absence of any body armor, provides further evidence that the Indus peoples were unaccustomed to close combat tactics. Archaeologists also found representations of horses and horse bones.[14] However, there is no evidence that indicates that the Indus peoples used horses for military purposes. Thus, the residents of the Indus valley were concerned primarily with static defenses and had little if any experience in mobile warfare.

The lack of an offensive war-making ability coincided with early interpretations of the Rig-Veda that suggested that "Aryan invaders" destroyed the Indus civilizations. The Aryan Rig-Vedic literature describes the Aryan battle god, Indra, as "destroying fort after fort with strength . . . as age consumes a garment."[15] The literature also refers to Agni, the god of fire, as the destroyer of forts.[16] The Vedas also describe land battles between the Aryans and the Dasyus. The Aryan armies invariably routed the hated Dasyus with their "invincible" battle chariots. All this was accepted as evidence that Aryan invaders destroyed the Indus cities. In recent times revisionists like Romila Thapar have questioned the Vedas' early translation, arguing that no firm evidence exists to suggest that invading Aryans destroyed the Indus cities or that these cities were non-Aryan in the first place. Revisionists also dispute the archaeological data once put forward to support the theory that the invaders destroyed the Indus cities.[17] As has Colin Renfrew, Thapar and other researchers have noted the mistake made by earlier researchers who viewed the term *Aryan* as describing a race or ethnic group rather than a language.[18] Some researchers suggest that the terms *Aryan* and *Dasyus* actually refer to behavior and not race.[19] They contend that Aryan speakers lived in the Indus region long before the Indus civilization declined and that Aryan cultural and linguistic influences spread gradually from their point of origin in Anatolia to Iran and North India. They point out that there has been evidence of commerce between India, the Middle East, and Anatolia since "earliest times."[20]

The later Vedic Aryans, or Indo-Aryan speakers, as Thapar prefers to call them, engaged in a form of mobile warfare. Although they used cavalry, their chief weapon was the horse-drawn battle chariot, or *ratha*. Aryan infantrymen carried swords, axes, maces, and daggers in addition to bows and arrows. Vedic infantrymen were also equipped with protective clothing and armor.

Kurukshetra

The migrating Vedic tribes gradually spread south and east toward modern-day Bengal. Vedic literature speaks of a number of tribal kingdoms throughout the north.[21] The literature also mentions the many battles fought between these expanding tribes, the most famous being the Bharata War, which was fought in the area of Kurukshetra and a description of which is better known in its epic form as the *Mahabharata*. Although the *Mahabharata* is an epic poem, historical events and personalities probably influenced it.[22] Kurukshetra is thought to be only a few miles from Panipat, a medieval Indian battlefield. The area is of strategic importance because it controls the entrance into the fertile Gangetic Plain from northwestern India. In addition to the evidence in the Vedic literature, archaeological evidence suggests that the lifestyle and culture depicted in the epic existed during the Bharata War. The lifestyle of the people who created Painted Grey Ware pottery and who lived in the region between approximately 1100 and 1000 BC shares many similarities with the lifestyle of the people depicted in the epic, and the period coincides closely

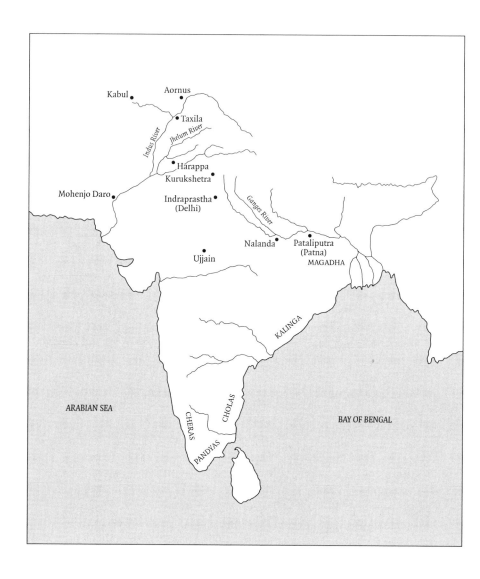

Political map of South Asia 3500 BC–AD 1000

with the estimated time frame of the Bharata War (1424–1000 BC). However, many versions of the *Mahabharata* exist, the earliest of which was probably created some five hundred years after the Vedic period (c. 1700–900 BC).[23]

An examination of the accounts of the battles establishes that they were based upon battle tactics utilized in India during the Vedic period. The most important evidence is that all the important elements of an ancient Indian army are present in the armies depicted in the *Mahabharata* – infantry, chariots, cavalry, and elephants. Furthermore, the battle accounts conform closely to descriptions in the Vedas. The primary weapon in the *Mahabharata* is the bow and arrow, which again is the same as in the Vedas. In the epic the phrase "science of warfare" is referred to as *dhanurveda* (knowledge of the bow). Mastery of all weapons is generalized under the term *dhanurveda*, and, according to E. W. Hopkins, "it embraces all the fighting knowledge."[24] Furthermore, as in the Vedas, the *Mahabharata* gives the chariot the pride of place in the army's battle order. By comparison, the infantry was mere fodder for the chariot-mounted warrior. The epic describes the construction, design, and types of chariots.[25] There are many examples in the epic of lone chariot-mounted warriors taking on and defeating entire bodies of foot soldiers. While this may be an exaggeration, it confirms the infantryman's inferior position. Along with the infantry, the cavalry too had little influence in the epic battles. The lack of a fighting saddle and the all-important stirrup limited the Vedic cavalryman's ability.[26] The *Mahabharata* frequently notes that cavalrymen often fell off their mounts. One important aspect where the epic differed from the Vedas is in the mention of war elephants. The Vedas do not specifically mention the use of elephants in battle, although the Nikayas (the Pali texts) state that armies used elephants in warfare during the sixth and fifth centuries BC.[27] According to Thapar, this period (c. 600–400 BC) is the second phase of urbanization – the Gangetic Plain. (The first phase is the urbanization of the Indus valley.)[28] It is possible that the introduction of the war elephant coincided with the evolution of urban states. The *Mahabharata* describes elephants as the occasional mounts of kings and princes, yet, despite their fearsome reputation, they did not replace the chariot-mounted warrior in importance.

A hallmark of the battles described in the *Mahabharata* is the elaborate battle formations, or *vyuhas*, which are consistent with those described in Vedic literature.[29] These battle formations are extremely elaborate and take the shape of groupings of animals, weapons, and man-made objects. However, they probably never saw utility in the battlefield. Nevertheless, their mention indicates that Indian armies deployed in large, complex, and unwieldy formations prior to battle. These formations were not dissimilar to those that Alexander the Great and other invaders would confront in the centuries to come. A typical formation consisted of chariots, elephants, cavalry, and infantry deployed in a complex and cumbersome mass. Such formations were suitable only for static confrontation in an open field. The introduction of mobile tactics would throw such formations into chaos.

From the time of the later Vedic civilization to Alexander's invasion in 327–26 BC Indian battle tactics saw little change in terms of mobility. The one major change that did occur, the introduction of the war elephant, served only to bring further stagnation to battlefield mobility. The chariot continued to dominate the battlefield. It remained the Indian armies' main fighting arm, albeit with the support of growing numbers of war elephants. The infantry and cavalry remained ineffectual, almost useless appendages for Indian armies. During most battles the outcome hinged upon a small elite group of chariot- and elephant-mounted warriors.

These stagnant battle tactics differed dramatically from the lessons being learned outside India and could only develop in sheltered isolation from external influences. The Indian kingdoms and tribes that fought each other utilized identical military tactics, and this partly explains their armies' massive and complex battle formations. Their immobility meant that the very deployment and shape of a formation could spell victory or defeat before the start of the battle. Such engagements often involved heavy casualties, especially for the losing side. For all their stage-managed appearance, battles in ancient India were extremely bloody affairs.

The Macedonian Invasion

Prior to the Macedonian-led invasion of India, the Persians under Cyrus II (c. 585–c. 529 BC) and Darius I (522–486 BC) subdued western India's border regions. Cyrus II subjugated the Indian tribes of the Paropanisus (Gandhara/Hindu Kush) and the Kabul River valley, while Darius I advanced up to the Indus River. According to Herodotus, this part of India formed the twentieth satrapy (the jurisdiction of a satrap, or governor) of the Persian Empire. It was also the richest, providing Darius I's tax collectors with no fewer than 350 talents of gold dust.[30] Darius I's successor, Xerxes I (ruled 486–465 BC), used Indian soldiers in his wars against the Greeks, giving the latter their first glimpse of Indian soldiers. Herodotus noted, "The Indians clad in garments made of cotton carried bows of cane, the latter tipped with iron. . . . [The Indian cavalry were] . . . armed with the same equipment as in the case of the Infantry, but they brought riding horses and chariots, the latter being drawn by wild asses."[31]

In Herodotus's account we see confirmation of the information in the *Mahabharata* and the Vedas, namely, that the primary weapon was still the bow and arrow and that chariots still played a central role in Indian armies. Darius III also used Indian troops against Alexander the Great in 330 BC. The chronicler Arrian notes that "Darius's army had been reinforced by the Sogdians, the Bactrians, and Indian tribes on the Bactrian border. . . . Darius' total force . . . [included] a few elephants. . . . [T]he Indian troops from the hither side of the Indus had about fifteen of them."[32]

After defeating Darius's army Alexander began his invasion of India during the spring of 327 BC. He directed his first attacks against the fortified local cities of the Aspasians, Assakenians, and Gouriains. Alexander also took the cities of Massaga, Bazira, and Aornus.[33] It is ironic that the descendants of the Aryan invaders found themselves being overrun in the same manner that their ancestors had once overcome the original inhabitants of northern India. It was only on the banks of the Hydapses (Jhelum) that an Indian ruler, Porus (Paurava), dared to confront Alexander in the open field.

The battle of the Hydapses is the first military action in ancient India documented by contemporary observers, all of whom were Greek or Macedonian. In sharp contrast, no equivalent Indian account of this famous battle exists. By the end of June 327 BC, Alexander's army was camped near the town of Jhelum on the west bank of the river.[34] Porus and his army stood on the east bank ready to oppose any crossing. The precise number of troops deployed by both sides continues to be a mystery, with differing accounts from Arrian, Diodorus, Plutarch, and Curtius. The general consensus is that Alexander commanded about 11,000–15,000 men.[35] Porus led at least 20,000 infantry, fewer than 4,000 cavalry, approximately 100 elephants, and some 300 chariots.[36]

After Alexander's initial deployment a brief period of movement and countermovement followed during which Alexander moved his troops up and down the riverbank, looking for a suitable place to cross, while Porus countered his every move. Alexander then split his army, and, under the cover of darkness and rain, the Macedonian main force effected a crossing using a wooded midriver island to further shield them from the Indians.[37] Unsure if this was the main attack or a feint, Porus dispatched a small contingent to confront the Macedonian bridgehead, but Alexander made quick work of this small force.[38] Porus then moved most of his army to meet Alexander after leaving a small contingent to guard the Haranpur ford, where he had been standing vigil. According to the Greek observers, the two forces confronted each other on the Karrai plain. The Macedonians deployed in their traditional formations, with their heavy infantry drawn up in phalanxes in the center

9

and the cavalry on the flanks. Porus's army lined up in a similar fashion, with the added presence of chariots and elephants. Each commander placed his elephants in front of the infantry in the center of the army and deployed the chariots on the flanks with the cavalry.[39]

Alexander maintained the initiative by attacking the Indian forces with his cavalry. He first unleashed his mounted archers on the Indian cavalry's right flank. While coping with this barrage, he ordered his lieutenant, Coenus, to strike the Indian cavalry with his cavalry squadrons. Alexander led the remainder of his cavalry to crush the Indian cavalry on the other flank on the inland side.[40] With Porus's cavalry and chariots routed, Alexander ordered his heavy infantry to advance upon the Indian center. The mighty Macedonian phalanxes advanced but soon recoiled when they confronted the Indian elephants.[41] Porus seized this opportunity and ordered his forces to attack the Macedonian cavalry and infantry. However, the Macedonians recovered quickly and began to engage the pachyderms, soon driving them from the battlefield. Without the support of the elephants, the disorganized Indian militia were helpless against the Macedonian phalanx. A Macedonian cavalry attack to the Indians' rear compounded their problems. Alexander's forces encircled and captured the remnants of Porus's army after hours of bloody conflict.

In many ways, Alexander's military genius and the effectiveness of his veterans made the battle's end result a foregone conclusion. But this need not necessarily have been the case. This engagement was the most difficult of all of Alexander's battles. The Greek chroniclers vividly describe the fierceness of the fighting. Their estimate of a thousand Macedonian dead and several thousand wounded is one of the highest casualty rates that any of Alexander's armies suffered, especially in proportion to the number of troops engaged (11,000–12,000). Although Porus is not known as a great military captain, he was an adequate commander. Never letting Alexander's reputation overawe him, he maneuvered his army with a firm hand prior to the battle, matching all of Alexander's moves on the west bank of the Hydaspes. When the Macedonians destroyed his son's small force, he did not panic but instead quickly moved to meet what he correctly perceived to be Alexander's main force. Porus's deployment prior to the battle (the infantry and elephants in the center flanked by the chariots and the cavalry) was the best under the circumstances. Even when the Macedonian cavalry swept away his cavalry and chariots, Porus not only maintained his formation but also managed to launch a quick attack when he saw the vaunted Macedonian phalanx waver. In this phase of the battle Porus experienced his best chance to claim a victory and inflict the heaviest casualties upon the Macedonians. According to

Arrian, Alexander remarked, "I see at last a danger that matches my courage. It is at once with wild beasts [elephants] and men of uncommon mettle that the contest now lies."[42]

Thus, Porus's defeat cannot be blamed on his poor leadership. He did make some serious tactical errors: his decision to oppose Alexander's river crossing, which gave the initiative to the Macedonians, and his decision to fight on the rain-soaked and muddy riverbanks, which robbed his chariots of their limited mobility. But it is also clear that Porus's fate was sealed long before he faced Alexander's veterans. The roots of his army's demise lay in the centuries of military stagnation prior to the Macedonian invasion. The organization, equipment, and battle tactics that constituted Porus's army ensured its destruction on that fateful day.

Macedonian and Indian Military Organization

Porus's army was organized along the *cahturanga* concept, dating back to the days of the *Mahabharata*. This arrangement involved the army's fourfold division into elephants, chariots, cavalry, and infantry. The only change that had taken place since that time was that the elephant had displaced the chariot as the choice mount of the king and his elite officers. The militia infantry continued to be the least significant element in this organization. The Macedonians approached battle in a completely different manner. For them, the heavy infantry phalanx was an important offensive weapon. The Macedonians drew their heavily armored infantry into a modified version of the Greek phalanx in a tighter and more cohesive formation bristling with the dreaded 24-foot-long *sarissa* to present an almost impenetrable and unstoppable mass of men and spears on the move. The Macedonian infantry elite, the famous Hypaspists, were less heavily armored and as a result more mobile. They formed a link between the slower phalanx and the more mobile cavalry on the flanks.[43]

In contrast, the Indian infantry simply did not deploy in such a compact mass or move with such precision. Its main role was to serve as a mopping-up force for a successful elephant and/or chariot attack. Indeed, the Indian infantry's poor equipage seems to support this follow-up role. The Indian infantryman carried a sword and spear approximately 9 feet in length. With the exception of senior commanders, no one wore any metal armor.[44] An infantryman probably had some cloth protection (a wadded turban or some sort of leather corselet and guard), but this was far inferior to the armor of even the Macedonian light infantry, the Hypaspists. Such a force could and did melt away in the face of the advancing Macedonian phalanx. The lack of armor and the absence of swords and heavy spears among the Indian infantrymen were not the result of an ignorance of metallurgy in India. Indeed, India was well known in the classical world for its skills in iron making.[45]

The main difference between the Macedonian and Indian infantries lay in their social composition and training. Indian infantry forces consisted mostly of peasant levies constituted hurriedly to meet the invader. These forces lacked the Macedonian heavy infantry's cohesiveness, training, and discipline. The latter had been a professional military force since Philip II (Alexander the Great's father) replaced his tribal militia with standing infantry units composed of peasant conscripts. After the Peloponnesian War (431–404 BC), a large number of impoverished and landless farmers were readily absorbed into the army, which lessened the financial burden of maintaining such a large force; presumably, they did not cost as much as peasant conscripts. Later, successive wars of conquest continued to support the army.[46] The constant training and campaigning enabled it to function as a well-disciplined, unified force "with a cohesiveness and weight of armament that was unmatched in the contemporary world."[47]

The Indian infantry's only saving grace was its archers, who fought with a very powerful long bow. According to the Greek historian Megasthenes (c. 350–c. 290 BC), the Seleucid ambassador to Chandragupta's court, the Indian infantryman carried a bow approximately as long as himself. The arrow is described as being little shorter than 3 yards, "and there is nothing which can resist an Indian archer[']s shot, – neither shield nor breastplate."[48] As in Vedic times, the bow and arrow continued to be the personal weapon of choice with Porus's soldiers. He even armed his chariot- and elephant-mounted warriors with bows. A significant number of the Macedonian dead was among their cavalry.[49] Since the Indian cavalry or chariots could not have caused these casualties, the bowmen must have inflicted this damage. The Macedonian death rate might have been far greater if the soggy, rain-soaked ground had not prevented many Indian bowmen from notching their powerful weapons.[50]

Thus, the Macedonians hopelessly outclassed the Indians in cavalry, infantry, and battle tactics. The only offensive weapons at Porus's disposal were his war elephants. Not even the vaunted Macedonian phalanx could stand up to the charge of these martial pachyderms. But by themselves, the elephants could not decide the battle's outcome, for, like the tanks of today, they too needed infantry support to protect their flanks and rear. In this regard the Indian infantry failed miserably. The Greco-Macedonians, after recovering from their initial shock, quickly surrounded the elephants and assailed them from all sides, stabbing, hacking, and even burning them. Although the elephants were well armored and trained to meet frontal attacks, the attacks from the rear, sides, and below must have panicked them. In the final analysis, the Indian infantry's inability to follow through and support the elephants' initial assault doomed any hopes Porus had of reinforcing his counterattack.

Chandragupta Maurya

For reasons still not entirely clear, Alexander ended his campaign in India and left the subcontinent in 325 BC. By doing so he avoided an inevitable confrontation with the most powerful kingdom in northern India, that of the Nandas. The Nanda dynasty were initially rulers of Magadha but had gradually expanded their power from the central Gangetic Plain to the entire valley in addition to substantial territories in the south up to the Godavari River.

Soon after Alexander's departure, Chandragupta Maurya (died c. 297 BC), the founder of the Mauryan dynasty, overthrew the Nanda dynasty. According to Plutarch, a youthful Chandragupta had actually met Alexander between 326 and 325 BC.[51] Considerable confusion exists as to how exactly Chandragupta ascended the throne in Magadha about 320 BC. According to Plutarch, he first overthrew Alexander's prefects in northwestern India and then seized power in Magadha. However, when and how Chandragupta seized the throne and defeated Alexander's prefects is still a mystery.

While Chandragupta consolidated his newfound power, Alexander's successors fought over his satrapies, and by 312–311 BC Seleucus Nicator (thereafter known as Seleucus I), one of Alexander's generals, had won control of the eastern satrapy. This brought Seleucus into confrontation with Chandragupta, and the two fought a series of battles in 305 BC. The classical writers are completely silent about the details of this war, but it appears that Chandragupta gained the upper hand.[52] This is significant because it is the first instance of an Indian army defeating a major foreign power. Because details of this war are virtually nonexistent, we cannot know how Chandragupta may have matched and even defeated the mighty Greco-Macedonian phalanx.[53]

In India, meanwhile, the elephant continued its reign as the Indian armies' dominant offensive feature. In fact, the organization of Indian armies, including those of Chandragupta, who probably witnessed firsthand the effectiveness of the Greco-Macedonian military system and even confronted it under Seleucus I, showed little evidence of change. Megasthenes described the Mauryan army as comprised of 600,000 infantry, 30,000 cavalry, 9,000 elephants, and a large number of chariots.[54] While these numbers were no doubt exaggerated, the important point is that the Mauryan army still utilized the traditional cahturanga, or fourfold division of the army into elephants, chariots, cavalry, and infantry.

The *Arthashastra*

Chandragupta's reign was perhaps witness to the genesis of one of the most remarkable works on statecraft in the ancient world, the *Arthashastra*, reputedly the work of a Brahmin named Kautilya (c. 321–296 BC), variously described as the advisor and mentor of Chandragupta Maurya. Puranic texts describe Kautilya as having helped Chandragupta overthrow the Nandas.[55] Thomas Trautmann's study of the *Arthashastra* suggests that it has no single creator.[56] In its present form it can be dated, at the earliest, to the second century AD, or some five hundred years after Chandragupta.[57] Some of the later additions to the work could be descriptive of the Gupta dynasty, founded by Chandragupta I in AD 320. Nevertheless, the core of the text may have been based on Kautilya's understanding of the Mauryan state.

Part of this treatise (book 10) is one of the few works on warfare in ancient India. The book begins with elaborate instructions for setting up a fortified encampment during a campaign, followed by similar instructions on how to conduct a route march. An army on the march was a huge and cumbersome affair, not least because of the large number of camp followers. The *Arthashastra* is replete with accounts of how and where to place women within an army and in camp. Given the size of Mauryan armies, the *Arthashastra* advises commanders to plan their route marches through villages and forests, where supplies would be plentiful. It also places great stress upon choosing the right kind of terrain to fight upon. A suitable battleground would be "level, firm, clear, not causing jolting, not causing wheels or hoofs to get stuck, not obstructing axles."[58] A portion of the book that discusses battle formations is an almost exact replica of the battle formations described in the *Mahabharata*. The *Arthashastra* sees battle formations as being the most important part of an engagement and explains that no action could be initiated without close attention to the disposition of the appropriate formation. The elephants and the chariots still had pride of place. The weak part of an enemy's formation was analyzed as that which lacked "elephants and horses."[59]

The *Arthashastra* assigns great importance to elephants in warfare because their purpose was "breaking up, scattering or trampling down the hostile forces."[60] It also gives detailed information on special breeds of elephants, those best suited to warfare, and instructions for training them.[61] According to the *Arthashastra*, "Victory (in battle) for a King depends principally on elephants; for elephants being possessed of very big-sized bodies and being capable of life-destroying activities, pound troops, battle-arrays, fortresses and camps of the enemies."[62] Unsurprisingly, the *Arthashastra* recommends the death penalty for killing an elephant. It was not alone in its high regard for elephants, as other Indian writers were equally vocal in their praise. Pala-kyapa, the author of the Hastyayur-Veda, noted, "Learning is the ornament of the world, the moon of the night, and the elephant of the army. . . . [W]here there is truth there is religion; where there is religion there is prosperity; where there is beauty there is nobility; and where there are elephants there is victory."[63]

The *Arthashastra* offers compelling evidence that military tactics had re-mained essentially stagnant since the epic period. The Greco-Macedonian intervention in India made no impression upon Chandragupta and his suc-cessors.[64]

North and South India, AD 186–1079

At its zenith, the Mauryan dynasty controlled almost all of the Indian subcon-tinent with the exception of pockets in the east and the south. When the em-pire collapsed in AD 186 a number of smaller empires and kingdoms emerged in northern and southern India. They formed the last of the great Hindu king-doms prior to the Muslim invasions. During the interregnum these powers fought many wars. Although many Indian accounts discuss these conflicts, the works give few details of the battles.[65]

Nevertheless, the evidence suggests that Indian military organization, if not tactics, had changed a little. During the reign of Harshavardhana, also known as Harsha, the ruler of a considerable empire in northern India (c. AD 606–47), such changes became evident.[66] A Chinese traveler named Hsüan-tsang who visited Harsha's kingdom gave a remarkably detailed description of the king's army, which consisted of foot soldiers, horses (cavalry), and elephant soldiers.[67] Although his account also mentions the use of chariots, other evidence suggests that the chariot was disappearing from the Indian armies. Hsüan-tsang, who also visited the court of Pulakeshin II, a powerful ruler of southern India (AD 610–42), mentioned noticing only infantry, cav-alry, and elephants but no chariots.[68] The chariots that Hsüan-tsang referred to probably were the military commanders' personal transport. He described them as carrying an officer and being drawn by four horses with infantry guards on both sides.[69]

However, the abandonment of the chariot did not signify a new approach to warfare, since the elephant retained its role as the primary offensive weapon. Hsüan-tsang stated that Harsha subdued India in six years with

5,000 elephant soldiers, 20,000 cavalry, and 50,000 infantry. Following this success, his forces increased to 60,000 elephant soldiers and 100,000 cavalry.[70] These numbers may have been exaggerated, but Harsha did employ elephants in large numbers. According to the *Harshachirata*, Harsha obtained elephants by every means possible, including during forest roundups and as presents, revenue, booty, fines, audience fees, essential gifts of an embassy, circus beasts, and special consignments from officers of elephant reserves and the Vindhyan Sabara settlements.[71] Battlefield immobility, however, remained the hallmark of Indian armies, including those of the mighty Harsha.[72] As for the infantry, nothing suggests an elevation in its lowly status. Hsüan-tsang states, "They carry a long spear and a great shield; sometimes they hold a sword or saber, and advance to the front with impetuosity. All their weapons are sharp and pointed. Some of them are these – spears, shields, bows, arrows, swords, sabers, battle-axes, lances, halberds, long javelins, and various kinds of slings. . . . These weapons they have used for ages."[73]

The bas-reliefs of Bharut and Sanchi in north-central India (c. 200 BC) show the majority of the soldiers carrying bows.[74] Alexander Cunningham depicts one soldier who is not wearing a helmet and whose hair is bound by a headband. His dress consists of a tunic with long sleeves, reaching nearly to midthigh, that is tied in two places by cords, at the throat by a cord with two tassels, and across the stomach by a double-looped bow. A dhoti (an Indian wrap cloth usually made of cotton) covers his loins and thighs, reaching below his knees in stiff, formal folds. His boots, which come high up his legs, are fastened by a cord with two tassels like those on the neck of the tunic. His short and straight sword, about 2.5 feet long, is "monstrously broad" and is sheathed in a scabbard.[75] Greco-Macedonian accounts corroborate much of this information.[76]

The sculptures of armed men in the Purana Mahadeva temple at Harsanath, Rajputana, dating from the mid–tenth century AD, show that there had been little if any evolution in the equipage of the soldiers. These soldiers are depicted without any battle dress except a loincloth ending in a tail between their legs. They wear their hair in a bun and carry bows with a quiver of arrows on their backs, leaf-shaped daggers, straight swords, and small round shields.[77] Similarly, the paintings and engravings found in the rock shelters in the Mahadeo Hills around Pachmarhi in Madhya Pradesh also depict Indian foot soldiers wielding swords, spears, shields, and bows with little or no clothing except for a loincloth.[78]

The cavalry of this period was somewhat better equipped. The bas-reliefs at Sanchi and Mathura (1 BC) show what appear to be a saddle and a stirrup.[79] Sir John Marshall describes the Sanchi relief as the "the earliest example by some five centuries of the use of stirrups in any part of the world."[80] Whether this particular representation was a fully fledged "true metal stirrup" is questionable; some scholars suggest that no concrete representation of a true stirrup exists before the ninth century AD.[81] The saddle was infrequently used in India at this time. An Arab traveler in AD 11 remarked that the Indians "ride without a saddle, but if they put on a saddle, they mount the horse from the right side."[82] Perhaps using a saddle or stirrup was confined to the Indian elites. One would assume that the cavalry would use such vital pieces of equipment, yet no evidence for their use exists. Mounted archers, whom Alexander used with such great success against Porus, were found in the Gupta army.[83] But the end of the Gupta era (c. AD 600) also saw the end of the army's use of mounted archers. Neither Hsüan-tsang nor Bana, an author who resided at Harsha's court, made any reference to them. Also, there is no information to suggest that awareness of the stirrup led to the establishment of heavy armored cavalry, as in Europe. Some of the Gupta coins depict riders clad in chain mail, but such armor was restricted to commanders.[84] The all-important stirrup, which so radically altered warfare throughout the world, had almost no equivalent impact in India. Some historians have blamed the Indian cavalry's sorry state on the lack of a good breed of horse in India, but Indian rulers imported horses from distant lands.[85] The Indian armies' inability to take advantage of the stirrup, which was in use in India centuries ahead of any other region in the world, remains one of Indian warfare's great mysteries.

In southern India warfare progressed along similar lines as in the north, with no major tactical innovations. However, unlike their northern contemporaries, the southern dynasties maintained substantial naval forces, although until the arrival of the Cholas these navies were mainly coastal in nature. The imperial Cholas were the most powerful of all the southern dynasties in ancient India. Founded on the Coromandel Coast sometime before AD 850 by Vijayalaya, the Chola Empire lasted until AD 1279.[86] At its height the empire controlled most of southern India. Despite tremendous military successes on land, the Cholas are best remembered for their remarkable series of long-range naval conquests. The Cholas' rise came during the reign of Rajaraja I, the greatest of all the Chola kings (AD 985–1014). Under his leadership, the Chola navy conquered northern Sri Lanka and the Indian Ocean islands of the Maldives.[87] His son and successor, Rajendra, launched the largest and most successful long-range naval expedition of any Indian ruler, sending it against the Sailendra rulers of Malaya and Sumatra in an amphibious operation of considerable magnitude.[88]

The imperial Chola fleet represented the zenith of ancient Indian sea power. Its naval operations were a stupendous effort, given the primitive nature of the technology and the long distances involved. The only naval battles that the Cholas fought were against the Cheras, another powerful Tamil dynasty. The Chera fleet, however, was no match for the imperial Chola navy and suffered frequent defeats at the hands of the Chola king Rajadhiraja (reigned AD 1042–52), especially during the battle of Kandalursalai.[89] No detailed account of this battle describes the types of ships, weapons, and tactics used.

In addition to a powerful navy, the Cholas could call on a substantial army, including an elephant corps, cavalry, and infantry, a threefold division that is referred to in an inscription from Tiruvalisvaran near Ambasamudaram in the Tinnevelly District. The inscription described the army as *munrukaimahasenai*, or the "great army of the three arms."[90] The army, which was spread all over the country, was stationed in local garrisons or military camps known as *kodagams*. Scholars know little about the Chola armies' recruiting, training, and tactics, although the establishment of the kodagams indicates some sort of permanent military organization. Nilakanta Sastri believes that the army possessed at least two types of soldiers, the *kaikkolars* (regular salaried imperial soldiers) and the *nattuppadais* (local militia forces).[91] Elephants formed a vital part of the military as with any other major army in the subcontinent. Indeed, one of the most detailed accounts of the battle use of elephants comes from a Chinese traveler who witnessed the Chola war elephants in either battle or exercise. This traveler, writing in 1178, noted, "The Government owns 60,000 war-elephants, everyone seven or eight feet high. When fighting, these elephants carry on their backs houses, and these houses are full of soldiers who shoot arrows at long range, and fight with spears at close quarters. When victorious, the elephants are granted honorary names to signalize their merit, and there are some who bestow upon them embroidered housings and golden mangers. Everyday the elephants are taken into the presence of the King."[92]

The battle tactics of the south also appeared similar to those of the Vedic and epic period. A Chola inscription gives the following account of a battle between the Rashtrakuta ruler Krishnaraja and his Chola counterpart, Rajaditya, in 949: "The heroic Rajaditya, the ornament of the solar race, having shaken in battle the unshakable Krishnaraja with his forces, by means of his sharp arrows flying in all directions was himself pierced in his heart while seated on the back of a large elephant by the sharp arrows of the enemy."[93]

Because of the almost total reliance placed upon the war elephant in ancient Indian armies, those kingdoms and empires that were military powers maintained large numbers of elephants. Foreign observers, including the classical and Chinese writers and Arabic visitors, corroborate this. The Arab merchant traveler Sulaiman, referring to the king of Ruhmi (during the post-Gupta period), stated, "When he goes out to battle, he is followed by 50,000 elephants."[94] While these figures were exaggerated, Indian armies maintained huge numbers of fighting elephants. Indian colonists also spread the credo of the war elephant to Southeast Asia. According to Chinese sources, the Hindu Khambuja Empire, based in Laos (c. 802–1296), under Surya-Varman II (c. 1113–50) had a force of no fewer than 200,000 elephants.[95] Other colonial Hindu empires, including the Sailendras in the Malay Archipelago and the Champa Empire in central and southern Annam, used war elephants extensively.[96]

Warfare and State Formation

The art of war in ancient India shows remarkable consistency from the Vedic period to AD 1000 as successive empires employed the same tactics with minor changes. A significant reason for the static nature of military tactics is the subcontinent's geographical isolation, which kept India in the dark about changes in the warfare elsewhere. The local Indian powers, even the mighty Mauryas and Guptas, perceived little need to change their traditional way of fighting. The brief interlude of Alexander the Great's invasion and the introduction of the latest Mediterranean heavy infantry tactics had no impact upon the subcontinent's military evolution. Even Chandragupta Maurya, who allegedly witnessed Alexander's military organization firsthand, saw no need to adopt a similar system. In fact, the Greeks who settled the eastern satrapy, including Persia and northwestern India, adopted the use of war elephants for their armies.

But geographical isolation alone is too simplistic an explanation, since many Indian empires, like the Mauryas, Guptas, and Cholas, had extensive contact with foreign lands. The Periplus of the Erythraean Sea, written by an anonymous Greek merchant in the second half of the first century AD, recorded extensive trade between Rome under Emperor Augustus (reigned 27 BC–AD14) and southern India.[97] Thus, it is unlikely that the Indian empires would have been unaware of military developments in the rest of the world. Successive dynasties imported the best Arabian stallions for their imperial stables, yet cavalry played no important role in the army. More baffling perhaps was the possible introduction of the stirrup, which appeared in India long before the rest of the world. This simple piece of equipment revolutionized the role of the cavalry in Europe, yet no Indian equivalent to the heavily armored knight existed. The Indians must have been aware of the mounted archers of the Scythians and the Parthians, but again, no Indian equivalent developed.

Thus, the stagnation in Indian military tactics was not due to isolation and ignorance. In his comparative analysis of European and Indian armies, Stephen Rosen suggests that the Macedonian (and Spartan and Roman) armies' ability to divorce themselves from their surrounding societies made them more cohesive and effective fighters. Their system of intense drill, iron discipline, and constant deployments created a professional military organization. In contrast, the Indian armies maintained close links to their societies and thus reflected the divisions (the protocaste structures) and lack of cohesion in Indian society. The Indian militia armies could not evolve into a professional military force and as a consequence lacked the military effectiveness of the Macedonian armies.[98] However, this does not explain why Indian society, in which social divisions were no more or less defined than in its European counterparts, failed to develop a professional military force. To address this issue we must delve into aspects of state formation in ancient and early medieval India.

Traditionally, historians have perceived the ancient Indian state as a centralized entity along European lines. In 1980 Burton Stein's theory of the segmentary state in southern India challenged this view. In *Peasant State and Society in Medieval South India* Stein studies hundreds of local societies in the Chola Empire called *nadus*, noting that they are organized pyramidally in relation to central authority.[99] The nadus were stratified and ranked, occupationally diverse, and culturally varied territories. Furthermore, they had autonomous administrative and coercive capabilities while at the same time recognizing a ritual center – an anointed king. This resulted in three different types of localities – central, intermediate, and peripheral – with the central power of the Cholas diminishing as one moved farther away from the center. The Kaveri River basin formed the core of Chola political authority from the tenth to the thirteenth centuries. It is from here that the Chola rulers drew their small standing army under royal control. On the other hand, the entrenched, communally organized local societies maintained the local militia, which formed the bulk of the army.[100]

Other scholars have challenged Stein's thesis, but they too have developed variants of the decentralized state. According to Herman Kulke, the process of integrative state formation in early medieval India pertained to three concentrically connected geographical areas and accordingly went through three chronologically distinct stages of development that can be characterized by three key terms: *rajavamsa*, *samantachakra*, and *mandala*. Rajavamsa pertains to the chiefdom and the establishment of local rule under a "royal" lineage in the nuclear area from where the political development ensued. Samantachakra refers to an early kingdom and the process of extending political authority within the nuclear area and the establishment of tributary relations within the circle of formerly independent neighbors without, however, annexing them. Mandala refers to the imperial kingdom and the process emanating from the central nuclear area of agrarian extension, social stratification, political hierarchization, and cultural integration. Kulke believes that the mandala, or imperial kingdom, represented the third and final stage in Hindu statehood development before the founding of the Indian Islamic Empire. However, he also points out that few Indian kingdoms were able to reach this third and final stage.[101] The Gupta and Mauryan Empires came closest to developing strong and viable mandalas. However, they continued to evolve as patrimonial empires and were unable to restructure the political and economic links with their peripheries to any significant degree. Although the king taxed and controlled large regions, the local caste groups continued to wield a tremendous amount of self-regulation.[102]

The segmentary and mandala concepts confirm the view that the major center of Indian civilization was not political but religious-ritual. S. N. Eisenstadt and Harriet Hartman note that the center was not organized into a homogeneous, unified setting but instead consisted of a series of ritual subcenters such as pilgrimage shrines, networks, temples, sects, and schools spread throughout the subcontinent and often cutting across political boundaries.[103] Crucial to understanding this regional subdivision was the relationship between the castes, which were local units brought together in a combination of ritual, economic, and political ways. However, intercaste relations were also constructed upon countrywide cultural premises that possessed many local variations.[104] Such intercaste relations were built in hierarchies and/or in terms of center-periphery relations. These relations often manifested themselves in public ceremonies with gifts and presentations where differences in ritual power and economic relations were symbolized.

The king was the central and complex figure within this system. While some authors have suggested that his symbolic authority was derived from Brahmanic legitimation, recent research suggests that both the Brahmin and the Kshatriya (warrior) *varnas* (classes) exercised lordship and mastery over their respective ritually defined domains. As Eisenstadt and Hartman suggest, the order lies not "in one fixed or internally consistent ranking, but in a pragmatically constituted set of shifting meanings and configurations of castes."[105] Thus, there developed in India a concept of sovereignty that emphasized the multiple rights of different groups and sectors of society and not the existence of a unitary concept of the state. In turn, Indian politics developed patrimonial characteristics whereby rulers relied upon personal loyalty and bonds to control officials and to communicate with the regional peripheries. Assuming, then, that the decentralized state thesis was the norm in ancient and early medieval India, this explains why these kingdoms could not harness the resources necessary to maintain and train a professional army. Furthermore, the Indian empires' short-lived nature in comparison to that of the Achaemenians in Persia, the Hans in China, and the Romans also meant that they had few opportunities to restructure the economies in the areas under their control.

CHAPTER 2

Warfare in Medieval India

Harshavardhana was the last of ancient northern India's great Hindu rulers. After his death in AD 647 northern India disintegrated into many smaller kingdoms. According to the Chinese traveler Hsüan-tsang, three powerful Hindu kingdoms, Kapisi to the north, Sindhu or Sindh to the south, and Tsao-Kutaor or Tsay-li in between, dominated the westernmost region.[1] The territory of these and other Hindu kingdoms in western India also included much of modern-day Afghanistan.[2] Thus, the small westernmost kingdoms of Kabul and Zabulistan first bore the brunt of the Arab incursions from AD 606–47.[3] Soon after, the larger kingdom of Sindh also began to feel pressure from the Arabs. The Arab push into Sindh resulted in the first recorded clash between the Indians and the Arabs. As had the Macedonians, the Arab invaders kept numerous accounts of their expeditions into India, the most detailed being the *Chach-Nama*, an Arabic account of the Sindh conquest translated into Persian by Muhammad Ali bin Abu Bakr Kufi.[4]

During the reign of the Umayyad caliph Mu'awiyah I (661–80) the Arabs launched a successful series of offensives against Sindh. Al-Hajjaj, the governor of Iraq, appointed Muhammad Kasim as the commander of his armies in Sindh and made elaborate arrangements to ensure the success of the campaign. Al-Hajjaj ordered 6,000 Syrian warriors to join Muhammad's forces. After further preparation, Muhammad advanced into Sindh and toward Debal, the capital of the Hindu ruler Dahir, which he captured after a brief struggle. He then moved on to the banks of the Indus, where Dahir confronted him on the opposite bank in 712.

The stage was thus set on the banks of the Indus for yet another confrontation between an Indian army and an invading foreign army. The similarities between this battle and the battle of the Hydaspes are amazing. Like Alexander, Muhammad too successfully effected a river crossing, and, like Porus, Dahir also dispatched a contingent of troops (probably cavalry) to meet this attack. Muhammad easily dealt with this small force, and the two armies finally faced each other near the fortress of Raor. Unfortunately, the *Chach-Nama* is scant on battle-related details. It appears that, like Porus before

23

him, Dahir, mounted on his elephant, led a charge against the Arab forces. However, the Arabs were prepared for an elephant charge, as they set fire to Dahir's howdah with naphtha balls or arrows and killed Dahir when he dismounted. In true Indian tradition, Dahir's remaining army fled to Raor, which then fell to Muhammad's victorious forces.

The Arab conquest of Sindh was one of the last victories in the Arabs' efforts to spread the influence of Islam. Soon afterward the Abbasids (c. 750–1258), who began a new caliphate based in Baghdad, pushed aside the Umayyads. The Arab governor of Masurah, or Sindh, isolated from these events, managed to survive the Abbasid takeover and ruled independently of the caliph's control. With the passage of time, the Arabs in Sindh soon ceased to be a major political or military force and began to coexist peacefully with the Rajput kingdoms to the east.

The Gurjara Pratihara dynasty, founded by Nagabhatta (reigned 725–40), revived to some extent the glory of Kanauj, the former capital of Harshavardhana in the heart of the Gangetic Plain. This dynasty survived until Mahmud of Ghazni overthrew it in 1018–19.[5] Most of northern India, however, was fragmented into more than a hundred smaller kingdoms under rulers who called themselves Rajputs.

The Rajputs emerged around the seventh century after the Gupta Empire collapsed. They were descended from the Huns and the central Asian tribes that invaded and settled India following the collapse of Guptan power.[6] Initially, four clans, the Pratiharas or Pariharas, the Chauhans, the Solankis, and the Paramaras, emerged. The Rajput clans perceived themselves as Kshatriyas (warriors) descended from a mythical hero who emerged from a huge sacrificial fire at Mount Abu. What made the Rajputs stand out from the rest of Indian society was not their foreign origins but their fanatical attempts to assert their Kshatriya status. Over time, other Indian groups followed their example and claimed descent from the solar and lunar races, establishing themselves as Rajputs in various parts of western and central India.[7]

The clan remained the central focus of all the Rajputs' politics. A Rajput chief, or raja, ruled not only because of his ability as a warrior and a leader but also because of his ability to sustain his kinsmen's support and loyalty. His death signaled the start of a significant power struggle between clan factions for control of the throne. The Rajput administrative system was also intimately tied to an individual raja's fate: if he fell, so did they.[8] The Rajputs also directed their loyalties to subregional varnas and caste identities rather than to a territorially defined state. According to Richard Fox, "This continued ideological identification at regional levels could never be effaced by the state in traditional northern India."[9]

These traditions prevented the Rajput clans from establishing permanent political systems, let alone creating a united Rajput Empire. In the midst of this continuous clan conflict a new wave of powerful foreign invaders planned to invade northern India.

The Turkish Invasions

In 962 Alaptagin, a former Turkish slave of the Samanid ruler Abdul Malik (946–61), founded the kingdom of Ghazni.[10] In 977 he was succeeded by another former slave, Sabuktajin, who founded the Yamini, or Ghaznavid, dynasty. Sabuktajin began a series of confrontations with the Hindushahi dynasty, led by Jaipal (960–1002), who lost considerable territory, including portions of Afghanistan, the northwestern frontier, and the Khyber Pass.[11] In 998 Abu Qasim Mahmud, Sabuktajin's eldest son, ascended the throne of Ghazni.[12]

Like his father before him, Mahmud, after consolidating his hold over Ghazni from local rivals, quickly turned his attention to India.[13] During his second expedition Mahmud confronted the Hindushahi ruler Jaipal and his army at Peshawar on 28 November 1001.[14] The battle of Peshawar was the first major clash between the Turks and the Indians and was the precursor of conflicts to come. The Muslim chronicler al-Utbi left a fairly detailed account of this battle in his *Tarikh Yamini*, noting that Mahmud had a force of 15,000 select cavalry and a large force of Ghazis (Muslim volunteers paid in loot). On the opposing side, Jaipal fielded a force of 12,000 cavalry, 30,000 foot soldiers, and 300 elephants.[15] Mahmud's forces initiated the action (probably with a barrage of arrows), and Jaipal's forces advanced to engage them. According to al-Utbi, fifteen elephants fell as archers shot their legs and swordsmen severed their trunks. The Turks came well prepared to deal with the Hindu war elephants. By noon the battle was over, and 15,000 Indians lay dead. Jaipal had been captured.[16] Although the chronicler exaggerated the number of Indian casualties, Mahmud's army had little difficulty in defeating the Indian force. With Jaipal's elephants quickly immobilized, his army was no match for the smaller, more mobile, and better organized Ghaznavid cavalry. The impact of Mahmud's irregular Ghazis is questionable, but the Indian infantry was equally ineffective.

Jaipal's defeat left the way clear for Mahmud to carry out several more expeditions in northern India. But the other northern Indian rulers now realized that they could stop Mahmud's rampaging armies only if they established a united front.[17] The ruler who led this alliance was Anandpal, Jaipal's son and successor. Contingents from the rulers of Delhi, Ajmer, Kalingar,

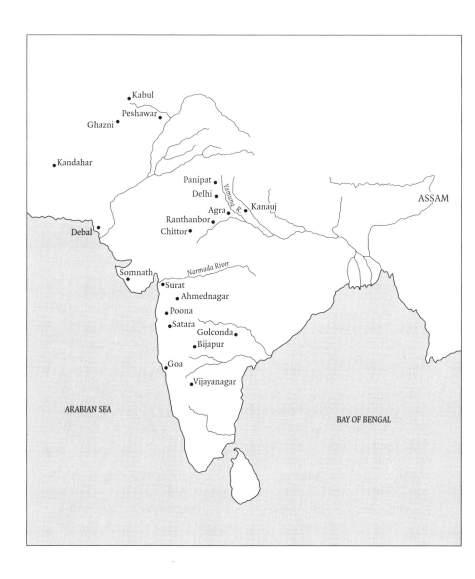

Political map of South Asia AD 1000–1760

Gwalior, and Kanauj joined his forces. The Indian army that eventually took the field was, according to some contemporary writers, the greatest Indian force fielded against the Turks. With Anandpal in the lead, the massive army moved into the Punjab, where it faced Mahmud's well-entrenched forces on the banks of the Indus. According to Muslim chroniclers, the two sides faced each other for forty days, an unlikely period given the size of the forces and the logistical and troop morale problems this would create. Mahmud then ordered 6,000 archers (probably mounted) to move to the front of the Indian forces and attack them. At this point the battle seems to have swung against the Turks, for a force of 30,000 (obviously an exaggerated figure) barefooted Gakkar tribal warriors forced their way into Mahmud's cavalry and reportedly killed 3,000–4,000 Muslims in a few minutes. If this is accurate, it is one of the rarest instances in which infantry managed to defeat an elite cavalry force. The Gakkars may have surprised the Ghaznavid cavalry, but the details of this Gakkar attack are scant. The Indians' advantage did not last long, however, as the effect of naphtha balls and arrows overwhelmed the Indian war elephants, causing them to flee the field. Six thousand Arab cavalry and 14,000 Turks, Afghans, and Khiljis pursued the Indians for two days and nights, during which they slaughtered at least 8,000 of them.[18]

According to Muslim accounts, the Indians fought a determined battle that almost overwhelmed Mahmud's cavalry. However, Indian tribals probably could not cause so much damage to Mahmud's vaunted cavalry forces. The main Indian force could not launch its own attack, indicating that Anandpal had little control of the united forces under him. The collapse of the Indian army after the departure of Anandpal and his elephants was no surprise, since it remained a recurrent theme in Indian warfare.

The defeat of Anandpal marked the end of any organized attempt to defeat Mahmud of Ghazni, and he continued to launch his devastating expeditions into India. During his many raids he sacked the holy cities of Thaneshwar (1012–13), Mathura (1018–20), and Somnath (1025–26) and defeated the Jats in the Jud Hills (1025–26). During the attack on the last city Mahmud mobilized the largest army he had ever used to raid India. It included 30,000 cavalry in addition to an indeterminable number of Ghazi volunteers. He also made elaborate plans to support his troops with 30,000 camels loaded with water and corn.[19] After this raid he returned to Ghazni, where he died in 1030 at the age of sixty-one.[20]

Mahmud's brilliant organizational and tactical abilities exposed the many serious flaws in the Indian armies confronting him. To begin with, his armies' significant strike element was the handpicked cavalry. These varied in number depending upon the nature of his operation. During Mahmud's expedition to Kanauj and Mathura, for example, Firishtah, a Muslim historian, states that he had no fewer than 100,000 picked cavalry and only 20,000 "northern" foot.[21] Using a cavalry-dominated army with an efficient baggage train composed mainly of camels enabled Mahmud to maneuver at will throughout northern India. With the possible exception of the battle against the Hindu confederacy in 1008–9, Mahmud always took the initiative and decided when, where, and how to confront the Indian powers. The Hindu armies, moving sluggishly with their war elephants and large baggage trains, could not hope to match Mahmud's speed. As a result, Mahmud usually engaged in sieges against forts and cities. The Hindu armies were almost always on the defensive against the Ghaznavids.

Once battle commenced the disparity in the abilities of the opposing forces became all the more apparent. Mahmud learned how to deal effectively with the threat from the elephants with flaming naphtha balls and showers of arrows. His forces became adept at singling out and isolating the Indian leader's mount. Once he had been disposed of, the army usually disintegrated. Without their war elephants the Hindu forces were no match for Mahmud's cavalry.

The Ghori Invasion

From 1027 to 1275 northern India was spared further western invasions. During this time the Ghaznavid dynasty collapsed, and the Ghori dynasty replaced it in 1158. In 1173 Muhammad Ghori became the ruler of Ghazni. After consolidating his power he turned his attention to India. By 1187 he had conquered the Ghaznavid Empire in Afghanistan, Sindh, and the Punjab.[22]

Ghori then moved against Prithviraj Chauhan Delhi and the ruler of Ajmer. In 1189 Prithviraj's army confronted him at Tarain.[23] According to the *Tabakat-i Nasiri*, a Muslim chronicle, Ghori was carried off the battlefield after Govind Rai, the younger brother of Prithviraj, wounded him. In a reversal of their usual roles, the Muslim forces, upon seeing their leader fall, fled the battlefield. The Rajputs had a golden opportunity to decisively crush the retreating Ghori army, but they did nothing. Prithviraj seemed content to lay siege to the fortress of Bhatinda, which he recaptured after thirteen months.[24] Repossessing his lost territories was probably Prithviraj's major strategic objective.

Muhammad Ghori, however, was not ready to concede defeat, and he immediately began to assemble a large army for another invasion. The *Tabakat-i Nasiri* lists his army as comprised of 120,000 armored cavalry and several "divisions" of elephants.[25] Once again, the two armies met at Tarain. Ghori left his main army to the rear and had a force of 10,000 mounted archers deploy among the Indians to harass them. It is not clear what happened after this, but it appears that Prithviraj's forces moved against the archers, and in response the main Ghori army attacked and defeated them. Prithviraj was captured and put to death.[26] Using his mounted archers to draw out the Indians enabled Ghori to choose the time and place of his counterthrust to smash the Indian forces. His most effective weapon was not the divisions of war elephants but his feared armored cavalry.

The Delhi Sultanate

Muhammad Ghori was killed in 1206 in Dhamyak near the Jhelum River by Gakkar tribals, whom he had crushed in a recent campaign.[27] After his death, one of his trusted generals, Qutubuddin Aibak, inherited his Indian possessions. Qutubuddin became the first ruler of the so-called slave dynasty (members of which were former slaves like himself), which ruled northern India from 1206 to 1290. The slave dynasty in turn laid the foundation of the Delhi sultanate, a series of mainly Turkish dynasties (Afghan toward the end) that ruled much of India from Delhi until 1526.

The greatest of all the Delhi sultans was Alauddin Khilji of the Khilji dynasty, who ruled between 1296 and 1316. Alauddin extended his empire to include most of southern India in addition to most of northern India, making it one of the largest since the days of Chandragupta Maurya. He also maintained one of the most formidable military establishments of any Indian empire. Thus it is not surprising that a series of spectacular military campaigns marked his reign. He also has the rare distinction of being one of India's few rulers to defeat a major foreign invader, the Mongols. The Mongol invasions began soon after Alauddin ascended the throne when a Mongol army of ten tomans (one toman equals a division of 10,000 men), under the leadership of Kadar Khan, invaded Sindh and the Punjab in 1296–97. However, two Khilji generals, Zafar Khan and Ulugh Khan, intercepted and defeated them. In 1298 another Mongol army invaded Sindh and captured the fortress of Siwistan. Once again Zafar Khan defeated it.[28] Undeterred, the Mongols returned in 1299 under Qutulugh Khwaja with a huge force of twenty tomans. On this occasion, Alauddin met the Mongols on the outskirts of Delhi. According to the Muslim chronicler Ziau-d Din Barani, Alauddin deployed his army in three wings, the center under his command, the right flank under Zafar Khan, and the left under Ulugh Khan. During the bloody battle Zafar Khan broke through the enemy lines but was then cut off and killed. The Mongols, however, eventually retreated from the field. Details are sketchy, but Alauddin used war elephants, which were part of the force under Zafar Khan that the Mongols cut off and destroyed. According to Barani, the elephants "were wounded and their drivers killed." In 1303 another large Mongol force, led by Targhi Beg (the same warrior who killed Zafar Khan), laid siege to Delhi while Alauddin was busy besieging the Rajput fortress of Chittor. Delhi, however, withstood the attack, giving Alauddin time to organize his forces and plan for the inevitable confrontation. In the long campaign that followed in the next few years, Alauddin's forces were totally victorious. The battles that occurred throughout the campaign resulted in a tremendous slaughter of the Mongols. In time, the Mongols developed a great fear of the Khilji army, its cavalry in particular, and "all fancy of coming to Hindustan was washed clean out of their breasts."[29]

A measure of Alauddin Khilji's military genius was that, even as he conducted a successful campaign against the invading Mongols, he also waged a war against India's surviving Hindu kingdoms. This campaign began in 1297 with the easy conquest of Gujrat, after which he turned his attention to the powerful Rajput kingdoms of Ranthanbor and Chittor. After capturing the former in 1300–1301, he laid siege to the formidable fortress city of Chittor, which he captured after eight months; he then ordered its population of 30,000 massacred.[30] The conquest of Ranthanbor and Chittor destroyed the two most powerful Rajput strongholds and broke Rajput power in northern India. Although Alauddin continued to wage war against other Rajput kingdoms, none would henceforth offer any serious opposition.

Having suppressed much of Hindu northern India, Alauddin turned his attention south, establishing a southern command under Malik Kafur, a general who quickly conquered Devagiri and made it a vassal state. (It was later annexed.)[31] In 1309 Malik Kafur marched on Telengana and laid siege to its capital, Warangal. He raised the siege, however, when the ruler, Rai Pratap Rudra Deva II, surrendered 100 elephants, 7,000 horses, and a huge amount of treasure, including the famed Koh-i-Noor diamond.[32] Taking advantage of the internal feuding among the Pandyan dynasty, Malik Kafur captured the city of Maura in 1311. He returned to Delhi on 18 October with 612 elephants, 20,000 horses, 96,000 mounds of gold, and many precious stones.[33] By the end of 1311 the Khilji Empire stretched from the Indus in the northwest to Bihar in the east and from the Himalayan foothills in the north to Rameshwaran in the south. Not surprisingly, the Khilji army under Alauddin was one of the most effective armies in Indian military history. Alauddin maintained a tight grip over a centralized military structure by no longer assigning revenue collection tasks to his officers (giving them virtual land grants) and instituting, in its place, a system of cash payment for services.[34]

The Delhi sultanate's armies, including those of the Khiljis, consisted of cavalry, elephants, and infantry. As it had with Mahmud of Ghazni and Muhammad Ghori, the cavalry continued to be the lynchpin of the armies, although elephants gradually gained importance. Alauddin Khilji himself secured thousands of elephants as war booty from defeated enemies. It appears that the Turks who settled India, like the Greco-Macedonians before them, succumbed to the lore of the war elephants and incorporated them in large numbers into their armies. Despite having devastated Hindu armies equipped with elephants, the Turks were still impressed with the military potential of the pachyderms. Indeed, Mahmud of Ghazni, who never settled in India, had no fewer than 2,500 elephants in his army.[35] Yet despite this acquired affection for the war elephant, the sultanate armies did not lose their ultimate faith in their excellent cavalry. They continued to lavish attention on their horses, which were only the best imports from Arabia. Continued reliance upon a hard-hitting mobile cavalry force, bolstered by elephants and infantry, enabled the sultanate armies to vanquish all Hindu opposition. Alauddin's superb cavalry alone enabled him to outmaneuver and defeat the Mongols' highly mobile cavalry.

The well-oiled military machine that Alauddin Khilji created, however, did not survive after his death. One successor, Firoz Tuqhluq (1351–86), began to grant land in lieu of cash to his commanders, which had an immediate negative impact upon the imperial army's professionalism and central authority. What had once been a powerful partially centralized military machine broke up into many feudal levies.

At this particularly vulnerable juncture, the great Samarkand Turkish chieftain Timur-i-Lang, known in English as Tamerlane, invaded northern India in 1397 to wage a holy war against the infidels and to obtain the region's fabulous wealth.[36] Since a Muslim dynasty ruled northern India, an interest in wealth was probably the primary reason for Timur's decision to invade. Timur began his attack in March 1398 by crossing the Indus. By September he had defeated many local Hindu rulers. He then captured Multan and ravaged the Punjab. In December 1398 he found himself in front of Delhi facing Nasir al-Din Mahmud Tuqhluq's army. The *Tuzuk-i Timuri*, or chronicle of Timur, gives Mahmud's strength as including 10,000 cavalry, 40,000 infantry, and 125 armored elephants; no figures are given for Timur's forces. Timur first launched his right wing against Mahmud's left wing, which was defeated after a bloody battle. Mahmud in turn attacked with his main force, led by the elephants, against Timur's center. The Timurids immediately fell upon the elephants, killed their drivers, and harried the animals with swords and darts. Timur then launched his own counterattacks and eventually crushed Mahmud's army.[37]

Timur's relatively easy victory indicates a serious decline in the Delhi sultanate's capabilities. In the first place, the army that faced Timur was smaller than the earlier Khilji armies, was heavily dominated by infantry, and possessed an ineffective cavalry. Indeed, like the Hindu armies so easily defeated by his predecessors, Mahmud's army had become closely tied to the elephant. During the battle his only offensive action was a charge into the center of Timur's army.

After completing his rampage of northern India, Timur crossed the Indus in 1399 and returned to Samarkand. His invasion dealt the deathblow to the weak sultanate empire because Mahmud's defeat swept away the sultanate's elaborate administrative structures. In 1451 the Afghan Lodhi dynasty came to power in Delhi, and under Lodhi's successors a measure of the sultanate's glory was restored, but Delhi exerted scarcely more influence than the surrounding Rajput and Hindu kingdoms. The way into India was open for yet another invader.

The Mughals

In October 1504 Zahir ud Din Muhammad Babur, son of a petty chieftain of Ferghana, captured Kabul from the Arghun chieftain Muhammad Muqim, which gave him overlordship over Ghazni.[38] After consolidating his grip on Afghanistan, Babur turned his attention to India, where he launched a series of four invasions from 1519 to 1524. During the fourth he succeeded in wresting control of the Punjab from Ibrahim Lodhi, the last of the Delhi sultans.[39] Having now secured a firm foothold in India, Babur resolved to overthrow the sultanate.

On 20 April 1526 Babur's forces met Ibrahim Lodhi's army near the town of Panipat. The *Babur-Nama* estimates Ibrahim's forces as 100,000 men and 1,000 elephants.[40] Babur did not mention the number of his army, but it included cavalry, formations of matchlock-equipped infantry, and several cannons.[41] Babur was the first commander to introduce massed artillery in an effective manner onto the Indian battlefield. However, considerable controversy exists as to how many cannons he brought with him, with estimates ranging from 700 (an unlikely figure) to 2 (equally unlikely).[42] Ibrahim's army opened the battle by advancing rapidly but at the last moment hesitated or failed to close with the enemy. Babur then launched his own attack with archers (probably mounted) against Ibrahim's flanks, while his artillery bombarded the center. Babur then recounts that Ibrahim's army, after making two weak counterattacks against Babur's flanking forces, collapsed toward its own center in a critical mass that was unable to move in any direction (not unlike the Romans at Canae). By midday the battle was over, with thousands of Lodhi troops dead upon the field, including Ibrahim Lodhi.[43]

This first battle of Panipat was significant not only because it destroyed the Delhi sultanate but also because the first large-scale use of artillery in India contributed to ending the reign of the war elephants. Although Babur mentioned a Lodhi force of 1,000 elephants, Ibrahim was unable to launch an attack against Babur's center. In all previous attacks against foreign invaders, whatever the outcome, Indian elephants had charged the enemy center. Ibrahim's considerable elephant force (even allowing for exaggerated numbers) could not do this because of Babur's artillery, which panicked the unfortunate pachyderms. Without the elephants to give them the forward momentum they so desperately needed, Ibrahim's forces were hemmed in by Babur's more mobile army and massacred. From the period of the epics, the war elephant had formed the main offensive element in all the "traditional" Indian armies. Babur's cannons put an end to one of the most outdated trends in Indian warfare.

With the Lodhi dynasty's weak Turko-Afghan survivors unable to exercise much control over northern India after the first Panipat battle, the Rajputs showed signs of rejuvenation under the banner of Rana Sangha of Mewar. Babur immediately recognized the rana as his main threat and prepared to confront him. On 17 March 1527 the two armies met at Khanua, 35 miles east of Agra. Rana Sangha had welded together an unlikely military confederacy, including a number of Muslim chieftains from northern India. Babur estimated the confederacy's total strength at 201,000.[44] According to Babur, the Rajputs advanced behind their elephants. Babur deployed his cannons and matchlock men in a line behind a wall of carts chained together. He commanded the center, while two trusted lieutenants commanded his flanks. As he had done at Panipat, Babur deployed his flanking forces on both his right and left wings. As Rana Sangha advanced, the forces engaged on all the fronts. In the center Babur and his matchlock men, with the support of his cannons, engaged the rana (presumably, his charging cavalry and elephants). Babur then ordered his elite Royal Corps, waiting in the van of his center, to advance. Babur's artillery commander, Ustad-ali, supported this attack by pounding the "iron-mantled forts [elephants?] of the infidels."[45] At this point, the matchlock men also advanced from behind the cover of the carts to fire upon the enemy at close range. The battle reached a critical stage when Rana Sangha's larger army pressed in upon Babur's flanks, especially the left. However, they were repulsed, according to Babur (there are no details in the *Babur-Nama*), and the entire enemy force was defeated.

The battle of Khanua bears more military significance for medieval India than does the battle of Panipat. Unlike the ill-organized and small force thrown up by Ibrahim Lodhi to confront Babur, Rana Sangha created a formidable military force. Not only did the Hindu chiefs join his ranks, but so did a number of Turko-Afghan and Indian Muslim chiefs. Although Babur does not give the number of troops he had on the field, it appears that the confederacy outnumbered him, which explains why he could not develop his dreaded flanking movement. Furthermore, the rana's army had a large cavalry force, about 100,000 (if Babur's figures are accurate), which enabled the rana to mount a significant attack against Babur's flanks. The main battle, however, took place in the center, and here Babur's artillery saved the day. The collapse of the Indian center demoralized the more successful flanking Indian forces (mainly cavalry) and resulted in them fleeing the battlefield – "the absurd (batil) Hindus, knowing their perilous position, dispersed like carded wool before a wing."[46] Had it not been for Babur's cannons and ultimately superior tactics, the rana might have achieved an historic victory.

The Mughal Emperors

After a few more battles that helped consolidate his power in northern India, Babur died on 26 December 1530, naming his son, Humayun, as his successor. While Humayun was an ineffectual ruler, his son, Jalal ud Din Muhammad Akbar, laid a solid foundation for the Mughal Empire in India.[47] He established a highly centralized government and a uniform administrative system, much of which he borrowed from the earlier ruler of Delhi, Sher Shah Suri. The power and glory of the Mughal Empire continued to grow under his successor's leadership. Arguably, the most militarily capable of all the great Mughal emperors was Muhiuddin Muhammad Aurungzeb, who succeeded to the throne in July 1658. During his reign the Mughal Empire reached the zenith of its territorial expansion. Unfortunately, his hunger for territory and his unwillingness to compromise with local Hindu rulers resulted in many rebellions, chief among them being the Rajputs in northern India and the Marathas in the west. Aurungzeb's reign was marked by a series of military campaigns that toward the end were increasingly unsuccessful. These incessant wars hastened the collapse of India's last great empire. However, they left behind a possible renaissance in the military evolution of the subcontinent.

The Mughal Military

As it had in the Delhi sultanate before it, military force established and maintained the Mughal Empire. All the Mughal rulers from Akbar onward supported formidable military establishments. The *Ain-i-Akbari* (Almanac of the Empire) divides the Mughal military into four classes: *mansabdars* (officers) and their men, cavalrymen without mounted followers, independent cavalry, and infantry. The word *mansab* is derived from the Arabic *mansib*, which means office or rank; hence, a mansabdar is an officer.[48] All of the Mughal Empire's officers, including civil, were mansabdars belonging to one of sixty-six grades.[49] Cavalry comprised the army's second class after the *mansabdari* forces. These were single men who did not command followers and thus could not get mansabdari rank. Since most of them were men of talent and birth, the emperor kept them to be assigned at will. The army's third class also consisted of single cavalrymen, but the state had to support them through land or cash grants since they were too poor to own horses and equipage. Of the nine types of infantrymen listed, only the matchlock men saw action. The rest included porters, runners, guards, gladiators, wrestlers, slaves, and laborers who worked as support personnel. The core of the Mughal military, however, was inextricably interwoven and indeed sustained by the mansabdari system.

The imperial treasury paid the mansabdars a salary to maintain their soldiers as well as their personal lifestyles and status, which determined their rank, or *zat*. In the eleventh year of Akbar's reign, he instituted a second rank (and salary) known as the *sowar* rank, which specifically stated the number of horses and amount of equipment each mansabdar had to maintain. He based the sowar gradations upon the number of soldiers each mansabdar was allowed to recruit, ranging from a low of 10 to a high of 10,000 men. Actual figures represent a low of 20 and a high of 7,000.[50] Thus, a mansabdar got two salaries, zat for his personal use, and sowar for maintaining his troops. If the zat and sowar ranks were equal, the mansabdar was designated a first-class officer. If the sowar rank was less than half of the zat rank or there was no sowar at all, he was a second-class officer. The zat rank was usually accompanied by the sowar rank, and rarely was it found alone. Furthermore, it was either equal to or more than the sowar rank but never the reverse. If the government wanted to raise the sowar rank over the zat, it conferred the status of *do aspah* (two-horse trooper) or *seh aspah* (three-horse trooper). This gradation was based on the number of horses a trooper had at his disposal during a march or campaign.

Although the monetary gains of such a rank were great, the officer's pay and allowances being doubled, the real benefit lay in a tremendous increase in the officer's status. These ranks were endowed with tremendous prestige and honor and were reserved for only the most senior officers.[51] The mansabdars were from the Mughal court aristocracy and owed their exalted positions in society to the emperor; thus, they were totally dependent upon him. Under a strong emperor this elaborate system functioned reasonably well and enabled the Mughal Empire to maintain large armies. In addition to the mansabdari forces the Mughal emperors maintained their own imperial standing armies, although these were quite small in number. Akbar's regular standing army numbered only about 25,000, including a force of 12,000 cavalry, with the rest being matchlock men and artillerymen.[52] The small numbers involved indicate that this was an elite unit that probably functioned as the emperor's personal guard.

The Mughal army's strongest and most important arm was the cavalry. All the mansabdars maintained cavalry, and the cavalry also formed a substantial element of the imperial army. There was no shortage of good horses. They were divided into seven classes, led by those from Arabia and Turkey, referred to as Buhri and Tazi.[53] Next in value came the Turki from wider Turkistan and Afghanistan, the Kohi from Kohistan, the Buldasti from East Punjab, and the Alaghi from Sindh. The Mughals considered these horses to be of high quality, while they considered all the native breeds to be bad, especially the little pony type Tattu, which they thought was the worst.[54] In fact, the latter has become a popular term of slander in Urdu. Elephants had finally ceased to play an important role in offensive operations, being used mainly for transport, as load carriers, as "artillery towers," and to batter down the gates of a fort or city. Few accounts exist of elephants charging enemy formations in Mughal warfare. On the battlefield Mughal commanders used elephants as observation towers.[55]

The Mughals had many cannons, the weapon that finally put an end to the elephant's reign as India's primary battlefield offensive weapon. The Mughal army's artillery wing was called the *top-khanah* (literally, cannon house). It included a manufacturing and magazine department and was headed by an official called the *mir atish*.[56] The Mughals built a wide variety of cannons from heavy (20 tons) to light pieces and even *bans*, or rockets. They generally made the cannons by crushing brass, bronze, or copper and sometimes by rolling wrought iron. In addition to cannons, the Mughal foundries produced many handguns. These were not matchlocks but the more primitive and bulky arquebus type that fired manually like a cannon. By the 1590s the Mughals had adopted the buttonlock, a matchlock-type mechanism invented in Germany in the 1510s.[57]

During Akbar's reign the Mughals made many advancements in artillery technology and tactics. Abul Fazal describes a cannon that could be dismantled for a march and then reassembled when needed for action. Akbar's armies even had light artillery pieces that could be carried by elephants and even smaller guns that could be carried by single men. Akbar is also said to have organized batteries of seventeen cannons that could be fired with one match.[58] In addition to cannons the Mughals also extensively used bans, one of the earliest and probably the only indigenously developed firearm in India. It consisted of an iron tube about 1 foot long and 1 inch in diameter attached to a bamboo rod some 12 feet long.[59]

The infantry was the Mughal army's weakest arm, and in this respect it did not differ from the traditional Hindu armies. The infantry's most important component was the arquebus carriers, or *banduq-chis*. Akbar had at least 12,000 of them.[60] The state gave the mansabdars a fixed number of infantry in addition to the imperial infantry. It is not clear how the rulers maintained or armed these troops, but their inferior position to the cavalry is clear because of their official description in the payroll, which is given as *nima suwaran*, or half-troopers.[61]

Warfare in Mughal India

Up until the latter half of the 1600s the Mughal military establishment remained the most formidable of its kind in India. Not only did it outnumber its Muslim and Hindu opposition, but it also had a marked qualitative edge in its artillery and cavalry, the latter arguably being the finest in Asia. This overwhelming advantage is closely reflected in the Mughal armies' tactics during their innumerable conflicts to sustain and expand their control of the subcontinent.

Few other Indian powers had the ability to confront the military might of the Mughals in open battle. Most resistance came from fortified cities and forts or in the form of guerrilla warfare. Of the former, the most notable example is Akbar's siege and investment of the Rajput fortress of Chittor in 1567–68. Although Akbar had secured an alliance with the Amber Rajputs, most of the other clans remained hostile to Muslim rule. Most prominent among them were the Rajputs of Mewar, who were confident in the invincibility of their famous fortress and capital, Chittor. Many considered the fortress to be one of the most formidable in India, situated as it was upon the tallest hill in the region with a plentiful supply of running water.

Akbar's campaign against the Rajputs in Chittor provides us with a model study of Mughal siege operations. He began by collecting some 5,000 builders, carpenters, and stonemasons, whom he ordered to build trenches all the way to the walls of the fortress. As the workers toiled, wooden planks covered with rawhide protected them in the trenches. At the same time, miners constructed mines at the feet of two important bastions and filled them with gunpowder. Unfortunately, when the commander had them blown up, the explosion killed 500 Mughal infantry who were waiting to storm the breach.[62] The royal battery then commenced a fierce bombardment that expanded the breach. Mughal troops poured into the breach and overwhelmed the defenders on 25 February 1568.[63] The siege of Chittor illustrates the effective way that the Mughals used gunpowder and cannons to reduce the walls of a fortress.[64]

On the battlefield the Mughals usually easily defeated the few armies that dared to confront them. In June 1576, for example, Rana Pratap, the indomitable Rajput chieftain of Mewar (now without Chittor), attacked the imperial forces with a small force of 3,000 cavalry at Haldi Ghati, a mountain pass in the Aravalli Range. Despite a heroic fight, the vastly superior Mughal forces crushed the rana's small army.[65] In fact, the largest conventional confrontation involving imperial forces was a fratricidal war for the throne after Shah Jahan's illness in September 1657. Aurungzeb allied with his brother Murad to defeat their eldest brother, Dara, at the battle of Samugarh in 1658. Both sides were similarly armed and equipped, but Aurungzeb won the day with his superior generalship, especially the excellent use of his artillery.[66]

The rare occasions when non-Mughal forces defeated the imperial armies usually happened when an enemy succeeded in nullifying the Mughals' numerical and technological advantages. During Jahangir's reign, for example, the Abyssinian slave ruler of Ahmednagar, Malik Ambar, waged a highly successful guerrilla campaign against the imperial armies from 1608 until his death in 1626.[67] Malik Ambar used masses of light cavalry, mainly Maratha, not only to cut off and isolate Mughal armies but also to strike deep into Mughal-controlled areas.[68]

During Aurungzeb's reign in 1661 the emperor dispatched an imperial army under Gen. Mir Jumla to conquer the Hindu kingdom of Assam, ruled by the Ahoms.[69] After suffering defeat at the hands of the imperial armies in conventional warfare, mainly in a series of futile attempts to defend their fortresses, the Ahoms took to guerrilla warfare. In anticipation of the rainy season, they withdrew to Assam's jungle-clad hills, from where they conducted a series of surprise attacks against the Mughals, repeatedly ambushing them whether they advanced or retreated. The Ahoms were particularly adept at interdicting the Mughal supply system and succeeded in starving many Mughal garrisons. When retreating under attack, the Ahoms adopted a scorched-earth policy, destroying crops, stores, equipment, and dwellings and moving the local populace from the area abandoned to the Mughals. In doing so, the Ahoms evolved a classic form of guerrilla resistance to counter the Mughal military superiority in conventional warfare. In addition to losses suffered in these attacks, the Mughal forces suffered immensely from malaria and the lack of food supplies.[70] Eventually, the Ahom king signed a peace treaty acknowledging his subordinate status to Delhi, which enabled a desperate Mir Jumla to withdraw the imperial army with some semblance of honor to Dacca, where he died of fever in March 1663.[71] Attempts to rejuvenate the offensive in 1670 under Raja Ram Singh, the son of Jai Singh, proved equally futile.[72] Guerrilla warfare thus became the most successful means by which the Mughal Empire's enemies could hope to defeat the imperial troops. In the end, such tactics would finally destroy the empire when a Maratha chieftain of the Bhonsle clan, Shivaji, refined his warriors' guerrilla fighting skills to a fine art.

Shivaji and the Rise of the Marathas

When the western Chalukya kingdom split during the twelfth century it evolved into two distinctive linguistic areas, the Marathi-speaking areas of Maharashtra and the Kanada-speaking area of Karnataka. In Maharashtra the new Yadava dynasty used the vernacular Marathi as its official language and patronized the important pilgrimage sites in Maharashtra.[73] In 1526 the Bahamani Empire, which controlled much of the Deccan that belonged to Maharashtra, dissolved, and in its place arose five separate kingdoms, of which three survived to become regional powers: Ahmednagar, Bijapur, and Golconda.[74] Through patronage of these three Muslim kingdoms several Maratha families rose to power. Many of these clan leaders became mansabdars, or *deshmuks* (a category of landlord), for the Muslim Deccan kingdoms, receiving jagirs, or land grants, that enabled them to maintain their troops.[75] These Maratha clans frequently fought amongst themselves, often as a result of being on opposing sides within the Deccan Muslims' power struggles or frequently due to blood feuds among themselves. The Marathas were at this time little different from their Rajput counterparts in the north.[76]

Nevertheless, toward the end of the sixteenth century the power of the Maratha chieftains grew considerably. The Mughals, who for some time had sought to subdue and control the Deccan Muslim kingdoms, realized that the Maratha chiefs were a powerful military tool of these kingdoms and sought to woo the Marathas to their side. In 1621 the Mughals enjoyed their greatest success in this venture when one of the Marathas' most powerful chiefs,

Lakhuji Jadhav, defected to their side. The Mughals immediately rewarded him with an impressive mansab of 24,000 men.[77] In 1626 the last powerful Maratha chief still loyal to the Deccan Muslim rulers, Shahaji of the Bhonsle clan, came over to the Mughals. He was given a mansab of 6,000, including 5,000 horses.[78] However, he soon grew dissatisfied with the Mughals and set about creating his own independent principality.[79] Shahaji broke with the Mughals and joined the kingdom of Bijapur in its struggle against the latter; however, the Bijapuris, suspecting that "Shahaji Bhonsle has become a real threat to this court," imprisoned him in Bijapur on 28 July 1648.[80] His son Shivaji (born in February 1630) retaliated with a series of successful campaigns against the Bijapur army, forcing it to release his father in October 1649.

Shivaji's father had given him the two districts of Poona and Supe. He quickly consolidated his hold on them by capturing fortresses in those areas not yet under Bhonsle control and by building new forts. With the capture of the fortress of Purandhar, Shivaji had by 1649 established total control over the Poona region.[81] These campaigns established Shivaji as a formidable military leader and enabled him to take over the reins of power from his ailing father. Shivaji continued his campaign against the Bijapuris when in November 1656 the Mughal emperor Shah Jahan ordered the imperial armies to invade and seize Bijapur. This quickly resulted in a confrontation with Shivaji, who appeared to have similar designs. The situation was diffused when Shah Jahan ordered a cessation of hostilities against Bijapur in August 1657, leaving Shivaji to recommence his campaign against Bijapur. In November 1659 Shivaji defeated the Bijapur army in a surprise attack after killing their commander, Afzal Khan.[82] In the course of this great victory, Shivaji captured 65 elephants, 4,000 horses, 1,200 camels, and large numbers of cannons and guns.[83]

These military actions perturbed the Mughals, and their viceroy in the south, Shaista Khan, marched on Poona "to put down Shivaji, capture his territory and clear the region of disturbances."[84] Shivaji, realizing that he could not defeat the imperial armies in a conventional confrontation, quickly adopted guerrilla tactics. He further reinforced this tactic by removing all grain and fodder from the region. Despite these setbacks, a determined Shaista Khan continued the campaign and used his heavy artillery to batter down the defenses of a number of Maratha fortresses and take them. By November 1660 he had occupied most of the Poona region. Undeterred in the face of imminent defeat, Shivaji struck back. On the night of 5 April 1663 he attacked Shaista Khan in his encampment with a small band of men in what can only be described as a classic commando-style raid. Shaista Khan was wounded, and dozens of his men were killed. Then early the next year, on 6 January 1664, Shivaji struck deep into Mughal territory and ravaged the city of Surat, forcing the governor, Inayat Khan, to flee in panic. Shivaji returned from this expedition with tremendous amounts of booty.[85] An enraged Aurungzeb (now emperor) transferred Shaista Khan to Bengal and in 1665 directed the Mughals' most able general, a Rajput chieftain named Mirza Raja Jai Singh, to the south to crush Shivaji.

Jai Singh's campaign is a textbook example of a successful counterguerrilla operation. His first act was to ensure that no local chief would help Shivaji. He sent a Portuguese artillery officer in Mughal service, Nicolo Manucci, to the rulers of Ramnagar, Pent, and Chintia to warn them that they would suffer dire consequences if they aided Shivaji.[86] With Shivaji isolated, Jai Singh quickly occupied Poona and had moved on to the formidable fortress of Purandhar by 30 March 1665. Once there he set fire to the adjoining hamlets, thus denying the defenders outside help. With this done, he moved in his heavy siege equipment. The stronghold of Purandhar is actually two fortresses, Purandhar and Rudramal, atop a hill 4,500 feet above sea level. In the course of his careful preparations to take the fortress, Jai Singh wrote to Aurungzeb, requesting bigger cannons.[87] Early in the battle Rudramal quickly fell, but Purandhar remained the focus of a prolonged siege operation. In the meantime Jai Singh dispatched troops to devastate the countryside, capture the inhabitants, and confiscate their livestock, all aimed at further isolating Shivaji.[88] His forces also continued to invest other minor forts in the region. Whenever a Maratha force came out to oppose the imperial army it was defeated; for example, during a battle near the fortress of Lohagad the Mughals captured 300 Maratha men and women and seized 3,000 head of cattle.[89] In the meantime, the siege of Purandhar approached its climax as Mughal trenches approached the walls of the fort. Jai Singh ordered gun platforms to be placed in front of the ramparts, which were then bombarded. The defenders manning them had to flee to the inner wall, and the ramparts were seized.[90] Faced with the imminent collapse of his most powerful fortress and the ravaging of his territories, Shivaji sued for peace on 20 May 1665.[91]

In the Treaty of Purandhar Shivaji agreed, among other concessions, to surrender no fewer than twenty-three forts to the Mughals and to promise military service to the emperor in the Deccan.[92] Jai Singh laid down the clauses of the treaty, thus managing to convince Aurungzeb (who thought the treaty was too lenient) and Shivaji (who did not trust the Mughals) to accept it.[93] With Shivaji out of the way, the Mughals invaded Bijapur once again in November 1665. Beholden to the treaty, Shivaji fought on the Mughal side. After a period of ineffectual campaigning, Aurungzeb, on Jai Singh's advice, summoned Shivaji to Agra, ostensibly to bestow honors upon him that would further ensure his loyalty.[94] Then, on the pretext of taking offense at Shivaji's attitude, Aurungzeb placed him under house arrest and demanded the surrender of his forts. Shivaji stalled for time and managed to escape Agra in September 1666.[95]

After Shivaji's escape a period of uneasy truce followed. Jai Singh had failed to conquer Bijapur, and a disappointed Aurungzeb ordered him to return to the imperial court, but he died en route in August 1667.[96] Although Aurungzeb made both Shivaji and his son mansabdars in the Mughal army, the peace did not last, and by February 1670 Shivaji was again at war with the Mughals. The catalyst for the latest confrontation was Aurungzeb's rejuvenated anti-Hindu policies, during which he destroyed the temples of Vishwanath and Benares. Shivaji began his campaign when his general, Tanaji Malasure, captured the fortress of Simhagad on 4 February 1670.[97] The great fortress of Purandhar was also recaptured from the Mughals on 8 March.[98] In an unstoppable campaign Shivaji's forces swept on to capture the fortresses of Kalyan, Bhiwand, and Mahuli. He also raided and plundered Chandwad, Talkonkan, and Nander.[99] In Berar the Mughal governor stayed pinned down in the fortress of Ausa while Shivaji's forces plundered the province.[100] Between 4 and 5 October 1670 Shivaji sacked Surat for the second time. The Mughal garrison fled into the fort, and, according to English observers, "in the interim the enemy ransack[ed] the great houses at leisure."[101] Virtually unopposed, Shivaji's forces rampaged through the Deccan, subduing Mughal forts and collecting *chauth*, or tax, from the region. While fighting the Mughals, Shivaji also took on the Muslim kingdom of Bijapur and managed to wrest substantial territory from it. Noting Shivaji's fight on two fronts, an admiring if apprehensive Englishman based in Bombay stated, "He [Shivaji] despiseth and beareth himself manfully against all enemies."[102] The Mughal armies' desperate generals tried unsuccessfully to run Shivaji down. Yet even when they did catch up with his forces, the outcome did not favor them. At the first big confrontation at the battle of Salher in February 1672, Shivaji's forces soundly defeated the imperial armies. The Marathas captured 6,000 horses, as many camels, 125 elephants, and the entire Mughal supply train.[103]

On 6 June 1674 Shivaji, now the most prominent Hindu chieftain in India, was crowned king of Satara in an elaborate and lavish ceremony.[104] After his coronation, Shivaji sought to consolidate his power in the Deccan. He continued to engage in a successful military campaign against the Bijapuris and initiated the conquest of Karnataka in 1677. The Mughals, now thoroughly terrified of his growing power, worked desperately to stem his advances. They first made an alliance with Bijapur and even managed to make Shivaji's son

Shambaji defect briefly to their side, but they failed miserably to make any military headway against him. Shivaji's forces continued to raid and plunder Mughal territory until his death after a brief illness on 3 April 1680.[105] At the time of his death, Shivaji's territories extended from Ramanagar near Surat in the north to Karwar near Goa in the south along the western seacoast. He also controlled territory in the Deccan plateau and in Karnataka on the east coast, part of the Maratha homeland. In addition to areas directly under his control, Shivaji also obtained land revenue from Bijapur and Golconda, both part of the Mughal territory.

Following Shivaji's death, the power of the Maratha monarchy declined, and the Maratha Empire fragmented into a confederacy of regional powers under important sirdars, or military chiefs, all under the tenuous leadership of a peshwa, or chief minister. These divisions were reflected in the establishment of various armies by the peshwas and the sirdars. Most Maratha soldiers now preferred to fight as light cavalry, and indeed, the Maratha sirdars almost exclusively employed masses of light cavalry to oversee the vast areas under their control. Only the peshwa's army, much to the consternation of the sirdars, began to raise new European-style infantry battalions, which had tragic repercussions when the Maratha confederacy later confronted the Afghans at Panipat.

By the early eighteenth century, the Maratha military system was in a state of limbo, suspended somewhere between the sirdars' traditional system and the peshwas' partially Westernized system. The degree and the speed by which the army transitioned from the former to the latter would determine the fate of the Maratha Empire in the forthcoming conflict with the British. Equally important would be the political resilience of the Maratha confederacy and its ability to act against a common enemy.

Shivaji's Military System and Tactics

The earliest mention of the Maratha military dates back to ancient times, when the Chinese traveler Hsüan-tsang described the inhabitants of the region as "proud spirited and warlike," although he also pointed out that "their martial heroes who led the army in battle went into conflict intoxicated, and their war elephants were also made drunk before an engagement."[106] The region's harsh terrain and climate made the Marathas an insular and self-dependent community. The *watan*, or hereditary land, was of primary importance to a Maratha, not unlike the *bapoti* of the Rajput. Not surprisingly, the Maratha clans, like their Rajput counterparts, were constantly feuding. It took Shivaji's iron will to provide the foundation for a future Maratha Empire and war machine.

43

Shivaji maintained a small but effective standing army, something few medieval Hindu rulers managed to achieve for any prolonged time span. In order to accomplish this, Shivaji first abolished the jagir for military officers and instead regularly paid them in cash.[107] During campaigns all the spoils belonged to the state and not the army. After the campaign the state provided the army with housing in barracks.[108] The strength of Shivaji's army was relatively small compared to that of the Mughals. Maratha chroniclers put it at above 100,000, a rather optimistic figure.[109] The two main components of his armies were cavalry and infantry. In a marked divergence from most Hindu and, for that matter, Mughal armies, Shivaji maintained more infantry than cavalry. The extremely broken and hilly terrain under his control and the many forts he had to garrison probably account for this. Also, Shivaji's inability to access the great northern horse-trading markets, which were controlled by the Mughals, led him to rely more on infantry. Shivaji's armies were known for their remarkable mobility due to the cavalry's and infantry's extremely light personal equipment. An English observer, John Henry Grose, noted in 1757 that Shivaji's troops wore no armor, had a cloth turban for a helmet, and wore little more than a loincloth and a mantle over their shoulders.[110] The Marathas' logistics were equally sparse, especially in comparison to that of the Mughal armies. Another European visitor, Francis Gemelli Careri, who visited India in 1695, noted that the Marathas were able to field "50,000 horse, and as many or more foot, much better soldiers than the Moguls, for they live a day upon a piece of dry bread, and the Moguls will march at their ease carrying their women, abundance of provisions, and tents so that their army looks like a moving city."[111]

The Marathas' weapons were no different from those of the rest of the country. They used muskets, matchlocks, swords, spears, daggers, clubs, and bows. Grose also noted that the Marathas favored close combat with the sword and target (shield). Grose believed that the small, round Maratha shield could deflect musket balls at a distance.[112] The Marathas were less proficient in the use of firearms, artillery in particular. The very nature of Shivaji's lightly equipped mobile forces probably left little place for cumbersome artillery. What artillery he possessed he deployed in his numerous fortresses. These fortresses were strategically located and usually built on virtually inaccessible hilltops. They had immensely strong stone walls and an adequate supply of water and provisions to withstand long sieges. Their main weakness, however, was in their artillery, which could not keep the larger Mughal artillery at a distance. If the Mughals threatened one of his fortresses, Shivaji had to remove artillery from nearby fortresses to strengthen the firepower of the fortress under attack. Despite these weaknesses, the Maratha fortresses formed a formidable obstacle to Mughal control of the Deccan, and they could only be overcome after lengthy and costly sieges and/or large payoffs to the garrison commanders. Shivaji is said to have constructed 100 forts throughout his territories.[113]

Maratha military tactics revolved around raids, skirmishes, and fortifications. Only rarely did Shivaji confront Mughal main force armies in the field. Their highly mobile infantry and cavalry worked effectively as raiders to neutralize the Mughal siege-warfare tactics that had been used so successfully against the Rajputs. Mughal superiority in artillery and cavalry proved to be too weak to enable the empire to gain total military domination over its domestic opponents. The end result was that the Mughal emperor's centralizing efforts were doomed by the close of the seventeenth century.[114] Indeed, as Stewart Gordon notes, the Marathas had won the war by 1705 merely by avoiding defeat.[115]

Mughal Warfare and State Formation

The Mughal Empire achieved an impressive degree of centralization, yet it would be inaccurate to assume this was a precursor to British India's highly rationalized and structured military, administrative, and legal framework. Stephen Blake, drawing heavily on Max Weber's work on the patrimonial state, suggests that Mughal India was a patrimonial-bureaucratic state not unlike Ottoman Turkey, Safavid Persia, Tokugawa Japan, and Ming China. According to Weber, patrimonial domination originates in the patriarch's authority over his household; it entails obedience to a person not an office. Patrimonial states rise when lords and princes extend their control in areas beyond the patriarchal domain, which involves a change in authority from the patrimonial (domestic and personal) to the political (military and judicial).

Blake goes on to suggest that patrimonial armies consist of troops who owe primary allegiance to an individual rather than to a dynasty or an office. In patrimonial kingdoms the military consisted of the ruler's household troops. In patrimonial-bureaucratic empires, in contrast, armies were large and complex. As a result, they split into two types: the household troops, which functioned more as a palace guard, and the soldiers, which were raised by the major subordinates and made up the bulk of the army. These men, however, were more bound to their own commanders than to their emperors.[116] The Mughal administrative system followed a similar pattern: candidates for posts in the patrimonial-bureaucratic administrations had to demonstrate personal qualifications of loyalty, family, and position in addition to technical qualifications such as the ability to read and write.[117]

45

However, as the patrimonial empire grew it became impossible for the rulers to personally maintain all members of their administration, and they began to give officials benefices and prebends. In time this led to a situation where the rulers increasingly assigned the state's revenues to soldiers and officials. Since these revenues bypassed the rulers entirely and since most of the lands concerned were at a considerable distance from the capital, this resulted in the emperors having less control over their officials. Under such conditions the personal, patrimonial authority began to wane, and officials began to appropriate prebends and declare themselves independent.[118] To prevent this, the patrimonial emperors traveled constantly to maintain the personal bonds on which the state was founded. The emperors required that soldiers and officials visit the court regularly and even leave family behind as hostages. They were also periodically rotated from post to post, and the emperors created offices with overlapping interests to check the power of their subordinates. Finally, a network of spies outside the regular channels reported directly to the emperors on the officers' activities. In the Mughal system, in addition to regular court appearances, the emperors required that mansabdars present themselves at court after a change in assignment, after a change in jagir posting, during promotion time, and if possible during cele-brations. The Mughals also appointed officers with cross-cutting areas of re-sponsibility; for example, the finance officer and the military officer relied on each other for efficient governance. Finally, Mughal emperors spent nearly 40 percent of their time during the empire's 200-year period on tour.[119]

The Mughal patrimonial-bureaucratic empire was a significant step up in centralization from ancient and early medieval India's state structures. How-ever, it was based upon the authority of the emperor's person and not the state. As a result, it could not make the transition to the modern state, as was the case in contemporary Europe. There the "military revolution," the massive increase in armies' firepower made effective by intensive drilling of infantry and refined tactics, resulted in the enhancement of centralized power, as the massive costs and organizational efforts to deploy and main-tain vast standing armies spurred centralization. But this military revolution could not have been possible without a corresponding "bureaucratic revolu-tion." As Bruce Porter notes, on average the size of central state bureaucracies probably quadrupled during this period (1559–1660).[120] Rationalized civilian bureaucracies sprang up to manage the immense problems of military pro-duction and supply. These professional and permanent bureaucracies were independent of the royal household and became a force for political central-ization in their own right.

A military or a bureaucratic revolution did not occur in the Mughal Empire.

The Mughal introduction of massed artillery had a great impact on the Indian battlefield, but it did not lead to an increase in the firepower or the effectiveness of the infantry. The cavalry continued to dominate the infantry. Without any significant military innovation, the Mughals could not monopolize and, as a consequence, demilitarize the subcontinent. As Muzaffar Alam points out, "In a highly differentiated society, the expansion of artisanal production, urban development and the regions' integration into a wider network in the seventeenth century was to the upper strata of local communities. The strength acquired following the prosperity of their regions enabled them to challenge the Mughal claims in the face of declining imperial authority. They were now rich enough to afford the weapons and the provisions necessary to wage a long war against the Mughals."[121]

The Mughal army became one of many competing military powers in India, albeit the largest one. The Mughal army itself was decentralized, for with the exception of the small imperial army, the armies were loyal to their mansabdars rather than to the emperor or the Mughal state. As a consequence, the armies' contributions to the centralized state were nullified. Similarly, the patrimonial bureaucracy encouraged decentralization as the bonds between the ruler and the subordinate continued to weaken over time in spite of the ruler's best efforts.

The Mughal state's failure to monopolize military power on the subcontinent meant that vast groups of armed peasants operated independently of imperial control. Dirk Kloff suggests that the prospect of service with various armies attracted millions of farmers, Mughal or other, for reasons of social mobility and because they were the state's rivals rather than its subjects.[122] Statistical comparisons with European armies also suggests that limited Mughal control of the vast Indian military labor market hampered its efforts at centralization. Stephen Rosen's calculations show that even the most conservative figures for Indian soldiers per capita are at least as high as those for Europe at the end of the Thirty Years' War (1650), that is, 550,000, or 0.5 percent of a population of some 105 million (Europe west of the Urals, including Scandinavia, Britain, European Russia, Spain, and the Balkans). He also states that the actual numbers may be closer to ten times the incidence of soldiers per capita in Europe during that war. Furthermore, in sharp contrast to European states, the Mughals controlled only a small proportion of the total military forces in India. The *Ain-i-Akbari* gives the empire's total number of soldiers in the 1590s as 4.4 million, which includes local militia, consisting mainly of foot soldiers outside of Mughal control. This represents 3 percent of an estimated population of 135 million in 1600. The Mughal numbers do not mention the forces fighting for the Marathas, the

Deccan sultanates, and the Rajput clans opposed to the Mughals. With them included Rosen notes that 4 percent of the population was engaged in local warfare.[123] Without the resources to maintain a competitive military force, let alone the ability to control a growing regional military labor market, the once-mighty Mughal imperial army became just another small contender in the forthcoming struggle for political power in the subcontinent.

Part Two

CHAPTER 3

The Marathas at Panipat

After a series of increasingly ineffective campaigns to suppress the Marathas, Aurungzeb died in February 1707 in Ahmednagar while the very Maratha armies he had tried to eliminate besieged the city. His son, who replaced him, was followed quickly by a succession of extremely incompetent rulers, while intense feuding occurred within the imperial court. With its center paralyzed and unable to command the loyalties of its mansabdars, the Mughal Empire began to break up. Aurungzeb might have taken comfort in the fact that his rivals in the south, the Marathas, fared little better after Shivaji's death. The latter's son, Shambaji, had taken over the crown after a brief power struggle following his father's death, but Aurungzeb captured him and put him to death in 1689. In 1707, when his son Shahu, a captive of the Mughals, was released to create dissension among the Marathas, the stratagem worked. Shivaji's younger son, Rajaram, ruled the Marathas until his death in 1700, after which his wife, Tarabai, took control. Although she opposed Shahu's succession, he was crowned king in 1708 after a brief civil war during which he succeeded in driving Tarabai and her supporters south of the river Krishna, leaving Shahu in control of the northern territories.[1]

During Shahu's struggles, Balaji Vishwanath, a Chitpavan Brahmin from the Konkan, greatly assisted and advised him. A grateful Shahu appointed Balaji as his peshwa, or chief minister, in 1713. Balaji thus became the first of many Chitpavan Brahmins who as peshwas became indispensable to Shahu in running the Maratha Empire. With the passage of time, the Chitpavan elite, which monopolized the hereditary office of the peshwa, became the true architects of a mighty Maratha Empire that dominated much of northern India. The Maratha kings became titular figureheads with no real power. Yet even as Balaji aided Shahu to the throne, he ultimately laid the groundwork for the increased independence of a new generation of Maratha military leaders, or sirdars. Shivaji had paid his officers in cash and abolished the system of land grants, or jagirs. However, Rajaram had reversed this policy, and his wife, Tarabai, utilized the jagir system to garner support for her cause. When Shahu took over Balaji advised him to expand the jagir system. Under Balaji's direction the jagirs were even made hereditary. The system's main beneficiaries were the new sirdars, who derived their power not from the traditional title of deshmuk, or district representative, but from the number and quality of troops they maintained under their personal banners. As the Maratha territories expanded under the peshwa's direction, so too did these military leaders' power and prestige. Although the peshwa maintained a strong army, he could not control the independent aspirations and activities of the sirdars as they gradually gained control over tax collection.[2] After Shahu's death in 1749 these chieftains became virtually independent rulers. The leading sirdars established their own subinfeudatory domains, thus making the Maratha Empire a loose confederacy of fiefdoms under the nominal direction of a central power now completely in the hands of the peshwa.

The post-Aurungzeb Mughal Empire's self-destructive tendencies greatly facilitated the rise of Maratha hegemony in northern India. Because Peshwa Balaji Vishwanath was certain of the imminent collapse of the Mughal Empire he tried to consolidate Maratha power in the wake of its demise. In the absence of a strong and capable successor to Emperor Aurungzeb the imperial court in Delhi dissolved into self-serving cliques dependent on the support and recognition of the regional viceroys, who by now had the Mughal Empire's only viable military forces. Not surprisingly, one by one these viceroys began to assert their independence from Delhi.[3]

The Marathas, of course, were deeply embroiled in the breakup of the empire.[4] Peshwa Balaji Vishwanath died on 2 April 1720, and Shahu appointed Balaji's young son, Bajirao, as his successor.[5] Under his guidance the Marathas launched a series of military campaigns to secure more territory and taxes. During these campaigns Bajirao subdued the nizam of Hyderabad (formerly a Mughal viceroy) and forced upon him a favorable treaty for the Marathas in 1719.[6] In 1735 the Marathas surrounded Emperor Muhammad Shah's Mughal army and forced him to pay chauth, or tax, for the Malwa region. Additional campaigns to collect chauth from the Mughal emperor continued until 1737, with Delhi practically coming under Maratha siege.[7] Bajirao died in April 1740, and his son Bajirao II, better known as Nana Saheb, succeeded him.[8] Like his predecessors Nana Saheb continued to profit from the hostility between the new nizam of Hyderabad (Nasir Jung, son of Nizam-ul-Mulk) and Delhi. He also meddled in and contributed to the infighting in Delhi between the emperor, Ahmad Shah, and his wazir, or chief minister, Safdar Jang. The intrigues climaxed when a Maratha army occupied Delhi for much of 1754 and assisted (maybe even directed) an internal coup that deposed Ahmad Shah and placed the prime minister, Imad-ul-Mulk, upon the throne.[9]

The Marathas were not only intimately involved in the Mughals' affairs, they were also embroiled in the internal feuding of the Rajput clans. With the collapse of the Mughal Empire internal dissension and rivalries amongst the Rajput clans and families reached new heights. Because the Marathas were the predominant military power, the Rajputs frequently sought them as allies in the innumerable power struggles in Rajputana. Between 1733 and 1759 the Rajput kingdoms of Jaipur, Jodhpur, Bundi, and Udaipur closely involved the Marathas in their internal conflicts. At the same time, the Marathas fought the Jats, who inhabited the Indus valley across the Punjab to the river Ganga in the east and Gwalior to the south. They also took on the Afghan settlers, known as Rohillas, of the Roh region, an area covering parts of Afghanistan and northwestern India.[10] Despite the occasional defeat, the Maratha armies dominated their opponents, frequently by sheer force of numbers.

Maratha Warfare and State Formation

The rise of the Marathas' military power coincided with the development of the Maratha state. Indeed, by the 1730s the peshwa's armies had openly confronted and defeated the Mughal armies. As the embattled Mughal court ceded more and more territories to the Marathas the latter had to devise more efficient and permanent means to extract revenue from the areas under their control. At the regional level the Marathas divided their territories into subahs, or provinces, like the Mughals before them. The subahs were usually assigned as land grants to pay the cost of troop maintenance (saranjams) for military service to various Maratha sirdars. Rajaram, who succeeded Shivaji's son Shambaji in 1689, first introduced the land grants. Shahu continued this practice of granting saranjams. In theory they could be transferred or confiscated at the discretion of the peshwa, and Peshwa Balaji Bajirao reportedly used military force to confiscate Sirdar Damaji Giakwad's land grants. Generally, the sirdars viewed the land grants as their patrimony, and they jealously guarded them against the encroachment of the peshwa.[11]

Below the subahs, the next level of administration was the pargana, or district, level. Here the main revenue official was the kamavisdar, who collected revenue. The primary tax collected was khandani, or tribute payment, which could be collected for a few years or in perpetuity. The rate of tribute was based on the individual power of the zamindars, or revenue collectors, rather than on the potential of the land. The peshwa specified in a contract the number of troops a kamavisdar could recruit and maintain. In addition, an auditor, or *mazumdar*, reported directly to the peshwa and regularly examined the kamavisdar's books as well as the troops and garrison stocks.[12]

By 1745 the Marathas had established an administration system similar to the Mughal system it replaced. The extent to which the peshwa adopted and modified the Mughal Empire's patrimonial bureaucracy to his own needs can be judged by the Mughal terms of reference used in the interaction between the Marathas and their conquered subjects. Taxes were called by Mughal terms, assessed in Mughal manner, and paid in customary Mughal months. Maratha revenue demands never exceeded the preexisting Mughal settlement. Furthermore, when the Marathas gave replacement sanads to zamindars, they described their duties and responsibilities in Mughal terms. Finally, the Marathas' apparatus of law and order – the courts and the rural and urban police – reflected that of their Mughal predecessors in both terminology and function. Differences were small but significant. The Marathas did not have a system of ranking and a hierarchy like the mansabdari system. The military and civilian leadership was strictly divided between non-Brahmins and Brahmins. Also unlike that of the Mughals, Maratha power was not concentrated in *sarkars*, or government towns. Finally, Maratha influence shifted urban and commercial development in favor of Maratha-settled towns such as Indore and Gwalior. Financial networks shifted from Agra, the Mughal capital, to Poona, the peshwa's capital. New bankers, many of them Deccani Brahmins, moved the revenue south rather than north. Trade routes were similarly diverted to Poona and Bombay.[13] As Maratha administration increased in its scope and complexity, the aggregate *jama*, or revenue contract, multiplied rapidly. At its peak in 1755–57, the revenue of 3.3 million rupees from Malwa was surprisingly close to the comparable Mughal revenue of 5 million rupees for 1700. The total revenue from all twenty-two subahs actually increased from 300 million rupees in Shivaji's and Aurungzeb's days to about 500 million rupees by 1789.[14]

Skirmishes

It was during this tumultuous period when northern India existed in a power vacuum, caught between a dying Mughal Empire and a rising Maratha Empire, that Persia's ruler, Nadir Shah, invaded.[15] He easily defeated Muhammad Shah's forces in 1739 and left India with substantial booty. During the raid the Marathas engaged in a campaign against the Portuguese at Bassien, taking the port city on 12 May 1739, by which time Nadir Shah had left northern India. Almost ten years later Ahmad Shah Durrani, one of Nadir Shah's generals, now the ruler of Afghanistan, invaded India.[16] Once again the Persians easily defeated the pitiful Mughal forces, and Durrani raided northern India at will. He had annexed Punjab, Kashmir, Lahore, Multan, and Sarhind by 1757 and also exacted tribute from Delhi. At this point the Mughal emperor called on the Marathas for help. At that time the only Maratha force in the region was a small contingent of 3,400 men (probably all cavalry) under Antaji Mankeshwar, and the superior Afghan forces defeated them at Narela some 16 miles from Delhi on 16 January 1757. In early March Durrani sacked the holy cities of Brindaban and Mathura, slaughtering the hapless population. According to a Muslim who survived the sack of Mathura, the Yamuna River was stained with blood for more than two weeks. In fact, after the massacre at Brindaban a dam of human bodies blocked the Yamuna River. So great was the carnage that cholera broke out in the Afghan camp located at Mahaban some 13 miles downstream. With about 150 of his men dying daily, Ahmad Shah Durrani decided to return to Afghanistan.[17]

The Marathas reacted to this setback in the north slowly and deliberately. By March 1758 a Maratha Grand Army under Raghunathrao, the peshwa's younger brother, and Malharao Holkar, an influential sirdar, had invaded Afghan-controlled Punjab. In Punjab the Sikhs were in open revolt against Afghan authority and had defeated the governor, Jahan Khan, by February 1758. The Marathas attacked soon after and, with some help from the Sikhs, managed to capture Attock, Peshawar, and Multan between April and May 1758.[18] Ahmad Shah Durrani reacted swiftly. In September 1759 he left Kandahar with a strong army, swept Maratha garrisons out of the northwest region near Afghanistan and the Punjab, and crossed the Indus on 25 October.[19] In India the trans-Ganga Rohilla chiefs joined him.

Dattaji Sindhia led the first Maratha force to meet Durrani, an advance guard that he defeated at Tararoi on 24 December 1759.[20] Dattaji then fell back toward Delhi and tried to stop the Afghans on the dry bed of the Yamuna at Banari Ghat on 9 January 1760.[21] In the ensuing battle Dattaji was killed, and the Maratha force had to flee beyond Delhi.[22] Durrani then plundered and looted Delhi and the adjoining region, brushing off feeble Maratha counterattacks led by Malharao Holkar. The initial clash at Banari Ghat was an ominous portent of future events. The Afghans' superior firepower in the shape of Rohilla (Indo-Afghan) matchlock men repelled repeated charges by the Maratha light cavalry, who were armed with swords and spears.

The death of Dattaji Sindhia, one of the ablest Maratha generals, came as a shock to the peshwa. Up until that time Maratha military prowess had been at its zenith, virtually unchallenged in northern India.[23] Soon after Dattaji's death, Peshwa Nana Saheb directed the victorious Sadashiv Rao Bhau to lead a new Maratha campaign into the north to recover lost ground from the Afghans. The peshwa's seventeen-year-old son, Vishwasrao, who was to be the army's nominal commander, accompanied him. On the Maratha side the stage was set for the historic third battle of Panipat.

With conflict imminent, both the Afghans and the Marathas started to woo the other major powers in India that had watched the conflict from the sidelines. The most powerful northern Indian ruler was Shuja-ud-Daulah, the nawab of Avadh and Allahabad. He controlled the richest and most populous part of the country and had a considerable treasury at his disposal. His powerful army also included thousands (10,000 by some estimates) of semi-naked Gosain (Hindu Nagas) warriors who were fanatically devoted to him and would even kill their fellow Hindus on his behalf.[24] Despite the fact that he was a Shiite of Iranian descent and little liked by the Afghans, who were Sunnis, Durrani persuaded Shuja-ud-Daulah to join the Afghan cause. The next important ruler in northern India was the Jat king Raja Surajmal of Bhuratpur. Although he favored the Marathas, he remained neutral as a result of inept Maratha diplomacy. The Rajputs, the only other significant military power in northern India in any position to aid the Marathas, also stayed neutral.[25] The Marathas entered into a major confrontation without allies to support them.

The Maratha Military Organization on the Eve of Panipat

The Maratha Grand Army that took the field at Panipat was very different from Shivaji's armies. To begin with, its sheer size alone set it apart from the comparatively smaller forces fielded by Shivaji. Furthermore, the peshwa's army was a combination of several independent forces and not the united organization that Shivaji had welded. Although Sadashiv Rao Bhau, the peshwa's appointed commander, led the army, the force included several independent contingents under the control of their respective sirdars. The political fissures that made up the Maratha Empire reflected themselves in the Maratha Grand Army at third Panipat.

Another big difference between the two Maratha armies at Panipat was the Maratha infantry's tremendous decline under the peshwas. Shivaji's fleet-footed Mawali (from the Mawal region) light infantry quickly vanished after his death. In the list of the military saranjams there is no mention of infantry (*pavlok* or *payade*) at all. A British observer noted that very few Marathas took to the field as infantry.[26] Although these observations come after the battle of Panipat, they do reflect the Maratha armies' composition prior to and during the conflict. The Maratha move toward large cavalry forces is not surprising. First, as Maratha power and influence in northern India expanded the Marathas gradually controlled and absorbed the traditional horse trade in India. Second, given the long-distance campaigns undertaken by the Marathas, it comes as no surprise that they preferred cavalry. Finally, the overwhelming prestige and status a cavalryman enjoyed over his infantry counterpart probably induced most Maratha soldiers to acquire horses.

Despite this overwhelming reliance on cavalry, the peshwa did not altogether abandon the infantry. Indeed, the example of European-style infantry in the neighboring state of Hyderabad most impressed him. It was the nizam's call for French military aid that prompted Nana Saheb to investigate European military organization. Convinced of its worth, the peshwa in 1752 brought into his service Muzaffar Khan, a *gardi* officer whom the French general Charles de Bussy, in the service of the nizam, had trained.[27] Nana Saheb probably established a few infantry units trained along European lines. Evidence exists of increased recruitment of Sikhs, Arabs, Abyssinians, Siddis, and other non-Marathas to build up the infantry during the reigns of his successors.[28]

The gardi infantry were trained and equipped to fight along European lines, and the peshwa armed them with muskets and the paraphernalia to carry the balls and powder. The introduction of these troops marks the Marathas' first definite move to keep abreast of European contemporary battle tactics and weaponry as practiced by the French, who were starting increasingly to flex their military muscles in India. Indeed, the gardi troopers' performance in the battle of Udgir on 2–3 February 1760 against the nizam of Hyderabad had justified the peshwa's confidence in them.[29] The peshwa's gardi force, although small in number, was a significant military innovation for an Indian state. For the first time an Indian ruler had a military capability that was significantly greater than that of his subordinates or enemies on the subcontinent.[30] Indeed, the peshwa's new model infantry force preceded by almost half a century the Ottoman sultans' establishment of a similar unit.[31]

The establishment of a gardi corps required tremendous fiscal reform. They had to be paid regularly, since they were professional soldiers. The increased costs of pay, military equipment, and administration of this new force placed a great strain on the peshwa's government. Revenue extraction through the patrimonial bureaucratic institution proved to be inadequate for the task at hand. Between 1752 and 1760 the gardi corps witnessed only a moderate expansion, to 9,000 men. In contrast, the centralized Ottoman state increased its Nizam-i Cedid force from 2,536 men in 1797 to 9,000 men in 1801 and to 25,000 by 1807.[32]

The gardis received preferential treatment from the peshwa and usually received pay on a regular basis from the peshwa's treasury. The peshwa diaries give us some indication of the payment system. In 1758 the peshwa fixed the gardis' wages for a service period of a month and a half. The government supplied the soldiers with ammunition for their matchlocks and gave them carts in which to carry their wounded. The latter privilege signified the importance and special nature of their close combat tactics.[33] This special treatment earned them the resentment of the Maratha cavalry, who rarely received regular pay from the peshwa and never during campaign, the expectation being that they would live off the booty acquired during raids, although the peshwa's own *huzurat*, or household cavalry, was probably an exception to this rule. The Maratha cavalry often contemptuously referred to the gardis as *topeewallahs*, or cap wearers, because of their distinctive headgear.

In contrast, during the era of the peshwa, the cavalry formed the core of the Maratha armies and was divided into two types. The largest contingent was the saranjami cavalry, which the sirdars raised with their saranjam land grants. The second type was the *italakhi* cavalry, who received pay directly from either the peshwa or the sirdar.[34] There were four classes of cavalry, the *khasgi pagga, silhedars, ekas,* and *pendharis.* However, the quality of these categories differed substantially. Highest in status were the khasgi pagga, the peshwa's household cavalry (they fell into the italakhi category), who were probably the best cavalry in India at the time. However, their elite status also meant that they were few in number compared to the sirdars' massive formations of silhedars and ekas. According to Kashi Raj Shivdev Pundit, an eyewitness of the third Panipat battle, their strength was 6,000 out of the peshwa's force of 38,000 soldiers.[35] The last category, the pendharis, were little more than camp followers utilized mainly to loot and raid enemy camps and territories. The cavalry's equipment differed little from Shivaji's time.[36] Although the peshwa could easily acquire firearms, a British observer noted that the Maratha cavalrymen were adept at fighting with swords.[37]

Artillery continued to remain the Maratha military's weakest arm. Unlike Shivaji, the peshwas extensively used artillery in their campaigns. Although Bajirao had his own gun foundry, he imported considerable cannon, shot, and powder from various foreign sources.[38] His successor, Peshwa Madhavrao I, established a cannon factory at Ambegavan, near Votus, and at Poona. However, Maratha foundries produced guns of inferior quality. According to a British observer, "A few days' march shakes the [gun] carriage to pieces." He goes on: "The cannon are never made to any precise caliber, but are cast indifferently by all diameters and the ball afterwards adapted to the bore."[39] The Marathas used local iron smiths to cast their cannons. Because their techniques were inferior, the guns often exploded when fired.[40] Also, the guns and gun carriages were heavy, bulky, and extremely difficult to move;

often, a hundred or more draft animals were required to move just one gun.[41] Initially, Portuguese and Indian Christians manned the peshwa's artillery, but by Panipat gardi officers and men had replaced them.

Panipat, 1760

Sadashiv Rao Bhau left the town of Patdur (north of Udgir) on 14 March 1760 with an immense army. This moving city, complete with soldiers' families and traders, had more in common with the traditional Mughal imperial armies than with Shivaji's swift and lightly loaded armies.

According to James Grant Duff,

> the appearance of this army was more splendid in appearance than any Maratha force that ever took the field. The camp equipage, which, in the former expensive campaign had been brought back from Hindustan by Raghunath Rao, was employed as part of the decoration. The lofty spacious tents, lined with silks and broadcloths, were surmounted by large gilded ornaments, conspicuous at a great distance; immense parti-colored walls of canvas enclosed each suit of tents belonging to the principal officers; vast numbers of elephants, flags of all descriptions, the finest horses magnificently caparisoned, and all those accompaniments of an Indian army which give such an imposing effect to its appearance, seemed to be collected from every quarter in Bhow's camp. Cloth of gold was the dress of the officers, and all seemed to vie in that profuse and gorgeous display characteristic of wealth lightly acquired. It was, in this instance, an imitation of the more becoming and tasteful array of the magnificent Moghuls in the zenith of their glory.[42]

Although the Marathas still had excellent light cavalry, concern about protecting the many slow-moving camp followers seriously limited their overall mobility. The army's slow progress can be judged by the fact that only on 1 August did Bhau recapture Delhi from a small Afghan garrison.[43] At about the same time, the Afghans' Indian allies, mainly the Rohillas, moved onto the banks of the Yamuna opposite Delhi, where Ahmad Shah Durrani and his army joined them between 5 and 6 October. Bhau stayed in Delhi from 22 July to 10 October 1760. He quickly discovered that his food and fodder supply was running low, as the fertile Doab, from where such provisions normally came into Delhi, was now in Afghan hands. To add to his problems, Bhau found himself running short of money, as the kamavisdars did not send money to him in the city. Nor could he borrow cash, as the traditional moneylending family, the Ranagades, had fled Delhi. By August the letters from Delhi to the peshwa had an increasing note of desperation, describing both men and horses on the verge of starvation. In a letter to the peshwa on 15 September 1760 Bhau noted that there was no time to forage or raid for money and supplies, as the start of the big battle was fast approaching.[44]

With the peace negotiations going nowhere, Bhau struck first. He discovered that one of Durrani's officers, Abdus Samad Khan, had arrived at the fort of Kunjpara, 93 miles north of Delhi on the west bank of the Yamuna, with vast amounts of supplies for the Afghans and was waiting to cross the Yamuna when it subsided. Bhau left Delhi on the 10th, had surrounded the fort by the 16th, and stormed it on 17 October 1760. His gardi troops under Ibrahim Khan devastated the Afghan cavalry, which tried to support the garrison with controlled musket fire. Along with the garrison, many supplies fell into Bhau's hands.[45] Bhau's bold maneuver, reminiscent of Shivaji's lightning raids, enabled the Maratha army to replenish temporarily its rapidly diminishing supplies. Before Bhau could return to Delhi with his vast camp, however, Durrani crossed the Yamuna and blocked his way. Both armies then moved on to the plain surrounding Panipat. The Marathas occupied the town itself on 29 October, while the Afghans set up camp some distance away on 1 November. Both armies then remained stationary for more than two months. In this game of wait and see, the Marathas came off the worst. Their vast camp could not sustain itself for such a long period without extreme hardship. Local rulers, who normally feared the Marathas, did not offer support. The Afghans, on the other hand, thanks to the support of their Indian brethren, the Rohillas, managed to establish relatively secure supply routes to their forces. The attempt by a Maratha chieftain, Govindpant Bundele, to cut off Durrani's supplies eventually ended in defeat when an Afghan cavalry force surprised and killed Govindpant and most of his troopers.[46] Govindpant's mission had been central to Bhau's plan to cut off and starve out the Afghans instead of directly confronting them.[47] In the wake of this disaster the Afghans slaughtered some 20,000 Maratha camp followers when they left the shelter of the camp to forage for desperately needed food.[48] Until the last moment both sides tried to conclude a treaty rather than fight, with the Marathas being most flexible. According to Kashi Raj, Bhau had sent a letter to him through Bhau's secretary, Ganesh Pundit, on the eve of battle stating his willingness to submit to any conditions that would preserve his army.[49] While the Afghans argued at length over whether to accept or refuse the proposal, Bhau decided to attack on 14 January 1761.

Out of a total population of 300,000 (some estimates say 800,000) in the village of Panipat, only some 50,000 were soldiers. Out of this number, 8,000–9,000 were gardi infantry under Ibrahim Khan, while the remaining force was cavalry. The Marathas also had some 200 cannons ranging from heavy fieldpieces to light camel- or elephant-mounted zambaruks, or swivel guns.[50] The Afghans and their Indian allies had about 41,800 cavalry and about 38,000 infantry, mostly Rohilla matchlock men under the Indo-Afghan chief Najib-ud-Daulah, who had invited the Afghans into India to confront the Marathas.[51] The Rohillas were equipped mainly with matchlocks, which, although heavier and with a slower rate of fire than the Maratha gardis' muskets, nevertheless fired a heavier ball to a greater distance.[52] The Afghans had fewer heavy artillery pieces than the Marathas but had an overwhelming superiority in the camel-mounted swivel guns.

The Maratha deployment was as follows. The Marathas located their left flank, which consisted mainly of Ibrahim Khan's gardis (8,000–9,000 men) lined up behind the heavy artillery, in the village of Nimbdi to the southwest of Panipat. Damaji Giakwad's and Vithal Shivdeo's light cavalry and other smaller contingents (4,000–5,000) supported him. In the center stood Bhau and Vishwasrao together with the peshwa's household cavalry, the dreaded huzurat (about 10,000). To the right and almost touching the Panipat camp stood the Maratha cavalry's main mass (approximately 18,000) under the sirdars – Antaji Mankeshwar, Yaswantrao Pawar, Jankoji Sindhia, Malharao Holkar, and other minor captains. The commanders placed the light artillery in front of this wing.[53] All the camp followers remained behind the battle line, mainly to the rear of the right wing.

The Afghan battle array took a crescent shape whose right wing faced the Maratha left wing. This wing consisted mainly of Rohilla matchlock men, numbering approximately 14,000, under Hafiz Rahmat Khan and Dunde Khan. Approximately 4,000 infantry and cavalry under Barkhurdar Khan and Amir Beg supported them. In the center stood Shah Vali Khan with 15,000 cavalry, about 1,000 Kabuli (from Kabul) infantry, and up to 2,000 camel guns.[54] On the Afghan left wing, which faced the Maratha right wing, stood Najib-ud-Daulah with 15,000 infantry and dismounted cavalry, Shah Pasand Khan with 5,000 Persian horse, and Shuja-ud-Daulah with some 3,000 horse and infantry. The Afghan left and the Maratha right stood approximately 3 miles away from each other, much farther than the other opposing wings. Ahmad Shah Durrani stood behind his battle line with his elite slave cavalry, the bashgulls, numbering some 6,000, of which 3,000 stayed in reserve in the camp.[55]

The battle began at about 9:00 AM with an ineffectual Maratha artillery bombardment, after which Ibrahim Khan ordered his infantry to move forward and engage Hafiz Rahmat Khan's and Dunde Khan's Rohilla matchlock men. As soon as the gardi advanced in front of them, the Maratha heavy guns fell silent and took no further part in the battle. The well-trained gardi infantry had an immediate effect. Their controlled volleys decimated the Rohillas' front ranks and began to force them back. In the meantime, the Maratha cavalry, supporting Ibrahim Khan, tried to charge the Rohillas but were repulsed by heavy fire. Nevertheless, Ibrahim Khan continued to fire and move, and the Rohillas, suffering tremendously under this barrage, began to waver and flee to the rear. Meanwhile, in the center Bhau and the huzurat launched a fierce cavalry assault on the Afghan center, yelling their famous war cry "Har! Har! Mahadev!" [Hurrah! Hurrah! Great God!]. Despite being subjected to a punishing hail of defensive fire from the camel-mounted zambaruks and the Kabuli infantry, the huzurat closed in with their spears and swords. The charge of the Maratha light cavalry, especially that of the elite huzurat, was so swift and spontaneous that it could be likened to the sudden movement of a shoal of fish; the cavalry, with its glittering array of spears and swords, moved as one body rather than in a gradually rapid advance from front to back. The Afghan cavalry could not react fast enough and was almost stationary when the huzurat hit it. Thousands of Afghans died in this attack. From the center Afghan units began to panic and retreat, at which point Ahmad Shah moved in his *nasaqchis*, or military provosts, to round up the fleeing soldiers and reinsert them into the battle. The embattled Hafiz Rahmat also received an infusion of 7,000 men, while the Afghan center received an additional 4,000 men. This timely reinforcement immediately stabilized the Afghan right wing, which now began to exchange fire with Ibrahim Khan's much-depleted gardi infantry. The Maratha cavalry on this flank, after its initial repulse, did not intervene as the Rohilla infantry's superior numbers gradually annihilated the gardi infantry.

In the center, a desperate struggle continued until 1:00 PM, at which point the peshwa's son, Vishwasrao, was killed, either struck by a zambaruk ball or wounded by a sword and an arrow. The news of his death spread like wildfire through the Maratha ranks, and Bhau himself was distraught. At this vital moment Ahmad Shah fortuitously threw his elite slave cavalry, the bashgulls, into the fray along with an additional 1,000 camel guns. The course of the battle now turned decisively in the Afghans' favor.

The battle on the Afghans' right flank and the Marathas' left took longer to develop, as a distance of about 3 miles separated them. Najib-ud-Daulah and his Rohillas on this flank advanced by throwing up earthen breastworks at intervals as they approached to within matchlock range of the Maratha cavalry. Rockets fired into the cavalry's massed ranks created tremendous confusion among the Marathas. The two sides clashed at about the same time as Vishwasrao fell. Najib-ud-Daulah drove a wedge between Jankoji's cavalry and the Maratha center under Bhau. At this critical juncture the Maratha cavalry under Malharao Holkar fled the battlefield.[56] The remnants collapsed into the Maratha center, which the Afghans completely encircled.

The Maratha left wing had by this time been completely eliminated. The Afghans wiped out to a man the gardi infantry and captured their commander, Ibrahim Khan. The Maratha cavalry's left flank had followed the right flank in flight. The Afghan right wing now began to turn to the Maratha left flank or, rather, to complete the encirclement of the Maratha center. Undaunted, Bhau continued to make desperate charges with the depleting huzurat. Ahmad Shah, sensing victory, threw in the remainder of his bashgull cavalry. Surrounded on all sides and spurning all entreaties from his lieutenants to flee, Bhau fought to the last with the huzurat. By 3:00 PM the battle was over, and the great slaughter of the fugitive Marathas, especially the hapless camp followers, began. Even conservative estimates of the Maratha casualties state that 30,000 soldiers died. The numbers among the camp followers, who did not have any horses upon which to flee, can only be imagined.[57] The peshwa, who was crossing the Narmada River in mid-January on his way into Hindustan with reinforcements, received news of the disaster in an eloquently coded message: "Two pearls [Bhau and Vishwasrao] have been dissolved, twenty-seven gold-mohurs [Jankoji and other slain sirdars] have been lost, and of the silver and the copper [soldiers and camp followers] the total cannot be cast up."[58] The peshwa, who was devastated, never recovered from the shock, dying within months of his return to Poona. The entire region was plunged into despondency, as every military family had lost at least one member at Panipat.[59]

Panipat represents a remarkable contrast in the command and control abilities of the opposing leaders. On the one hand, Ahmad Shah Durrani had a remarkable degree of control over his forces as he stood to the rear of his battle line, probably mounted on a camel or an elephant. As his right wing and then center began to crumble, he could direct the roundup of deserters and reinsert them into the line. He then ensured that all fronts maintained constant pressure on the Marathas. His subordinates, including his Indian allies, faithfully carried out his orders. Bhau, in contrast, lost control of the battle the moment it began. While the gardi forces went ahead as planned, Bhau could not ensure that the light cavalry under Vithal Shivdeo would maintain formation with the slow-moving infantry and support them. On his right, Bhau had no control of the cavalry under Jankoji Sindhia and Malharao Holkar. At no point in the battle did either captain choose to engage the advancing Rohillas under Najib-ud-Daulah. The moment they came under matchlock fire, and probably coinciding with Vishwasrao's death, they fled the battlefield.

In reality, the Maratha army at third Panipat was an imperfect alliance of two distinctive forces. The first was the peshwa's force under Bhau's own command, the gardi infantry, and the huzurat cavalry. The second was the numerous contingents of Maratha sirdars, the largest under the command of Holkar and Jankoji. These cavalry units were similar to those maintained by Shivaji, being light and highly mobile, designed to strike the enemy on the move, to take him by surprise, or even strike when he was wavering under artillery fire. Such cavalry could not face well-organized infantry armed with muskets or matchlocks and with substantial artillery support. The peshwa's infantry, on the other hand, was designed just for this task. His household cavalry, the huzurat, although still light cavalry, was far more disciplined, but its chief deficiency was its small size.[60] There is little doubt that Bhau, like the peshwa, was a convert to European-style, infantry-dominated battles, particularly after the battle of Udgir. He placed great faith in Ibrahim Khan, and it was the latter who laid out the tactical plans during the campaign, first at the battle of Kunjpara and then at Panipat itself. Their reliance upon Ibrahim Khan caused resentment among the Maratha sirdars, who perceived themselves to be sidelined during the campaign. The highly centralized and professional gardi corps was vastly superior to the militia and mercenary levies of the Maratha sirdars. They could not help but notice the increasing reliance that the peshwa placed upon this force. Its very presence represented the implicit if unarticulated threat of domineering force that the peshwa held over them. Not surprisingly, throughout the Panipat campaign the sirdars expressed distrust and contempt for the gardi corps.

A defeat at Afghan hands at Banari Ghat and in the engagement just before Panipat also demoralized the sirdars. Even the Maratha hit-and-run tactics had little effect on the Afghans. Afghan cavalry, mounted on superior horses, hunted down and killed Govindpant Bundele, who was engaged in just such a campaign in the rear of the Afghan position prior to the main battle. The Maratha sirdars' lack of confidence in Bhau's battle plans and the belief that their cavalry could not match the Afghan cavalry resulted in the most important sirdars deserting halfway through the battle.

Ahmad Shah Durrani faced no such problem with his united forces, including those of his Indian allies, which had adapted to fight a battle dominated by firearms. In addition to Rohilla and Kabuli infantry armed with matchlocks, the cavalry was armed with pistols and muskets, and many cavalrymen fought dismounted. This large infantry force, combined with several thousand mobile camel guns, enabled Ahmad Shah to wipe out the peshwa's small though superbly trained gardi infantry and the huzurat cavalry by the sheer weight of numbers. Panipat was essentially a battle of firepower. The

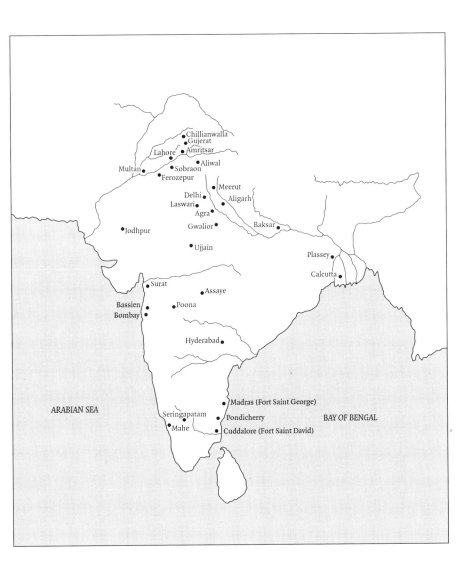

Chillianwalla
Gujerat
Lahore • Amritsar
Aliwal
Multan
Sobraon
Ferozepur
Meerut
Delhi
Aligarh
Laswari
Agra
Jodhpur
Gwalior
Baksar
Ujjain
Plassey
Calcutta
Surat
Assaye
Bassien
Poona
Bombay
Hyderabad
ARABIAN SEA
Seringapatam
Madras (Fort Saint George)
Pondicherry
BAY OF BENGAL
Mahe
Cuddalore (Fort Saint David)

Political map of South Asia 1760–1850

side with greater firepower, the Afghans, won the day. This battle ended the cavalry's dominance over the infantry on an Indian battlefield. Long the underdog, the infantry, in the shape of the Rohilla matchlock men and the peshwa's gardis, had finally become a force with which to be reckoned. As they fled the battlefield, the surviving Maratha sirdars, including Holkar and Jankoji, carried with them indelible images of the gardi musketeers and the Rohilla matchlock men who had played such a decisive role in the campaign. In time these sirdars and their successors would become the chief proponents of this new form of warfare, which they at one time had so bitterly opposed.

Despite the devastating losses suffered at Panipat, the Marathas recovered politically and militarily. Soon after the battle Durrani left for Afghanistan, never to return, while the resurgent Marathas subjugated his Afghan allies, the Rohillas.[61] None of the participants experienced Panipat's true impact, except for one rather interested observer – the British. The East India Company had gradually become a substantial political and military power in eastern and southern India. The company had waged successful campaigns against the French and the Muslim rulers of Karnatik (spelled Carnatic by the British) and Bengal with an army composed mainly of sepoys, or British-trained Indian soldiers.[62] Yet for all of their success, they, like the other lesser Indian powers, had respected the Marathas' mighty armies. Panipat had shattered this aura of invincibility, and the British were ready to begin their struggle for empire in India confident of their ability to take on the Maratha confederacy.

CHAPTER 4

Colonial Warfare in Bengal and Mysore

After Aurungzeb's death, the European powers began to compete openly for territory and concessions in India. Although not the first to make their presence felt in the region, by the end of the eighteenth century the British had become the dominant European power in the subcontinent. On 31 December 1600 Queen Elizabeth granted a charter to the "Governor and Company of the Merchants of London trading into the East Indies."[1] The next year a 300-ton-sail ship under Capt. William Hawkins reached Surat, where Hawkins established the company's first Indian factory. From this minuscule beginning the company, better known as the East India Company, began to expand its foothold in India. In 1615 James I sent Sir Thomas Roe as ambassador to Emperor Jahangir in Agra, where he received a firman, or legal document, acknowledging the British presence in Surat.[2] To the south Capt. Anthony Hippon founded a factory in Masulipatam, the port city of the Muslim Deccan kingdom of Golconda, in 1611. However, Dutch pressure forced the British to evacuate it in 1628. They then secured rights from a petty Hindu raja to establish Fort Saint George some 230 miles south of Masulipatam. This post soon developed into the town of Madras and became the base of British operations in southern India.[3] From this fort the British moved into the northeast in 1633, when an expedition established stations at Hariharpur in the Mahanadi delta and Balasore on the boundary between Bengal proper and Orissa.[4]

From the moment they set foot in India in 1612 the British became embroiled in conflicts with the other European powers in India – the Dutch, the French, and the Portuguese. Furthermore, they also fought local powers like the Marathas. Matters came to a head in 1744 with the declaration of war in Europe between England and France. The French, led by the energetic Joseph-François Dupleix, governor-general of all French possessions in India, seized Madras from the British in October 1746, only to return it in 1748 under the terms of the Aix-la-Chapelle treaty.[5] At about the same time the French in India began to focus on local politics. When Nizam-ul-Mulk, former Mughal viceroy of the Deccan and later an independent ruler, died in 1748, the French supported Muzaffar Jang, one of the claimants to the throne, and waged a successful campaign against the challenger, Anwar-ud-Din, the ruler of Karnatik. The French then turned their attention to the second challenger, Nazir Jang, the de facto ruler of the Deccan who had British support, led by Maj. Stringer Lawrence. Muzaffar Jang defeated and killed Nazir Jang, and the French then installed Muzaffar as the ruler of the Deccan in their stronghold of Pondicherry. A grateful Muzaffar Jang bestowed upon the French considerable territories in southern India.[6]

In 1751 the British, by then under the leadership of Robert Clive, struck back by installing their own puppet, Muhammad Ali, as the nawab of Karnatik.[7] Although the French eventually managed to establish a firm presence in the court of Hyderabad, they found themselves on the defensive; Dupleix himself was recalled to France in 1754.[8] But in 1756 the Seven Years' War broke out in Europe, and the French renewed their efforts against the British in India under Thomas-Arthur de Lally, who had been sent to India in 1758. Unfortunately for the French, Lally's campaigns were a series of disasters and blunders. His first mistake was to recall Gen. Charles de Bussy from Hyderabad just when the general had all but taken over this powerful kingdom. On the battlefield Lally suffered constant defeat at British hands, culminating in the disaster at Wandiwash in January 1760. The French navy too made little headway against a smaller British fleet and ultimately let the British capture Pondicherry in January 1761. With the fall of Pondicherry all French hopes for an Indian empire were dashed. The British were now the lone European power in the subcontinent.[9]

While the British fought the French in southern India, they also carried out a protracted campaign in Bengal to expand their territories and influence. Bengal was a province of the Mughal Empire, and an appointed military governor, or faujdar, oversaw its administration. After the fall of the Mughal Empire the governor of Bengal, Ali Vardi Khan, broke away from Delhi's weak control in 1742. He ruled until his death in 1756, after which his son Siraj-ud-Daulah succeeded him. Both father and son maintained extremely rigid control of the Europeans at the trading posts in Bengal. The British, who had the largest presence in the region, resented this control. In 1752 Robert Orme, in a letter to Clive, noted that the company would have to remove Ali Vardi Khan in order to prosper.[10] Under Siraj-ud-Daulah relations were even worse, and finally the nawab decided to expel the British from his domain. After a brief siege the British garrison in Calcutta fell on June 1756. Subsequently, some British prisoners died while being held in the fort. This incident, later propagandized as the infamous "black hole of Calcutta," gave the company the perfect excuse to engage in a protracted campaign against the nawab. Clive was given command of this expedition.

Clive moved out of Madras in October 1756 and by January 1757 had captured Calcutta. A treaty with Siraj-ud-Daulah followed in February in which he restored the British presence in Bengal. The treaty was a stroke of luck for the British, who were now in a fierce conflict with the French. The French, who had a presence in Bengal in Chandranagar, could ally themselves with the nawab at any moment. But the British moved fast; they had forced the French garrison to surrender by March 1757.[11] All this time Siraj-ud-Daulah had hesitated. In January Ahmad Shah Durrani had sacked Delhi, and the nawab, fearing his Afghan brethren more than the British, sought peace with the British. But the British had disposed of the French and were in no mood to compromise. Despite the treaty they wanted to renew the conflict and found an excuse when another member of the nawab's family requested British aid to overthrow Siraj-ud-Daulah and claim the throne for himself. Clive immediately agreed, noting that the "universally hated [nawab] would be overthrown whether we gave our consent or not."[12] Charging the nawab with violation of the February 1757 treaty, Clive moved out of Chandranagar with approximately 3,000 troops and established himself at Plassey (Palashi in Urdu), 23 miles south of Murshidabad, where the nawab was already stationed with 50,000 men.[13]

Despite the overwhelming odds Clive decided to attack because he knew beforehand that Mir Jafar, one of the nawab's commanders, would not fight. In fact, only one of the commanders, Mir Muin-ud-Din, remained loyal to the nawab. Siraj-ud-Daulah himself had only a small contingent of 2,000 soldiers. At the start of the battle, when the British attacked, only Muin-ud-Din's unit moved to challenge them. Although damp gunpowder and devastating British fire hampered his efforts, Muin continued the advance until he was killed. Nevertheless, he managed to force the British to retreat to the mango groves from where they had started their advance. If the nawab's entire army had advanced at the same time, the British might have been crushed, but two other commanders, Yar Lutf Khan and Rai Durlab, along with Mir Jafar, kept their forces out of the fray. At this point the nawab fled the field, and the conspirators later murdered him as he fled Bengal.[14] In due time, Mir Jafar was established as nawab and a British puppet. With total control of Bengal, the British had the foothold they needed to consolidate and expand their gains in India.

The military engagement at Plassey is not particularly notable in military terms; nevertheless, it further reinforced the superiority of the British commanders and soldiers (there were only 1,000 British soldiers at Plassey) over the disorganized Indian forces.

The Establishment of the British Military System in India

Besides securing the British right to establish a trading post in Surat, Sir Thomas Roe's successful visit to Emperor Jahangir in Agra also resulted in permission for British merchants to bear arms.[15] Gradually, the British employed large numbers of local peons, or guards, to protect their factories.[16] As British posts spread to the south and the east, large forts, including Fort William in Calcutta and Fort Saint George in Madras, came into being, and, as a consequence, royal charters granted in 1661 and 1669 allowed the company to enlist soldiers locally.[17] Bengal was the first Presidency to establish its own native forces. Between 1668 and 1683 it created two companies of native soldiers with twenty-one cannons.[18] Bombay followed suit with two Rajput companies. In 1661 400 royal troops were sent to the city for its protection, and Bombay formed the first European regiment in India, the Bombay Fusiliers, in 1668.[19] Madras experienced a similar evolution at a later date. Madras began setting up large military forces only in the eighteenth century during the Anglo-French wars. In 1748 Major Lawrence received command of all of the East India Company's forces in India. He established a Madras European regiment and recruited 2,000 Indian sepoys, which he used only for guard duties.[20] Bombay too began to raise large local forces, recruiting up to 2,000 men in Surat, mainly Arabs and Turks.[21] Bengal followed suit with a force of between five and seven companies. The British also created an artillery company to support each of the Presidency (Bengal, Bombay, and Madras) armies, with Bengal getting the first in 1749.[22]

However, from 1757 to 1767, under Clive's leadership, the company's military organization, beginning with that of the Bengal Presidency, underwent a dramatic expansion and modernization. After the battle of Plassey Clive realized that the local infantry, commanded by Indian officers, was an ill-trained and undisciplined force.[23] He established a regiment of Bengal native infantrymen known as the Lal Paltan (literally, the "red bunch" because of their red uniforms), commanded exclusively by Europeans.[24] In 1761 the Bengal army had 1,200 Europeans and 8,500 sepoys.[25] Madras partially copied this system by using European and local officers to command its nine battalions of sepoys.[26] By 1759 the Madras army consisted of two European battalions, six sepoy battalions, and two artillery companies supported by a regiment of British regulars.[27]

The evolution of the cavalry occurred slowly largely due to shortages and the tremendous costs involved in obtaining good horses. The British controlled only the fringes of the prime horse-trading areas in western and central India and thus relied upon the few horses that trickled down to them after the Marathas, Mughals, and Rajputs had their pick of the best horses. Nevertheless, in 1760 the company financed two troops of dragoons and one of hussars, comprising about 200 men, under Maj. John Caillaud in Bengal.[28] In 1762 the company recruited two risalas, or squadrons, of mainly irregular Mughal cavalry.[29] Madras formed its own regular cavalry in 1784, and by 1788 it had four regiments of Madras native cavalry.[30]

However, Clive's infantry reforms within the Bengal army had the greatest long-term impact upon the Indian army.[31] He established the principle that Europeans exclusively would command local soldiers, a formula the army strictly adhered to until the end of World War I. The "new" army Clive organized met its first real test in 1764 in the battle of Buxar, the Britishers' first act of open military conquest in India.

Buxar, 1764

In the aftermath of the battle of Plassey, the British installed Mir Jafar on the throne of Bengal. Unfortunately for them, this erstwhile puppet soon set about establishing his independence. In 1759 he concluded a treaty with the Dutch when they invaded Bengal with a force from Batavia. The British, however, defeated the Dutch on the Bedara plains on 25 November 1759.[32] The British then replaced Mir Jafar with his son-in-law Mir Kasim as the new nawab in September 1760. But matters only worsened, as the British treated their new puppet ruler in an even more humiliating manner. A Mr. Ellis, the British agent in the state of Patna, seized control of the city of Patna in June 1763 to stifle the nawab's bid for independence. In response, the nawab recaptured the city and put to death the unfortunate Ellis and his English compatriots. The English in Calcutta then reestablished Mir Jafar on the throne, making him nawab once again. At the same time, the company sent out an army under Maj. Thomas Adams to defeat Mir Kasim. Adams quickly took Murshidabad on 23 July. Additional forces joined him there, bringing his strength to 1,000 Europeans and 4,000 sepoys. On 2 August 1763 Adams's army reached the plain of Gheria some distance from Sooty, where Mir Kasim had entrenched himself. However, upon seeing the small size of the British forces, Mir Kasim's army of approximately 30,000 men marched out to give battle. Sumroo, the Indian name of an Alsatian mercenary named Walter Reinhardt, and Marak, an Armenian mercenary, commanded the force.[33] Their regular infantry brigades stood in the center. On their right stood some 8,000 cavalry and 12,000 irregular infantry, while on their left, almost standing in the Bhagirathi River, stood a small body of irregular horse. The British deployed with their European infantry in the center and the sepoys on either flank. As the two sides engaged in an artillery duel, a force of Mir Kasim's cavalry attacked the British left flank, shattering a sepoy battalion and almost wiping it out. Through this gap more cavalry poured in and attacked the European infantry from the rear, seizing two guns. But the British quickly countered, recovered the guns, and launched a charge. The nawab's forces broke under this impetuous assault and fled the field, leaving twenty-three guns and much munition.

Mir Kasim then decided to face the British from a well-fortified position at Oundha Nala, a pass 5 miles south of Rajmahal between the Rajmahal Hills and the Ganges. The pass itself was a mile wide. Within this narrow strip of land Mir Kasim threw up massive earthworks, up to 60 feet thick and 10 feet high. To complicate matters for an attacker, the earthworks were positioned in front of a deep morass. After months of preparation, Adams placed a battery 500 yards from the fortifications and opened fire on 3 September. The bombardment had little effect, and all seemed lost until a European deserter from Kasim's camp showed the British a path through the impenetrable morass that led to the nawab's right flank. On the night of the 4th Adams sent a portion of his army through the morass and captured the stockade, dominating the fortifications. The remaining British forces then followed. Taken completely by surprise, the nawab's army was slaughtered and dispersed. Mir Kasim fled with the survivors to the neighboring kingdom of Avadh (British spelling, Oudh or Audh).[34]

When Mir Kasim's army retreated into Avadh the state's nawab, Shuja-ud-Daulah, agreed to cooperate with Mir Kasim in return for monthly payments and the promise that he could use Mir Kasim's army in time of need. With this agreement signed the two allies marched on to Banaras, where the local raja joined them, and prepared to cross the Ganges in March 1764. After some confusion in their own ranks, the British forces, under the command of Maj. John Carnac, moved out to confront the allies.[35] However, the British army failed to prevent the allied army from crossing the Sone River, and Carnac fell back on Patna on 24 March. Mir Kasim and Shuja-ud-Daulah followed closely and took up positions right against the city's defenses. In Patna Carnac had 19,000 men, including 1,000 Europeans, 12,000 of Mir Jafar's soldiers, and 6,000 sepoys. When the allies learned that additional British forces were on their way they initiated the battle on 3 May 1764. Shuja-ud-Daulah's forces, with little if any support from Mir Kasim's regulars, launched the attack. Despite many concerted attempts, Shuja could not overwhelm the British defenses. On 30 May his forces suddenly broke and fell back on the village of Buxar, but, inexplicably, Carnac did not pursue them.

On 28 June Maj. Hector Munro, who brought fresh troops with him, replaced Carnac. He gave the order to advance on 6 October, and by the 22nd the two armies confronted each other on the Buxar plain. The situation for Mir Kasim had changed rather dramatically in the interim. He had run out of money, his forces had joined Shuja's army, and Shuja had imprisoned him. The joint army, now under Shuja, was joined by about 40,000 men and the raja of Banaras. Shuja deployed this new allied army behind strong entrenchments, with the Ganges River securing the left flank and the Torah Canal securing the right. Munro's army consisted of 1,000 Europeans, including 70 horse (probably scouts), 5,500 sepoys, and 1,000 Mughal cavalry. The British deployed in two lines, with British units in the center and two sepoy battalions on each flank. The cavalry was divided into two divisions; one guarded the baggage (supported by two sepoy companies), while the other, along with a small European force, formed the reserve behind the center and the front line. The commanders deployed the artillery in batteries interspersed among the lines. Shuja, noting the small size of the British army, moved out to meet it. His right flank rested on the banks of the Ganges and occupied the fort and village of Buxar. It consisted of a division led by Beni Bahadur with several infantry battalions led by European officers. A contingent of Shuja's household cavalry, the Sheikzadi (descendants of Muslims who colonized India from the twelfth to the sixteenth centuries), commanded by Sheikh Ghulam Khadar, supported them. In the center were located the trained brigades of Sumroo and Marak, consisting of eight infantry battalions with artillery deployed on either flank and 6,000 irregular cavalry and infantry commanded by Kuli Khan. The raja of Banaras was located on the right flank with a large force of Rohilla horse and foot and some 5,000 Afghan cavalry, many of whom had fought at Panipat in 1761.

The battle commenced with both sides advancing on each other after an artillery bombardment. Shuja's Sheikzadi cavalry attacked and captured the British baggage train, but the British, although suffering heavy losses, repulsed the Afghan cavalry. In the center a ferocious confrontation developed, with Sumroo and Marak's regular battalions standing their ground against the British. Shuja had also deployed a strong force in a grove of trees, and this unit shattered a sepoy battalion, seriously threatening the British advance. But Munro quickly secured the threatened right wing with some first-line European infantry and two additional sepoy battalions and then cleared the grove with their bayonets. At this point, without any orders or warning, Kuli Khan, who was supporting the center, flung himself and his cavalry at the

British left wing. He was quickly killed, and his cavalry were flung back in disorder. This spectacular defeat caused Shuja's line, which up until that time had been standing firm, to retreat. Munro, sensing victory, gave the order for a general advance. Shuja desperately tried to form a new line to the rear, but Beni Bahadur's units were in full flight by this time. The retreat quickly turned into a rout as the defeated army tried to cross the Torah stream.[36]

An examination of the campaigns of Mir Kasim and Shuja-ud-Daulah reveals that Indian armies increasingly relied upon artillery and musket-armed infantry rather than the traditional cavalry, a trend that had been established at Panipat. Significantly, the presence of infantry trained and led by Europeans in Mir Kasim's army indicates that Indian rulers were rapidly utilizing such formations. This practice, which originated with the nizam of Hyderabad, spread to the major Indian powers as they came under increasing British pressure and sought to emulate their highly successful military organization. In spite of these changes, the campaign in Bengal had shown that British infantry, especially the all-European units, were markedly superior to the Indian allies' European-led and -trained units. Despite having a tremendous superiority in artillery, approximately 100 to 28, Shuja's guns had little impact upon the battle due to the poor training of the Indian gunners. The Indian infantry also was poorly trained and was reluctant to close in with bayonets when the British attacked in similar fashion.[37] Indeed, the hallmark of these battles is the tremendous success achieved by even small units of organized European infantry when they advanced with bayonets. The Indians, in contrast, preferred to engage in close individual combat with the tulwar, or curved scimitar, a slashing weapon that created a offensive-defensive slashing zone to their front and sides. The disadvantage of this weapon is that it prevented the Indians from operating in concert and in closely ranked formations, thus considerably diminishing their effect on disciplined European troops. The latter used the shock effect (and flank security) of closed ranks and the longer reach of their pikelike bayonets to sweep the Indians' loose formations from the field. Finally, the bayonet as a stabbing weapon was more likely to create a mortal wound than the slashing sword. The latter, unless it was used by an attacker against an unprotected neck or head, usually left the victim with horrible, albeit survivable, lacerations and cuts.

The one area where the British suffered a distinct disadvantage compared to the Indians (in addition to numbers) was in cavalry. Although the Indian light cavalry could do little against even the hastily constructed British infantry square (infantry units formed a square shape with bayonets presented to repel cavalry charges), it did highlight the British need for their own cavalry. Buxar also established the reputation of the Indian sepoy units, who suffered more casualties in proportion to their numbers than their European counterparts (approximately 5,800 to 800). Clive's military reforms had paid off handsomely: the British no longer hesitated to thrust their sepoys into the thick of even the most desperate battles. In the House of Commons, Munro declared that "sepoys properly disciplined and led on with the Europeans are good soldiers and will do anything."[38] Buxar was also the first battle that the British fought for territory in India. Unlike Plassey, it was not a battle to install a favorite nawab on the throne; instead, it was an outright attempt to seize control of Bengal. Acquisition of this populous and lucrative region gave the British the ideal base from which to conquer the remainder of India.

Buxar, however, did not automatically signify the capitulation of the surviving powers in northern India. The rulers of Avadh and powerful zamindars like the raja of Banaras began to expand and reorganize their forces to match the British. Shuja-ud-Daulah, appalled by his Mughal cavalry's ineffectiveness against the British, began to reduce their numbers in favor of infantry.[39] He organized these soldiers along European lines and hired French officers to train them. They were subject to strict discipline and paid regularly, the latter a requirement in order to compete against the British, who offered the most stable careers for Indian recruits.[40] By 1768 Shuja had 70,000 sepoys in seventy *paltans* (groups), which were grouped into divisions called Telingas and Jhelingas.[41] He armed the troops with firelocks, matchlocks, and cannons, all made near his palace in Faizabad under French supervision.[42] Military governors, or faujdars, received orders to dispatch a certain number of recruits (mainly Hindu peasants) from each pargana, or district, for military service.[43] In addition to these peasant sepoys, Shuja also employed mercenary clans such as the Gosains (warrior ascetics) and the Mewatis, whom the Mughals had periodically employed as auxiliaries.[44] However, the new army never saw combat against the British. The latter quickly imposed a number of treaties on Shuja and his successor, Asaf-ud-Daulah, thereby considerably emasculating the budding army and ultimately rendering it ineffective.

More effective opposition to the British domination of northern India came from the powerful Hindu zamindari, or landowning, family in Banaras. Mansa Ram, an assistant to the Mughal governor of Banaras, Meer Rustam Ali Khan, founded the "kingdom" of Banaras. Using his newfound power, Mansa Ram gradually put his clansmen into positions of power and soon controlled the district. He proved so influential that Rustam Ali got him the title raja from the Mughal emperor Muhammad Shah.[45] Like the Mughal and the Maratha armies, the Banaras zamindari recruited its forces from a broad base, which reduced the raja's dependence on his immediate clansmen.[46] The Banaras army was based on three tiers. The Bhumihar elite and the recruits from the raja's Bhumihar Brahmin kin network occupied the highest position. The second tier consisted of Afghan and Rajput risaldars, or troop leaders, most of whom had served in the Mughal army. The third tier, or the rank and file, consisted of the zamindar auxiliary forces. This heterogeneous force helped balance the various ethnic groups within and outside of the army. It also aided the raja in keeping control over these disparate forces. The drawback to the system was its decentralized nature, with recruitment and training falling in the hands of the risaldars, who were mostly clan leaders.[47] Cheyt Singh, Mansa Ram's grandson, expanded the army's peasant base by extending his recruitment to the Bhumihar zamindaris of Banaras and northern Bihar in order to diminish his Bhumihar kinsmen and the power of the Afghan risaldars. According to C. A. Bayly, as many as 100,000 Bhumihar Brahmin clansmen militarily supported the Banaras raja.[48] Later, Cheyt Singh extended his peasant recruitment to the Rajput zamindaris of Banaras and Avadh.[49] Seema Alavi believes that the Banaras raja's expansion of peasant levies partly was in response to similar recruitment carried out by Shuja-ud-Daulah in neighboring Avadh. However, whereas Shuja used the administrative institutions of the faujdar and the aumil to raise his army, Cheyt Singh utilized his clan and religious affiliations in the countryside to recruit his soldiers.[50] On the eve of his rebellion against the East India Company, Cheyt Singh's forces stood at 7,690 men, including 700 household troops, both horse and foot, 1,150 *sipahis* (soldiers), 1,800 matchlock men, a large number of important levies armed by the zamindars, and 1,700 Afghan cavalry. During the insurrection, his army rose to 22,190, with most men coming from the region's various Rajput lineages and Bhumihar zamindaris.[51]

Hyder Ali and State Formation in Mysore

On 20 February 1772 Warren Hastings arrived in Calcutta to begin his appointment as governor, and he immediately started consolidating the East India Company's hold over the region. Together with the nawab of Avadh, the British fought a war in 1774 against the Afghans of Rohilkhand to the north of Avadh, which they subsequently annexed. The British, in the meantime, took advantage of internal dissensions within Avadh and gained control over the administration until the nawab, Asaf-ud-Daulah, paid off his debts to the British and committed himself to a firm alliance with them. The British then installed his successor, Nawab Saadat Ali Khan (1798–1814), the son of the late nawab Shuja-ud-Daulah, on the throne, and thus he remained under their complete control.[52] With Bengal now completely secure, the British turned their attention to southern India, where Hyder Ali, the ruler of Mysore, challenged their forces.

Hyder Ali was a soldier of fortune who had entered the service of Nanjraj, Mysore's Hindu ruler. By 1761 Hyder had taken over the reins of power from Nanjraj. The latter had exhausted his treasury in a fruitless alliance with the British during a war (1750–55) against the neighboring kingdom of Karnatik, in whose territory Madras was situated. As soon as he took over the throne, Hyder began to consolidate his power base through a process of conquest and subjugation of the region's *polygars*, or local warlords. He extended his kingdom from 84 *gulies*, or districts, to 144 gulies. He then subdivided this area into Mughal-style subahdaries of varying size. The governing subahdars had full power, military and civil, to govern their respective provinces. In every district, an aumil and a deputy subahdar assisted them.[53]

However, establishing a strong military force remained Hyder's immediate and main concern. Just prior to taking power, Hyder had clashed briefly with the British in 1760 when they tried to assist his rivals in Mysore. Although his reign began amid tension with the British, Hyder tried to enlist their help in his war against the Marathas in the north that began in October 1763. The war ended in 1765, with Hyder receiving no aid from the British. He also wanted to parley with the British in order to obtain European firearms with which to equip his rapidly expanding army. In 1763 he promised to continue the privileges the British had enjoyed under the Wodeyar dynasty provided they supplied him with 7,000 muskets.[54] The company stalled for time, noting its long-term policy of never selling arms to Indian powers or assisting them with arms. Undaunted, Hyder directly applied to the Bombay government for 3,000–4,000 muskets.[55] The Bombay government decided that it would supply Hyder with a token 500 muskets to prevent him from "throw[ing] himself into the arms of the French."[56] Hyder continued to ask the British for more muskets, but he did not receive further supplies. The British disregard for their various treaty agreements with Mysore and the growing distrust between the British government in Madras and Hyder eventually propelled Hyder into a French alliance, just as the British had feared.

The First Anglo-Mysore War

Although relations with Hyder had deteriorated, the British achieved success in Karnatik. Fortunately for them, the nawab, Muhammad Ali, placed by the British on the throne, proved rather pliant and allowed the British to dictate his foreign policy. Because Hyder's rise to power in Mysore made the nawab apprehensive, he put together an alliance with the nizam of Hyderabad and the Marathas to crush the upstart Hyder. However, Hyder was a consummate diplomat: he bought off the Marathas with money and territory and convinced the nizam to come over to his side.[57]

On 25 August 1767 the combined armies of Mysore and Hyderabad entered Karnatik with some 65,000 men. Hyder had at his disposal 12,800 cavalry, 18,000 infantry, 210 Europeans, and 49 cannons.[58] Throughout the campaign Hyder's forces bore the brunt of the fighting, while the nizam's forces took little part in the engagements. The British, who were the real military power in Karnatik, had only 600 European soldiers, 5,000 sepoys, 30 cavalry, and 14 cannons under Col. Joseph Smith.[59] Despite this, they inflicted a sharp defeat upon Hyder on 2 September at Changama, causing 1,500 casualties to 170 of their own. On the 25th Smith, who had been reinforced by Col. James Wood and now had a combined force of 1,300 Europeans, 8,000 sepoys, and 30 guns, inflicted another defeat upon the allies at Tiruvannamali.[60] The nizam again took no part in the battle and in fact joined the British after Hyder retreated. In January 1768 the British, operating in two divisions under Colonels Wood and Smith, forced Hyder onto the Bangalore plain and reduced many of his forts. Following the defeats of Changama, Tiruvannamali, and Vaniyambali, Hyder avoided direct confrontation with the British and turned instead to a campaign based upon seizing British supplies, burning crops and villages, and seizing cattle. So accomplished was he in the latter that he rendered vast areas surrounding Karnatik desolate with "not an inhabitant or hut . . . seen in a day's journey."[61] Not wanting to directly confront the British forces, Hyder tried to draw out smaller contingents from the main body to wipe them out. He almost managed to accomplish this when a contingent under Colonel Wood was sent to recapture the mountain fortress of Malwagal. Hyder cut off and isolated Wood's detachment of 4,000 sepoys and 700 European soldiers along with their supplies and artillery. Wood, fearing encirclement, panicked, dumped his stores, and retreated rapidly. On the 21st, however, Hyder surrounded him. Only the timely arrival of a relieving force under a Major Fitzgerald prevented the certain annihilation of the British force. Col. Ross Lang, who replaced the panic-stricken Wood, dispatched a force of 5,000 men under Fitzgerald to track down Hyder. This plan proved to be a mistake, for not only did Hyder easily evade Fitzgerald, but he also isolated and wiped out a force of 50 Europeans and 200 sepoys. The tide of the war appeared to shift in Hyder's favor, and he soon recovered most of the territories he had lost to the British. The latter, seemingly stunned at this sudden reversal, tried to seek peace, but the war resumed on 6 March 1769. Hyder, now possessing a good understanding of his British foe, reacted with alacrity. He positioned most of his force 140 miles south of Madras to decoy the British army under Colonel Smith while he marched north with 6,000 cavalry and only 200 picked infantry to Madras, where he amazingly arrived in less than three days, on 29 March 1769. With the defenseless city at his mercy, he negotiated a very favorable peace treaty, bringing to a conclusion the first Anglo-Mysore War.[62]

The Second Anglo-Mysore War

In the wake of the treaty Hyder once again found himself embroiled in conflict with the Marathas. The British immediately violated the terms of the Madras treaty by refusing to give him aid. Nevertheless, Hyder, by using his diplomatic and military skills, managed to keep the Marathas at bay. The Marathas' severe internal conflict in 1775, stemming from British support for the pretender to the office of peshwa, Raghunathrao or Raghoba, also aided Hyder. The British were also occupied by other problems. As a result of the American Revolution, by 1778 the British were again at war with the French. In India the British captured Pondicherry on 19 October 1778. Flush with victory over the French, the British governor of Madras, Stephen Rumbold Lushington (appointed 13 February 1778), proposed capturing French-controlled Mahe on the west coast. Hyder could not allow a British conquest at his own doorstep. Furthermore, he placed tremendous strategic importance on Mahe because he obtained his French-supplied arms and munition from this port. Ignoring Hyder's concerns and warnings, Rumbold captured Mahe on 19 March, just before Hyder's army was due to arrive to support the French.[63] Hyder now set about forming a confederacy against the British. He already had French support, but now the Marathas also joined him. Even the pretender Raghunathrao, angered by the lack of British support for his cause, joined the alliance. In the face of such overwhelming support for Hyder, the opportunistic nizam of Hyderabad decided to quickly follow suit. A thoroughly alarmed Madras government sent an emissary, a Mr. Gray, to Hyder's capital in Seringapatam to negotiate a new treaty. Hyder now had little confidence in treaties with the British and with Rumbold in particular, and he did not respond to Gray's entreaties. In Madras Governor Rumbold was dismissed for starting the war.

In July 1780 Hyder invaded Karnatik with an army of 80,000, mostly cavalry.[64] The total forces available to the British in Madras amounted to 26,065 men, of whom 15,000 belonged to the nawab of Karnatik.[65] Hyder initiated the war by laying siege to some British forts in northern Arcot. In response the British sent a force of 5,209 men to Arcot to raise the siege. Hyder then sent part of his army under his son Tippu to intercept Col. William Baille at Guntur, some 145 miles south of Madras, and prevent him from joining with now Col. Hector Munro, commander in chief at Madras. Tippu's cavalry attacked Baille on 5 September at Parambakam but was beaten off.[66] On

79

the 9th a Lieutenant Colonel Fletcher joined Baille with 1,007 men of the Seventy-third Regiment, including 301 Europeans.[67] On hearing this, Hyder reinforced Tippu with his main army the very same night. Because Baille now had a total of 3,820 men, including 86 European officers and 508 European soldiers, he was confident of victory.[68]

The following morning Baille broke camp and moved out, only to come under heavy fire from Hyder's guns. Baille then formed his force into a long oblong "square," with all the baggage in the middle, and slowly began to move forward. At first the formation beat off all attacks, but an explosion in the munition tumbrels within it caused the formation to waver. Hyder's Maratha light cavalry attacked the square in a flash and broke the formation's front. Hyder's remaining cavalry poured through, and within moments the battle was over and Baille had surrendered. His casualties were heavy; 36 of 86 European officers died, as did 300 out of 508 European infantry.[69] The losses notwithstanding, this was the British army's most crushing defeat in India at that time. Other British forces reacted instantaneously. Munro re-treated rapidly to Madras, abandoning his baggage and throwing his cannons into the Conjeeveram water tank to speed his retreat in addition to losing some 500 men. At this point when he had the British at his mercy, Hyder for some inexplicable reason refused to march on Madras but turned instead to capture the fortress of Arcot, which he did on 3 November.[70]

Hyder's decision gave the British time to shore up their forces in the south. Hastings, reacting quickly to the frantic appeals from Madras, dispatched Sir Eyre Coote with all available men to Madras; the force arrived there on 5 November.[71] On the 17th he moved south, retook Pondicherry from the French, and also lifted the sieges on several British forts in the area. Hyder followed Coote's army and learned on the 25th that a French fleet under Chevalier d'Orves had arrived off the coast, thus cutting off Coote's over-seas supply line to Bengal. Hyder then positioned himself to cut off Coote from the grain-producing interior and simply waited to starve out the British. He almost succeeded; in the first half of 1781 Coote's army, which required 450,000 bags of rice to feed the men, received only 125,000. The situation in the second half of the year was even worse, with the army obtaining only 90,000 bags of rice.[72] Unfortunately for Hyder, the French fleet suddenly de-parted from its blockading position on 15 February, and the British rushed in the desperately needed supplies from Madras.[73] Coote then moved close to the village of Porto-Novo near the sea on the northern banks of the Vallar River. On 27 June he learned that Hyder had arrived there with an army of 40,000. Hyder deployed his army astride the Cuddalore road, with the right wing resting on a height and the left hugging the sand banks near the coast.

Coote had at his disposal 8,476 men, of whom 2,070 were Europeans. After careful inspection Coote saw that Hyder's left was very weak, since it was unfortified. He immediately dispatched Gen. James Stuart with the second column to turn this flank while he sought to engage the enemy's attention with the first column. The British carried out the deployment with precision, but Hyder, immediately recognizing the British tactics, reinforced the weak point. Stuart attacked twice but was repulsed. Hyder launched a cavalry counterattack, which Stuart repulsed with great difficulty. Just as a second such attack was begun, the cavalry commander, Mir Sahib, was killed, and a British schooner engaged the massed cavalry with cannon fire. These events broke up what could have been an overwhelming cavalry charge. Stuart attacked again and this time succeeded in breaking Hyder's left flank, leaving Hyder with little option but to retreat.[74]

Porto-Novo was an important battle, for it decided once and for all the fate of Madras.[75] Although Hyder fought on, the aging warrior never again directly confronted the British. On 7 December 1782, at the age of sixty, an ailing Hyder Ali passed away. After his death the war continued until the Treaty of Mangalore on 11 March 1784 ended the hostilities.[76] The Marathas had already made peace with the British in May 1782, as had the French in 1783. According to the terms of the treaty the British agreed to evacuate the territory of Mysore, while Tippu did the same with Karnatik.

The Third Anglo-Mysore War

After his father's death Tippu inherited a war-ravaged kingdom. After a brief war against the Marathas and the nizam of Hyderabad in 1786–87, he was once again drawn into conflict with the British, who were determined to eliminate Mysore. The conflict was caused by a third party – the small kingdom of Travancore on the southwestern tip of India. The king of Travancore, Raja Rama Varma, provoked Tippu by allowing British forces to be stationed on his soil. Matters came to a head in 1788–89, when the raja gave safe haven to rebels from Mysore. After a series of border clashes, Tippu invaded Travancore on 12 April, brushing aside its ineffectual army. The two British battalions in Travancore, which had been reinforced with three more battalions under a Colonel Hartley from Bombay, were forced to fall back on Travancore as its army dissolved at the border. Tippu continued to reduce fort after fort until he heard that the British planned to invade Mysore, at which point he returned home.

This latest British attempt to crush Tippu had its roots in British prime minister William Pitt's India Act, which passed Parliament in 1784. This act greatly strengthened the post of the governor-general in India, an appointment that was henceforth solely the Crown's prerogative. Accordingly, King George III appointed Charles Cornwallis as governor-general, and he arrived in India in September 1786 armed with considerable powers and a desire to redeem his honor, which had been lost to the "colonials" at Yorktown. Despite specific advice from the board of directors of the East India Company "to adopt a pacific defensive system," Cornwallis decided to cut Tippu down to size.[77] However, realizing the extent of Tippu's military prowess, he sought "to form an alliance with the Marattas against Tipoo our common enemy."[78] At the same time, he began overhauling the company's military establishment so that by December 1787 he could write, "The company's armies are ready in all the provinces."[79] Meanwhile, Sir Charles Malet, the British agent in Poona, had by 1 June 1790 managed to secure an offensive-defensive alliance between the peshwa, the nizam of Hyderabad, and the company. All of these moves coincided well with Tippu's attack on Travancore, a British ally. According to the terms of the alliance, the Marathas and the nizam were to invade Mysore immediately with an army of at least 25,000; furthermore, should Cornwallis request cavalry, they were to provide him with such a force within a month.[80]

Tippu stood alone. Even the French dared not intervene on his behalf. However, in spite of the alliance against Tippu, the British initially fought the third Anglo-Mysore War without their allies. The British, having long plotted a careful offensive plan, made the first move. According to their plans, Gen. William Meadows, the governor of Madras, would enter western Mysore through the Gajalhati Pass and occupy Coimbatore Province. General Abercrombie, the governor of Bombay, was to attack from the coast and occupy Kanara and Malabar. Finally, a third force under Colonel Maxwell would invade Baramahal in northwestern Mysore. Initially, everything went according to plan, as General Meadows's advance force under Colonel Floyd drove back Tippu's garrisons through the Gajalhati Pass and occupied Satyamangalalm. Several forts in the area had fallen to the British by 22 August 1790. Tippu's reaction was characteristically swift and forceful. Having arrived back in Seringapatam from Travancore, he mobilized his forces and with an army of 40,000 men sans baggage force-marched to the Gajalhati Pass, descending it swiftly and undetected.[81] He surprised Colonel Floyd at Satyamangalalm and forced him to retreat to Coimbatore. On 13 September he again attacked Floyd's force and inflicted some 550 casualties but failed to follow and crush the retreating British. At this point all the British forces in the region, including Meadows, Floyd, and Stuart, fell back on Coimbatore.[82] Tippu then turned his attention to Colonel Maxwell in Baramahal, but Meadows joined

Maxwell with his forces, and brief skirmishing was all that came of this move. With all of his attention absorbed on the east Tippu was unable to prevent General Abercrombie from taking Malabar after a sea landing at Tellicherry in December 1790. Despite this success, the main British attack in the west was a disaster, as Cornwallis, who dismissed Meadows and took personal command of all forces in the field, had concentrated all of his forces in the west at Vellore and had issued marching orders on 11 February 1791.[83] The British Grand Army moved against Bangalore, which fell to it on 21 March 1791. Here Cornwallis established a temporary cantonment, and the nizam of Hyderabad joined him on 13 April with some 15,000 men. The joint force left Bangalore on 4 May 1791, but Mysorean light cavalry constantly harried them, and a series of short actions were fought in the Karighatta Hills some 9 miles from Seringapatam, an island fortress in the Kaveri River. Tippu's forces then retreated into the Seringapatam fortress, which the British tried unsuccessfully to storm, suffering heavy losses in the process. By now Cornwallis's supply situation was becoming rather acute, forcing him to lift the siege on 20 May and leave for Bangalore. He had to abandon most of his supply train, as all of his cattle had starved to death or had been slaughtered for food. Despite appeals from his officers, Tippu did not march out of Seringapatam to attack the retreating British forces.

As Cornwallis established his temporary camp in Bangalore in April the Marathas finally opened their northern offensive. Nana Phadnavis sent a force of 12,000 cavalry and 5,000 infantry to open the offensive. The Marathas laid siege to the northern fortress of Dharwar, which fell to them after a six-month siege on 4 April 1781. With Dharwar captured, the Maratha army, with new forces under Raghunathrao, stormed into northern Mysore. At this time Cornwallis's forces were in dire straits and were overjoyed to join up with the Marathas at Melukote.[84] The Marathas, with their vast stores and mobile bazaars, provisioned Cornwallis until he received much-needed supplies from Madras. On 31 January 1792 the combined allied armies, now under Cornwallis, were reviewed in Bangalore. The British had 22,000 men and 86 guns, including 42 siege pieces. The nizam's forces under Prince Sikander Jha had 18,000 men, and the Marathas under Haripant had 12,000 men (mostly cavalry), but Parashuram Bhau was to join them with 20,000 men.[85]

Tippu awaited the attack in a prepared position to the north of his island fortress with some 40,000 infantry and 100 cannons. On the night of 6 February 1792 Cornwallis gave the order to attack.[86] The attack met with total success, and Tippu's forces retreated into the fortress. Surrounded on all sides, he began peace negotiations on 24 February 1792 and then signed the Treaty of Seringapatam.[87] The treaty was a devastating blow to Tippu. At one stroke he lost his kingdom's significant revenue-producing districts, including the Baramahal, Dundigal (which included the fertile region of the Doab), and Salem. In the west he lost the spice-rich Malabar, which included the important ports of Calicut and Cannanore.[88]

The Fourth Anglo-Mysore War

In May 1798 India's new governor-general, Richard Colley Wellesley, 2nd Earl of Mornington, arrived to assume his office. His overall mission was to consolidate the East India Company's position in India. The one perceived obstacle to this goal was, of course, Tippu Sultan, the "Tiger of Mysore." In the aftermath of the harsh Treaty of Seringapatam, Tippu had managed to engineer a partial recovery, especially with his army. At the same time he reestablished contact with France, this time dealing with the Jacobins, who referred to him as their "citizen Prince."[89] On hearing of this relationship Wellesley, who probably had been waiting for just such an excuse, ordered General Harris, the commander in chief of the Coromandel Coast, to begin gathering an army.[90] As Cornwallis had done before him, Wellesley easily secured the cooperation of the nizam of Hyderabad, who by this time was a British dependent.[91] The Marathas, however, were a different case altogether. Although the peshwa had agreed to an alliance, none of the sirdars wanted to leave their provinces. Finally, Parashuram Bhau agreed to join the British war effort in exchange for territory captured from Mysore.[92] With his military preparations and alliances secure by November 1798, Wellesley openly confronted Tippu about his so-called alliance with the French.[93] The governor-general knew that the French could not send aid to Tippu because of the destruction of their fleet in Alexandria.[94] Without waiting for a reply, Wellesley left for Madras, from where on 3 February 1799 he ordered Generals Harris and Stuart to invade Mysore and lay siege to Seringapatam.[95]

Harris and the Madras army set out from Vellore on 14 February 1799 with 15,000 infantry, 2,600 cavalry, and 100 cannons.[96] Arthur Wellesley, the governor-general's brother, joined him at Ambur on the 20th with a force of 10,000 infantry and 6,000 cavalry from the nizam of Hyderabad. The Bombay army under Stuart moved out of Cannanore on 21 February with 6,420 men. The British commanders also expected the ni-zam of Hyderabad and the Marathas to provide some 25,000 men each. As the Madras army advanced into Mysore, Tippu's lieutenants, Sayyid Sahib and Purniah, proved unable or unwilling to hinder Harris's advance. Indeed, evidence suggests that the British had bought off these and many other important officials in Tippu's government.[97] Tippu himself marched out of Seringapatam to confront Harris at Malvalli on 18 March. Tippu first attacked the British right wing with cavalry and the left with infantry, but the British repulsed these, and Tippu had to retreat into Seringapatam, which the British surrounded by mid-April. On the 21st, after Tippu refused to reply to a humiliating treaty that the British sought to impose upon him, the British began to bombard the fort.[98] A breach was created on 3 May, and General Baird was ordered to storm it the next day with his unit of 2,494 European soldiers and 1,892 sepoys. Despite stiff resistance, the breach was carried at the point of the bayonet. Tippu died fighting on the ramparts alongside his men.[99]

The Mysore Army under Hyder and Tippu

Hyder Ali's military system, which had so terrified the British, was based upon light cavalry. Of all the Indian rulers who set up European-style units with the help of the French, none enjoyed a closer relationship with the French than Hyder and his son Tippu. Yet Hyder did not adopt a European-style, infantry-dominated army. This is not to say that Hyder did not use his French connection: he relied on French help to establish his artillery and munitions foundries. He also employed French officers in his army, but they and other Europeans served in self-contained units.[100] With the exception of some artillery and infantry units, Europeans commanded few of the Mysore army forces. At the start of the first Anglo-Mysore War in 1767, Hyder invaded the British-controlled province of Karnatik with a combined army of 18,000 cavalry, 8,000 Maratha Pindhari (irregular light cavalry), 20,000 infantry, 750 Europeans in two companies of dragoons, and 250 artillerymen.[101]

The Mysore army reached the zenith of its power under Hyder's son Tippu Sultan. Between 1761 and 1792 the Mysore army developed into one of the most formidable in the Indian subcontinent. The rise of so powerful a force in the span of thirty years is surprising when one considers that both Hyder and Tippu were patrimonial monarchs. Despite the inbuilt weaknesses of the patrimonial bureaucratic kingdom he inherited, Tippu undertook drastic measures to centralize his state's war-making potential. He required all amildars to ascertain the exact distance between every town and village throughout his kingdom as well as all landmarks on the way, including streams, plains, hills, and wells. He reserved all resins such as wax, lac, dammar, and agalloch for the magazine at Seringapatam. Trees such as teakwood and acacia required for making the wheels of gun carriages were not to be felled for any other purpose. The amildars were also held personally responsible for requisitioning bullocks for the war effort. Every district paying 1,000 pagodas or more in taxes was required to keep four brood mares, which were mated with government-owned stallions. As the war effort gathered pace, the number of iron foundries in each district was ordered doubled. Iron *dubas*, or shells, and steel *khutties*, or cutlasses, were to be sent to Seringapatam when needed. All trade with Madras was halted. Even personal travel to the area could result in property confiscation. Lastly, Tippu made captive all Christians in Mysore and handed their lands over to the ryots, or peasant farmers, of other religions.[102]

Unlike other contemporary patrimonial Indian rulers, Tippu did not establish his army along militia lines. His army was highly centralized, and salaried officers headed most of his commands. The exceptions to this rule were his most trusted aides, Puraniya and Muhammad Reza, who were given land grants in lieu of a salary.[103] Tippu also constantly shuffled his officers from place to place to make sure no officer established a power base in the area he commanded.[104] Tippu recruited his infantry, or *jaish*, from both Mysore (called *zumra*) and from outside his kingdom (called *ghair zumra*).[105] These soldiers formed a centralized monarchical army; they were long-service volunteers, and even the troops recruited outside Mysore had to bring their families to live with them in Mysore.[106] Tippu's infantry were trained along European lines, mainly by the French, and used Persian words (the Mughal practice) of command.[107] They were organized into *cutcheris* (brigades). Each cutcheri was comprised of six *cushoons* (regiments), and each cushoon was divided into four *juqs* (companies).[108]

The cavalry could be divided into two categories, *askar* (national or regular) and *silhedar* (mercenary or irregular). In the first case, the government owned the horses and supplied and paid the riders. In the latter case, the horses belonged to the mercenary captains or the individual mercenary soldiers. The government paid a monthly salary to these captains and paid for the loss of a horse while it was still in Mysore service.[109]

Like his father before him, Tippu continued to use European, mainly French, mercenaries organized into a separate unit. However, during Tippu's reign in 1794 the number of mercenaries he employed constantly fell. The unit totaled twenty Europeans and two hundred Indian Christians, mainly artillerymen, or *topasses*. By 1799, prior to the fall of Tippu's capital, Seringapatam, this unit consisted of only four officers and forty-five other ranks.[110] The lack of European officers in their military is indicative of the tactics that Hyder and Tippu favored in their wars against the British – cavalry skirmishing rather than pitched infantry battle.

The Anglo-Mysore Wars stand out among the many wars that the British fought in India. For the first time an Indian power successfully dictated the character of the conflict with the British. In this case the tactics were uniquely

Indian: the use of light cavalry. By refusing to meet the British in a set-piece battle, both Hyder and Tippu fragmented the British and destroyed their forces piecemeal. But their most favored tactic was to starve out the British by cutting their supply lines and denying their draft animals access to forage.

The immense supply trains of draft animals that accompanied every British force proved to be a major liability. In the early campaigns in Karnatik, Hyder controlled much of the region and could easily deny the British access to draft animals. One way he achieved this aim was to raze the thousands of villages from which the British could requisition or buy these animals; of the 2,290 or so villages that surrounded Madras, Hyder destroyed 2,000.[111] The British needed tens of thousands of cattle for even minor operations; during the siege of Arcot Coote needed 35,000 cattle to carry his supplies.[112] As the campaigns against Mysore progressed, the British found that they needed more and more draft animals. In 1781 an army of 11,000 men required 30,000 cattle, but estimates for the very next year for a force of the same size projected a requirement of 40,000 cattle.[113] The company's emphasis on infantry in part required it to engage a massive train of draft animals. Infantry-dominated armies stayed in the field much longer, they moved more slowly, and they were more dependent on the rations they carried with them. Lt. Thomas Munro of the Madras army noted with disgust that the European troops were less hardy than the sepoys and required far greater logistical support to maintain them in the field.[114] Similarly, the lack of cavalry also compelled Coote to take more cannons with him to beat off enemy cavalry; in January 1781 he had forty-four, but in April 1781 the number had risen to sixty.[115] Each additional cannon of course meant dozens of additional draft animals. To compound the company's problems, it often received bullocks of poor quality partly as a result of the conditions that Hyder and Tippu imposed and partly because of the conduct of bullock contractors (mostly British) who were entirely dishonest and exploitive in their dealings with the company's agents. The British noted with some dismay that this want of good quality bullocks meant that while their forces could manage only 15 miles a day (under optimum conditions), Hyder could easily do 30 miles.[116] This logistical problem meant that the British suffered constant shortages of provisions, which probably helps explain why Munro preferred to protect the supply depot at Conjeeveram rather than march to Baille's relief.

The British problems with their bullock supply trains persisted even during the campaigns under Wellesley, when the tide of the war had shifted decisively against Tippu. When Wellesley renewed his campaign during the third Anglo-Mysore War the British army with its supply train of 60,000 cattle ran into tremendous difficulties. The presence of 35,000 bullocks belonging to the nizam's army further enhanced the problem. Even before the joint army was well under way cattle began to die in thousands. Foraging alone consumed several days and at one point imperiled the campaign itself; in the end the British advanced only 5 miles a day, and this without the slightest hindrance from the Mysore cavalry.[117]

The main problem that the British faced in the Anglo-Mysore Wars, however, was a lack of cavalry. Coote complained that even the worst of Hyder's cavalry were better than nothing, for they cut off intelligence and supplies to the Madras army.[118] The fact that "the best Indian soldiery had sought service in the Mysore cavalry" compounded his problems.[119] The ability of Hyder's cavalry to range at will across Karnatik hamstrung the British forces. In February 1782 Hyder seized a replenishing force of 3,000 bullocks under a Major Byrne, which resulted in Coote being inactive from February to May.[120] The British eventually redressed this imbalance with the aid of Maratha light cavalry (who had in the first place originated the very raiding tactics that the Mysorean cavalry used) and by substantially increasing their own cavalry forces. The British ability to adapt to their enemy's tactics first by using Maratha cavalry and second by giving priority to the problems of supply in the harsh terrain of the Deccan enabled them to achieve victory in the Anglo-Mysore Wars. While the Mysoreans relied upon traditional Indian cavalry tactics to combat the British, another Indian power, the Marathas, would try to beat the British at their own game: the set-piece European-style infantry battle.

CHAPTER 5

Fauj-e-Hind, the Army of Hindustan

With the destruction of Mysore the Marathas remained the only significant indigenous military threat to British hegemony on the subcontinent. Follow-ing the disastrous campaign against the Indo-Afghan alliance, however, the Marathas underwent a period of political upheaval and resurgence. Peshwa Nana Saheb died soon after the battle of Panipat. His second son, Madhavrao, succeeded him in July 1761 at the age of seventeen. An energetic and worthy heir, the young peshwa quickly suffered endless intrigues at the Maratha court. The chief instigator of these plots was Madhavrao's father's brother, Raghunathrao, also known as Raghoba. Madhavrao soon managed to sub-due Raghunathrao (he imprisoned him in 1768) and turned his attention to reestablishing Maratha power in North India. Following the disaster at Pani-pat the local zamindars, or landlords, south of the Yamuna and the Chambal had stopped paying revenues and tribute to the Marathas and had even dared to occupy Maratha-administered villages. Madhavrao sent Malharao Holkar, one of the few Maratha leaders to survive Panipat, to subdue the north. Dur-ing his campaign Holkar captured Gangurni in Malwa in June 1761 and de-feated the Jaipur army of Raja Madho Singh on the 29th at Mangrol.[1] The powerful Jats proved to be more problematic, especially after the aged Holkar died on 20 May 1766. However, Maratha forces under Mahadji Sindhia and Tukoji Holkar renewed the northern offensives in early 1769, defeating the Rohillas in 1770 and gradually subduing the Jats.[2] Madhavrao's biggest suc-cess came when he succeeded in inducing the Mughal emperor Shah Alam to leave British "protection" and return to Delhi to Maratha "protection," upon which the unfortunate Shah Alam became a virtual prisoner of the Marathas.[3] Unfortunately, the young peshwa died in 1772 as a result of an accident and was succeeded by his brother Narayanrao. He too was subject to plots hatched by Raghunathrao, who succeeded in having the new peshwa and ten of his associates murdered on 13 August 1773. Raghunathrao then declared him-self peshwa, but a coalition led by Nana Phadnavis (spelled Farnavis by the

British), Trimbakrao Pethe, Haripant Phadke, and others opposed him. His cause received a further blow when Narayanrao's widow, Ganga Bai, gave birth to a son, Savai Madhavrao. Nana Phadnavis and his associates, known as the Barbhais, or seniors, ordered the arrest of Raghunathrao and invested the young infant as the peshwa. Raghunathrao immediately fled to the British and sought their protection. They readily provided sanctuary in exchange for the Treaty of Surat, which stated that the British would help Raghunathrao regain the office of peshwa in return for substantial monetary and territorial gains.

In the wake of this treaty, a period of brief skirmishing followed that resulted in the Treaty of Purandhar in March 1776. However, in March 1778 Raghunathrao's meddling once again forced the British into war against the Poona government. This time the Marathas, under Nana Phadnavis's able leadership, easily defeated the British at the battle of Vadgaon on 19 January 1799.[4] A series of skirmishes followed in which the Marathas thoroughly defeated the British. Finally, under severe pressure from London, the British sought peace.[5] A new treaty, the Treaty of Salbai, was signed on 17 May 1782. It forced the British to return territory they had gained after the Treaty of Purandhar.[6] However, Nana Phadnavis, who ran the Poona government, agreed not to ally himself with other European powers.[7]

In Hindustan to the north, however, Maratha power once again expanded under the aegis of Mahadji Sindhia, Dattaji Sindhia's nephew and successor.[8] It was Mahadji Sindhia who became Shah Alam's chief protector and who managed to crush all opposition in Delhi from Muslim chiefs such as Ismail Baig and the Rajputs.[9] During these struggles Mahadji raised a force of European-trained infantry under a remarkable European mercenary, Benoît de Boigne. The success of his forces, which soon came to be known as Fauj-e-Hind, the Army of Hindustan, became the focus of other Maratha chieftains' envy. Maratha leaders, especially Tukoji Holkar, soon became resentful of Mahadji's tremendous success in North India. The latter sought to thwart Mahadji's attempts to control this region, and the two fought a battle at Lakheri in May 1793, during which Mahadji's infantry-based army under de Boigne thoroughly trounced Holkar's forces.

While Tukoji Holkar and Mahadji fought, relations between Poona and the British had briefly become better. As a result of the alliance against Hyder and Tippu, the British were able to besiege Seringapatam in 1792 and impose a crippling treaty on Tippu.[10] However, with Tippu eliminated, the traditional rivalry between the Marathas and the nizam of Hyderabad resurfaced. Although the British attempted to mediate, both sides moved inexorably toward war.[11] The young peshwa, Savai Madhavrao, took personal command of the Maratha army on 15 December 1794 and issued a call to all the sirdars to join him. In response to his call a great host of Maratha armies, the likes of which had not been seen since Panipat, began to gather.[12] Estimates of the Maratha force vary from 100,000 to 200,000.[13] The nizam assembled a force of about 130,000, including 12,000 gardi, or European-style infantry, under a Monsieur Raymond.[14] In the first week of March both the armies confronted each other near the village of Kharda. After some minor skirmishing the battle began on 11 March. The decisive engagement took place between Mahadji's forces under Jivba and Perron and Raymond's gardi. These opposing infantry formations battled with musket volleys and cannon fire, after which Raymond launched a fierce attack that was repulsed with heavy losses. At this point the rest of the nizam's forces fled to the fortress of Kharda. Negotiations immediately began, and a treaty was concluded in April 1795.[15]

The battle of Kharda firmly reasserted the ascendancy of the Marathas, which had been lost after Panipat. The Maratha coalition harked back to Baji Rao and Nana Saheb, when all the Maratha sirdars universally acknowledged and respected the peshwa. Of particular significance was the fine leadership display of the young peshwa, Savai Madhavrao, during the campaign. His actions suggested he might assume the reins of power and establish the peshwa's leadership over a reinvigorated Maratha confederacy. Unfortunately, this was not to be. Kharda was the Maratha confederacy's last great combined military endeavor.

The first blow to the newborn post–Kharda Maratha alliance came when the young peshwa, Savai Madhavrao, died suddenly on 27 October 1795 at age twenty-one. (There is some debate if his death was an accident or suicide.) Baji Rao II, the son of the archintriguer Raghunathrao, succeeded him. Unfortunately, Baji Rao II, like his father before him, turned Poona into a den of political infighting and destroyed the facade of unity that had existed since the battle of Kharda. He allied with the volatile Daulatrao Sindhia, nephew and successor of Mahadji Sindhia. The elder Mahadji had died on 12 February 1794 while visiting Savai Madhavrao in Poona to obtain a settlement with Holkar. Daulatrao then attacked the Holkars and killed one of the three brothers, Malharao Holkar, in September 1797. Emboldened by his success, he occupied Delhi and imprisoned Nana Phadnavis. The peshwa, thoroughly alarmed by Daulatrao's actions, began to seek help. In October 1798 Lord Wellesley, who had been waiting for such a moment, instructed Colonel Palmer, the British resident in Poona, to obtain the peshwa's support against Tippu in exchange for British aid for the peshwa against Daulatrao.[16] The Maratha confederacy's final blow came when Nana Phadnavis passed away on 13 March 1800. Regarded by the British, French, and Indians alike as the era's greatest statesman, Nana Saheb alone had the ability to unite the various Maratha factions to face the impending British threat.

Adding to this chaos, the surviving Holkar brothers, Vithoji and Yaswantrao, launched a military campaign against the peshwa and Daulatrao Sindhia. In April 1801 the peshwa captured and killed Vithoji. Yaswantrao, however, achieved some success against Daulatrao's European-trained infantry by sheer dint of his personal leadership and determination. On 23 October 1802 he dispatched his now-famous letter to Baji Rao II, asking him to stay out of the conflict with Daulatrao: "My dispute is with [Daulatrao] Sindhia only, which I am prepared to settle in my own way. You are playing into Sindhia's hand and ruining the State." In the same letter he added, "The English are waiting at the gates for a chance to seize the Maratha state."[17] The prophetic warning had little effect on the peshwa. Fearing his fate at the hands of the victorious Yaswantrao, he fled to Mahad, from where he sent a letter to Jonathan Duncan, the governor of Bombay, requesting British aid.[18]

With the peshwa now completely at his mercy, Wellesley made him sign the historic Treaty of Bassein, which stated that in return for British protection Baji Rao II would subsidize and maintain a company force of 6,000 in his domain.[19] Baji Rao II's actions stunned the Maratha chieftains, including Daulatrao. Although Yaswantrao Holkar departed from Poona on 13 March 1803 to avoid an immediate confrontation with the British, war seemed imminent. Wellesley had obviously foreseen opposition from the Maratha chiefs. He wanted to prevent them from forming a coalition against the British, and in this he was eminently successful. Raghoji Bhonsle and Daulatrao Sindhia immediately joined forces and called on Yaswantrao Holkar to join them. He was about to do this when Wellesley forwarded to him letters between Daulatrao and Peshwa Baji Rao II in which they discussed their plan to defeat Holkar after dealing with the British.[20] As a result, Yaswantrao Holkar, the Marathas' most able sirdar, stayed neutral during the first phase of the Anglo-Maratha conflict. By successfully rupturing the Maratha confederacy, Wellesley greatly reduced the tremendous odds against the British. Their troubles, however, were by no means over, since they still had to deal with the Army of Hindustan, northern India's most formidable military force.

The Evolution of the Fauj-e-Hind

The story of the Army of Hindustan is also the story of Mahadji Sindhia's rise to power in North India. To this we must also add the incredible adventures of Benoît de Boigne, a European mercenary who helped create the Army of Hindustan. De Boigne was born on 8 March 1751, the son of a Monsieur la Borgne, a hide trader in Chambéry, Savoy. In 1770, thirsting for an army officer's career and having been spurned by his native Savoy, he was commissioned into the French army's Clare Regiment of the Irish Brigade at the age of nineteen. (At this time he also changed his name to the more "respectable"-sounding de Boigne.) After six years of boring garrison duty, he obtained a commission in Admiral Orloff's battalion of Greeks, raised by the Russian army to fight the Turks. Unfortunately for de Boigne, the Turks imprisoned him. During his Turkish captivity he heard stories about India. After his release he immediately set off for India. In Madras he joined the Sixth Native Infantry in time to see action against Hyder Ali.[21] De Boigne's career in the company army suddenly ground to an ignominious halt, however, after an indiscreet dalliance with an officer's wife. With his hopes for a promotion dashed, de Boigne resigned, apparently with the intention of going back to Europe through India and Russia. During his journey through Hindustan, however, he caught the attention of Mahadji Sindhia, who immediately recognized that the Savoyard was a breed apart from the many European freebooters who sought to sell their doubtful military skills to various Indian chiefs. In 1784 he hired de Boigne to raise, train, and command two large battalions with artillery.[22] Mahadji's estimate of de Boigne's character was not misplaced. The Savoyard worked day and night to establish a force of about 1,700 men. The soldiers received the same pay as the company's soldiers, and de Boigne saw to it that all the pay reached the men and that no middleman siphoned off a cut. He also never defrauded the men or withheld their pay in long arrears, as was the practice in many other Indian armies, including that of the company. His honesty paid off, as the Army of Hindustan never mutinied. Much of de Boigne's success in recruiting and maintaining a first-rate army was due to Mahadji's tremendous revenue resources. Although de Boigne hired few Europeans, he selected the best available. His first senior European officer was a Scotsman named Sangster who was at the time employed in Madec's Old Corps in Gohad. Sangster was responsible for equipping the vast force de Boigne planned to establish. For battalion commanders he hired Hessing, a Dutchman, and Frémont, a pro-Royalist Frenchman. To train his new force de Boigne relied exclusively on British manuals, with which he had become familiar while in the Madras army.[23]

De Boigne's artillery was part of his battalions and consisted of light three-pounders and six-pounders drawn by eight bullocks or by gangs of laborers (*kelasis*).[24] The use of light artillery was in marked contrast to the unwieldy artillery pieces Indian armies normally carried. (Later de Boigne added a separate train of heavy siege guns while still maintaining his light guns.)[25]

De Boigne had scarcely set up his forces when Mahadji ordered him to move toward Agra, ostensibly to restore Shah Alam II to the throne. Many Mughal nobles who sought alliances with the disaffected Rajput houses in an attempt to hold off renewed Maratha attempts to subdue them obviously did not appreciate Mahadji's role in Delhi. The problems with the Rajputs began when Mahadji, as the emperor's protector and the Mughal Empire's regent, demanded that the Rajput kingdoms pay the traditional tribute and taxes due to the Mughal Empire.[26] The raja of Jaipur, Pratap Singh, refused to pay the taxes, and he persuaded Raja Bijai Singh of Marwar to support his cause. He even went so far as to buy British support.[27] It was against the Rajput armies that the Army of Hindustan first bloodied the steel of its bayonets. Mahadji marched to confront the Rajputs with Mughal forces by his side. However, when he reached the plain of Tunga some 14 miles northwest of Laslot village, his Mughal "allies" led their cavalry across the battlefield to join the enemy, as per a prearranged agreement. The same cavalry then attacked and dispersed Mahadji's own cavalry, while the remaining Mughal infantry, with Mahadji, withdrew from the field. Left alone in the battlefield was the Maratha artillery under Khandoji Appa and de Boigne, with a pitiful number of red-coated infantry. A huge mass of Rajput cavalry of the Rathor clan faced them. While Mahadji desperately tried to get the Mughal infantry to reenter the battlefield, de Boigne calmly formed a hollow square with his 1,700 men.[28] When de Boigne saw the Rathors preparing to charge, he ordered the men forming the front face of the square to retire behind the gun line, exposing eight six-pounder guns. The moment the charge began, the guns opened fire. Despite horrendous casualties, the Rathors closed around the fire-spitting square, where the infantry greeted them with a devastating volley from 320 muskets before presenting bayonets. Despite their best attempts, the Rathor cavalry could make no impact upon the hedgehog of bayonets. Within moments the charge was over and the field was covered with dead, dying, and wounded Rajput warriors and their mounts.[29]

But de Boigne was not done. As the Rathor cavalry re-formed at some distance he ordered his men to attack. The rear wall of the square smartly turned about, while the sides pivoted around until they formed an open column and were in line with the front of the square. Thus in a single line some 300 yards wide and incredibly vulnerable to cavalry attack, the column advanced. The guns, which the surviving gunners and kelasis had quickly wheeled into new positions, belched out supporting fire, while the infantry fired, loaded, and moved ahead in perfect order. The Rathor cavalry, amazed at this display, once again came under withering fire and fled the field.[30]

Despite having won the field, de Boigne learned to his chagrin that Mahadji had decided to retreat after all. His Hindustani infantry (not de Boigne's) rebelled after not receiving pay for seven months. After a very tense standoff, Mahadji allowed them to join the Rajputs.[31] It took eight days for Mahadji's armies to reach Alwar, all the way under ferocious attack from the Mughal cavalry, whom de Boigne's forces kept at a distance. Mahadji then secured as an ally Raja Ranjit Singh of Bharatpur (spelled Bhurtpore by the British), ruler of the Jats. With his aid Mahadji bided his time, gathering strength.

However, Mahadji Sindhia's failure to subdue the Rajputs immediately led to his power unraveling in Delhi.[32] The hostile Mughal noble Ismail Baig found a new ally in the brutal Ghulam Kadir, a Rohilla, and the two besieged Agra. Agra's defenses had been entrusted to Lukhwa Dada, a Maratha Brahmin who easily held the fortress until help arrived. During the first relief attempt a combined Jat and Maratha force was met by the rebels at Chaksama, where three battalions of de Boigne's infantry repulsed several cavalry charges. Unfortunately, the remaining Maratha cavalry once again left the battlefield, and de Boigne had to conduct a carefully coordinated fighting retreat under immense pressure that ranks as perhaps the Army of Hindustan's greatest achievement. On 18 June 1788 the Marathas and the Jats tried to relieve Agra again, this time with de Boigne in total command of the battle. Ismail Baig fought by himself as Ghulam Kadir returned to his home base, Saharanpur, which Sikh and Maratha light cavalry were attacking. The forces met just outside Agra, and de Boigne's infantry repelled Ismail Baig's ferocious cavalry charges and then dispersed his infantry, capturing his guns and camp.[33]

Meanwhile, in Agra Ghulam Kadir had imprisoned and blinded the old emperor and terrorized the Mughal nobles while his troops sacked the city. When de Boigne led Mahadji's forces into the city, Kadir tried to flee; however, he only got as far as Ghaurgarh near Meerut, where he was captured, tortured for his unspeakable crimes against the Mughal emperor, and finally decapitated. His remains were put on display in Delhi.[34] Mahadji was once again the undisputed master of Hindustan.

In 1790 Mahadji Sindhia negotiated a new contract with de Boigne. The Savoyard was given a jagir consisting of the huge Aligarh Province. From the immense revenue from this jagir de Boigne could keep 2 percent, or 48,000 rupees (15,000 pounds), per year. Under his new contract de Boigne reengaged the Scotsman, Sangster, whom he placed in charge of the arsenal in Agra. There Sangster immediately set about casting the best cannons made in India. He also made muskets (for 10 rupees each), gunpowder from a mixture of sulphur and saltpeter from Bikaner, and cannon shot from excellent Gwalior iron. As the Agra arsenal grew, Sangster ultimately managed five factories, each under the management of a superintendent.

De Boigne also established a cavalry force of one regiment with 500 men per brigade.[35] He hired the cavalry on the traditional silhedar basis, whereby the cavalry troopers obtained and owned their own horses and weapons. The fact that Mahadji Sindhia controlled some of the most important horse-trading routes and marketplaces did not make this much of a problem. De Boigne also equipped his infantry platoons with one camel each to carry the soldiers' backpacks. This freed the men to conduct prolonged forced marches, for which they soon became extremely famous in Hindustan and were known as the Cheria Fauj, literally, the bird army. De Boigne's force initially consisted of eight British-style regular infantry battalions of 700 men each, with two Rohilla matchlock men battalions. Each battalion had a battery of two three-pounders, two six-pounders, and one howitzer.[36] Rarely did the entire brigade fight as a unit. Instead, it usually detached independent groups of single or multiple battalions to carry out individual assignments spread out all over northern India.[37] To command his battalion de Boigne relied on European freebooters available in Hindustan; they included John Hessing (Dutch), Baours, Pedron, and Rohan (French), Roberts (English), Sutherland (Scots), and Pierre Cuiller, or "Perron" (French).[38]

While de Boigne toiled to set up his new army, Ismail Baig once again sought willing Rajput help to stir up trouble for Sindhia. In May 1790 Baig's and the Rajput princes' combined armies assembled at Patun near Delhi.[39] Mahadji sent Lukhwa Dada with the Maratha cavalry and de Boigne with the Army of Hindustan to meet the enemy. As before, the Maratha cavalry stood on the sidelines while de Boigne's regulars confronted an enemy force of 55,000 (mainly cavalry) and 129 cannons. De Boigne won yet another victory, losing only 129 dead and 472 wounded. He captured 107 pieces of artillery, 6,000 stands of arms, 252 colors, 15 elephants, 200 camels, 513 horses, and 3,000 precious bullocks.[40] Mahadji immediately capitalized on this victory and sent de Boigne and Lukhwa Dada in pursuit of the retreating Rajputs. Raja Pratap Singh surrendered at once when de Boigne came calling at Jaipur, but Bijai Singh was determined to continue the fight. He reassembled his army after a massive recruiting drive of all able-bodied men in Jodhpur and placed himself on the road to Jodhpur near the town of Mertah.

De Boigne, after another of his famous forced marches, placed himself outside the Rajput camp, unbeknownst to them, at dawn on 10 September. Everything was going according to plan when his left wing under Rohan advanced without orders. At this time the Rathor cavalry surged out of the camp and hit Rohan's forces while they were in open column.[41] The sudden shock of the attack had its effect, and the Rathors, recovering from their own surprise, quickly cut down the sepoys. De Boigne in the meantime quickly formed a hollow square and readied to meet the Rathors when they turned to him. The result was another devastating repulse of the Rajput cavalry. The Rathors, having been forced to run twice in the past, perished to a man on de Boigne's bayonets. A British officer in de Boigne's brigade noted: "It is impossible for me to describe the feats of bravery of the *zard-kapra-wallas* or forlorn hope of the enemy. I have seen, after their line was broken, fifteen or twenty men only return to charge one thousand infantry, and advance to within fifteen paces of our line, before they were all shot."[42] The disastrous defeat at Mertah ended Rajput opposition to Mahadji Sindhia in Hindustan. Bijai Singh sued for peace, losing the rich province of Ajmer and millions of rupees.

On his return Mahadji Sindhia gave de Boigne a salute with hundreds of cannon shots and ordered him to raise a second brigade. He was given a larger jagir, and his own pay was raised from 4,000 to 6,000 rupees per annum. While de Boigne built up the Second Brigade, Perron took the First Brigade and hunted down Ismail Baig.[43] De Boigne, happy with his subordinate's work, gave him command of the Second Brigade, which had been raised by 1791. In 1793 he established the Third Brigade. De Boigne now had a considerable army under him. Along with three brigade commanders – Frémont (First Brigade), Perron (Second Brigade), and Sutherland (Third Brigade) – each brigade was a self-contained force with its own artillery, engineers, cavalry, and supply train. He designed the infantry battalions on the British model, with eight companies each, fifty men in each company, and an attached battery of three-pounder and six-pounder guns and a howitzer. The Rohilla battalions now became skirmishers. De Boigne lavished close attention on his cavalry, equipping them with "galloper" guns (horse-drawn light artillery) almost a decade before British forces in India obtained such weapons (in 1800). The Army of Hindustan's total strength now stood at 27,000 men. They were housed at a massive cantonment built at the fortress of Koil outside Aligarh.

With Mahadji Sindhia at the zenith of his power, Tukoji Holkar, who had become jealous of his rising star and fearful of Mahadji's influence and control over the peshwa, decided to initiate a confrontation.[44] He mistakenly believed that his own sepoy brigade under a French mercenary, Chevalier Dudrennerc, was the equal of de Boigne's army. He immediately began to stir up trouble for Mahadji in Rajputana. Matters came to a head in May 1793, when Tukoji's son Malaharao, determined to initiate hostilities, demanded tribute from Sindhia's possessions in Malwa and also threatened Ujjain and Mainpur.[45] After a period of marching and countermarching the two armies confronted each other at Lakheri. The First Brigade, led by de Boigne, supported the Maratha cavalry under Lukhwa Dada. The two armies confronted each other in a narrow pass held by Tukoji. As de Boigne advanced, his forward units were thrown into confusion as their ammunition tumbrels exploded under heavy fire from Tukoji's artillery. When de Boigne retreated briefly into the forest to rally his men, Tukoji's cavalry, sensing an opportunity, immediately rushed out onto the plain below. De Boigne advanced on them with his re-formed infantry, forcing "[Tukoji] Holkar's rabble on horseback . . . to scatter like chaff before the wind."[46] Only his infantry brigade, under Dudrennerc, fought to the bitter end, although de Boigne's regulars hemmed them in in front, and Gopal Bhau's cavalry, with sixty guns firing on them at point-blank range, shut off their rear and flanks.[47] Tukoji fled the field. In reward for his actions Mahadji awarded de Boigne the position of *subedar*, or commander, of Hindustan. Soon afterward, in February 1794, Mahadji died in Poona.[48] The reins of power passed on to his fourteen-year-old nephew, Daulatrao Sindhia, whom he had adopted as his own son a few months before his death. De Boigne, realizing that he could never achieve the same rapport and trust with the young Daulatrao and suffering from deteriorating health, obtained permission to resign and set off in December 1795 for Calcutta, from where he sailed for Europe with his vast treasure.[49] Mahadji's death and de Boigne's departure ended the Marathas' hope of victory in the forthcoming conflict with the British.

Death of an Army

With the young Daulatrao at the helm matters began to deteriorate rapidly. Hindustan's impulsive and impressionable new ruler proved pliant to intrigues amongst the court factions, and he soon managed to alienate the old leaders who had fought loyally with his adopted father, most notably, Lukhwa Dada, the Marathas' ablest general. Daulatrao also found himself engaged in a bitter conflict, known as the "Bais War" (*bai* means "lady"), with two of Mahadji's widows who had garnered the support of many sirdars formerly loyal to Mahadji.[50] The Army of Hindustan found itself being utilized against its former Maratha sirdars. Furthermore, there were the usual bloody engagements against the Rajputs and against the Holkars, reinvigorated under the leadership of Yaswantrao Holkar. The latter, recognizing the futility of going against the Army of Hindustan in the open field, bided his time by reinventing the Marathas' traditional cavalry-raiding tactics. In July 1801, when the Army of Hindustan was widely dispersed, Yaswantrao struck at Ujjain, Daulatrao's capital. There he pulverized and massacred an independent sepoy brigade (four battalions) under George Hessing. After sacking the city he attacked another independent force under Macyntyre and forced it to surrender. Finally, he clashed with the First Brigade of the Army of Hindustan under Brownrigg. The Cheria Fauj proved to be a force very different from the independent brigades. They repulsed Yaswantrao's fierce attacks, including those by his own sepoy brigade under a Major Plummet, with heavy losses. In October the First Brigade, under its commander, Robert Sutherland, forced Yaswantrao into a confrontation by threatening his capital at Indore. In the ensuing battle the First Brigade completely crushed Holkar's forces.[51]

While the First Brigade dealt with Holkar, Perron reduced the forces of the amazing George Thomas, a mercenary who had made himself an independent ruler in Hariyana, southwest of Delhi.[52] When attempts to win over the fiery Irishman failed, Perron sent his Third Brigade under Louis Borquin to subdue "King" Thomas. Borquin, however, was an inept commander, and the two sides fought to a standstill at Jehazgar. The action was the Army of Hindustan's most desperately fought engagement to date, and at one point the sepoys broke under the relentless fire from Thomas's experienced artillerymen. Fortunately for the Third Brigade, just as its own commander lost his nerve, so did the redoubtable George Thomas. The latter hid himself in his tent, immersed in a drunken stupor, for the next two weeks. When he finally emerged, he found that Perron's reinforcements, including the Fourth Brigade and the Third Brigade under the command of Colonel Pedron, completely surrounded him. Thomas fled to Hansi, his home base, where he finally surrendered to the incompetent Borquin on 20 December.[53]

After Thomas's defeat Perron began to distance himself from Daulatrao's future military activities. Meanwhile, in the Deccan Yaswantrao Holkar decided to break Daulatrao's power by forcibly detaching the peshwa from his influence.[54] He had rebuilt his army and had set up three new brigades under British commanders Vickers, Harding, and Armstrong. The opposing forces met at Hadapsar outside Poona on 25 October 1802. Four battalions of the First Brigade under Captain Dawes represented Daulatrao's forces.[55] They bore the brunt of Yaswantrao's ferocious cavalry attacks. They repulsed the first charge, but Yaswantrao, rallying his men with the cry of "Now or never!" personally led a fierce charge that broke Dawes's square.[56] With Daulatrao's forces defeated, a terrified Baji Rao II fled into the waiting arms of the British, resulting in the signing of the Treaty of Bassein on 31 October 1802.

As mentioned earlier, Wellesley had succeeded in breaking up an impending alliance between Yaswantrao Holkar and Daulatrao Sindhia. He now had to confront only the Army of Hindustan, as Bhonsle's irregulars posed little threat. On paper, at least, it seemed that the two armies were evenly matched. The British put into the field eight cavalry regiments, including three British army light dragoon regiments. The infantry consisted of thirteen sepoy battalions and His Majesty's Seventy-sixth. All told, the British had some 50,000 men under arms throughout India. The army in the Deccan and the Gujrat totaled 35,596 men.[57]

Daulatrao Sindhia had with him in the Deccan the First Brigade under Col. Anthony Pohlmann. Perron had dispatched the Fourth under Dudren-nerc and the Fifth under Brownrigg along with Sumroo Begum's four battalions under Saleur.[58] Near Delhi he had the Second Brigade under Geslin, some 5,000 cavalry under Colonel Fleury, and the forces in the garrisons of Delhi (Drugeon), Agra (George Hessing), and Aligarh (Pedron). However, the Army of Hindustan's greatest weakness was not in its numbers or its fighting ability but in its midlevel officer corps. Most of these officers were British or Anglo-Indian. The British had already offered any European officer a handsome sum if he defected to their side.[59] Instead of countering the British offer, Perron dithered and finally dismissed all British and Anglo-Indian officers, including those who were still loyal.[60] Overnight the Army of Hindustan lost the bulk of its officer corps, which ensured that the outcome of the impending war against the British had already been decided.

On 23 August 1803 Gen. Arthur Wellesley confronted the combined armies of Daulatrao Sindhia and Raghoji Bhonsle at Assaye. Actual fighting took place only between Sindhia's First Brigade and the British. The rest of the Maratha army, mostly 50,000 cavalry, took no part in the battle. Wellesley's forces crossed the Katina River on the 24th, but he had personally reconnoitered the area and noticed that Daulatrao's regulars formed the Maratha left wing and had already deployed in good order, while the remaining Maratha force milled about in disorder. Wellesley immediately decided to attack the regulars of Daulatrao's First Brigade and directed his forces accordingly. When the First Brigade, the seniormost brigade in Daulatrao's army, deployed to meet the British, it did so very awkwardly by moving in a line formation rather than by marching in column and then deploying in line. The inability to execute such a simple maneuver indicated that the veteran brigade, which had conducted far more complicated maneuvers under intense fire and cavalry attack, had lost most of its command element. In fact, as Shelford Bidwell suggests, Pohlman, the German brigade commander, possibly was not even present at the battle.[61] Despite these problems, the First Brigade pivoted a complete 90 degrees from a front facing south to confront Wellesley's infantry advancing from the east. Two British regiments, the Twenty-fourth and the Seventy-eighth, spearheaded the British attack. The Seventy-eighth, advancing smartly with the support of its sepoy battalions, quickly overran the Maratha artillery and closed in on Daulatrao's infantry. After a brief exchange of volleys and a determined bayonet charge by the Seventy-eighth, two battalions of the First Brigade broke and retreated. However, the attack on the left of the Maratha wing did not go as smoothly, and the Seventy-eighth suffered upward of 50 percent casualties. Wellesley immediately sent in cavalry under Colonel Maxwell to aid the Seventy-eighth, but the Maratha gunners, whom the Seventy-eighth had overrun, returned to their pieces and poured fire into the rear of the British cavalry. At this point the Seventy-eighth reversed its front to reengage and recapture the guns, which gave the battered First Brigade time to reconfigure its line and repulse two attacks before its survivors retired from the field. Leaderless and alone, most of the Cheria Fauj's 6,000 men fought to the last by their guns and gave the Duke of Wellington one of his hardest fights.[62] Total British casualties amounted to 1,778 dead and wounded, not including the loss of some 79 officers. After the debacle at Assaye, Daulatrao Sindhia and Raghoji Bhonsle withdrew northward toward the Ajanta Hills. Wellesley followed them after a few days, during which Colonel Stevenson's forces joined him. Battle was joined once again on the 29th on the Argaum plain. Here the Maratha forces, bereft of Daulatrao's regulars, were decisively defeated.

In the north the same story repeated itself. Perron made no move to concentrate his two brigades, the Second and Third. Instead he fought a hopeless cavalry action against Lake on 29 August and then defected to the British.[63] With Perron out of the way, Lake destroyed the Second and Third Brigades with ease outside of Delhi. As at Assaye, the poor handling of these veteran brigades revealed the lack of an effective command element. The British similarly attacked and dispersed the officerless Fifth Brigade outside Agra. The Fifth Brigade was undoubtedly the best formation in Daulatrao's regular army. It consisted of twelve infantry battalions and was under Dudrennerc's command, but Lake enticed him and the unit's European officers to defect to the British. Command of the Fifth Brigade then passed to Ambaji Ingle, who, upon hearing of the fall of the Agra fortress, halted his advance and withdrew to the mountainous Mewar region.[64] Lake immediately set off in pursuit, leaving behind his baggage and heavy guns. After an exhausting forced march, he ran down the last of Daulatrao's brigades at Laswari on 1 November 1803, only 8 miles from the pass in the Mewar Hills. A swift cavalry attack halted the Marathas, and Lake waited for his remaining forces to catch up.

Meanwhile, Ingle deployed the Fifth Brigade between the village of Laswari and a rivulet. In this position he beat back the first cavalry attack. He then left Laswari and deployed his forces in two columns straddling the nearby village of Moholpur and with all his cannons in front. By the 2nd Lake had been reinforced by most of his infantry and decided to attack. Since he had only light galloper guns he decided to avoid the mass of Maratha guns in the center and instead attacked the Marathas' right flank. Ingle reacted instantly by pivoting his right flank, bringing it parallel to the rivulet and placing his left wing upon Laswari, thus once again presenting his front to the British. The ability to complete a complicated maneuver involving some seventy cannons indicates that despite the total loss of its high and midlevel command elements the Fifth Brigade could still maneuver in the field.

The famous British Seventy-sixth Regiment launched the attack. Daulatrao's regulars resisted fiercely, and only after the sepoy battalions joined in the fray did the Fifth begin to fall back, losing its guns in the process. Although the regulars sought to retreat in good order, the Twenty-seventh Dragoons and the Sixth Native Cavalry Regiment attacked and dispersed them. Of the 9,000 men who comprised the brigade, only 2,000 survived. The British did not escape lightly, though, losing some 824 dead and wounded.[65]

With the main Maratha threat eliminated, the British turned on Yaswantrao Holkar, the last surviving Maratha sirdar of any note. Realizing that he could never hope to prevail against the British in an open confrontation, Yaswantrao reverted to a mobile campaign, relying primarily on his cavalry. His biggest success came when he forced a large British regiment under Brig. Gen. William Monson to retreat and then wiped it out in August 1804.[66] Although Yaswantrao fought an excellent mobile campaign against the British, the British eventually forced him to sign the Treaty of Rajghat on 5 January 1806.

Unlike their wars with Mysore, the British entered the Anglo-Maratha Wars well prepared. Through their agents in Delhi (William Palmer) and Poona (Charles Malet) they had gauged correctly the Marathas' strengths and weaknesses. Using political intrigue and bribery, they first split up the Maratha confederacy and then bought off Daulatrao's European officers. By themselves these tactics are not surprising, for the Indians and especially the Marathas used them constantly. What is surprising is the degree to which the British had also mastered these Indian stratagems. If the Marathas in the shape of Mahadji Sindhia's Army of Hindustan had come the closest to mastering the European military system, the British had completely mastered Maratha politics. Once again it was the British ability to recognize the formidable threat of Daulatrao Sindhia's regulars and to readapt their methods to deal with it that saw them through the Anglo-Maratha Wars.

CHAPTER 6

The Anglo-Sikh Wars and Pax Britannica

Guru Nanak (1469–1539) established the Sikh religion in the Punjab. He preached a religion based upon the universal brotherhood of mankind without distinction of race, class, or creed. In 1604 his successor, Arjan Singh, completed the construction of the magnificent Harimandir, or Golden Temple, in Amritsar to give the rapidly growing community a geographical focal point. Although the new religion mainly attracted lower-caste Hindus, it also appealed to Muslims, which brought the wrath of the Mughals down upon the Sikhs. Emperor Jahangir put Guru Arjan to death and viciously persecuted the Sikh community. Under their new leader, Guru Hargobind, the movement took on a decidedly militant characteristic to combat Mughal oppression. After the Mughals executed Guru Tegh Bahadur in 1675, the militancy of the Sikhs reached a new level under his son and successor, Guru Gobind Rai. Gobind initiated a military community known as the Khalsa, or pure. Henceforth all male Sikhs engaged in the profession of arms, and rules that invoked strict discipline controlled their conduct. Although Emperor Aurungzeb initiated a new campaign against the Sikhs, Guru Gobind managed to evade the imperial armies. However, one of the last Mughal emperors, Farukh Siyyar, managed to capture and kill Gobind's successor, Banda Singh, along with thousands of his followers in 1715.

Fortunately for the Sikhs, this was the last gasp of the once-mighty Mughal Empire, and they began to flourish in the 1730s and gradually asserted their independence. Their main enemy was no longer the Mughals but the Afghans, who under Ahmad Shah Durrani waged a constant war against them from 1747 to the early 1760s. However, after his victory over the Marathas at the third battle of Panipat, Durrani quickly recognized Sikh influence in the Punjab. Much of the region at this time was divided between several Sikh clans, or misls, led by chieftains. In addition, a number of Hindu and Muslim chiefs, who combined outnumbered the Sikh chiefs, also ruled in this area. These clans constantly fought each other and the Afghans. (Ahmad Shah Abdali, the Afghan leader, was considered the Punjab's nominal ruler.) Veena Sachdeva has identified 125 political units in the Punjab in the eighteenth century. None of these principalities were large, and most collected revenues of less than 500,000 rupees, with a few even struggling to bring in 20,000 rupees a year.[1]

The Punjabi chieftains' armies were also quite small. The strongest of the chiefs could field a temporary army of 5,000–15,000 men with great difficulty. Of this force, only a small proportion would be under his direct control (the Fauj-i-Khas). Most of the soldiers were militia provided by landlords. Light cavalry, known as *ghorchurra*, dominated Punjabi armies, with infantry used mainly for garrison duty. By the late eighteenth century many of these armies also used firearms of all types.[2]

Ranjit Singh

On 13 November 1780 a son, Ranjit Singh, was born to Maha Singh, the leader of the Sukerchariya misl. At the age of five the boy was married to the grand-daughter of Jai Singh, the chief of the most powerful Sikh misl, the Kanhaya. When Jai Singh died in 1787 the two clans united under Ranjit Singh, and the united clan flourished under his energetic leadership. When the Punjab was invaded by the Afghan leader Zaman Shah (1796–99), Ranjit Singh was the only Sikh leader to confront him in open battle, and he managed to defeat him in 1799 by capturing Lahore. From then on Ranjit Singh's preeminence over the other Sikh chieftains was never questioned. In 1801 he proclaimed himself maharaja of Punjab and began to subdue other clans. He even seized the Afghan province of Multan in 1804. While Ranjit Singh consolidated his power base in the Punjab, the British were busy seizing Hindustan from the Marathas. Ranjit Singh closely followed their actions and was particularly impressed with General Lake's British infantry as they operated against Yaswantrao Holkar in the Punjab.[3]

By 1808 Ranjit Singh had extended his territories from Gujerat in the north to Ludhiana in the east and Multan in the west. He then turned his attention to Malwa in the south on the frontier with the British. In Malwa on the banks of the Sutlej River the independent Sikh chiefs approached the British for help. The latter sent a diplomatic mission led by Charles Metcalfe to Ranjit.[4] However, in September 1808 Ranjit crossed the Sutlej and occupied Malwa without informing Metcalfe. He also summoned his generals and chiefs and accelerated production of war matériel.[5] Stung by this action, the British threatened dire consequences, and in February Metcalfe's 200-man sepoy escort made short work of several hundred attacking Sikhs.[6] The sight of a handful of well-organized sepoys repelling hundreds of fanatical Akali, or religious, warriors left an indelible impression upon Ranjit. He at once recognized his military weakness and signed the Treaty of Amritsar in 1809. He withdrew his forces from Malwa and recognized the Sutlej River as his kingdom's southeast boundary.[7]

Blocked by the British in the south, Ranjit once again turned to the Punjab, subduing the remaining independent Sikh clans, and in 1810 he defeated the Gurkhas at Kangra and ejected them from the region. In 1818 he retook Multan, and in 1821 he drove the Afghans from Kashmir. Having established a firm grip on northwestern India, Ranjit began to modernize his army.

At the close of 1800 Ranjit Singh's army consisted primarily of a cavalry force of some 2,500 men. However, by 1803 he had established an infantry force by using deserters from the East India Company and by raising two Najib (Rohilla matchlock men) battalions.[8] His attempts to induce the Punjabis to give up their horses and join the infantry proved unsuccessful, and he had to turn to other sources. Fortunately, he found a ready supply from Mahadji Sindhia's disbanded Army of Hindustan as well as deserters from the British and local armies.[9] In addition to the regulars, Ranjit, like the Mysoreans and the Marathas, also maintained a substantial irregular army. In this case it was mainly a feudal army that by 1808 numbered approximately 15,000 men.[10] In the period following the humiliating Treaty of Amritsar in 1809 Ranjit expanded his infantry, and by 1821 he had fourteen battalions whose strength varied from 200 to 800 men.[11] At the same time Ranjit began to raise a body of regular cavalry, and by 1819–20 he had created three regiments of 100–600 men each.[12] In 1822 Ranjit's attempts to establish a professional army received a great boost when he hired two French officers, Capt. Jean François Allard, formerly of the Napoleonic Seventh Hussars, and Col. Jean Baptiste Ventura, a Napoleonic infantry officer.[13] He commissioned them to raise model infantry and cavalry units upon which he would pattern the regular army. The new force was called the Fauj-i-Khas and consisted of Ventura's four infantry battalions and Allard's two cavalry regiments.[14] In 1807 Ranjit established factories in Lahore to produce guns, but the quality of these guns was questionable.[15] Under the direction of European officers, however, the artillery and the associated gun foundries were overhauled and dramatically improved.[16] The impact of these French officers on the army was so positive that Ranjit gradually adopted the French method of training.[17]

In 1822 Ranjit made Allard commander of the regular cavalry, and by 1831–32 the army contained five *rajmans*, or regiments, of varying strength (226–650 men).[18] However, Ranjit continued to lavish great attention on his irregular ghorchurra cavalry, often at the expense of Allard's regulars. The ghorchurras were light cavalry in the same mold as the Maratha and Mysore light horse.[19] They, rather than Allard's regular cavalry, formed Ranjit's household cavalry. Ranjit continually strove to increase the discipline and efficiency of this 10,000-man corps by reorganization, training, and inspections. He armed the cavalry with 15-foot-long steel and bamboo lances.[20] Ranjit dressed the regular infantry in an impressive Western uniform (although the uniform included the traditional Sikh turban).[21] He armed them with a mixture of matchlocks and flintlocks (known as "Brown Bess"), with the latter becoming the standard issue by the 1820s.[22] The regular infantry continued to multiply, and by 1831–32 Ranjit had 20,000 men in twenty-one battalions.[23] Along with the regulars Ranjit also increased the irregulars so that by 1831 he had 23,950 irregular infantry (mainly garrison troops).[24] All Sikh soldiers, whether cavalry, infantry, or artillery, carried a tulwar, or scimitar, which was their weapon of choice for close-in fighting. As the regular army gained prestige, Sikhs began to enroll in large numbers. From 1822 onward they began replacing all non-Punjabi soldiers.[25] By 1835 the entire regular army, almost entirely Sikh, was organized along brigade lines, with each brigade comprising three to four infantry battalions, one artillery battalion, and a cavalry regiment.[26]

The Sikh army was superior to any other local Indian army in its command structure. Instead of relying exclusively upon European officers, Ranjit encouraged and selected the sons of Sikh chiefs to enroll as officers at an early age so that they could be trained comprehensively in European military tactics and drill.[27] These Sikh officers commanded the Sikh army in the impending conflict with the British.

The Anglo-Sikh Wars

Ranjit Singh died in 1839, leaving behind the most formidable military establishment in India outside of the East India Company. His weak and ineffective son, Kharrack Singh, succeeded him; however, he was murdered in 1840, and his death led to an internal power struggle among various court factions for the control of the throne. The Sikh army at the time of Ranjit's death numbered approximately 150,000 men, of whom some 60,000–65,000 were regulars.[28] Courted by different political factions, the army began to make demands on Raja Hira Singh and his successor, Jawahar Singh.[29] During this chaotic period, the army began to govern itself through a system of elected councils at company level, which in turn formed battalion or regimental committees.[30]

The British reacted quickly to the political instability in Lahore. They began to mass large numbers of troops at the Sutlej River, the border between the two powers, in complete violation of the 1809 treaty. In November 1843 Major Broadfoot, the new British frontier agent, unilaterally declared all Sikh territory south of Sutlej as a British protectorate.[31] In response to this and other British provocations, the Sikh army crossed the Sutlej in December 1845 and invested the town of Ferozepur, triggering the first Anglo-Sikh War. Despite prior intelligence of Sikh movements, the British force of eight infantry battalions (one British), twelve horse guns, and twelve field guns, totaling 7,000 men under Gen. Sir John Littler, was taken by surprise. The large force of 50,000 Sikhs would have easily overwhelmed the British but for the treachery of two Sikh leaders, the prime minister, Lal Singh, and the commander in chief, Tej Singh. They had been secretly in contact with the British and actually hoped that the British would destroy the Khalsa, thus allowing them and the Maharani Jindan to rule as dependents.[32] The traitors' delaying tactics enabled the British to muster all their forces. The commander in chief, Gen. Hugh Gough, left Ambala with an army of 12,000 men on 11 December and force-marched 114 miles in five days to reach Ferozepur. He reached Mudki south of Ferozepur on the 18th and stopped to feed and provision his forces. Soon afterward a small Sikh force of 2,000 infantry and 9,000 cavalry under Lal Singh advanced to probe the British lines, thus initiating the first round of battles.

Gough soon discovered that the Sikhs had deployed their main force in a forest near Mudki, and he immediately positioned his thirty six-pounder horse guns to engage them at 300 yards. The lighter British guns, however, soon received the worst of the exchange with the heavier Sikh guns. Meanwhile, a large mass of Sikh irregular cavalry threatened the British flanks, and Gough immediately ordered the British cavalry to attack. A force consisting of the bodyguard and the Fifth Light Dragoons under Gough, the Ninth Irregulars (Indian) and half of the Fourth Light Cavalry under Brigadier Mackier, and units of the Third Light Dragoons and the remaining half of the Fourth Light Cavalry charged the Sikh cavalry and forced them to fall back. The cavalry also succeeded in turning the Sikh position and temporarily silencing their guns. In the meantime, the twelve battalions of British and sepoy infantry formed up and began to advance. Artillery fire and musketry from the Sikhs immediately greeted them. Under such intense fire, the sepoy battalions wavered and stalled, but gradually the British Fiftieth and Thirty-first Infantry Regiments closed in and stormed the Sikh guns, using their five-to-one superiority in numbers to drive back the Sikh infantry. Gough attributed this success to the bayonet. After losing most of their guns, the Sikh force fell back to their camp in Ferozeshah, midway to Ferozepur. The

British won the field at a cost of 215 dead and 657 wounded in six hours of fighting.[33]

After the battle the British returned to their camp in Mudki, where His Majesty's Twenty-ninth Foot, the First European Light Infantry, two eight-inch howitzers, two eighteen-pounders, and two sepoy regiments joined them. At this point, Gough ascertained that Lal Singh with some 20,000 men was entrenched in Ferozeshah, while Tej Singh with 30,000 men was still "watching" General Littler and his garrison in Ferozepur. Gough immediately decided to attack Lal Singh before the two Sikh armies could unite. At 2:00 AM the entire British force, except for two sepoy regiments (left behind to guard the wounded and the baggage), marched out to Ferozeshah and had reached its outer defenses by 10:00 AM Soon afterward news came of Littler's movement out of Ferozepur to join Gough's forces. All seemed to be going well for the British until the governor-general, Sir Henry Hardinge, imposed his civil authority and forbade any action until Littler joined Gough. The Sikhs fared little better, since the treacherous Tej Singh ignored the Sikh junior commanders' requests to attack Littler's small force as it marched on Ferozepur. Littler finally joined Gough at 1:00 PM, and the combined force of 18,000 men, two howitzers, and sixty-three light guns massed some 3,000 yards from the southwest corner of the Sikh entrenchments. By 3:30 PM Gough had deployed his force in a large semicircle around the western entrenchments of Ferozeshah.

The British launched their attack at 4:00 PM and were immediately subject to heavy fire from the Sikh artillery. Brigadier Reed's brigade came under particularly intense fire as it, along with another brigade (Ashburn's), emerged from the woods some 300 yards from the Sikh guns. Reed, foreseeing the total destruction of his brigade, ordered an immediate charge at the guns. However, the two sepoy regiments and the British Sixty-second Foot, which continued the advance, had to drop to the ground short of the guns, with heavy losses. The British regrouped and deployed their own artillery in a more effective position, and the remaining infantry advanced on the Sikh guns. The Sikh gunners defended their guns to the bitter end, while their infantry fired a fierce volley on the British and then threw down their muskets, unsheathed their dreaded tulwars, and charged.[34] The British infantry met them with bayonets and pushed them back. By nightfall the British and the sepoy infantry had fought their way into the Sikh encampment when Gough sounded the recall, which enabled the Sikhs to regain their guns. They then began to fire on the British infantry squares outside the town throughout the night.[35] The next morning the attack was renewed, and, after a seesaw battle, the British captured the Sikh trenches and took their guns. With Ferozeshah in British hands, Lal Singh's remaining forces fled to the Sutlej. Cavalry on both sides had little effect upon the main battle. Although the British and Indian cavalry easily dispersed the Sikh irregular cavalry, they themselves made little impression on the well-disciplined Sikh infantry.

The battle, however, was not over. Even as Lal Singh's forces fled to the Sutlej, by 1:00 PM Tej Singh's larger army of 30,000 men had finally moved out of Ferozepur and toward Ferozeshah. The British did not want another confrontation against a powerful and fresh Sikh army because they were exhausted and running low on ammunition. Despite this, the British forces (two sepoy regiments and the Third Dragoons) managed to put the large mass of Sikh cavalry to flight after a hectic melee. In the meantime Gough had drawn up his infantry into a four-deep square (initially to face a possible Sikh cavalry charge) facing the enemy in the north. However, no sooner had the Sikh cavalry threat waned than the square came under artillery fire. With overwhelming fire support from their artillery, the Sikh infantry now attacked the British. At this delicate point Captain Lumley, the acting adjutant general, ordered the artillery to replenish their munition stocks at Ferozepur (Littler had left all his supplies there to fool the Sikhs), and he had the cavalry accompany them. To the incredulous Gough and the infantry, it appeared that the end was near as they awaited the Sikh artillery and infantry onslaught, but the Sikhs were denied victory once again when Tej Singh ordered a retreat.[36] Thus the remarkable series of events that constitute the battle of Ferozeshah ended at 4:00 PM on 22 December 1845. The British had lost 694 dead out of a total of 2,415 casualties.[37] The Sikh losses were much greater.

Battered but undaunted, the Sikh Khalsa soon recrossed the Sutlej and established a bridgehead at Sobraon. As they feverishly entrenched themselves Gough moved toward them after receiving a reinforcement of 10,000 men under Sir John Grey from Meerut. However, some 80 miles away another Sikh force under Gen. Runjur Singh crossed the Sutlej near Philaur. Gough immediately dispatched a force under Gen. Sir Harry Smith to stop Runjur before he cut off the British communication lines with the rest of India. After a brief skirmish at Bhudowal, the two armies met near the village of Aliwal on 27 January 1846. Smith had a force of 12,000 men in four infantry brigades and two cavalry brigades, twenty-eight field guns, and two eight-inch howitzers. Runjur's forces had grown to 20,000 men. The Sikhs stood with their backs to the Sutlej (a mile away) and with their flanks resting on the villages of Aliwal and Bhundri, which they linked by 3 miles of hastily dug trenches. The battle was a repeat of Ferozeshah: the British infantry formed up into lines and advanced, the Sikh guns opened fire on them, and the British guns replied. After a fierce melee the British took the Sikh guns and thrust back the

Sikh infantry, which had formed up in squares. The Sikh cavalry attempted a feeble charge, but the British cavalry scattered them. With less than a mile between their positions and the Sutlej River, the British gradually crowded in the Sikh infantry and broke its formations. At this point the Sikh forces began to retreat across the river. At a cost of some 151 dead and 413 wounded, the British captured sixty-seven guns, all the Sikh baggage, and 3,000 men.[38]

Near Sobraon a delighted and relieved Gough now prepared to attack the Sikhs. He already had a full description of the Sikh positions provided to him by the Sikh commander Tej Singh.[39] By 9 February he had a force of 20,000 (including General Smith's forces) in three infantry divisions, four cavalry brigades, fourteen horse and field artillery batteries, six eighteen-pounders, and eighteen heavy howitzers and mortars. At dawn on the 10th the British heavily bombarded the Sikh entrenchments, while the Sikh guns replied shot for shot. A little after 8:00 AM the order to advance was given. Brigadier Stacy's brigade led the attack on the Sikh right flank but was repulsed with heavy losses, and the division commander, Sir Robert Dick, was killed. A subsequent British attack on the Sikh left flank managed, however, to breach the Sikh defenses after a bloody struggle. The British attack in the center also met with similar success. After engineers made a gap in the fortifications, the British cavalry, under Gen. Sir Joseph Thackwell, poured through. Attacked from three directions and having been evicted from their gun lines and trenches, the Sikh infantry retreated slowly toward the river; but upon reaching the narrow bridge all order vanished, and the retreat turned into a bloody rout as the British brought their guns to bear upon the narrow causeway. By noon the battle was over. While suffering a relatively small loss of some 320 dead and 2,063 wounded, the British had killed some 10,000 Sikhs and captured sixty-seven guns.[40] In true form, the Sikh leader Tej Singh had fled the battle well before the end.

On 18 February 1846 the Sikhs signed a humiliating peace treaty on British terms. In addition to vast indemnities the Sikhs lost the fertile Jullundher Doab between the Sutlej and Beas Rivers. The Sikh army was drastically cut down to 32,000 infantry and cavalry.[41] The British also made Dilip Singh a puppet ruler along with his mother, Maharani Jindan.[42] The British rewarded the traitors Lal Singh and Tej Singh by once again installing them as prime minister and commander in chief.[43] However, the Sikh threat was far from dead, as the unemployed Sikh army formed a discontented body waiting to rise up in revolt. Their opportunity came in April 1848, when Mulraj, the Muslim governor of Multan (which Ranjit Singh had seized from the Afghans in 1819), rebelled against the British when they tried to replace him.[44] Almost immediately the Sikhs rallied to Mulraj's banner. The British added fuel to the fire when they exiled Maharani Jindan and Dilip Singh to Benares on 15 May 1848. Under such blatant provocation, the Sikhs in the north under Chuttar Singh joined Mulraj, thus triggering the second Anglo-Sikh War. Raja Shere Singh (part of the puppet government in Lahore), his son, and most of the Sikh army, which was supposed to be under British control, also joined Mulraj's cause.

After a brief skirmish at Ramnagar on the banks of the Chenab on 22 November, the British besieged the fortress of Multan, which fell to them following a siege operation on 22 January 1849. On the 10th General Gough marched with an army of 12,000 men and sixty-six guns to confront Shere Singh. Shere Singh's army was comprised of some 30,000 men with sixty-two guns. The Sikh commander, like those before him, had deployed his army with its back to a river, the Jhelum, and with a town, Chillianwalla, in front of it. Gough reached Chillianwalla on the 13th and deployed to attack with his infantry in a line in the center and his cavalry on his flanks. Although Shere Singh did not dig entrenchments, a dense growth of thorny brush protected his front, while the Chillianwalla forest protected his flank. After a brief cannonade, the British and sepoy infantry advanced along a 3-mile-wide front, but no sooner had they entered the dense brush when the units quickly lost cohesion. In the center the Twenty-fourth Foot outstripped its sepoy regiments and emerged in the clear to receive the full blast of the Sikh fire. A desperate rush with bayonets momentarily secured the Sikh guns, but the Sikh infantry countered and scattered the Twenty-fourth, which suffered some 231 dead (including its commander, Brigadier Pennicuick) and 236 wounded. The two sepoy regiments that were following, the Twenty-fifth and the Forty-fifth, also broke (the Twenty-fifth actually managed to hit the Sikh positions before retreating), and the entire force streamed back. More disaster followed. A large body of Sikh cavalry maneuvered in a manner menacing to the British flank. This resulted in some confused orders emanating from the commanders of the Second Cavalry Brigade, whose units turned their backs on a small body of Sikh cavalry.[45] The Sikhs' small force, reacting in the best opportunistic traditions of Indian light cavalry, immediately attacked and sent the entire British cavalry reeling into the hospital camp to the rear.

The tide of the battle began to turn in the British favor when their remaining infantry units captured most of the Sikh guns. The British cavalry brigade under General White now struck back and easily scattered the Sikh cavalry, but an attack on the Sikh infantry gained little but heavy casualties. Nevertheless, by nightfall the Sikhs were retreating toward the Jhelum. The British retired to Chillianwalla to tend to their wounded, having lost 2,331 killed, wounded, and missing.[46]

After this debacle Shere Singh tried to avoid another conflict with the British in the open. Instead he sought to entice the British into attacking him in the hills and ravines a few miles north of Chillianwalla, where the terrain would aid him against the dreaded British infantry. General Gough, however, forced Shere Singh to make a stand at Gujerat by blocking his retreat and thus cutting him off from Lahore. With the initiative totally on the British side, Gough slowly built up his forces to 24,000 men and 106 guns. Having assembled one of the largest British armies in India, Gough easily routed the weakened Sikhs at the cost of 96 dead and 670 wounded on 21 February.[47] On 9 March Shere Singh surrendered at Rawalpindi. The Punjab was annexed on the 30th, leaving the British as the sole military power in India.[48]

Under Ranjit Singh, the Sikh army reached a level of expertise second only to Mahadji Sindhia's Army of Hindustan and in artillery was second to none in India, including the British. The subsequent deterioration of the army's discipline and command structure, however, left it completely vulnerable to the East India Company's veteran armies. Furthermore, even if the Sikh army had emerged from the political chaos with its discipline intact, it would have faced the insurmountable task of overwhelming the company's huge forces. In other words, regardless of the strides the Sikhs made in adapting to European military tactics, they could not defeat the British, who controlled the Indian subcontinent's vast resources.

Pax Britannica

The three Indian armies that confronted the East India Company between 1769 and 1850 had the ability to inflict a crippling blow to the British military machine in India. Their failure to do so eventually resulted in their destruction and subsequent absorption into the British Empire. Despite the Indians' adoption of Western military strategy, the British overwhelmed them with their ability to adapt to Indian tactics and exploit Indian politics.

In Mysore, for example, neither Hyder nor his son Tippu transformed their army into a Western-style infantry army; they were more comfortable with their light cavalry tactics. Unfortunately for them, by the third Anglo-Mysore War, the British had adapted very well to their tactics. In the case of the Marathas, the change to a Western-style military system had begun long before the British were a military force in the subcontinent. Under Sindhia the Marathas made tremendous strides in catching up with the West. The British only dispatched the Army of Hindustan by isolating it from the rest of the Maratha confederacy and denuding it of its officer corps. The British achieved this victory through political intrigue and bribery, time-honored Indian (and

European) tactics that the British had learned (and then relearned) well. Without these measures the British would have stood little chance against the Marathas, a fact they readily acknowledged: "These battalions were the most uncommonly well-appointed and had a most numerous artillery, as well served as they can possibly be, the gunners standing to their guns, until killed by the bayonet, all the sepoys of the enemy behaved exceedingly well and if they had been commanded by French officers, the event would have been, I fear, extremely doubtful."[49] The Sikhs were the only Indian power that built up their army as a reaction to the British. Even in their case, the British extensively used subterfuge to secure the Sikh commanders' help against their own army.

The question that remains unanswered is, How did the Indian powers build up such formidable military establishments? The answer lies in the institutional evolution of the armies. The Indian armies under discussion incorporated elements of many different army styles: the centralized monarchical army, the national army, the mercenary army, the feudal army, and professional military organizations. What becomes problematic is how to allocate these terms to the state's various military organizations.

Of the three armies discussed, the Mysore army under Hyder and Tippu had the least time (thirty years) to implement changes in army style. At the beginning of the era the army's organization essentially reflected the late Mughal Empire's feudal military system. In fact, Hyder was the feudal governor under the Wodeyar rulers of Mysore before he seized power. Under Hyder and Tippu the army underwent a dramatic transition from a feudal to a centralized monarchical army. By Tippu's time the majority of the regular army and cavalry officers were paid in cash. However, Hyder and Tippu maintained a substantial mercenary cavalry as well as smaller units of European soldiers. Tippu did not make a complete transition to an all-national army because the light cavalry tactics upon which he relied forced him to call upon the services of mercenary cavalry.

The evolution of the Maratha armies spanned a far greater period (1664–1803). Like Mysore, the original Maratha military system was feudal in nature. Shivaji transformed the feudal armies into a centralized army for a brief period. After his death the military reverted to its feudal origins, with the sole exception of the imperial army under the peshwa's direct control. However, under Mahadji Sindhia the Maratha military system underwent a remarkable transition. Mahadji's army initially consisted of a feudal force of several thousand cavalry. From 1784 on he established a European-style mercenary infantry force under Benoît de Boigne. In 1791 this force became a feudal army of sorts when de Boigne received the rich province of Aligarh as a jagir to raise several infantry brigades that eventually became the Army of Hindustan. By 1803 this mercenary-feudal army had made the transition to a seminational army of long-service soldiers. It seems that these "mercenary" soldiers had begun to identify themselves with Mahadji Sindhia's cause, for even when their European officers and paymasters deserted them, most continued an obviously hopeless struggle against the British. Unlike their officers, they refused lucrative British offers to desert.[50] Such conduct is astonishing when one considers that mass defections by mercenary units were a common occurrence in India. Mahadji Sindhia's feudal cavalry levies, which were predominantly Maratha, played little or no role in his conquest of northern India or during the struggle against the British. Instead Mahadji and his successor, Daulatrao, relied on the Army of Hindustan, northern India's embryonic national army.

Ranjit Singh's Sikh army also evolved from a feudal background. Ranjit was fortunate because he had Maratha and British sepoy armies as models for his new regular army. Additionally, he built his first regular infantry force from the deserters of the East India Company and survivors of Sindhia's brigades. With considerable help from French Napoleonic-era officers, Ranjit established a formidable national army along European lines. By the end of his reign Ranjit had dispensed with most of his mercenaries and had replaced most of his European officers with Sikh officers. In this vital aspect of command and control the Sikhs achieved more progress than any other Indian power. Similar to the Marathas before them, the Sikh army's feudal element, the ghorchurra light cavalry, played a small role in the conflict with the British. Instead, the Sikh national army, under the command of local self-governing bodies of soldiers and junior Sikh officers, bore the brunt of the war effort.

The Indian armies between 1750 and 1850 made tremendous strides in military organization. Had the British not impeded this progress, these armies might have achieved a position equal to the best European armies. By anticipating and preempting the progress of the Indian powers, the British effectively stymied any decisive moves against them. The failure of the three Indian powers to counteract the British raises one question: Was there an inherent weakness within these states that hindered their efforts at adopting the Western military system? The answer is yes, for all these states were essentially feudal in origin and had little time to transition to a stable monarchy with a centralized bureaucracy. In contrast to the Indian powers, other non-European powers that sought to emulate the Western military system (e.g., Turkey, Egypt, China, and Japan) did so over a longer time span and without any substantial external interference.[51] But even with this handicap, the Indian powers successfully thwarted the Portuguese and the French from expanding their footholds in India.

One key component to the British success lies in their unique geographic position in India. The British had three centers of power: Bombay, Calcutta, and Madras. These cities straddle the subcontinent's three corners, enabling the British to establish an unrivaled intelligence network. Furthermore, defeat in any region did not mean annihilation for the British, as was the case with the French in Pondicherry; they merely retreated to the other two British strongholds. All these advantages, coupled with the British ability to adapt and innovate on the basis of a vastly superior centralized organizational and governmental infrastructure, led them to victory.

East India Company State Building and Warfare

All the advantages that the British enjoyed in their struggle against the Indian powers would have benefited them little had they not at the same time successfully harnessed the subcontinent's tremendous resources. The British were not the first to obtain more revenues to finance their war effort. The Indian powers, since the waning days of the Mughal Empire, had competed to gain more territories and hence revenue to finance their war establishments, which were the main props of their political power. In the post-Mughal era the competition became more intense not only because more regional powers existed but also because the transition to the new Western style of warfare involved considerably more expense. The units of trained Western-style infantry set up by the nizam of Hyderabad and the peshwa were in essence long-term professionals and not seasonal soldiers who could be hired for particular campaigns. The training and drilling required to maintain the skills of such a force required it to be supported all year long. Such units required uniform clothing, equipment harnesses, muskets, ball, and gunpowder, all of which cost much more than a sword and a target, the equipment of the traditional Indian foot soldier prior to the era of firearms. If artillery was added to the equation along with more gunpowder and shot, the price went up further. In the case of Mahadji Sindhia, who manufactured all of his equipment, including his cannons and shot, the capital investment was immense, which is why he assigned the revenues of the immensely rich province of Aligarh to de Boigne.

Mahadji Sindhia's expansion into northern India came about primarily due to his need for additional revenues to shore up his power base. To this end he was forced to make severe demands on all people under his nominal control, especially the Rajputs.[52] Even during peace Mahadji's armies needed substantial funds. During his visit to Poona his troops were in long arrears, and he had to borrow 7 million rupees from reluctant local moneylenders to pay them.[53]

Merely having the desire and the foresight to set up a European-style infantry did not in itself mean an instant military power base for an Indian ruler. He also had to have the finances to sustain such a force. Yaswantrao Holkar, undeniably the ablest of Maratha leaders after Mahadji, had difficulties setting up a single infantry brigade and was always bereft of money. He made severe revenue demands upon the Rajputs during his war with Mahadji Sindhia.[54] Holkar needed immense funds to maintain his new infantry-based army, and, after defeating the peshwa and Mahadji's combined armies outside Poona, he found himself desperately short of cash with his army in long arrears. His answer was to sack Poona.[55]

The British were late and somewhat reluctant entrants into the race for military dominance in India. Unlike the Indian powers, the East India Company for much of the eighteenth century had gradually expanded its military forces in India primarily to safeguard its economic interests and not, as the Indian powers had done, to expand a military power base in the region and thus enhance state formation. As far as the British were concerned, military power was a means to an end rather than an end in itself; it was a necessary expenditure. The company had originally set up sepoy forces to protect its trading locations in India, but gradually, as the company's armies expanded, they became the main drain of the company's financial resources. It soon became clear that the money extracted from trading alone could not support the company's military efforts. The main source of wealth in India lay in revenue or tax collection, which in turn demanded more and more territorial expansion. Indeed, one of the British leaders' first acts after capturing Calcutta in January 1757 was to order the neighboring zamindars to pay their respective districts' rents and revenues in lieu of having their country destroyed. By these payments the company hoped to finance its ongoing conflict against the nawab.[56] In Bengal in the 1770s the company's army of 4,000 Europeans and 26,000 sepoys required a budget increase of 8 million pounds over a ten-year period compared to the mere 5.3 million pounds being spent on trade. This forced the company to annex large districts in the region in 1760. In 1764 more money was required, and by 1765 the company had taken over the entire revenue system in Bengal.[57] Territorial expansion was often closely linked with military finances. The British often stationed troops in the client state's territories, forcing the rulers, as in the case of Avadh, to divert resources to the British garrison. The British adopted the same pattern in Bengal, Karnatik, Travancore, Poona, and the Punjab. The distribution of many troops to the territories of nominally independent Indian rulers was not only a strategic necessity but was also crucial to obtaining the necessary finances to support the company's rapidly growing sepoy armies.

The establishment of Bengal as a firm tax base for the company enabled it to pursue a prolonged war against Mysore. Neither the Madras government nor the puppet nawab of Karnatik had the funds to prosecute such a prolonged war and had begun to rely entirely upon Bengal, which sent 2,797,853 rupees between September 1780 and February 1781 to finance the war effort.[58] The Bengal government, appalled by what it saw as the Madras government's risky ventures, often threatened to stop sending financial aid and even suggested that the Madras government seize the Karnatik revenue from the nawab to finance the war.[59] In the end Madras could not sustain its war against Mysore without such massive support from Calcutta. In March 1781, during the second Anglo-Mysore War, Coote's army was already a month in arrears.[60] The war in Mysore forced the Bengal government to resort to drastic measures. Sevak Ram, the Maratha agent in Calcutta, wrote to Poona, noting that the British had resorted to forceful money collections. They canceled monetary concessions that many zamindars enjoyed in connection with market collections. This long-term aid from Bengal paid off, and the British soon turned the tables on Tippu Sultan. The Treaty of Seringapatam financially devastated Tippu. By the onset of the fourth and final Anglo-Mysore War Tippu's kingdom yielded a revenue of only 1 million pounds sterling, while the combined British revenue in India exceeded 9 million pounds.[61] In 1803 British estimates of the total jama, or legitimate assessments, to the major Indian powers broke down as follows: Peshwa, £124,220,916; British East India Company, £123,578,709.1; the nizam of Hyderabad, £34,673,304.7; Sikhs and others, £32,234,983.4; Abdali (Afghans), £16,301,500.[62] After the peshwa, the British were the second largest revenue collectors in India. However, the figures do not reflect the military reality on the ground (the virtual destruction of Maratha military power) or the company's rapidly growing tax base, as it continued to bring more and more local Indian powers into its political and economic sphere of control. Thus, in addition to their superior organizational and professional abilities, the company's commanders could maintain a large professional army only through the infusion of massive finances from a growing network of tax collection. The company's civil service at last provided the subcontinent with a rational professional and permanent civil bureaucracy independent of the royal household. This bureaucracy enabled the British to tackle the problems of maintaining a professional army in the field, something the Indian powers could not effectively achieve.

The British were not only more successful in cornering the subcontinent's revenues, they were also more adept at achieving this goal. The highly professional and competent East India Company bureaucracy instilled a continuity and stability in the revenue collection system that had not existed since the Mughal Empire's glory days.[63] No longer were the local rulers subject to the competing Indian powers with their often arbitrary and self-destructive demands but instead were subject to a new, more permanent system of regularized tax collection. The lack of continuity in the Indian powers' revenue collection system was a serious detriment to the smooth functioning of their new Western-style permanent armies. With the exception of Mahadji Sindhia's Army of Hindustan, most Indian powers, including Holkar, could only maintain token infantry-based armies in the field. Even the Army of Hindustan had to take to the field in fragments as a tax collection force to obtain the funds to maintain its existence.

The failure of the Indian powers to create and maintain a viable professional military in the field was rooted in the inability of the Indian states to develop centralized state structures. Since ancient times Indian states had created what Max Weber has deemed patrimonial characteristics, where rulers relied on personal loyalty and bonds to control officials and to communicate with their regional elites.[64] The Mughal patrimonial-bureaucratic empire was a significant step up in centralization from ancient and early medieval India's state structures. However, the emperor and not the state served as the basis of this centralization. As a result, the empire could not transition into a modern state, as happened in contemporary Europe. European centralization occurred as a result of a "military revolution" that involved a massive increase in armies' firepower along with significant advances in tactics, training, and strategy. The revolution triggered substantial growth in the size and complexity of European armies. Not only did armies become larger and need more expensive equipment and munitions, they also remained in the field much longer, thus making them a professional fighting force.[65] The massive costs and organizational efforts involved in deploying and maintaining these vast standing armies resulted in the enhancement of centralized power throughout Europe. But this military revolution could not have occurred without a corresponding "bureaucratic revolution." As Bruce Porter notes, European state bureaucracies quadrupled in size during this period (1559–1660), partly to manage the immense problems of military production and supply. These professional and permanent bureaucracies maintained their independence from the royal household and became a force for political centralization in their own right.[66] The Mughals and their successor states, including that of Mahadji Sindhia, could not put into effect a similar bureaucratic revolution and as a direct consequence found it impossible to sustain the tremendous costs of maintaining a professional European-style army.

Recent studies of the British conquest of India have rejected the state formation thesis outlined above. Seema Alavi, for instance, suggests that while superior military force served as the basis for the East India Company's political dominance of North India, British control was not predicated upon possessing a more advanced military organization, command of technology, or fighting skills. Instead, "it rested more on the fact that in the eighty years of Company rule its army had become the major guarantee of social and political stability. . . . [I]t was the incorporation of the Company's military institutions within civilian society rather than the overt use of violence which assured Company rule."[67] While this theory explains later consolidation of company rule, it does not illustrate the company's initial military and political domination of India. The British ability to dominate the battlefield and eliminate its competitors provided it with the opportunity and ability to shape the dynamics of Indian society.

In a recent book examining the historical relationship between society and armies in India Stephen Rosen presents an intriguing theory for the defeat of the Indian powers at the hands of the British.[68] He suggests that Indian armies were always weaker than British-led sepoy (and European) armies because they were essentially militia forces with close links to Indian society. As a result, these armies reflected Indian society's caste divisions and thus could not match the battlefield discipline of the British sepoys. Since the sepoy army was divorced from Indian society, it was a more professional and effective fighting force.[69] However, Indian leaders such as the Maratha chief Mahadji Sindhia and the Sikh Khalsa did in fact manage, albeit with considerable difficulty, to raise professional armies that the British envied. The failure of these forces to defeat the British had more to do with the inherent weaknesses of the Indian states than with the divisions plaguing Indian society. Similarly, Indian powers like Mysore simply avoided head-to-head confrontation with British armies. Their cavalry-raiding tactics rendered the superior discipline and cohesiveness of the British forces irrelevant. Success for the British, in this particular confrontation, came only when the company controlled and eventually decimated the once-thriving horse trade in northern India.

Of Men and Horses

The British gradually conquered India not only through their slow absorption of the subcontinent's territory and accompanying revenue resources but also by co-opting the Indian military labor market and inland trading routes.

In the decades following the collapse of the Mughal Empire a huge military labor market evolved with roots in the peasantry of Hindustan and southern India. In most cases the local zamindars recruited men who in turn sold their services to the regional ruler or warlord. In Mughal times the imperial armies recruited their troops directly from military labor markets like the Brahmanical pilgrimage site of Baksar on the Ganges.[70] As the Indian powers built up their own professional infantry armies, they relied increasingly upon this multilayered military labor market for their recruits. Mahadji Sindhia, when recruiting for his Army of Hindustan, bypassed the middlemen such as the zamindars and jemadars, or jobbers, who provided these recruits. De Boigne's ability to recruit directly from the labor markets such as Baksar enabled him to create a professional army based upon a steady stream of military labor relatively unaffected by the jobbers' interference. The British also tried not to rely on the middlemen and in the nineteenth century stopped the recruitment of Buxari (from Buxar) matchlock men under their own jemadars.[71] However, as the East India Company gradually extended its control over Hindustan, it dealt a severe blow to the military labor market, which up until that time had been predominantly a seller's market. Not only did the British become the sole "buyer" of military labor, but they also denied other Indian powers access to this market. Yaswantrao Holkar's almost total reliance on cavalry-based armies (mainly Maratha) in his campaigns against the British probably occurred because he no longer had access to the Hindustani military labor market. Similarly, Ranjit Singh's gradual reliance on Sikhs for his regular infantry units may have resulted from his inability to access the Hindustani military labor market. The devastation of the military labor market and the increasing bureaucratic centralization under the East India Company had a considerable impact on the once-independent zamindars and taluqdars, or district-level landlords, who in prior times had functioned as quasi kings or petty rajahs. These individuals, who had considerable local economic and military power, had frustrated all efforts at state centralization prior to the consolidation of British rule. However, the "revised" agrarian settlement of 1835 dramatically altered their power base. Not only were their possessions slowly whittled away, but the British stripped them of armaments and retainers and gave them only honorary magistrate capacity to try petty cases. As Thomas Metcalf noted, under the British the taluqdars became landlords rather than the quasi rulers they had once been.[72]

After the battle of Plassey in 1757, when the British began recruiting sepoys from rural Bengal, Burhanpur and Dinapur became important recruiting centers. However, many recruits failed to meet the minimum physical standards, especially height. Seema Alavi believes that this lack of good recruits forced the British to expand their recruiting to North India's wheat-growing areas, where the British focused their recruiting efforts on high caste Hindu peasants who embodied the subcontinent's "martial races." In other words, the recruiting imperative of the martial races was evident in the British-Indian armies as early as 1750.[73] However, the documentary evidence suggests that the British were doing nothing more than recruiting peasants who met the right physical characteristics.[74] It is clear that as the company brought more populous regions in the hinterland under its control, its options for military recruiting expanded, while the local Indian rulers' abilities to do the same decreased. Such a practice was evident in Bengal and Karnatik and later in Avadh, Banaras, and Hyderabad. In Avadh the company gradually replaced the local ruler, Asaf-ud-Daulah, as the region's primary military recruiter, thus taking over the same military labor market that Shuja had so painstakingly evolved during his reign.[75] A similar process took shape in Bihar, where the defeat of Raja Cheyt Singh in 1782 led to the appropriation of his military labor market. In both cases the company inherited rather than invented a tradition of recruiting high caste Hindus. By 1779 the company had established permanent recruiting centers in Budgepur, Patna, Baxar, Jaunpur, Ghazipur, Pratapgarh, and Azamgarh. The same year the British established a permanent coordinating center in Buxar to ensure smooth movement of these troops to fill the Bengal army.[76] Referred to by Dirk Kolff as the Bhojpur region, the eastern districts of Avadh and Shahbad and the districts of Champaran and Saran in northern Bihar became important recruiting areas for the Bengal army.[77] Brigadier Troup, the commander at Bareli, noted that the "Bengal native Infantry came chiefly from the provinces of Avadh, Buxar, Bhojpur and Arrah."[78] Over time the Bengal army attracted potential recruits from the Doab, Rohilkhand, and even west of the Indus River.[79]

In addition to absorbing traditional recruiting areas the company also had the advantage of being extremely well regarded as a stable and consistent paymaster. While the company's pay scale was not necessarily much higher than the other Indian powers, the certainty of receiving regular pay and even pension benefits made service in the company's armies very attractive. Few Indian powers could boast similar records. In most cases, financial stability in Indian armies depended solely upon the degree of oversight that individual leaders exercised. Generally, the Indian powers, with a few rare exceptions (e.g., Mahadji Sindhia's army under de Boigne), did not have consistent pay or pension plans.[80] In the service of the company soldiers serving for twenty years or more could receive a cash pension, and disabled veterans received land grants too.[81]

By the mid–nineteenth century the company had created and perpetuated a high caste Hindu army in Bengal. The Bombay and Madras armies continued to have units with both high and low castes, with more of the latter.[82] Within the army the company sought to instill in the soldiers an intense pride in their regiments while at the same time scrupulously giving every assistance to the soldiers to help them maintain their high caste rituals.[83] Alavi refers to the company creating a Hindu "sanctuary" within the cantonment. However, it is not clear if the British created these policies to deliberately remove the sepoys from the constraints and hierarchy of Hindu society in order to use them to police the Hindu population, as Alavi suggests.[84] The concessions to the Indian soldiers' high caste rituals may have been little more than an acknowledgment that supporting these practices enabled the soldiers to maintain their morale and the esprit de corps of the close-knit units. By the 1820s, as the company began to solidify its administrative control over North India, it realized that concessions to the soldiers' high caste status and the power-sharing agreements with local landlords with regard to military recruitment were detrimental to increased centralized control. As the company sought to increase its control of the sepoys, however, the latter began to react with increasing violence. Between 1822 and 1825 the number of desertions rose from 687 to 8,322. The Barrackpur mutiny in 1825, when the Forty-seventh Regiment refused to march to Rangoon during the Burma campaign of 1824–25, was a stark example of the sepoys' zealous defense of their perceived caste rituals. They were in fact precursors to the final conflagration of 1857.[85]

The same process of market domination and ultimate takeover is even better highlighted in the Indian horse-trading business. Horse-trading links between India and Central Asia had been established since ancient times.[86] As the need for more and more foreign breeds for cavalry-based armies grew, so did the horse trade. By the eighteenth century India was an important and possibly the largest horse-trading market in the Southern Hemisphere. Afghan merchants bought breeds from Central Asia, Eastern Europe, and the Middle East for a low price and then fattened them in the grasslands around Kabul and Kandahar before sending them to the great horse markets in India.[87] The influx of these horses into India often coincided with the annual fairs and the great religious festivals. Maratha and Sikh military commanders regularly attended these fairs to obtain the best war horses.[88] The British, with their main bases in Bengal and Madras, were the farthest regional power from these horse markets and were forced to make do with the leftovers. The Marathas and the Mysoreans frequently intercepted and bought off horses from traditional supply lines controlled by the nizam of Hyderabad and the Afghans of Bhopal, Kurnool, and Cuddapah.[89] Similarly, in North India Sikh agents for Ranjit Singh intercepted the supply of horses to Haridwar.[90] For these reasons, the British, particularly the Madras government, found themselves in desperate shortage of good cavalry horses during the Anglo-Mysore Wars. They had to rely upon local cavalry forces, and even upon Maratha cavalry, to protect their lines of communication, which proved to be tremendously expensive. In desperation, the British unsuccessfully tried to launch a breeding program at Pusa in Bengal in 1793.[91] But these ad hoc measures were insufficient to keep up with demand, and the British had to rely almost exclusively on "friendly" and locally hired cavalry forces. In 1793 the peacetime Bengal cavalry had only two native cavalry regiments of approximately 500 horses. Six years later this number had risen to 3,500 and by 1809 to 6,000. The Madras cavalry also could only increase its numbers substantially by incorporating cavalry from the nawab of Arcot and the nizam of Hyderabad. Bombay had no cavalry force until 1803, choosing to rely solely upon cavalry units from "friendly" local allies.[92]

In sharp contrast to the British weakness in cavalry, the Indian powers maintained huge cavalry forces. One British estimate noted that in 1778 Hyder's army in the Deccan had 28,000 horses, while the Marathas had 67,000 horses in the Deccan alone, not counting Hindustan.[93] Robert Orme placed the Hindustani cavalry's strength in 1760 at a conservative 200,000.[94] The British need for a steady supply of strong cavalry horses was not met until the nineteenth century, when regular exports of Iranian horses began to reach India via sea.[95] By that time, however, the British had taken over most of Hindustan, and the effect on the historic overland horse trade was similar to the effect on the military labor market; namely, what had been a seller's market quickly became a buyer's market, which the British, who were the only major military power in Hindustan, monopolized. As the British began to import more horses by sea, the great Indian horse markets withered. After the fall of the Sikh Khalsa, the huge flow of horses into India from western Asia slowed to a trickle. Warfare, state formation, and horse trading thus became the decisive ingredients that helped to establish the Pax Britannica in late-eighteenth-century India.

Part Three

CHAPTER 7

The Army of the Raj

During the incessant fighting in India from 1750 to 1850 the East India Company army proved to be a major military innovator. Additionally, British troops began to utilize Indian techniques in their European campaigns. Experience gained during the Anglo-Sikh Wars in particular affected the development of British tactics. At Chillianwalla and Gujerat, for example, the British used a combination of line and column infantry formations for the first time.[1] At Chillianwalla the British cavalry's stunning defeat prompted the adoption of the inversion drill (the about-face) for cavalry formations by entire divisions rather than by threes and twos. As one scholar has noted, "It required the Chillianwalla debacle, a far greater strain on the British cavalry than the charge of the Light Brigade, to ensure . . . [that] inversion was permitted."[2] Artillery went through a similar reform process. During the battle of Gujerat, the final large-scale engagement of the Anglo-Sikh Wars, the British, in reaction to the excellent Sikh artillery, deployed 100 guns, the largest British artillery concentration to date. The wars convinced the British that increasing artillery would reduce infantry casualties.[3] However, once the British firmly controlled India, the military emphasis changed from dynamic conquest to a more mundane policing effort.

After the rebellion of 1857 the Crown took control and immediately appointed a commission of inquiry to investigate the causes of the "mutiny" and to propose changes in the organization of the army. The chief recommendation of the Peel Commission (headed by Secretary of State for War Jonathan Peel) was that the proportion of Indian to British soldiers in India should not be greater than three to one.[4] The ratio was maintained by what became known as the Cardwell system. In the process of reforming the British army, Secretary of State for War Edward Cardwell introduced a twelve-year standard service to be split between active and reserve service. According to this system, short-service commission soldiers who came to India must be at least twenty years old. They would serve at least six years before returning to England on reserve status.[5] In practice, it was impossible to keep an equal number of battalions at home, and units could not maintain regular drafts. According to Brian Bond, the home units eventually became training battalions for their sister battalions overseas. One contemporary critic, Col. G. F. R. Henderson, went so far as to declare that the real army was in India![6] Ironically, the British leaders in India also disliked the Cardwell system. The government of India resented the cost of passage for recruits to and from England and the fact that India essentially had the job of training raw recruits for Britain. The government noted, "It was no consideration for the efficiency of the army in India that evoked the short service system, and its suitability to the conditions of Indian requirements had been gravely questioned on more than one occasion."[7]

In July 1879 the army in India consisted of 6,602 British officers, 60,341 British soldiers, and 123,254 Indian soldiers.[8] That year the specially appointed Eden Commission, whose mission was to examine the army's organization and expenditures, warned of the dangers in persisting with the Presidential armies. The commission proposed establishing four regional corps located in the Presidencies of Bengal, Madras, Bombay, and the Punjab. It also concluded that currently it was not possible to reduce the army. (Lord Roberts abolished the Presidential armies in 1895 in favor of a single army headquarters.)[9]

Under the energetic and ambitious leadership of Lord Kitchener, commander in chief India from 1902 to 1909, the Indian army experienced dramatic structural and doctrinal reforms prior to the Great War. Lord Kitchener primarily tried to deflect the Indian army from its increasing emphasis on internal security duties. Ever since the rebellion of 1857 the structure of the Indian army had been based on internal rather than external security concerns. Kitchener re-formed the army into nine divisions, divided between two commands, northern and southern, the latter having four divisions and the former five. He renumbered the regiments and eliminated the deficient ones. The old designations of Madras, Bombay, and Bengal were dropped from the regimental titles. In 1905 Kitchener undoubtedly hoped that the army would absorb the lessons of the Boer War, just as the British had attempted to do at their Staff College at Camberley. Because of his experience of fighting the Boers using high powered Mauser rifles, Kitchener decided to reequip the Indian army with the Enfield .303 magazine rifle. He also introduced the 2.75-inch mountain screw gun, a highly effective mobile support weapon that fired a ten-pound shell up to 6,000 yards and broke up into five mule-transportable loads.[10] The officers of the newly created Mountain Batteries were not from the Indian army but came from the Royal Artillery and spent several years in India. Kitchener's reforms helped establish a small, highly trained frontier army.[11]

Although Kitchener streamlined the army for frontier fighting, it had been engaged in frequent frontier conflicts long before his arrival. With few exceptions, warfare against the northwestern Pathan tribes was mainly a midlevel insurgency operation. Soldiers spent much time on endless patrols and garrison duties on forgotten hilltops and in valleys. Prevention of an uprising was preferred to battle. To this end, the government valued intelligence gathered by political officers and their agents. Since the tribes rarely confronted the British in open battle, it became vital to guard all lines of communication to garrisons and outposts from ambushes. To achieve this goal the government established high elevation posts to protect and support advancing troops and convoys. The 2.75-inch screw gun became the lynchpin of these posts, the forerunners of the firebases used in Vietnam. The punitive offensive operations launched by the British usually ranged from battalion- to brigade-level formations. The disorganized state of the northwest and Afghan tribes and their lack of modern armament allowed the British to control them with a small but highly professional army. The unique requirements of the frontier army had an impact upon the British home army. At a 1906 meeting to coordinate the practices of the home and the Indian armies, many on the Army Council favored dividing the British and Continental armies into large divisions as seen in India because they regarded them as more flexible and better suited to the British military's imperial requirements.[12]

The frontier army's recruitment system reflected both the Indian army's highly selective requirements and the "martial races" system. Soldiers already in the regiment typically encouraged relatives and friends to apply for entry. After medical examinations and interviews with Indian noncommissioned officers and the adjutant of the regiment, the commanders placed successful applicants on the *umedwar*, or hopeful list, to be called up when vacancies occurred. Training of the new recruits was usually done within the regiment. Toward the close of the nineteenth century, as martial races selection became the norm, recruiting officers roved a particular district looking for the right kind of recruit to be presented before the British officers. The elaborate selection process was heavily influenced by pseudosciences like anthropometry (race determination by physical measurements), which ultimately led to the creation of recruiting handbooks that conveniently highlighted a particular martial race's physical and mental traits. These handbooks, which the army regularly updated, became the recruiting officer's bible.[13]

The Indian Expeditionary Force in France

Early in 1914 the Indian army had about 150,000 men. When the war broke out the Indian government offered Britain two infantry divisions (consisting of three brigades, each brigade made up of one British battalion and three Indian or Gurkha battalions) and two cavalry divisions (with three brigades, each with one British and two Indian regiments). After some hesitation, the British government readily accepted this offer in August 1914.[14]

The Indian Corps disembarked in France in October 1914. The commanders hurriedly equipped the men with short Enfield .303 rifles, machine guns, and field artillery (British units) before being dispatched to the front.[15] The Indian Corps had been thrust pell-mell into a war the likes of which it had never seen before, and it had a devastating effect upon the men. Unit after unit, including the vaunted martial races (Gurkhas, Sikhs, Rajputs, etc.), broke and fled from the horror of the trenches. The fact that neighboring British units did not desert like the Indians made their actions all the more troubling for their commanders.

The official British explanation at that time blamed the desertions on the heavy officer casualties that had denuded the Indian units of their leadership element. The British high command believed that Indian soldiers were in effect lost without their white officers.[16] Jeffrey Greenhut attributes the destruction of the Indian Expeditionary Force in France to a traumatic form of culture shock. He explains the Indian soldiers' dependence on their white officers and their inability to take command by the fact that British officers were more than mere leaders: "They were the interpreters of a totally unfamiliar environment, of a military system so completely foreign that Indian soldiers could not function without them. . . . [T]hey fulfilled a role no uneducated peasant could hope to emulate."[17]

However, culture shock and a new military system do not entirely explain the Indian troops' total reliance on British officers. The real answer lies in the Indian troops' thorough indoctrination into a subordinate position within the army. No Indian officer wielded command over even the lowliest British ensign. As one British observer noted, "Native Indian officers['] . . . present position of subordination to British officers in the regiment is calculated to impair any initiative or leadership they may have originally possessed."[18] Sir Harvey Anderson, the lieutenant governor of Burma, noted that Indian officers in the war lacked initiative to command because they had never been taught to do so.[19] With no Indian role models who could stand alongside their white officers, Indian viceroy commissioned officers and noncommissioned officers had little or no self-confidence to take on any leadership role after their white officers died. Although the debacle at Kut in Mesopotamia captured the imagination of the British public and the postwar military reformers, it was the Indian Expeditionary Force's performance or lack thereof in France that had a significant long-term impact on the Indian army during the interwar period. In the years following the Great War, the Indian army embarked upon an ambitious plan to gradually Indianize the entire officer corps.

The Indian Officer Corps

The process of incorporating Indians into the army officer corps began in August 1917 when the War Cabinet formally agreed, in principle, to appoint Indians to the commissioned rank in His Majesty's Army.[20] The War Office's only stipulation was that all candidates take competitive exams at Sandhurst or in the officer training course at Sandhurst. Ten Indian candidates would be nominated per year.[21] The War Cabinet's decision, made under intense pressure from India, brought to an end decades of internal debate within the upper echelons of the Indian government and army on the Indianization of the officer corps. The Sandhurst scheme to train Indian officers began with a rocky start, as the British authorities in India tried to send only cadets from "acceptable" families, namely, those from a martial and royal background. Unfortunately, these candidates often were unable to handle the stresses of the Sandhurst program, and many dropped out. The authorities in India tempered these failures, however, when they opened the competition for the Sandhurst entrance exams to youths from the Indian middle class, who were better educated and more motivated for an officer's career. Problems persisted, however, as few Indian middle-class families could afford the substantial costs of sending and putting their sons through Sandhurst. Furthermore, Sandhurst itself could not take in an indefinite number of Indian cadets without losing its character as a British academy. The only viable option was to establish an Indian military academy.[22] In April 1932 the Indian government, acting upon the recommendations of a committee headed by the commander in chief, Gen. Sir Philip Walhouse Chetwoode, bought 155.3 acres of land in Dehra Dun and began constructing the Indian Military Academy (IMA).[23]

The IMA sought to emulate Sandhurst in all ways except one: the duration of its course. The Chetwoode Committee had recommended a three-year course for the IMA instead of Sandhurst's eighteen-month course. The army settled for two and a half years of instruction, since the military leadership recognized that cadets at the IMA needed academic preparation to make up for the deficiencies of the Indian school systems. In all other respects the IMA followed Sandhurst. For instance, the Federal Public Services Commission (India) conducted the entrance exams on the third Monday of October, similar to the system in England. The format of the exam also closely mirrored Sandhurst's entrance exam. While the IMA curriculum reflected greater academic emphasis than Sandhurst, the annual exam system was also very similar. The academy held one exam at the end of the term, and the entire course consisted of five terms over a two-and-a-half-year period with two main sections, general military education and detailed military education. As at Sandhurst, the commandant recorded and reviewed the company commander's grade for and remarks on each cadet at the end of each term.

The IMA was open to unmarried candidates who were British subjects of Indian domicile or a subject of a state in India (the princely states). The school routed applications through the local collector, the deputy commissioner, or the local police officer. Students from the Prince of Wales Royal Indian Military College had to send their applications via their principal, indicating the special status this school enjoyed over its civilian counterparts in India. A total of thirty vacancies would be opened every half year, fifteen by open competition and fifteen to Indian army cadets.[24]

Between October 1932 and May 1941 sixteen regular or "prewar" courses took place. Of the 693 cadets admitted, 535 were commissioned, giving a success rate of 85.72 percent, a remarkably high number when compared to the Indian Sandhurst cadets.[25] The first five of the sixteen courses have been recorded in the annals of the IMA: (1) pioneers (1 October 1932–22 December 1934); (2) immortals (1 March 1933–4 June 1935); (3) invincibles (1 October 1933–21 December 1935); (4) stalwarts (1 February 1934–3 June 1936); and (5) bahadurs, or brave ones (23 August 1934–29 December 1936). These five classes and the "pioneers" in particular represent the Indian Officer Corps elite in preindependent India. Not only did they have to set an example for future generations, but they were also the products of a rigorous selection process and a comprehensive one-and-a-half- to two-year training course. The Indian officers graduating from the officer training course during the Second World War received only a fraction of the attention and care lavished upon the prewar cadets.

The onset of the Second World War drastically changed the training at the IMA. Between February 1940 and January 1946 forty-nine "war courses" were offered.[26] The academy conducted war courses for Indians and Europeans residing in India. The general duration of these courses was six months. In all, the army commissioned 3,887 cadets, both Indian and British, during this period. Out of a total of 4,744 cadets entering the war courses, the army commissioned 3,013, reflecting a relatively low attrition of 14.31 percent.[27] In addition to Dehra Dun, three additional accelerated officer training courses opened up during the war, at Mhow, Bangalore, and Belgaum. The latter originally only trained British cadets but toward the end of the war trained four to five mixed batches of British and Indian cadets.[28] The IMA proved invaluable to the British war effort in the Southern Hemisphere. Without the invaluable work of the academy in churning out emergency commissioned officers, the Indian army probably could not have maintained its massive formations on the Burma front. The value of the academy was proven in that the British sent 727 British cadets directly from England to Dehra Dun to receive their emergency commissions.[29]

Armies and Budgets

During the First World War the critics of the Indian army and particularly the Cardwell system described it as an albatross around the British army's neck. When the government reintroduced the system in the 1920s a new generation of critics took up the anti-Cardwell torch. To many opponents it appeared that the British army was essentially "regulated by the conditions prevailing on a portion of one of the frontiers of the Empire's constituent parts."[30] The chief concern was that the Indian army, with its sights firmly set on frontier warfare, would hamper any progress the British army might make toward "mechanized warfare," the mantra of the "progressives" in the interwar British army. An older concern was that the imperial commitments and India in particular would sap the strength of the small postwar British army. Pessimism about the ties between the armies in India and England became the chief concern of a younger generation of British reformers, including J. F. C. Fuller, William Ironside, Percy Hobart, and Lindsay, who saw the Cardwell system as a major barrier to change in the British army.

The reformers blamed the slow pace of change on the Indian army general staff, whom they often portrayed as a group of old fogies far too enamored with the smell of leather and horses to ever contemplate any move toward mechanization, thus stymieing the efforts of the brave young reformers within the British army. Unfortunately, these reformers made little or no attempt to examine the strategic and doctrinal links between the Indian and the British armies. These linkages have often been taken for granted, as has the British army's "obvious technical and progressivist" superiority as well as its preeminence in determining the strategic posture of Indo-British imperial defense.[31]

The Colonial State and Military Modernization

The changing strategic and doctrinal relationship between the Indian and the British armies began during the aftermath of the First World War. Despite the pessimistic view many British officers held of the Indian army, many in the British government (primarily senior officials in Whitehall) regarded the Indian army as an indispensable partner to the smaller British army in defending the British Empire, a view no doubt consolidated by India's considerable contribution during the Great War. These optimists, who were able to neutralize the Indian army's critics, initiated events that not only helped to integrate the Indian army into the greater scheme of imperial defense but also dramatically influenced the military doctrines of the two armies.

In 1919 the British government appointed the Army in India Committee under Lord Reginald Esher to examine ways in which to increase integration between the armies in England and India. The committee also considered the impact of dominion status upon India's contribution to imperial defense. According to the committee's report, "India has now been admitted into partnership with the Empire, and the Indian Army has fought, alongside troops from other parts of the Empire, in every theater of war. Its responsibilities have thus been greatly widened, and it can no longer be regarded as a local force, whose sphere of activity is limited to India and the surrounding frontier territories. It must be treated as part of an Imperial Army, ready to serve in any part of the world."[32] The report, submitted in 1920, put forth the radical recommendation that the Indian army be made directly responsible to the British government rather than the viceroy. The report suggested that the Indian army could be used to bypass restrictions on the size of the British military as agreed in the postwar negotiations. The Esher Committee essentially called for the chief of the imperial general staff to make the all-important appointment of the military secretary to the India Office. Furthermore, the committee suggested that the appointment of the commander in chief India should be made only after taking the advice of the chief of the imperial general staff. These proposals only alarmed the Indian government, which did not intend to hand over control of the Indian army to the British government and the Committee for Imperial Defense.

Fortunately for the Indian government, unexpected help came from the nascent Indian Legislative Assembly. One of Esher's ill thought out plans was to extensively use the Indian army to police the British Empire and the mandated territories. Indian politicians opposed this proposal. Sir P. S. Sivaswamy Aiyer introduced fifteen resolutions that rejected the entire Esher Committee report and rejected any proposal to make the Indian government relinquish control of the army to Whitehall. The new assembly declared that "the Army in India should not, as a rule, be employed for service outside the external frontiers of India except for purely defensive purposes, or with the previous consent of the Governor General-in-Council in very grave emergencies, provided that this resolution does preclude the employment on garrison duties overseas of Indian troops at the expense of his Majesty's Government and with the consent of the Government of India."[33] Indeed, as far back as 1919, when the Esher Committee created its report, Lord Chelmsford, viceroy of India from 1916 to 1921, had insisted, "So long as India pays, – and I do not suppose the War Office are going to propose to the English treasury to take over the charges of the Indian Army, – India must control its own Army."[34]

The Indian government, under the leadership of Viceroy Lord Chelmsford, fully accepted the Sivaswamy resolutions passed by the assembly in 1921. Like the Indian politicians, the Indian government (and the Indian army) had no intention of paying to police the empire. In regard to this particular issue, at least, the two traditional rivals could agree fully. In fact, relations between the British-controlled Indian government and the Indian nationalist legislators were so good at this time that the commander in chief, Lord Rawlinson, believed that the Indian Legislative Assembly's attitude was one of "pleasing moderation." He noted that the budget, which included some extra taxation to fund army spending, passed through "without much serious difficulty."[35] The Indian legislators, however, had absolutely no control over the army. The military continued to be the sole responsibility of the viceroy and his hand-picked council. At no time could the Indian politicians have dictated to the army, even on the minutest aspect of military affairs. Although senior officers publicly expressed great concern over the pressure applied to the Indian politicians, their private correspondence shows a very casual disdain for the efforts of the Indian legislators.[36]

Despite this unlikely cooperation to defeat the Esher proposals, in reality the Indian government found itself under growing pressure to increase imperial defense commitments. By the 1930s the Indian army had been scattered in outposts ranging from the Far East to Africa, just the situation the Indian government had intended to avoid. Even worse, until 1933 the army had received no financial assistance from the British government. How did this come about? In order to answer this question we must examine the shift in the strategic perception of the Indian army during the interwar period.

The main stumbling block to any strategy for Indian involvement in imperial defense was the lack of funds. Indeed, in 1922 the Retrenchment Committee, led by Lord Inchcape, effectively froze plans for the army's expansion or modernization.[37] If, therefore, the army reformed for its role as an imperial defense force, the British treasury would have to help. A Committee for Imperial Defense subcommittee report on Indian defense requirements supported this view by noting in June 1922 that it "recognized that the Indian Army cannot be treated as if it were absolutely at the disposal of His Majesty's Government for service outside India." The subcommittee accepted the Indian government's view that "the Indian Army should not be required to permanently provide large garrisons." Moreover, the cost of such a garrison "should be borne by His Majesty's Government, or by the dependency or colony requiring their services."[38] In 1933 the Garran Tribunal, appointed by the British cabinet, allotted 1.5 million pounds to India from the British treasury to finance that portion of the Indian army that would act as an imperial police force.[39] With the British government potentially providing financial backing for a modern intervention force, the Indian government's attitude toward imperial defense softened considerably. As the viceroy, Lord Linlithgow, noted in 1937, "You have the money – we have the men."[40]

In March 1938, amidst a worsening security situation in Europe and at the urging of the secretary of state for war, Leslie Hore-Belisha, the Committee for Imperial Defense set up a committee under Maj. Gen. H. R. Pownall to look into the reorganization and modernization of the Indian army.[41] The Pownall Committee acknowledged that the collective security system had failed and that the Axis powers seriously threatened the empire. On the other hand, the committee noted that the frontier menace to India from Afghanistan and Russia had decreased. The committee noted that "there are grounds for the belief that on the present scale of her defense forces India is less under insured than are other parts of the British Empire. Moreover, the degree of readiness of the forces in India is in some respects higher than elsewhere, and she maintains a large standing army in peace."[42] The committee noted that the Indian government had agreed to place one division at Britain's disposal "contingent upon effect being given to certain measures" that would result in the reorganization and reequipment of the Indian army.[43] In order to successfully implement the Indian army's new role, the committee deemed it essential that those Indian units slated for the imperial reserve must adhere strictly to the standards of British home units. Thus modernization of a portion of the Indian army became imperative. For financing this modernization and reorganization, the committee drew attention to the government of India's belief that no increase could be made in the current (1938) estimates, amounting to Rs 45 crores (£33.75 million). The Pownall Committee concluded that the British government would have to provide an additional £2,285,000 annually and that a further sum of £870,000 from imperial funds might be needed each year.[44]

With general agreement on the Pownall proposal, further fueled by the deteriorating security situation in Europe, a committee established in the summer of 1938 under Admiral of the Fleet Lord Chatfield examined how to implement the modernization scheme. The Chatfield Committee, while agreeing with the general conclusions of the Pownall Committee's report, believed the whole Indian army and not just a single imperial reserve division needed to be modernized. In addition to proposing a thorough reorganization plan for the Indian army, the committee submitted an estimate of the finances needed to modernize and expand certain key defense industries: a metal and steel factory for the manufacture of heavy and light bombs, Rs 80 lakhs; a gun and shell factory, Rs 73 lakhs; a rifle factory, Rs 73 lakhs; an ammunition factory, Rs 10 lakhs; a gun carriage factory, Rs 6 lakhs; a cordite factory, Rs 24 lakhs; a filing factory, Rs 32 lakhs; and a TNT factory at Kirkee, Rs 70 lakhs. For the crucial financing estimate the committee calculated that the total cost would be Rs 36.26 crores (£27.2 million) for the army; Rs 6.21 crores (£4.66 million) for the air force; and Rs 2.62 crores (£1.96 million) for the navy (total: Rs 45.09 crores [£33.82 million]). The committee thought that while India should bear some of the burden, the bulk of the total initial modernization cost must come from Britain over a five-year period.[45]

India generally welcomed the Chatfield Committee's sweeping proposals. Gen. Sydney Frederick Muspratt and Gen. Claude John Eyre Auchinleck noted that the "conclusions of the Chatfield Committee are far reaching and the recommendations made in the report are likely to influence profoundly the future of the forces in India."[46] Their only objection was to the committee's proposal to reduce the size of the army, a longtime goal of British reformers, including the secretary of state for war.[47] As Muspratt and Auchinleck observed, "Coming at a time when the rest of the world is furiously increasing its armed forces, the proposed reductions of the army in India on the score of them being surplus are certain to prove controversial."[48] They were correct. With the imminent outbreak of war, the British general staff refused to approve any troop reductions. In June 1939 the British cabinet agreed to assume the added cost outlined in the Chatfield report. The same year the Indian general staff issued its first modernization plan. The scheme detailed the army's peacetime unit strength and allocated units for deployment in either the external defense force based in the Deccan or the general reserve headquartered at Meerut and Lucknow. The plan called for a major expansion and modernization of the defense-related production facilities, including gun, shell, metal and steel, ammunition, and explosives factories. It also called for an immediate conversion from the obsolete Berthier section machine gun to the more modern Czech-inspired Bren section machine gun.[49]

While the various official committees attempted to modernize and reorganize the Indian army within the existing framework of the Cardwell system, the reformers in Britain were in complete opposition to it. According to B. H. Liddell Hart, "So long as the Cardwell system is maintained they [British battalions in India] are worse than superfluous, since not only are they preserved in a form that does not meet the conditions of modern war, but a similar number of units of the same type have to be maintained at home."[50] The reformers' proposed remedy was the separation of the two armies. According to J. F. C. Fuller, "If mechanized arms cannot operate in this [Afghanistan] theater of war, the reorganization of the army at home will either be seriously delayed, or two armies will have to be maintained, one for European warfare and the other for Oriental."[51] The most common scheme proposed was to create two separate active armies, the first one of long service (twenty years) for colonial duty and the second of shorter service for European duty in the event of a major war.[52]

The reformers complained vociferously that the Cardwell system forced the British army at home to maintain similar units to reinforce those in India, thus deflecting it from mechanization. There is, however, no reason to believe that the reformers would have gotten their way had the British garrison (forty-five battalions) in India been drastically cut. After all, Indian taxpayer money wholly maintained the British battalions in India. If the battalions had been removed from India, they probably would have been disbanded, further reducing the emaciated British army. One British official noted morosely that a reduction in British units would throw those units "on to the Imperial Budget, or as the only alternative, force us to disband them and so to weaken the armed strength of the Empire as a whole without any relief to the British taxpayer."[53] So even without these battalions, no extra money or forces would be made available in Britain to contribute toward the military modernization program as the reformers had hoped. The main obstacle to the mechanization of the army was not the Cardwell system but the lack of funds.

When Lord Henry Seymour Rawlinson succeeded Sir Charles Monro as commander in chief India in the autumn of 1920 he was plunged into "the old problems of military efficiency and financial stringency."[54] Although Rawlinson considered that "the provision for internal defense is already dangerously small, he had reluctantly suggested a reduction in the British establishment of 6,000 troops to 59,000 in all, but this would not be possible before 1922. As it was the British contingent was under-strength and required an actual increase of 7,000 men to even reach the proposed reduction total."[55] Viceroy Chelmsford concurred with the above view, noting that the British army's recruitment and organization always considered the fact that India maintained a minimum strength of British troops, hence, reducing the British garrison in India would involve many difficult and complex questions.[56] The harsh reality was that India saved the British taxpayer from supporting no less than a quarter of the British army. Of the 252,000 British troops in 1921, 65,501 (26 percent) served in India (including Aden garrison) and were supported wholly by Indian tax money.[57] Not surprisingly, opposition to reducing the forces in India came not only from India but also from the British general staff. The chief of the imperial general staff, Gen. Sir Cyrill Deverell, opposed the attempts of the secretary of state for war, Hore-Belisha, to reduce the India garrison. In a letter to the prime minister in November 1937 Hore-Belisha noted, "The Indian obsession, which refuses to allow objective examination of the proper disposition and organization of our Imperial Forces, assumes that the Indian commitment is fixed for all on unchanging traditions and that it must govern the pace and capacity of development of the rest of the army."[58] In another letter he remarked, "A cardinal feature of re-adaption of the Army is an impartial examination of whether India's share of our personnel is not disproportionate. Such an examination he [Deverell] is unwilling to undertake."[59] Having reached an impasse with Deverell, Hore-Belisha replaced him with Gen. John Gort, "who is the most dynamic personality I have met in the Army, and who is bred in an independent school. He could devote most of his time to executive reorganization of the Army."[60]

With Deverell gone, an exuberant Hore-Belisha delivered his first army estimates speech in the House of Commons in March 1938. He outlined a total sum of £108.5 million, the highest since 1914–18, and repeated his view that "India must no longer govern Army organization and distribution. For this reason the Prime Minister was prepared to initiate discussions between the War Office and the India Office."[61]

In reality, the Indian army was never as averse to reductions as the critics made it out to be. In May 1921 the new viceroy, Lord Reading, appointed a committee under the commander in chief, Rawlinson, to examine Indian military requirements. Rawlinson, despite the objections of his general staff, acquiesced to the committee's plan for the removal of three British cavalry regiments and five British infantry battalions.[62] However, as soon as the committee submitted its report, the Muslims of the Madras Presidency began a violent anti-British agitation – the Moplah rebellion – that postponed its consideration.[63] The British cabinet also quickly rejected the proposal.[64] The cabinet's decision pleased Rawlinson, and with the help of the Inchcape Committee's report he pushed through some reductions in both the British and Indian armies. "It is," he argued, "more important for the internal peace of India that we should balance our budget, than we should keep extra troops."[65] By 1925 the army in India had been reduced to an establishment of 197,000: 57,000 British soldiers and 140,000 Indian troops, 24,000 and 12,000 fewer than in 1914.[66]

It is important to note, however, that India was neither the only nor the most draining region in terms of imperial commitment. Restoring order in Ireland remained the single largest burden that the British Army had to bear in the early 1920s. The Irish problem more than anything else prevented the Cardwell system from functioning effectively and upset traditional patterns of training and deployment. At the height of the Irish conflict, on 10 December 1920, when martial law was declared in four Irish counties (Cork, Tipperary, Kerry, and Limerick), fifty-one British battalions served in Ireland.[67] In August 1921 the British cabinet actually decided to hold back troops destined for India to deploy them in Ireland if necessary.[68] Only after the Anglo-Irish agreement in December 1921 did the government begin to remove the British garrison from the Irish Free State.[69]

Colonial Military Doctrine

Another favorite target of the Indian army critics was their perception that the army adhered to old doctrines and archaic techniques. But although the Indian army lagged behind the British army in terms of equipment, the same deficiency did not apply to training and doctrine, a fact that one of the staunchest anti–Indian army reformers grudgingly conceded. When Sir Giffard Martel arrived in India in the late 1920s prior to taking up an instructor's position at the Staff College at Quetta, he wrote to Liddell Hart – a fellow officer and staunch critic of the Indian army – that the "army in India is in no way the dud show that people at home suggest – real live show in many ways though short of equipment."[70] Even though the Indian army did not take to armored warfare as enthusiastically as the reformers wished, it did not stop its Staff College at Quetta from planning and war-gaming the latest theories in mechanized warfare doctrine.

In fact, ever since the Indian army had established the Staff College at Quetta, it had kept abreast of the latest European doctrines. A joint entrance exam for the Staff Colleges at Quetta and Camberley indicates that these two vital operational training centers closely coordinated their educational programs. Candidates had to be well versed in the latest debates on military modernization. The questions covered British military strategy during the Great War ("Westerners" vs. "Easterners"), the mobility of a fighting force, the role of armored fighting vehicles and planes in policing the empire, and the impact of the Cardwell system and ideas to change it.[71]

Significantly, many inter- and postwar British officers who propagated mechanized warfare doctrines had spent a significant part of their formative years at Quetta. Even Martel, who often chafed at what he perceived as the army's foot-dragging on mechanization, conducted numerous mechanized war games at Quetta. In 1932 he and his students drafted a bold plan for taking Kandahar, Afghanistan, in seventy days with light tanks and aircraft.[72] Gen. Sir John Burnett-Stuart, an influential British officer with regard to armored warfare, also spent much of his time in India. His biographer records that "he received a sound education in small-unit tactics during his service with the Rifle Brigade [1867–98] in India."[73] In 1920 Burnett-Stuart returned to India as general officer commanding Madras District and played an instrumental role in putting down the Moplah disturbance. During those operations he became probably the only interwar British officer to use highly mobile infantry columns, armored cars, and pack artillery on a large scale in an operational environment.[74]

Quetta contributed to the doctrinal maturation of another British officer – Gen. Bernard Law Montgomery. In June 1934, freshly promoted to full colonel, Montgomery assumed the post of chief instructor at Quetta. His brother Brian and close friend Gen. Dudley Ward believed that it was in Quetta that Monty's "tactical concept of war had . . . fully matured." General Ward noted, "People like Liddell Hart I think are vastly overrated. They are obsessed with mobility – which is fine if you can have it. But it isn't often so; and the only way you can win battles is to defeat the enemy who wants to deprive you of that mobility. It was Monty who taught us how to do this."[75]

Service in India tended to give many reformers a more realistic approach toward mechanization.[76] As commander of the Third Division in Britain (1926), Burnett-Stuart believed that mechanization was an inevitable but slow process. He recognized the Cardwell system's continued existence and favored partial mobility – four armored divisions with at least one in Egypt and India.[77]

Furthermore, the image painted by reformers and critics of the Indian army of an Indian general staff obsessed with frontier warfare soldiering is also inaccurate. Most of the interwar Indian army commanders, including Rawlinson, Chetwoode, Auchinleck, and Archibald Percival Wavell, were dynamic and progressive military leaders. Chetwoode, in fact, served as the general officer commanding Aldershot Command prior to becoming commander in chief India. In September 1925 Chetwoode led one side in Britain's first large-scale peacetime maneuvers since 1914 that tested the new concepts of mechanized warfare. Predictably, it turned into a fiasco and strengthened Chetwoode's caution against rapidly adopting new fighting methods without adequate training and preparation.[78]

As commander in chief India from 1930 to 1933 Chetwoode agreed with the cautious modernizers, but he did not intend to be a defender of the status quo. In his farewell address at the Staff College at Quetta, he bitterly criticized the intellectual stagnation of the officer corps in both the British and the Indian armies:

> I do not think that, as a class, they [officers] have improved in general education, or military instinct and leadership, since the war. . . . I have found men all over India who evidently scarcely read the papers, and are quite unaware of what is going on in India around them, and still less of the stupendous events outside this country. . . . I am rather afraid that quite a number of the average Staff College students aim at being correct, methodical, "sealed pattern" staff officers, ground out to pattern by the Quetta and Camberley mill. Am I altogether wrong in thinking that, to many Englishmen, to be independent in thought, to have imagination, to go outside the obvious, to be different to others, is to be almost un-English, or even that more frightful "not sound."[79]

Even Brian Bond, who labels Chetwoode as one of the conservatives on military modernization, described Chetwoode's September 1924 Quetta address as "the most devastating indictment of the military profession by a senior-ranking officer in the inter-war period."[80]

Prior to taking over as army chief in India, Wavell commanded the experimental Sixth Infantry Brigade, during which time he penned an article in the *Journal of the Royal Services Institute*, noting that while mechanization was inevitable, it would happen gradually. More importantly, Wavell noted that a mixed combined-arms unit of tanks and highly trained infantry would be the way of the future.[81] Wavell's emphasis on infantry support was actually a step ahead of his fellow reformers' belief in solely armor-based units and would play an important role in his efforts to modernize the Indian army during his tenure as its commander in chief from 1941 to 1943.[82]

Reformers and researchers have often seized upon these Indian commanders' caution toward rushing headlong into a new system of warfare as evidence of the Indian military leadership's lack of progressive ideas. In reality, the Indian general staff usually had a far better idea of the true capability of their army and its officers as well as their resource and financial limitations than did their British counterparts. They acquired this knowledge partly because the Indian army permanently served in operational conditions from the Far East to the Middle East. Constantly embroiled in coping with unexpected situations, the Indian general staff had to make the best possible use of a significantly smaller financial budget than its British counterpart. An excellent example of this commonsense approach is the debate over whether tanks should be used in India. Tanks, as Fuller pointed out, may have been useful on the North-West Frontier, but were they necessary? The Indian army had already secured firm control over the tribesmen with a combination of infantry, armored cars, and a few Royal Air Force squadrons. In view of the financial situation, would it have been possible or even desirable to establish tank regiments on the frontier with the tremendous costs such an undertaking would have entailed? Nevertheless, the metamorphosis of the strategic role of the Indian army to that of imperial defense necessitated a substantial move toward mechanization. Actual material change in the army was slow; the need to rearm the home army became first priority. However, the Indian army was already moving ahead with its own reorganization plans.

In December 1939, even as the Chatfield Committee worked through its report, the chief of the general staff's office sent a note to all regional command headquarters in India. It pointed out that the rapid mechanization of the European armies had "appreciably modified the theory and practice of warfare developed with older types of forces and now a tactical technique is rapidly being evolved."[83] The note called for closing the gap between the British and Indian armies. However, the note also stated that "stereotyped higher formations such as corps and divisions which form the basis of organization of European armies are not likely to be needed by a modernized army in India."[84] The Chatfield Committee, which had originally put forth the proposal, believed that such peacetime organization was wasteful and that in time of war these units could be specially created and organized.[85] The note indicated that future modernization plans would enable the cavalry light tank regiments to be equipped with the latest two-pounder gun tanks, the artillery would be fully mechanized with modern guns and tractors, and the infantry battalions would get sufficient transports to carry all weapons and unit equipment, bringing the army up approximately to the 1938 model for battalions based in Great Britain.[86]

These plans, coming to fruition on the eve of the war, did not, however, transform the Indian army into a well-equipped modern army overnight. Brian Bond points out:

> Clearly these decisions came too late for any real progress in the modernization of the army in India to be made before the outbreak of the Second World War. Indeed it was weaker and less prepared for war in 1939 than in 1914 with a total of 205,038 British and Indian troops as compared with 269,954 in 1914. As for up-to-date equipment, as late as February 1939 there was still one anti-aircraft battery in the whole of India. The Indian

forces fell far short of being able to fulfill the internal and external roles envisaged for them by the Chatfield Committee.[87]

Bond and other researchers, including Martin Wainwright, rightly believe that in terms of equipment in 1939 the Indian army was woefully short of the Chatfield Committee's lofty goals. But was the Indian army "less prepared for war," as Bond alleges? A detailed examination of the tactical doctrines of the British and Indian armies during the war years reveals that even if the Indian army lacked the material resources to wage a modern war, in doctrinal terms it entered the Second World War with a far more realistic appreciation of its capabilities and limitations than it had for the 1914–19 war. Indeed, the true dynamics of the military modernization programs in the Indian army are not found in the highly visible matériel sphere but rather in the army's ideology and mind-set.

CHAPTER 8

The Indian Army during the Second World War

On 3 September 1939 the viceroy, Lord Linlithgow, informed India over the radio of the circumstances in which "we find ourselves at war with Germany today."[1] The war itself came as no surprise to the Indian government. Feverish planning (if not action) had been under way for some time to transform the Indian army into a capable modern intervention force. Indeed, by the end of the war India had become the single largest manpower contributor to the Commonwealth war effort, managing to raise a professional military of 2.5 million soldiers, sailors, and airmen, the largest force of its kind in the world.[2] The first real test for the Indian army came in the desert in North Africa, where the British Commonwealth and the German armies pitted their imperfect warfare doctrines against each other. At the end of an immense struggle the British Commonwealth forces all but wiped out the Afrika Korps and through this process emerged with a radically different appreciation of how to wage "modern" war. In the East, in Burma and Malaya, this scenario repeated itself between the British Commonwealth forces and the imperial Japanese armies with the same results.

The Western Front

Much of the historical research done on the war in North Africa generally ignores the early campaigns against the Italians. Most research dwells upon Gen. Richard O'Connor's highly mobile campaigns against the Italians with his "Jock" columns. These small motorized infantry, artillery, and armor units wreaked havoc on the disorganized and retreating Italian forces. Many researchers, however, have ignored the British military's excellent use of Indian artillery during these campaigns in both the infantry and tank support roles. In December 1940, during battles against the fortified Italian camps at Nibeiwa and East Tumar, the Fourth Indian Division's chief of Royal Artillery, the famous "Red Eagles," used his entire artillery – fifty-six eighteen- and twenty-five-pounders, eight six-inch howitzers, and eight sixty-pounders – as a single grand battery to support each brigade's (three brigades per division) attack.[3]

The same coordination with the artillery was evident in the East African campaign, when the Fourth and Fifth Indian Divisions took on the Italians at their best, defending well-prepared defensive positions with elite troops.[4] Throughout the campaign the artillery worked in close conjunction with the Indian infantry. At the fall of Keren the British commander, Gen. William Platt, praised "the continuous support given to the infantry by the Royal Artillery."[5] The performance of the artillery was all the more commendable because the Commonwealth forces had a limited artillery park of only 124 guns.[6] Indeed, during the entire Eritrean campaign the Indian army displayed its traditional flair for effectively using limited resources.

The arrival of General Rommel and his Afrika Korps changed the complexion of the desert wars in more ways than one. Not only were the Germans a superior opponent compared to the Italians, but the Indian army no longer constituted the majority within the Eighth Army. The "new" British-dominated Eighth Army immediately revealed serious deficiencies in functioning as a cohesive combined-arms force, something at which the Germans were more successful. Furthermore, mobility – that long-sought-after goal and the core of many a Staff College war game at Quetta and Camberley – proved elusive. Successive Eighth Army commanders from Gen. Arthur Cunningham to Gen. Neil Ritchie failed to concentrate their forces at the decisive point. Even when they achieved such a rare concentration, British armor proved unable to work in concert with the artillery and the infantry, which led to German antitank defenses repeatedly mauling it.[7]

In his authoritative three-part study of British field artillery tactics in the *Journal of Royal Artillery* Brig. R. G. S. Bidwell comments extensively on the British army's misuse of artillery early in the North African campaign against the Germans. Yet he notes with some puzzlement: "This, however, does not explain why it was from India, the most starved and backward of commands, that two divisions [the Fourth and the Fifth] came who at Keren and in the early desert operations showed how artillery should be handled. It was later that the decline began."[8]

The obsession with mobility deflected the Eighth Army from appreciating the need for "true" combined-arms operations with infantry and artillery. Under the influence of radical reformers the British army entered the war with a gross overappreciation of armor-only formations capabilities. The British Seventh Armoured Division – a division trained by General Percy Hobart, who was a great believer in armored-only formations – entered the war in June

1940 with a ratio of about 330 tanks (two armored brigades) to only two infantry battalions and two artillery regiments. At the Sidi Rezegh battle, the
British had 500 tanks (three armored brigades) supported by only three infantry battalions.[9] After Sidi Rezegh General Auchinleck, Indian army officer
and commander in chief Middle East, proposed measures to create a parity
between armor and infantry. He specifically wanted to reduce the number of
armored brigades in a division to one and replace the ad hoc support group
with a full infantry brigade.[10] In addition, Auchinleck believed, "We must,
therefore, while retaining the divisional HQ organization, ensure that it is
capable of handling a collection of brigades of varying numbers and types.
That is to say, the real basic tactical unit must be the brigade group, whether
armored, motorized or lorried, and that each brigade group must be capable
of being transferred from one divisional commander to another as a matter
of course and habit, and without having to resort to a last minute improvi-
sation which must occur with our present divisional organization whether it
be armored corps or infantry."[11]

Auchinleck also proposed creating mixed armor and infantry mobile field
divisions to regain the initiative from the Germans.[12] His main problem,
however, was that Ritchie, his Eighth Army commander, could not carry out
his directives. Auchinleck finally sacked Ritchie and took personal command
of the army on 25 June 1942. With an Indian army officer in command, the
effect on the desert campaign was immediate. At the first battle of El Alamein the German commander, Rommel, noted, "General Auchinleck, who
had meanwhile taken over command himself at El Alamein, is handling his
forces with considerable skill and tactically better than Ritchie had done.
He seemed to view the situation with considerable coolness, for he was not
allowing himself to be rushed headlong into accepting a 'second best' solution by any move we made."[13]

Indeed, by June 1942 Auchinleck had stabilized a defensive line at El Alamein. Here he reverted to the positional warfare tactics utilized so successfully in the East African campaign against the Italians. For possibly the first
time in the campaign against the Afrika Korps, the Eighth Army successfully
concentrated its artillery resources in a major defensive battle. At the first
battle of El Alamein in July 1942 the Eighth Army coordinated the fire of nine
artillery regiments on more than one occasion. In the midst of the raging
battle on 15 July Eighth Army Chief of General Staff T. W. Corbett declared,
"The artillery is being restored to its rightful place in the battlefield."[14] Unfortunately for Auchinleck, Churchill and Chief of Imperial General Staff
Gen. Alan Brooke failed to see the true value of his achievement and sacked
him. The immediate reason given was his failure to punch through German

lines during the subsequent counterattacks. However, these counterattacks, launched under tremendous pressure from Whitehall, collapsed as a result of the demoralized state of the British armor, which simply refused to advance in support of the infantry. Brooke, who knew the tremendous difficulties confronting Auchinleck, was not prepared to confront Churchill on his behalf, as he would on many later occasions for Montgomery.

Nevertheless, Auchinleck's brief stint as Eighth Army commander marks a sea change in British military operations during the war. Henceforth all British operations centered on positional warfare tactics, the centerpiece of which was the battle of attrition. Massed artillery, airpower, and infantry dominated, with armor operating as an infantry support arm. This "change" represented a return to the operational style favored by the Indian army that was dictated not by any orthodoxy but by a realization that the British and Indian armies lacked the training and equipment to carry out complex combined-arms mobile operations.[15]

Historians are only now beginning to appreciate that Montgomery's assumption of the leadership of the Eighth Army was not a revolution in British military tactics but rather an evolution of the system that Auchinleck introduced when he was commander. Montgomery's first battle at Alam Halfa was essentially a repeat of the first battle at El Alamein and was based upon plans Auchinleck had drawn up for such a German attack.[16] The second battle at El Alamein was predominantly a British artillery and infantry offensive. The armor came into play much later in the battle, after the infantry had broken through the German defenses. Even with Rommel on the run, Montgomery dared not send his armor in pursuit, so complete was the British lack of confidence in their ability to conduct even basic maneuver operations with armor. It is not surprising that the artillery, which played such a vital role in the second battle, was literally a continuation of Auchinleck's organization. As Gen. Sir Francis Tuker recalled, "On the night of 23 October, 30th Corps attacked under a barrage on a four division front, the barrage coordinated by the good gunner, Brigadier Meade Dennis, the same officer who had well served Auchinleck as artillery commander on the northern sector of the Alamein front. He was now used to handling hundreds of guns."[17]

The second battle of El Alamein proved significant for the artillery as it saw the introduction of complex artillery fire control: "Fire-plans could be arranged quickly, and what is more important, modified in mid-career to match the ebb and flow of battle."[18] According to Colonel G. R. Stevens, official historian of the Fourth Indian Division, the new fire plan system had probably been devised by the divisional chief of Royal Artillery, Brigadier Dimoline, who by "constant training and experiment evolved a technique for crash saturation shoots well in advance of current practice. Gun surveys and the artillery communication grid were elaborated until the C.R.A. [chief of Royal Artillery] could sit in his battle headquarters with trace sheets which blended like musical scores, from which he could play his weapons singly, in unison or in harmony."[19] The effect on the battlefield was startling, as General Tuker noted:

> Lacking an efficient armored force, the Eighth Army was now using much of its field artillery in a mobile role to halt the axis advance, a role which was properly that of self-propelled artillery but nonetheless most effective in a country where few heights afforded such wide observation for the gunners and where mechanical traction enabled them to concentrate at speed. The records of the 9th Light and other [German] formations bespeak of the punishment they received from South African and British field and medium guns. The method showed a reading of circumstances, of ground, resources and enemy which was refreshing after so many months of neglect. Throughout July the application of artillery in the sector from Ruweisat northwards was about as good as it could be.[20]

Dimoline's techniques continued to evolve throughout the desert campaign. In fact, they represented the early manifestation of time-on-target synchronized shoots and seventy-gun battery (divisional artillery) stonks, which became very common in the European theater.[21]

The Eighth Army that Montgomery inherited from Auchinleck was by no means a lame duck. General Tuker, who commanded the Fourth Indian Division at the time Montgomery assumed command, agreed with Montgomery's assertion that the Eighth Army was ill trained but wondered to what he was comparing them, as troops from Great Britain were even less competent. Tuker thought that the best-trained Allied infantry came from Australia, New Zealand, India, and South Africa.[22] British units entering the North African theater showed considerable inexperience and doctrinal rigidity. Tuker noted that during the battle of Mejerda, Tunis, in May 1943 the British units refused to execute a night attack, a standard procedure for Indian units. During the same battle, the British First Army, who were strangers to Brigadier Dimoline's new artillery fire plans, hesitated before allowing him to take charge of a 400-plus artillery concentration.[23]

When the war moved from Africa to Italy, so too did the Indian army – with the Fourth, Eighth, and Tenth Infantry Divisions. Here too it became obvious that the Indian army's emphasis upon infantry was not misplaced. The campaign in Italy proved that "even in modern combat infantrymen were often more relevant than either tanks or planes."[24] Gen. Alphonse Juin, commander of the Free French Forces, even remarked, "The widespread mechanization of British and American forces constituted a serious obstacle to any swift progress up the Italian peninsula." [25] Under the circumstances, because the Indian infantry divisions represented some of the most experienced infantry divisions in the theater, they saw almost continuous action right up to the German surrender in Italy in September 1945. [26]

The Burma Front

The Indian army sent the vast bulk of its troops to the Southeast Asian theater during the war. Nine Indian infantry divisions and many independent brigades (armor and infantry) plus support groups fought in that theater of conflict. Included in this force were the only Indian tank units to see extensive action during the war, the Fiftieth, 254th, and 255th Indian Tank Brigades. [27]

Early in the conflict, the mobility of the veteran Japanese forces and their disregard for flanking security took the British and Indian forces completely by surprise. Hong Kong, Singapore, and Malaya fell in quick succession to the Japanese. Only in Burma did the British slow the Japanese momentarily and staged a fighting retreat. Outmaneuvered and outfought by a remarkably lightly armed, albeit experienced, Japanese army, the Commonwealth and Chinese forces fell back into India. The Japanese forces, in turn, paused to regroup and consolidate their overextended supply lines.

In India the weary Commonwealth forces built up their strength and planned for the next phase of the war under the guidance of Lt. Gen. Sir William Slim, an Indian army officer. The significance of Slim's assumption of the command of the Fourteenth Army is comparable to Auchinleck's takeover of the Eighth Army in North Africa. The effect of these generals, in terms of both the course of the war and Allied military doctrine, proved to be the same. However, Slim, unlike Auchinleck, was under less pressure from Churchill to produce instant victories and could mold his forces into the best possible condition before going on the offensive. One of Slim's first actions was to issue an eight-point training directive to his units to "get used to having Japanese parties in their rear, and when that happens, regard not themselves but the Japanese as 'surrounded.'" The directive's point five cautioned the infantry on Japanese-style tactics: "There should rarely be frontal attacks and never frontal attacks on narrow fronts. Attacks should follow hooks and come in from flank or rear, while pressure holds the enemy in the front." On the issue of armor, Slim sought to change the prevalent view that tanks were useless in the jungle. He argued: "Tanks can be used in most country except in close country they must always have infantry with them to defend and reconnoiter for them. They should always be used in maximum numbers available and capable of being deployed."[28] Slim was, in fact, laying the framework for the Allied tactics in the coming campaign, whereby superior Allied firepower and logistics would deflect Japanese mobility and ultimately destroy their lightweight infantry-based army.

In the Allied counteroffensive against the Japanese in Burma the commanders mainly used infantry to assault the enemy, with close tank support when available, and always with heavy backing from artillery and air strikes. Although artillery and air support never reached the numbers employed in North Africa and Europe, divisional artillery concentrations like those used to support the assault of the Thirty-seventh Brigade (belonging to the Twenty-third Indian Division) on Tamu in July 1944 became commonplace.[29] The Japanese, by contrast, rarely concentrated more than a battalion's worth of artillery. At Kangaw, for instance, the heaviest reported Japanese artillery concentration of the war consisted of only one battalion firing 600 rounds per day.[30] "Cab ranks" provided close air support whereby forward observers called down fire from fighters circling over the advancing troops.[31]

The campaign in Burma witnessed some of the best all-arms coordination by British and Commonwealth forces in the entire war. Undoubtedly, this was partly due to the weakness of the Japanese, since they could deploy only a fraction of the tanks and artillery the Germans had in Africa and Europe. As a result some observers concluded that due to the Commonwealth's overwhelming superiority in matériel and men "tactics were not so important as the logistics of maneuvering such a force into position."[32] Such a conclusion, however, is inaccurate, for merely sustaining logistics and the concentration of forces would not have been enough to defeat the extremely mobile Japanese forces. The Commonwealth forces achieved success through good coordination of air, artillery, tanks, and infantry, which allowed them to relentlessly pursue the enemy. Mobility – that much-sought-after quality in the pre-Auchinleck Eighth Army and a concept that found little place in Monty's set-piece battles – became a vital element in Slim's Burma campaign.[33]

Indian Officers at War

The Second World War was a defining moment in the military careers of the small group of Indian officers who fought in it. While peacetime training and education had given them a largely theoretical grasp of warfare, actual combat enabled them to mature as military leaders. The lessons that the young Indian officers learned during the war years formed the core of Indian military doctrine in the postindependence period and continues to play a major role in the evolution of the Indian army today. Individual Indian officers who later assumed senior positions in the independent Indian army participated in the often-painful learning process that the Indian and other Allied armies endured during the war. In the North African deserts Indian officers took part in the well-orchestrated campaign against the Italians. However, the primary wartime memory for most Indian officers who fought on the Western front and in the North African desert in particular involved defeat at German hands. These officers learned firsthand the disastrous consequences of a British-led Commonwealth army engaging the Germans without a coherent military doctrine. Undoubtedly, this experience molded their attitudes toward warfare in the postindependence Indian army. The underlying theme in all of the officers' actions and writings in the postindependence Indian army rested on a firm belief in the infantry-artillery, defensive-offensive doctrine that Auchinleck originated in North Africa. Officers such as Maj. K. S. Rajendra Sinhji and Maj. P. P. Kumaramangalam, who saw extensive action in North Africa, became the chiefs of the independent Indian army. Others, including Maj. S. D. Verma and 2nd Lt. Permindrah Singh Bhagat, became senior general officers.[34]

The main theater where most Indian officers saw action, however, lay in the East, with the Fourteenth Army. In this conflict against the Japanese Imperial Army, the future tactical doctrine of the independent Indian army emerged. The majority of the postindependence army's senior officers also gained their war experience on this front. Capt. S. H. F. J. Manekshaw became one of the few Indian officers to see extensive action against the Japanese throughout the war.[35] His tremendous drive and energy eventually resulted in the government awarding him a Military Cross in June 1942.[36] Manekshaw rose in the Indian army to become not only army chief but also India's first field marshal. He commanded the Indian army during its very successful campaign in East Pakistan in 1971. Interestingly, the tactics of that campaign bore remarkable similarities to Slim's successful campaign against the Japanese in Burma and Malaya.

Additionally, Indian officers commanded battalion- and brigade-level combat units in the Burma theater. These officers helped implement General Slim's radical eight-point plan to carry the war to the Japanese. The most visible example is that of K. S. Thimmaya. Soon after the war began the British promoted Thimmaya to lieutenant colonel and gave him command of the Eighth Battalion, Nineteenth Hyderabad Regiment, which served in the Twenty-fifth Indian Division, was stationed in Mungdaw, and soon faced the Japanese. Thimmaya went on to deftly handle the battalion in a series of complex operations along the Mayu Range.[37] Col. L. P. Sen and Col. S. P. P.

Thorat also commanded battalion-level formations in the field during the war.[38] Thorat ended his career as the chief of the independent Indian army. Thimmaya too became army chief, and Sen became a senior general officer.

Although infantry combat dominated engagements in the Burma theater, it was here rather than at the Western Front that the Indian Armoured Corps came of age. The Burma-Malaya campaign involved the only extensive use of the large brigade and regiment-size Indian tank formations in the entire war. Large tank divisions, so popular in Africa and Europe, were not useful in the East. A staff report in 1945 outlines the Indian army's approach to armored corps formations:

> As a result of the outstanding success of the German Panzer divisions in France in 1940, military opinion swung strongly in favor of the creation of numerous armored formations. Under pressure from the prevailing military thought, it was decided in India to embark on a program of mechanization and expansion which included the formation of an I.A.C. [Indian Armoured Corps] of 3 armored divisions. . . . [I]t was [then] decided in 1944, to abolish the remaining Indian armored division in the India Command, and to concentrate on the production of Indian tank brigades to suit conditions of possible actions against the Japanese.[39]

During the war the seniormost Indian cavalry officer was Lt. Col. J. N. Chaudhuri, who became the first and only Indian to command a cavalry regiment, the Sixteenth (armored cars).[40]

More so than North Africa, the fighting in Burma and Malaya laid the foundation for the future tactical doctrine of the Indian army. It was in Burma that the combined-arms battle concept reached its zenith for the British Commonwealth forces. Artillery, although fewer in number than in the European theater, played an equally crucial role. Many future senior Indian artillery officers learned their trade in Burma's jungles and mountains.[41]

The Second World War resulted in the British government lifting many of the constraints placed upon the Indianization process (e.g., limiting it to only eight units of the army). Thousands of Indian emergency commissioned officers (IECOs) now flooded the army. For many of them service in the war provided the ideal opportunity to consolidate and enhance their career prospects during the postindependence period. One such officer, S. K. Sinha, became the 11,555th IECO during the war. He joined the Fourth Battalion/Twelfth Frontier Force Rifles and took part in low-key operations until the war's end. After the war most IECOs were not given permanent commissions. Out of 13,000 IECOs the army selected only 450 for permanent commission. Sinha and Capt. B. N. Sarkar were the only two selected from their batch of forty.[42]

More often than not, only after the war did many permanently commissioned IECOs see action as peacekeepers. For example, the army posted Sinha as general staff officer grade III (operations) to the headquarters of the Fifteenth Indian Corps at Batavia (Jakarta), Indonesia.[43] The corps was originally ordered to take over from the Japanese forces and release the thousands of Allied POWs and civilian European captives. However, the mission soon turned into a war against the Indonesian nationalist forces under the leadership of Sukarno, who had no desire to see the Dutch reoccupy the islands. Since the Dutch divisions were still being raised and trained, the veteran Indian Fifth, Twenty-third, and Twenty-sixth Infantry Divisions led the fighting and secured the port towns of Batavia, Semarang, and Surabaya in Java; Medan, Pedang, and Pullenbang in Sumatra; and Macassar in Sulawesi. Here the Indian officers experienced intense guerrilla warfare, and several Indian officers, including Lt. Col. Sarvajeet Singh Kalha, who had won the Distinguished Service Order in Burma, were killed.[44] On the eve of independence, the Indian army was one of the few armies in the world that possessed extensive experience in guerrilla warfare. Later, such experience proved invaluable in enabling the postindependence Indian army to wage a successful protracted campaign against Communist separatist movements in Northeast India.

The Colonial Legacy

India emerged from the war as a regional military power. Its contribution to the British war effort and the resultant size of its military forces and defense infrastructure left it in an ideal position to fulfill the Chatfield Committee's goals, that is, becoming the bulwark of the British imperial defense. The subsequent onset of the cold war only further enhanced India's strategic potential in the eyes of British defense analysts in both New Delhi and Whitehall.

The volatile political situation in India, however, remained the main stumbling block to this rosy future. Political events in India fast outstripped the government's understanding. Britain's departure from India no longer remained doubtful; the Labour government, elected in August 1945, had already publicly declared its intention to give India independence. The problem looming was how to implement the transfer of power. Would there be one undivided India or two independent states of India and Pakistan? While the politicians attempted to thrash out this intractable issue, the soldiers, under the leadership of Commander in Chief General Auchinleck (reappointed commander in chief India in June 1943), worked feverishly to prepare the Indian army for independence. Initially, Auchinleck and his staff believed that the

Indian army would not be partitioned. A unified Indian army was, after all, the core of the Commonwealth's future defense strategy. The British, even at this eleventh hour, hoped that although India and Pakistan would be partitioned, the two dominions would maintain an undivided military establishment. Such thoughts, however, proved to be wishful thinking.

On 3 June 1947 Lord Mountbatten, the last viceroy, announced that power would be transferred to the two independent dominions of India and Pakistan on 15 August 1947. In May Jawaharlal Nehru rejected a last attempt to maintain an undivided defense establishment, giving Auchinleck little more than ten weeks in which to "reconstitute" (Auchinleck preferred this term to "partition") the armed forces between the two emerging nations. The Indian government established a Joint Defense Council to facilitate this task. According to Martin Wainwright, this was yet another last-ditch attempt by Mountbatten "to retain the unity of and British influence over the command structure of the two dominions."[45] The same month Mountbatten made this historic announcement he also set up the Armed Forces Reconstruction Committee to suggest how defense resources could be divided between the two dominions.[46] The Joint Defense Council, under the chairmanship of Lord Mountbatten, had supplanted this role by 15 August. It controlled all the military assets and manpower until they were divided between the two dominions.

On 30 June the interim cabinet accepted the chief of staff's proposal that the armed forces and defense assets be divided along a seventy-to-thirty ratio in India's favor. However, this clean mathematical divide proved difficult to implement. To begin with, many of the army regiments were ethnically diverse (there were no Muslim-only units). It was decided that while units would be divided along the seventy-to-thirty ratio, the personnel of these units would have the option of transferring to the armed forces of the other dominion. A different problem arose over the military's establishments. For various but primarily strategic reasons the British had located most of the defense establishments in the interior of the subcontinent. Because it would obviously be impractical to physically uproot these facilities and transfer them to Pakistan, the chief of staff decided that only movable assets would be divided. Consequently, India walked away from the partition with one of the largest defense-production establishments in the world.[47]

Once the division of political power had taken place, it became increasingly difficult for the Joint Defense Council to coordinate the division of military resources. One problem the council encountered was India's reluctance and slowness in complying with the redistribution of military stores. Auchinleck, however, considered this a minor point and believed that the council's task generally had been completed. Yet it increasingly became apparent that the council was becoming a defunct body. The two dominions simply could not agree on anything substantial. Any high hopes Mountbatten had for continued cooperation were finally dashed when Pakistan launched Operation Gibraltar on 22 October 1947, its covert guerrilla war to gain control of the princely state of Kashmir. In November, amidst escalating conflict in the Kashmir valley, the government dissolved the Supreme Commanders Headquarters, and Auchinleck left India.

The Indian army marched into independence a creature quite different from what the British had intended. Not only was this army no longer the bastion of a greater Commonwealth defensive alliance, it was no longer a single entity. In many ways the partition of the Indian army and not Nehru's decision to make India a republic came as the greater shock to the British. The division itself without a doubt weakened the subcontinent's military potential. Did this unforeseen calamity then destroy decades of painstaking British efforts to modernize the Indian army? The answer has to be no, for the Indian army emerged relatively unscathed from the partition. In regard to the most important asset of any emerging army – the officer corps – the Indian army easily emerged in a superior position compared to Pakistan. Not only did the new Indian army have many more officers than that of Pakistan, it also had the most capable and experienced officers. Indeed, the Indian Officer Corps reflects the true success of the British efforts.

Part Four

CHAPTER 9

Kashmir and the McMahon Line

Even as the Second World War raged across the globe, Gandhi and the Indian National Congress waged a relentless campaign under the popular slogan "Quit India" to force the British to leave India. By late 1942 Viceroy Lord Linlithgow's response was to deploy thousands of troops and quell the disturbances with tremendous violence. However, most British political leaders recognized that Indian self-rule was inevitable. The election of a new Labour government under the leadership of Clement Attlee made this opinion official. However, subsequent negotiations to create a unified India failed, and the British government decided to transfer power to two independent nations, India and Pakistan. Numerous semi-autonomous princely states, relics of the British conquest during the eighteenth and nineteenth centuries, were incorporated into the Indian union. Problems arose when two of them, Junagadh and Hyderabad, both under Muslim rulers, attempted to join Pakistan. Both states were deep within Indian territory and had overwhelmingly Hindu populations. In response, the Indian government sent troops to "reintegrate" the princely states with India. Pakistan protested the Indian police actions but did not act. A third such situation, however, proved to be far more contentious. The princely state of Jammu and Kashmir, often referred to as Kashmir, was ruled by a Hindu Dogra ruler who favored independence. The state's population was split between three groups: a Muslim majority in the west, a large Hindu minority in Jammu to the south, and a predominantly Buddhist population in Ladakh to the east. Further complicating the issue was that Kashmir, unlike landlocked Junagadh and Hyderabad, shared its borders with India, Pakistan, Tibet, and Afghanistan. Mohammed Ali Jinnah, the Pakistani president, was determined to absorb Muslim-dominated Kashmir while giving up the Hindu-dominated Jammu region. On the other hand, Nehru, the Indian prime minister and a member of the Kashmiri pandit, or teacher, elite, wanted the entire province to be part of India as a symbol of the secular aspirations of the new nation. While Kashmir's Hindu ruler, Hari Singh, dithered between independence and union with India, an enraged Jinnah decided to use force to settle the issue. After instituting an economic blockade Pakistan launched a full-scale invasion. Two months after becoming an independent republic on 15 August 1947 Indian troops flew into Srinagar, the capital of Jammu and Kashmir, to confront thousands of tribal raiders whom the Pakistani army had armed, trained, and coordinated. The attackers were not Pakistani army regulars but tribesmen recruited from northern Pakistan. On 26 October 1947 a desperate Hari Singh signed the Instrument of Accession, thereby handing over his kingdom to India. The very next day the headquarters of the First Sikh flew into Srinagar.

Kashmir

The first Indo-Pakistan War has been the longest war (October 1947–November 1948) fought between Pakistan and India to date. Coming as it did a mere three years after the conclusion of the Second World War, it showcased the capabilities of the newly independent Indian and Pakistani armies. At a tactical level it highlighted the use or attempted use of skills learned during that war, but the operational performance is probably of greater interest, as few Indian officers and even fewer Pakistani officers obtained hands-on experience commanding units above the battalion level.

Indeed, the independent Indian army's first battle experience came as a rude shock. Because the tribal Lashkars outgunned and outnumbered them, the First Sikh and later the 161st Brigade had to fight a desperate defensive action to save Srinagar. The outlying towns of Baramula and Bagdam fell on 28 October and 3 November, respectively. However, the Indian brigade commander, a decorated (Distinguished Service Order) World War Two veteran, L. P. ("Bogey") Sen, successfully organized a counterattack on the Lashkars who had closed in on the First Sikh at milestone 4 on the road from Baramula to Srinagar. The plan was a masterpiece of mobility and indirect approach. While the First Sikh held up the tribal column, Sen deployed the First Kumaon (parachute) to its southwest, flanking the roadbound enemy's right side. Additionally, he ordered two armored cars of the Seventh Cavalry to motor down the Sambal road to the enemy column's rear on the Shalateng-Baramula highway.[1] Sen launched that attack at 5:00 PM on 7 November with complete surprise, resulting in the total rout of the tribals.[2]

The battle of Shalateng was a turning point in the campaign against the raiders. By the 9th the Indians had taken Baramula, and Uri, the last major town in the Sri valley, quickly followed on the 13th. In a mere few weeks an Indian brigade had cleared the Sri valley of several thousand heavily armed raiders. Although the Indians had defeated largely undisciplined tribal forces, the campaign still reflects the 161st Brigade's strong performance, operat-

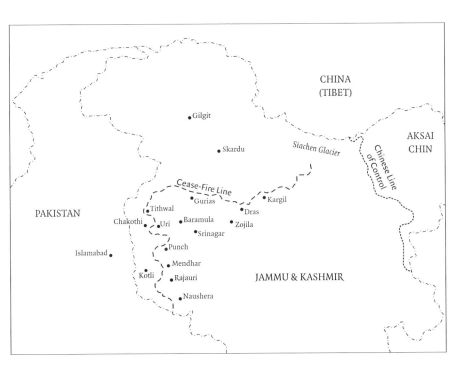

CHINA
(TIBET)

AKSAI
CHIN

Gilgit

Skardu

Siachen Glacier

Chinese Line of Control

Cease-Fire Line

Gurias

Kargil

PAKISTAN

Tithwal

Dras

Chakothi

Uri

Baramula

Zojila

Srinagar

Islamabad

Punch

Mendhar

JAMMU & KASHMIR

Kotli

Rajauri

Naushera

Kashmir-India-Pakistan conflict 1948

ing as it did amidst difficult conditions and relying solely on a tenuous air link for supplies and reinforcements. Its ability to react quickly to an enemy advancing in overwhelming numbers on multiple fronts, to retreat in good order despite heavy losses, and then to defeat the main enemy attack with a rapid concentration of meager resources are all hallmarks of a veteran force.

On 16 November 1947 Maj. Gen. Kalwant Singh, general officer commanding of the newly constituted Jammu and Kashmir (henceforth J&K) Division, issued orders to relieve other Kashmiri towns under siege by the raiders. His operational plan called for a two-pronged advance. From the south in Jammu the Fiftieth Parachute Brigade would advance in a northwesterly direction, relieving Naushera, Jhangar, Kotli, and Mirpur. From the north (Uri) the 161st Brigade was to strike toward Punch. Gen. Roy Bucher, the commander in chief and the commander of the Fiftieth Parachute Brigade, and Brigadier Paranjpe both thought that the plan was too risky and ambitious. Nevertheless, by 26 November Naushera, Jhangar, and Kotli had been taken, and Mirpur had been successfully evacuated. The advance from Uri, however, proved fruitless. The raiders adopted guerrilla tactics and decimated the 161st Brigade's support column, forcing it to return to Uri.[3]

With winter setting in both sides halted most offensive operations. On 26 November the joint planning staff, under orders from the chiefs of staff, prepared a paper on Kashmir.[4] The paper's gloomy conclusion was that during the winter months the army could hold on only to Jammu and Kashmir District. However, under political pressure from the Defense Committee, army headquarters finalized a more offensive plan by 10 December 1947 that envisaged regaining all territory still in the hands of the raiders. Logistics played a big role in the planning. Despite troop shortages, the commanders placed a ceiling of 4,000 men for the Kashmir valley operation.[5] The documents from this operation reveal much cooperation and understanding between the civilian and military leadership. The army's accession to Nehru's demands for more offensive action was tempered by the general staff's efficient and realistic appreciation of the complexities of the operation and of the limited resources available.

The preparations to regain lost territory began on a sour note when raiders recaptured Jhangar in a well-coordinated assault with the support and direction of the Pakistani army. The loss of Jhangar further reinforced the Indian army's belief that it was confronting the regular Pakistani army and not tribal hordes and that the enemy still had an overwhelming superiority in numbers and logistics. The Indian army's offensive began in January 1948. The first major operation (30–31 January) was aimed at capturing Kot, a primary concentration area for the enemy and a hilltop position dominating the

Naushera-Tawi valley and the town of Naushera. The attack plan reveals that the Indian army had realized the extent of Pakistani army involvement. The commanders not only assigned Indian air force Tempests to provide air support but used elaborate deception schemes to indicate that a counterattack against Jhangar was imminent. The actual attack on Kot was a total success, and the Indian army captured the position on the 31st.[6]

After the fall of Kot the Pakistanis attacked Naushera on 6 February 1948. The Indian artillery largely decimated this assault in what the official history describes as a "gunners battle."[7] Indeed, as logistics improved and troops and equipment flowed in, artillery began to play a key role. On 5 March Maj. Gen. Kalwant Singh launched Operation Vijay, a two-brigade (Nineteenth and Fiftieth) push down the Naushera-Jhangar road to recapture Jhangar. Infantry and artillery cooperation was excellent throughout the operation. At Pir Thal Hill, for example, twenty-four guns, the largest artillery concentration so far, pinned down the defenders while the Third Maratha Light Infantry and the First Patiala Light Infantry scaled the right and left slopes. The artillery fire had such a devastating impact on the enemy position and morale that the Pakistanis evacuated before the Indian troops could close in.[8]

While the Fiftieth Parachute Brigade and the Eightieth Brigade launched diversionary attacks, the Nineteenth Brigade, with the tanks of the Central Indian Horse supporting them, blasted through enemy roadblocks and advanced 48 miles in four days. Jhangar fell on the 17th, and the Indians captured Rajauri on 12 April.[9] As the Indian army's operations expanded, so did the command and control structure. On 1 May Maj. Gen. Kalwant Singh left Kashmir to take up his appointment as chief of general staff at army headquarters. The commanders subsequently split J&K Command between the Sri Division under Maj. Gen. K. S. Thimmaya and the Jammu Division under Maj. Gen. Atma Singh.[10]

On 22 May the 163rd Brigade secured the town of Tithwal with very little opposition, since the garrison had fled after being subjected to artillery fire from a battery that the Indians had manhandled into position over mountainous routes.[11] On 17 May the Sri Division began a 45-mile advance from Uri to take the town of Domel on the border with Pakistan. Sen's 161st Brigade took on the task of capturing Domel. However, Pakistan intervened in force with approximately a brigade's worth of troops, including the First and Fourth Frontier Force Rifles and the Fourth Battalion/Fifteenth and Sixteenth Punjab Regiments. Working closely with the tribals, they halted the advance of the 161st Brigade at Chakothi.[12] Thimmaya then ordered the Seventy-seventh Parachute Brigade to move out of Uri to sever Chakothi's road links to Chinari. This operation failed, and after the 161st Brigade again failed to outflank

Chakothi, the offensive was called off on 17 June.[13] In reaction, the Pakistani forces launched a counterattack in the Uri sector and by the 23rd had seized the important position at Pandu.[14]

Meanwhile, in the south the Jammu Division under Maj. Gen. Atma Singh was engaged in operations to relieve the garrison at Punch. On 20 November 1947 the First Kumaon fought its way into Punch to reinforce the 2,000 J&K soldiers already there. In January the Indian army flew in additional troops (two companies of Third Battalion/Ninth Gurkha Regiment) and artillery (the Fourth Mountain Battery). The remainder of the Third Battalion/Ninth Gurkhas arrived between 4 and 10 February.[15] The Punch garrison and 40,000 refugees were all supplied by air, a massive undertaking for the fledgling Indian air force but ably carried out with twelve Royal Indian Air Force Squadron C-47s and commanded by Air Commodore Mehar Singh, air officer commanding No. 1 (Operations) Group.[16] By May 1948 the Punch garrison (named the 101st Brigade) had taken the high ground overlooking Punch. An attempt in June to link up with the Nineteenth Brigade advancing from Rajauri failed. On 14 September Lieutenant General Shrinagesh, who had been appointed the overall corps commander of the J&K forces, initiated Operation Easy to relieve Punch. During the campaign the army captured a number of important heights and positions, including Pir Badesar, Pir Kalewa, Ramgarh fort, and Bhimbar Gali, in order to secure the route to Punch.[17] Unlike the rapid thrust attempted in June, this attack was a conventional advance with air support, tanks (one squadron of Central Indian Horse), and artillery.[18] The planning and preparation paid off, and on 19 November the Indians decisively broke the siege of Punch. The relief of Punch was the last major operation in the Jammu area. Before the Indian forces could recommence operations, the cease-fire came into effect in December 1948.

The conflict was not just confined to the Sri valley and its environs but also involved the inhospitable northern and northwestern regions. Kashmir's northern territory consists of two regions: Baltistan and Ladakh. The Indians lost Baltistan to Pakistan when the Gilgit Scouts, led by their British commander, Major Brown, overthrew Brig. Ghansar Singh, the maharaja's governor, on 1 November 1947. In Ladakh a small garrison under Lt. Col. Sher Jung Thapa of the J&K forces at Skardu blocked the advance of the tribals into the area. In the desperate fight to save western and southern Kashmir the Indians could spare little to stop the Pakistani attacks in the north. Although Skardu continued to hold out, Kargil fell to the raiders on 22 May, and Dras followed on 11 June. The result was that Leh, the capital of Ladakh, was cut off from the rest of Indian-controlled Kashmir. On 14 August Colonel Thapa surrendered Skardu to the raiders. The failure of the Indian troops to relieve Skardu reflects the ad hoc nature of these operations. Not only were the relief columns under strength, they also operated with minimal intelligence of enemy movements and worked along overextended supply lines.

Almost a week after the fall of Dras Thimmaya authorized Operation Erase, a two-battalion assault to recapture Gurias.[19] On 21 June the Second Battalion/Fourth Gurkhas began the advance, with the First Grenadiers following on a different axis. On the 28th the First Grenadiers established themselves on the heights outflanking Gurias. The raiders quickly abandoned their positions, and the Indian troops entered the town on the 29th. The Gurias operation secured the northern route into the Kashmir valley, but the situation in Ladakh remained critical. On 18 August Thimmaya sought and obtained approval from Western Command Headquarters to launch Operation Duck to retake Dras and Kargil.[20] Brig. K. L. Atal's Seventh Brigade opened the assault. After an initial two-pronged attack collapsed in the face of heavy defensive fire and extremely harsh terrain, he launched a frontal assault through the Zojila defenses under cover of darkness on 12 and 13 September. Not surprisingly, the two attacking battalions, the Fifth Maratha and the Third Jat, lost their way and were pinned down in the morning.[21] Thimmaya, apparently seeing similarities between the Pakistani defenses at Zojila and the Japanese positions in Burma, decided to bring in tanks to blast the Pakistani bunkers.[22] The ambitious Operation Bison swung into play. Working at a frantic pace, Indian army engineers improved the crude track from Baltal to Zojila to enable it to take tanks. A Stuart light tank squadron was then moved 276 miles from Akhnur under the greatest secrecy and arrived at Baltal on 15 October. When the Indians attacked on 1 November the raiders fled after the sudden appearance of the tanks.[23] The Indians maintained the momentum of the campaign, and, with artillery and tank support, the Seventy-seventh Brigade (First Patiala) seized the heights overlooking Dras. Indian troops entered Dras on 15 November and took Kargil on the 24th. Within days troops advancing from Leh met the Seventy-seventh Brigade, thus ending the long blockade of the town.[24]

Postmortem

The campaign in Jammu and Kashmir, the second longest military campaign waged by the Indian army to date, is also one of its most successful. The army's performance reflected the high state of combat efficiency achieved during the Second World War. More importantly, the Indian army's success vindicated the reforms carried out in the interwar British-Indian army. After initially experiencing shock at the strength and organization of the Pakistani-sponsored raiders, the general staff did not panic and flood Kashmir with troops. Instead, it carefully noted the logistical difficulties. As a result, when the Indian counteroffensive eventually opened in early 1948, it was sustained with minor hitches right up until the cease-fire. Despite numerical superiority and the advantage of operating close to its supply bases, the Pakistani army failed to make any substantial headway. The inadequacies that characterized most Pakistani operations can be traced to their depleted officer corps. As noted in the previous chapter, the Pakistanis suffered extreme officer shortages at the time of independence. The British refusal to allow its officers in the Pakistani army to serve in Kashmir further compounded this problem.[25]

At the tactical level, the Indian army followed the system learned during the Second World War; namely, whenever possible the commanders used artillery and air power to support the infantry. The Indian army, however, could not obtain the firepower available to the Commonwealth armies. During the Kashmir campaign the largest Indian artillery concentration, at Pir Thal, consisted of only twenty-four guns of various calibers. Air support too was largely symbolic, with pairs of Tempests or Spitfires entering the fray and with the odd converted C-47 "bomber" joining in as well. To make up for these deficiencies, the Indian army attacked predominantly under the cover of darkness. Despite the broken and heavily wooded terrain, they usually pressed home these attacks successfully. Not surprisingly, infantry shouldered the main weight of the campaign. The leadership of the officers and the noncommissioned officers particularly helped secure the often seemingly impossible goals set. Of the 400-plus gallantry awards given for the campaign, most went to the noncommissioned officers.

At the operational level, the army showed a remarkable degree of adaptability and innovation under adversity, the best example being the movement of light tanks up to the Zojila Pass to destroy the Pakistani bunkers located there. The Indian army also used tanks and armored cars aggressively throughout the campaign. However, more than any other operation in Kashmir, the campaign in Ladakh typifies the operational and tactical excellence achieved by the Indian army.

The army's rank and file predominantly consisted of veterans, and as such its performance came as no surprise. If there was ever a doubt, it concerned the Indian Officer Corps, which, although far larger than its Pakistani counterpart, still lacked field command experience. There too, however, the success of the interwar reforms shone brightly. From the general staff down to the junior officers, the performance level was, with few exceptions, above average.

The Nehruvian State and the Military

On 14 August 1947 Jawaharlal Nehru became the prime minister of independent India. Not since the Mughal era had an Indian inherited such a vast "empire." Of course, the major difference was that, unlike the Mughals, the challenges confronting Nehru were not so much state formation as they were state building. It was a task he applied himself to with characteristic zeal and dedication. Although Nehru technically worked within a "consultative" cabinet government responsible to a parliament, he led the nation virtually single-handed for the next seventeen years. Aiding him in this task were the formidable leaders of the Indian National Congress, the British Empire's oldest and best-prepared political party. To Nehru poverty and underdevelopment were the greatest problems confronting the nation. His formula for eradicating them was centralized economic planning. In 1948 he chaired the Congress Party's Economic Program Committee and launched a series of five-year plans to meet his goals. In 1954 the Congress Party officially declared its goal to establish a socialist India. The government paid little attention to the modernization and expansion of the defense forces in the three five-year economic plans launched before 1962.

In the immediate postwar period India enjoyed (albeit briefly) a fiscal windfall for its defense budgeting because the government did not have to spend its scarce foreign exchange to procure much-needed equipment. Since India obtained much of its equipment from Britain, it could draw funds from the debts Britain had incurred during World War Two.[26] These sterling balances, however, were only a short-term solution to India's defense procurement problems. Soon after independence the Indian government asked the noted British physicist Patrick Maynard Stuart Blackett to prepare a report outlining how India could achieve defense production self-sufficiency in the shortest possible time. Well aware of the many weaknesses in India's economy, Blackett proposed a modest plan to indigenize defense production. Although the Indian government publicly accepted the Blackett report, it never implemented it. Indeed, future Indian defense officials, including Dr. V. S. Arunachalam, scientific advisor to the Indian Ministry of Defense, noted in 1984 that the Blackett plan was a "ruse" to retard development in India.[27] Blackett, however, had correctly gauged the tremendous financial problems any military modernization program would entail. By 1950 the government was spending 29 percent of its annual budget on the armed forces. The cost in foreign currency terms amounted to approximately $50 million. This figure rose to $210 million in 1959.[28]

In the 1940s and 1950s the government granted the most equipment procurement money to the Indian air force. Between 1948 and 1956 the air force acquired 104 Dassault Ouragon and 110 Dassault Mystère IV fighter-bombers from the French and 100 Spitfire and Tempest piston-engined fighter-bombers, more than 100 Vampire jet fighter-bombers, 54 Canberra bombers, and 182 Hawker Hunter fighter-bombers from Great Britain as well as an agreement with the British Folland company to license-produce the diminutive Folland Gnat fighter in India.[29] To promote the defense indigenization plan, in 1956 the government launched the HF-24 jet-fighter program under the direction of Dr. Kurt Tank, designer of the Focke Wolfe F-190 fighter. The inability to obtain an adequate jet engine for this fighter, however, delayed its deployment until 1965.[30] In October 1960 an Indian mission in Moscow signed an arms deal for twenty-four IL-14s (transports), twenty-six MI-4s (helicopters), and sixteen AN-12 (medium transports), all to be delivered in 1961–62. In May 1962 the Indian government bought a small number of MiG-21 supersonic fighters and also concluded an agreement to license-manufacture them in India.[31]

The navy was the smallest arm of the military at independence. The government, however, had ambitious plans for it. In 1947 Blackett, with the help of Vice-Adm. William Edward Parry from the Royal Navy, drew up a ten-year naval plan.[32] The plan called for the government to build a fleet consisting of two light fleet carriers, three light cruisers, eight to nine destroyers, and necessary support vessels. At the time of independence India had a small coastal navy of four frigates, six minesweepers, and a survey ship. In July 1948 the government acquired a light cruiser – the INS Delhi (formerly the HMS Achilles) – from Britain, which greatly boosted the firepower of the fleet. In 1950 the naval expansion program continued when the navy acquired three R-class British destroyers. In 1953 it also bought three Hunt-class British destroyers. Almost a decade after the Blackett report the Indian government finally acquired a light aircraft carrier, the INS Vikrant (formerly the HMS Hercules) from Britain and Seahawk naval jet fighters for it. The same year the navy inducted another ex-British light cruiser, the INS Mysore. Between 1957 and 1959 it also acquired five coastal minesweepers. In 1960–61 the government launched the first major naval ship production program under an agreement with the British to license-build four to eight Leander-class frigates at the Mazagon docks in Bombay.[33] Despite these periodic acquisitions, the Indian navy still remained short of the Blackett report's modest goals.

The government, however, granted the lion's share of the budget to the army, with most of the funds going to pay and pensions. Equipment procurement suffered greatly, with only the absolutely necessary items being purchased in small quantities. The army's most significant purchase was over

200 Centurion tanks from Great Britain in 1956–57. To help reduce army expenditure, Nehru cut the size of the army by 50,000 men to about 500,000 in 1950.[34] However, the army's main problem was not its deficiencies in manpower and material resources but rather its inability to maintain the operational skills learned during the Second World War. Budgetary restrictions meant that all aspects of peacetime operational and even tactical training had to be severely curtailed. Maj. Gen. R. M. Rau, who had served in the First Armoured Division from 1956 to 1959, noted that during exercises "a column of 40 bridging vehicles was represented by a single lorry flying a checkered flag . . . a minefield was represented by two tapes laid on the ground . . . sometimes even this was not done . . . time was merely added on paper."[35] During another exercise in 1959 Brig. D. K. ("Monty") Palit, commander of the Seventh Infantry Brigade (part of the Fourth Indian Division) at Kameng on the Indo-Tibetan border, had his proposal to train his troops for mountain warfare rejected because his troops had to build their own housing at Towang. The defense minister, Krishna Menon, ordered this as yet another economizing measure.[36] So complete was the government's indifference to and ignorance of an army's basic peacetime functions that Nehru tried to stop the army's routine acquisition of intelligence on the People's Liberation Army of China (PLA) in Tibet.[37] Nevertheless, despite these setbacks, the army managed to move ahead with plans to introduce new training programs. In 1958 the army established the Jungle Warfare School at Dehra Dun and began a course on counterinsurgency warfare at Mhow (the College of Infantry Combat). But for every two steps the army took forward the government took another back. In 1960 the government finally allowed Army Chief General Thimmaya to make a long-desired study of mountain warfare in the Italian Alpine region at the invitation of the Italian government. Upon returning to India he proposed raising mountain divisions to carry off a Himalayan defense scheme that would deploy lightly equipped mobile infantry in forward areas with backing from strong, highly mobile mechanized infantry in the plains. Both Menon and Nehru rejected this proposal, as it would "constitute a basic shift in strategy with far-reaching and unwelcome repercussions on foreign policy."[38]

Although budgetary considerations and government indifference to the army's peacetime needs crippled its readiness, the blatant attempts of senior government and army officials to politicize and fictionalize the Army Officer Corps directly contributed to the 1962 debacle. The process began when Menon, a close friend and confidant of Nehru, took over the defense portfolio in 1957. Up until that time the position of defense minister had little priority and influence in the cabinet. Menon, with his close access to the prime minister, changed this. His abrasive style and refusal to heed the advice of the army general staff, in particular that of the army chief, Thimmaya, resulted in bad blood between the two. In 1959 Menon appointed Maj. Gen. Brij Mohan Kaul to the post of quartermaster general over and above Thimmaya's recommendation that Maj. Gen. P. S. Gyani be appointed to that position.[39] To make matters worse, Kaul was a highly ambitious officer who had enjoyed close relations with Nehru (a Kashmiri Brahmin like himself) since 1945. In August Thimmaya and Menon met to sort out their differences. However, when Thimmaya realized that Menon did not intend to back down, he resigned. As a professional military officer Thimmaya had made the correct choice to resign as a result of irreconcilable differences with his civilian leadership. Unfortunately, on the 31st he allowed Nehru to talk him into withdrawing his resignation. The very next month Nehru, speaking to Parliament about the issue, described Thimmaya's actions as "peculiarly unwise and a most extraordinary thing to do" and dismissed the army chief's differences with Menon as being "trivial and of no consequence."[40] This episode dealt a devastating blow to Thimmaya while at the same time greatly strengthening Menon's position. When Thimmaya's tenure as army chief ended in 1961, as was the custom he recommended to the government the name of his successor: Lt. Gen. S. P. P. Thorat, the general officer commanding Eastern Command. Once again, in a final humiliating act Menon overruled him and appointed Lt. Gen. P. N. Thapar, general officer commanding Western Command, as the new army chief. More significantly, he made Lieutenant General Kaul the chief of general staff over Thimmaya's strong objections.[41] Kaul's appointment to this prestigious position was seen as a scandalous action, since he had spent most of his formative years in the Army Service Corps, a noncombat unit. As a result of this appointment, the Army Officer Corps broke into pro- and anti-Kaul cliques. Most senior officers disliked Kaul's appointment, none more so than Maj. Gen. Sam Manekshaw, commandant of the Indian Military Academy. The Menon clique retaliated quickly. In 1961 a military board summoned Manekshaw to answer charges that he had publicly criticized his superior (Kaul) and the civilian leadership (Menon). The inquiry board not only cleared Manekshaw of these charges but recommended action be taken against the junior officers who had reported Manekshaw's alleged indiscretions.[42] The Manekshaw affair represents a low point in the history of the Indian army, with officers turning against each other. However, the worst impact of the Menon-Kaul era was the total emasculation of the army chief, which began with the appointment of General Thapar, who in the coming conflict with China proved to be little more than an errand boy to Kaul.

Even as the Menon-Kaul team contributed to undermining the army's morale and operational ability, Nehru embarked upon a dangerous game of diplomatic brinkmanship with the Chinese. Frustrated at China's refusal to accept the British McMahon Line as the dividing line between India and Tibet and China's subsequent establishment of border posts and rail lines in the disputed territory, Nehru instituted his "forward policy" on 2 November 1961. According to the new policy, Indian forces would greatly expand their patrols in the disputed region and establish posts to regain Indian territory. Nehru and his close advisors, including Menon and Kaul, genuinely believed that such a move would not lead to an actual military confrontation.[43] Nehru's actions in the months leading up to the border war with China represented a monumental strategic blunder exceeding Stalin's actions in the months preceding Nazi Germany's invasion of the Soviet Union.

The Forward Policy

From Ladakh to the North East Frontier Agency (NEFA), Indian troops and police, on orders from Delhi, created isolated posts to make contact with the Chinese.[44] The latter reacted immediately with a major military buildup and accelerated the development of roads and bunkers. Gen. Daulat Singh, the general officer commanding Western Command and responsible for the Ladakh region, urged Delhi to back down because of the Indian army's lack of preparedness, but the government overruled him.[45] As the Indian forward policy gathered momentum, the Chinese decided to launch a preemptive attack to crush Indian "expansionism."

The Chinese chose to strike first in the NEFA. In the first half of 1962 India had succeeded in setting up twenty-four new posts in this area.[46] Chinese preparations reached a high point when the government drafted thousands of Tibetans into labor battalions to build up supply stocks. According to one source, Beijing sent a Chinese general from the Korean theater to take charge of the offensive against India.[47] The Indian army seemed oblivious to this buildup. Even as late as August 1962 Brig. D. K. Palit, director of military operations, while on a visit to the Fourth Indian Division deployed against the Chinese at Kameng, stated that a war with China would not occur for the next few years until the Chinese rail link to Lhasa was established sometime in 1964.[48]

But if Delhi continued to ignore the looming danger, the Indian field commanders in the NEFA certainly were not complacent. Brig. John Dalvi, commander of the Seventh Brigade at Towang, Maj. Gen. Niranjan Prasad, commander of the Fourth Indian Division, and Lt. Gen. Umrao Singh, commander of the Thirty-third Corps, had no illusions about India's ability to evict the Chinese from the imposing Thag La Ridge, which the Indians claimed. On 29 September Umrao Singh protested in writing the impossible task facing the Fourth Indian Division. In an unprecedented move his note also criticized Lt. Gen. L. P. Sen, general officer commanding Eastern Command, for mishandling the whole situation.[49] This dramatic move should have cautioned the general staff in New Delhi. Instead, in reaction it created a new Fourth Corps to implement the forward policy and, of course, to bypass Umrao Singh. The commander of the corps was none other than Lieutenant General Kaul, who left vacant the post of chief of general staff in New Delhi.

On 5 October Kaul flew into Lumpu to see for himself the progress of the Fourth Indian Division. By 7 October, after reconnoitering the Indian positions, he finally agreed with Brigadier Dalvi's and General Singh's views that the Indians were hopelessly unprepared to meet a Chinese counterattack. Yet, even with this realization, Kaul decided to go ahead with the operation. To take Thag La Ridge, Kaul had at his disposal Dalvi's Seventh Brigade with four battalions. The Chinese defended the ridge with at least a regiment of troops (about the size of the Indian brigade) on reverse slopes, well supported with artillery and backed by a road system.[50] On the 10th the Second Rajput crossed the Namka Chu River below Thag La in an attempt to outflank the Chinese. In response the latter attacked the forward Indian position of Tseng Jong across the Namka Chu, held by fifty-six men of the Ninth Punjab. The Indians immediately halted their thrust, and the Punjabis withdrew across the river. Kaul, suddenly realizing that the Chinese meant business, decided to leave for Delhi to give the army chief and the government a personal appraisal of the situation.[51]

Even at this late hour Delhi did not appreciate the gravity of the situation. Brigadier Dalvi's appeals to withdraw to a more defensive position were ignored. According to Kaul, the authorities in Delhi, both civil and military, demanded that Tsangle, the last Indian position in the disputed Namka Chu area, be held at all cost.[52] By 19 October the Chinese had concentrated an entire regiment in full view of the Indians at Tsangle, and it was obvious to Brigadier Dalvi that the Chinese were about to launch a full-scale attack. In the meantime, Kaul, who was suffering from high-altitude sickness, had retired to his residence at 5 York Road, New Delhi, from where he continued to issue orders to the Fourth Corps via telephone.[53] On the 18th he ordered Dalvi to reinforce the Tsangle position and to patrol the area. Dalvi pointed out that the Chinese were about to attack in overwhelming numbers and protested his orders, only to have army headquarters via General Prasad inform him that he would be court-martialed if he protested any further.[54] The forthcoming battle for the NEFA was to be waged in the map rooms of Delhi rather than by the field commanders on the ground.

The War in the NEFA

The Chinese commenced a divisional strength attack at Namka Chu on the 19th with a one-hour artillery bombardment. The Seventh Brigade's only artillery was a two-gun battery of 3.7-inch howitzers based at Tsangdhar. The brigade could not take part in the battle, however, due to severed communication lines. Furthermore, overextended defensive positions lacking mutual support also hampered the brigade. Using the same infiltration tactics that had proved so successful in Korea, the Chinese easily surrounded the Indian positions and overwhelmed them. The Chinese had wiped out the Rajput battalion on the Namka Chu by 9:00 AM, and the same fate befell the Gurkhas at Tsangdhar at 12:30 PM The destruction of the Gurkhas was a deathblow to the Seventh Brigade, for Dalvi had hoped to use Tsangdhar as his second line of defense. With its fall the brigade ceased to exist as a cohesive fighting force. Of the surviving battalions, the Ninth Punjabis and Fourth Grenadiers retreated through Bhutan, as the Chinese had cut off all withdrawal routes through Indian territory. The Chinese captured Dalvi on the 22nd as he attempted to join up with the headquarters of the Fourth Indian Division, which had moved to Ziminthang.

The Fourth Indian Division's headquarters had, however, withdrawn on the 21st from Ziminthang to Towang, where General Prasad desperately sought to erect a defensive position. The newly inducted Sixty-second Brigade was still being brought up to strength, and its battalions were thrust into the front line piecemeal. When the Chinese recommenced their assault on the 22nd, the only real opposition came from the First Sikh, covering the Bum La approach and supported by eight guns from the Ninety-seventh Field Battery. However, after repeated assaults the Sikhs had to withdraw. At 11:00 AM on the 23rd General Sen finally visited Towang and gave orders for a withdrawal from Se La. After abandoning all the artillery and mortars and most of its heavy stores, the headquarters of the Fourth Indian Division established itself at Driang Dzong, some 40 miles southeast of Se La, on the 24th. The same day army headquarters finally began to awaken to the scope of the disaster. Lt. Gen. Harbaksh Singh took over the Fourth Corps, and Maj. Gen. A. S. Pathania replaced Maj. Gen. Niranjan Prasad. Incredibly, five days later Kaul returned to the Fourth Corps to replace Harbaksh Singh.

After capturing Towang the Chinese temporarily halted their advance, providing a much-needed respite to the Indians, who utilized this time to con-

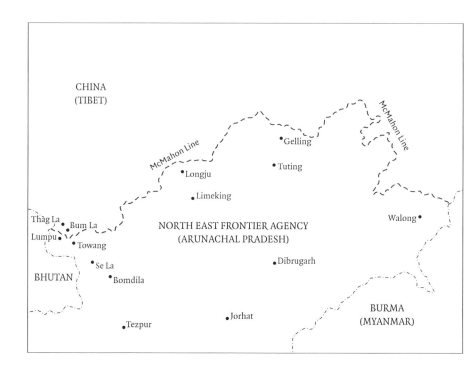

CHINA
(TIBET)

McMahon Line

•Gelling

McMahon Line

•Longju

• Tuting

•Limeking

Thàg La
Lumpu•   • Bum La

NORTH EAST FRONTIER AGENCY
(ARUNACHAL PRADESH)

Walong •

• Towang

•Se La

•Dibrugarh

BHUTAN

•Bomdila

•Tezpur

•Jorhat

BURMA
(MYANMAR)

NEFA-India-China conflict 1962

tinue a desperate buildup. By 17 November the Sixty-second Brigade had established itself at Se La with five infantry battalions, three field batteries, and two heavy mortar batteries. The Sixty-fifth Indian Brigade formed up at Ewang, north of divisional headquarters at Driang Dzong, with two infantry battalions and one artillery battery. The Forty-eighth Brigade established itself at Bomdi La with three battalions, two artillery batteries, and two tanks of the Seventh Cavalry.[55] When the Chinese did attack they ignored the road route (west) from Towang and struck instead from the northeast via the Bailey trail. Pathania immediately dispatched the Fifth Guards from Bomdi La to stop the Chinese thrust, but the guardsmen came under heavy attack at Thembang on the 17th and were stopped well short of their objective, the post at Poshing La, which a small unit of the Assam Rifles (a paramilitary frontier force) defended. By evening the Fifth Guards, having suffered some 160 casualties, fell apart. At the same time the Chinese also attacked the Sixty-second Brigade at Se La and prepared to cut it off from the rest of the Fourth Indian Division. The brigade's commander, Brig. Hoshiar Singh, had prepared for a siege, but Pathania, unnerved by the threat to Bomdi La, ordered the Sixty-second Brigade to withdraw to Driang Dzong. According to the new plan, the Sixty-second Brigade, the Sixty-fifth Brigade, and divisional headquarters would meet at Driang Dzong and then fight their way to Bomdi La.

The change in plans proved to be disastrous; the withdrawal of the Sixty-second Brigade on the 18th quickly turned into a rout as the Chinese pursued the main column. On the 27th the Chinese ambushed and killed Brig. Hoshiar Singh and most of his headquarters at Phutang.[56] The previous afternoon Pathania had evacuated Driang Dzong without waiting for either brigade. However, this evacuation too turned into a rout when the Chinese attacked and Pathania and his staff fled on foot. Kaul then ordered the Forty-eighth Brigade, still at Bomdi La, to send forces to Driang Dzong. Just as it was in the midst of shuffling its forces, the Chinese attacked, and the brigade disintegrated, even as the commander ordered a retreat to Rupa, some 9 miles south of Bomdi La. One battalion, the First Madras, did not receive the order to pull out, and the Chinese wiped it out. To compound the disaster, the Sixty-seventh Brigade, which had been moving up to reinforce Bomdi La, became caught up in the retreat and confusion. Brig. Gurbaksh Singh, the commander of the Forty-eighth, tried to reestablish the Bomdi La defenses, but the confusion thwarted his efforts. By now it was too late to establish a position in Rupa, which the Chinese had occupied, and the brigade had to fall back to Tenga with elements of the Sixty-seventh. From there they received orders from the Fourth Corps to fall back to Chaku. During this retreat the

Chinese attacked yet again, and the demoralized troops broke up into small units and fled south to the foothills. The Fourth Indian Division, the famous "Red Eagles," had ceased to exist.

While the Fourth Indian Division's main force fell apart in the Kameng sector of the NEFA, the same fate befell its Fifth Brigade (five dispersed battalions), which had been deployed in the eastern half of the NEFA. In this sector the Chinese began their attack on the night of 20–21 October. The Sixth Kumaon, which was deployed on the McMahon Ridge (the Lohit Frontier Division), managed to beat them off, but by morning the Chinese had infiltrated their flanks and rear. With no hope of support from the Fifth Brigade, the battalion withdrew to Walong. At this time the newly raised Second Infantry Division controlled the Walong sector, and Brig. N. C. Rawlley, commander of the Eleventh Brigade, was given temporary command.[57] Rawlley ordered the Sixth Kumaon to take to features "green pimple" and "yellow pimple" (referring to hills), which afforded the Chinese artillery observers an excellent view and was an obvious base for further Chinese attacks. The attack, which the Seventy-first Heavy Mortar Battery and the Seventeenth Parachute Field Regiment weakly supported, failed. In fact, a Chinese counterattack surrounded the leading Kumaon companies and forced them to retreat.[58] On the 16th the Chinese began an all-out assault against Walong from both sides of the Lohit River. They supported heavy frontal attacks with an enveloping move from the west. By 11:00 AM Rawlley had ordered a retreat, but this order did not reach the Third Battalion/Third Gurkhas, who held positions in the rock face along the west bank of the Lohit. As a result the Chinese methodically blasted them out of their bunkers with antitank rockets and recoilless rifles.[59] Rawlley tried to make a stand at Yepak, but the Chinese had already occupied it. On the 27th the remnants of the Eleventh Brigade, some 1,843 men, stumbled into Teju.[60] The Chinese were equally successful in their attacks on the NEFA's remaining two divisions. In the Siang division they seized Gelling, Tuting, and Limeking Posts.[61] The Indian posts in this division were even more isolated from supply bases than forces in the Kameng and Walong divisions. As a result better sense prevailed, and the commanders allowed them to pull out before the Chinese attacks.[62]

The War in Ladakh

The border war was not restricted to the NEFA region alone. In Ladakh China already possessed a vast tract of land claimed by India. The territory in question, the Aksai Chin plain, lay some 100 miles east of Leh, the capital of Ladakh. In October 1958 an Indian patrol confirmed that the Chinese had built a roadway through the Aksai Chin, which prompted Delhi to take a no-compromise stance with Beijing.[63] The forward policy in Ladakh began with the 114th Brigade's move to Leh in May 1960. Using the village of Chushul 182 miles southeast of Leh as a base, Indian patrols were sent forward throughout 1961–62 to establish posts along a 300-mile front from the Karakoram Pass in the north to Demchuk in the south. In response, the Chinese set up their own forward positions to outflank the Indian posts and enlarged their forces in the region to a division with a base at Rudok.[64] Lt. Gen. Daulet Singh, general officer commanding Western Command, advised army headquarters that the forward policy should be curtailed until Indian strength in the Ladakh had been built up to a division, but they overruled him.[65]

As in the NEFA, the Chinese began their attack on 19 October after careful preparation. In the north the Indian posts at Parmodak, Bishan, Chandani, and Bhujan had fallen by the 22nd. On the 23rd the larger Indian position at Daulet Beg Oldi, held by 125 men of the J&K Militia, was withdrawn. In the central sector the forward Indian post at Galwan, held by sixty men of the Fifth Jat, fell on the 20th.[66] Other positions held by the Fifth Jat at Post Patrol Base, Kongama, and Nulla Junction had fallen by the 23rd. The sector commander, Brig. T. N. Raina, decided to withdraw the Fifth Jat base from Hot Springs, which was about to be encircled, and move it to Lukung.[67] In the Chushul sector the posts at Sinjap I and II fell on the 22nd. The remaining Indian posts were withdrawn before the Chinese overran them. In the southernmost sector near Demchuk, the Chinese took Chang La and Jara La on the 27th.

Thus in a little more than a week the Chinese had seized most of the posts the 114th Brigade had established so laboriously over a span of two years. Yet, unlike in the NEFA, the local field commander did not panic. Brigadier Raina withdrew his primary positions before the Chinese could encircle them. As they had done in the NEFA after their first push, the Chinese now halted momentarily. The Indians in Ladakh also began to build up their defenses at a feverish pace. On the 26th Gen. Daulet Singh visited Chushul to appraise the situation himself. He returned to his headquarters convinced that the Chushul airfield and its environs would be the next target of the Chinese military.[68] Subsequently, the headquarters of the Fifteenth Corps informed Brigadier Raina that he was to hold on to Chushul at all cost.[69] Soon afterward Maj. Gen. Budh Singh's newly raised Third Indian Himalayan Division assumed responsibility for Ladakh. The Fifteenth Corps brought the 114th Brigade up to strength with the induction of the Thirteenth Kumaon and First Jat.[70] It deployed the Seventieth Brigade at Dungti to the south of Chushul and flew the 163rd Brigade into Leh to complete the establishment of the

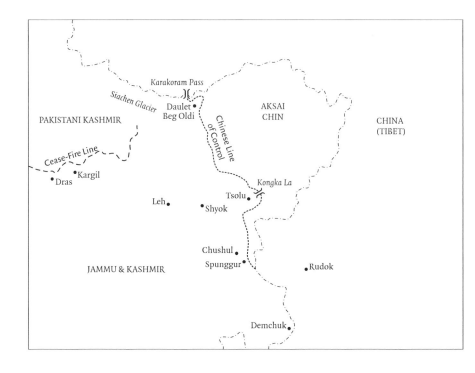

Ladakh-India-China conflict 1962

Third Division. In addition to these troops, the Twentieth Lancers with AMX-13 light tanks (squadron headquarters and two troops), a battery of the Thirteenth Field Regiment, and the Thirty-second Heavy Mortar Regiment were also flown in.[71] The entire responsibility for transporting these forces lay in the hands of the Indian air force, as the land route via Zoji La was closed. American-built Fairchild Packets, Russian-built MI-4 helicopters, and AN-12 transports ferried a constant stream of men and matériel into Leh.

The 114th Brigade now directed most of its firepower against the Spunggur Gap, a 1-mile opening in the eastern ranges of the Chushul valley. The First Battalion/Eighth Gurkha Rifles deployed a company in the gap and two companies on Gurung Hill to the north. The Thirteenth Kumaon established a company at Rezang La in the southeast and two companies on Gurung Hill to the east and just south of the Chushul airstrip. The brigade dispatched the remaining Kumaonis to Chushul village and the Fifth Jat to Taska La to the south and on the Leh-Chushul road.[72] The brigade emplaced the tanks of the Twentieth Lancers on Gurung Hill with their guns trained on the Spunggur Gap along with the artillery. All the support weapons of the brigade were provided with first-line and second-line scales of ammunition. The Kumaoni company at Rezang La, for instance, had 1,000 mortar rounds onsite.[73] The 114th Brigade also prepared dummy guns and tanks to decoy the Chinese artillery spotters. The brigade's four twenty-five-pounders and four 3.7-inch howitzers were registered on the Chinese army's likely ingress routes.[74]

The Chinese recommenced their attack on 18 November, choosing to concentrate initially on Rezang La and Gurung Hill. At Rezang La the Thirteenth Kumaon's C Company did not get any artillery support or fire support from adjacent Indian posts. The Chinese attacked at 3:00 AM and overwhelmed the post after a furious bombardment with 132 mm rockets, 76 mm field guns, and numerous heavy and medium mortars.[75] The Kumaoni 3-inch mortar section had only seven rounds left after having fired 944 in a span of six hours.[76] Although the Gurung Hill defenders had artillery support, it consisted of only two twenty-five-pounders. When the Chinese attacked on the 18th, the artillery spotter, 2nd Lieutenant Goswami, called down fire from these guns until the Chinese overran his position. The fire from these two Indian guns caused heavy casualties among the Chinese, who could only overrun the position on the 19th after bitter fighting.[77]

That night the 114th Brigade began to withdraw its forward troops, including the forces on Magar Hill, to in-depth positions near Chushul village. Most of the brigade's transport withdrew to Dungti to prevent it from falling into Chinese hands.[78] The confusion and disintegration that had characterized the withdrawal of the Sixty-second Brigade from Se La and the Forty-eighth

Brigade from Bomdi La in the NEFA was not repeated here, since this withdrawal had been preplanned and was efficiently performed. But there were no more Chinese attacks; on 21 October the Chinese declared a unilateral cease-fire.

Postmortem

The performance of the Indian army in the 1962 border war with China represents a dramatic reversal of the operational capabilities demonstrated during the 1947–48 war in Kashmir. The apathy of the civilian authorities toward the peacetime Indian army's requirements and some officials' attempts to politicize the officer corps played a significant role in this turnaround. Nevertheless, in the final analysis the major responsibility for this sorry state of affairs rests with the Indian general staff. Well aware of the dangers inherent in the Indian cabinet's strategy for evicting the Chinese from areas claimed by India, none of the officers in question, from the army chief, General Thapar, down to the field commander, Brigadier Dalvi, sought to confront the civilian authorities with the blunt realities of their ill-thought-out actions.[79] Only Brigadier Dalvi, at the eleventh hour, offered to resign rather than order his troops to advance into pointless disaster.

The chaos and indecision that characterized the Indian general staff's strategy toward China in its pursuance of the forward policy also affected the Indian army's tactical performance. After the initial shock of the Chinese NEFA invasion the Fourth Indian division commander, Maj. Gen. Niranjan Prasad, and his successor, Major General Pathania, were unable or unwilling to issue orders to enable the surviving Indian brigades to pull back and consolidate their defenses. As a consequence, the Chinese had little trouble infiltrating the widely dispersed Indian battalion and even brigade positions. The lack of adequate artillery and heavy mortar support and the total absence of air support doomed the Indians' attempts to stem the Chinese advance.[80] Much has been made of the Indian soldiers' poor equipment, particularly in terms of small arms, which forced them to rely on bolt-action Enfield .303 rifles against the Chinese AK-47s. But the real advantage that the Chinese enjoyed was their ability to concentrate their firepower and manpower resources at the point of attack. There was, however, an overwhelming Chinese superiority in recoilless guns and mortars. However, it was the loss of confidence in their military leadership that had the most devastating effect on the Indian soldiers' morale and discipline. After a long and arduous retreat into the lowlands of Assam (Bhairograh), the soldiers of the Forty-eighth Brigade, exhausted and demoralized, discovered that no provision had been made for shelter. In reaction to their commander's ineptitude, the soldiers smashed their rifles and used them as match wood. Not a single Indian officer dared to intervene.[81]

In the Ladakh sector the performance of the Western Command was much more professional. After the first Chinese attack Western Command Headquarters, without succumbing to pressure from Delhi, issued timely orders for many of the surviving posts to withdraw. In the subsequent buildup to meet the renewed Chinese offensive the Indian forces in this area concentrated on smaller and more defensible positions. The one puzzling drawback in the actions of the Indian forces in this sector was their failure to garrison the Chushul defenses with adequate artillery. In the buildup after the initial Chinese attack the Indian air force flew in AMX-13 light tank squadrons but no additional artillery to back up their four twenty-five-pounders and four 3.7-inch howitzers. A substantial artillery firebase could have saved the heights around Chushul from falling to the Chinese. Instead, the latter suffered tremendous casualties in taking the Indian positions at Rezang La and Gurung Hill.

Lacking supporting fire power (air and artillery) and the ability to choose its own battleground, the Indian army in 1962 was essentially fighting a battle without any operational doctrine. Positional warfare, which had served the army so well in the Second World War and in the first Kashmir War, had been thrown out the window. The end result, in retrospect, was not at all surprising.

CHAPTER 10

The Second Indo-Pakistan War

The border war with China marked the end of the Nehru era in more ways than one. Rigid adherence to a nonaligned foreign policy, partnership with China, and limited military spending, the centerpieces of Nehruvian foreign and defense policy since independence, essentially came to an end. Even before Nehru's death in 1964 the Indian government had embarked upon a massive expansion and modernization program for the armed forces. The army and the air force mainly benefited from the new five-year defense plans. The former had its strength immediately increased by at least six divisions, a process to be completed over several years. Two of the new divisions would be infantry, with the remaining four to be classified and equipped as "mountain divisions."[1] These mountain divisions would be provided with animal transport and light artillery with an emphasis on increased firepower.[2] The Ishapore 7.62 mm semi-automatic rifles (a licensed copy of the Belgian FN-FAL) replaced the old bolt-action .303s. The army introduced a new British 81 mm mortar. Indian armor was equipped with more Centurion tanks, and, for the first time, Soviet T-54/55s were introduced.[3]

The move to buy more Soviet equipment reflected economic and political limitations. Although India found it difficult to obtain the latest Western arms, ostensibly because of its nonaligned foreign policy, the high cost of the hardware also drove the Indians to purchase Soviet weaponry at bargain-basement prices. The government implemented this policy even though, in the immediate aftermath of the 1962 border war with China, the United States and Great Britain both extended grants worth $60 million for military equipment. Canada, France, and Australia also contributed supplies worth some $10 million.[4] However, the Western bloc did not back up this initial military aid with a long-term defense procurement relationship between India and itself.

India's first five-year plan (1964–69) led to the army doubling in size to about 825,000 men and the air force to forty-five squadrons. Total expenditure on defense during the plan period totaled Rs 50 billion ($10 billion at a pre-1966 rupee devaluation rate), with a foreign exchange content of Rs 7 billion (a little over Rs 41 billion).[5] The first annual budget after the 1962 war planned to double the defense expenditure from Rs 4.73 billion to Rs 8.67 billion. In March 1962 the army budget, which had stood at Rs 2.45 billion, more than doubled its allocation, to Rs 5.71 billion.[6] However, the defense budget as per percentage of the GNP stayed around 3.8 to 3.6 percent between 1962 and 1965.[7]

By 1965 the total strength of the Indian armed forces stood at 869,000, out of which 825,000 belonged to the army.[8] The army was organized into sixteen infantry divisions, four mountain divisions, one armored division, one independent armored brigade, and two light armored regiments.[9] The Pakistani strength in 1965 stood at about 200,000, with 160,000 men in the army, organized into six infantry divisions, two armored divisions (the Sixth Armoured was still forming), and some independent regiments.[10] Although India enjoyed an overwhelming numerical superiority over Pakistan, the latter had a considerable qualitative edge in terms of equipment. For instance, in the case of tanks the Pakistanis had 1,050 to India's 1,150, but the Pakistani strength included 594 modern M-47/48 Patton tanks to India's 270 Centurions. Pakistan's two armored divisions had three armored brigades compared to India's one armored division with one armored brigade and one motorized brigade.[11] Furthermore, all the Pakistani divisions had their own mobile and hard-hitting integral reconnaissance and support battalions.[12] In all, the Pakistanis received some $1.3 billion worth of logistics, training and arms, including M-47/48 tanks, F-86 Sabres, and F-104 Starfighters, from the United States.[13]

With the considerable military aid acquired through its membership in the South East Asia Treaty Organization (SEATO) and the Central Asia Treaty Organization (CENTO), both anti-Communist military alliances, Pakistan had built up a considerable superiority in armored and mobile formations over India.[14] It appears that the Pakistani general staff, not unlike their Israeli counterparts, had come to the conclusion that preemptive deep-strike mechanized operations were the only way of offsetting the enemy's (India) vast numerical superiority in infantry.

Confrontation

In December 1964 the Indian government granted special status to Kashmir, placing it on par with other states in the Indian union. In April 1965, in an apparent response, Pakistani armor and infantry struck at a number of Indian border posts in the Rann of Kutch to the south. This brief skirmish ended on 1 May, and in June India and Pakistan signed an agreement at the conference of Commonwealth prime ministers in London.

It is not entirely clear if Pakistan's operation in the Rann of Kutch was an attempt to evaluate its new armored formations, especially the Patton tank, against India. At least one scholar believes that "it was clear that Pakistan used the conflict as a low-cost test of Indian wills and capabilities." [15] What is indisputable is that the Pakistani high command was pleased with its army's performance. As Gen. Muhammad Musa, then Pakistan army chief, notes, "India's rout in the Rann of Kutch proved that our troops were better trained and their technique of fighting and professional qualities were superior to the enemy's." [16]

On 7 August 1965 the Pakistani army commenced Operation Gibraltar against Indian Kashmir. The plan envisioned 7,000 lightly armed guerrillas infiltrating the Kashmir valley to disrupt communications and sabotage military and power installations. The primary objective, however, was to foment an uprising among the local Kashmiris against India. [17] The Indian army reacted violently and swiftly, indicating it had prepared for such an eventuality. In addition to quickly stamping out the guerrilla bases in Indian territory the Indian army launched a series of limited offensives into Pakistan-occupied Kashmir to seal the guerrillas' invasion routes into India. In Kargil and Tithwal the Indian forces captured a number of Pakistani posts, thus sealing off the Guraiz valley to the intruders. On 27 August the First Parachute Battalion launched an attack against the Haji Pir Pass and had seized it by the morning of the 28th. By the end of August all the guerrillas had either been killed, captured, or driven out of Indian Kashmir.

The Pakistani high command was surprised that the Indians would willingly cross the cease-fire line and seize strategic Pakistani positions. The loss of the Haji Pir bulge (a salient or hump that protrudes into foreign or enemy territory) particularly angered the Pakistanis, as it enabled the Indians to reopen the Uri-Punch road, closed since 1947. With its plans for a covert war thwarted in Kashmir, the Pakistani high command initiated Operation Grand-Slam on 31 August–1 September, a full-scale Pakistani offensive to capture the Chaamb-Akhnur salient in southern Kashmir (Jammu). [18] It was the Indians' turn to be surprised.

Chaamb and Akhnur

The move against Chaamb and Akhnur was a superb strategic and tactical choice. The Pakistanis could cut road links from Jammu to Rajauri and from Naushera and Punch to the north. The terrain favored a Pakistani attack in many ways. First, it lay close to the Pakistani bases in Sialkot and Kharain, while the Indians had to rely on a single 111-mile-long roadway to Pathankot.

India-Pakistan conflict 1965

Furthermore, the bridge at Akhnur over the Chenab River could take the weight of only the light AMX-13 tanks. But the most damaging factor to the Indian defenses in this sector was the 1949 cease-fire agreement, which limited the number of troops either side could deploy in Kashmir. Pakistan had an international border with the southern part of Chaamb and was thus not subject to such restrictions.

Under the circumstances, Pakistan's move against Chaamb should have come as no surprise to the Indians. According to Maj. Gen. Joginder Singh, chief of staff for the Western Command in 1965, exercises in 1956–57 and 1958–59 had clearly indicated Chaamb as the most likely area for a Pakistani offensive.[19] General Singh blamed the general officer commanding Western Command, Lt. Gen. K. S. Katoch, for dismissing the possibility of a strong Pakistani attack against Chaamb.[20] When the Pakistanis attacked in force the Indians were completely unprepared. The Pakistani Twelfth Infantry Division and two regiments of medium tanks, mostly M-48 Pattons, led the attack. Maj. Gen. Mohammed Yahya Khan, general officer commanding Seventh Infantry Division (a corps-sized formation), led the attack.[21] A single Indian infantry brigade, the 191st, supported by the Twentieth Lancers' single AMX-13 tank squadron, opposed them.[22] To make matters worse, the Indian command structure was in transition, as the Tenth Infantry Division was given the responsibility for the Chaamb-Akhnur sector. Maj. Gen. D. B. Chopra and a skeleton staff had moved into Akhnur on 28 August just days before the assault.[23]

The Pakistanis launched a three-pronged attack, with the main thrust aimed at Dewa Mandiala. Air strikes by Indian air force (IAF) Vampires succeeded only in hitting more Indian than Pakistani targets, and the army never again utilized the air force in this sector. By late evening on the 1st the Pakistanis had driven a wedge between Mandiala and Chaamb. On 2 September the Pakistanis paused while Maj. Gen. Yahya Khan and his headquarters (Seventh Division) replaced the Twelfth Division headquarters and its commander, Maj. Gen. Akhtar Hussain Malik, as the commander of the Chaamb operation.[24] On the 3rd the Pakistanis attacked Jaurian, and on the 4th they forced the Forty-first Indian Brigade, which defended the area, to withdraw to Akhnur. The 161st Indian Field Regiment abandoned its guns during this retreat. The Indians, hampered by treaty restrictions, could not commit more armor to Chaamb. To offset the Pakistani advantage in Chaamb, the Indian general staff launched a counteroffensive into the Lahore-Sialkot sector. The attack had an immediate effect on the Pakistani army in Chaamb. By 9–10 September the Pakistanis had pulled back the Eleventh Cavalry, the Tenth Infantry Brigade, and the entire Fifteenth Infantry Division's artillery to meet the Indian counteroffensive.[25] By the 5th the Twenty-eighth Indian Brigade had established positions between Jaurian and Akhnur, thus bringing a complete halt to the Pakistani offensive in this sector.

The Lahore Front

The Eleventh Indian Corps opened the Indian counteroffensive on the Lahore front with the Fourth Mountain Division, the Seventh Infantry Division, the Sixty-seventh Infantry Brigade, and the Second Armored Brigade. At a commanders conference in May 1965 the army chief, General Chaudhuri, defined the role of the Eleventh Corps in the event of a war: (1) protect Indian territory from Pakistani aggression and occupation; (2) pose a threat to Lahore by securing the Ichogil Canal; and (3) destroy enemy forces, particularly the Pakistanis' newly acquired armor.[26] On 6 September at about 5:00 AM the Eleventh Corps launched a three-pronged attack. To the south the Fourth Mountain Division under Maj. Gen. Gurbaksh Singh struck along the Khem-Karan-Kasur axis. To the north Maj. Gen. H. K. Sibbal's Seventh Infantry Division attacked along the Kharla-Burki road. Farther to the north the Fifteenth Infantry Division under Maj. Gen. Niranjan Prasad struck eastward on the Old Grand Trunk Road from Amritsar to Lahore. The Indian thrust surprised the Pakistanis, as they had not expected the Indians to attack outside the Kashmir theater. Initially, the Indian forces faced only two Pakistani infantry divisions: the Tenth under Maj. Gen. Mohammad Sarfaraz defended the Lahore front, and the Eleventh under Maj. Gen. Abdul Hamid defended the Kasur-Hussainiwalla axis. The powerful Pakistani First Armored Division was concentrated near the Changa Manga forest.[27]

The Fifteenth Indian Division made many gains on the first day of the offensive. Not only did the division succeed in crossing the Ichogil Canal at Dograi, it reached Battapore on the outskirts of Lahore.[28] The Pakistanis reacted swiftly, beginning with a number of fairly effective air strikes against the Fifty-fourth Brigade on the Grand Trunk Road. The Fifty-fourth had been given the task of capturing two bridges across the Ichogil Canal at Dograi and Jallo. The Thirteenth Punjab, advancing toward Jallo, bore the brunt of the Pakistani air strikes, and this, combined with some heavy shelling, brought their advance to a halt. By midday on the 7th Pakistani armor had forced the Third Jat, which had taken the bridge at Dograi, back to the east bank. It also forced back the Fifteenth Dogra, which was to follow up the Third Jat's attack. The divisional commander, Niranjan Prasad, informed the corps commander, Harbaksh Singh, that he could not advance farther due to heavy casualties. The latter, after visiting the Fifteenth Division headquarters at Atari, ordered Prasad to immediately resume the attack. When the division's Thirty-eighth Brigade failed to make any headway, Harbaksh Singh ordered Maj. Gen. Mohinder Singh to replace Prasad.[29] After some additional planning he once again ordered the Third Jat to attack Dograi. The entire divisional artillery was supposed to support this attack, which started on the 21st at 1:00 AM While the Fifteenth Indian Division engaged the Tenth Pakistani Division's artillery, the Jats attacked Dograi, which the Pakistani Sixteenth Punjab held. After bitter hand-to-hand fighting, Dograi fell to the Jats at 6:14 AM on the 22nd.[30] Two companies from the Fifteenth Dogra reinforced the Third Jat, and, despite many Pakistani counterattacks, Dograi remained in Indian hands.

In the south the Seventh Indian Division advanced along the Bhikwind-Kharla axis to take the bridge over the Ichogil Canal at Burki. By 10:30 AM the Forty-eighth Brigade's Sixth Battalion/Eighth Gurkhas had reached the bridge across the Hudiria Drain halfway between the international border and Burki. The Pakistanis had blown up the bridge, which meant that Indian army engineers had to construct a Bailey bridge that afternoon under air and artillery attack. After the Sixty-fifth Brigade cleared the area around Barkha Khurd toward Burki, the Fourth Sikh was ordered to attack Burki on the night of 10–11 September. The Sixteenth Punjab (Indian), which would seize the bridge over the Ichogil Canal, was to follow the Fourth. Because the Pakistanis had heavily fortified Burki, a squadron of the Central Indian Horse gave the Fourth Sikh fire support. According to the attack plan, the Fourth Sikh would launch a night attack on the 10th with armor support from the Central Indian Horse. Not surprisingly, the armor failed to make contact with the infantry, and the attack had to be launched without tank support. Under the cover of artillery fire, the Fourth Sikh machine guns were deployed forward to suppress the Pakistani bunkers, while the infantry, using fire and movement tactics, closed in on them. Burki had fallen to the Fourth Sikh by 8:45 PM, and the Indian forces had reached the Ichogil Canal by 9:30 PM[31] The Pakistanis, however, had blown up the bridge just before the Indian forces reached it. Nevertheless, the capture of Burki was the Eleventh Corps's most trouble-free operation. Its early capture enabled the Seventh Division's Twenty-ninth Brigade to be transferred to the Fourth Mountain Division to assist it against superior Pakistani forces.

Of the three divisions in the Eleventh Corps, the Fourth Mountain had the most difficult task. The corps commander ordered the division to destroy the bridge over the Ichogil Canal on the Khem-Karan-Kasur axis to contain a possible attack by the powerful Pakistani First Armored Division.[32] The Fourth Mountain Division began its advance to the Ichogil at 5:00 AM on the 6th. By midday the Seventh Brigade had reached the canal. Elements of Pakistan's Eleventh Infantry Division, which was launching its own counterattack into Indian territory, met the division. According to the Pakistani plan, the First Armored Division's Fifth Armored Brigade and the Eleventh Division's 106th Infantry Brigade would capture Khem-Karan to establish a bridgehead/base for the eventual advance of the First Armored Division toward Amritsar.[33] On the 7th the Fourth Indian Mountain Division, under heavy Pakistani infantry and tank attack, began to fall back. During the withdrawal its Sixty-second Brigade lost cohesion and began to trickle back into Valtoha, well inside Indian territory. Maj. Gen. Gurbaksh Singh immediately ordered his artillery commander, Brig. J. S. Sandhu, to bring down heavy fire on the bridge spanning the Ichogil and also on a smaller bridge spanning the Rohi Nalla, a stream, to stop the Pakistani offensive.[34] The Pakistani First Armored Division had to spend the entire night of 7–8 September building a new bridge across the Ichogil.[35] This twenty-four-hour respite allowed the Fourth Indian Division time to regroup.[36] According to Pakistani plans, the First Armored Division's Fourth Armored Brigade was to advance northeast, taking the bridge over the Sutlej at Harike (south of Amritsar). The Fourth would then continue its advance and take the bridge over the Beas, effectively severing Amritsar's major road link with India.[37] In doing so the Pakistani high command expected to encircle the Eleventh Indian Corps along the Lahore front and Amritsar, thus bringing a successful end to the war.[38]

However, the break in the Pakistani operations on the 7th enabled the Fourth Indian Division to redeploy the Sixty-second Brigade in the area between Asal Uttar and Chima, thus blocking the proposed route along which any Pakistani attack would come. The division also laid extensive minefields.[39] Just before the Pakistani attack began at 2:30 PM on the 8th Indian tanks belonging to Lt. Col. Salim Caleb's Third Cavalry and Lt. Col. A. S. Vaidya's Deccan Horse deployed to meet the advance of the Pakistani First Armored Division. The Third Cavalry's Centurions stopped the Pakistani advance at Chima. That night the Pakistanis halted their operations in Khem Karan to concentrate on the Asal-Uttar/Chima area. On the Indian side, the Second Armored Brigade finished deploying to cover the front from Harike to Kharla.[40] On the 9th the Pakistani armor attacked in force, but the Fourth Indian Division's antitank defenses, the divisional artillery, and the tanks of the Second Armored Brigade confronted them. By 10:00 PM the Pakistanis had withdrawn from the battlefield, leaving the battlefield littered with their destroyed, damaged, and abandoned tanks. On the 10th the Pakistani Fourth Armored Brigade, which included an infantry battalion (Tenth Frontier Force) mounted on M-113 armored personnel carriers (APCs), tried to advance up the Khem-Karan-Taran axis, only to have the Third Cavalry's Centurions stop them at Chima by midday.[41] With their outflanking attack having failed, the Pakistani First Armored Division commander, Maj. Gen. Nasir Ahmed, ordered one final attack to break the Indian defenses, this time at Mehmudpara and Lakhna, but once again the Third Cavalry's Centurions stopped them.

By this time the First Indian Corps offensive in the Sialkot sector was making headway, and a worried Pakistani army headquarters ordered most of the First Armored Division to move to Prasur. The Indians similarly moved the Second Armored Brigade, less the Third Cavalry, which was seconded to the Fifteenth Indian Division. The Indian headquarters now concentrated its attention on retaking Khem Karan from the Pakistani Eleventh Infantry Division. The Fourth Indian Division's general officer commanding, Maj. Gen. Gurbaksh Singh, asked for reinforcements and received two infantry battalions, the Second Mahar and the Fourth Sikh, on 11 September. On the 12th the Fourth Sikh, as part of the Seventh Brigade, moved forward into position less than a mile from Khem Karan. In doing so it stumbled upon a Pakistani tank laager. During the ensuing battle the Pakistanis captured much of the Fourth Sikh along with its commanding officer, Lt. Col. Anant Singh.[42] The Second Mahar, supported by a squadron of Deccan Horse Sherman tanks, had also moved out by 5:00 AM on the 13th, only to have strong Pakistani defenses and air strikes halt them.[43] Gurbaksh Singh's attempts to reinforce the attack with additional armor from the Third Cavalry and two companies from the Ninth Jammu and Kashmir Light Infantry proved futile. On the night of 21–22 September the Indians launched a last desultory attack, ordering the First Battalion/Eighth Gurkhas and Fifteenth Kumaon to take Khem Karan from the northwest. Like the Fourth Indian Division's earlier assault, little reconnaissance of the enemy positions was made before the attack. As a result, unexpected minefields and Pakistani defenses disrupted the cohesion of the attack, which Pakistani air and artillery strikes finally stopped.[44] The cease-fire came into effect at 3:30 AM on the 23rd, bringing all fighting to an end in this sector.

Sialkot

According to Gen. Joginder Singh, chief of staff Western Command, Lt. Gen. Sam Manekshaw, general officer commanding-in-chief Western Command in 1963–64 (then field marshal), first raised the possibility of an Indian offensive in Sialkot. Army headquarters shelved the plan due to lack of forces but revived it when Lt. Gen. Harbaksh Singh became general officer commanding Western Command. In August 1965 the army chief, General Chaudhuri, created the First Army Corps under Lt. Gen. O. P. Dunn to fulfill this goal.[45] The plan was to cut off Sialkot from Lahore by first taking Phillora, Chawinda, and Pagowal and then advancing some 22 miles west of Chawinda to cut the Sialkot-Gujranwalla road near Daska.[46]

Prior to the main offensive, the Sixth and Twenty-sixth Divisions secured the advance's flanks by taking Maharajke-Charwa and Anula-Bajragrahi, respectively, on 8 September. At 6:00 AM the First Armored Division moved out of its assembly area at Samba. It consisted of the First Armored Brigade and Forty-third Lorried Brigade. Its armor strength included the Fourth Horse, Sixteenth Light Cavalry, and Poona Horse, all armed with Centurion tanks; the Second Lancer with up-gunned Shermans; and the Sixty-second Cavalry with Sherman MK-4s.[47] The commanders assigned different routes to the Forty-third Brigade and the First Armored, but both came short of their objectives, the lorried brigade due to rain and mud and the armored brigade due to opposition from Pakistan's Twenty-fifth Cavalry, dug in at Pindi-Bhago/Narsing Chobara. This slowdown enabled the Pakistani commanders to hurriedly move their new Sixth Armored Division to the Daska-Chawinda area.[48] On the 9th the First Corps spent the entire day establishing a firm base for further offensive actions, thus sacrificing the element of surprise so essential to the plan. On the 10th General Dunn gave the order to capture Phillora. The First Indian Armored Division's general officer commanding ignored the direct route to Phillora from the Sabzipur axis and tried instead an approach from the north in the direction of Rurki-Khurd/Rurki-Kalan. He directed one armored regiment, the Sixteenth, to Khakanwalla to the west of Phillora to prevent Pakistani reinforcements reaching Phillora. Infantry and two armored regiments of Patton tanks defended Phillora. Despite a strong fight the Indians seized the town on the 12th.[49] On 13 September the Sixth Mountain Division, with the support of the Sixty-second Cavalry, moved against Pagowal and captured it by last light.[50] On the 14th the First Armored Division struck at Chawinda, which Pakistani armor heavily defended. Since the First Armored Division was unable to suppress Pakistani armor, the commanders did not commit the Forty-third Lorried Brigade's infantry into the battle. On the 16th the general officer commanding, First Armored Division, ordered the Seventeenth Horse and Ninth Dogra to establish blocking positions to the rear of Chawinda southwest of Butur Dograndi.[51] Despite heavy Pakistani counterattacks they accomplished this, and by 3:00 AM on the 17th the general officer commanding had ordered the lorried brigade to attack. He called off the attack, however, due to a lack of reinforcements, which he had expected from the Sixth Mountain Division.

After some further delays the Fourteenth Division's Thirty-fifth and Fifty-eighth Brigades launched an attack on 18–19 September. Despite the corps's artillery support, the Pakistani counterbombardment pinned down and scattered the attacking infantry, and the assault was called off at first light.[52] On the 21st the First Armored Division was withdrawn for refitting, and all offensive operations ceased on this front.

The Air War

Aside from the three major theaters of ground conflict described above, minor clashes occurred to the north in Kashmir and to the south in the Rann of Kutch. In addition to the combat on the ground, the 1965 war represents the first large-scale use of air power in anger in the subcontinent since the Second World War. In October 1932 the Indian Legislature passed an act creating the Royal Indian Air Force (RIAF). It actually came into being on 1 April 1933 at RAF Drigh Road, a neighborhood of the city of Karachi. During the Second World War, approximately ten RIAF squadrons operated in the Burma theater equipped with a mix of obsolete Vultee Vengeance and Hurricane fighter-bombers.[53] In 1947 the RIAF's assets were divided in much the same way as the army had been between India and Pakistan, with some 80 percent going to India and 20 percent to Pakistan.[54]

During the 1948 war in Kashmir the C-47s (Dakotas) and Tempests of the IAF provided fairly effective transport and close air support to the Indian troops. Indeed, it is doubtful if Srinagar could have been saved without the intrepid efforts of the IAF C-47 "drivers." During the border war with China the newly acquired Soviet-built AN-12 medium transports were instrumental in sustaining and thus saving the base at Chushul. In 1965 the IAF, in addition to its many transport missions, also made a major contribution of its combat capabilities to the war effort.

At the outbreak of the 1965 war the IAF consisted of 28,000 personnel in forty-five squadrons. These included 8 MiG-21s, 110 Mystère IVAs, 50 Gnats, 56 Ouragons, 132 Vampires, 53 Canberras (including 7 configured for photoreconnaissance), and approximately 50 Hunters. The Pakistani Air Force (PAF), with 110 F-86F Sabres, 25 B-57BS, 12 F-104A and B Starfighters, 12 T-33A trainers, and 1 B-57 Reconnaissance plane, opposed it.[55] The commanders of both air forces began their careers with the RIAF. The PAF's air marshal, M. Asghar Khan, was the commanding officer of the Ninth Squadron in 1946, while Air Marshal Arjan Singh of the IAF won his Distinguished Flying Cross during the Second World War as the squadron leader of No. 1 Squadron in the Arakan. At the time of independence he was a group captain.

Unlike the Indian army, the IAF appears to have done little in the way of contingency planning for a coherent war strategy against Pakistan, which was most apparent in the IAF's dismal conduct in the close air support role. In Chaamb, for instance, the IAF sent its obsolete Vampires and later Mystères to stop the Pakistani advance. These fighters mistakenly strafed and rocketed Indian ground formations instead. The Indian ground forces in this theater never again requested air support. This scene repeated itself in the Lahore sector, where Gen. Mohinder Singh, the general officer commanding Fifteenth Infantry Division, told the IAF to hold its ground-attack missions to the west bank of the Ichogil Canal or they would be fired upon by his troops.[56] The IAF, however, claims that the Indian army entered the war without making any attempt to seek a joint army–air force battle plan.[57] This view receives some support from Lt. Gen. S. K. Sinha, who noted that the chief of army staff, General Chaudhuri, only asked for air support when Pakistani forces threatened the Jammu-Srinagar highway in the Chaamb-Jaurian sector. Similarly, he notes that the army operations in Punjab and Rajasthan were carried out with minimum coordination with the IAF.[58]

It is difficult to get a clear picture of the IAF's deep-strike, interdiction, and air-superiority operations. Both sides' considerably divergent and exaggerated claims make it impossible (without access to government documents) to do so at present. The IAF did launch a concerted counterair effort against the PAF air bases, particularly against their primary base at Sargodha. It conducted these operations by using Hunters and Mystères during the day and Canberras by night. According to Pakistani claims, these attacks met with little success and resulted in heavy losses to the IAF at the hands of the defending PAF Sabres and Starfighters.[59] In addition to the counterair effort, both sides targeted each other's radar stations. Here the IAF proved to be the more successful in its attack against the Pakistani radar station at Badin.[60] Interdiction efforts by both sides against communication hubs, military bases, command posts, and war industries appear to have been minimal. In fact, both air forces essentially fought a battle of attrition during the seventeen-day war.

According to the Pakistanis, the Indians were apprehensive about taking on the American-built F-86 Sabres and F-104 Starfighters (the Pakistani had two squadrons) armed with sidewinder air-to-air missiles. Yet IAF combat reports state that both the Hunter and the Gnat did well against these Pakistani front-line fighters. The IAF observed that the automatic cannon was still an important element in air combat, a fact later confirmed by the Americans in Vietnam. After the war the PAF claimed 113 Indian aircraft downed, while the IAF claimed 73 Pakistani aircraft destroyed.[61] Both sides also claim to have achieved air superiority over each other, although over the battlefield, at least, the Indian army would agree with the PAF's assertion that it had control of the skies.

The Naval War?

The only naval activity during the war was the Pakistani destroyers' brief bombardment of the Indian posts at Dwarka and Okha. The Indian navy restricted itself to general patrolling, and its vaunted light carrier, the INS Vikrant, remained stuck in the Bombay dry dock due to a damaged boiler.

Conclusion

Unlike the 1962 border war, the rapid onset of the 1965 War did not paralyze the Indian army. The army's reaction to Pakistan's Operation Gibraltar was immediate and decisive. The Indian government did not intend to allow the guerrillas safe haven in Pakistani Kashmir and struck across the ceasefire line at will. Indeed, as a result of war games and exercises the Northern and Western Commands had contingency plans in case Pakistan attacked in Kashmir, Chaamb (Jammu), and Amritsar. The Indian strategy was primarily defensive. The Indian offensives toward Lahore and Sialkot were intended to draw out Pakistani forces from Chaamb and Amritsar, a task in which they succeeded. The Pakistani claim that India intended to capture Lahore is unlikely because the army headquarters deployed the premier Indian strike formation, the First Armored Division, in the Sialkot sector.

The Indian strategy of limited probing attacks to offset Pakistani pressure on other fronts was suited to its positional warfare doctrine. In the defensive battles in which they engaged, Indian forces used their superiority in infantry and artillery to offset the Pakistani advantage in armor. At Khem Karan, for example, dug-in Indian tanks, recoilless guns, and artillery of the Fourth Indian Division stopped Pakistan's First Armored Division with its formidable force of four Patton tank regiments, five mechanized battalions mounted on M-113 APCs, and one M-24 Chaffee light tank regiment. In fact, the Indian battle plan used at Khem Karan was not very different from the plan that the Eighth Army had used in the battle of Alam Halfa against Rommel's Afrika Korps.

The Indian offensives were mainly infantry and artillery operations. Even in the Sialkot front, the First Indian Armored Division's First Armored Brigade generally operated without its infantry component, the Forty-third Lorried Brigade. Pagowal and Phillora fell to infantry attacks, while the armor provided flank antitank security. The main attack against Chawinda, which failed, was also an infantry attack by the Sixth Indian Infantry Division with corps artillery support. Armor and infantry operating as a combined-arms team is not very evident in the Indian army's 1965 operations, which is not surprising, because the Indian army possessed no APCs in 1965. In fact, no Indian division possessed the same mobility as a first-line, World War Two British or American division. The limited nature of the Indian offensive indicates that the Indian general staff recognized this weakness.

In sharp contrast to the Indians, the Pakistanis opted for an offensive strategy based on mobile warfare tactics. Aware that India possessed a huge advantage in infantry, the Pakistanis sought to develop a qualitative edge in firepower and mobility. Their First Armored Division had three armored brigades with a mix of M-47/48 tank regiments and M-113-tracked APCs. They were establishing a second such division when the war broke out. Unfortunately for the Pakistanis, two weaknesses hamstrung them. First, they did not have enough armor and mechanized infantry assets to offset the Indians' numerical superiority. Second, and probably more importantly, the Pakistanis could not execute the combined-arms campaign of high mobility needed to encircle and neutralize the Indian Eleventh Corps. Maj. Gen. Nasir Ahmed, the commander of Pakistan's First Armored Division, held back his division's leading elements on 7 September so that a bridge could be built over the Ichogil Canal, thus enabling the rest of his division to cross over. The delay and the practice of concentrating before any new advance meant that the Pakistani armor could not exploit the conditions that the disorganized retreat of the Fourth Indian Division created. When the attack recommenced on the 8th it ran headlong into newly prepared Indian defenses. The predilection of the First Pakistan Armor to stick to regular roadways in the course of its advance eased the task of the Indian defenders. The First Pakistani Armored Division made few attempts to use its tremendous mobility to outflank the defensive positions of the Fourth Indian Division and the Second Indian Armored Brigade. The Pakistani attacks against these Indian positions involved minimal tank-infantry cooperation. According to Indian sources, the Pakistani infantry was usually pinned down by Indian artillery fire or left behind by advancing Pakistani armor. The Pakistanis appeared unwilling or unable to operate their tanks and M-113 APCs as a combined-arms force.

Forced by strategic circumstances to take on an armored warfare doctrine they were not prepared or equipped to fight, the Pakistanis suffered heavy losses at Amritsar and Khem Karan. Despite the early Pakistani success at Chaamb and the similar Indian success at Sialkot, the 1965 war was essentially a static war. With the Indians falling back upon their traditional positional warfare doctrines, the advantage rested with India in all the combat theaters except Chaamb. Neither the Indians nor the Pakistanis had the requisite know-how to engage in a war of maneuver. The Indians, even if they did not publicly acknowledge this weakness, did not engage in any ambitious operations. On the other hand, the Pakistanis' acquisition of modern mechanized military hardware (the tank and the tracked APC) appears to have lulled them into a false sense of security. Their attempts to emulate the textbook guidelines for combined-arms warfare without having rigorously exercised and adapted this doctrine to their own needs resulted in the near destruction of their vaunted First Armored Division.

CHAPTER II

The Third Indo-Pakistan War

The 1965 war represented the last opportunity for the Pakistan military to win a quick victory against an Indian military in transition. By the time the two armies clashed again in 1971 the Indian military machine had matured into one of the world's largest and most professional fighting forces. The most visible aspect of this change was the induction of many weapon systems, mainly Soviet, to replace the outdated and obsolete equipment in the army, navy, and air force. A hidden and no less significant aspect of this maturation was the evolution of an air, naval, and land warfare doctrine. The land warfare doctrine essentially continued the positional warfare doctrine evolved during the Second World War. The navy and the air force, on the other hand, embarked upon new and bold strategies.

These changes occurred despite the economic decline of the 1960s due to the severe droughts from 1965 to 1967 that devastated the agricultural productivity of the country. The failure of the agricultural sector caused inflation in the economy and increased the nation's reliance on food aid.[1] The Indian prime minister, Indira Gandhi, like her father, Nehru, wanted to steer India toward a socialist pattern of development. Eradicating poverty thus remained a central plank of the Indira government, as did self-sufficiency in food production. The introduction of new strains of wheat and rice, which increased food production to almost 100 million tons in 1968–69 (the so-called Green Revolution), made the plan reasonably successful. Poverty eradication proved far more difficult, as radical measures such as nationalizing more industries and centralizing food-grain markets gradually crumbled due to nepotism and corruption. The economic problems no doubt contributed to the fact that between 1966 and 1971 the government never spent more than 3.5 percent of its annual budget on the military.[2]

Confrontation and Buildup

The 1971 war, although initiated by Pakistan, did not come as a surprise to the Indian government. Indeed, Gen. Sam Manekshaw, the army chief of staff and chairman of the Joint Chiefs of Staff, controlled the escalation

197

of pressure on East Pakistan that led to the Pakistani counterstrike in the West. In December 1970 Sheikh Mujibur Rahman, the leader of the Bengali Muslim Party, won an overwhelming victory in the East Pakistan elections. Gen. Yahya Khan, the Pakistani military dictator, was unwilling to accept this popular vote and declared martial law on 17 February 1971. On the night of 25–26 March the Pakistani garrison in East Pakistan under Maj. Gen. K. H. Raja commenced a brutal crackdown on Bengali dissenters, beginning with the arrest of Sheikh Mujibur Rahman. The Bengalis resisted as much as they could, with the best opposition coming from the local police and the East Pakistan Rifles. As a result of the bloody fighting that followed, millions of Bengali Muslims fled into India.

Staggering under an immense refugee problem and at the same time sensing a weakness in the Pakistani position vis-à-vis Kashmir, the Indian government began to back the Bangladeshi freedom fighters, the Mukti Bahini. The latter, however, failed to make an impression on the Pakistani army, and as the flood of refugees grew the Indian government decided to act. On 28 April 1971 the Indian cabinet, headed by Prime Minister Indira Gandhi, met General Manekshaw. The cabinet members told the general of their decision to intervene militarily in East Pakistan. Manekshaw insisted that operations begin only after careful planning and preparation. He noted that the month of May was during the monsoon season and that this would bog down any Indian offensive into East Pakistan. He also wanted to insure that all units were fully equipped, especially the First Armored Division, which suffered from a lack of spare parts for its new Vijayanta (Vickers) tanks.[3] Like Montgomery before him, Manekshaw proved to be the master of the set-piece battle. With the strategic initiative on the Indians' side, Manekshaw would set the ball rolling only after he had every conceivable card stacked in his favor.

Even before frantic activities began in the months preceding the December conflict, the Indian armed forces had undergone substantial modernization between 1965 and 1971. The air force was the main beneficiary. The program to manufacture Soviet MiG-21FL fighters was well under way, and the government equipped seven squadrons with this aircraft. There were three ground-attack squadrons equipped with the indigenously designed and built HF-24 Marut fighter. Another six squadrons were rebuilt with the newly inducted Soviet Sukhoi SU-7 strike fighter. The air force's largest number of aircraft was the seven squadrons of Gnat fighters. Still in service were six Hunter squadrons, two Mystère IV squadrons, and three Canberra bomber squadrons. In total the IAF had 625 combat aircraft and 80,000 men at the start of the conflict.[4]

Pakistan too had initiated its own air force modernization program, despite the cutoff in U.S. military aid after the 1965 war. By December 1971 the PAF consisted of thirteen combat squadrons and 17,000 personnel. The aircraft strength included forty F-86F Sabres, ninety Sabre MK-6s (ex-Luftwaffe, acquired from a Swiss arms dealer), seventy F-6 (Chinese MiG-19) fighters, twenty Mirage IIIE fighters from France, seven F-104 Starfighters, sixteen B-57 bombers, and two RB-57 reconnaissance aircraft.[5]

The Indian army also went through a modernization program during this period. It license-produced the British-designed Vickers medium tank as the Vijayanta, a replacement for the Centurion. The army also inducted the Soviet-built T-54/55 medium tanks to replace the aging Shermans. The First Armored Division's lorried infantry and the independent armored brigades obtained Polish-wheeled (SKOT) and tracked (TOPAS) APCs along with a number of Soviet BTR-60 wheeled APCs. The Indian artillery received a tremendous boost with the induction of the Soviet 130 mm field gun, which had a range of 17 miles. The army strength saw a modest increase to 850,000 men. It included twelve infantry divisions, one armored division, ten mountain divisions, three independent infantry brigades, one parachute brigade, and four independent armored brigades.[6] Pakistani army strength saw a dramatic rise in this period to about 365,000 men in two armored divisions, thirteen infantry divisions, two armored brigades, and one independent infantry brigade.[7] In 1971 India not only continued to maintain an overwhelming superiority in numbers, but it had overtaken Pakistan in terms of the quality of its armored forces.

As the Indian military buildup along the border with East Pakistan gathered momentum, so did the likelihood of border skirmishes. On 30–31 October Indian and Pakistani troops clashed at Kamalpur. The situation worsened between 20 and 27 November, when additional clashes took place at Bogra and Hilli. With the Russian veto at the UN Security Council shielding India from international pressure, the Pakistani military junta began to turn to a military option. On 3 December at about 5:45 AM Pakistan launched preemptive air strikes at Indian airfields. The Pakistanis planned to seize territory in the west as bargaining chips for any Indian gains in the east. According to the Pakistani army's public relations officer, Lt. Col. Siddiq Saliq, "the defense of East Pakistan lay in the West."[8]

The Campaign for Bangladesh

Lt. Gen. Amir Abdullah Khan Niazi, the general officer commanding, Pakistani Eastern Command, formulated the plans for the defense of East Pakistan. Niazi adopted a "fortress" concept of defense, that is, converting border towns into strongholds, especially those that lay along the most likely routes of an Indian advance. They included Jessore, Jhenida, Bogra, Rangpur, Jamla-pur, Mymensingh, Sylhet, Bhairab Bazar, Comilla, and Chittagong. The army would provision these fortress towns with munitions and rations to undergo a two-month siege. Troops in the fortresses could not fall back without the general officer commanding's permission, failing which they were to fight to the end. The Pakistani chief of army staff, Lt. Gen. Abdul Hamid Khan, approved this plan with slight modifications.

The Pakistani army distributed resources in East Pakistan as per the plan. The Ninth Division under Maj. Gen. M. H. Ansari deployed its headquarters at Jessore with the 107th and Fifty-seventh Brigades at Jhenida.[9] The Six-teenth Division, led by Maj. Gen. Nazar Hussain Shah, was responsible for North Bengal, with its headquarters at Nator, while its Twenty-third Brigade was at Rangpur and its 205th Brigade was sent to Bogra.[10] The Fourteenth Division under Maj. Gen. Abdul Majid Qazi was responsible for the east-ern border and had its headquarters at Dacca. Its 117th Brigade garrisoned Comilla, its Twenty-seventh Brigade was stationed at Mymensingh, and its 212th Brigade was at Sylhet.[11] The Ninety-third Independent Brigade, com-manded by Brigadier Ataullah, was stationed at Chittagong. As the prospect of hostilities approached, Niazi created two ad hoc divisions, the Thirty-sixth and the Thirty-ninth. He initially established them by milking the existing units, especially the Twenty-seventh Brigade and the 117th Brigade, and by in-ducting new units, the Fifty-third Brigade (stationed at Feni). During the last week of November Pakistani general headquarters dispatched five additional brigades to Niazi.[12]

According to Colonel Saliq, the strategy for the defense of East Pakistan rested on the premise that India would only seize chunks of territory to estab-lish a foothold for the new government of Bangladesh.[13] In fact, Pakistani intelligence had correctly assessed India's strategy toward East Pakistan right up until July 1971. Lt. Gen. K. K. Singh, the director of military operations at army headquarters who planned the forthcoming operation in East Paki-stan, believed that, given the Indian army's inability to conduct a mobile campaign, there would not be enough time to take Dacca (the capital of East Pakistan) before international pressure forced India to halt all offen-sive operations. (Indians planners estimated a twenty-one-day window of opportunity.) With this in mind, the military initially limited its plan to cap-turing significant territories, including Chittagong, Chalna, and Khulna.[14] By November, however, the Indian high command had decided to capture all of East Pakistan. Several factors influenced this change in plans. On 9 Au-gust 1971 India signed a treaty of friendship with the Soviet Union that

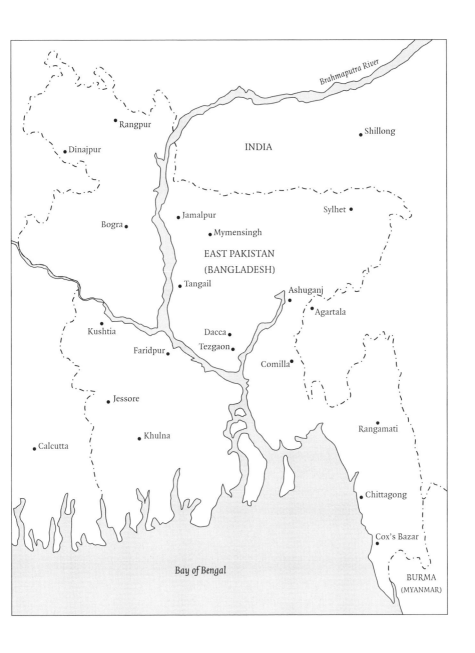

Eastern Front–India–Pakistan conflict 1971

reduced the possibility of Chinese intervention on Pakistan's behalf. War games conducted in October indicated that if the Indian army took to country tracks, thus bypassing the Pakistanis' fortified towns, it could speed up the operation. Furthermore, experience had shown that attacks on these fortified towns would be expensive and time-consuming; in other words, they would play into Pakistani hands. Lastly, the junior and midlevel officers wanted a more aggressive mobile operational style, which had indicated a high success rate in the October war games.[15]

The inability of the Pakistani high command and intelligence services to foresee a possible scenario for a full-fledged Indian conquest of East Pakistan resulted in their Eastern Command preparing for a hopeless confrontation. For example, General Niazi, still working on the original intelligence estimates of India's intentions, ordered his units not to withdraw until they had suffered at least 75 percent casualties, which in effect meant the unit's destruction.[16] This order, combined with the lack of adequate planning for in-depth and fall-back defensive positions, made the task of the attacking Indian commander – Lt. Gen. Jagjit Singh Aurora, general officer commanding Eastern Command – all the easier.

To accomplish his goal Aurora had at his disposal three army corps. The southwestern sector near Calcutta was the responsibility of the Second Corps under Lt. Gen. T. N. Raina.[17] The northwestern sector to the west of the Brahmaputra River became the responsibility of the Thirty-third Corps under Lt. Gen. M. L. Thapan.[18] The region between the Brahmaputra and the Meghna Rivers came under the aegis of a static headquarters formation, the 101 Communications Zone, with headquarters in Shillong. Its commander, Maj. Gen. Gurbaksh Singh Gill, controlled the Ninety-fifth Mountain Brigade. The region to the east of the Meghna River, the eastern sector, came under the banner of the Fourth Corps, led by Lt. Gen. Sagat Singh.[19] The IAF allotted eleven squadrons to the eastern theater, including four Hunter, one Sukhoi-7, three Gnat, and three MiG-21 squadrons. A single Pakistani F-86 Sabre squadron confronted the IAF, thus ensuring total Indian air superiority.[20]

The Jessore Front

Major General Ansari's Ninth Pakistani Division was responsible for the Jessore sector. He faced the daunting task of defending the area against Lieutenant General Raina's Second Indian Corps. The latter's offensive plan called for Maj. Gen. M. S. Brar's Fourth Indian Division to advance on Magura via Majdia, Jibanaggar, Kotchanpur, and Jhenida. From there, the division would be ferried across the Madhumati River and advance toward Faridpur. Maj. Gen. Dalbir Singh's Ninth Indian Division was to advance on the fortified city of Jessore. From there, one brigade would advance south to Khulna, while the remainder of the Ninth Division would assist the Fourth Division.[21] The Pakistani plan for its Ninth Division was simple enough: delay the enemy on the border as long as possible before falling back to prepared positions at Jessore and Jhenida.[22] Unfortunately for the Pakistanis, border skirmishes in the months leading up to the Indian attack had enabled the Fourth Indian Division to secure a substantial foothold in the villages of Jibanaggar and Uthali in East Pakistan. When the main Indian attack began, the Sixty-second Indian Brigade took Kotchandpur on 4 December, while the Forty-first Indian Brigade's Fourth Battalion/First Gurkhas took Darsana on the northern flank of the Fourth Indian Division's advance route. The Fifty-seventh Pakistani Brigade, led by Brig. Manzoor Ahmed, apparently surprised that the Indians had broken out in a direction that ignored the road axis, fell back on Chaudanga.[23] However, the Fourth Indian Division, headed in the direction of Jhenida, had established a roadblock on the Chaudanga-Jhenida road. By 9:30 AM on 7 December the Ninth Dogra had reached Jhenida. The swift Indian advance prevented Brigadier Manzoor from falling back to Jhenida as planned, and the defenseless town fell to the Indians at 2:30 PM.[24] The Sixty-second Indian Brigade captured Kaligunj south of Jhenida on the 7th and took Magura the next day. With the advance progressing better than expected, Lieutenant General Raina released the Seventh Brigade to the Fourth Indian Division to seize Kushtia and to cut off the Pakistani retreat to Faridpur.[25]

Brigadier Manzoor, upon learning that the main defensive position of Jessore had fallen to the Ninth Indian Division on 6–7 December, moved the Fifty-seventh Pakistani Brigade to Kushtia. There elements of Pakistan's Eighteenth Punjab and two troops of M-24 light tanks managed to ambush elements of the Seventh Indian Brigade and throw them back in confusion.[26] The Indians overreacted to this setback, and by 10 December most of the Fourth Indian Division had assembled in front of Kushtia. This force included the Sixty-second Brigade, which the commanders diverted from its assigned task of advancing on Faridpur after crossing the Madhumati and Garai Rivers. Brigadier Manzoor's Fifty-seventh Pakistani Brigade retreated across the Hardinge bridge over the Ganges on the 10th and blew up two spans of the bridge. The next day the Fourth Indian Division entered Kushtia, and the Sixty-second Indian Brigade resumed its original mission of crossing the Madhumati toward Kamarkhali and Faridpur. At the same time, the Seventh Indian Brigade advanced along the Harinadanga axis. The Thirty-eighth Pakistani Frontier Force Rifles and the Fiftieth Punjab tried and failed to stop the Indian advance. They were forced to retreat and suffered heavy losses in the process when the Seventh Indian Brigade established a roadblock behind them on the Faridpur road.[27] Major General Ansari and the rest of the Ninth Pakistan Division surrendered to Lieutenant Colonel Torpy, commander of the Fifth Maratha Light Infantry, on 16 December.[28]

Like the Fourth Indian Division, Maj. Gen. Dalbir Singh's Ninth Indian Division had managed, in the months leading up to the war, to obtain a considerable foothold (58 square miles) in the Garibpur area. Brigadier Makhmad Hayat's 107th Pakistani Brigade defended the area. By 6 December the Forty-second Indian Brigade had punched out toward Afra with the Thirty-second Indian Brigade following through. That evening at about 5:30 Hayat evacuated Jessore for Khulna to avoid being cut off.[29] By 7 December the Indians had captured both Jessore and Jhenida, the stated lynchpins of the Ninth Pakistani Division's defenses. Although the Thirty-second Indian Brigade pursued the 107th Pakistani Brigade, its commander, Brigadier Hayat, managed to conduct a fairly effective fighting retreat toward Khulna till the cease-fire on 16 December.[30] General Dalbir Singh's insistence on following a cautious advance with overwhelming firepower to batter down roadblocks facilitated Hayat's retreat.[31]

The North Bengal Sector

The North Bengal sector, or the northwestern sector, as it was known to the Indians, fell under the aegis of Lt. Gen. M. L. Thapan's Thirty-third Indian Corps. He confronted Maj. Gen. Nazar Hussain Shah's Sixteenth Pakistani Division. In an attempt to cover all possible routes for an Indian advance Shah had deployed his units close to the border. The 205th Brigade with the divisional headquarters was at Bogra, the Twenty-third Brigade was at Rangpur, and the Thirty-fourth Brigade was at Nator.[32] He divided the Twenty-ninth Pakistani Cavalry Regiment (M-24s) amongst the brigades. As in the Jessore sector, Indian troops had been nibbling away at Pakistani territory in the months leading up to the full-scale war on 4 December. Particularly heavy clashes had taken place in Hilli, and the Indians took the village of Morapara on 22–23 November.[33] The Thirty-third Indian Corps's plan was to protect the Siliguri corridor in the north while at the same time capturing Gaibanda and Bogra with an exploitative thrust toward the Ganges.[34]

When hostilities began on the 4th Pakistani troops pulled back from Kurigram, Lalmonir Hat, and Domar and moved into a new defense line on the Dinajpur-Saidpur-Rangpur axis. The first Indian attack came from the west when the Sixty-sixth Indian Brigade (part of the Twentieth Mountain Division) took Charkhai on the 4th.[35] On the 6th the brigade struck toward the Rangpur-Bogra highway and captured Nawabgunj. The 340th Indian Brigade followed through on the 7th and captured Pirganj, thus cutting the Rangpur-Bogra highway.[36] The Indian advance surprised the Pakistanis, and Major General Shah had a narrow escape when advancing Indian tanks shot up his convoy, which was returning from Rangpur to Bogra. Maj. Gen. Lachman Singh, general officer commanding Twentieth Indian Mountain Division, then ordered his three brigades to advance. The 202nd Brigade advanced via Khetal, the Sixty-sixth via Bhaduria-Ghraghat-Gobindganj, and the 340th via Gobindganj. The Indian advance toward Bogra along the Pirganj-Bogra axis split the Sixteenth Pakistani Division. Its Twenty-third Brigade was isolated on the Dinajpur-Rangpur axis, having failed to fall back in time, while the 205th Brigade managed to retreat into Bogra.[37] After this success the Indian advance slowed; the 202nd Indian Brigade could only clear the Fourth Frontier Force Rifles (Pakistan) from Hilli on the 11th and was ordered to head back to Rangpur.[38] The Sixty-sixth Indian Brigade also had great difficulty in securing Bhaduria on the 11th, suffering some 132 casualties (in the Seventeenth Kumaon) in the process.[39] The 340th Brigade managed to take Gobindganj with a flanking attack with PT-76 amphibious light tank support. The Pakistanis had blown the bridge to the north but were surprised to find the Indians established in a blocking position behind them. The Pakistani garrison at Gobindganj fled on the night of 11 December, abandoning their equipment. Mahastan fell the next day to the 340th Brigade.[40] The Sixteenth Pakistani Division then moved to Nator, leaving the 205th Brigade to defend Bogra. Lachman Singh attacked Bogra on the 14th. The Sixth Guards and the Sixty-ninth Armored Regiment established a roadblock to the rear of the town, while a squadron of the Sixty-third Cavalry and the Second Battalion/Fifth Gurkha Rifles attacked frontally. Excellent close air support missions and artillery strikes preceded the attack.[41] Bogra fell on the 14th, but elements of the 205th Pakistani Brigade continued to fight on until the cease-fire on the 16th. To the north the Twenty-third Pakistani Brigade, which was deployed along the Dinajpur-Saidpur-Rangpur axis, held off the Seventy-first Indian Brigade. The 202nd Indian Brigade and the newly inducted Sixth Indian Brigade did not reach Rangpur from the south until the 16th.[42]

The Comilla-Sylhet Sector

Lt. Gen. Sagat Singh's Fourth Indian Corps in the Comilla-Sylhet sector was the strongest Indian corps on the eastern front. It was also responsible for the longest and most sensitive border area between India and East Pakistan.

The capital of East Pakistan, Dacca, lay only 50 miles from the Indian border town of Agartala. However, in order to get to Dacca, the Fourth Corps would have to cross the 4,000-yard-wide Meghna River, which was spanned by a single railway bridge at Bhairab. Pakistan had deployed its Fourteenth Division, under the command of Maj. Gen. Abdul Majod Qazi, to defend the Sylhet sector.[43] As with the other sectors, Indian troops and Mukti Bahini guerrillas had been very active in the month of November, undermining Pakistani border positions. General Qazi planned to withdraw his forces to the west bank of the Titas River but failed to blow up the bridge, which fell to Indian forces on 3 December.[44]

Maj. Gen. B. F. Gonsalves's Fifty-seventh Indian Mountain Division had the task of advancing to the Meghna River via Daudkandi in the Akhaura area. The commanders ordered Brigadier Tulli's Seventy-second Brigade to neutralize Gangasagar, while they told Brigadier Misra's 311th Indian Brigade to take Akhaura itself. Gangasagar fell to the Fourteenth Guards on 3 December, and Akhaura fell to the Eighteenth Rajput on the 5th.[45] With the Titas bridge under its control, the Fifty-seventh Indian Division was ordered by its corps commander to strike for the Bhairab rail bridge along the Brahmanbaria-Ashuganj axis.[46] The Seventy-third Brigade now attacked the Twenty-second Pakistani Brigade, which was holed up at Brahmanbaria. The Indian attacks, from the front and the rear, surprised the Pakistanis, who withdrew on the night of 7–8 December to Ashuganj.[47] The 311th Indian Brigade, however, had to wait for its heavy equipment to catch up, and this pause allowed the Twenty-seventh Pakistani Brigade to dig in at Ashuganj. At this time General Qazi suddenly decided to blow up the Bhairab bridge on 9 December. The Twenty-seventh Pakistani Brigade crossed the river and reached Bhairab Bazar, where it remained for the rest of the war.[48] The Twenty-seventh Pakistani Brigade made no attempt to move to the aid of Dacca, which was defended by a single regular Pakistani army battalion and some paramilitary elements.

Undeterred by the destruction of the Bhairab bridge, General Gonsalves decided on a heli-borne crossing of the Meghna River. The operation commenced on the 9th at Brahmanbaria, from where the air force moved the 311th Brigade troops to Raipura some 9 miles from Bhairab Bazar. During the following days it flew troops into Narsingdi. Meanwhile, the Seventy-third Brigade crossed the Meghna on river craft. The Twenty-seventh Pakistani Brigade allowed only two Indian battalions and some air strikes to bottle it up in Bhairab Bazar.[49] By 14 December both the Seventy-third and 311th Indian Brigades were en route for Dacca, and the first Indian artillery fire began to hit the city the same day.

To the north of the Sylhet sector Lt. Gen. Sagat Singh ordered Maj. Gen.

K. V. Krishnarao's Eighth Indian Division to secure Samshernagar airfield and Maulvi Bazar. He ordered the division to follow this action up by investing Sylhet itself.[50] Prior to hostilities, the Fifty-ninth Indian Brigade had attacked and eliminated a Pakistani post at East Atgram on 20–21 November. Another Indian force, including the Fifth Battalion/Fifth Gurkhas, probed Pakistani positions to the north of Sylhet.[51] As a result, Pakistani forces fell back to a new defensive line from Charkhai in the east to Hemu in the north to Chhatak in the west.[52] In addition to his primary objectives, Major General Krishnarao also aimed to prevent the 202nd Pakistani Brigade at Sylhet and the 313th Pakistani Brigade at Maulvi Bazar from coming to the aid of the beleaguered Twenty-seventh Pakistani Brigade in the south.

By 4 December the Eighty-first Indian Brigade had seized Samsher Nagar and Ghazipur. Kulaura fell on the 6th, and the brigade moved on to Fenchuganj. Acting on a wireless intercept that revealed that the Pakistanis were withdrawing from Sylhet to join the Twenty-seventh Pakistani Brigade at Ashuganj, Major General Krishnarao ordered the heli-lift of the Fourth Battalion/Fifth Gurkhas (the Eighty-first Indian Brigade) to the north bank of the Surma River about a mile from the railway bridge. Some ninety men, including Lieutenant Colonel Harolikar, landed under fire on the 7th. Fortunately for the Indians, the Pakistanis did not attack this small landing party. The commanding officer of the Twenty-second Pakistani Baluch refused to attack the small Indian airhead, claiming his troops were exhausted. The commander of the Thirtieth Frontier Force Rifles gave the same excuse on the 9th. Finally, the Thirtieth Frontier Force Rifles and the Thirty-first Punjab launched a weak attack on the 10th but were easily repulsed.[53] On the 14th the Sixth Rajput linked up with the Fourth Battalion/Fifth Gurkhas on the south bank of the Surma. The 313th and 202nd Pakistani Brigades sat out the remainder of the war in Sylhet.

When the conflict began the 313th Pakistani Brigade was stationed at Maulvi Bazar, and its commander, Brigadier Rana, had withdrawn the Thirtieth Frontier Force Rifles and the Twenty-second Pakistani Baluch from their border posts to the town proper. On 6 December the Pakistani commanders ordered the 313th Brigade to join the Twenty-seventh Brigade at the Akhaura–Bhairab Bazar axis. Rana replied that he could not do this, as he was under heavy Indian air attack. On the evening of the 7th the Thirtieth Frontier Force Rifles was withdrawn to Shadipur Ferry and from there to Sylhet on 8–9 December with the remainder of the 313th Brigade.[54] There they joined the 202nd Pakistani Brigade to sit out the war. Major General Krishnarao's Eighth Indian Mountain Division had succeeded (with the help of Indian air power) in isolating the 313th Pakistani Brigade and preventing it from intervening in the crucial battle along the Akhaura–Bhairab Bazar axis.

South of Sylhet lay the Comilla sector. On the Indian side Maj. Gen. R. D. Hira's Twenty-third Indian Mountain Division oversaw the area. Maj. Gen. Mohammed Rahim Khan's Thirty-ninth Pakistani Division opposed him. His Fifty-third Brigade was deployed at Feni, and the 117th Brigade was at Comilla, while the divisional headquarters was also at Comilla. The Pakistanis planned to pinch out from the flanks (Feni and Comilla) any Indian attack up the Chandpur road, which the Pakistani headquarters at Dacca considered to be the most likely route for an Indian attack.[55] Brigadier Ataullah's Ninety-seventh Independent Pakistani Brigade, along with two commando battalions, defended the Chittagong hill tract, which lay to the south of Comilla.

During November Major General Hira managed to secure the Belonia bulge, a strip of Pakistani territory some 6 miles wide and 16 miles long that jutted into India.[56] His main objective, as the Pakistani headquarters had rightly estimated, was Chandpur.[57] The Twenty-third Indian Division's schedule was quite flexible – Comilla by D+14 and Feni by D+18. After the fall of Comilla, the Fifty-seventh Indian Mountain Division would join the Twenty-third Division in operations against the Pakistani defenses in the Lalmai-Myanmati Hills. Following this attack, they would advance toward Chandpur via Laksham and to Daudkandi via Comilla, thus severing Dacca from Chittagong.[58]

On 3 December the Fourteenth Jat led the 301st Indian Brigade as it struck toward Main Bazar just south of Comilla. By the 4th they had captured their objective along with two companies of the Twenty-fifth Frontier Force Rifles and their battalion commanding officer.[59] On 5 December the 181st Indian Brigade followed the 301st Brigade and cut the road and rail links between Laksham and Lalmai. The same day the 301st Brigade took Muzafarganj.[60] As a result of the Indian advance, most of the Twenty-third Punjab (Pakistani) was cut off on the west bank of the Dakatia River. On 5 December Brigadier Aslam received orders to withdraw the Fifty-third Pakistani Brigade to Laksham, where the Indian forces subjected the Pakistani garrison to constant artillery and air strikes. On the 9th the Pakistani commanders ordered the garrison to join the 117th Pakistani Brigade at Maynamati-Comilla. The brigade left Laksham on the night of the 10th after destroying most of its heavy equipment. However, only a small portion made it to Maynamati, as Indian troops rounded up most of the brigade on the 12th between Ram Mohan and Chandina.[61]

On 8 December the Fourteenth Jat captured Comilla when the 117th Pakistani Brigade withdrew to the Maynamati cantonment as a result of intense pressure from the Sixty-first Indian Brigade on the city of Maynamati.[62] A column from the Sixty-first Indian Brigade reached Daudkandi on the 9th, while the rest of the brigade maintained pressure on the Maynamati cantonment, where the 117th and Seventy-third Pakistani Brigades were holed up. The Sixty-first and 181st Indian Brigades moved to Maynamati, while the 301st Indian Brigade crossed the Meghna River and reached the Lakhya River southeast of Dacca on the 15th. The next day the Pakistani forces surrendered. In the Chittagong sector Indian forces, including the Eighty-third Brigade and "Kilo" Force under Brigadier Anand Swaroop, engaged the Ninety-seventh Pakistani Brigade and its two supporting commando battalions up until the surrender.[63] In the south the Indians launched an amphibious operation against Cox's Bazar. "Romeo" Force, a 1,550-man unit comprised of the First Battalion/Third Gurkha Rifles (formerly with the Ninth Division), two companies of the Eleventh Bihar, the 881st Light Battery, an ambulance platoon, and an Army Service Corps detachment, was loaded on to a merchant vessel, the *Vishwa Vijay* (15,000 tons). On the night of 13–14 December the First Battalion/Third Gurkha Rifles was transferred to two landing ship tanks, the INS *Gharial* and the INS *Guldar*. An unexpected sandbar forced the men to swim ashore in 9 feet of water. Not surprisingly, two men drowned, and the commanders called off the entire operation.[64]

The Northern Sector: Mymensingh-Tangail

On the Indian side the 101st Communication Zone, with headquarters in Shillong, secured the responsibility for this sector. Its normal peacetime duties involved the logistical support for all Indian army units in the northeast. As hostilities became imminent, its initial duty was to contain the Pakistani troops in the area while the Second and Fourth Indian Corps struck out for Dacca. The underdeveloped communications infrastructure on the Indian side precluded any extensive troop deployments, and the only Indian force in this sector was Brig. Hardev Singh Kler's Ninety-fifth Indian Mountain Brigade. The overall sector commander was Maj. Gen. Gurbax Singh Gill. However, as operational plans continued to evolve in November, the commanders assigned the Ninety-fifth Indian Brigade the task of destroying Pakistani forces in the Tangail and Mymensingh Districts, which would deny the Dacca garrison any substantial reinforcements. General Gill planned to take Tangail with paratroopers since helicopters were in short supply. The town formed the critical bottleneck for Pakistani forces retreating from Jamalpur and Mymensingh to Dacca.[65]

The Pakistanis were not concerned that the northern sector could become a major line of Indian advance into Dacca. The Pakistani Eastern Command placed this sector under Major General Jamshed's Thirty-sixth Pakistani Division, which had only two battalions, the Thirty-third Punjab and the Thirty-first Pakistani Baluch, grouped under Brigadier Qadir's Ninety-third Brigade. When hostilities occurred, the two battalions, trading space for time, were to fall back on Jamalpur and Mymensingh, the two fortified towns on the south bank of the Chotta (small) Brahmaputra River, which would form the line of no penetration.[66] When the Indians attacked in this sector on the 4th, according to plan, the Thirty-first Pakistani Baluch (minus a company that fell with the Kamalpur border post) withdrew to Jamalpur, reaching it on the 6th. The Thirty-third Punjab also fell back on Mymensingh. On the Indian side, Maj. Gen. G. C. Nagra took over from General Gill, who had been injured in a mine explosion. Nagra decided to take Jamalpur from the right flank while at the same time maintaining frontal pressure. The First Maratha Light Infantry and the Thirteenth Guards crossed the Chotta Brahmaputra some 5 miles to the west of Jamalpur. But the temporary reliance on draft animals to move heavy equipment meant that the force could only cut the Jamalpur-Tangail road by first light on the 9th.[67] The Sixth Sikh Light Infantry from the 167th Mountain Brigade reinforced these soldiers on the 10th.[68] The Indian attack on the Pakistani defenders was planned for the same night; coincidentally, it turned out to be the same time that the Thirty-first Pakistani Baluch intended to break out of the Indian encirclement and head for Dacca under new orders.[69] During the ensuing break-out attempt, Indian forces captured most of the Thirty-first Baluch.[70] However, the Thirty-third Punjab managed to withdraw unmolested from Mymensingh and reach the Madhupur junction.[71]

On the afternoon of 11 December the Second Indian Parachute Battalion dropped some 5 miles northeast of Tangail. Its objective was the five-span concrete bridge on the Madhupur-Tangail road. Capturing this bridge would cut off the Ninety-third Pakistani Brigade from Dacca.[72] However, by the time the Indian paratroopers had deployed, some elements of the Thirty-third Punjab had managed to pass through to Dacca. The remainder, after unsuccessfully trying to dislodge the paratroopers, took to cross-country pathways to avoid the roadblock. On 12 December at about 5:00 PM the Ninety-fifth Indian Brigade linked up with the Second Parachute. General Nagra now decided to move directly on to Dacca. The Sixth Sikh Light Infantry led the advance and took Kaliakair on the 13th. On the 14th the 167th Indian Brigade joined the Ninety-fifth Indian Brigade at Turag. By 10:00 PM on the 15th the paratroopers had reached Mirpur. Dacca was virtually defenseless, and the only organized forces were the exhausted remnants of the Thirty-third Punjab. No other Pakistani forces had managed to fall back on Dacca. The next day General Nagra drove across the Mirpur bridge to General Niazi's headquarters at about 11:00 AM The Second Parachute Battalion, the first Indian unit into Dacca, escorted him.[73] At 1:00 PM General Niazi signed the instrument of surrender in the presence of Lieutenant General Aurora, general officer commanding Eastern Command. Some 90,000 Pakistani regulars and irregulars surrendered to the Indian army.

The Western Front

A preemptive attack into western India formed the lynchpin of Pakistani strategy when the 1971 war began. Pakistan was going to nullify Indian gains in the relatively weakly defended East Pakistan with gains in the west. To accomplish this goal Pakistan had three army corps at its disposal (the First, the Second, and the Fourth), with two armored divisions, ten infantry divisions, two armored brigades, two artillery brigades, and one independent infantry brigade. They deployed two corps-sized divisions, the Twelfth and the Twenty-third, in Kashmir; these powerful "divisions" had eleven infantry brigades between them. According to the offensive plan, Pakistan's Twelfth Infantry Division would start the campaign with a limited offensive to capture Poonch. The Twenty-third Pakistani Infantry Division, with additional infantry, and the Second Independent Armored Brigade would hold Chaamb up to and including Akhnur. Pakistan's First Corps, with the Eighth and Fifteenth Infantry Divisions, was responsible for defending the Shakargarh bulge, extending from the Chenab River to the Ravi River. The Fourth Pakistani Corps held the area from just north of Lahore (Maqbulpura) to the southwest of Bhawalpur with the Tenth and Eleventh Infantry Divisions and an independent infantry brigade. The Eighteenth Infantry Division, deployed along the Sind border, was to advance from Rahim Yar Khan and capture Ramgarh to threaten Jaisalmer. The powerful Second Corps, with general headquarters reserves, would launch the main Pakistani offensive. The general headquarters included the First Armored Division, the Seventh Infantry Division, and the newly raised Thirty-third Infantry Division. The main Second Corps strike force included the Sixth Armored Division and the newly raised Seventeenth Infantry Division in the Montgomery-Okhra area and the Eighth Independent Armored Brigade in the Gujranwalla-Daska area. (The latter was nominally under the control of the First Corps, ready to react to an Indian thrust into Shakargarh.) According to Indian sources, considerable debate occurred in the Pakistani general headquarters over whether to launch an immediate offensive with the Pakistani First Corps or strike after India had shown its intentions.[74]

The Indian operational plan on the western front was primarily defensive with two exceptions, both apparently having been insisted upon by Prime Minister Indira Gandhi (under advice from the army, no doubt). The first was that several strategically important positions along the Kashmir cease-fire line that had been seized during the 1965 war but handed back to Pakistan under Soviet pressure in the 1966 Tashkent Agreement should be occupied once again and this time retained. Second, India was to launch a limited offensive to threaten lines of communication between Karachi and Lahore to deter Pakistani offensives in Kashmir, the Punjab, and Rajasthan.[75]

India had three army corps deployed on the western front. Lt. Gen. Sartaj Singh's Fifteenth Corps with five divisions was responsible for J&K. Its Third Indian Mountain Division faced both Pakistan and China to the north from Ladakh. The Nineteenth Infantry Division, headquartered in Srinagar, held the Uri and Tithwal sectors. The Twenty-fifth Infantry Division was responsible for Poonch, Rajauri, and Jhangar. The Tenth Infantry Division, along with the Deccan Horse, was responsible for Chaamb and the approaches to Akhnur. The Twenty-sixth Infantry Division was responsible for the defense of Jammu. The Third Armored Brigade was to be the backup for both the Tenth and Twenty-sixth Divisions.

Lt. Gen. K. K. Singh's First Indian Corps, headquartered at Samba, controlled the area from Samba to Madhupur and the border in the Pathankot and Gurdaspur areas.[76] Lt. Gen. N. C. Rawlley's Sixteenth Corps controlled the border area between Dera Baba Nanak to the Anupgarh-Suratgarh axis in Rajasthan. Its Fifteenth Infantry Division was responsible for the Dera Baba Nanak, Gill Ferry, Grand Trunk Road, and Raja Tal approaches to Amritsar. The Seventh Infantry Division, along with the Third Cavalry, was responsible for the Kharla–Khem Karan and Hussainiwalla axis, while the Eighteenth Cavalry, the Seventieth Armored Regiment, the Ninety-second Independent Recce Squadron, and the No. 4 Independent Armored Squadron supported them. The Sixteenth Corps was also allocated the use of the Fourteenth Independent Armored Brigade. In addition to these forces, army headquarters had its own reserve, including the First Armored Division and the Fourteenth Infantry Division, located in the southern area of the Eleventh Corps's sector. The remainder of the western border came under Lt. Gen. G. G. Bewor's headquarters, Southern Command, with the Twelfth and Eleventh Infantry Divisions responsible for the defense of the Jaisalmer and Barmer sectors.[77]

India's posture in the west proved to be primarily defensive. K. K. Singh, the director of military operations at army headquarters prior to taking over command of the First Corps, devised a plan that envisaged three possible scenarios for a Pakistani offensive. With its First Corps, Pakistan could strike between Kathua and Samba and cut the new rail link between Pathankot and

Jammu and then strike deep into the Shivalik Mountains.[78] The second scenario foresaw the First Corps striking in the north across the Ravi River in the Deva Baba Nanak–Gill Ferry area and in the south with the Second Corps attacking across the Sutlej River in the Kasur area. As a third option, Pakistan's Third Corps could strike either in the Jalalabad area or in the Ganganagar-Anupgarh area.

Indian forces had been deployed to meet these possible attacks. The commanders deployed the First Indian Corps in the Samba-Pathankot-Gurdaspur area, while army reserve headquarters moved to the Faridkot-Abohar area, and the Fourteenth Independent Armored Brigade moved to Ajnala. The Indian counteroffensive plan involved having the First Indian Corps attack the Shakargarh bulge. A limited offensive in the Jammu sector by the Tenth and Twenty-sixth Indian Infantry Divisions north and south of the Chenab River could decoy the Pakistani forces that reacted to this strike. If the Shakargarh offensive succeeded in drawing the Pakistani reserve Second Corps from Okhra-Montgomery, then the Indian reserve, including the First Armored Division and the Fourteenth Infantry Division, could attack across the Sutlej toward the Upper Bari Doab Canal.[79]

Chaamb

Both India and Pakistan had fortified their positions in Kashmir greatly since the 1965 war, so neither side wanted to risk a major offensive in the Kashmir region. During the fourteen-day war both sides launched minor localized attacks to gain better ground. Lightly defended Jammu, however, was a different story, as both sides prepared to launch major ground offensives in this area. The sensitive Chaamb area came under the aegis of the Tenth Indian Infantry Division, itself part of the Fifteenth Indian Corps. Maj. Gen. Jaswant Singh, the divisional commander, planned to advance along the northern bank of the Chenab River. The Twenty-eighth Indian Brigade was deployed in the hill sector northeast of Chaamb; the 191st Brigade held the plains west of the Munawar Tawi (rivulet); the Sixty-eighth Brigade, which was to spearhead the attack, was near Akhnur; and the Fifty-second Brigade was deployed near Jaurian. The Tenth Indian Division hoped to establish a firm foothold on the cease-fire line from where the Third Indian Armored Brigade could strike into Pakistan. In November the Seventy-second Armored Regiment from the Third Armored Brigade joined the Tenth Division's integral armored unit, the Ninth Horse, to boost the division's strike potential.

Unfortunately for Gen. Jaswant Singh, his Pakistani counterpart had his own plans for an offensive into Chaamb that preempted the Tenth Indian

CHINA
(TIBET)

AFGHANISTAN

Risalpur
Chakala
Peshawar

Srinagar
Punch

Mianwali

Sialkot

Chaamb
Akhnur

Sakesar

Chawinda

Samba

Sargodha

Shakar Garh

Pathankot

Lahore

Amritsar

Khem Karan

Sehjra

Jullundher

Kasur

Ferozepur

Halwara

Quetta

Fazilka

PAKISTAN

Bhatinda

Bhawalpur

Sirsa

IRAN

Sukkur

Bikaner

Khairpur

Jaisalmer

INDIA

Jodhpur

Gwader

Pasni

Karachi

Arabian Sea

Rann of Kutch

Jamnagar

Western Front–India–Pakistan conflict 1971

Division's own attack and completely surprised the Indians. The Pakistani division facing the Tenth Indian Division was Maj. Gen. Efthikar Khan's Twenty-third Pakistani Infantry Division. Its Fourth Azad Kashmir Brigade oversaw the area from Uparla to Bakan, the Twentieth Pakistani Brigade held the area from Bakan to Mattewalla, and the Seventh Azad Kashmir Brigade defended the Bhimbar and Mirpur areas. The Sixty-sixth and 111th Brigades, located at Daulat Nagar and Jalapur Jattan, formed the divisional reserve. The division's armor support came from the Twenty-sixth Cavalry (Sherman MK-2s). The Eleventh Cavalry (T-59s) joined it in October, at which point head-quarters Second Armored Brigade took over both regiments. When hostilities broke out, the Twenty-sixth Armored Regiment and the Twelfth Independent Squadron (M-36B2s) supplemented these armored forces.[80]

Unlike his Indian counterpart, Maj. Gen. Efthikar Khan had devised a pre-cise and coherent plan for his divisional attack into Chaamb. The offensive was to open at 9:00 PM on 3 December. At first light on 4 December the Sixty-sixth and 111th Brigades would strike along the Moel-Chaamb axis and secure the area from Nala to Barsala. The 111th Brigade's Eleventh Cavalry would then thrust through Munnawali and secure the home bank (west) of the Tawi River near Mandiala. The 111th Brigade would then advance and cap-ture Chaamb. The Twentieth Brigade, operating in the south, was to feint at the Burgail, Manawar, and Nadala enclave. Its primary role was to halt any Indian counteroffensive from Jhanada, Manawar, and Chimival. If the 111th Brigade succeeded, then the Twentieth Brigade would try and take all of these areas.[81]

The Tenth Indian Division operated on the assumption that the best way to defend Chaamb was to go on the offensive and as such had made no prepa-rations to guarantee the defense of Chaamb. It made little or no attempt to prepare in-depth defenses, particularly on the west bank of the Tawi River. The commanders deployed the 191st Brigade on the west bank only during the night of 2–3 December. On 2 December they made last-minute attempts for a better defensive posture when the Deccan Horse (T-54s) deployed a single squadron on the west bank. But by and large, the Tenth Indian Division re-mained concentrated in marshaling areas in preparation for its own offen-sive. Significantly, a dummy minefield covered the area between Barsala and Jhande, which the divisions planned to use as an invasion route into Paki-stan.[82]

When the Pakistani offensive opened as planned, the Indians were com-pletely surprised. By 4 December the Eleventh Pakistani Cavalry had suc-ceeded in taking the Mandiala North crossing. The Indian commanders rushed troops and tanks piecemeal into the battle.[83] Although initial attempts to retake the Mandiala North failed, the Indians repulsed all Pakistani attempts to exploit the area east of the Tawi. The Pakistanis now increased their pressure in the south and by the 6th had taken the Mandiala South crossing. The same day, at 9:00 PM, Maj. Gen. Jaswant Singh ordered the abandonment of the west bank of the Tawi and had all the bridges blown.[84] The Pakistani thrust in the center was fast approaching Chak Pandit and threatening the 191st Indian Brigade's flank. Fortunately for the Indians, the Pakistanis could not maintain their momentum. The 111th Pakistani Brigade and the Second Pakistani Armored Brigade failed to concentrate for an attack on Palanwala on the east bank, which gave the Indians time to prepare their defenses on the east bank.[85] The Indian commanders rushed the Sixty-eighth and Fifty-eighth Brigades along with the Seventy-second Armored Regiment up to new positions. When the Pakistanis attempted to establish a foothold on the east bank on 7–8 December, Indian forces threw them back. On the 8th, however, Pakistani forces took Dewa, thus securing their northern flank against an Indian offensive. On 9–10 December the Twenty-eighth Pakistani Cavalry and the 111th Brigade secured the crossings at Darh and Raipur.[86] That afternoon elements of the 168th Indian Brigade retook Darh, while the Third Battalion/Fourth Gurkhas from the Fifty-second Brigade, along with two troops from the Deccan Horse, retook Raipur.[87] At this point all Pakistani offensives to cross the Tawi ceased after the death of Maj. Gen. Efthikar Khan in a helicopter crash on 9 December.[88] The only Indian success in Jammu came in the sector under the Twenty-sixth Indian Division. Maj. Gen. Zorawar Bakshi planned a highly effective attack to take the "chicken's neck," a narrow strip of Pakistani territory jutting toward Akhnur. Brig. Mohinder Singh's Nineteenth Indian Infantry Brigade was to strike south and cut off the neck at the shoulders. The attack began on 5 December and successfully seized the salient, although delays allowed the defending Pakistani troops to escape.[89]

Shakargarh

Shakargarh is a large bulge of Pakistani territory jutting into India between the Chenab and Ravi Rivers. On the Indian side the First Indian Corps held the area. The corps commander, Lt. Gen. K. K. Singh, formerly (until October 1971) the director of military operations at army headquarters, was well versed with the offensive plans, having formulated them himself. He deployed his corps as follows. Maj. Gen. Balwant Singh's Thirty-sixth Indian Infantry Division was sent to the southeast bank of the Ravi River to guard the approach to Pathankot in the general area of Thakurpur-Gurdaspur-

Dinanagar. Maj. Gen. B. R. Prabhu's Thirty-ninth Indian Infantry Division was deployed in the Madhopur-Bamial-Dayalchak area to cover Madhopur's approaches and communication lines. Maj. Gen. W. A. G. Pinto's Fifty-fourth Indian Infantry Division was deployed between the Bein River and Degh Nadi. If a Pakistani offensive did not materialize in this sector, then Gen. K. K. Singh planned an offensive into the Shakargarh bulge. In accordance with Manekshaw's wishes, the Indian army first ensured the security of Akhnur, Jammu, Samba, Madhopur, Gurdaspur, and Amritsar. Once the army achieved this goal, the next objective was to engage the Pakistani strike force and if possible destroy it before it could be committed to an offensive. According to the Indian army planners, this could be best achieved with an offensive into the Shakargarh bulge.[90]

The initial plan for the Shakargarh offensive called for the First and Fifteenth Indian Corps to launch a joint attack into the bulge. However, the preemptive Pakistani offensive into the Chaamb meant that only the First Corps could strike into the bulge. Gen. K. K. Singh proposed a two-pronged attack. The northern prong would include the Fifty-fourth Indian Infantry Division and the Sixteenth Indian Armored Brigade. From the south in the area between Bein and Degh Lake the southern prong would include the Thirty-sixth Indian Infantry Division and the Second Indian Armored Brigade. The Karir Lake would form the interdivisional boundary line, and the initial objectives were Zafarwal (the Fifty-fourth Division) and Shakargarh (the Thirty-sixth Division). The Thirty-ninth Indian Infantry Division, along with the Scinde Horse (from the Sixteenth Armored Brigade), held the Samba-Ramgarh area to deny the Pakistani advance to Jammu.[91]

On the Pakistani side the defense of the bulge belonged to Lt. Gen. Irshad Ahmed Khan's First Pakistani Corps. Its Fifteenth Pakistani Infantry Division under Maj. Gen. Abid Ali Zahid oversaw the Sialkot border. Maj. Gen. Abdul Ali Malik's Eighth Pakistani Infantry Division defended Shakargarh. The Eighth Pakistani Armored Brigade provided armored support for both these divisions. In addition to its defensive tasks, the First Pakistani Crops also had the secondary duty of eliminating all Indian enclaves and "stimulat[ing] offensive actions in order to draw enemy forces into the Shakargarh area."[92] The First Pakistani Corps did not have to worry about this last requirement, because on 5 December it had all the Indian forces it could handle.

The basic Pakistani defensive plan for the bulge was to hold all major towns and communication hubs, including Narowal, Shakargarh, and Zafarwal. The Indians were aware of this and knew that Pakistan intended to use mobile forces to defend the gaps between these static points. Armored strike forces would engage and destroy Indian forces in a "killing ground" between these strong points. The Eighth Pakistani Armored Brigade would provide the bulk of the counterattack force. After it had inflicted suitably heavy attrition on the Indian attackers, the Sixth Pakistani Armored Division and the Seventeenth Pakistani Infantry Division would attack the Ganganagar area.[93] A major from the East Pakistani Brigade, Eighth Pakistani Infantry Division, who defected to the Indian side before the battle provided valuable intelligence on the Pakistani plans.[94]

On the evening of 5 December the Seventy-second Indian Infantry Brigade (part of the Thirty-ninth Division), with the support of the Seventh Cavalry, began the advance toward Shakargarh between the Bein River and the Karir Lake. The Second Indian Armored Brigade and a mechanized battalion (the Eighth Dogra) backed these advance units. By the 7th Pakistani minefields had halted the division's thrust at Harar Kalan. The divisional commander, Major General Prabhu, ordered an outflanking move from the direction of Shabazpur, but this attack failed on the 8th, when an attempt to trawl through the minefields failed. The Thirty-ninth Division's failure to take Dehrla and Chakra exposed the Fifty-fourth Division's eastern flank as it advanced west of Karir. To compensate, the First Corps ordered the Fifty-fourth Division to take Dehrla-Chakra, which it did on the 10th.[95] The Seventy-second Brigade also managed to capture Harar Kalan on the 10th.[96]

The corps commander then decided to place the responsibility of taking Shakargarh with the Thirty-sixth Indian Division. He sent the Thirty-ninth Division headquarters to take over the Ramgarh-Samba area and sent most of its combat strength to the Thirty-sixth Division, while its Seventy-second Brigade came under the Fifty-fourth Division.[97] The Fifty-fourth Division, with four infantry brigades and the Sixteenth Armored Brigade, moved to take Zafarwal-Dhamtal, with the latter intending to advance toward Deoli-Mirzapur. It faced the Twenty-fourth Pakistani Infantry Brigade, the Eighth Armored Brigade, and part of the Pakistani First Corps Reconnaissance Regiment.[98] The Seventy-fourth Indian Brigade took Chakra after a night attack led by the Eighth Grenadier with a squadron of support from the Fourth Cavalry, while Dehrla fell to the Sixth Kumaon.[99] The divisional commander, Major General Pinto, then ordered the Ninety-first Brigade to follow through and exploit south. By 15 December the Ninety-first Brigade was less than a mile away from the Shakargarh-Zafarwal road at Ramri Barwal Chanda. While the Ninety-first Brigade advanced, the Seventy-fourth and Forty-seventh Indian Brigades prepared to cross the Supwal ditch and turn the Pakistani positions on the Basanthar River. With the Ninety-first Brigade providing a firm base and fire support, the Sixteenth Madras and the Third

Grenadier took Saraj Chak, Jarpal, and Lohal to establish a bridgehead on the night of 15–16 December.[100] The Seventeenth Horse and the Sixth Madras reinforced them at first light. On the morning of the 16th the Sixteenth Pakistani Infantry Brigade and the Eighth Pakistani Armored Brigade launched a violent counterattack from the direction of Laliar-Ghazipur. Lt. Col. Hanut Singh's Seventeenth Horse's (Poona Horse) Centurion tanks repulsed the counterattack, with heavy losses. It also smashed the Thirteenth Pakistani Lancers and the Thirty-first Cavalry's repeated attacks. The B Squadron of the Poona Horse virtually annihilated the Thirty-first Pakistani Cavalry at Saraj Chak-Jarpal.[101] Indian artillery played a significant supporting role. On the 17th the Pakistanis rushed in the 124th Brigade all the way from Rahim Yar Khan and launched a desperate counterattack via Barapind that the Indians also repulsed with heavy losses.[102] Up until 8 December Maj. Gen. B. S. Ahluwalia's Thirty-sixth Indian Division had a primarily defensive role in its sector – to guard the approaches to Pathankot. When the corps commander gave it an offensive role, the division received the Eighty-seventh Infantry Brigade and the Second Armored Brigade to add to its Eighteenth and 115th Infantry Brigades. Its artillery included two medium regiments, one heavy mortar battery, one air defense battery, and three Engineering Regiments.[103]

South Punjab

The area south of the Shakargarh bulge and up to Rajasthan came under Lt. Gen. N. C. Rawlley's Eleventh Indian Corps. Its Fifteenth Indian Infantry Division, with the support of the Sixty-sixth Armored Regiment's Vijayanta tanks, defended Amritsar and was deployed to cover the Dera Baba Nanak–Gill Ferry axis. The Eighty-sixth Brigade with the Seventy-first Armored Regiment manned this area. South of the Gill Ferry and short of the Grand Trunk Road was the Fifty-fourth Brigade. The Sixty-sixth Brigade held the Grand Trunk Road itself and the Raja-Tal axis. The Ninety-sixth Brigade was deployed in the rear Chagwan area. The Seventh Indian Infantry Division with the Third Cavalry (Centurion) held the Kharla-Lahore, Khem Karan–Kasur, and Ferozepur-Kasur axis and was also responsible for the border up to Jalalabad. F sector, a divisional-level formation, was in charge of the area south of Jalalabad to Anupgarh. This area had seen ferocious fighting in 1965, and, as a result, the Indian commanders concentrated most of the Indian armor in the sector of the Eleventh Corps.[104]

The Fifteenth Indian Division and the Tenth Pakistani Division fought over small enclaves on the Ravi River. The Pakistanis took Kassowal, while the Indians took Jassar and Dera Baba Nanak. The Seventh Indian Division and the Eleventh Pakistani Division fought similar small-scale actions, with the Pakistanis seizing Hussainiwalla and the village of China Bidhi Chand, while the Indians took the Sehjra salient.[105] In the ad hoc F sector (under Maj. Gen. Ram Singh, raised in July 1971) three Indian infantry brigades faced the Pakistani 105th Brigade at Sulaimanake and the Twenty-fifth Pakistani Brigade at Bhawalnagar.[106] In this sector the 105th Pakistani Brigade managed to capture some Indian border posts west of the Sabauna distributary.[107]

Rajasthan

The border of the Indian Southern Command with Pakistan consisted of four sectors: Bikaner, Jaisalmer, Barmer, and Kutch. The two sectors that saw action during the war were Jaisalmer and Barmer. Major General Khambatta's Twelfth Indian Infantry Division (headquartered at Tanot) and Maj. Gen. R. D. R. Anand's Eleventh Indian Infantry Division (headquartered at Ranwar) defended these areas. Armor support came from the Twentieth Lancers (AMX-13s) for the Twelfth Division and the No. 3 Independent Squadron (T-55s) for the Eleventh Division. General Bewor, the general officer commanding Southern Command, planned to take Rahimyar Khan some 40 miles deep in Pakistani territory and thus cut off Karachi's rail link to Lahore. He assigned the task to the Twelfth Division, while he ordered the Eleventh Indian Division to advance toward Naya Chor–Umarkot and threaten Hyderabad.[108]

However, on 5 December, the same day the Indians began their offensive, the Eighteenth Pakistani Division struck at Longenwalla with its Fifty-first Brigade, supported by the Twenty-second Cavalry (T-59s). The IAF reacted swiftly, and by midday Hunter fighter-bombers from Jaisalmer had wreaked havoc on the Pakistani armored columns, bringing the entire Pakistani attack to a halt. The Twelfth Indian Division, which was diverting its forces to Longenwalla, now went on the defensive.[109] Despite the urging of the army chief, General Khambatta, with Bewor's backing, did little more than follow the retreating Pakistanis, thus capturing more than 250 square miles of the Thar Desert on the Pakistani side.[110]

The Eleventh Indian Division had begun its advance on 4 December. Very quickly, however, the commanders discovered that divisional engineers could not cope with the deep desert sand. After an Army Engineering Regiment and a Railway Engineering Group (Territorial Army) rushed in to help, the advance continued. By the 8th the leading brigade had reached Parbat Ali, the outer perimeter of the Pakistani defensive ring around Naya Chor.[111] It took Parbat Ali on the 13th.[112] While the Indians reinforced for another attack, the

Pakistanis rushed in a brigade group from the Thirty-third Infantry Division and a T-59 Tank Regiment from the reserve corps and managed to stabilize the front until the cease-fire. However, even as the Eleventh Indian Division conducted its ponderous advance to Naya Chor, the Indian paracommandos launched successful raids against Chachro, Virwah, Nagar Parkar, and Islamkot.[113]

The Air War

In 1971 both the IAF and the PAF planned and mounted major air campaigns against each other. The greatly increased air activity during the 1971 war reflects the substantially larger air fleets maintained by both air forces since the 1965 war. In 1966 the PAF began to receive the first of seventy Chinese F-6 fighters, a Chinese copy of the MiG-19 fighters.[114] The same year the PAF also began to receive ninety ex-Luftwaffe Sabre MK-6 fighters.[115] In 1968 the PAF obtained its most potent strike aircraft yet, the French Dassault Mirage IIIE. Twenty Mirages equipped the No. 5 Squadron based at Sargodha. In addition to these new acquisitions the PAF continued to maintain forty F-86 Sabres, one squadron of seven F-104 Starfighters, and one squadron of B-57 bombers, all obtained earlier from the United States. The PAF also bolstered its aircraft acquisition program with a number of new airfields equipped with dispersed and hardened shelters. Many U.S. .50-caliber quad-mounted machine guns, supplemented with Chinese-built 14.5 mm and 37 mm automatic guns, also protected all Pakistani airfields. Extensive radar network, including Soviet P-35 ground control intercept radars, Plessey (British) AR-1 low-level radars, and Marconi (British) Condor radars, reinforced the PAF's extensive ground observer network.[116] By December 1971 the PAF had a total of thirteen combat squadrons manned by 17,000 personnel. It had deployed all but a single squadron in West Pakistan.

The IAF too underwent a substantial modernization and expansion program during the interwar period. In 1966 the IAF, which up until then had been a branch of the army, became an independent service with separate commands in central, western, and eastern areas along with training and maintenance commands. In 1971 the IAF had some 625 combat aircraft in thirty-three combat squadrons and a manpower strength of 80,000. The most numerous aircraft type was the diminutive Gnat, which equipped seven squadrons. The license-built MiG-21 fighter was the second most numerous combat aircraft. Although the IAF was extremely happy with the performance of the Soviet fighter, it had some concerns about the fighter's lack of an automatic cannon. The IAF correctly believed that the Soviet K-13A (NATO code name "Atoll") infrared homing air-to-air missile was too unreliable and large to be the fighter's only armament. As a result of the Indian insistence, the Soviets developed the GP-9, a twin 23 mm cannon gun pack that could be carried on the MiG-21 FL's belly. The Soviets also added to the MiG-21 an Indian-developed lead-computing gun sight. During the 1960s the IAF also acquired a large number of short-range Soviet Sukhoi-7 fighter bombers, which equipped six squadrons in 1971.[117] Two fighter squadrons and a conversion unit were equipped with the locally designed and built HF-24 fighter-bomber. Six Hunter squadrons continued to serve in the IAF, as did three Mystère IVA squadrons and three Canberra bomber squadrons.

As had the PAF, the IAF too constructed new airfields along with dispersed and hardened shelters.[118] In addition to extensive anti-aircraft artillery, the IAF also deployed twenty batteries of Soviet SA-2 surface-to-air missiles. Equipped with the latest version of the "Fan Song E" (NATO code name) fire-control radar, the missile could engage targets flying as low as 1,000 feet.[119] The IAF also made considerable efforts to improve the level of air and ground cooperation and air and naval cooperation.[120] Air Chief Marshal P. C. Lal, IAF commander during the 1971 war, attributes the poor ground support performance of the IAF during the 1965 war to its emphasis on deep-strike bomber offensives. This doctrine, Lal noted, was copied from the RAF, despite the fact that during the Second World War the RIAF had operated almost exclusively in a close air support role. The big change in doctrine came in 1969 during an air commanders conference, when it was decided that after air defense, close air support for the army would have priority over bomber offensives.[121] To facilitate close cooperation with the army, an advance headquarters of Western and Eastern Commands operated within their army counterparts headquarters. An air commodore who provided the air support that his army command needed led these units. At the corps level, each corps headquarters had its own Tactical Air Center commanded by a group captain, and further in the field there were forward air controllers responsible for directing air strikes against the enemy. In 1971 the commanders assigned specific aircraft types and squadrons their own areas of ground support operations.[122]

As in the case with the ground war, the preliminary clashes between the opposing air forces occurred well before 4 December. On 22 November four PAF Sabres from Dacca clashed with four IAF Gnats of the Twenty-second Squadron. After a dogfight the Indians claimed three Sabres downed for no loss to the Gnats, while the PAF claimed two Gnats downed for the loss of two Sabres.[123] The main air war began on the evening of 3 December, when PAF Sabres and B-57s launched preemptive air strikes against Indian airfields, railway stations, and suspected troop concentrations. The Pakistanis struck the Indian airfields at Pathankot, Amritsar, Avantipur, Srinagar, Uttarali, Agra, and Ambala.[124] Unlike in 1965, the PAF met with little success, as the IAF had dispersed its planes in concrete shelters, resulting in only a few aircraft suffering minor damage. The IAF struck back immediately, attacking the Pakistani airfields in the east (Tezgaon) and the west (Peshawar, Sargodha, Shorkot, and Mauripur).[125]

On the eastern front the IAF concentrated its initial effort against the sole Pakistani combat airfield at Tezgaon. MiG-21s of the No. 28 Squadron eventually put the airfield out of action by using rocket-assisted M-62 1,100-pound bombs to make deep craters in the runway.[126] The lone PAF No. 14 Sabre Squadron fought back valiantly and downed some Indian aircraft, but repeated IAF strikes against the Tezgaon runway finally grounded the PAF Sabres for good. This left the IAF free to concentrate on ground support missions. The IAF also carried out a massive helicopter lift mission to move the Fourth Indian Corps across the Meghna River. The commanders entrusted the airlift operations in this sector to the No. 110 Helicopter Unit, with twelve MI-4 helicopters, including two from the No. 105 Helicopter Unit.[127] Between 7 and 11 December the twelve MI-4s of the No. 110 Helicopter Unit transported some 4,500 troops and 515 tons of equipment, providing the Fourth Indian Corps with tremendous mobility to neutralize the Pakistani defenses.[128] On the 11th IAF transports dropped the Second Indian Parachute Battalion near Tangail. The IAF close air support missions reached a zenith on the 14th, with MiG-21s rocketing the governor's mansion in Dacca, which prompted the governor of East Pakistan, Dr. A. M. Malik, to write out a hasty resignation letter while cowering in a bunker. The next day General Niazi signed the instrument of surrender.

On the western front the IAF flew a combination of deep strike interdictions and close air support missions throughout the fourteen-day conflict. In addition to attacking Pakistani airfields, the IAF, in conjunction with the Indian navy, struck repeatedly at Pakistan's oil storage facilities in Karachi. Canberras and Hunters carried out these strikes. At the same time Hunters, Gnats, Mystères, SU-7s, and HF-24s flew constant close air support missions from Kashmir in the north to the Rajasthan Desert in the south. The PAF tried to follow a similar pattern of air strikes but concentrated mainly on close support and air defense missions. Heavy air combat engagements occurred throughout the war, with both sides claiming exaggerated kill ratios. At the height of the air war on 15–17 December, both sides threw considerable air power into the crucial battles of the Shakargarh bulge and the Naya Chor in the Sind.

At the end of the war the IAF had flown almost 6,000 sorties. In the east

1,178 of the 1,978 sorties were ground support missions, indicating the IAF's new mission emphasis. Similarly, about half of the 4,000 sorties flown in the west were also ground support missions.[129] India claimed to have destroyed 94 PAF aircraft while losing some 54 of its own planes. The PAF claimed 106 Indian aircraft destroyed for a loss of only 25 PAF planes.[130] The IAF's campaign in the east was a predictable success, but the west was a different matter altogether. Here, despite the PAF's ferocious opposition, the IAF's two-pronged strategy of attack and close air support worked reasonably well. A primary goal of the IAF after the ground support mission was to destroy the Pakistani energy, industrial, and communications infrastructure. In this regard the IAF claimed much success, and U.S. intelligence documentation has backed its claim. According to U.S. State Department documents, within a few days of the outbreak of the war India had destroyed 40 percent of Pakistan's total oil supplies, leaving the country with an estimated two weeks' worth of petroleum stocks.[131] Pakistani sources also corroborate this account.[132]

The Naval War

Following its nonperformance in the 1965 war the Indian navy sought to develop a more effective fighting force. In the late 1960s two successive chiefs of naval staff, Adm. A. K. Chatterjee and Adm. S. M. Nanda, made a strong case for a blue-water (oceangoing) navy. The naval lobby argued that India's geostrategic location required it to maintain a strong navy. They pointed out that in 1965 the Indonesian president, Achmad Sukarno, bolstered by $1 billion worth of Soviet-built ships and equipment, including the most powerful gun cruiser in the region, had offered to seize the Andaman and Nicobar Islands in the Bay of Bengal to aid Pakistan.[133] The naval lobby also noted the obvious, that India's seaborne trade and offshore resources needed naval protection.[134] Although many people within the government and the other two branches of the military opposed naval expansion, a blue-water navy remained a popular issue for politicians. In 1968 the government elevated the chief of naval staff to the rank of admiral, thus bringing the navy in line with the other two services with regard to its leader's seniority. And even though the defense minister, Swaran Singh, opposed a blue-water fleet, the routine modernization of the current fleet became an inevitable process. Navy expenditure ballooned from a mere 7.8 percent of defense capital expenditure in 1966–67 to 34.3 percent in 1971.[135]

When the 1971 war started the Indian navy had a total of 40,000 men in uniform. Its main surface combatant fleet included one light aircraft carrier, four

Soviet-built "Foxtrot"-class (NATO code name) diesel patrol submarines, two light 6-inch gun cruisers, twenty-one destroyers and frigates, ten patrol craft (including six Soviet Osa-class missile boats), and eight coastal and inshore minesweepers. The carrier *Vikrant* and the Indian Naval Air Stations also hosted some thirty-five Seahawk jet fighters, twelve Alize antisubmarine warfare planes, two SeaKing antisubmarine warfare helicopters, and ten Allouette helicopters. The Pakistani navy numbered some 10,000 men, with four French Daphne-class diesel patrol submarines, one light anti-aircraft gun cruiser, seven destroyers and frigates, six patrol boats, eight coastal minesweepers, and two UH-1 "Huey" helicopters.[136]

The Indian Naval Command deployed its lone carrier (the *Vikrant*), four destroyers, and one submarine with the Eastern Fleet. The Western Fleet consisted of the cruiser *Mysore*, twelve destroyers/frigates, three submarines, and six Osa missile boats. It also deployed two destroyers with the Southern Fleet. The Indian navy's objectives included destroying Pakistani shipping, blockading East and West Pakistan, and protecting Indian ports.[137] The Indian navy's involvement in the East Pakistani civil war began as early as mid-1971, when it established a training camp south of Calcutta to train East Pakistani freedom fighters to become naval saboteurs.[138] These naval commandos began their operations on 15–16 August with a coordinated attack on the East Pakistani seaport of Chittagong and the river ports of Chalna, Chandpur, and Barisal. The commandos timed their assaults with the help of coded messages sent out on regular All Indian Radio broadcasts.[139] These and other operations were so successful that when the war began on 3 December the naval commandos had imposed a virtual naval blockade on East Pakistan.

At the commencement of hostilities the Indian carrier battle group under Rear Adm. V. K. Sarma, consisting of the *Vikrant*, two air defense frigates (ex–Royal Navy type 14), and two Soviet Petya-class antisubmarine warfare corvettes, left its base in the Andaman Islands and sailed for the East Pakistani coast. From there the *Vikrant*'s Seahawks and Alizes launched 400 sorties against Chittagong and other coastal and riverine ports.[140] The force sank three of the four Pakistani naval boats as well as several merchant vessels. The naval air operations brought a complete halt to all sea and riverine activities in East Pakistan, cutting the Pakistanis off from the rest of the world.

In the west the Indian navy maintained a fairly effective if not total blockade of the Pakistani port of Karachi. On 3–4 December Indian Osa missile boats and two Petya-class corvettes left Bombay. They refueled at Diu, and, after a brief wait at Dwarka, three of the Osas moved out to attack Karachi. Some 40 miles off Karachi they detected and sank the Pakistani destroyer PNS *Khaiber* (ex–Royal Navy battle class) with two SSN-2 "Styx" (NATO code name) antiship missiles. They also sank the Pakistani minesweeper, the PNS *Muhafiz*, when it moved in to pick up the survivors from the *Khaiber*. On the 8th the Osas attacked Karachi again, damaging the naval tanker the PNS *Dacca* and sinking and damaging several merchant ships. On the 9th other Indian surface combatants shelled the Makran coast, including the ports of Pasni, Gawder, and Jiwani.[141] The three Indian submarines operating in the Arabian Sea with support from the submarine depot ship the INS *Amba* (based in Cochin) met with no success, which was not surprising, since they operated under extremely strict rules that required a Pakistani warship to be positively identified before attack.

The Pakistani navy could only strike back with its submarines, outnumbered as it was on the surface. On the evening of 8 December the Pakistani Daphne-class submarine the PNS *Hangor*, operating off the Rann of Kutch, spotted two Indian frigates, the INS *Kirpan* and the INS *Khukri* (ex–Royal Navy type 14). The *Hangor* sank the *Khukri* with a salvo of three homing torpedoes, thus giving the Indian navy the dubious reputation of being the first navy since the Second World War to lose a warship to a submarine.[142] In the east the Pakistanis had sent their only long-range submarine, the U.S.-built PNS *Ghazi*, to locate and sink the *Vikrant*. While patrolling off Vishakapatnam harbor on 3 December the Indian destroyer the INS *Rajput* surprised the *Ghazi* with a routine drop of depth charges outside the harbor. Soon afterward the Indians heard a loud explosion, and days later naval divers confirmed that the *Ghazi* had indeed been sunk.[143] The Indian navy's own Russian-built Foxtrot-class submarines remained silent during the war; however, recently it has been revealed that the Indian navy submarine the INS *Karanj* shadowed and obtained several torpedo-firing solutions on the USS *Enterprise* as it steamed past the Bay of Bengal as part of Task Force 77. After the 4 December attacks on Karachi, the main Pakistani surface combatants did not venture out of port. Control of the seas had passed to the Indian navy.

Postmortem

Raymond Aron has described the 1971 Indo-Pakistan War as a prime example of a "Classic War" in the Clausewitzian tradition. India struck a direct blow at Pakistan's armed forces to produce an immediate political goal.[144] Indeed, the Indian government under Prime Minister Indira Gandhi controlled and engineered all the events leading up to the outbreak of the war after the Pakistani crackdown in East Pakistan. In marked contrast to the events in 1962 and 1965 the Indian government, operating this time from a position of strength vis-à-vis Pakistan, seized the military initiative after having garnered all possible international and domestic political support.

The war itself is a startling example of how successful the postindependence Indian army has been in implementing the defensive-offensive military doctrines it imbibed during the Second World War. Beginning with his point-blank refusal in April 1971 to launch a "speedy" offensive against East Pakistan to his careful buildup and preparation in the months leading to the escalation of border conflicts in November, the chief of army staff, Gen. Sam Manekshaw, proved to be the master of the set-piece battle plan. The planning by army headquarters for the offensive into East Pakistan was deliberate and methodical. The director of military operations, Lt. Gen. K. K. Singh, well aware of the army's inability to conduct "true" mobile operations, had initially opted for a limited border offensive. Only when Mountain Divisions deployed against China could be diverted to the East Pakistan offensive as a result of the Indo-Soviet treaty and a substantial ground superiority was apparent did planning for an all-out offensive to take East Pakistan begin. Overwhelming superiority in troops and firepower and air and naval supremacy in the Bay of Bengal thus lay at the roots of Indian offensive planning. However, this does not diminish the excellent operational and tactical abilities of Lt. Gen. Jagjit Singh Aurora, general officer commanding Eastern Command, and his subordinate commanders. Their skill in adapting their operational plans to the rapidly changing situation in the field brought the war to a spectacularly swift end. East Pakistan's dense forests and riverine terrain are excellently suited to the Indian army's light infantry formations. Nevertheless, the heli-lift operations in Sylhet and the parachute drop in Tangail also reveal the army's (and the air force's) willingness to experiment with highly complex types of air-land mobile operations. The success of the First U.S. Air Cavalry Division in Vietnam particularly influenced the heli-lift operations.

In the west the Indian army had mainly defensive objectives, and in these, with the exception of the loss of Chaamb, it was remarkably successful. The Western Command's ability to strike telling blows at the Shakargarh bulge in the Punjab while the Southern Command struck out toward Naya Chor in Rajasthan kept the Pakistani high command off-balance and prevented them from throwing in their powerful strike corps, the Sixth Armored Division and the Seventeenth Infantry Division. Although the commanders primarily used semistatic infantry formations for military operations in the west, the army also obtained significant experience in combined arms mechanized warfare. The Eighteenth Rajputana Mechanized Battalion worked closely with tanks to overwhelm Pakistani positions in the Lalial forest across the Basanthar River. These minor but significant experiences with helicopters and armored personnel carriers have had a significant impact on the army's doctrinal evolution in the 1980s and 1990s.

The 1971 war also saw the IAF emerge as a mature and independent fighting arm. A defensive-offensive doctrine, similar to the army's, replaced the air force's earlier "bomber only" offensive doctrine. Despite some blemishes, the IAF's close air support performance in 1971 was a vast improvement of its performance in 1965. Not only did the air force and army cooperate on fire support missions, but the IAF also provided excellent transportation support for the army with efficient heli-lift and paradrop missions. Significantly, even though its fleet of obsolete and short-range strike planes hampered the IAF, it managed to sustain a remarkably effective strategic air campaign against Pakistan.

The Indian navy underwent a complete metamorphosis in 1971 compared to its total inaction in 1965. The navy made effective use of its Osa missile boats and its light carrier, the *Vikrant*, which represented two of its three most potent offensive weapons, the third being the four Foxtrot-class submarines. Much of its spectacular successes came about as a result of the overwhelming superiority it enjoyed over its Pakistani counterpart. Yet its performance in 1971 was a battle against internal enemies within India as much as it was against the Pakistani navy. At the end of the 1971 war domestic critics of the blue-water navy were mostly silenced, and the navy could pursue its long-cherished modernization and expansion program with relatively little political opposition. The postwar reaction to the navy, then, became symptomatic of the national reaction to the Indian military as a whole. India was now a regional power, having decisively neutralized for the moment at least the direct military threat from its South Asian rival. A strong Indian armed force would henceforth form the bedrock of India's continued rise to power in Asia.

Part Five

CHAPTER 12

Insurgencies, Interventions, and High Altitude Warfare

The 1971 war with Pakistan was the Indian armed forces' last major conventional war. Prior to and after that conflict the armed forces and the army in particular have seen almost constant action in a variety of low intensity, primarily internal conflicts. India's northeast has been and continues to be a hotbed of ethnic, religious, linguistic, and economic tensions. In recent times the burgeoning population growth in South Asia has meant that these previously isolated tribal regions have come under severe migratory pressure from people moving out of Bangladesh and West Bengal in India. These new pressures have exacerbated the preexisting tensions mentioned above, resulting in many tribal insurgencies with objectives ranging from local autonomy to outright independence.

Insurgency in Northeast India

Tribal insurgency in Northeast India arose almost on the heels of independence. In 1947 the Naga National Conference, under the leadership of Zaphur Phizo, demanded Naga independence and dispatched many telegrams to the Indian government and the UN secretary general. The Indian government responded initially with mediatory efforts but quickly switched to a military solution. Between 1956 and 1958 intense combat took place between Indian soldiers and Naga rebels. In 1955 Phizo began to attack Assam Rifles posts in the remote Tuensang Division. The rebels followed up these attacks by massacring villagers who did not support their cause. In response, the Indian government dispatched an army battalion into the area. The move succeeded in dislocating Phizo's operations for the time being. He responded by establishing the Naga Federal Army, later the Naga Home Guard. The rebels tried to organize along conventional lines with companies, battalions, and brigades and at their peak had a strength of 10,000. Initially, their equipment was quite primitive and included bows and arrows, *morungs*, or clubs, and dahs, or large hacking knives. Abandoned Japanese weapons and equipment that the British and Americans supplied to the Nagas supplemented these weapons. Later, as Pakistan and China began to support the rebels, they began to get modern small arms. The rebels also supplemented their stocks with weapons and ammunition seized from Indian security forces and from police and Assam Rifles armories that they raided. The Nagas also established strong defensive and ambush positions in the jungle and in fortified hilltop villages using sharpened *punji* (bamboo) sticks embedded in camouflaged ditches.

Phizo utilized murder and intimidation to obtain recruits, logistical support, supplies, and intelligence from the local population. The heavy-handed tactics of the security forces and, in particular, the Assam police undoubtedly aided his cause. By 1956 Nagaland was almost ungovernable. The rebels derailed trains, ambushed convoys, and murdered government and security personnel. In April that year the government finally committed an army brigade, the 181st Independent Infantry Brigade, to full-time counterinsurgency operations in the area.[1] The government gave the general officer commanding Assam, whose headquarters was at Shillong, about 400 miles from Kohima (later the capital of Nagaland), responsibility for counterinsurgency operations.[2] Although the army had to wait for the monsoon season to abate at the end of the year before it could begin operations, it conducted an intensive counterinsurgency campaign in the winter. During these operations the army arrested 1,000 rebels, while 3,000 surrendered voluntarily. The army suffered 300 casualties.[3] The successful operations of the Indian army resulted in some moderate Naga leaders opening negotiations for local autonomy with the government. In August 1957 moderate Naga leaders held a Naga people's convention in Kohima and demanded further autonomy in return for giving up the demand for independence. The Indian government accepted the majority ruling of the 1957 convention and set up the Naga Hills–Tuensang Division. The government followed this decision by granting a general amnesty to all Nagas in government detention.

Phizo and the other hard-liners reacted with predictable violence, targeting any Naga suspected of government sympathies. To enhance security, the Indian government began to group the population into large "supervillages." It provided these centers with water, medical facilities, provisions, a double stockade, and armed guards. The government apparently borrowed this idea from the massive British relocation scheme in Malaysia. However, it applied the conditions only to one area in the Naga Hills, and the rebels simply moved to another area. Furthermore, the villagers preferred to stick to their cultivable fields rather than relocate to the security of the stockade.[4] Further negotiations with the moderate Naga leaders followed, and in 1963 Nagaland, carved out of the state of Assam, became the Indian Union's sixteenth state.[5] Radical Nagas under Phizo's leadership rejected this accord and continued to fight for an independent Nagaland, this time with Chinese support and from safe bases in East Pakistan. In May 1963 the Eighty-first, 192nd, and 301st Infantry Brigades moved into the Naga Hills, and Nagaland headquarters came into being, with Maj. Gen. K. P. Candeth as general officer commanding. For administrative reasons the military named the new formation the Eighth Indian Mountain Division.[6] In 1968 the army resumed intensive operations, attacking and destroying several rebel camps and hideouts. Several internal divisions hamstrung the rebels, which resulted in the rebels splintering into opposing groups. The army had in the meantime greatly refined its counterinsurgency operations. It extensively used helicopters to speed up movement and rotated the region's infantry battalions through the Counter-Insurgency School at Varingete in the Mizo Hills. Helicopter operations began in earnest in 1964 with the IAF's No. 105 Helicopter Unit (MI-4s) supporting army operations in the North East Frontier Agency, Nagaland, and Manipur.[7] The commanders used the helicopters to move troops at short notice, which proved very effective in cordon and search operations. As the army's regional infrastructure solidified and expanded, it took a long-term look at its strategy and evolved local welfare, health, and sporting activities to win the "hearts and minds" of the locals. The army also had the Eighth Mountain Division soldiers introduced to Naga customs, language, and lifestyle. At the same time, engineers improved paths and roads and constructed playing fields, cinemas, and canteen facilities.

The rebels suffered a major blow during the 1971 Indo-Pakistan War when the Indian army overran their East Pakistani bases in the Chittagong Hills, capturing several Naga and Mizo rebels. In 1972 the Naga rebels, lacking their East Pakistani bases and under heavy pressure from the Indian army, agreed to a cease-fire. In 1974 the moderate Naga party, the United Democratic Front, won the state elections and sought to bring about a rapprochement between the rebels and the government. Renewed Indian army operations finally resulted in the Shillong Accord in November 1975. Although many militants accepted the Indian constitution and surrendered their arms, hard-liners such as Phizo and later the groups based in Myanmar (Burma) such as the Muaviah group continued armed struggle. In the early 1990s the Nationalist Socialist Council of Nagaland (NSCN), led by Isaac Swu and T. H. Muviah, consolidated its cadres and launched a very successful campaign against security forces, resulting in heavy casualties for the latter.[8] Negotiations remained locked in a stalemate. In 1991 the Eighth Mountain Division, which oversaw most of Northeast India, including Nagaland, Tripura, and

Mizoram, became the Indian army's largest division in terms of the area of responsibility and troops under its command.[9]

In 1960 the Mizos, another northeastern tribe, began agitating for independence under the banner of the Mizo National Front (MNF). More so than the Naga rebels, the MNF received considerable aid from Pakistan and China. The Mizo leader, Laldenga, formed the Mizo National Army (MNA) with their assistance. The actual armed struggle began in February 1966 when thousands of MNA rebels began a coordinated attack against the treasuries and armories at Aizwal, Lungleh, Demagiri, and Marapara. At the same time, they besieged Assam Rifles and Border Security Force (BSF) posts, and by November the MNF had the entire Mizo area under its control.[10] In reaction, the government sent in the army. The latter quickly dispersed the MNA, but the Mizo insurgency continued in spurts and jerks with increasing help from China and Pakistan. The Eighth Infantry Division conducted several successful operations against the MNF, especially with helicopters. In 1967 special heli-borne operations involving the Fifth Parachute Battalion captured the MNF home and defense ministers.[11] The same year the 101st Special Communication Zone's lieutenant general, Sagat Singh, launched a special heli-borne operation to destroy Mizo training camps in East Pakistan; however, the mission failed.[12]

The Indian army's successful campaign in East Pakistan in 1971, however, severely dislocated the movement. Both the MNF and the Nagaland National Front received a further blow in the late 1970s when China terminated all covert aid to Indian underground forces. The Indian government continued its carrot-and-stick approach with the MNF, granting Mizoram statehood along with considerable local autonomy in 1971. At the same time, the Indian government granted statehood to Meghalaya, Manipur, Tripura, and Arunachal Pradesh (formerly the North East Frontier Agency) in an attempt to preempt demands for political autonomy from the region's major tribes. At the same time the government maintained military pressure. In September 1980 the Armed Forces Special Powers Act of 1958 was made applicable to Manipur. The Mizo unrest continued until 1986, when Laldenga came to an agreement with the Indian government, securing special status and safeguards similar to Jammu and Kashmir. Laldenga eventually assumed the chief ministership of Mizoram state on 21 August 1986.

No sooner had the Mizo issue reached a settlement when the Nepali Gorkha National Liberation Front (GNLF) of West Bengal's Darjeeling district began to agitate for a separate state of Gorkhaland. Although the GNLF agitation has not blossomed into a full-scale insurgency, sporadic violence continues, with the Indian government standing firm in its refusal to grant the region statehood.

In addition to demands for independence and local autonomy, insurgency in the northeastern states has also been aimed against illegal immigrants from Bangladesh. After the 1971 war hundreds of thousands of Bangladeshi migrants flooded into Assam.[13] The Congress government welcomed these immigrants as a "vote bank." With the Bangladeshis taking over much of the local industry and even dominating many urban areas in the Brahmaputra valley, the Assamese launched their first antiforeigner movement in 1967.[14] In 1979 the movement became violent as further evidence of government complicity in rigging the voter registers emerged. The All Assam Students Movement and the All Assam Gana Sangram Parishad (Assam People's Council) agitated intensely for the deportation of all foreigners. In 1983 almost 4,000 people died when Prime Minister Indira Gandhi called for state elections. In August 1985 the Rajiv Gandhi–led Congress (I) government reached an agreement with the agitation leaders to delete from the election rolls all immigrants who came to Assam between 1 January 1966 and 24 March 1971. Despite this agreement the problems in Assam continue to this day, with Assamese demands now moving on to independence from India. The Assamese groups participating in the armed struggle are many and varied; they include the United Liberation Front of Assam (ULFA) and, more recently, the Bodo Security Force (BDSF). The Bodo Student Union was formed in 1971 with the demand for a separate "Bodoland" for the northern Brahmaputra valley. The BDSF has established close ties with the NSCN, and army operations (during which the army captured 170 Bodo militants, including 38 hardcore members) have established the existence of substantial training and supply links between the two organizations.[15] During the first half of 1991 the army's Fifty-seventh Mountain Division conducted Operation Bajrang and Operation Rhino to root out ULFA militants. During Operation Bajrang the army operated largely on its own and was hampered by political opposition that eventually led to its premature recall to barracks. In Operation Rhino the government gave the army a free hand, and the army assumed control of paramilitary and armed police units combating the militants. The army also coordinated all intelligence to prevent the duplication of efforts and confusion. The commander of the Fourth Corps, Lt. Gen. Ajay Singh, oversaw the direction of the operation. Operation Rhino proved to be a success, netting the army 136 militants from fifteen different hideouts scattered all over the state. By 16 November Rhino had nabbed fifty hard-core ULFA members.[16] Within a month of Operation Rhino ULFA's back had been temporarily broken, and the desperate group sued for peace to buy time. The state politicians once again prevailed, and the government called off the army, allowing many desperate militants to finally escape into Bangladesh.[17] Since then the army has followed a carrot-and-stick approach with the ULFA movement, which has evolved into a major security threat in Assam. While aggressive army operations netted 150 ULFA militants, including 62 hardcore members in 1994 (742 surrendered), the chief of army staff, General Shankar Roy Chowdhury, referred to the "ULFA boys" as "our own children and not enemies."[18] Such an attitude was apparent in the next major military operation against the rebels from 13 April to 14 May, code-named Operation Flushout in some areas and Operation Hiphazat in other areas, "depending on the psyche of the local population." Troops from the Second and Twenty-first Mountain Divisions fanned out in areas of upper and lower Assam along a 500-mile axis. According to army sources, the counterinsurgency operations in Assam reached a critical phase, with unrelenting pressure being applied on the militants on the north, south, east, and west banks of the Brahmaputra River, forcing the militants to the peace talks. The operation specifically targeted ULFA cadres returning from their cross-border camps in Bhutan to be with their families during the Assamese harvest festival, Rongali Bihu. As a calculated gesture of goodwill, the Fourth Corps's general officer commanding, Lt. Gen. D. B. Shetkar, announced a cease-fire for three days in May.[19]

Insurgency in the Punjab

Although the northeastern insurgency is the oldest and most costly in terms of resources and lives lost, the Punjab and Kashmir insurgencies have captivated both domestic and international attention. The Punjab is one of the Indian Union's most important states in economic and strategic terms, the former because it is the country's granary and the latter because it shares a border with Pakistan. Also, the army recruits 8–10 percent of its soldiers from the Punjab. As a result of its strategic location, the Punjab is the home of the army's Western Command, with the Tenth Corps based at Bhatinda and the Eleventh Corps at Jalandher. Traditionally, the Hindus in Punjab have been urban traders and industrialists, while the Sikhs made up the rural community. This situation has often led the Sikhs to accuse the Hindus of monopolizing the state's vital economic spheres.[20] These complaints stem from the Sikhs' fear that the Hindu majority will dominate and subjugate them, a fear that has gained ground since Indian independence.

Matters came to a head on 8 September 1981, when the main Sikh political party, the Akali Dal, submitted many grievances to Prime Minister Indira Gandhi's Congress (I) government. When negotiations failed to produce a settlement, the government decided to back an obscure Sikh religious leader, Jarnail Singh Bhindranwale, as a counterpoise to the Akali Dal. The tactic worked remarkably well, except that the center never exerted total control over him. By 1982 Bhindranwale was operating independently from the center and developing his own antigovernment message. Bhindranwale and his supporters launched a terrorist campaign in the Punjab to create an independent Sikh state, Khalistan. After a spate of massacres that saw the massive exodus of Hindus, the government cracked down and called in the army. On 5 June 1984 the government launched Operation Bluestar to evict Bhindranwale and his followers from the premises of the Golden Temple in Amritsar, where they had taken refuge from the security forces. The army's assault on the Golden Temple resulted in a bloody battle that lasted twenty-four hours. Casualties were heavy: the army suffered more than 200 dead and wounded, while Bhindranwale was killed along with 1,500 supporters. Several hundred trapped pilgrims also died in the crossfire. Collateral damage to the temple complex was considerable – during the height of the battle the army used Vijayanta tanks to blast the extremists out of the Akal Takht, a holy shrine. In retrospect, it is clear that neither the government nor the army expected such fierce and coordinated opposition. The army simply did not know of the militants' heavy armaments, which included mortars, antitank rockets, and machine guns.

The assault on the Golden Temple sent shock waves through the Sikh community. Moderate Sikh Parliament members were aghast at what they saw as a gross desecration of the very heart of the Sikh religion. But the most crucial Sikh reaction, and potentially the most dangerous, came from Sikhs in the Indian army. On 7 June, a day after the battle, the Sikh Regiment's Ninth Battalion mutinied in Ganganagar. Six hundred soldiers, almost the entire "other ranks" strength, broke into the armory and then left the cantonment for the border with Pakistan and for Delhi. Troops of the Rajputana Rifles rounded up most of the mutineers.[21] The largest mutiny took place in Ramgarh Bihar, the Sikh Regimental Center, where recruits for the Sikh Regiment are trained. The soldiers mutinied a day after the Ninth Battalion's mutiny, the news of which they heard from the BBC. The next day at about 10:00 AM they stormed the armory. When the camp commandant, Brig. S. C. Puri, drove in to investigate, they shot him dead. The mutinous troops, 1,461 in number, then set out for Amritsar in a convoy. They were stopped and rounded up after firefights with other army units during which five soldiers died. Yet another Sikh Regiment battalion mutinied in Jammu near Punjab, and a series of smaller mutinies occurred in various other units scattered across the country. Although the mutinies were relatively isolated and involved mainly impressionable raw recruits, they were the most serious crisis for the postindependence Indian army, hitherto immune to the ethnic conflict that frequently ravaged the country, and shocked both the army and the government.[22]

The army followed up Operation Bluestar with Operation Woodrose to flush out terrorists from the countryside surrounding the Golden Temple. The army apparently jettisoned its hard-learned hearts-and-mind strategy from the northeastern insurgency and instead behaved in a very heavy-handed manner with the locals. The end result was that the surviving militants could recruit a new generation of disenchanted youths to fight the government. Between 1985 (Prime Minister Indira Gandhi was assassinated in 1984) and 1990 the army stayed out of counterinsurgency operations in the Punjab. Although the police received special powers, the violence continued to increase dramatically after 1984. In 1988 paramilitary commandos successfully besieged the Golden Temple in Operation Black Thunder, which flushed out more terrorists taking refuge there. At this time, the insurgents' weaponry began to get more and more sophisticated, with AK-47s, RPG-7 rocket launchers, general purpose machine guns, sniper rifles, and explosives. Most troubling was the fact that the insurgents felt free to attack army units. They obtained most of these weapons in Pakistan, whose government did not cooperate with the Indian authorities.[23] The government's attempt to grant amnesty to several jailed militants and then hold state elections back-fired, with the violence escalating to a zenith in 1990–91, when more than 6,000 people died in the conflict.[24] The police, totally demoralized by the conflicting signals of the center and the constant attacks of the insurgents against them and their families, had all but given up the fight.

In 1990 the government sent in the army once again to save the situation. The latter responded with Operation Rakshak I, a massive three-division effort aimed at sealing the border with Pakistan and helping the police regain the initiative lost to the terrorists. The operation, however, proved unsuccessful and only dispersed the insurgent groups around the state. Further Sikh dissatisfaction with the government's tactics only helped the insurgents establish footholds outside the Punjab.[25] The failure of Rakshak I and the subsequent withdrawal of the army led to a further escalation of the conflict, this time throughout the Punjab. In 1992 the army reentered the fray with Operation Rakshak II, which not only involved the Punjab but included sealing off the entire border with Pakistan to the Arabian Sea. In addition to the army's 120,000 men, the government placed 53,000 Punjab police, 28,000 Home Guards, 10,000 special police officers, and 70,000 paramilitary personnel in the Punjab in February 1992.[26] As before, the major goal of the army operation was to rebuild the shattered morale of the police and paramilitary forces. To this end, the army deployed Quick Reaction Teams, which could deploy within fifteen minutes to any part of the state to support the police. The army primarily operated in the rural areas, where a new "gentler and kindlier" attitude toward the locals (as in the northeast) included helping them restart schools, medical facilities, and agricultural projects.[27] It reinforced these actions with aggressive patrolling and cordon and search operations to keep the insurgents on the run. At the same time, the army paid particular attention to sealing the border area, with 900 border villages being placed under a dusk-to-dawn curfew.[28] All told, the army committed not only the Tenth and Eleventh Corps but also its Strike Corps, the First, to this operation. Even the First Corps Armored Division took part in the operations, without its armor. By June 1992 (after starting in November 1991) the army had participated in some 1,334 cordoning operations and had carried out 121,465 patrols, or about 600 to 700 patrols a day. Each brigade patrolled an area of 40 square miles. The army's actions were mainly preventative, but it succeeded in killing 120 insurgents, capturing 175, and accepting the surrender of 56.[29]

Rakshak II marked the definitive turn in the Punjab conflict. The reinvigorated police and paramilitary soon captured or killed many Sikh militant leaders. Between 1981 and 1992 the army killed 6,000 terrorists and captured 20,000. In the latter half of 1992 only 650 militants remained, divided between some 90 gangs.[30] By now the insurgents had lost much support from the local populace, who saw them as common criminals.[31] Although sporadic violence continues in the Punjab, the government has mostly reestablished law and order.

Intervention in Sri Lanka

On 31 June 1987 India and Sri Lanka signed an accord that allowed Indian troops to land on the Jaffna Peninsula in order to act as peacekeepers between the Sri Lankan government forces and the Liberation Tigers of Tamil Eelam (LTTE), a violent separatist group founded on 5 May 1976 that had been fighting for independence from Sri Lanka for a decade. Initially, the LTTE welcomed the Indian Peace-Keeping Force (IPKF) as liberators, but within months the IPKF and the LTTE were engaged in a bloody war. India's Sri Lankan misadventure lasted for almost four years and is the Indian armed forces' longest sustained conflict. Its impact on the Indian security establishment has been profound and ranges from a rethinking of strategic planning and intelligence gathering to the reassessment of small unit tactics and firepower.

The Sri Lankan crisis erupted in the early 1980s, when elements of the minority Tamil population (who make up roughly 20 percent of the population)

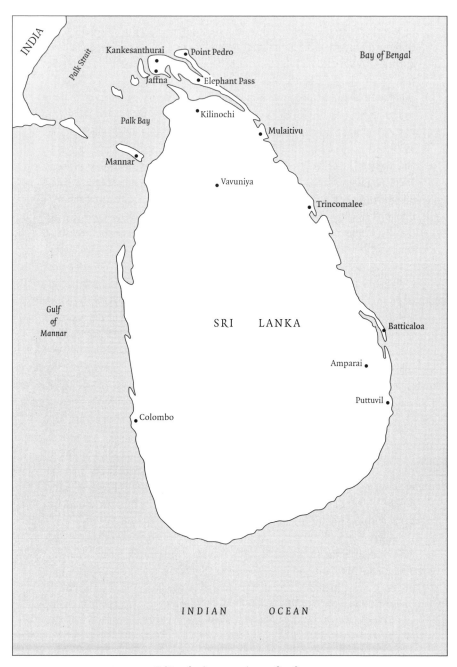

Sri Lanka intervention 1987–89

took up arms against the Sri Lankan government. The Jaffna Tamils, long suffering under a government controlled by the Sinhalese majority, began to mobilize under the banner of the Tamil United Liberation Front for greater autonomy. In December 1982 the ruling Sinhalese United National Party, under the leadership of President Julius Jayewardene, held a referendum instead of an open election and extended its term in office. Opposition-led violence in the streets of the capital, Columbo, quickly snowballed into an anti-Tamil pogrom, during which hundreds if not thousands of Tamils were killed.[32] The spark that ignited the anti-Tamil violence was the ambush and massacre of fifteen Sri Lankan army soldiers by members of the LTTE on 23 July 1983.[33]

The plight of the Sri Lankan Tamils did not go unnoticed in the southern Indian state of Tamil Nadu. Indeed, the Sri Lankan government's handling of the Tamil issue became a prime political issue for local Tamil politicians in India. Political parties in Tamil Nadu, especially the ones in power, sought to outdo each other in their attempts to aid their brethren in Sri Lanka. At the same time as the Columbo massacres, M. G. Ramachandran's Tamil Nadu government began to funnel arms and cash to the Tamil rebels, especially the LTTE. In Tamil Nadu itself Tamil refugees from Sri Lanka, many of them rebels and rebel sympathizers, engaged in gun running, drug running, and money laundering to funnel aid to the Tamil fighters in Sri Lanka. The Indian Tamils did not favor this open flaunting of the law-and-order situation in Tamil Nadu, but the Indian Tamil politicians were not dissuaded. Although the Tamil politicians pressured the Indian government to take action, it too was concerned about the escalating violence in Jaffna and about reports that foreign intelligence agencies were aiding the Sri Lankans. In the aftermath of the 1983 Columbo riots the Indian government decided to act, hoping to maintain leverage over the Tamil Nadu government's actions. The Research and Analysis Wing (RAW), India's external intelligence agency responsible to the cabinet secretariat, trained Tamil rebels at Chakrata, north of Dehra Dun in India.[34] The Chakrata base was a top secret military complex known as Establishment Two Two (written as Establishment 22) where RAW and CIA instructors jointly trained Tibetan fighters to operate in Chinese-occupied Tibet.[35]

In April 1987 the Sri Lankan armed forces began a major offensive against the Tamil-held Jaffna Peninsula. The unsuccessful operation resulted in considerable death among the civilian population. A subsequent land and sea blockade cut off 800,000 Tamils, including 200,000 in the city of Jaffna, from all food and fuel supplies. The Indian government decided to act. In early June it sent a mercy convoy of small ships out from southern India to Jaffna, but the Sri Lankan navy forced it to turn back. Two days later, in an openly defiant act, the Indian government sent in air force AN-32s escorted by Mirage 2000 fighters to drop food and medical supplies on Jaffna. When it became obvious to Sri Lankan president Jayewardene that the world community would not aid him against his giant neighbor, he signed the Indo–Sri Lankan Accord with Indian prime minister Rajiv Gandhi in July.[36]

A month earlier the director general of military operations, Lt. Gen. B. C. Joshi, had initiated planning for the upcoming Sri Lankan intervention under the title of Operation Pawan. The general officer commanding Southern Command, Lt. Gen. Depinder Singh, oversaw the operation. The forces at his disposal included the Fifty-fourth Infantry Division (which had been undergoing training for amphibious and air assault operations), the Thirty-sixth Infantry Division, the Second Armored Brigade, and the 340th Independent Infantry Brigade Group. First Corps headquarters in Jaffna with an overall force commander in Madras administered this force, with substantial air force and naval support. Within forty-eight hours of the accord being signed some 3,000 Indian troops had been airlifted into Palaly Airbase in the Jaffna Peninsula. When the IPKF moved into Jaffna in August, its main function as per the terms of the accord was to disarm the Tamil rebel groups, a precondition to uniting the northern and eastern provinces and to holding elections for a joint provincial council.

However, the LTTE, the most powerful rebel military group, reneged on its earlier agreement to surrender its arms and began a violent terror campaign against Sinhalese civilians and opposing Tamil rebel groups. Indeed, by the time the IPKF took over from the Sri Lankans, the LTTE, led by its leader, Prabhakaran, who had returned to Jaffna from Delhi, where he had been virtually under house arrest, had all but wiped out all other Tamil rebel groups. As the IPKF sought desperately to regain some semblance of control, the LTTE continued to flaunt its power. On 7 October LTTE cadres opened fire on the IPKF personnel in Trincomalee. New Delhi immediately issued orders to the IPKF to crack down on the LTTE and remove its forces from Jaffna, and the next day it directed the Indian navy to establish a naval blockade of Jaffna. Undeterred, the LTTE deliberately escalated the confrontation by capturing and burning alive five Indian commandos who had been shopping in Jaffna. The LTTE's actions surprised the IPKF and the Indian government, despite the fact that the Indian intelligence community – RAW, the Intelligence Branch (IB), and "Q Branch" (intelligence) of the Tamil Nadu police, who had worked closely with the Tamil militants – had predicted that the accord would collapse, especially in the face of LTTE opposition. It did not help matters that these intelligence organizations deeply resented the fact that the Ministry of External Affairs and the prime minister's office had drawn up the accord without any input from them.[37] Far worse was the lack of cooperation between the army and the civilian intelligence agencies. Lt. Gen. S. C. Sardeshpande, former general officer commanding Jaffna area, remarked, "We heard little from the representative of RAW. . . . Perhaps RAW saw us as not quite ripe to deserve sharing their findings! As events forced themselves from mid '89 onwards we differed with their assessment, sometimes radically. . . . They seem to permit themselves the luxury of over-enthusiasm, over-optimism and the virtue of meeting other demands and compulsions better known to them. Our 'pulse' of the people proved right in the end. . . . Contributions from RAW, IB and the Indian High Commission was limited and seldom helped us."[38]

The Indian plan for Operation Pawan included capturing Jaffna and seizing the LTTE leader, Prabhakaran. Maj. Gen. Harkirat Singh's Fifty-fourth Infantry Division had the responsibility for capturing Jaffna. Although missing most of its heavy weapons, the division planned a multipronged four-brigade assault to take the city of Jaffna. The Ninety-first Brigade, based at Kankesanthurai on the northern coast, would move south toward Jaffna along the Mallakam-Kakuvil axis. The Seventy-second Brigade, based at Palaly Airbase, would also move south toward Jaffna via Urumparai. The 115th Brigade, based at Point Pedro, was to advance along the Atcheveli-Putte axis toward Jaffna. The Eighteenth Brigade was to move west from Navatkuli toward Jaffna. Along with the main operation to seize Jaffna, the army planned a heli-borne raid to destroy the LTTE headquarters at Jaffna University and if possible to capture Prabhakaran. The air operation commenced at dusk on 10 October. In the first phase three IAF MI-8s put down seventy paracommandos in the university football field adjacent to the LTTE headquarters. The LTTE immediately subjected the commandos to a hail of ground fire, killing six and wounding nine. The commandos then conducted a fighting retreat until finally a force, including the three T-72 tanks (the only Indian armor in Jaffna) that had advanced along the Palaly-Jaffna railway line to avoid mines, rescued them.

The second phase of the operation involved a similar drop of thirty men from the Thirteenth Sikh Light Infantry to a more distant school playing field. The hurried insertion of the Thirteenth Sikh Light Infantry into the battle is symptomatic of the errors that dogged these early IPKF operations. The unit initially moved from its base in Gwalior, 149 miles south of Delhi, to the airhead at Bangalore in southern India for an onward flight to Jaffna in August. On 7 October the battalion flew back to Gwalior, only to be sent back to Bangalore the next day. The tired troops finally arrived in Jaffna on 11 October; the commanders then sent them into battle.[39] This first platoon came under heavy fire even before landing, losing its radio and radio operator almost at once. This force, still believing it was securing the perimeter for follow-on forces, continued to fight until the next afternoon, when, out of ammunition, its three survivors fixed bayonets and charged the LTTE positions. One man survived the debacle. Only later did the Indians discover that the LTTE had been listening in on their carelessly uncoded radio transmissions and had set a trap for them.[40]

Meanwhile, the main Indian advance on Jaffna had been reduced to a crawl on the roads, mainly because of mines and snipers. Initially, the Indian brigades had advanced in an advance-to-contact formation. But as the resistance increased along the approaches to Jaffna, they reverted to the slower fire-and-movement formation. At the same time, the IPKF, realizing that the LTTE had wired mines to the electric supply, cut off all power to Jaffna. The proposed three-day operation to take Jaffna had turned into a bloody battle. By day six the LTTE had stopped all the Indian brigades. The Ninety-first Brigade had halted at Inuval, the Seventy-second was stopped at Urumparai, and the 115th Brigade had halted north of Kopai North. The advancing Indian troops had suffered terribly. One of the hardest hit was the Fourth Battalion/Fifth Gurkhas, part of the Seventy-second Brigade. The battalion, like many before it, had been moved into Sri Lanka on the 11th and had been launched into action within hours. The commanders assigned the Gurkhas to follow the tanks into Jaffna University and to link up with the para-commandos, but enemy fire pinned them down. Within hours the battalion had lost three majors, including its battalion adjutant, Maj. N. D. Singh. An old Tamil woman shot dead one of the company commanders, Major Verghese (the only Tamil speaker in the unit), when he went into a house to comfort a group of panic-stricken civilians. The final blow came when the commandant, Lt. Col. I. B. S. Bawa, was shot and mortally wounded. It was days before the battalion was ready to fight with new officers flown in from India.[41] Finally realizing the scale and extent of the LTTE's strength and determination, the Indians began to rush in heavy weapons and armored vehicles. In round-the-clock sorties that eventually resulted in the partial collapse of Palaly's concrete airstrip, IAF IL-76s brought in artillery, BMPs, and even T-72s. The army's advancing columns urgently needed ammunition and supplies, which the IAF helicopter pilots delivered with great tenacity under heavy ground fire. Between 11 and 31 October the IAF flew 2,200 tactical transport and 800 assault helicopter sorties.[42] While the columns regrouped and reequipped, the commanders ordered the Forty-first Infantry Brigade into Pandittarippu on the Jaffna Peninsula on 17 October to reinforce the pressure on Jaffna. On the 19th the Indian advance resumed. The Eighteenth Brigade cleared Tellupillai, entered the outskirts of Jaffna, and engaged the

LTTE in hand-to-hand combat. The Seventy-second Brigade cleared Urum-parai and advanced on Kopai North. The 115th Brigade closed in on the Nullur temple complex, and the newly inducted Forty-first Brigade moved into Jaffna from the northwest. Meanwhile, in the city itself, Indian paracommandos from the Tenth Battalion and soldiers from the First Battalion Maratha Light Infantry moved out of the old Dutch fort and seized the town hall, the clock tower, the library, the theater, and the Ashok hotel. At the same time, artillery and naval ships shelled the causeway linking Jaffna Peninsula to Karaituvu Island to prevent the LTTE fighters from escaping. By the 22nd the Indian army had moved in with a pincer formation on the main LTTE defenses around the general hospital. On the 29th the IAF used its MI-25 attack helicopters for the first time when they delivered rockets and heavy machine gun fire to destroy a LTTE position in Chavackacheri, thus enabling the Eleventh and Twelfth Madras Battalions to complete a successful link-up.[43] The LTTE, surprised by the Indian army's willingness to smash its way into Jaffna despite heavy casualties to itself and the civilian population, began to launch desperate suicide missions. Volunteers strapped bombs onto themselves and then threw themselves at the advancing Indians, but to little avail; the inexorable Indian advance continued. For the first time the LTTE fighters, who had become used to conventional battles with the Sri Lankan security forces, found themselves forced to revert back to guerrilla tactics in the face of superior Indian firepower and tactics. That night Ajit Mahattaya, the LTTE Jaffna area commander, ordered his fighters to evacuate the city. Divesting themselves of their uniforms and arms, many fighters escaped the Indian cordon amidst the flow of refugees.

At a cost of 319 dead and 1,039 wounded, the Indian army had wrested control of Jaffna from the LTTE. The latter's casualties are unknown, but they were certainly heavy, as the LTTE fighters took on the Indians in conventional close-in urban combat right up until the withdrawal order. As a shocked IPKF assessed the situation, it quickly opened battle schools in Palaly and Trincomalee to brief newly arrived units. For the first time since the 1962 war with China, Indian troops had found an opponent that had superior close support weaponry. The LTTE's AK-47s outperformed the standard Indian Ishapore self-loading rifle (FN-FAL) in close combat amidst the streets and ruins of Jaffna. In desperation, RAW imported 70,000 AK-47s from Poland and flew them directly into Jaffna.[44] According to Lieutenant Colonel Katoch, commander of the First Paracommandos, many soldiers preferred to use captured AK-47s.[45] Furthermore, the LTTE had an abundance of grenade and rocket launchers, sniper rifles, mines, and mortars, which it used to devastating effect. Only toward the end of the Jaffna battle did the Indians rush in BMPS, T-72S, and 105 mm light field guns to tilt the firepower balance in their favor. Even then the LTTE mines posed a serious threat to the armored vehicles. Mines weighing up to 220 pounds could literally catapult 42-ton tanks into the air. Such a mine killed Col. D. S. Saraon, deputy commander of the Seventy-second Brigade, when it blew his BMP to bits, killing him and the entire crew.[46]

Although Operation Pawan centered around the seizure of Jaffna, two Indian brigades deployed in the eastern province of Trincomalee and Batticaloa sought to clear LTTE rebels from the area. Here the latter kept a lower profile and quickly reverted to guerrilla tactics rather than face the Indian army in the open. Their main weapon was the land mine, which caused the most casualties amongst the Indians. On 12 October twenty-one Indian soldiers died in Batticaloa when a remote-detonated mine blew up their truck. The main Indian actions consisted of massive cordon and search operations such as the one that 300 paracommandos conducted on the 19th in Batticaloa.

Indian operations resumed in the Jaffna Peninsula on 3 November as troops swept through the Mullai region, killing twenty-five LTTE rebels. Another operation on the 14th in the Vandramalai area killed fifteen Tiger rebels, including their commander, "Chandran." The LTTE, which had melted into the countryside, launched hit-and-run attacks, including frequent mortar attacks on the Indian camp at Kankesanthurai. On the 19th, in a well-planned publicity stunt, the LTTE high command released eighteen Indian POWs at Chavackacheri. The Indians responded with a cease-fire on 20–21 November, hoping that the Tigers would lay down their arms. LTTE attacks resumed on the 29th with vigor, and the IPKF replied with more sweep operations that unearthed supplies of arms and equipment in the Chavackacheri temple on 16 December. The Indian army launched an equally massive cordon and search operation in the eastern province. In a major operation on 5 November involving 2,000 troops and IAF helicopters, the Indians captured 150 LTTE men and two commanders. As the IPKF stepped up aggressive patrolling, several clashes occurred with LTTE groups in Batticaloa. The Fifty-seventh Mountain Division's massive house-to-house search of the town of Batticaloa and thirty surrounding villages in February–March 1988 resulted in ten dead rebels and forty captured. This operation and additional reverses caused the LTTE to evacuate Batticaloa. In preparation for the LTTE retreat the IPKF blockaded the Elephant Pass route to Jaffna. An IPKF ambush killed twenty guerrillas retreating south toward Amparai. As a result, most LTTE cadres retreated westward into the forests beyond Vavuniya.

By March 1988 the Indian buildup in northern Sri Lanka amounted to about 65,000 men, including army, navy, air force, and paramilitary forces.

Southern and central army commands had contributed six divisional head-quarters to the conflict. The logistical effort involved in transporting so many men and their equipment across the Palk Straits was immense. Almost all of the IAF's transport fleet participated in keeping up the air bridge, while the government pressed the state-owned Indian Airlines into a troop transport role. In addition, No. 19 Squadron's AN-32s, Nos. 109 and 119 Helicopter Units' MI-8s, and No. 125 Helicopter Unit's MI-25s also took part in the campaign. The Indian army's No. 664 Air Observation Post (AOP) Squadron, with Nos. 10, 26, and 31 Flights flying Chetaks and Cheetahs, and the Indian navy's No. 321 Squadron with Alizes supplemented these air elements.[47] The Indian navy, while primarily maintaining a naval blockade of Jaffna, also transported some heavy equipment. By May 1989 the IPKF strength had stabilized at 48,000 men.[48] Most of these units lacked their heavy equipment, including armor and artillery. However, the IPKF deployed the Sixty-fifth Armored Regiment with a few artillery regiments. In addition to these forces, the army deployed all three paracommando battalions, the First, Ninth, and Tenth, in Sri Lanka.[49]

Indian operations now concentrated on the Vavuniya jungles. In May 1988 Operation Checkmate located a massive LTTE hideout in the Wanni jungle to the west of Vavuniya. Forces used in this battle (mainly the Fourth Infantry Division) included the Forty-first Infantry Brigade from Vavuniya, the 167th Mountain Brigade from Mulaitivu/Vavuniya, the Seventh Infantry Brigade from Mulaitivu, the Ninety-third Field Regiment, and elements from the Sixty-fifth Armored Regiment (T-72). From 2 to 6 March 1989 the action shifted to the Nittikaikulam jungles northeast of Vavuniya. In March 1989 the IPKF's Operation Baaz was in full swing when two Gurkha companies on an in-depth reconnaissance from their base southeast of Alampil with forty-eight hours' worth of rations and munitions came under heavy fire in the Nayaru Lagoon area. Fighting continued through the night as it became obvious that the Gurkhas had stumbled upon a major Tiger base. After sending back for reinforcements and munitions, the commanding officer, Col. V. K. Bakshi, led his men into close combat with kukris, or curved short swords. By dawn Bakshi was mortally wounded, and the Gurkhas were confronting the LTTE along a 2.5-mile-long front. Soon five Indian battalions ringed the area. When the battle ended on the 7th the LTTE had lost seventy men. The IAF played a vital role in the Nayaru Lagoon action. No. 109 Helicopter Unit's MI-8s from Vavuniya and Palaly ferried in troops, ammunition, equipment, food, and supplies, while MI-24 gunships operating from China Bay in Trincomalee and from Vavuniya flew repeated sorties to support the infantry columns. The army used Chetak helicopters for AOP tasks and casualty evacuations, while it flew most casualties to base hospitals on MI-8s.[50] By the 9th an entire division was conducting "jungle-bashing" operations in the Nayaru Lagoon area.[51] Photographs published in 1989 in an Indian magazine showed that Nittikaikulam forests were the hideout for the LTTE leader, Prabhakaran, and many of his senior aides.[52] Intensive patrolling and repeated cordon and search operations, ranging from small infantry sections to multidivisional efforts like the one described above, became the daily routine for the 50,000-man IPKF force. The mission's success or failure usually lay in the level of training, tactical and operational ability, and innovativeness of individual units. Lieutenant General Sardeshpande, a former IPKF Jaffna area commander, recalled that most Indian casualties came about due to weaknesses in training and leadership.[53]

Although the army bore the brunt of the war effort, the Indian navy also played a significant role in the conflict. In addition to a coastal blockade, navy aircraft, including Alize ASW patrol aircraft, flew day and night to maintain a stranglehold on all LTTE marine activities. Between November 1987 and March 1988 the Alizes sank forty-seven LTTE boats, inflicting 264 casualties.[54] Naval commandos from the newly raised Indian Marine Special Forces (IMSF) unit (now the Marine Commando Force) carried out many raids on LTTE coastal positions. The IMSF was an all-volunteer force set up in February 1987 and modeled after the U.S. Navy SEALs. Two Indian naval officers who underwent the SEAL training program in the United States started the unit. Among the many successful missions conducted by the fledgling IMSF in Sri Lanka was a daring midnight operation on 21 October 1987 to destroy the heavily defended LTTE Guru Nagar jetty. Lt. Arvind Singh, who took part in the eighteen-man operation, was later awarded the Maha Vir Chakra (the "great bravery medal," the second highest combat decoration).[55]

Meanwhile in Columbo, a new president had been elected on 19 December 1988. President Ranasinghe Premadasa did not favor his predecessor's Indo–Sri Lankan Accord and made repeated calls for the IPKF's withdrawal. Soon after coming to power, Premadasa initiated talks with the LTTE and began to send arms to them, ostensibly to counter a Tamil police force, the Tamil National Army, that the Indians established in Jaffna.[56] With a new Sri Lankan government now cooperating closely with the LTTE and literally rescuing it from the brink of obliteration, the Indian government decided that the time had come to leave Sri Lanka.[57] On 18 September 1989 India and Sri Lanka signed a join communiqué declaring that all IPKF operations would come to a halt at 6:00 AM on 20 September 1989 and that India would withdraw all troops by 31 December 1989. After losing 1,150 dead and 2,984 wounded in a bloody two-and-a-half-year conflict, the last batch of over 2,000 IPKF soldiers left Sri Lanka on 24 March 1990.[58] While the pull-out came as a relief to the IPKF, one divisional commander believed that "the IPKF had inexhaustible man-power resources, no American type public hysteria over the dead or wounded and given time would have emerged on top. What it needed from its highest military and political hierarchy was a single-minded pursuit of it and orchestration of other actions alongside and in tune with military operations."[59]

Renewed Insurgency in Kashmir

Since 1989 the most pressing insurgency issue has been the reigniting of the Kashmir problem. Thanks to government mismanagement at the center and a corrupt state government, the long-standing tensions in the valley exploded into violence in mid-1989. Within two years insurgent groups based mainly in Pakistan-held Kashmir began violent campaigns against the Indian government and Hindu locals in Kashmir.[60] The army has always maintained a large presence on the line of control on the Kashmir border, and it immediately tried to seal off the border. However, the rugged terrain makes a complete seal-off, as in the Punjab, extremely difficult. Perhaps the most disturbing fact for the government is that unlike in 1947 and in 1965 the present insurgency in Kashmir is primarily homegrown.

The various separatist groups, however, receive substantial support from their bases in Pakistan. The latter denies aiding the guerrillas, but the sheer number of insurgents and the large supplies of sophisticated weaponry, organization, and training indicate some sort of Pakistani government involvement. A 1991 report to the U.S. Department of State noted that Pakistan's official involvement in this second round of infiltration (the first being in July–August 1965) was far from insignificant. The report noted that Pakistan supplied substantial political, diplomatic, and material support to the Kashmiri uprising and that the material support took various forms, including the training, indoctrination, arming, and cross-border movement of the infiltrating forces. Furthermore, the passing of Kashmiri Muslims across the line of control into Pakistan-controlled Kashmir and their covert reinfiltration following training in light arms and guerrilla tactics has played a very important role in maintaining the tempo of the insurgency. Finally, the report also pointed out that the support was planned and coordinated in large part by Pakistan's Inter-Services Intelligence Directorate (ISI) and that all this was carried out with the full knowledge and under the auspices of the Pakistan army.[61]

From 1990 on the insurgents have shown little hesitation in fighting against army units that tried to stop them from entering Indian Kashmir.[62] By May 1990 the army was seizing antipersonnel and antitank mines in addition to the usual haul of AK-47s, RPG-7s, and RPDs. The army's efforts to ensure tight border security, including random ID checks, have alienated the locals.[63] Perhaps in response to the crackdown on the Indian side and the more aggressive border patrolling of the Indian forces, the Pakistanis beefed up their own forces on the line of control. The resultant tension and the greatly increased incidents of cross-border firings and artillery duels led to a near state of war between the two sides. In April 1990 the Pakistani prime minister, Benazir Bhutto, speaking in Larkhana in Sind province, declared that Pakistan was embarking on a 1,000-year war to wrest Kashmir from India. Governor Shri Jagmohan's draconian measures with the support of paramilitary and army forces dissuaded Pakistan from launching another massive Operation Gibraltar–type infiltration scheme.[64] On 5 July 1990 the government placed the state under emergency rule, which brought into effect many statutes, including the Terrorist and Disruptive Activities Prevention Act, the Armed Forces Special Powers Act, and the Public Safety Act, that gave the security forces and the army in particular substantial immunity from prosecution.

In May 1991 the Indian government stated that it had information about thirty-eight training centers for militants in Pakistan-occupied Kashmir and another forty-two in different parts of Pakistan. The statement went on to note that an estimated 4,000–5,000 militants had crossed the border for training.[65] Throughout the early 1990s the Indian government blanketed the state with army and paramilitary personnel and waged a relentless battle against the insurgents. In 1993 Pakistani Military Intelligence estimated that the Indian army had 300,000–400,000 troops deployed in Kashmir, although third-country observers put the figure at 150,000. In the same year the army had one of its five regional commands (the Northern Command), two of its ten corps (the Fifteenth and Sixteenth), and seven of its thirty infantry divisions deployed in Jammu and Kashmir.[66]

By the mid-1990s the fighting in the valley itself had become very intense, with government personnel only being able to venture out in large armed convoys. Although the situation shows little sign of easing in the near future, the security forces are gaining the upper hand, and morale remains high, partly because the army has controlled all aspects of this latest campaign against the insurgents. However, the successes of the security forces have also resulted in tremendous human rights violations in Kashmir, bringing them under unprecedented worldwide scrutiny.[67]

By 1994 the renewed Kashmiri insurgency had become the most intensive and violent uprising the Indian security forces had to combat since independence. As local support for the militants grew and as the security forces applied intense pressure on groups that operated in the countryside, the insurgents began to move into the cities and towns. Although the army continues to play a crucial role in the conflict, particularly in the countryside and on the line of control, that year the BSF deployed 45 of its 148 battalions in Kashmir.[68] Of this number, it deployed fourteen battalions in Srinagar. The locals often accused the BSF soldiers, who operate twenty-four hours a day, often from small bunkers amidst a hostile population, of human rights abuses. Despite the negative publicity, the BSF managed to secure areas that the insurgent groups had previously "liberated." Their most successful tactic was repeated cordon and search operations, carried out between 3:00 and 4:00 AM, to flush out the guerrillas. Most of the BSF's casualties resulted from hand-grenade attacks and explosive devices.[69]

In 1993 the army implemented a counterinsurgency doctrine in Kashmir that was based on the army's long experience in the northeast and Sri Lanka. The centerpiece of the doctrine is the grid system. In Jammu and Kashmir the grid consists of forty-nine sectors. The army placed security force units in each grid area to dominate it. Each grid also has a Quick Reaction Team ready to react instantly to an ambush or large-scale confrontation. The second part of the doctrine established a dedicated, locally recruited counterinsurgency force such as the Assam Rifles to bolster and eventually replace the army in counterinsurgency roles. In response the army formed the Rashtriya Rifles.[70] The rapid expansion and maturation of the Rashtriya Rifles, the involvement of Special Forces units from the National Security Group and the Marine Commando Force, and the rebuilding of an effective intelligence network have resulted in the dramatic attrition of the insurgent forces. The army claimed that by 1997 militants were being picked off at will.[71]

The increased counterinsurgency activities and the vigil against infiltrators have created a warlike situation along the line of control. By 1998 regular artillery duels occurred between Indian and Pakistani gunners across the line of control.[72] Lt. Gen. Krishen Pal, commander of the Fifteenth Corps (headquartered in Srinagar), stated that the Pakistani reaction was a desperate attempt to avert the destruction of the terrorist forces in the valley.[73] Significantly, Pakistani-based insurgents started to operate in the Jammu region. From April 1998 onward the insurgents have been active in Rajouri, Poonch, and Udhampur, areas previously unaffected by the insurgents. In response the security forces stepped up counterinsurgency operations in the area and set up local Village Defense Committees, consisting of armed and trained villagers to confront the insurgents.[74] The ISI-trained insurgents also used the latest "burst" and frequency-hopping high frequency radio gear to communicate with their handlers in Karachi and Kabul and ISI-developed matrix codes for communication. Monitoring, deciphering, and locating signal sources represented a major challenge to the army's Signals Intelligence Units. In 1998 400 calling stations existed in the Kashmir valley alone. Since the army's electronic equipment was largely obsolete by comparison, the government instituted an action plan to provide state-of-the-art direction finders and interception equipment to the counterinsurgency forces in the state.[75]

In December 1998, with almost half a million troops and security force personnel engaged in round-the-clock counterinsurgency operations, the army chief, General Malik, declared that militancy in Jammu and Kashmir had been reduced to a trickle despite the intense efforts of Pakistan's ISI to push more militants into the region. Malik noted that many Kashmiri locals were, for the first time, coming forward to help the army nab foreign mercenaries. He noted that "the cycle of militancy is over now and it is happy time in the Valley again. Now the Army, besides fighting insurgency is helping the civil administration in organizing medical camps, education trips for students and also make the public aware of the menace of militancy."[76] In 1999 the army's socioeconomic role in stymieing the insurgency was codenamed Operation Sadhbhavna (an extension of an earlier operation codenamed Goodwill). According to Lt. Colonel Anandan of Military Intelligence, the role of the psychological operations was to "win the hearts and minds of the people[,] . . . create confusion among the militants[,] . . . and push fence sitters among the locals against the militants."[77] The army believes it has been helped in its efforts by the large numbers of foreign militants, who are increasingly unpopular among the locals for preying upon their women and introducing drugs to the area. However, in the wake of the Kargil confrontation (see below) the insurgents launched a number of spectacular suicide attacks against paramilitary and army posts in the valley, indicating that the militants are willing to continue the fight despite heavy losses.

The Siachen Glacier

When the United Nations Commission on India and Pakistan delineated the cease-fire line between Indian and Pakistani Kashmir in 1949, it stopped its work 40 miles short of the northern border with Kashmir. The Karakoram Range and the rugged mountainous Siachen Glacier dominate this area. The Siachen Glacier is 47 miles long and 1–5 miles wide, the longest glacier outside the polar regions. Since 1949 the region has become a source of dispute between India and Pakistan. India claims that the language of the commission's document implies that a tacit extension of the boundary exists all the way up to the Chinese border. Pakistan rejects this, noting that the 1949 delimitation agreement contained no reference to the boundary's extension beyond NJ-9842.[78] This disputed border region was never contested during either the 1965 or the 1971 war and remained on the back burner until the mid-1980s.

On the Indian side the military became concerned about the region in 1978 when the director of military operations, Gen. M. L. Chibber, received information that German mountaineers had been climbing in the Karakoram Range from the Pakistani side and that an American tourist map showed the 1,500 square miles of territory surrounding the Siachen Glacier as belonging to Pakistani Kashmir. At General Chibber's urging, Gen. T. N. Raina, the chief of army staff, authorized an operational reconnaissance patrol into Siachen. The army expedition did not discover any Pakistani presence, but it did find debris left behind by Japanese climbers. The Indians now began to send in their own tourist groups, with much fanfare.[79]

In 1983 the Indian authorities concluded that Pakistan was planning to mount a major operation to seize the region. Indian intelligence reported that a column of two companies supported by mortars was on the move in September–October 1983 to occupy the passes of the Saltoro Range. Further intelligence reports that stated that Pakistan was trying to buy large quantities of special snow equipment from Europe for its troops confirmed Indian fears. Pakistan had also launched a special training program for a unit called the Burzil Force to occupy the glacier. The Indians decided to preempt the Pakistanis with Operation Meghdoot, a heli-lift operation involving a battalion of Kumaon infantry. On 13 April 1984 the Indian air force flew a platoon into the Bilafond La Pass. On the 17th, following a suspension of the operations due to a blizzard, it flew a platoon into the Sia La Pass. With this daring move the Indians bought a week's worth of time to consolidate their positions before Pakistan's Burzil Force could reach the passes. The Indians sighted the first Pakistani troops near Bilafond La on the 24th. The next day these Pakistani forces opened fire on the Indian positions and then withdrew when the Indians retaliated. The Burzil Force then probed along the remaining Saltoro Range routes into the Siachen Glacier, and the Indians opposed it. The end result was that India now holds a dominating position over a length of almost 50 miles on the Saltoro Range, effectively controlling the Siachen Glacier.[80]

Since the initial buildup the two sides have been engaged in a high altitude conflict of varying intensity. The Indians note that the Pakistanis made

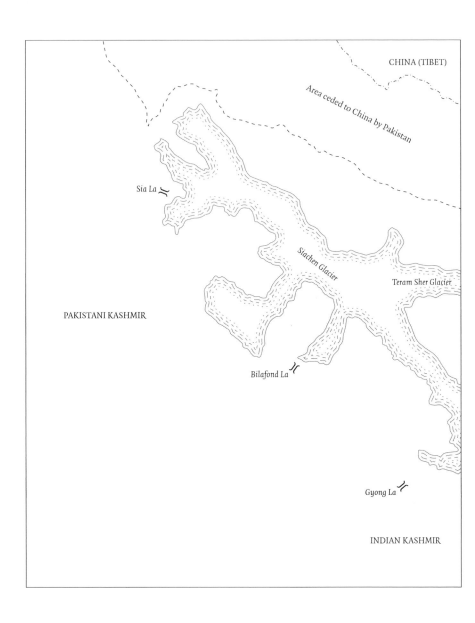

CHINA (TIBET)

Area ceded to China by Pakistan

Sia La

Siachen Glacier

Teram Sher Glacier

PAKISTANI KASHMIR

Bilafond La

Gyong La

INDIAN KASHMIR

Siachen Glacier area

an attempt in June 1984 to take Bilafond La and another attempt in February 1985 to capture the heights overlooking Sia La; both attempts failed. The nature of the terrain and the tremendous logistical difficulties mean that it is almost impossible to dislodge a strongly defended position. The only exception has been the Eighth J&K Light Infantry's capture of the Pakistani Qaid Observation Post in June 1987. After their failure to take Bilafond La in 1984 the Pakistanis established Qaid Post during the winter of 1986–87. The small post, located at a height of 21,600 feet, dominates the entire Indian complex at Bilafond La.

Artillery has proved to be the most effective weapon that either side has used in this conflict. Any movement that the artillery spotters can see on the opposing side is often brought under accurate and devastating fire. As both sides consolidated their gains, they correspondingly improved their firepower and spotting capabilities. In 1987, for example, Indians using night vision goggles spotted a Pakistani resupply team moving forward in the Gyong Sector at night to resupply camps at a height of 19,000 feet. In the ensuing artillery strike the Indians killed seven and wounded fifteen.[81] Artillery has also played a crucial role in the numerous offensive-defensive battles fought for the many heights on the Saltoro Range. The battle for Qaid Observation Post is a good example. The Pakistani army manned the post with eight men from Pakistan's elite Special Service Group (SSG) commando unit on a plateau not more than 50 feet in radius. Indian attempts to scale the slopes to the post began on the night of 23–24 June 1987 and only succeeded on the morning of the 27th, when artillery had all but wiped out the defenders.[82]

Pakistani retaliation for the loss of Qaid was substantial. In September an SSG battalion launched an all-out attack to take the Indian posts Sohrab and Ashoka (Pakistan names them Rana and Akbar), which dominate Bilafond La Pass. In preparation, Pakistani artillery pounded the Indian positions in the days preceding the attack. The Indians, expecting an attack on Qaid Post (now called Bana Post after Subedar Bana Singh, who captured it), developed artillery fire to cover all approaches. In the meantime, Pakistani artillery fire was falling at a rate of 3,000–4,000 shells per day on the Indian positions. The Third Battalion/Fourth Gurkhas, who had been inducted into the area to take up garrisoning duties, lost seven men between the 19th and the 23rd. The Pakistani assault on Sohrab and Ashoka began at 6:00 PM on 22 September 1987 with TOW antitank guided missile fire. Individual twelve-man teams under SSG captains began to scale the slopes. After Indian defensive fire checked their initial advance, the SSG assault teams regrouped at the foot of the Indian positions. On the 23rd the commander of the Third Battalion/Fourth Gurkha Rifles, Maj. Krishna Gopal Chatterjee, led a thirty-five-man relief platoon up to Sohrab Post. When the men reached the post they spotted SSG commandos less than a mile below climbing to the post. Chatterjee called in artillery fire and began to fire his own rockets (probably Carl Gustaf 84 mm RCLS). At 8:00 PM the Pakistanis attacked Ashoka Post, and the Indians finally beat them back with air defense gun (probably 23 mm) fire. On the 24th the attack resumed. A TOW missile destroyed a bunker on top of Ashoka Post, but the Indians continued to resist. Despite heavy losses, the SSG teams closed in once again at 12:30 AM on the Indian positions, and a desperate close combat began with guns and grenades. As the Gurkhas stood up in their trenches to fire down on the attackers, SSG snipers picked them off. A third attack came at 1:30 AM with the Pakistanis closing in to 55 yards. At least one Pakistani soldier made it to the post only to be killed by a blow from a kukri. Finally, Major Chatterjee called down "SOS fire" directly on the Indian position. The result was a hail of air-burst shells that finally eliminated the bulk of the SSG attackers. The Indians claim to have suffered 23 dead and 27 injured while inflicting some 150 casualties on the Pakistanis.[83]

The Pakistani attempts to seize Sohrab and Ashoka are the last known major offensive actions to be mounted by either side. Although smaller actions have been fought for other posts and peaks along the range, the conflict has essentially stalemated to an exchange of artillery and small arms fire. Despite these constant clashes, most Indian casualties on the glacier have come about due to natural causes. Many soldiers succumb to high altitude pulmonary edema, which fills the victim's lungs with fluid. Others are lost to hidden crevasses, blizzards, and avalanches. In 1991 an avalanche triggered by the vibrations of a helicopter almost wiped out Bana Post. Temperatures on the high posts are extreme, and minus 45 degrees Fahrenheit is standard. Windchill factors of up to 3,000 are common, and a recording was once made of 4,000. At a windchill factor of 1,400 any exposed flesh will freeze within minutes. With the exception of rum and kerosene, everything freezes and has to be thawed out. Contact with metal on exposed flesh results in the skin being peeled off. On an average day at least one soldier is evacuated from the glacier. The High Altitude Medical Research Center treated 450 high altitude pulmonary edema cases in three years, a world record. In 1989 Indian officials admitted that during the first few years of the conflict noncombat casualties accounted for almost 80 percent of total attrition. In the 1990s this figure had risen to 97 percent as both sides ceased major offensive activity.

Before being inducted into the high altitude posts, soldiers undergo a brief period of training and acclimatization at the Siachen battle school located in the base camp (12,000 feet) on the banks of the often frozen Nubra River. Instructors from the high altitude warfare school at Gulmarg run the program. Here "green" inductees not only get acclimatized to the high altitude but also learn about the lay of the land and become accustomed to working in the bulky clothing they will have to wear for the next three months. Only when the soldiers have become experts at tying knots, fixing ropes to ice walls, making ice caves, scrambling over vertical walls, and traversing crevasses will they be trained to use special weapons such as the Russian Dragunov 7.62 mm sniper rifle and the AGS grenade launcher, both weapons chosen no doubt for their excellent winter performance record. From base camp the soldiers make a four-day trip to the supply camp at Kumar (16,000 feet). Before doing so they take a ceremonial last bath and shave, knowing they cannot partake of this luxury for the next six months. Then, loaded with rucksack, sleeping bag, and the all-important kerosene stove (which keeps them warm and melts snow for water), they begin the trek to Kumar.[84] From this post the soldiers make the final ascent to the forward positions deployed along the Saltoro Ridge. Space in these posts is at a premium, as the post is sometimes too small to install the standard issue fiberglass huts. At Billa Top (18,600 feet), a post perched at the junction of the Bilafond La Glacier and the Lolofond Glacier, the soldiers have the luxury of a width of half a mile. But in winter the fiberglass huts are buried under snow, and the soldiers have to crawl through a 15-foot-long tunnel to get in and out. At the Bana Post space is so limited that to prevent contaminating the snow around the post, which serves as the drinking water supply, the soldiers have to hold a rope and lean over the cliff sides to defecate. Unlike most Western armies, Indian troops cook their food, even under the most arduous combat conditions. On the glaciers, cooking the staple food of lentils and rice takes hours because of the rarefied atmosphere.

Groups of about ten men take supplies to the posts, each carrying about 22 pounds and moving by starlight along a marker-dotted path to avoid detection by Pakistani observers. High altitude means that after every five steps in the knee-deep snow most men have to stop to catch their breath. However, two posts, including Amar (at 20,500 feet), rely completely on Cheetah helicopters for their supplies. All told, the Indians have about 2,000 men all along the actual ground position line. The helicopters (MI-17s and Cheetahs) that maintain the supply and transportation lines also struggle to stay in the air. Because of the high altitudes they can carry only one fourth their normal payload. On a regular day with good weather the base camp logs in about seventy helicopter takeoffs and landings, making it one of the busiest helipads in the country. In addition to their transport and evacuation role, the army's AOP Corps's Cheetahs also fly as high as 25,000–26,000 feet for a "shoot" – designating targets for the artillery. So arduous is the tour of duty on Siachen that Indian soldiers returning from the three-month stint receive a new ribbon – the coveted "glacier pin."[85]

On the Pakistani side the same conditions prevail, as attested to by Jean-Jacques Cécile, a French correspondent for the Paris-based RAIDS military enthusiast magazine. (He is one of the few qualified foreign military observers ever to be allowed into the area.) In 1995 the bulk of the forces for Pakistan's glacier force came from the 323rd Brigade, based at Dhansam. The 102nd Brigade, based at Pratapur, some 62 miles from the glacier, has set up a base camp and a glacier warfare school at the foot of the glacier. The Pakistanis have deployed their men along 200–300 strong points along the confrontation line. Although the Indians control most of the high ground, the Pakistanis boast the world's highest garrison, the soldiers who occupy Conway's Saddle, a rocky outcrop in the northern region of the glacier. Cécile also noted that the military situation was deadlocked and that, "badly demoralized after losing so many men for practically no territorial gains, the Pakistanis have given up hope of flushing out the Indians, and are contenting themselves with simply holding their ground."[86]

In the meantime, talks have been going on between the two sides to try and settle the conflict. Between January 1986 and June 1989 India and Pakistan held five rounds of talks on the Siachen Glacier. These talks failed, as did a military commanders conference held in Delhi on 9–10 July 1990. The outbreak of a new Kashmiri insurgency and the renewed tension between India and Pakistan have meant that both sides remain dug in along the glacial heights.

The Battle for National Highway 1A: The Kargil War

In November 1998 Pakistani Northern Light Infantry Regiment soldiers infiltrated across the 11,483-foot-high mountain passes along the line of control to occupy high ridges in Batalik, Kaksar, Dras, and the Mushkoh valley.[87] The intrusions would enable the Pakistanis to dominate and control the Srinagar to Leh Highway 1A. According to the Indian army, the Pakistani incursions into the Kargil sector were a desperate attempt to internationalize the Kashmir issue in the wake of the collapsing ISI-backed militancy in Jammu and Kashmir. The operation was the brainchild of the Pakistani chief of army staff, Gen. Pervez Musharraf, and his chief of general staff, Lt. Gen. Mohammed Aziz. To support its claims, the Indian army released intercepts of telephone conversations between Generals Musharraf and Aziz while Musharraf was visiting Beijing.[88] Ghulam Hasnain, a *Time Magazine* reporter who covered the conflict at its most intense phase from the Pakistani side, reported that early in the operation Pakistani Northern Infantry troops crossed the line of control without weapons to prevent arousing suspicions among the local Pakistanis. Their job was to build bunkers along the four ridge lines in Batalik, Kaskar, Dras, and the Mushkoh valley. On one of the ridges (9,842 feet high) overlooking the town of Kargil, the Pakistanis placed a Chinese-made 57 mm anti-aircraft gun in a cave protected by steel girders and concrete to shell Indian troop convoys on National Highway IA.[89] The Pakistani infiltration was possible during the winter because the Indian army abandoned its forward positions during harsh winter months and remanned them in the summer when the Zoji La Pass, the only mountain pass connecting Kargil to the Kashmir valley, opened. The Pakistanis estimated that they would have until the end of May 1999 or even early July, but the pass was opened in early May, leading to a confrontation earlier than the Pakistanis expected.

Indian army intelligence indicated that the four areas of infiltration were the responsibility of four Pakistani Northern Infantry Battalions: the Fourth, located in Gilgit; the Sixth (previously the Sixty-second Brigade), located in Skardu; the Fifth (previously the Eighty-second Infantry Brigade), located in Minimarg; and the Third, located in Dhansam. Two companies of SSG commandos were allotted in smaller teams of thirty-four to ninety-four among the four battalions. All twenty batteries of the Pakistani army's artillery in the area would provide fire support to the intruding forces.[90]

The Pakistanis completely surprised the Indian army. The Indians first detected the infiltrators on 14 May 1999, when the Pakistanis ambushed routine patrols, causing heavy casualties. In response the Indians sent in more patrols, only to face a similar fate. Only when reconnaissance flights overflew the area on 21 May did the Indian army realize that the Pakistani-backed "intruders" were some 300–400 in number entrenched on 14,000–16,000-foot-high ridges. The chief of army staff, General Malik, on a trip to Czechoslovakia returned to India and flew to Kargil to receive an on-the-spot assessment.[91] Conceding that it had suffered a major intelligence failure, the army began a massive troop buildup to eject the intruders, who it now assessed were Pakistani regulars.[92] With the intruders deeply entrenched, the army requested air support. The Cabinet Committee on Security initially denied this request. However, Malik invited Air Chief Marshal Tipnis to join him in the operations room at army headquarters on the 24th. Tipnis was convinced of the gravity of the situation, and on the 25th the army and air force chiefs made a successful joint appeal to the committee for air support.[93] On 26 May IAF MI-17 gunships and MiG-21 and MiG-27 fighters launched six sorties against the Pakistani intruders.[94] On the 27th the IAF lost a MiG-21 to engine failure, and the Pakistanis captured the pilot, Flight Lieutenant Nachiketa,

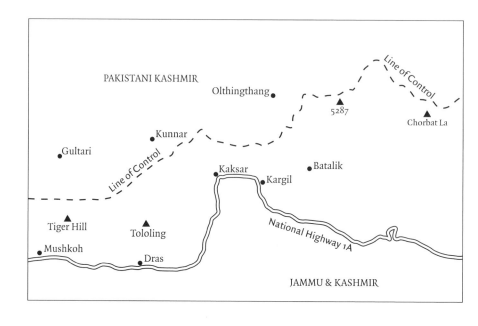

Kargil conflict 1999

after he ejected. Using a surface-to-air missile, the Pakistanis shot down a second Indian fighter, a MiG-27 attempting to locate the downed pilot, and they shot dead its pilot, Squadron Leader Ahuja, on the ground.[95] On the 28th the IAF lost an MI-17 helicopter with all of its crew.

On the ground, direct assaults against the well-entrenched Pakistanis resulted in heavy Indian casualties, prompting the army's additional director general of military operations, Maj. Gen. J. J. Singh, to state a change in army tactics. Henceforth, the army planned to "hold them [the Pakistanis] from the front and isolate them from the rear (the Pakistani side of the LOC) and then roll up their positions one by one."[96] The operation, now named Vijay (victory), led to a gradual troop buildup. By the first week of June almost 25,000 additional troops had been massed to evict the intruders.[97] On 10 and 11 June the Desert Scorpions Paracommando Unit advanced on Point 5203, a commanding position along the Yardol Ridge in the Batalik subsector. The seventy-five paracommandos took ten days to encircle the Pakistani bunkers on the peak and then seized it in a surprise assault on the night of 23 June with support from the Ladakh Scouts, which thwarted a Pakistani attempt to cut off the Siachen sector.[98] The Indians repulsed Pakistani counterattacks after a major battle resulting in fifteen dead on the Indian side and twenty-three dead on the Pakistani side.[99] Earlier, on 31 May, thirty soldiers of the Ladakh Scouts, under the leadership of Maj. Sonam Wangchuk, captured a vital mountain ridge in the Chorbat La subsector near Batalik, giving the Indian army a foothold for future operations and cutting off a major infiltration route for the Pakistanis.[100] On 13 June the army achieved its first major success when troops from the Second Rajputana Rifles captured Tololing Peak, which dominates the Dras sector.[101] A massive artillery strike involving all the guns in the Dras sector, including the formidable Bofors FH-77B 155 mm guns, preceded the attack.[102] The next day, the Second Rajputana and Ninth Grenadiers captured Point 4590, the nearest point that overlooked National Highway IA. The forces suffered seventeen killed and forty injured in the process, the highest casualty numbers incurred in a single battle. Pakistani positions remained strong in the Kaksar, Mushkoh valley, Batalik, Chorbat La, and Turtok areas. On 28 June companies from the Maratha Light Infantry and Dogra Regiment seized Point 4700.[103] A few days later Point 5100 (the Knoll, Three Pimples, and Lone Hill) fell. These advances in the Dras subsector paved the way for an assault on the imposing Tiger Hill, which dominates the area.[104] Based on the documents found on the bodies of the Pakistani fighters, the Indian army determined that troops from Pakistan's Second, Third, Fourth, Fifth, Sixth, Seventh, and Twelfth Northern Light Infantry Regiments took part in the operation.[105] Naik Inayat

Ali, a soldier of the Fifth Northern Light Infantry captured on the Batalik heights on 2 July, verified this. Inayat Ali stated that relentless Indian air and artillery fire wiped out his unit of 200 men.[106]

As the Indian army operations gathered momentum, the IAF conducted day and night air assaults on Pakistani positions, with the most successful wiping out a Pakistani supply base in Muntho Dalo southwest of Kaksar. A subsequent army sweep of the area recovered the bodies of thirteen dead Pakistanis.[107] On 4 July the Indian army gained its most significant victory when it captured the imposing 16,500-foot-high Tiger Hill in Dras with a loss of only five killed and ten wounded. Preparation for the attack began as early as 24 June, with IAF strikes on the Pakistani positions with laser-guided bombs.[108] The Eighteenth Grenadiers cleared the position after an eleven-hour operation that was preceded by an intense artillery strike involving some 140 guns.[109] As a result of its relentless "accurate and devastating fire," the army chief awarded a unit citation to the 108th Medium Regiment.[110] An intense operation to take Point 4875, Point 4927, and Point 5287 in Batalik and Dras followed the seizure of Tiger Hill. For the first time Pakistani forces launched counterattacks to regain the lost positions. According to Indian army sources, ninety-two Pakistani and thirty-eight Indian soldiers fell during the fighting.[111] The IAF continued close support and attack operations with a flight of eight MiG-23BMs and MiG-27s bombing Pakistani supply camps and positions in the Dras sector.[112] All told, the IAF flew 550 strike missions, 150 reconnaissance missions, and 500 fighter escort flights. Furthermore, it flew 2,185 helicopter sorties in 925 flying hours for casualty evacuations and logistical support.[113]

On 11 July 1999 the Pakistani foreign minister, Sartaj Aziz, announced that the Indian and Pakistani directors general of military operations had agreed on a sector-by-sector cease-fire to end the hostilities along National Highway 1A. Pakistan would withdraw the intruding forces.[114] Operation Vijay cost the Indian army 333 dead (including 25 officers), 520 wounded, and 15 missing in action, including 2 officers.[115] Pakistani casualties remained unclear (the Indian army estimated them at 679 dead, including 30 officers), and the Pakistani army continued to insist that the intruders were *mujahedeen*, or freedom fighters.[116] However, the Indian army claimed to have identified the bodies of thirty Pakistani officers, including a brigadier (Nusrat Sial of the Sixty-second Pakistani Infantry Brigade), and thirty-eight soldiers.[117] The scale of the Pakistani army's involvement in the conflict became clearer on 14 August, when President Rafiq Tarar announced the Operational Awards for "conspicuous courage and supreme sacrifice made for the honor of Pakistan." The list included ninety-seven men, including thirty-nine officers, and seventy of the awards were posthumous. Most soldiers came from the Northern Light Infantry, but officers and men from the Punjab Regiment, Frontier Force Rifles, Baluch Regiment, Sindh Regiment, and various support arms were also involved.[118]

The Kargil operations had repercussions in both Pakistan and India. In Pakistan the prime minister's decision to withdraw from the heights did not enjoy popular support. The army especially made clear its displeasure.[119] As relations between the current army chief, Gen. Parveez Musharaaf, and Prime Minister Nawaz Sharif deteriorated, the prime minister attempted to fire the army chief, only to be overthrown in a military coup in October. On the Indian side, after some initial embarrassment Prime Minister Atal Behari Vajpayee's Bharahija Janata Party (BJP), or National People's Party, government garnered much public support for the Indian army's successes. Although the BJP coalition was removed from office after failing a no-confidence vote in Parliament, the BJP once again returned to power after general elections in September–October 1999.

The political repercussions for the Indian army, however, have yet to be determined. In August 1999 the government announced the formation of a committee of inquiry to probe into the military handling of the Kargil crisis.[120] However, the controversy over the failure to react to the early intelligence and signs of Pakistani intrusions has spilled over into the press. The two main protagonists are Maj. Gen. V. S. Budhwar, commander of the Leh-based Third Infantry Division, and his subordinate, Brig. Surinder Singh, commander of the 121st Infantry Brigade in Kargil. Surinder Singh, who had initially commanded operations, was removed on 6 June. The brigadier, claiming he was a scapegoat for inaction on the part of Major General Budhwar, released to the press a communication sent by him to Third Division headquarters on 1 September 1998 outlining substantial infiltration activity in the region.[121] Major General Budhwar responded with his own press interview, rejecting the brigadier's claims and stating that "Singh was removed for his inept conduct."[122] Although the number of press interviews and judicial filings carried out by aggrieved armed forces officers increased dramatically in the 1990s, the Budhwar-Singh imbroglio is unprecedented. For the first time, senior army officers publicly aired their grievances, revealing details of military activities soon after a military confrontation. The "press war" reveals, among other issues, a serious lapse in communication within the military chain of command. It also reflects the growing ability of a bolder and more enterprising Indian news media and the new communication technologies in breaking down the hitherto unassailable walls of secrecy surrounding military high command in India.

In operational terms, the Kargil conflict has reinforced and perhaps even refocused the army's traditional expertise in positional warfare with an emphasis on artillery and infantry formations. In September 1999 press reports noted that the Indian army would establish a new corps, the Fourteenth, comprising the Third Infantry Division based in Leh and the Eighth Mountain Division based in Nimu. In addition to managing the 87 miles of the line of control in the Kargil sector and the disputed Siachen Glacier, the corps is also responsible for security along the disputed border with China. The new corps takes considerable pressure off the Fifteenth Corps based in Srinagar, which previously oversaw the entire Kashmir operational area. To make up for the permanent redeployment of the Eighth Mountain Division, the army raised a new infantry division to take the division's place in Sharifabad, Kashmir, where it had been heavily involved in counterinsurgency operations.[123] Equally significant has been the army's reappraisal of its artillery doctrines. Prior to the Kargil conflict, the army placed great emphasis on the acquisition of tracked self-propelled 155 mm howitzers for its mechanized formations. In the aftermath of the Kargil War the army's Field Artillery Rationalization Plan called for the replacement of the fourteen different calibers it uses currently with 155 mm/52 caliber weapons. Furthermore, the army is now more interested in wheeled 155 mm self-propelled guns, which have better strategic mobility and offer highly mobile shoot-and-move capability.

Kashmir continues to present the Indian armed forces with differing and challenging conventional and unconventional war scenarios, and as this book goes to press it is undoubtedly the most dangerous flashpoint for war in the subcontinent.

Part Six

CHAPTER 13

The Evolution of a Regional Military Power

Following the 1971 war India enjoyed relative political and economic stability. The exception was the late 1970s, when the beleaguered prime minister, Indira Gandhi, declared emergency rule. The first-ever rejection of the Congress Party by the Indian electorate and the election of the Bharatiya Janata Party (BJP), which controlled the government from 1977 to 1979, followed this action. Indira Gandhi returned to power in 1980, and the Congress (I) Party essentially governed the country until the general election in May 1996. During this time the Indian economy grew at a modest rate, although in the post-1990 era the last Congress (I) government's radical economic liberalization policies opened the floodgates of economic growth.

For the military this has meant that although modernization and expansion programs have evolved slowly, the steady economic growth has resulted in many of the seemingly ambitious goals set in the 1940s finally coming to fruition. These goals have been achieved despite the outlay for defense hovering at around 3.5 percent of the GNP. However, because the Indian economy has grown at an average rate of 5 percent of the GNP since 1979 and 9 percent since 1988, the amounts allocated to defense since 1979 are far greater than in the 1960s and 1970s. Taking inflation into account, there was a 27.3 percent increase in defense allocations in 1985–86 and a 21.1 percent increase in 1986–87.[1] Indian defense expenditure peaked in 1987–90, reaching $8.5 billion, or roughly 5.5 percent of the GNP. The defense budget increases were mainly due to the economic success that India enjoyed in the mid-1980s, with low inflation being supplemented by a 5 percent rate of growth in the GNP. A steady increase in the GDP also offset defense-spending increases.[2]

By the early 1990s a severe budget problem had developed as India's foreign exchange reserves plummeted. Although defense spending was only 4 percent of the GNP, it had to be reduced to about 2.5 percent. In fiscal year 1991–92 the defense budget increased by about 7 percent but actually fell in real terms, given the 17 percent inflation rate and the devaluation of the Indian rupee.[3] The problems appeared as early as 1988, when the government cleared the Seventh Defense Plan late that year; however, this was the plan's fourth year with little if any funds to pay for it. The budgetary cuts had reduced the army to near bankruptcy, with no funds to pay salaries for almost three months.[4] So precarious was India's financial situation that critics of the Narasimha Rao government alleged that it showed the World Bank a draft of the Eighth Five-Year Plan in mid-1992 (presumably to get loan approvals) before the Indian Parliament could debate it. By the mid-1990s, however, the economic liberalization policies of the Narasimha Rao government began to bear fruit. A reinvigorated foreign exchange reserve and the influx of foreign investment enabled an increase in defense spending. In 2001, according to the World Bank's world development indicators, India was the world's fourth largest economy after the United States, China, and Japan.[5]

All three armed services have benefited from the increased levels of defense spending over the decades. The distribution of the defense budget between the services approximates to 70 percent for the army, 20 percent for the air force, and 10 percent for the navy. Since the late 1970s, however, the distribution ratio has altered in favor of the air force and the navy at the army's expense.[6] In 1970–71, for example, the army received 74 percent of the defense budget, but by 1980–81 it received only 66 percent. During the same period the capital allocation for the army also saw a drop, from 51 percent to 36 percent. To make matters worse, manpower costs (pay and pensions) absorbed an increasingly large portion of the army's budget.[7] The 1995 defense budget amounted to Rs 255 billion ($8.1 billion), a real increase of about 6 percent over the 1994 budget (Rs 235 billion, or $7.5 billion). By this time, however, the army's budget had fallen 50 percent (Rs 125 billion), the air force budget stood at 16.3 percent (Rs 41 billion), while the navy got 12 percent (Rs 15 billion). The largest part of the procurement budget (part of the capital outlay) was spent on aircraft and aero-engines ($820 million). The navy received $330 million in 1994 for its procurement, or capital outlay. These figures represent a substantial increase from previous years. According to the U.S. Arms Control and Disarmament Agency, India's weapons imports declined from a high of $4.3 billion in 1988 to $2 billion in 1990, to $615 million in 1991, and to an all-time low of only $10 million in 1993.[8] The projected defense budget for the fiscal year 1996–97 called for an increase of 9 percent to Rs 278.19 billion, or $8 billion. This figure, however, represented a drop in real terms as a result of inflation and the rupee's decline in the international market. The army received an increase of 4.3 percent, while the navy budget increased by 1.7 percent plus an additional 0.9 percent increase to replace its aging fleet. The air force, on the other hand, saw its budget drop 5.4 percent. However, specific air force funding for new aircraft and aero-engines increased by 35.3 percent to Rs 26.55 billion, mainly to pay for fifteen to twenty Sukhoi SU-30 fighters. The budget for armed forces pensions maintained its ominous upward spiral, with an increase of 3.2 percent to Rs 33 billion.[9] The actual spending figures for 1996–97 turned out to be Rs 294.98 billion.[10] The 1997–98 defense budget, however, saw a substantial increase to Rs 360.99 billion (revised estimate). A substantial portion of the 20.75 percent increase, Rs 36.2 billion, went toward meeting the obligations of the Fifth Pay Commission. Major defense projects included importing two submarines, the indigenous construction of another two, and the purchase of an air defense ship, frigates, advanced jet trainers, and T-72 tanks for the army.[11] The rapid growth in the defense budget accelerated in 1998–99, with the defense ministry allocating Rs 412 billion, an increase of 14.13 percent over the last allocation. The Parliament's Standing Committee on Defense noted that most of this increase would, like the last increase, help meet the outflow of the Fifth Pay Commission's recommendations and pension augmentation for defense personnel. The rupee's devaluation had also eroded the budget, so in real terms the provision for items other than salaries remained static. The committee also noted that, "keeping in view the current security environment in the region, the committee feels that as reflected by the budget allocations the defense of the country is yet to receive the due priority it deserves from the government."[12] With inflation and increases in pay and pensions eating into the budget increases, the BJP government in 1998 estimated the defense budget for 1999–2000 at Rs 457 billion, the largest expenditure ever undertaken by the central government. The 11 percent increase in the budget during 1998–99 just matched the 9 percent inflation rate and the sliding rupee exchange rate, which had declined by 10 percent. Furthermore, pay and allowances would eat up some 25 percent of the entire budget, and another 50 percent would go toward maintenance costs, leaving only 25 percent for modernizing the armed forces. The budget constituted 2.4 percent of the GDP, a figure that remained constant for most of the decade.[13] Following the Kargil War the government stated that the defense budget would see a hike by about Rs 80 billion, bringing the revised estimate to approximately Rs 500 billion. The single largest beneficiary would be the army and in particular the infantry, which would receive a new weapon systems, ammunition, communications systems, training equipment, and clothing for mountain warfare on a priority basis.[14]

The Army

A major reason for the army's declining budget was the acquisition by the air force and the navy of high value foreign currency loaded weapon systems. By the 1980s indigenous production had met a substantial portion of the army's equipment requirements. Even when equipment had to be imported, the army usually obtained it from the Soviets on very favorable rupee-ruble exchange rates. In the late 1970s the army imported a number of T-72 battle tanks from the Soviets. After this purchase an agreement followed to license-produce more than a thousand T-72MI tanks at Avadi.[15] The T-72 project came about as a stopgap measure to compensate for the innumerable delays in establishing the indigenous main battle tank project. A deal to license-produce the Soviet BMP-2 mechanized infantry combat vehicle at Medak soon followed the T-72 deal. During the 1980s Indian army units also received a potent boost to their air defense capabilities when they pressed into service the SA-6 self-propelled surface-to-air missile system and the ZSU-23 Shilka self-propelled anti-aircraft artillery system (sixty units). Modest numbers of SA-8, SA-9, and SA-13 self-propelled surface-to-air missiles and the SA-14 hand-held surface-to-air missile later supplemented these purchases. In the 1990s the Indian army acquired the powerful Tunguska self-propelled missile/gun anti-aircraft system from the newly formed Commonwealth of Independent States (CIS). The Indian army also obtained antitank guided weapons (ATGW) – the AT-3 Sagger – from the Soviets in the 1970s and 1980s. The army installed them on BRDM reconnaissance vehicles and the BMP-I mechanized infantry combat vehicle. In the late 1980s the Indian government obtained a licensing agreement from the Soviets to manufacture the AT-4 Spigot ATGW. In the late 1970s and 1980s the Indian army also acquired Soviet and later CIS artillery pieces. These included 152 mm and 180 mm guns, 160 mm mortars, and the BM-21 truck-borne rocket launcher system.[16]

During the same period the Indian army also acquired Western weapon systems. The army's single largest order came in 1986, when it signed a deal for the 410, FH-70, and 155 mm howitzers from the Swedish firm Bofors. The deal, worth some $3.5 billion, also involved a license-production agreement, but the army dropped this agreement when a major scandal erupted over the commission payments (by Bofors) to middlemen and unnamed Congress (I) party chiefs.[17] The army also made many smaller purchases from the West. They included a deal with a Dutch company to produce 250 Signaal Flycatcher radar fire-control systems for army and air force air defense units. The army also concluded a deal with the Euromissile Conglomerate to license-manufacture the Milan I and II ATGW. In 1999 the Indian army reinstated a long-delayed search for a 155 mm self-propelled artillery system for its armored and mechanized divisions and brigades. This deal, which involves license-producing 400–500 systems and their accompanying support vehicles, is expected to be one of the largest contracts of its kind in the world, and many international manufacturers are competing for it. The Ministry of Defense annual report in 1999 indicated that the army wanted to acquire either the South African LIW T-6 155 mm/52 caliber turret system to mount on the Arjun tank chassis – tested in Rajasthan – or a 155 mm/52 caliber version of the Russian 152 mm 2S19 gun turret mounted on locally made T-72 chassis.[18] The Kargil conflict might have changed this decision; the army is now expressing an interest in wheeled self-propelled 155 mm guns such as the Bofors FH-77B self-propelled howitzer, which has greater mobility and can be deployed in greater numbers.[19] In 2002, under the Field Artillery Rationalization Plan, the army planned to replace an assortment of guns ranging from 75 mm to 130 mm with 155 mm/52 caliber weapons. These would include several thousand guns in towed, wheeled, and tracked configurations. Israeli, Swedish, and South African manufacturers were competing for the largest ever artillery contract in August 2002.[20]

The army's indigenous production programs have evolved at a much slower rate than expected. The much-heralded main battle tank project, slated for production in the 1980s, is just beginning to materialize, with a preliminary order for some 150 preproduction tanks placed in February–March 1996. The Defense Research and Development Organization (DRDO) designed and developed the tank (named the Arjun after a mythical Vedic warrior), which weighs 59 tons. It mounts a 120 mm rifled tank gun, which is constructed out of long-life electro-slag refined steel. The gun has a thermal shroud to shield it from the warping effects of heat and cold and fires a wide range of munitions with combustible cartridges. The most advanced aspect of the tank's development is its Kanchan composite armor, which compares very well with the latest armor from Great Britain, the United States, France, and Germany and has aroused considerable international interest. Despite the many locally designed features, the preproduction vehicles and possibly the early tanks will use German fire-control systems, tracks, engines, and transmissions. This was made necessary due to the delays in getting locally designed systems ready for production.[21] The emphasis on German equipment reflects the Indian army's long-standing regard for German armor systems ever since it was denied the West German Leopard I battle tank in the 1950s in lieu of what it considered to be the grossly inferior British Vickers MK-I battle tank, the Vijayanta. However, the main battle tank project has been over budget and behind schedule. The 1999 Ministry of Defense annual report revealed that the army was acquiring 300 Russian T-90 main battle tanks in addition to placing the Arjun into serial production, even though the army saw the Arjun as unacceptable.[22]

The second major indigenous weapons project for the army is also being developed jointly for the air force and the navy. Called the integrated missile development program, this ambitious plan involves developing a complete family of surface-to-air, surface-to-surface, antitank, antiship, and air-to-air missiles. The first success for this program will come when the army deploys a fourth-generation long-range (2.5–4 miles) fire-and-forget millimeter wave homing Nag antitank missile on modified BMP fighting vehicles. Similarly, the army (to be followed by the navy and air force) expects to deploy the Trishul short-range quick-reaction and Akash medium-range surface-to-air missiles and their fire-control systems. The indigenous phased array Rajendra radar system designed for the Akash can simultaneously track up to sixty-four aircraft at ranges of 31–37 miles.[23] In 1999 press reports suggested that the army would obtain six Russian S-300V (SA-12 Gladiator) antiballistic missiles (a deal worth $1 billion) to raise an independent missile defense shield. The DRDO would integrate the S-300V system with the Akash missile and Rajendra radar systems.[24] The project that has garnered the most international interest, however, is the Prithvi surface-to-surface guided missile. This potent weapon, first flown in March 1988, is deployed on a locally built version of the Czech Tatra all-terrain truck and has a range of 93–155 miles, depending on the size of the warhead.[25] It has an advanced strap-down inertial navigation system that gives it a circular error of probability of less than 275 yards.[26] In 1999 the army deployed the missile with the 333rd Artillery Regiment, which was reportedly based – in nonoperational status – at Jalandher in northern Punjab state to counter Pakistan.[27] In addition to the medium-range Prithvi, the army will also deploy a locally designed unguided rocket artillery system known as the Pinaka that will eventually replace the Russian BM-21 systems. The military battle tested a single launcher successfully for the first time during the Kargil conflict in 1999.[28]

The missile program has overshadowed other successful army projects, such as the 105 mm light field gun and the design and production of the family of 51 mm, 81 mm, and 120 mm mortars. The army has also helped develop a new generation of 5.56 mm rifles and machine-guns known as the Indian small arms system to replace the FN-FAL-derived Ishapore rifle.[29] However, these weapons have yet to prove reliable in exhaustive army trials, and as a stopgap measure the government has acquired 100,000 AK-47s from the Russians and the former Eastern Bloc. It was only during the fighting in Kargil in the spring of 1999 that the army reequipped significant numbers of troops with the new rifle. In the transport field the army hopes to soon deploy a new family of four-wheeled and eight-wheeled trucks. They will be backed up by a license-produced version of the Czech Tatra heavy eight-wheeled truck-tractor. In August 1998 the army chief, Ved Prakash Malik, said that the army would acquire ninety antimine Casspir armored personnel carriers from South Africa to equip troops engaged in anti-insurgency operations in Kashmir and the northeast.[30] Similar progress has also been made in the less visible but important field of electronics. The Army Radio Engineering Network, under development for some two decades, was finally completed in 1988 at a cost of Rs 5 billion. The system is already being modernized with the addition of the Integrated Digital Network.[31] In 1999 the army allocated Rs 6.20 billion to link the army with the private and public sectors and develop EW, IW, C3I, and C4I systems. During the same year the army began to develop the Combat Information Decision Support System (CIDSS) and space-based surveillance assets supplemented by unmanned aerial vehicles.[32] A senior army officer noted that "our effort is to create a seamless link from the bottom to the top."[33] At the core of the system is the Army Strategic Operational Information Dissemination System (ASTROIDS), which will connect army headquarters with the various theater commanders and downward to the operational corps. A C4I2 (command, control, communication, computers, information, and intelligence) system, ASTROIDS will be the operational system between the national and army authorities. Functioning below ASTROIDS is the Tac C3I (tactical, command, control, communication, and information) system. Designed as the primary functioning system for the field formations, Tac C3I, in turn, has other components under design, including the CIDSS.[34] Following the Porkhran II nuclear tests in 1998, the army's Corps of Signals also initiated a program to create firewalls to deal with the electromagnetic pulses of nuclear explosions.[35]

More significant has been the evolution of the army's warfare doctrines. On 20 March 1979 the army inaugurated the Mechanized Infantry Regimental Center at Ahmednagar. At about the same time it formed the first mechanized infantry division, which became operational in the early 1980s. The government's decision to license-manufacture the Soviet BMP-2 infantry fighting vehicle (the first one rolled out in August 1987) placed the mechanization program on a firm footing. Nevertheless, the army's move toward mechanization has been and continues to be cautious. Rather than opt for a complete conversion of its infantry divisions to mechanized units, the army has experimented with Reorganized Army Plains Infantry Divisions (RAPIDS). These divisions have two regular infantry brigades and a single mechanized infantry brigade.[36] The army tested the divisions extensively in the massive Brasstacks military exercise, but then interest waned until Gen. Sunith Francis Rodrigues became the new army chief in 1990. In addition to gradually increasing mechanization the army succeeded, despite heavy opposition from the air force, in creating an Army Aviation Corps (AAC) in mid-1986. This force has developed slowly, and it was only in 1991 that the AAC took over the ground control operations and maintenance of its helicopter squadrons from the IAF and began operating them as an integral part of army divisions. The army's regular infantry divisions too are undergoing a thorough revamping to prepare them for a wide range of operations, from counterinsurgency to nuclear, biological, and chemical warfare. According to the director general of infantry, Lt. Gen. Gurpreet Singh, the changes would significantly boost the surveillance, antitank, firepower, communications, and mobility of the infantry.[37] The conflict in Kargil also reinforced the efficacy of the Indian conventional forces. Defense Minister George Fernandes noted that the Kargil crisis had revealed that India's conventional forces "can fight and win a limited war, at a time and place chosen by the aggressor."[38]

The Air Force

The IAF began replacing its obsolete fighter fleet in the late 1970s and the 1980s. The first major acquisition was the Anglo-French Sepecat Jaguar International strike fighter to fulfill the deep penetration strike aircraft requirement. The Janata Dal (National Front Party) government in 1978 originally signed the deal. When the new government of Indira Gandhi took over, it decided to proceed with the 1-million-pound deal in 1980. The final agreement called for the direct purchase of 40 aircraft and the licensed assembly and eventual production of 120 aircraft (more were produced in the early 1990s to serve as attrition replacements). Since then the IAF has placed orders for additional batches of attrition replacement aircraft and two seat trainers. From the mid-1990s on all Jaguars have been receiving several avionics and sensor upgrades, including the Israeli-made Litening all-weather navigation and targeting pod.[39] In 1982 India signed a deal worth some $1.3 billion with the French Dassault company to supply forty Mirage 2000 fighters along with spare parts and technical support. In August–September 1999 news reports emerged suggesting that India was seriously negotiating with France to purchase at least one squadron of the two-seat Mirage 2000D strike fighter.[40]

For the ground attack role, the IAF decided to replace its aging SU-7s with the Soviet MiG-23/27 family of swing-wing fighter bombers. After the IAF placed an initial order for 100 MiG-23BN strike fighters and MiG-23 trainers, an agreement followed to license-manufacture 165 MiG-27 strike fighters.

Although cost was a determining factor in the new MiG deal, the IAF holds the aircraft (despite their short range) in high regard for their armor protection, their high sea-level speed, and their simple but accurate fire-control systems.[41] In December 1998 the IAF revealed that it had begun a plan to equip its MiG-27s with the latest Israeli-made airborne electronic warfare suite. According to the IAF,

> the improved avionics of the MiG-27 will be used in a battle manoeuver called cooperative engagement capability. The MiGs fitted with the electronics systems will be used as a behind-the-lines aircraft which will jam enemy radars, disable electronic systems and even target and prioritize enemy aircraft and weapons systems. . . . [I]deally, about eight MiG 27s fitted with the electronic warfare system, flying about 150 km [93 miles] behind the front-line aerial attack, will detect enemy radars and electronic devices, jam them and intimate a ground based vector control team. The vector control team will in turn intimate the front-line attack, in India's case, the SU-30s or MiG-29s, of targets and incoming aircraft. The combined efforts of the Electronic Warfare System as the early warning system, the ground control as the trigger and the front-line fighters as the fire power, constitutes a cooperative engagement.[42]

Although the Israelis sent back the IAF team working in Israel in December 1998 following postnuclear sanctions on India led by the United States, the Israelis delivered the first system to India in April 1999.[43] The IAF also obtained fifty-five MiG-23MF interceptors in 1983–84 as an interim counter to Pakistan's new F-16 Fighting Falcons.[44] In August 1989 the Indian government concluded an agreement to purchase forty MiG-29 fighters from the Soviets. Additional deals to purchase more of these air superiority fighters followed, and the IAF currently has eighty to ninety MiG-29s of various types in service.[45] Despite strong pressure from the Soviet government and later from the Russian government, the Indian government has rejected the option to license-produce the MiG-29 in favor of the indigenous light combat aircraft (LCA) project. Local production of the MiG-21BIS variant continued until the late 1980s with some 150 aircraft being delivered to the air force.[46] Most of these aircraft will undergo an extensive overhaul and be refitted with new avionics with the aid of the Russian MiG Bureau to tide the IAF over until the LCA goes into production.[47] In 1981 the IAF replaced its aging Canberra reconnaissance planes with eight MiG-25R Foxbat high-altitude, high-speed reconnaissance aircraft.

During the 1980s the IAF also overhauled its entire air transport fleet. Between 1980 and 1985 the IAF acquired 120 Soviet-built AN-32 medium transports. It purchased twenty-four IL-76 heavy-lift transports from the Soviets from 1985 to 1989. Between 1984 and 1989 the air force acquired 100 MI-17 helicopters to replace the MI-8s. It also obtained ten of the heavy-lift MI-26 helicopters in 1992. Additionally, the IAF purchased twelve MI-24 Hind and twenty MI-35 Hind attack helicopters in 1983 and 1989. In 1983 the Indian government signed a contract with Dornier of Germany to license-build more than a hundred DO-228 light transports.[48] The local design and production of transport aircraft does not seem to be a priority for the Indian government. Throughout the 1990s the IAF also had a long-standing requirement for sixty to seventy advanced jet trainers, which it desperately needs to replace the aging Hunter and MiG-21 trainers currently being used. Reports in August 1999 suggested that a decision to purchase either the British Hawk or the Franco-German Alphajet was near.[49]

The long-delayed LCA project continues to be the IAF's main focus for future acquisition plans. This combat aircraft should be the air force's standard ground attack and air superiority fighter well into the twenty-first century. Often described as a pilot's dream by the press, the diminutive fighter has tremendous capabilities.

Full engine power four seconds after idle. Subsonic to high supersonic speed in less than 100 seconds. Airborne after a 500-meter run. An "L" turn in three seconds. A radar that spots enemy aircraft flying below normal detection range and also identifies and tracks ground targets at night. And missiles guided to hit hostile planes 60 km [37 miles] away or lock on to targets with laser beams and bomb them with pin-point accuracy. In fact the only thing light about India's light combat aircraft (LCA) is really its weight. Shaped like a moth and small enough to sit on a badminton court, the aircraft weighs barely eight tons. That puts it in the bantam breed of fighters. But in performance it is intended to match the best in the world.[50]

The air force always expected the cost to be high, and by 1990 the project had cost taxpayers Rs 12–15 billion.[51] The government established a special task force, the Aeronautical Development Agency, to channel the country's research and development effort into this vital project. The LCA soon ran into an old problem familiar to the Indian aircraft industry when the locally designed Kaveri jet engine failed to meet development deadlines. The government then decided to power the prototypes with the American General Electric F-404 turbofan. In 1992, as the cost of the program skyrocketed, the Indian government decided to welcome foreign collaboration and investment.[52] The date for the first flight keeps being postponed, and the first prototype only rolled out in early 1996. The nuclear tests in 1998 resulted in the suspension of all U.S. military assistance programs, with the result that the LCA has experienced further delays. In December 1999, on the eve of dynamic testing of the aircraft, the DRDO declared that the first flight test would take place "sometime in 1999." [53] Despite the chronic difficulties and glitches associated with the LCA project, it appears to be finally on the track to completion. The willingness of the government to accept the cost of buying foreign components – especially the avionics and flight-control systems – means that the project has a better chance of coming to fruition. On 4 January 2000 the LCA prototype finally took to the air, sparking hopes that it would be inducted into service by 2005.[54] Should the LCA become operational, it likely will be equipped with the Astra beyond visual range air-to-air missile. The missile is 12.5 feet long and has a solid propellant charge, an active radar seeker, and a 33-pound high-explosive warhead activated by a proximity fuse. The missile will approach the target (up to 62 miles away) at Mach 4 and can undertake 40-g turns close to sea level.[55]

The second major indigenous project for the IAF is the advanced light helicopter (ALH) project, later named Dhruv. In 1978 the IAF issued an air staff requirement for a twin-engine helicopter. However, by 1982 the project was still on the drawing board, and in 1984 the "light" helicopter was transformed into a "medium" helicopter with a take-off weight of 8,818 pounds and an ability to transport some ten to twelve passengers. In 1992 the Indian government contracted MBB of Germany to obtain its excellent rigid rotor-head design. The ALH prototype finally flew in 1995. This helicopter will form the mainstay of the three services' vertical-lift fleets. The army in particular hopes to equip its fledgling AAC with hundreds of the new helicopter. In army service the ALH would serve in both transport and attack roles. The Indian navy will use the ALH as its main antisubmarine warfare platform in addition to transport roles. Hindustan Aeronautics Limited (HAL) also hopes to sell these advanced helicopters to the rapidly growing Indian air transport industry.

Following the nuclear tests in May 1998 the United States imposed sanctions on all defense cooperation with India, which resulted in several programs related to the LCA and the ALH being terminated. Indian scientists in the United States working with Martin Marietta on the LCA digital fly-by-wire system were sent back to India, and American engineers working in Bangalore on the Light Helicopter Turbine Engine Company engines for the ALH were recalled to the United States.[56] A decision to immediately utilize French Turbomecca TM-333 engines offset these sanctions in the case of the ALH.[57]

At the same time, the French company Sextant Avionique offered to help HAL develop flight control software for the LCA.[58]

As with the army, the air force too has benefited tremendously from the success of the integrated missile development program. The short-range Trishul and the medium-range Akash surface-to-air missiles will provide a potent air defense for the IAF's airbases. The long-range version of the Prithvi surface-to-surface missile (155 miles) will give the IAF deep-strike capability without jeopardizing its planes and pilots. The IAF is also slated to take delivery of the new Agni intermediate-range ballistic missile (IRBM), with a range of 1,553 miles. This missile completed its first test firing on 22 May 1989, thus making India only the sixth country in the world to successfully produce an IRBM with indigenous technology. On 19 February 1994 Agni completed a third successful launch from the Chandipur at-sea test range in Orissa, delivering a dummy warhead some 984 feet off the target at a distance of 1,242 miles.[59] The key to Agni's success lies in the locally developed ablative carbon reentry shield and a sophisticated strap-down inertial navigation system. Space technology is also being used to bolster the military's surveillance capabilities. Soon after the Kargil conflict the Indian Space Research Organization (ISRO) announced that the next remote sensing satellite, Cartosat-1, will carry two panchromatic cameras to provide better than 2.7-yard spatial resolution with a steerable swatch of 19 miles. At the same time, the DRDO announced that it had proposed to the government an ambitious plan for a space-based reconnaissance and intelligence-gathering hypersonic test vehicle that would cruise at speeds of Mach 7 at a height of 19 miles, giving it a surveillance, reconnaissance, and intelligence-gathering capability unmatched by satellites.[60]

A vast Air Defense Ground Environment System (ADGES), consisting primarily of an array of radars, will control the IAF's national air defense network. Under development and construction since the 1970s, the system coordinates all air defense activities in the subcontinent.[61] After the First Gulf War the Eighth Defense Plan called for the substantial improvement of the ADGES. The air force added advanced locally designed and built Indra I and II low-level radars to the network, greatly increasing its detection capabilities. A Troposcatter Communication System linked all principal operational commands and the air headquarters at Delhi. The air force had also introduced microprocessor-based message-switching systems and linked all different command headquarters and the air headquarters with an advanced digital-processing system by 1994. The ADGES received a significant boost in 2001, when India and Russia signed a deal to supply India with a network of long-range S-300 surface-to-air missiles capable of intercepting and destroying aircraft and ballistic missiles at ranges up to 124 miles.[62] In September 1999 P. H. Ron, head of the Bhabha Atomic Research Center accelerator and pulse-power division, revealed details of the KALI-5000 (kilo-ampere linear injector), a "soft-kill" weapon system that was being readied for testing. The system was packed with gigawatts of power and could use microwave bursts to destroy incoming aircraft and missiles by crippling their electronic systems and computer chips.[63]

The IAF sees itself as playing a decisive role in any future conflict in the subcontinent. In addition to adding to and refining its air defense and ground attack capabilities, the IAF has made significant strides in developing a formidable strategic deep-strike capability. The first step was the acquisition of the Anglo-French Jaguar in the 1970s and 1980s. In 1998 deliveries of the first forty Russian SU-30MK multipurpose aircraft began.[64] This formidable machine has impressed IAF pilots with its long range, large payload, and advanced avionics. Its acquisition and licensed production would provide the IAF with a quantum leap in its already formidable deep-strike capabilities.[65] In a speech to the 162nd graduating class of the pilots course at Hyderabad on 20 December 1998 Air Chief Marshal S. K. Sareen stated that the multirole SU-30 would form the backbone of the IAF's air defense and strike forces for the next three decades. The IAF's strategic strike capabilities have also received a boost with the deployment of the Prithvi surface-to-surface missile. And the future acquisition of the Agnis will launch the IAF into the exclusive IRBM users club. Furthermore, if the government decides to install a nuclear warhead, the IAF will have to evolve a new strategic doctrine.

These moves toward new doctrines and force structures have generated considerable debate within the air force. In a hard-hitting article in the 1994 *Vayu Aerospace Review*, Air Marshal C. V. Gole noted that the challenges facing the IAF at the turn of the century include

1. Absence of deep knowledge and awareness of the adversaries' capabilities.

2. Outdated operational thinking.

3. Obsolete/Obsolescent weapons.

4. Paucity of funds.

5. Disinclination of the military bosses to face the politico-bureaucratic combine and to accept some bitter, but necessary measures specially related to reductions in force levels.[66]

Although financial stringency remains a constant problem for the IAF, as it does for the other services, it seems unlikely that the IAF will reduce its force structures. Reduction, if it comes at all, will probably occur at the expense of the air force's inflated manpower. On the whole, the IAF has entered the twenty-first century as the most powerful air arm in the Asia-Pacific region.

The Navy

Although the buildup of the army and the air force has been quite substantial, the ongoing and proposed expansion program of the navy has overshadowed them. Key to the naval expansion program was the development of the navy's air power projection ability. In January 1983 the navy placed an initial order for five Sea Harrier Fleet Readiness Squadron MK-51 fighters along with two Harrier trainers. In April 1986 India decided to purchase the British carrier Hermes (renamed Viraat) for $94 million. The government followed the Hermes deal with another order for sixteen Sea Harrier fighters (delivered between 1988 and 1992). The Sea Harriers were equipped with the British Aerospace Sea Eagle antiship missiles and French Matra 550 Magic dogfight air-to-air missiles.[67] The navy also acquired twenty additional Sea King HAS-5 antisubmarine warfare helicopters between 1985 and 1990.[68]

To significantly upgrade its submarine arm, the Indian government signed a deal with HDW of Germany to acquire two Type-209 SSK-1500 diesel patrol submarines. Plans to license-produce four submarines in India were later cut down to only two boats, which the Mazagon docks in Bombay completed. Between 1986 and 1991 the navy acquired eight Russian Kilo-class diesel patrol submarines.[69] Substantial orders for Soviet and later CIS naval vessels preceded the Kilo submarine deal. Between 1980 and 1988 the navy obtained five Kashin-class destroyers. Other purchases from the Russians include eight Osa II missile boats (1976–77), five Pauk-class antisubmarine warfare corvettes (1989–91), three Nanuchka II missile corvettes (1976–78), twelve Polcocny-class LSTs, twelve Natya-class oceangoing minesweepers, and five Tarantul-class missile corvettes (1987–90; twelve more were built in India). In 1996–97 India ordered two more improved Kilo-class submarines and even placed an order for at least one 1,700-ton Amur-class diesel electric submarine. The submarine represents the latest Russian advances in nonnuclear submarine technology and may incorporate an air independent propulsion system.[70] In 1997–98 the navy placed an 816-million-rupee order for three Russian-built improved Krivak-III class frigates. The 4,000-ton frigates are being built at Saint Petersburg's Baltiisky Zavod shipyard, and the Russians have described them as "warships of the next century," incorporating the latest in Russian weapons, sensor, and stealth technology.[71] The ships will be the first in the world to be equipped with eight vertical-launch Novator P-10 Alfa universal cruise missiles – the supersonic cruise missile has a range of 186 miles and has not yet been deployed by the Russian navy.[72] The navy also obtained Russian naval weapon systems, including guns, missiles, and sensors, to mount on to Indian-designed and -built ships.

One of the most sensitive naval acquisitions from the Soviets has been the leasing in 1988 of a Charlie I–class nuclear attack submarine, the INS Chakra. In 1990, however, the Indians handed the submarine back. It now appears that Indian scientists and naval technicians utilized the nuclear-powered attack submarine (SSN) to gain firsthand experience in working with a nuclear submarine's power plant. In the mid-1990s the design and construction of a nuclear submarine had the highest funding priority in the navy's construction program. The submarine project, in fact, is on track and progressing well. Indeed, the Indian navy believes that the nuclear submarine program is so important that it has given it precedence over the long-desired aircraft carrier program. Press reports in mid-1999 suggested that the first Indian nuclear submarine was months from construction and might even be launched in 2006 or 2007.[73] The submarines would, among other requirements, serve as launch vehicles for the Sagarika, a naval cruise missile that was "in an advanced stage of development."[74] However, Adm. Vishnu Bhagwat, the chief of naval staff in January 1999, denied the existence of the missile but noted that a naval version of the Prithvi was instead being readied for sea trials aboard ship.[75]

Details on the carrier program continue to be confusing and at times contradictory. The navy appears to be resisting pressure to settle for a small helicopter carrier. Instead, it prefers to wait for funds to build a medium-sized carrier of about 40,000 tons. In fact, in 1989 the navy signed a memorandum of understanding with France to engage its help in designing and building a 30,000–35,000-ton carrier. It is also possible that the navy is delaying the carrier construction program to use the experience gained in designing a submarine nuclear power plant to build a similar system to power the carrier. In June 1999, during the commissioning of the destroyer Mysore, the prime minister, Atal Behari Vajpayee, announced that the Indian government had authorized the construction of an "air defense ship" weighing 32,000 tons to be built at the Cochin shipyard. The navy received a formal letter from the cabinet Committee on Security on 14 June 1999 sanctioning the construction of the carrier. The ship could fly either the naval version of the LCA or the latest naval version of the MiG-29 SMT.[76] In January 1999 Admiral Bhagwat stated that the navy was awaiting cabinet clearance to build the carrier, which was expected to cost approximately Rs 16 billion. Studies conducted indicated that the carrier would be five times the cost of the indigenously built destroyer the INS Delhi. Bhagwat reaffirmed that "the aircraft carrier is a very versatile weapon. It is not the navy's hobby-horse. An aircraft carrier will last one-and-a-half-times more than a destroyer does. It absorbs more punishment and delivers a punch 50 times deadlier than the destroyer."[77] Details also emerged of negotiations in 1999 for the purchase of a completely refurbished Russian carrier, the 40,000-ton *Admiral Gorshkov*, and a squadron of naval MiG-29 SMT fighters.[78] In October 1999 press reports suggested that the navy had finalized a deal for a total package that involved the thorough overhaul and modernization of the carrier and the acquisition of MiG-29K multirole carrier fighters.[79]

The nuclear submarines and the aircraft carriers constitute two legs of the navy's three-legged blue-water construction program. The third leg is made up of a variety of corvettes, frigates, and destroyers slated to support the carriers and to carry out independent patrol tasks. In 1980 the Mazagon docks in Bombay completed the last of six Leander-class frigates for the navy. Following the construction of the frigates, the docks built three Godavari-class frigates, an improved version of the Leanders weighing 3,500 tons. In 1987 the navy announced plans to construct a new class of destroyers – Project 15, weighing 6,000 tons. The Mazagon docks laid down the first ship of this class, the INS *Delhi*, in early 1991, and the navy commissioned it amidst great fanfare in 1997. At 6,500 tons the *Delhi* was the biggest and most powerful ship built in the Indian Ocean region. Its main missile suite included a battery of sixteen KH-35 Uran antiship missiles (Russia's variant of the highly successful U.S.-built Harpoon) with a range of more than 62 miles. Medium-range (19–31 miles) Russian Shtil surface-to-air missiles provided anti-aircraft defense. The weapons and sensors are a remarkable blend of Western, Russian, and Indian systems. Notable among them are the HUMVAAD, the Indian-designed and -built hull-mounted and -towed array sonar system, and the Ajanta electronic warfare system.[80] The navy commissioned the INS *Mysore*, the second ship of the class, in June 1999.[81] In February 1999 the Indian government issued a letter to construct three "futuristic" Project 17–class frigates. Although smaller than the Project 15 class at 4,600 tons, the new ships are slated to have even greater firepower and will incorporate stealth technology. The Mazagon docks laid down the first Project 17 frigate keel in July 2001.[82]

In the meantime, the Garden Reach shipyard in Calcutta has begun construction on a new class of frigates known as the Project 16A, or Brahmaputra, class.[83] On 23 August 1989 the Mazagon docks completed the INS *Khukri*, the first of a dozen or more corvettes. Armed with guns, missiles, and sensors, these ships have been designed to serve on extended patrol and to guard coastal installations. The *Khukri* carries many Indian-designed and -built sensors and equipment, including the Bharat Electronics Ajanta Electronic Support Measures System, which can detect and identify all electronic transmissions and store up to 1,500 of them in its memory. Bharat Electronics also supplied the sophisticated Action Information Organization System and a state-of-the-art communication system. The Khukri also carries an underwater towed decoy designed by the Naval Physical and Oceanic Laboratory of Cochin. The corvette's later antisubmarine warfare versions will carry the HAL-built ALH for antisubmarine warfare.[84] These heavily armed patrol corvettes will be supplemented by the Sukanya-class patrol corvettes, three of which have been acquired from South Korea (1990–92). The navy's amphibious capabilities also received a boost with the acquisition of the INS Magar, a 5,000-ton LST. Garden Reach, which built the Magar, is also constructing the large oceangoing Deepak-class replenishment ships.[85]

To support its massive shipbuilding program the navy unveiled plans in 1986 to build a huge naval base near Karwar in Karnataka. The facility will cover 1,409 square miles and will have 1.7 square miles of berthing space. In addition to functioning as the main naval base, the facility will handle shipbuilding, maintenance, and refitting requirements.[86] The entire building plan, named Project Seabird, began in August 1998 with a memorandum of understanding signed between the Defense Ministry and the state government of Karnataka, where the proposed base is located.[87] In 1987 the prime minister, Rajiv Gandhi, laid the foundation stone for a naval academy at Ezhimala in Kerala's Cannanore district. The state-of-the-art 2,300-acre coastal facility will be the finest naval academy in Asia.[88] In addition to naval vessels and shore facilities, the navy has also developed, in its various laboratories and related defense production units, naval weapon systems. These include homing torpedoes (NST-48s), radars, naval fire-control systems, advanced ship-borne sonars, and communication systems. In June 1998 the navy began testing a vertical-launch version of the short-range Trishul surface-to-air missile from the INS Dronacharya in Cochin.[89] Recently, the navy also opened a shore-based very low frequency communication system. All in all, the Indian navy, the least developed of the three services at independence, appeared to be the most self-sufficient military branch in indigenous production at the turn of the century.

The Nuclear Weapons Issue

India's governments since Jawaharlal Nehru have been ambivalent about nuclear weapons. Nehru, while championing world nuclear disarmament, liked to keep India's nuclear weapons option open in case "the need should arise."[90] Dr. Homi Bhabha, the father of India's nuclear industry, actively pushed nuclear weapons. The internal debate on nuclear weapons only intensified after China exploded a nuclear device in 1964. Not surprisingly, when the West introduced the Nuclear Non-Proliferation Treaty in 1968 Indian refused to sign until all nuclear weapons states had disarmed. India appeared to be on the verge of gate-crashing into the nuclear club when it exploded a plutonium device with a yield of 12–15 kilotons of TNT equivalent in the Phokran test range in Rajasthan on 18 May 1974.[91] Although India quickly labeled the test a "peaceful nuclear explosion," the United States cut off all nuclear assistance. In the 1980s the Pakistanis, under the dictatorship of Gen. Zia-ul-Haq, made tremendous strides in acquiring nuclear bomb–making ability, so for India nuclear weapons capability was fast becoming a necessity.

By the late 1980s the international community suspected that India had enough plutonium stockpiled to make eighty warheads. In this context India's missile program, and its Prithvi and Agni surface-to-surface missiles in particular, take on added significance. The successful development of these advanced delivery systems means that India does have an IRBM nuclear strike capability. Such nascent capability would be a significant strategic bargaining chip in any future confrontation with China. In recent times, however, tensions over nuclear weapons has been most acute with Pakistan. In 1995 rumors abounded that India was preparing the Phokran test site for a second nuclear test. The disclosure that India had gathered its top nuclear scientists to carry out a series of tests triggered intense international pressure (from the United States in particular), and Prime Minister Narasimha Rao's government backed down.[92] The successor governments of Prime Ministers Deve Gowda and I. K. Gujral maintained the test ban. In April 1999 the new government of Prime Minister Atal Behari Vajpayee gave the go-ahead for the suspended tests. This time the government went to great lengths to keep the tests a secret. The stratagem worked. On 11 May at approximately 3:45 PM India Standard Time India detonated three nuclear warheads, including a hydrogen warhead of 45 kilotons, in sequence in an underground shaft at Phokran. Two days later it tested two additional warheads, signifying India's decisive commitment to nuclear weaponization. A few weeks later Pakistan responded with nuclear tests at the Chagai test range.

The program was further consolidated almost a year later in April 1999, when India carried out a successful test of its Agni II IRBM from its missile test base in Chandipur, Orissa. The missile, with a range of 1,242 miles, improved upon the earlier version by utilizing solid state fuel for the rocket's upper stage in place of the earlier liquid fuel. The missile guidance system can also use a Global Positioning System for conventional warhead delivery to enable it to receive satellite feeds of its position in flight and a high-speed onboard computer to enable it to make corrections to its flight path.[93] In May the ISRO deployed three satellites (including one German and one South Korean) using its polar satellite launch vehicle C-2. The launch not only marked India's entry into the hotly contested satellite launch market but also confirmed its potential to build ICBMs.[94] Press reports in October 1999 indicated that India had already spent $50 million developing a 3,107-mile-range missile named Surya. A Russian cryogenic engine would power the prototype in lieu of an Indian cryogenic engine expected to be ready by 2001.[95]

With nuclear weapon deployment imminent, the Indian government and defense establishment wrestled with creating a command and control system to manage the new capability. In July 1999 a parliamentary Standing Committee on Defense asked Defense Ministry officials if a command and control system had been put into place to control nuclear weapons. Had the procedure for the safe handling and storage of the nuclear weapons been finalized? Their responses, not surprisingly, were less than satisfactory. Nevertheless, press reports in 1999 suggested that the government was setting up a national command post outside Delhi that would have not only all communication and radar facilities but also the strength to withstand a nuclear attack. The report also indicated that the military had evolved a system of codes that could be sent over a separate communications channel to the branch of the armed force in charge of a particular nuclear weapon. A consensus was also emerging over divided control of the weapons. The weapons launcher – missile or launcher – would be under the charge of either the navy, the air force, or the army, but the warhead's nuclear core would be held in a separate establishment during peacetime.[96]

On 17 August 1999 the government released a six-page preliminary draft nuclear doctrine prepared by the twenty-seven-member National Security Council advisory board. The draft outlined the broad principles for the deployment and employment of the nuclear force. Although the government would work out the policy and strategy details later, the draft indicates that the authority to release India's nuclear weapons rests with the prime minister or his or her designated successors. The draft declared the need to maintain a credible minimum nuclear deterrence so as to "deter the use and threat of use of nuclear weapons by any state or entity against India and its forces."[97] India's nuclear forces would be based on a triad of aircraft, mobile land-based missiles, and sea-based assets. The command and control system and the weapon systems would be set up to survive any surprise attack and could endure any "repeated attrition" attempts with adequate retaliatory capability to inflict a punishing second strike that would be unacceptable for the aggressor.[98]

Defense Policy Making

The defense policy–making apparatus that India inherited from the British had invested a considerable degree of autonomy with the army high command, the navy and air force having just recently been created. The commander in chief India controlled the Ministry of Defense. At independence, control of the Ministry of Defense passed from the commander in chief to the defense minister. However, at this point, the Defense Ministry's role was limited to passing on the government's orders as agreed upon by the army headquarters and the military finance department. At this time the senior-most civil servant in the ministry, the defense secretary, who had been the chief's subordinate, still ranked junior to all the principal staff officers at army headquarters.[99]

Soon after independence, on the advice of Lord Mountbatten and Lord Ismay (once secretary to the British cabinet's Defense Committee), the Indian government introduced a three-layered committee system for defense planning. It included the Defense Committee of the Cabinet (DCC), the Defense Minister's Committee, and the Chiefs of Staff Committee. Specialized bodies, including the Joint Intelligence Committee, the Defense Science Advisory Committee, the Joint Planning Committee, and various interservices organizations to deal with personnel and pension matters, aided in the decision-making process.[100] The service chiefs played a central role in the three committees, which were under complete political control, yet with minimal bureaucratic interference. The latter stipulation would change dramatically in 1952, when the Ministry of Defense's entire office manual was rewritten "to make the three wings of the armed forces report, not directly to the political authority but to the civilian bureaucracy."[101] The process of whittling down the military hierarchy began on 25 March 1955, when Prime Minister Nehru announced to Parliament the change in the designation of the commander in chief to chief of staff.[102] While this was primarily a symbolic change, the 1962 war with China resulted in the cabinet secretary being given a higher protocol status than the service chiefs.[103]

In 1962, after Krishna Menon's resignation, the DCC became the crucial body for decision making about defense-related issues. The government renamed it the Emergency Committee of the Cabinet (ECC) and then the Cabinet Committee of Political Affairs. The service chiefs no longer had to be present during all the meetings and sometimes were even absent when the committee discussed defense matters.[104] In 1966 the government established the Policy Planning Review Committee (PPRC). It was primarily a Ministry of External Affairs committee, although the defense secretary joined it in 1969. Its role was to evaluate India's foreign policy in relation to the international environment with due regard to the politico-military and politico-economic situation.[105] By 1971 the PPRC and the Joint Intelligence Committee (JIC) aided the Cabinet Committee on Political Affairs (CCPA), which replaced the DCC/ECC as the major decision-making body. The prime minister chaired the CCPA, and its usual members came from the ministers of defense, external affairs, home affairs, and finance. By the late 1970s, however, the body had become little more than a rubber-stamp institution, with the politicians giving their approval to complex proposals that the bureaucrats passed on to them with little or no review of the accompanying data. By 1983 Prime Minister Indira Gandhi and her security advisor, Ram Nath Kao, former director of the Research and Analysis Wing (RAW), had created a "core group." This new body, which included the government's principal secretaries, the director of the Intelligence Bureau, the director of RAW, and the chairman of the Joint Chiefs of Staff Committee, was responsible for all security and defense issues.[106]

In 1986 interest arose in re-creating a chief of defense staff position, which had existed under the British. The same year, integrated planning took place under the aegis of a Defense Planning Staff (DPS) under the leadership of an army lieutenant general. In April 1986 the defense minister, Arun Singh, established the DPS, and the CCPA approved several functions for it:

1. Carry out threat analysis and formulate threat assessments for various time frames.

2. Evolve military aims.

3. Conceive and recommend balanced force levels to achieve military aims.

4. Carry out joint training and joint logistics management.

5. Coordinate perspective planning for fifteen to twenty years.

6. Interact closely with research and development, defense production, industry, and finance.[107]

Unfortunately, the short-lived success of the DPS ended with the departure of two key members. The first was the defense minister, Arun Singh, who resigned in the wake of the Bofors scandal in July 1987, and the second was the army chief, Gen. Krishnaswamy Sundarji, after his retirement in early 1988. The DPS soon became a bone of contention between the Ministry of Defense and the services. At the same time, deep-rooted interservices rivalry prompted the services, especially the navy and the air force, which had always suspected army hegemony, from cooperating with the DPS. When the DPS visited the various formations and units of the three services and made recommendations, the government shelved the recommendations due to its unwillingness to commit funds beyond a yearly schedule.[108] The DPS's primary contribution was its Defense Perspective Plan 1985–2000. For the first time, the military had prepared a defense plan on the assumption that the government would allocate 4 percent of the GDP to defense prepared-ness. Another first was the willingness of the army and the air force to accept budget cuts so that the government could send additional funds to the navy and provide more funding for research and development. The chiefs of staff and the Ministry of Defense approved the plan. K. C. Pant, who took over from V. P. Singh as defense minister in April 1987, announced the plan to Parliament. A renewed tussle between the Chiefs of Staff Committee and the Ministry of Defense for control of the DPS followed this high point, however. Matters came to a head in 1989, when N. N. Vohra became the defense sec-retary and General Rodrigues served as the chairman of the Chiefs of Staff Committee. Hereafter, the DPS "was marginalized to routine duties, nowhere near the charter approved by the CCPA."[109]

The defense chiefs also became isolated from the decision-making pro-cess with the establishment in 1986 of the Policy Advisory Committee under the chairmanship of M. G. Parthasarathy, whose purpose was to take a long-term view of foreign policy and national security.[110] However, the committee was dissolved after the Sri Lanka intervention and the political demise of the defense minister.[111]

In a 1989 election campaign manifesto the Janata Dal accused the incum-bent Congress (I) government of endangering Indian security and promised to set up a National Security Council (NSC) to evolve an Indian security doc-trine. However, even after a National Front government came to power, the NSC proposal remained stillborn amidst widespread criticism that it was essentially the old system under a different name.[112] The CCPA continued to be the only institutional establishment for defense- and security-related de-cision making in the country. Even in this case, the prime minister's office made the important decisions at the cabinet's expense. Intelligence gather-ing, coordinating, and disbursement of real-time intelligence continued to remain inadequate, with the possible exception of data on Pakistan. The im-broglio in Sri Lanka is a classic example of intelligence failures and the lack of coherent strategic planning.

The nuclear tests on 11 May 1998 added a new urgency for the establish-ment of the NSC. The BJP government, which approved the nuclear weapons tests, had promised to establish the NSC. On 14 April 1998 the government created a task force under former defense minister K. C. Pant to present a report to the prime minister.[113] The group met with nearly 230 officials, ex-officials, and experts who, according to the task force, were unanimous "on having a system for managing national security in an integrated and coherent manner. Especially so after the May 11th nuclear blasts and the world wide reaction that followed." [114]

The national security advisor (of cabinet rank) would have three divisions reporting to him or her. One would work on long-term strategic planning and strategy development. The second would coordinate decision making and monitor policy implementation. The third would coordinate intelligence assessments for national security planning and management. The task force also insisted that the NSC must be kept at the minimum possible size. The task force made its recommendations on the basis of two principles: First, national security was not just about the military. It included the fields of domestic peace, economic well-being and financial viability, trade policy, technological strength, and foreign policy. Second, the NSC must be firmly situated within the constitutional and political framework. The organization should therefore function within the government and be answerable to the cabinet and the parliamentary system.[115]

The task force presented its report to the prime minister on 26 June 1998. In November 1999 press reports suggested that the NSC had finally been established. As expected, the prime minister headed it. The Union home minister, the defense minister, the foreign minister, and the deputy chairman of the planning commission constituted the council's other five permanent members. The prime minister's principal secretary is the national security advisor and the channel for servicing the organization. The backup structure to the NSC includes three elements. The Joint Intelligence Committee acts as the NSC's secretariat. The Strategic Policy Group, which includes the cabinet secretary, the three service chiefs, the foreign secretary, the home secretary, the defense secretary, the secretary of defense production, the finance secretary, the revenue secretary, the governor of the Reserve Bank of India, the director of the Intelligence Bureau, the secretary of the cabinet secretariat, the secretary to the Department of Atomic Energy, the scientific adviser to the defense minister, the space secretary, and the chairman of the Joint Intelligence Committee, provides interministerial coordination and backup for the NSC. The third and final element is the NSC advisory board, which consists of eminent persons outside the government. They are chosen from among experts in external security, strategic analysis, foreign affairs, defense, the armed forces, internal security, science, technology, and economics. The board meets once a month or more frequently if needed. It provides long-term prognosis and analysis to the NSC and offers solutions and policy options to the issues of concern. The new body's first task was to undertake a strategic defense review, which assumed great importance after the 11 May nuclear tests. As part of this exercise the NSC had to design a command and control system for India's nuclear capability.[116]

Welcome though the newly created NSC may be, its burdensome structure has left room for doubt as to whether it will achieve success where similar organizations have failed. Indeed, defense analyst and former director of the Institute for Defense Studies and Analysis (IDSA) K. Subrahmanyam described the newly formed NSC as "nothing more than old wine in a new bottle."[117] Among the problems Subrahmanyam sees with the newly formed NSC is the plan to convert the JIC into a secretariat for the NSC. Such a move, he believes, would lead to the neglect of long-term intelligence collection. Furthermore, Subrahmanyam thinks that mixing intelligence assessments with policy making is a negative step. He is also critical of combining the jobs of principal secretary and national security advisor, noting that the twin responsibilities would be beyond the scope of any one individual.[118]

In the aftermath of the Kargil conflict, the government appointed Subrahmanyam to lead a four-person committee to investigate why the Pakistani moves so surprised the Indian government and military. After its investigation, the committee laid the blame on poor intelligence gathering and information coordination. The Subrahmanyam committee noted that the intelligence agencies shared only eleven out of the forty-five inputs considered vital to assess Pakistani moves in Kargil with the newly formed National Security Council Secretariat (NSCS). In response to the Subrahmanyam committee's report, the government dismantled the NSCS and replaced it with an "all-powerful" Intelligence Coordination Group (ICG) under the aegis of the national security advisor. All intelligence agencies have to answer to the NSA under the rubric of the ICG, which in turn prepares the strategic intelligence assessment report for the government.[119] Furthermore, the government streamlined the intelligence-gathering network within the armed forces with the establishment of the Defense Intelligence Agency (DIA), headed by a three-star general or his naval or air force equivalent. The DIA would collate army, air force, and naval intelligence and assess the threat along the borders. The DIA was scheduled to hold monthly meetings with the NSA and the ICG. The culmination of the intelligence revamp was the creation of the chief of defense staff position, a recommendation of the National Task Force on Defense Management.[120]

Whether the newly created ICG will achieve success remains to be seen. As Subrahmanyam has pointed out, certain glaring structural flaws need remedying, not least among them being the many bureaucrats who dominate the proposed Strategic Policy Group. What stands out in the decade's long strug-gle to create an enduring and centralized defense policy–making organiza-tion is not the inherent schism in civil-military relations but rather the lack of trust between the politicians, the military, and the bureaucrats. The poli-ticians are loath to hand over control to either the bureaucrats or the mili-tary, while the military is squabbling over which of the three services has greater priority in budgetary and policy-making matters.[121] However, it is the unique role of the bureaucracy that has seriously hampered (many would say crippled) any effective defense policy making in India. Rather than func-tion as a conduit between the political leadership and the military, the de-fense ministry bureaucrats operate as an independent policy-making insti-tution in their own right. Their control over the Indian armed forces is, in all likelihood, unparalleled in any other country.[122] In June 1998 army officers expressed their outrage when Ministry of Defense bureaucrats questioned the army's usage of 23 mm ZSU-23-4 air defense guns to destroy Pakistani bunkers across the line of control, suggesting instead that the army could have made do with the cheaper light and medium machine-gun ammuni-tion. The bureaucrat in question, the additional financial advisor, defense ser-vices, in the Defense Ministry's Finance Division, is reported to have asked, "Under whose authority did the army use the ZSU-23 guns on ground target-ing roles?" To this the army replied, "How we conduct our operations, and what weaponry we use to execute those operations is really only our busi-ness. After all we live there, fight there and know best how to tackle the situation."[123] An angry defense minister, George Fernandes, ordered the bu-reaucrat and others in the ministry who delayed the army's request for snow-mobiles for operations in the Siachen Glacier region to go on a "familiariza-tion" tour of the Siachen Glacier.[124] While the growing bureaucratic role has come at the expense of both the politicians and the military, it is the military that has been virtually eliminated from the policy-making process.[125]

Strategies and Doctrines

The confusion in determining defense policy making is reflected in the con-troversy regarding Indian strategic thinking. In his 1992 essay "Indian Stra-tegic Thought: An Interpretative Essay" (written for the undersecretary of de-fense for policy in the administration of George Bush), George Tanham states that four factors have accounted for Indian strategy or the lack thereof.[126] The first is geography, which has caused Indians to see the subcontinent as "a single strategic entity" and to be fundamentally inward looking. The second factor, the reconstruction of Indian history, has emphasized integration under great empires such as the Mauryan and Mughal. The third factor, Indian culture, has reinforced the unifying process by stressing unity in diversity and the accommodation of differences. The fourth and final factor is the British Raj, which passed on its legacy of a unified India protected by land and sea barriers and the existence of smaller buffer states at the periphery of the subcontinent. Using these four factors as a template, Tanham then assessed India's threats and opportunities using the mandala concept of concentric circles.[127] He noted that, as per the mandala scheme, Indian domestic policy constituted the first circle, the smaller (friendly or neutral) neighbors made up the second circle, and Pakistan, China, and the former Soviet Union made up the third. Indian strategic responses as derived from this concept then sought to deny the smaller neighbors access to the great powers; contain Pakistan's influence in the region; prevent Chinese intervention with military and diplomatic means; cultivate relations with the former Soviet Union to neutralize the Pakistan-China nexus; develop naval, nuclear, and missile forces to maintain control over the Indian Ocean; and develop a deterrent capability against immediate and distant superpowers. Tanham concluded that India is concerned primarily with internal security rather than external security, which explains why it is predominantly a land-based power with heavy investment in its army. India's inward-looking strategic thinking has led it to be defensive in orientation rather than offensive. Finally, Tanham concluded that the small role played by the military in defense policy making, the lack of a stable political leadership at the center, and the lack of initiative on the part of the bureaucracy have made Indian strategic thinking ad hoc and imprecise.

In a 1996 sequel, "Indian Strategy in Flux?" Tanham noted some dramatic events in 1991 that may have altered patterns in Indian strategic thinking.[128] India's economic and political crisis in early 1991 and the collapse of the Soviet Union spearheaded these events. The Persian Gulf War and the rapid growth of the Chinese economy and military further accentuated India's insecurity. In response, India began to liberalize its command economy, slowly relying more on the market economy, trade, and foreign investments. At the same time, India sought to work more closely with the United States and to develop closer ties with the East Asian economic powers, particularly Japan. However, despite these changes, Tanham believes that ad hoc policy making still persists and may even have become "institutionalized," enabling India to adjust its "strategies and policies despite some shortcomings in the strategy-making process."[129]

The Tanham essays have generated a considerable and long-overdue debate on Indian strategic thought. His main and most provocative contention – that India lacks a tradition of strategic thinking – has generated considerable discussion.[130] Many Indian experts share this view but differ from Tanham in interpreting its scope and causes. Amitabh Mattoo acquiesces to a lack of military strategy but thinks that India does have a well-developed grand strategy that includes both domestic and international strategies that will help the country achieve its security goals.[131] Kanti Bajpai too concedes Tanham's point but rejects the causal factors put forth by him, namely, geography and culture. Bajpai claims instead that after the Peace of Westphalia (1648), which resulted in the rise of the nation-state, Europeans essentially engaged in "constant and unlimited war" and had to develop a tradition of "systematic and rigorous inquiry into strategy." In contrast, India, Bajpai argues, did not develop a similar approach to strategy not because of "Hindu culture" but because India entered into the European kind of international and domestic society only recently, in 1947. Bajpai believes that only after 1947 did India enter a state system in which war and the preparations for war are incessant.[132] Indeed, Tanham's cultural causation theory has come under considerable fire. Varun Sahni notes that the mandala concept of foreign policy is hardly uniquely Indian; rather, it is the "bedrock" notion of how many countries today view their place in the world. Similarly, Sahni rejects Tanham's contention that the Hindu caste system encourages a "peculiarly Indian" hierarchical worldview. He notes that the world is a hierarchical place and that all nations understand this reality in conducting their foreign policy.[133]

These scholars have rightly rejected Tanham's cultural causation thesis. However, their dismissal (see Mattoo's essay, "*Raison d'etat* or Military Adhocism") or downplaying of Tanham's contention that geography and the British Raj played a significant role in determining Indian strategic thinking deserves more scrutiny, as the earlier chapters of this book indicate. The general consensus in Tanham's landmark work, however, is that Indian strategic thinking is decentralized and ad hoc in nature. What is not answered by either Tanham or any of his critics is how postindependence India's lack of strategic planning has affected the evolution of sound military doctrine.[134] In other words, the debate on strategy and policy making does not fully explain the Indian state's ability to effectively wage war by ground, sea, or air.

Operational Doctrines

The operational doctrines of the army, navy, and air force have remained autonomous and institutionally secure despite the problems in strategic planning and policy making. In the case of the Indian army, this has meant a cautious evolution of the infantry-oriented defensive-offensive doctrine inherited from the British-Indian army. In the three major campaigns that the Indian army has fought since independence it has relied almost exclusively on the positional warfare or defensive-offensive tactics perfected during the Second World War. During these conflicts the army succeeded in attaining the Indian government's limited military-political objectives, namely, defending Indian territorial integrity.[135] On the whole, however, the army's operations have been reactive in nature. Even the campaign to liberate Bangladesh was a painstakingly planned operation that was executed in a "controlled military environment" extremely favorable to the attacking Indian forces.

The reasons for the army's continued adherence to what many see as an obsolete infantry-based fighting doctrine are quite complex. First, the army's main opponent has been the Pakistani army, which evolved from the partition of the British-Indian army in 1947. From the early 1960s onward, however, the Pakistani army shifted its doctrinal sights from positional warfare to offensive warfare based on highly mobile mechanized forces. Consequently, prior to the 1965 war the Pakistanis amassed a reasonably powerful armored strike force with U.S. M-47 Patton tanks and M-113 armored personnel carriers. The reasoning behind this change was that the more mobile Pakistani forces could outmaneuver the larger infantry-based Indian forces. The tactic failed, however. The Indian forces, operating behind an antitank defense screen that included dig-in tanks and recoilless guns with artillery support, devastated the attacking Pakistani armor. This scenario was essentially repeated in 1971 on the Western Front in the Punjab. The Pakistani failure to successfully integrate and put into effective use the complex mechanisms of a highly mobile mechanized doctrine no doubt strengthened the Indian general staff's cautionary approach to such doctrine. On the other hand, the Indian army has taken an evolutionary approach to mechanized warfare. Successive seminars conducted at the United Services Institute, Delhi, in 1973 and 1976 reveal a general satisfaction with the structure of the Indian infantry divisions.[136] At the same time, the Indian infantry formations have continued to evolve to meet changing conditions. An expert independent research team noted that "there are a number of variations in the organization of India's infantry divisions, based on their roles. Weapons and equipment have kept up with modern technology and modern war fighting skills [have] been assimilated as they emerged."[137]

Rather than transform its infantry divisions into mechanized formations, the Indian army has adopted RAPIDS. The single mechanized brigade and two infantry brigades of these divisions retain a strong link to the past infantry-dominated armies and doctrines. In fact, the Mechanized Infantry Regiment is one of the newest arms of the Indian army, having been established in 1979. Most of the Indian armored forces continue to be deployed in a defensive role to the infantry divisions and in independent brigades.[138]

This army's cautious approach (some have referred to it as stagnation) to mobile warfare is very much in character with the mindset of the army general staff during the interwar period (1919–38), and, like the latter, the doctrine of the independent Indian army too has critics both within and without the army. Regardless, the Indian army has had its greatest operational successes when it has carried out carefully planned defensive-offensive movements. In 1962, when the ill-prepared Indian army sought to confront the veteran People's Liberation Army along the Himalayas, the result was a humiliating defeat. Similarly, in 1988, when the army initiated a hurried offensive against the Tamil Tiger rebel army in northern Sri Lanka, it found itself embroiled in a bloody and indecisive three-year guerrilla campaign. Offensive-defensive military operations as described above have not been the Indian army's strong points. The 1999 Kargil conflict also vindicated in part the army's emphasis on positional warfare. After some initial miscalculations of the scale of the Pakistani incursions, the army swiftly adapted its resources and tactics to bring the maximum firepower (both air and artillery) to bear on the entrenched intruders.

However, it would be unfair to characterize the army's current operational doctrine as being totally influenced by positional warfare considerations. Furthermore, the doctrinal conservatism of the Indian army general staff has partly arisen from the constant paucity of funds to carry out the sweeping reequipment and, more important, the frequent military exercises needed to transform units into effective mechanized fighting forces. Thus, in many ways the budgetary problems confronting the postindependence Indian army are similar to those faced by its interwar colonial predecessor. Military innovation and modernization, even when attempted on a modest scale, have often depended upon the availability of funds rather than on the willingness of the general staff to accept change.

When funds and the political will have been forthcoming the army has been eager to experiment and imbibe new operational methods. Such was the case during Exercise Shiv Shakti, which took place between 2 and 7 December 1998 near Barmer, Rajasthan. This military exercise was the largest conducted since Brasstacks and involved 72,000 personnel from the army and air force. According to the general staff, the aim of the operation was "to validate new concepts that have emerged from changes in the battlefield environment and by the induction of new technology."[139] Among the technologies used were fourth-generation night vision devices (thermal imagers and image intensifiers) on tanks and helicopters to enable the army to carry out maneuvers at night. The military also used Global Positioning System receivers to make navigation in featureless terrain easier. The Russian-built Tunguska self-propelled gun/missile air defense system was used, as was the Stentor battlefield surveillance radar. The military also deployed the Israeli-built Searcher unmanned aerial reconnaissance vehicle along with the latest generation electronic warfare equipment to intercept and jam enemy communications. For the first time the army used the powerful Prithvi battlefield missile.[140]

Although government officials denied that the exercise had a nuclear factor, the general officer commanding Southern Command, Lt. Gen. H. M. Khanna, acknowledged that "we are validating the relevance of conventional capability in the nuclear era. . . . [T]he validity of conventional capability and its perceived effectiveness would have overreaching significance to prevent an escalation."[141] The exercise's nuclear "factor" was evident in the army's mechanized forces, which operated in a buttoned-down protective environment as if under nuclear attack. The Army Medical Corps too has revealed its plans to revamp its training to meet a nuclear war. Lt. Gen. R. Jaswal, director general of the Armed Forces Medical Services, noted that "medical personnel must . . . be prepared to tackle mass casualties as a result of NBC [nuclear, biological, and chemical] weapons." According to Jaswal, the corps was training doctors and medical personnel in three phases. The system, along with a new syllabus, is available to officers and junior commissioned officers and other ranks at Pune and Lucknow. All personnel would be trained for all three types of warfare. Some officers had already been sent to Europe for additional training.[142]

The exercise also highlighted the army's awareness of the revolution in military affairs (RMA), a concept that has gathered momentum since the 1990 Gulf War. The RMA began in the digital communications revolution of the 1990s and seeks to maximize the latest advances in remote sensing technologies and weapon systems with the aid of microchips to greatly advance the operational flexibility of an army. To this end, the Indian army and air force used the Indian satellite IRS-IC during Exercise Shiv Shakti to take detailed pictures of the battle zone and transmit them to the commanders in real time. In the words of one officer participating in the exercise, "We can get the satellite images about enemy movements wherever and whenever we ask for them. . . . [T]he corps commander in an area would get the pictures of the large theater, we can even provide pictures of the smaller tactical area right down to every battalion commander, or even further down to every tank commander."[143] The lessons learned from the exercise are available in two computerized war games called CDR-1 and CDR-2 developed by the Army Training Command. Gen. K. Sundarji, commandant of the College of Combat at Mhow, initiated interest in computer-assisted war-gaming in the early 1980s when he headed a team to study the subject.[144] Indeed, Sundarji is in many ways the originator of the army's desire to adapt to twenty-first-century warfare techniques. In 1980–81 he circulated his now-famous Combat Papers I and II, which deal with strategy and tactics in the nuclear age. Exercise Brasstacks, conducted under his guidance, was the first in India to take into account the impact of nuclear weapons on the conventional battlefield. Ironically, it was Sundarji's Army Plan 2000, formulated in the late 1980s, that had to be revamped after the second nuclear test at Phokran. Army Plan 2000 envisaged large armored and mechanized formations striking deep into Pakistan, reaching and even crossing the Indus River in Sindh, effectively slicing the country in two. Air Commodore Jasjit Singh, director of the IDSA, noted that under current circumstances such an offensive could elicit a nuclear response, so "the armed forces would have to evolve war-fighting doctrines for a limited war."[145] The emphasis would be on small, highly mobile battle groups designed to engage and destroy the enemy's combat assets rather than hold on to territory.

In a talk titled "The Indian Army in the 21st Century" delivered in February 1999, Army Chief Gen. V. P. Malik noted that the army needed "quality" soldiers with the right doctrines and organizations who can handle technologically advanced equipment and weapon systems. In order to address the needs of the RMA in the force, an affordable, long-term technological plan would have to be developed. Such a plan would seek to build space-based surveillance assets, theater assets, theater surveillance smart weapons, precision guidance systems, antimissile defense, and information superiority.[146] With regard to information technology, Malik declared that "cyberwar" is to the twenty-first century what blitzkrieg was to the twentieth. The army knows that modern-day communication and power grids can be brought to a halt with "virus" strikes. To better prepare the army for the twenty-first century, the commanders are creating a computer-literate force. In 1998 a classified IT [Information Technology] Roadmap 2000 laid out a plan to spread information technology throughout the army. The plan aimed to ensure that all officers and junior leaders would be computer literate by 2002. The military has set up a Junior Leaders Academy in Bareilly to upgrade the skills of junior commissioned officers and noncommissioned officers. In 1999 the Army Institute of Information Technology began its first course to teach combat leaders the rudiments of information technology warfare. Simultaneously, three army technology institutes, two in Secunderabad and one in Poona, began to incorporate information technology into their syllabus. Malik also began a restructuring program to cut troop numbers while boosting existing capabilities, the aim being to fight a "hyper" war where combat is so intense that an adversary is pummeled day and night without respite. Long-range sensors and accurate missiles will direct the battle, which will eliminate the difference between front lines and rear areas, and neither night nor bad weather would offer any respite.[147] In early March 1998 Malik made an official visit to Israel to gain firsthand knowledge of the "Israeli Army's strategy and tactics, its organization and training and the environment that produces its first-rate defense industry."[148] Despite many weaknesses in strategic policy making, the Indian army appears to be headed into the twenty-first century with a clear operational and force-composition goal in mind.

In order to make the army organizationally compatible with the new doctrine, the army is streamlining its force structure. By 2005 the army hopes to have cut 170,000 personnel. The process began in 1999, with the army reducing its noncombat and static unit strength by 50,000, thus enabling it to save around Rs 60 billion ($1.4 billion). The army also plans to disband and amalgamate regiments and mothball equipment to sustain war wastage reserves, cut costs, and increase overall efficiency. Besides manpower cuts, the Army Training Command in Shimla, 155 miles north of Delhi, has suggested restructuring the system of dedicated strike and holding formations, three strike and eight reserve corps, by training each force to perform the other's task. It also recommended reducing the number of formations by transforming them into "task-oriented" operational maneuver groups. Force Structure 2015 has recommended reshaping the 1.2-million-member army into a "lean, mobile and technologically oriented force."[149] Since the army's 38.5-million-rupee drive, launched in 1997 to make up the shortfall of 13,000 officers, has slowed down, the army will instead seek to train noncommissioned officers and junior commissioned officers as junior leaders (at the junior leader's academy in Bareilly) to command groups of 150 men, particularly in COIN operations in Kashmir and in northeastern states. Furthermore, under Plan 4B, introduced in 1998, the army is upgrading all 350 infantry battalions with enhanced firepower for COIN operations and surveillance assets to detect the flow of militants across the border with Pakistan. The units will use South African Casspir II mine-protected armored personnel carriers, man-portable Global Positioning Systems, and vehicles with antitank missile launchers. Despite the push toward improving COIN capabilities, General Malik has reiterated the army's concern that sustained COIN operations reduce the army's combat readiness and deplete its resources. Malik was also concerned with the army's adverse image presented abroad due to the deployment of 250,000 troops in COIN operations in Kashmir in addition to the 130,000 paramilitary personnel. Although the 36,000-man Rashtriya Rifles (National Rifles) raised in the early 1990s as a dedicated COIN force have proven effective, army units continue to be needed in Kashmir.[150]

The Indian air force did not emerge from the colonial period with a primary operational doctrine. It had neither the manpower nor the equipment to fulfill anything but the most rudimentary needs of air defense and logistical support for the army. However, in the half-century since independence it has emerged as the fourth largest air force in the world and potentially the most powerful in Asia. Not surprisingly, its operational doctrines have matured rapidly to keep pace with this growth.

The Indian air force did not participate in significant combat operations until the 1965 war. In 1948 it used its C-47s as improvised bombers, but its main contribution was the effective use of its transport aircraft. The same was the case in 1962, when the IAF provided effective logistical support for the army. The 1965 war was the first major combat engagement for the IAF. However, it entered the conflict without a clear operational doctrine or failed to follow up effectively on one. Air Chief Marshal P. C. Lal states that the IAF did have a deep-strike "bomber offensive" doctrine borrowed from the RAF.[151] However, the IAF conducted its attacks deep into Pakistan in a piecemeal manner that was largely ineffective. Ground attack missions to support the army were minimal and ineffective. The IAF's poor performance in 1965 stems partly from the rapid expansion program instituted after the 1962 war. Many units and pilots were still in training and had not developed full combat proficiency. Furthermore, neither the army nor the government attempted to consult or keep the IAF informed of contingency military planning in the days leading up to the Pakistani attack.[152] In the 1971 war the air force greatly improved its preparedness level and operational planning. It placed emphasis on close support for the army and air defense operations. The IAF's deep-strike operations into Pakistan again met with limited success (mainly in the East). Its primary achievement was the destruction of Pakistan's petroleum reserves.

The IAF's conduct in the two wars reveals a force still searching for an operational doctrine. Its early emphasis on deep-strike bomber missions was ineffective for various reasons, including the lack of a strategic bomber force to conduct such missions. Under Air Chief Marshal Lal an operational doctrine emerged prior to the 1971 war, when air defense, counter–air strike operations, close air support for the army and navy, and logistical airlift support became the air force's priorities. Strategic deep-strike missions now occurred within the counter–air strike missions. However, even by 1971 the

IAF lacked the proper aircraft to effectively carry out deep-strike missions. Its Hunters, Maruts, and Sukhoi-7s were short-range battlefield support aircraft. On the other hand, air defense and close air support requirements were partially met with the existing aircraft. Overall, the primary restraint to the evolution of an operational doctrine for the air force from independence until the 1970s appears to have been the lack of a suitable aircraft. In the late 1970s this problem dissipated when the IAF sought and obtained government authorization to acquire a deep penetration strike aircraft. The aircraft selected was the Anglo-French Jaguar strike fighter, which would be license-produced in India. The Jaguar was the first strike aircraft with the range and payload capability to fulfill the deep-strike or strategic bombing capability for which the IAF had long yearned. A similar agreement to license-produce the Soviet (later Russian) MiG-27 close air support strike fighter quickly followed this acquisition. Directly purchasing several squadrons of the advanced Mirage 2000 and MiG-29 in the late 1980s and 1990s substantially upgraded the IAF's air defense potential. By the 1990s the IAF had the necessary tools to fulfill its major operational roles.

Major air operations since 1971 have primarily involved the air force's airlift capabilities. During the intervention in Sri Lanka from 1987 to 1990 the air force showed itself capable of transporting large numbers of men and matériel to foreign and at times hostile operational theaters and maintaining them there over a substantial period of time. During the 1988 crisis in the Maldives the air force flew in, at short notice, an Indian paratrooper battalion and its equipment, revealing its rapid intervention capability in the immediate Indian Ocean region. The true extent of the IAF's strategic airlift capability was quietly demonstrated in the 1991 Gulf War, when it, along with commandeered civilian airliners, evacuated 155,000 Indians from Iraq and Kuwait. The swift and smooth operation revealed that the IAF had exponentially evolved effective command and control mechanisms for large-scale operations. If the airlift operations are an indicator of the IAF's operational doctrine in the twenty-first century, they prove the air force's ability to amass power projection capabilities throughout the Indian Ocean region.

In the late 1990s the acquisition of the Sukhoi-30 MKI two-seat long-range strike fighter resulted in a quantum leap in the IAF's deep-strike potential. The induction of the Prithvi surface-to-surface missile and the impending production of the Agni II IRBM have also transformed the IAF's strategic strike potential. The IAF has the ability to strike deep into China with aircraft and missiles. The air force's new capabilities have led to tension with the army over who would control the country's nuclear delivery systems. The air force has suggested the establishment of a Strategic Command based on its su-30s, Agni, and Prithvi.[153]

Tensions with the army over this issue, however, have not prevented the air force from working closely with the army to develop its twenty-first-century concept of "air land battle." The doctrine was validated during Exercise Shiv Shakti, conducted in December 1998. Since then the Army Training Command and the air force's Air War Strategy Cell have been refining the doctrine, which calls for the complete integration of the air force and army in a future conflict. The aim is to destroy the enemy force's middle echelon and to simultaneously engage the enemy's front-line troops through the use of long-range missiles, strike aircraft, and ground forces. NATO established this doctrine to take on the numerically superior Warsaw Pact forces, which favored attacking in echelon formations. It depends on using emerging technology weapon systems and sensors such as remotely piloted vehicles, satellite imagery, and precision-guided munitions to see behind enemy lines and deliver precise firepower to the enemy's choke points such as bridges, ammunition dumps, marshaling yards, and dams.[154] Indeed, the air force component of Exercise Shiv Shakti, code-named Exercise Gajraj, is a good indicator of the IAF's current operational capabilities. In what the air force described as a "routine annual exercise" 125 combat planes and 30 transports and helicopters manned by 300 pilots, 2,300 technical and support staff, and an operational crew numbering 1,300 flew 2,300 sorties.[155] The exercise, which was also the first to include the newly acquired su-30, was fully computerized, with computers being used not only for inventory, management, and support services but also for air-space management, missile safety, and mission analysis.[156]

As in the case of the air force, the Indian navy emerged from colonial rule with few resources and little operational experience with which to formulate a cohesive doctrine. These problems existed despite the fact that in August 1947, barely ten days after India gained independence, the First Naval Plans Paper (Paper No. 1), created by senior Royal Navy officers still guiding the Indian navy, called for a naval fleet to be centered around two light fleet carriers.[157] Although the Nehru government approved the plan's objectives, it would be fourteen years until the navy obtained its first light carrier, the *Vikrant*. To further complicate matters, Nehru's nonaligned foreign policy cut the navy off from much-needed British naval expertise soon after independence. The Royal Navy had hoped that the Indian navy, along with the Canadian, Australian, and New Zealand navies, would form the bulwark of a British-led Commonwealth naval force that would serve the Allied cause. India's independent stance, however, caused the Royal Navy to reconsider its relationship with the Indian navy. At the same time, throughout the 1940s and 1950s the Royal Navy was willing to support the navies of Australia, Canada, and New Zealand and "was prepared to 'carry' developments in these services to a greater extent because of their integration into the overall British and Allied concepts of naval defense. . . . India, by pursuing a policy of non-alignment with the Western Alliance was not committed to these arrangements."[158] Furthermore, in India the navy remained the juniormost of the three services in terms of size and priority. Only in 1968 was the navy chief of staff elevated to the rank of admiral, bringing the navy in line with the other three services. During the 1960s and 1970s successive naval chiefs and even politicians harped on the need to create a blue-water navy. The navy's shining moment came in the 1971 war, when it utilized its resources effectively to blockade East Pakistan and to severely restrict maritime traffic into the main West Pakistani port of Karachi. Two factors emanating from the 1971 conflict have had a considerable impact on the continuing development of Indian naval doctrine. First, the effective use of its lone aircraft carrier, the INS Vikrant, to blockade East Pakistan and the threat of the possible intervention of the task force led by the USS Enterprise convinced the navy of the need to obtain aircraft carriers if it was to have a blue-water navy. Second, the destruction of the INS Khukri by the Pakistani submarine Hangor and the mining activities of the Pakistani submarine Ghazi have made it abundantly clear that the modern diesel electric submarine is a tremendous force multiplier and could pose a potent threat to an enemy force no matter its size. The experiences of this conflict helped revitalize a debate about the relevance of large-surface combatants, like the carrier, with the tremendous technological advances in submarine development. One example of the debate is discussed in the 1995 article in the air force journal Vayu. In it Vice-Adm. Subimal Mookerjee, arguing against the carrier, noted, "Aircraft carriers dominated the oceans during the Second World War. Developments in naval technology since then – submarines, precision guided munitions and shore based high performance aircraft – have tilted the crucial offense-defense balance decisively against aircraft carriers. They retain their value in non-belligerent roles such as port visits, disaster relief and peace keeping, but their role and performance in war-like operations against credible new threats have not received objective evaluation."[159] On the other hand, Air Commodore Jasjit Singh made the following four points in support of an Indian carrier fleet:

1. The only effective approach to defend against the threat of anti-ship cruise missile is to intercept the launch platform (whether aircraft, surface ship, or submarine) before the missile can be launched.

2. Essentially, the solution for adequate defense of warships and merchant

fleets lies in area air defense capabilities and area anti-submarine warfare capabilities to meet traditional challenges and the new parameters imposed by the induction and proliferation of anti-ship cruise missiles. . . . In short, what India needs is air defense as well as anti-submarine capability in the Arabian Sea and the Bay of Bengal if it is to protect even the minimal key interests.

3. Given the shape of peninsular India and the Indian territories in the Andaman and Car Nicobar group (over 1,200 km [746 miles] from the mainland) and the Lakshadweep group in the Arabian Sea, a land based air power solution would require an extensive chain of radars, fighter interceptor bases, and a large contingent of fighter interceptors and anti-submarine aircraft. The carrier solution is far more cost-effective. Even if India were to go in for a land-based air power solution, the fighter-interceptors will be severely limited in the cover they can provide. This is why an integral air-defense and anti-submarine warfare capability is an operational necessity.

4. Can India afford not to have aircraft carriers for air defense and anti-submarine roles? The survival of the surface fleet in the modern world is highly suspect without carriers for their defense. Technology has altered the equation and the carrier is (now) needed to protect the surface fleet.[160]

In 1978 a government report indicated the navy would launch a twenty-year expansion program to give the navy true blue-water capability.[161] The proximate objectives of the plan included establishing a "sea power" befitting a nation of India's size and peninsular location; defending India's growing seaborne trade; improving India's coastal defense capability within its 12-mile territorial waters; and protecting its potential mineral resources within its 200-mile exclusive economic zone (EEZ).[162] The plan envisaged by 2000 a force of 250–300 vessels built around a fleet of 3–4 aircraft carriers and up to 20–24 submarines along with the necessary shore and seaborne support and logistical facilities.[163] Some analysts have argued that the 1978 naval plan is a continuity of the British naval strategy for India whereby India's security interests in the Indian Ocean region encompass not only Indian territory and the EEZ but a substantial area where the neighboring states acquiesced to India's security interests.[164] Jerold Elkin and Ashley Tellis perceive this security area as concentric zones emanating from the Indian mainland.[165] D. N. Christie notes that some interesting if inexact parallels exist between India's naval strategy and Australia's layered defense and denial concepts as presented in the 1986 *Review of Australia's Defense Capabilities* and the 1987 White Paper *The Defense of Australia*.[166] However, both Christie and Gordon believe that the goals of the 1978 Naval Plan are grossly unrealistic: "maximalist projections by 2010–25 of a blue-water navy capable of 'hemisphere

power projection,' was grossly unrealistic even under the most benign budgetary assumptions. Simple calculations based on construction rates, personnel development, the imperatives of modernization and replacement cy-
cles, compounded by the problems of block obsolescence and rising unit cost
of replacement (as demonstrated by both the Soviet and Chinese maritime
experiences), should have sufficed to produce a measured assessment much
earlier."[167] What these assumptions ignore is that throughout the 1980s and
1990s, the navy's acquisitions reflected a two-pronged approach. On the one
hand, the navy continued to pursue a long-term blue-water capability by purchasing a second light carrier, the ex–Royal Navy carrier *Hermes*, and Sea Harrier vertical jump jets with which to equip it and the *Vikrant*. The two light carriers give the navy minimal power projection capability in the Indian Ocean
region. Other surface combatants such as the Russian Kashin-class destroyers, the Krivak III–class frigates, the indigenous Godavari-class frigates, the
Delhi-class destroyers, and the proposed Type 17 frigates are multipurpose
vessels designed for independent deployment or as part of a carrier battle
group. The second prong of the navy's doctrine includes developing a powerful coastal warfare fleet built primarily around Russian-designed Trantul-
class missile corvette squadrons and Indian-designed Khukri- and Kora-class
corvettes. The navy's rapidly expanding submarine fleet also reflects this approach. The German-designed HDW submarines and several Italian mini-
submarines take on coastal and medium deployment missions, while the
larger Russian Kilo-class submarines can take on longer-range missions. The
lease of the Soviet Charlie-class nuclear submarine in 1988 and the ongoing
project to build an indigenous nuclear submarine reflect the navy's commitment to develop a long-range strike capability. The draft nuclear doctrine
also opens the possibility of the navy deploying nuclear-armed missile submarines in the twenty-first century.

In December 1998 the naval chief, Admiral Bhagwat, stated that the navy
would test launch a naval version of the Prithvi from a ship in January 1999.
(The test occurred on 11 April 2000 from the INS *Subhadra*.) Admiral Bhagwat declared that the naval Prithvi and a newer aircraft carrier would greatly
enhance India's force projection capability, adding that "it is a national requirement on the strategic frontier, not at the doorstep."[168] Furthermore, if
Christie's "maximalist" projection until 2010–25 is considered, then at the
current building rate in both Indian and Russian shipyards India may have
two conventional takeoff and landing carriers, three destroyers, nine frigates, four to six conventional submarines, and possibly a nuclear submarine
added to its fleet. Although the goal of a 200–300-ship navy will still be un-

attainable, these modern and vastly more capable warships will enable India to possess the most capable navy in Asia.

Besides unit acquisitions, other factors point to the navy's long-term commitment to obtaining a credible blue-water status. The navy's sealift capabilities were highlighted in 1992–94, when the Sixty-sixth Independent Indian Infantry Brigade took part in peacekeeping operations in Somalia. After the American pull-out in March 1994 the Indian government decided to send a naval task force to bring the Indian brigade back. Between 11 and 23 December an Indian task force that included the frigates INS *Ganga* and INS *Godavari*, the support ship INS *Shakti*, and a roll-on-roll-off cargo ship from Bombay evacuated the brigade with no casualties or damage to property. The expedition marked the first instance in the UN's history that a naval task force from Asia had been deployed for such a task.

Similarly, army and air force joint exercises in the Rajasthan Desert in November–December 1998 were preceded by a navy-led amphibious exercise called Triamph-98 (Tri Services Amphibious) off the Goa coast.[169] The war game involved 10,000 personnel and an aircraft carrier task group of some twenty-five ships, forty fighter planes (air force and navy), T-72 tanks, and army and marine infantry units. The exercise incorporated four distinct phases, beginning with the assembly phase in Mangalore, a training and work-up phase, the tactical phase, and the deinduction phase and dispersion after the objectives had been achieved.[170] As a result of the lessons learned during the exercises, the navy commissioned its first dedicated squadron for information warfare equipped with aircraft and sensors to obtain and transfer information with real-time connectivity to either shore- or sea-based facilities.[171] According to Admiral Bhagwat, the navy's enhanced power projection capabilities are "a national requirement of the strategic frontier."[172]

Unlike the army and the air force, the navy has generally been tightlipped about its operational and strategic goals. Beyond the obvious role of protecting the coastline and offshore resources, the navy has expressed an interest in taking on the principal role in the Indian Ocean region in combating piracy and protecting trade routes. However, it undoubtedly has an interest in creating a carrier-based expeditionary force in the region. In October 2000 the Indian navy carried out an unprecedented unilateral naval exercise in the South China Sea. The move expands the Indian navy's operational area from the Arabian to the South China Sea and toward a possible confrontation with China.[173] The architect of the navy's expanded role, Adm. Sushil Kumar, declared in July 2000 that the Indian navy's "formal" doctrine had three priority areas: naval diplomacy, creating a force with concentrated firepower and the ability to react rapidly to contingencies, and the acquisition of land-attack capability.[174]

All three services have shown themselves to be remarkably independent and decisive in creating their own operational doctrines. This trend has come about despite the bureaucracy's attempts to micromanage defense policy making and the civilian leadership's lack of strategic planning. In doing so the services have laid down an organizational and tactical foundation for an Indian strategic vision in the twenty-first century.

NOTES

Introduction

1. McNeill, *The Pursuit of Power*; Porter, *War and the Rise of the State*.

2. Hanson, *The Western Way of War*, xii, 227–28.

3. Parker, *The Military Revolution*, 118.

4. Parker, *The Military Revolution*, 130.

5. Keegan, *A History of Warfare*, 387–91.

6. Hanson, *Carnage and Culture*, 5, 440–41. This book is fraught with contradictions and unsubstantiated statements, including the lumping of Western and non-Western military evolution into stereotyped packages. Hanson's argument that Western military and political culture from the Greeks to the present has followed a clearly defined linear progression is patently false. Similarly, his argument that non-Western military systems (Asians in particular) failed to develop similar military systems is also weak. For a detailed dismantling of Hanson's book see Lynn, *Battle*, 12–27.

7. Although Lynn's work concentrates primarily on European military culture, his two chapters dealing with Indian and Chinese military culture offer some interesting insights into the evolution of differing Asian military systems. See Lynn, *Battle*.

8. Rosen, *Societies and Military Power*, 258–61.

9. Alavi, *The Sepoys and the Company*, 4, 1–3.

10. Keegan, *The Face of Battle*.

1. Warfare in Prehistoric and Classical India

1. Organized research on the Indus valley civilization remains scant, with few attempts at a detailed and in-depth reconstruction of the archaeological evidence. See Thapar, *Interpreting Early India*, 114.

2. Wheeler, *Early India and Pakistan*, 106–7; Wheeler, *The Indus Valley Civilization*, 15.

3. See Wheeler, "Harappa, 1946," 59.

4. Wheeler, "Harappa, 1946," 64; Wheeler, *The Indus Valley Civilization*, 20, fig. 4, and plan facing p. 20.

5. Wheeler, *The Indus Valley Civilization*, 27, fig. 6.

6. Stein, *An Archeological Tour in Gedrosia*, 60; Stein, *Archeological Reconnaissances*, 70–71.

7. McIntosh, *A Peaceful Realm*, 93–94.

8. Kenoyer, *Ancient Cities*, 56.

9. Kenoyer, *Ancient Cities*, 56.

10. Kenoyer, "The Indus Valley Tradition."

11. Wheeler, *The Indus Valley Civilization*, 61.

12. Wheeler, *The Indus Valley Civilization*, 58. See also MacKay, *Further Excavations*, 1:461, 2:pl. 121, 13–14, pl. 128, 7–11, pl. 131, 18, and pl. 132, 28–30. See also Vats, *Excavations at Harappa*, 1:391, 2:pl. 125, 13–14.

13. MacKay, *Further Excavations*, 1:459. See also Pant, *Studies*, 19–27.

14. Stein, *An Archeological Tour in Waziristan and North Baluchistan*, 38, 54.

15. Griffiths, trans., *The Hymns of the Rigveda*, 1:R.V. I-53.7 (cf. I-32.6), I-33.12, I-61.5, I-130.7, I-131.4, I-174.2, II-20.7, III-34.1, IV-16.13 (cf. I-53.8), I-54.6, II-14.6, I-130.3.

16. Griffiths, trans., *The Hymns of the Rigveda*, 1:R.V. VI-16.39, VII-6.2.

17. Thapar, *Interpreting Early India*, 101–3.

18. Renfrew, "Archaeology and Linguistics," 15–24. See also Renfrew, *Archaeology and Language*; Thapar, *Early India*, 13.

19. Feuerstein, Kak, and Frawley, *In Search*, 114.

20. The Anatolia location of the earliest Aryan speakers is Colin Renfrew's thesis and is partly adopted by Feuerstein, Kak, and Frawley, *In Search*, 54–55.

21. Thapar refers to this period as the era of chieftainships and kingships, 1600–1200 BC (*Early India*, 31).

22. The Sankhayana Svauta Sutra (Puranas) is the first to speak of a climactic struggle that proved disastrous for the Kaurava tribe. See Winternitz, *A History*, 470–71.

23. For more information on the historical accuracy and the possible time frame of the *Mahabharata* epic see Sircar, *The Bharata War*; and Roy, *Date*. Roy gives

a precise time frame of 1424–1414 BC (*Date*, 148). See also Thapar, *From Lineage to State*, 16–17.

24. Hopkins, *The Social and Military Position*, 253–54.

25. Hopkins, *The Social and Military Position*, 150–63, 179–203.

26. Hopkins, *The Social and Military Position*, 263–64.

27. Singh, *Ancient Indian Warfare*, 175.

28. Thapar, *Early India*, 31.

29. Thapar, *Early India*, 31.

30. Herodotus (born c. 490–480 BC), *The Histories*, bk. 3, 97, in Majumdar, *The Classical Accounts*, 1.

31. E. Mayer, *Geschichte des Altertums*, 3:128, quoted in Majumdar, ed., *History and Culture*, 2:40.

32. Selincourt, *The Life of Alexander the Great*, 98.

33. Arrian (Flavius Arrianus, AD 96–180), *Anabasis Alexandri*, bk. 4, chaps. 26–30, in McCrindle, *The Invasion of India*, 67–78; also Majumdar, *The Classical Accounts*, 12–19.

34. Selincourt, *The Life of Alexander the Great*, 171.

35. Hans Delbruck estimates 11,000, including 5,000 cavalry. See Delbruck, *Antiquity*, 220. Tarn, "Two Notes on Selucid History," estimates 15,000 infantry alone.

36. Delbruck, *Antiquity*, 221.

37. McCrindle, *The Invasion of India*, 205.

38. Fuller, *The Generalship* (1958), 191.

39. Delbruck, *Antiquity*, 221–25.

40. A detailed discussion of this controversy can be found in Delbruck, *Antiquity*, 225–28.

41. The Macedonians were no strangers to elephants by this time; after the capture of the rock of Aornus, Alexander sent out two of his officers to survey the region and to specifically learn of elephants. Subsequently, Alexander captured or hired a number of Indian elephant hunters or trainers whom he used to capture elephants, which were pressed into service with his army, probably as load carriers. Alexander is also supposed to have received thirty elephants as a gift from the ruler of Taxilla. Arrian, *Anabasis Alexandri*, bk. 4, chap. 30, in Majumdar, *The Classical Accounts*, 9–19.

42. McCrindle, *The Invasion of India*, 209.

43. Delbruck, *Antiquity*, 178–79.

44. Singh, *Ancient Indian Warfare*, 116.

45. According to D. H. Gordon, the evidence from Greek sources, including Ktesias and Herodotus, indicates that iron must have been in use in most of the urban centers in India by 450 BC. Ktesias, for instance, makes special mention of the excellence of two swords made of Indian steel presented to Artaxerxes

Mnemon. Indeed, Gordon feels that the famous crucible steel known by the Telegu name of *wootz* was in all probability invented by Indian iron smiths in the fifth century BC. See Gordon, *The Prehistoric Background*, 155, 162; see also by the same author "The Early Use of Metals," 55ff. Archaeological excavations in northern India have unearthed iron implements that date back to before the Painted Grey Ware pottery period (c. 1000 BC).

46. Fuller, *The Generalship*, 15, 42–51; Bosworth, *Conquest and Empire*, 243. Philip II's reform of the Macedonian army was preceded by similar reforms carried out by the Greek city-state of Sparta. The Spartans freed their hoplites from agricultural tasks by supplying them with rural, disenfranchised servants, known as helots, who worked their farms. This enabled the Spartan hoplites to train and stay in the field as a permanent army. See Hanson, *The Western Way of War*, 38.

47. Bosworth, *Conquest and Empire*, 261.

48. Arrian, *Indika*, chap. 16, in Majumdar, *The Classical Accounts*, 230. In fact, it was an Indian arrow that inflicted a near-fatal wound upon Alexander when he fought the Malloi. An arrow about "two cubits" long penetrated his breastplate and severely injured him. See Plutarch, *Life of Alexander*, Oration 2, in Majumdar, *The Classical Accounts*, 204; see also Arrian, *Anabasis Alexandri*, bk. 6, chaps. 10–11, in Majumdar, *The Classical Accounts*, 70–71; also Herodotus, chap. 7.65, in Schoff, "The Eastern Iron Trade," 231. Other Greek states did not create permanent military barracks like Sparta by forbidding their male citizens to engage in commerce or agriculture. However, they did require all male citizens between age seventeen and fifty-nine to be liable for service, and they had regular training programs to keep the infantry in a state of battle readiness. See Ferrill, *The Origins of War*, 106.

49. Delbruck, *Antiquity*, 224.

50. This same ground also immobilized the Indian chariots. The Indian cavalry too proved no match for the heavier armored Macedonian cavalry, which operated in very effective squadron, or *ilai*, formations. Delbruck, *Antiquity*, 127. The core of Alexander's cavalry force were his elite companion cavalry, or *hetairoi*, led by Alexander himself. At the battle of the Hydaspes Alexander also made extensive use of mounted archers to disperse the Indian cavalry.

51. Perrin, trans., *Plutarch's Lives*, vol. 2, chap. 62.

52. According to the Roman historian Justin, Sandracottus (Chandragupta) established his Indian empire while Seleucus was busy consolidating his claim to the eastern satrapy. Justin [Junianus Justinus], *Historiarum Philippicarum of Justinus*, bk. 15, chap. 4, in Majumdar, *The Classical Accounts*, 192–93.

53. What is known, however, is that the Selucids, led by Seleucus I, did alter their traditional Greco-Macedonian military organization to accommodate the Indian war elephant. Strabo states that in 302 BC, on the eve of the battle of Ipsus

against his rival Antiogonos, Seleucus received 500 elephants from Chandragupta for bringing a halt to the war between them. Although the exact numbers are disputed, the elephants played a decisive role in this battle. At Ipsus, Seleucus used the elephants in a defensive role, interdicting and preventing the return of Demetrius's cavalry to the battlefield. The Selucids, in addition to using the elephants mainly for defensive purposes, also supported them with light infantry, unlike the Indians. According to Appian, a unit known as the *stiphas* always accompanied the elephants into battle. Despite such judicious use of the elephants, they ultimately formed a weak link in the Selucid military organization, which became very apparent in Antiochus III's campaigns against the Romans. At the battle of Thermopylae (191 BC) their presence did little to deter the more mobile Roman legions from overcoming the slower Selucid phalanx. Furthermore, during the battle of Magnesia (190 BC) Selucid elephants, driven mad by a shower of Roman projectiles, actually broke the Selucid phalanx. Bar-Kochva, in his excellent study of Selucid military organization, suggests that the Selucids were innovative tacticians, but their move to incorporate elephants into their armies was a major tactical blunder. In terms of mobility the Romans totally outclassed them, and this was not attributable to rough terrain (favoring the lighter-equipped Romans), for as Bar-Kochva points out, the battlegrounds at Thermopylae and Magnesia were flat. Bar-Kochva suggests that Antiochus III's poor generalship and the poor quality of his phalangites caused him to lose the battle. Certainly, this may have contributed to the Selucid defeat, but the presence of the elephants, even in a defensive posture, could only have hampered the Selucid army's mobility. See Bar-Kochva, *The Selucid Army*, 76–77, 87, 171, 203, 205; Tarn, "Two Notes on Selucid History," 84–89.

54. McCrindle, *The Invasion of India*, 141, 161. Romila Thapar points out that the figure of 600,000 is double that of the Roman infantry before Diocletian increased it in the sixth century AD, thereby shaking the economy of the empire. Since the economic base of the Mauryan Empire was smaller than that of the Roman Empire, this figure is highly doubtful. See Thapar, *The Mauryas Revisited*, 16–17.

55. Shamasastry, *Kautilyas Arthashastra* (1929), 5; also Roychaudhuri, *Political History*, 121.

56. Trautmann, *Kautilya*, 186.

57. The palm-leaf parchments were discovered in 1904 when an anonymous Brahmin (who subsequently vanished) handed them over to Dr. R. Shamasastry, the chief librarian of the government of Mysore.

58. Book 10.3.50 quoted in Kangle, *The Kautilya Arthashastra*, 2:433–53.

59. Book 10.5.38, in Kangle, *The Kautilya Arthashastra*, 2:448.

60. Shamasastry, *Kautilya's Arthashastra*, bk. 10, chap. 4, p. 399.

61. Shamasastry, *Kautilya's Arthashastra*, bk. 2, chaps. 2, 31, 32, pp. 151–55.

62. Shamasastry, *Kautilya's Arthashastra*, bk. 2, chap. 32, p. 49.

63. Palakapaya, *Hastayayur-Veda*, chap. 1, sec. 5, vv. 23, 29. Another Sanskrit text, the *Nitisara Kamandaka*, states: "The Kingdoms of Kings depend upon elephants [and] one elephant, duly equipped and trained in the methods of war, is capable of slaying six thousand well caparisoned horses [cavalry]." See Sastri, ed., *Nitisara Kamandaka*, chap. 16, pp. 10–12, chap. 20, p. 61. The views of the Indian writers are backed by the Greek ambassador Megasthenes, who notes, "It is the elephant which in India carries the royalty. The conveyance which ranks next in honor is the chariot." He also notes that Indian women, while possessed of "uncommon discretion," would not consider it a disgrace (nor would society) to grant their favors for an elephant. See Arrian, *Indika*, chap. 16, in Majumdar, *The Classical Accounts*, 23.

64. The *Arthashastra* also gives us a rare glimpse into the finances of the Mauryan army. It notes, for instance, that an army is dependent on the treasury, for without pay an army might defect to the enemy or murder the king. Revenue extraction itself seems to have evolved from the concept of *bali*, or oblation to the gods, which later also became an offering to the king for protecting the people. Bali is also mentioned in the Rig-Veda and is the oldest Indo-Aryan term for royal revenue. In Mauryan times land revenue was usually charged to individual holdings and based on the quality of the land. The main item of land revenue appears to have been the *bhaga*, or the customary share of the agricultural produce first mentioned in the Arthashastra. See Spellman, *Political Theory*, 176, 79, 190–97; Jha, *Economy and Society*, 46–49, 50–57.

65. Take, for example, Skandagupta, one of the great rulers of the Gupta dynasties who controlled northern India from AD 455 to 467. He waged a successful campaign against Epthalite or Hepthalite invaders from Afghanistan. The Bhitari stone pillar, which describes this conflict, merely states: "By whose two arms the earth was shaken, when he the creator of a terrible whirlpool [Skandagupta] joined in conflict with the Hunas." See "Hunair yyasa Samagatasaya samare dorbhyam dhara kampita bhim-avartta-karasya," in Fleet, ed., *Corpus Inscriptionum Indicarum*, 315. A rare exception is the quote in the *Milindapanho*, which gives us an instantly recognizable image of an infantryman at war: "But surely then O King, why is it that when their frontier provinces have broken out in revolt, the Kings, to the end that they may bring the inhabitants of those provinces in subjugation again, leave their homes, attended by their ministers and chiefs, their soldiers and their guards, and marching over ground even and uneven, tormented the while by gnats and mosquitoes and hot winds, engage in fierce fights and suffer the presentiment of death." See Spellman, *Political Theory*, 149.

66. Devahuti, *Harsha*.

67. Watter, *On Yuan Chwang's Travels in India*, 1:171.

68. Watter, *On Yuan Chwang's Travels in India*, 2:239. Similarly, Bana, a famous Indian poet of this period who wrote the *Harshacharita*, or chronicle of King Harsha, makes no mention of war chariots while describing the imperial army. See Bana, *Harshacharita*, chap. 7.

69. Beal, trans., *Buddhist Records*, 83; Watter, *On Yuan Chwang's Travels in India*, 1:171. The Madhuban copper plates from Harsha's time also make no mention of chariots when referring to the various arms of the imperial army. See Buhler, "The Madhuban Copper-Plate."

70. Beal, trans., *Buddhist Records*, 213; Watters, *On Yuan Chwang's Travels in India*, 1:343.

71. Bana-Bhatta, *Harsha-Charita*, 68; Bana, *Harshacharita*, 55.

72. Harsha's armies appear to have been heavily weighted down with a large number of camp followers, including women and a vast kitchen, complete with its own livestock and cooking implements. Bana's description of an imperial army on the march could be mistaken for the mass migration of an entire community. See Bana-Bhatta, *Harsha-Charita*, 205–11; Bana, *Harshacharita*, 200–208.

73. Beal, trans., *Buddhist Records*, 83; Watters, *On Yuan Chwang's Travels in India*, 1:171.

74. Cunningham, *The Stupa of Bharut*, pl. 32, fig. 1; also Maisey, *Sanchi*, pl. 20.

75. Cunningham, *The Stupa of Bharut*, pl. 32, fig. 1, pp. 32–33.

76. Nearchus noted that "all [infantrymen] wear swords of vast breadth, though scarce exceeding three cubits in length. Those, when they engage in close fight . . . they grasp with both hands, that their blows may be stronger." Quoted in Strabo, *Geography*, chap. 16.1.52, in Majumdar, *The Classical Accounts*, 230, 279.

77. Gordon, *The Prehistoric Background*, 108, pl. 20.

78. Gordon dates these paintings and engravings to the "early centuries AD." They depict fierce battle scenes with mounted men (frequently riding caparisoned horses), archers, spearmen, and swordsmen, all engaged in fierce if confused close combat. Gordon, *The Prehistoric Background*, 105–6, pls. 18, 19.

79. Cunningham, *The Stupa of Bharut*, pl. 6, fig. 2, pl. 9, fig. 2, pls. 11, 20, 22; Maisey, *Sanchi*, pl. 32; see also Ghosh, ed., *An Encyclopedia*, 2:301.

80. Marshall, *A Guide to Sanchi*, 138 n. 3.

81. Coomaraswamy, "Horseriding." In a comparative context, Coomaraswamy notes that in China the metal stirrup does not come into evidence until after the Han period.

82. Suchaus, *Alberuni's India*, 1:243.

83. Allan, *Catalogue*, pl. 13, pp. 11–19.

84. Allan, *Catalogue*, pl. 22.

85. Many of these historians cite Herodotus, who noted that the animals in India, with the sole exception of the horse, were much larger than those found

in the rest of the world. Herodotus, *The Histories*, bk. 3, chap. 106, in Majumdar, *The Classical Accounts*, 4. Bana notes that Emperor Harsha filled his royal stables with horses from Sind, Punjab, Waziristan, the Pamir region, and Persia. See Bana-Bhatta, *Harsha-Charita*, 206; Bana, *Harshacharita*, 201. Horses were also obtained from Kamboja or Afghanistan. For more information on horse trading in ancient India see Gupta, "Horse Trade."

86. Sastri, *The Cholas*, 116.

87. *South Indian Inscriptions*, 1:v.

88. According to the Tanjore inscriptions made in 1030–31 AD, "[who] having despatched many ships in the midst of the rolling sea and having caught the Sangramavijayottunga-Varman, the King of Kadaram [Keddain Malaya Peninsula] together with elephants in his glorious army." See Hultzch, ed., *South Indian Inscriptions*, vol. 2, pt. 1, no. 20, p. 109. The Sailendra Empire was one of the most powerful Hindu colonial empires in Southeast Asia. See n. 86.

89. Hultzch, ed., *South Indian Inscriptions*, vol. 2, pt. 2, no. 59, p. 241, n. 1. See also *Miscellaneous Inscriptions*, 4–6.

90. K. A. Nilakanta Sastri believes that the inscription refers to a regiment of the Chola army. According to Sastri, the inscription belongs to the period of Rajaraja and Rajendra I. Another inscription from Sermadevi dated AD 1096 also refers to "the several armed thousands of the great army of the three divisions [kai]." See Sastri, *The Cholas*, 454–55.

91. Sastri, *The Cholas*, 456–57.

92. Chinese traveler Chau Ju-Kua quoted in Sastri, *The Cholas*, 457–58.

93. The disastrous battle of Takkolam devastated Chola power in southern India until the accession of Rajaraja I in AD 985. See Sastri, *The Cholas*, 131–32.

94. Sulaiman (his book bears the date AH 237, or AD 851) also stated that the king of Ruhmi only took to the field in winter "because the elephant cannot endure thirst." See *Salsilatu-T Tawarikh* of the merchant Sulaiman with additions by Zaidu-L Hasan, in Elliot, *The History of India*, 1:5, 25.

95. The Khambuja Empire was initially based around Vat Phu Hill near Bassac in Laos. It eventually became the most powerful of all the Hindu colonial empires in Indochina. According to Chinese sources Khambuja extended suzerainty over a vast region of central Indochina to the east of Burma, the south of China, and the west of Annam. It controlled the Hindu kingdoms along the upper valley of the Mekong, including Alavi-rashtra, Hari-bhunjaya, and Svarna-grama. At its zenith under Jaya Varman the Khambuja Empire included nearly all of Indochina from the Sea of China to the Bay of Bengal. Its territories included parts of Annam to the east, lower Burma, and parts of the Malay Peninsula. The physical legacy of the Khambujas lives on in the magnificent temple of Angkor-Vat in Laos built by Emperor Surya-Varman (died shortly after AD 1145). See Majumdar, *Ancient Indian Civilization*, 25, 57.

96. Other dominant Hindu empires in the southeast included Fu-Nan (its Chinese name), based in the delta and lower valley of the Mekong River; the Champa Empire, based in central and southern Annam; and the Sailendra Empire, based in the Malay Archipelago. An inscription composed in Sanskrit and written in Indian script engraved on two faces of a block of granite was found close to the village of Vo-Chanh near Nha-Trang in the province of Kanh-Hoa in southern Annam. See Majumdar, *Ancient Indian Civilization*, 22, 26; Barth and Bregaigne, *Inscriptions sanscrites*, Champa, inscription no. 1. Chinese sources in the fourth and fifth centuries speak of a Brahmin named Chu Chan T'an who usurped the throne of Funan. See Pelliot, "Le Fou-nan," 269.

97. Schoff, trans., *The Periplus*, 44ff. In 1945 Sir Mortimer Wheeler discovered a large number of Roman items near the ancient fishing village of Arikamendu some 2 miles south of Pondicherry. They included sherds of Roman ceramics traceable to Arezzo in Italy produced between 30 and 45 BCE. Indians imported very few goods but were eager to get their hands on Roman gold. Eleven hoards of Roman gold coins have been found in the area around Coimbatore (first century CE). Texts from the Sangam age speak of *yavana*, or Greek- or Roman-built ships, that came with gold and returned with pepper. See Wheeler, *Rome*, 133. See also Van Leur, *Indonesian Trade*.

98. Rosen, *Societies and Military Power*, 91, 102–3.

99. See Stein, *Peasant State*, 265–85.

100. Stein, "The Segmentary State Revisited," 137, 146–47.

101. Kulke, "The Early Imperial Kingdom," 233, 250, 262.

102. As Ronald Inden has stated, "They had an inherent, but limited and partial capacity to combine within and among themselves and order their own affairs" (*Imagining India*, 220).

103. Eisenstadt and Hartman, "Historical Experience," 39.

104. Eisenstadt and Hartman, "Historical Experience," 38; see also Beteille, *Caste, Class and Power*; and Mandelbaum, *Society in India*.

105. Eisenstadt and Hartman, "Historical Experience," 39–41; see also Bayly, *Saints, Goddesses and Kings*; Dirks, "Political Authority"; Rahaya, "India"; Rao and Subrahmanyam, *Symbols of Substance*.

2. Warfare in Medieval India

1. Beal, trans., *Si-Yu-Ki*, 188.

2. Cunningham, *The Ancient Geography of India*, 19–20.

3. The chief source of information on these expeditions is the *Futhu-ul Buldan* of Al-Biladhuri. See Jabar, *Kitab Futuh al-Buldan*, 1:113–30.

4. *Chach-Nama or Tarikh-i-Hind Wa Sind*, in Elliot, *The History of India*, 1:131–211.

5. See Tripathi, *History of Kanauj*.

6. Baden Powell, "Notes on the Origin."

7. They included the Chandellas, prominent during the tenth century in the region of Khajurao, and the Guhilots, or Sisodian, clan of Mewar. The latter came into power only during the fourteenth century but nevertheless claimed descent back to 1000 BC from Rama, the mythical Kshatriya prince of the Hindu epic Ramayana. See Bhandarkar, "The Guhilots"; also Sharma, Social Life, 21.

8. A. C. Lyall notes that it is universally assumed in every clan in Rajputana that the chief and ruler of the state is the only primus inter pares ("The Rajput States of India").

9. Fox, Kin, Clan, Raja and Rule, 169.

10. Nazim, The Life and Times, 25.

11. Al Utbi, Tarikh-Yamini, in Elliot, The History of India, 2:14–24.

12. Minhaju-s Siraj, Tabakat-i Nasiri, in Elliot, The History of India, 2:269; see also Habibullah, The Foundation of Muslim Rule, 22–24.

13. The exact number of these expeditions is still debated, but Sir H. M. Elliot, after carrying out a detailed analysis of numerous accounts, estimates it to be seventeen. See Elliot, The History of India, 2:434–78.

14. Elliot, The History of India, 2:438.

15. Al Utbi, Tarikh-Yamini, in Elliot, The History of India, 2:25; see also Bosworth, The Ghaznavids, 114.

16. Al Utbi, Tarikh-Yamini, in Elliot, The History of India, 2:26.

17. It was only during Mahmud's sixth invasion that the Hindu rulers decided to unite and confront him.

18. Al Utbi, Tarikh-Yamini, in Elliot, The History of India, 2:447–48.

19. Ibn Asir, Kamilu-t Tawarikh, in Elliot, The History of India, 2:469.

20. Minhaju-s Siraj, Tabakat-i Nasiri, in Elliot, The History of India, 2:270.

21. Elliot, The History of India, 2:460.

22. Minhaju-s Siraj, Tabakat-i Nasiri, in Elliot, The History of India, 2:280–94.

23. Firishtah places it on the banks of the Sarsuti 14 miles from Thaneshwar and 80 miles from Delhi. See Elliot, The History of India, 2:295 n. 3.

24. Minhaju-s Siraj, Tabakat-i Nasiri, in Elliot, The History of India, 2:295–96.

25. Minhaju-s Siraj, Tabakat-i Nasiri, in Elliot, The History of India, 2:296.

26. Minhaju-s Siraj, Tabakat-i Nasiri, in Elliot, The History of India, 2:296–97.

27. Taju-l Ma-Sir, in Elliot, The History of India, 2:235–36.

28. Ziau-d Din Barani, Tarikh-i Firoz Shahi, in Elliot, The History of India, 3:165.

29. Ziau-d Din Barani, Tarikh-i Firoz Shahi, in Elliot, The History of India, 3:199.

30. Amir Khusrau, Khazaiu-L Futuh, in Elliot, The History of India, 3:77.

31. Firishtah, History of the Rise of Mahomedan Power, 210.

32. Firishtah, History of the Rise of Mahomedan Power, 213; see also Ziau-d Din Barani, Tarikh-i Firoz Shahi, in Elliot, The History of India, 3:203.

33. Ziau-d Din Barani, Tarikh-i Firoz Shahi, in Elliot, The History of India, 3:204.

34. Day, *The Government*, 150. Alauddin's achievements even won grudging praise from Hindu chroniclers in Rajasthan. A Sanskrit inscription from the period remarked, "There, is, was, and shall be no king who can match the Sultan Alaud-Din-Khalji" (Burgess, Hultzch, and Fuhrer, eds., *Epigraphica Indica*, 20:189–90).

35. Firishtah, *History of the Rise of Mahomedan Power*, 40.

36. *Tuzuk-i Timuri*, in Elliot, *The History of India*, 3:397.

37. *Tuzuk-i Timuri*, in Elliot, *The History of India*, 3:439–41.

38. Ghazi, *Babur-Nama*, 1:199. Babur's family tree can be traced back to Genghis Khan and Timur-i-Lang. See Roux, *Histoire*, table 1.

39. Ghazi, *Babur-Nama*, 2:441.

40. Ghazi, *Babur-Nama*, 2:471.

41. The sultanate armies did not utilize large organized units of firearm-equipped infantry.

42. Ghazi, *Babur-Nama*, 2:468–69 n. 3.

43. Babur's account of the battle. See Ghazi, *Babur-Nama*, 2:423–74.

44. Ghazi, *Babur-Nama*, 2:562.

45. Ghazi, *Babur-Nama*, 2:570.

46. Ghazi, *Babur-Nama*, 2:572.

47. *Tazkiratu-L Wakiat*, in Elliot, *The History of India*, 5:141–42; see also Ambasthaya, *Decisive Battles*, 31–129. Bayram Khan, Akbar's uncle, who ruled as regent, fought the second battle of Panipat on 5 November 1556 to reclaim Delhi from yet another Suri-inspired insurrection led by Hemu, chief minister of the Suri dynasty.

48. Most mansabdars were members of the ruling Mughal elite, including the nobility, the emirs. However, a number of loyal Rajput and Afghan chiefs were also inducted into this body by Akbar.

49. Allami, *Ain-i-Akbari*, 1:248. Abu'l Fazal is the author of the imperial memoir the *Akbar Nama*, a yearly account of Akbar's reign that in its English edition ran to over 2,500 pages. He also put together an almanac of the empire of Ain-i-Akbari that runs to 1,500 pages in English. Abul Fazal was a senior officer of the imperial army at the time of his death in 1605. He was murdered by Prince Selim (who later became emperor with the title of Jahangir) during his rebellion against his father.

50. Irvine, *The Army*, 4.

51. The few officers who did obtain a land grant, or jagir, could not pass it on to their children. It reverted back to the emperor after their deaths. See Ali, *The Mughal Nobility*, 38–43.

52. Allami, *Ain-i-Akbari*, 1:256.

53. Allami, *Ain-i-Akbari*, 1:243.

54. Chakravarti, "Horse Trade."

55. Irvine, *The Army*, 175–81.

56. The mir atish (a Turkish term for artillery commander) was in charge of the administration and field command of the royal batteries. In the provinces, the qiladar, or fort commander, was in charge of the artillery. Artillery production in the karkhanas, or royal factories, came under the supervision of the khansamah, or lord steward, who maintained the foundry and directed the manufacture of guns and munitions.

57. Zaman, *Mughal Artillery*, 9–20, 23, 26–27. Sir Thomas Roe, an English envoy who visited the karkhana in Burhanpur in 1617, was not impressed by the quality of the guns.

58. Allami, *Ain-i-Akbari*, 1:119.

59. Khan, "Origin and Development," 27. The ban would be used extensively against the British in India and inspired their own Congreave rockets.

60. Abul Fazal states that Akbar was most impressed with matchlocks, and the *Ain-i-Akbari* goes into detail describing how they were made and subsequently tested by Akbar. Fazal describes at least three different types of matchlocks. Allami, *Ain-i-Akbari*, 1:120–23.

61. The quota of Dakhili infantry was composed of one quarter matchlock men and three quarters bowmen. Allami, *Ain-i-Akbari*, 1:264.

62. It appears that Mughal sapping and mining technology was little improved from the inefficient methods used by the Delhi sultanate. See Khan, "Origin and Development," 26–27.

63. According to the *Tabakat-i Akbari*, a huge sabat, or trench, was constructed from the Royal Battery (Morchai-i Badshahi) to the walls that was wide enough for ten horsemen to ride abreast. See Bakshi, *Tabakat-i Akbari*, 148–50.

64. Indeed, Aurungzeb would use the very same methods to destroy the forts of Ahmednagar, Golconda, and Bijapur in southern India.

65. Akbar realized that the Rajput chiefs had the potential to make important allies. Accordingly, he worked out an agreement whereby he acknowledged them as rajas in their domains and kept out of their internal affairs, in return for which the Rajput chiefs agreed to serve as mansabdars in the Mughal army. See Hallissey, *The Rajput Rebellion*, 26, 40–83.

66. Aurungzeb's artillery, in addition to being more mobile, was directed by the very able Suf Shikan Khan. See Ghauri, *War of Succession*, 137; Manucci, *Storia De Mogor*, 1:245–78; Khalifi Khan, *Muntakhabu-L Lubab*, in Elliot, *The History of India*, 7:220–25.

67. Mohamad Khan, *Waquia-i Jahangari*, in Elliot, *The History of India*, 6:380; see also Shyam, *Life and Times*.

68. The Persian term bargir means a soldier who has enlisted without his own horse and equipment and obtains the same from his employer. He is inferior

to the silhedar, who brings his own horse and equipment with him. See Sen, The Military System, 4–5.

69. Khan, Muntakhab-ul-Lubub, 2:130.

70. The Mughal operations in Assam also involved the entire Mughal coastal and riverine "navy," which, with the considerable help of Dutch and Portuguese sailors, managed to crush the Ahom riverine navy at the battle of Kallibar on 3 March 1662. Yet the losses suffered during the duration of the campaign were such that the Mughal coastal fleet in the east was all but devastated for some time to come. See Roy, A History, 48, 117–21.

71. Khan, Ma'asir-i-Alamgiri, 45; Sarkar, The Life of Mir Jumla, 302–3, 330–36.

72. The five surviving firmans, or decrees, from Aurungzeb to Ram Singh (now in the Rajasthan State Archives in Bikaner) reveal the immense interest the emperor maintained in all aspects of the campaign. In a letter written on 7 March 1670 Aurungzeb instructs Ram Singh on the siege of the Assamese fortress at Gauhati. He orders his commander to build a series of surrounding entrenchments and to place his camp on high ground in order to escape the monsoon floods, which had devastated Mughal encampments during the previous season. He also instructed Ram Singh to pay special attention to the establishment of supply dumps along the army's route of march. See Sarkar, "Some Little Known Facts," 58–59. For more information on the Mughal campaigns in the east see the following articles by Jadunath Sarkar: "The Conquest of Chatagaon," "Assam and the Ahoms," and "Shaista Khan in Bengal." See also the diaries of the Mughal military commander Mirza Nathan, Baharistan-i-Ghyabi. The original manuscript is in Paris at the Bibliothèque nationale, sup. pers. MS no. 252. (A photocopy is available in the Jadunath Sarkar Collection, no. 60, acc. no. 1327, National Library, Calcutta.)

73. Gordon, The Marathas 1600–1818, 12.

74. According to Stewart Gordon, the term Maratha came about as a result of military service to the Bahamani Empire by a new elite of Maratha chiefs who brought in bands of armed followers. He suggests that the word was used to differentiate all Marathi-speaking units in the Bahamani Empire and its successor states. Gordon, The Marathas 1600–1818, 15.

75. Duff, A History of the Marathas, 3:67–69.

76. In fact, the evolution of the term Rajput has a similar origin to that of Maratha, as it came about due to military service under the Mughals. See Gordon, The Marathas 1600–1818, 16.

77. Nadkarni, The Rise and Fall, 28.

78. Elliot, The History of India, 7:15. Shahaji's father, Maloji, was a petty cavalryman in the service of a Maratha clan, the Jadhavs of Silkhed, who had grants for military service under the Ahmednagar kingdom.

79. Elliot, The History of India, 7:36–37.

80. Sarkar, "An Early Supporter."

81. Duff, *A History of the Marathas*, 1:114.

82. Khobrekar, ed., *Tarikh-i-Dilkasha*, 16–17.

83. Wakaskar, ed., *Sabhasad Bakhar*, 21.

84. Kazim, *Alamgirnama*, 578.

85. For details see *English Records on Shivaji*; see also Sarkar, *Shivaji and His Times*, 97–108. M. N. Pearson argues that Shivaji's attacks on Surat and Shaistakhan marked the beginning of the Mughal decline, for the attacks forced them to concentrate on a futile and costly series of campaigns to crush Shivaji in order to maintain their military prestige ("Shivaji and the Decline").

86. Manucci, *Storia De Mogor*, 1:132.

87. Kazim, *Alamgirnama*, 891.

88. Sarkar, *The Military Despatches*, 50.

89. Khafikhan, *Muntakhabulluhab*, 180.

90. Wakaskar, ed., *Sabhasad Bakhar*, 40–41.

91. Military dispatch from Jai Singh to Aurungzeb, 19 June 1665, in Sarkar, *The Military Despatches*, 51.

92. A detailed version of the treaty can be found in letters from Jai Singh to Aurungzeb in Udiraj Tala-Yar, "Insha-i-Haft Anjuman," transcript, Jadunath Sarkar Collection, Indian National Library, Calcutta. The author was the son of the secretary to Jai Singh. His text is a compilation of letters between Jai Singh and Aurungzeb. This invaluable collection was discovered by Jadunath Sarkar in Benares; see Sarkar, *Shivaji*, 123–26.

93. Sarkar, *The Military Despatches*, 10.

94. Sarkar and Sinha, "Shivaji's Visits," 22.

95. Sarkar and Sinha, "Shivaji's Visits," letter 44, p. 53.

96. Udiraj Tala-Yar, "Insha-i-Haft Anjuman," 60; and Sarkar, *The Military Despatches*, 42.

97. Wakaskar, ed., *Sabhasad Bakhar*, 56–58.

98. Khan, *Masire Alamgiri*, 62.

99. Newsletter of 7 April 1670, in *Shivkalin Putrusar Sangarha*, letter 1298, 1:362.

100. Newsletter of 24 January 1670, in *Shivkalin Putrusar Sangarha*, letter 1298, 1:358.

101. *English Records on Shivaji*, 173.

102. *English Records on Shivaji*, 283.

103. Sardesai, *New History of the Marathas*, 1:196–97.

104. A British guest, Henry Oxonden, gives a description of the event in Sardesai, *New History of the Marathas*, 1:375.

105. Wakaskar, ed., *Sabhasad Bakhar*, 109.

106. Watters, *On Yuan Chwang's Travels in India*, 2:239.

107. Sen, *Siva Chatrapati*, 38. It is unclear as to how Shivaji financed this new

military system or if, in fact, this was a regularized system during the latter half of his reign.

108. Sen, *The Military System,* 13.

109. *Krishnaji Anant Sabhasad,* quoted in Sen, *The Military System,* 17. Stewart Gordon suggests that prior to the peshwas Maratha armies rarely numbered more than a thousand men. However, this figure seems too low. See Gordon, *Marathas, Marauders and State Formation,* 58.

110. Grose, *Voyage to the East Indies,* 1:126.

111. Careri, *A Voyage Round the World,* 4:212.

112. Grose, *Voyage to the East Indies,* 1:124–25.

113. Foss, *The Forts of India,* 196.

114. Pearson, "Shivaji and the Decline"; and Richards, "The Imperial Crisis."

115. Gordon, *Marathas, Marauders and State Formation,* 28.

116. Blake, "The Patrimonial-Bureaucratic Empire," 280–82.

117. Blake, "The Patrimonial-Bureaucratic Empire," 282.

118. Saberwal, "A Juncture of Traditions"; and Hardy, "Decline of the Mughal Empire."

119. Blake, "The Patrimonial-Bureaucratic Empire," 283, 297–99.

120. Porter, *War and the Rise of the State,* 67.

121. Alam, *The Crisis of Empire,* 304.

122. Kolff, *Naukar, Rajput and Sepoy,* 7, 58, 71–73, 84.

123. Rosen, *Societies and Military Power,* 129–36. The center's desire to control the regional militia was especially acute during Aurungzeb's reign. Jean de Thevenot, a French visitor to Aurungzeb's empire, noted that the emperor and his mansabdars could field 300,000 horse. However, many of the mansabdars could "hardly keep on foot one half of the men they are appointed to have, so that when the great Mogol marches upon any expedition of war, his army exceeds not a hundred and fifty thousand horse, with very few foot, though he have betwixt 300,000 and 400,000 mouths in the army [camp followers?]" (Jean de Thevenot, "The Third Part of the Travels," in Sen, ed., *Indian Travels,* 7).

3. The Marathas at Panipat

1. Sardesai, *Main Currents,* 87–92.

2. Sen, *Administrative System,* 275–76.

3. The first to go was Nizam-ul-Mulk Asaf Jah, viceroy of the Deccan from about 1712. He laid the foundation of the nizamat of Hyderabad. That very same year the viceroy of Avadh, S'aadat Khan (Burhan-ul-mulk), followed suit. A decade later the powerful viceroy of Bihar, Bengal, and Orissa, Murshid Kuli Khan, was succeeded by his son-in-law, Shuja-ud-Din Muhammad Khan (1727), who governed independently of Delhi.

4. In his attempt to rid himself of Delhi's control Nizam-ul-Mulk was aided by Shahu; their combined armies defeated the imperial army under Muhariz Khan, allowing the nizam to take firm control of Hyderabad in 1725. See Irvine, *The Army*, 146.

5. Nadkarni, *The Rise and Fall*, 172.

6. Sardesai, *New History of the Marathas*, 2:100.

7. Sardesai, *New History of the Marathas*, 2:151–54.

8. Duff, *A History of the Marathas*, 2:492.

9. Sardesai, *New History of the Marathas*, 2:324, 362, 367–79.

10. The Rohillas were Yusufzai Afghans of Roh, a region covering portions of Afghanistan and the Northwest Frontier Province. The Afghans had twice established empires in India under the Lodhis and the Suris only to have them both destroyed by the Mughals. After Aurungzeb's death more and more Afghans came into India to settle the rich territory that forms an irregular triangle between the Siwalik and Kumaon mountain ranges to the south, Avadh in the east, and the Ganges in the west. This area came to be known as Rohilkhand after the Rohilla Afghans and comprised a total area of about 186 miles long and 93 miles wide. See Hamilton, *Geographical, Historical and Statistical Description*, 1:31, 427.

11. Kadam, *Maratha Confederacy*, 18–28.

12. Stewart, *Marathas, Marauders and State Formation*, 38–39, 43.

13. Stewart, *Marathas, Marauders and State Formation*, 54, 60–61.

14. Stewart, *Marathas, Marauders and State Formation*, 54; and Kadam, *Maratha Confederacy*, 74–75.

15. Born in a poor Turkoman family in Khorasan in 1668, Nadir Shah took over the throne after Shah Tahmasp was deposed in 1732. In 1736 he was crowned Sahanshah Nadir Shah.

16. Ahmed Shah Durrani hailed from the Sadozi clan of the Abdali tribe of the Afghans who lived in the province of Herat. He served in Nadir Shah's army. When the latter was murdered in 1747 Ahmad Shah Durrani returned to Afghanistan, where he was crowned king, and took the title of *durrani padshah*, or pearl among kings. He was the first king of an independent Afghanistan. See Singh, *Ahmad Shah Durrani*, 27.

17. *Indian Antiquary*, 64–65; Sardesai, ed., *Selections*, 21:111, 27:146.

18. Apte, ed., *Selections*, letter 49, p. 56.

19. Singh, *Ahmed Shah Durrani*, 226.

20. I have used the British spelling since the descendants of the main Sindhia clan spell their names in the same manner – Sindhia – rather than the Maratha "Shinde."

21. Delhi was abandoned by the wazir Imad-ul-Mulk, who was running the affairs of state after murdering the emperor, Alamgir II.

22. Duff, A History of the Marathas, 1:604.

23. Indeed, a few months earlier, the peshwa's sirdars, including Dattaji, had carried the Maratha banners right up to and even beyond Attock in the northwest. In the south his officers Balvantrao Mehendele, Gopalrao Patwardhan, Malhar Naik Raste, and Visaji Krishna Baniwale had extended Maratha conquests south of the river Krishna. That very year, on 3 February, the peshwa's cousin Sadashiv Rao Bhau had won a decisive victory over the forces of Nizam Ali of Hyderabad at Udgir, as a result of which the nizam surrendered territory to the Marathas. See Shejwalkar, Panipat 1761, 31, 34; see also Persian Manuscripts no. 696, 20 December 1758, BISM; Sardesai, ed., Selections, xxviii, 200–202, 204, 210, 216–17, 266.

24. Srivastava, Shuja-ud-Daulah, 84–85.

25. Gupta, Marathas and Panipat, 137–39, 155.

26. Tone, Illustrations, 44.

27. The term gardi is derived from the word "guard" in its English, French, and Portuguese forms and refers to soldiers trained to fight as European infantry. See Elliot, The History of India, 3:155 n. In a document dated 1753–54 the peshwa mentioned the enlistment of a gardi officer named Muzaffar Jang (Muzaffar Khan). See Vad, Selections, 3:178. According to Duff, he had been dismissed from Salabat Jang's service. History of the Marathas, ed. Guha, 1:364.

28. Vad, Selections, 9:386.

29. Rao, "Maratha-Nizam Relations."

30. While it is true that the gardi infantry lacked the precision drilling of their European counterparts, their ability to deliver reasonably effective and sustained firepower on the battlefield was revolutionary for an Indian infantry force.

31. Selim III, utilizing the skills of German and Russian mercenaries, established his Nizam-i Cedid, an infantry regiment of some 2,536 men, in 1797. See Shaw, "The Origins." Egypt's Muhammed Ali was to follow with the establishment of his own Nizam-i Cedid in 1815. In China the scholar-official Li Hung-Chang would implement Western military reforms in the early 1860s as part of China's self-strengthening movement. In Japan the Choshu clan established its Western-style infantry in the early to mid-1860s in direct response to European attacks and the threat of the Tokugawa Shogunate. See Ralston, Importing the European Army, 85, 118–25, 154–55.

32. Shaw, "The Origins," 300–304.

33. Vad, Selections, 3:93.

34. Parasnis, ed., Peshwa Daftaratil Nivadak Kagadpatra, 60–61.

35. Pundit, An Account, 20. Kashi Raj Shivdev Pundit, a Deshantha Brahmin official in the service of Siraj-ud-Daulah, has left the only known eyewitness account of the entire third Panipat campaign and battle. Jagdish Narayan Sar-

kar also translated parts of the Kashi Raj manuscript and published it under the title "Panipat: 1761" as well as "Events Leading up to the Battle of Panipat, 1761." Lt. Col. James Browne is credited with the original translation in 1791, which was subsequently published as Kashi Raj Pandit, "Ahwal-i-Jang-i-Bhau va Ahmad Shah Durrani," trans. Lt. Col. James Browne, *Asiatic Researches* 3 (1799): 13ff.

36. Grose, *Voyage to the East Indies*, 1:124–25.

37. Tone, *Illustrations*, 47–48.

38. The foundry was visited by Capt. William Gordon in 1739. See Forrest, *Selections*, 79.

39. Grose, *Voyage to the East Indies*, 1:108–9.

40. Apte, "The Maratha Weapons of War," 118. For more details on Maratha weaponry see pp. 106–24.

41. Apte, "The Maratha Weapons of War," 118; Dirom, *A Narrative*, 10–12.

42. Duff, *History of the Marathas*, ed. Guha, 1:399.

43. Sardesai, ed., *Selections*, 27:258.

44. Sardesai, ed., *Selections*, 2:131, 144, 27:257, 247.

45. Sardesai, ed., *Selections*, 21:191–93, 197–98.

46. Duff, *History of the Marathas*, ed. Guha, 1:402.

47. Indeed, the aged (his age has been estimated as sixty-five to eighty) Govindpant's depredations in the Doab resulted in immediate hardships in the Afghan camp, causing food prices to soar. Pundit, *An Account*, 23.

48. Pundit, *An Account*, 27; Duff, *History of the Marathas*, ed. Guha, 1:404.

49. Pundit, *An Account*, 27–30; Duff, *History of the Marathas*, ed. Guha, 1:403.

50. According to Kashi Raj, the Marathas fielded 55,000 cavalry, 15,000 infantry, and 200 cannons. Pundit, *An Account*, 18, 20. Duff quotes roughly the same figures and adds 200,000 as the number of pendharis and camp followers. He also notes that the number of gardi infantry had been doubled by the peshwa after the successful campaigns against Salabat Jang and Nizam Ali. Duff, *History of the Marathas*, ed. Guha, 1:399, 402.

51. According to Kashi Raj, these were the regulars alone. The Afghan irregulars were not mustered. See Pundit, *An Account*, 18; Duff, *History of the Marathas*, ed. Guha, 1:399, 402.

52. Gupta, *Marathas and Panipat*, 221.

53. Gupta, *Marathas and Panipat*, 216–17.

54. According to Kashi Raj, the camel-mounted zambaruks and shuternals (types of swivel guns) were the main strength of the Durrani army. Pundit, *An Account*, 18.

55. Gupta, *Marathas and Panipat*, 218–19.

56. According to Duff, Bhau had sent a message to Holkar saying "to do as he had directed." Whether the message reached Jankoji is not known, but he

fled the battlefield soon after, followed by Damaji Giakwad and his cavalry, thus resulting in the complete collapse of Maratha resistance. See Duff, *History of the Marathas*, ed. Guha, 1:407. Rawlinson, who has edited Kashi Raj's memoirs, feels that the message from Bhau to Holkar was in fact a warning to extricate himself from the battle before he too was trapped. Pundit, *An Account*, xii.

57. Details of the battle have been gleaned from the collective works of James Grant Duff, Hari Ram Gupta, Casi Raja Pundit, and T. S. Shejwalkar. See also Sane, ed., *Bhau Sahebanchi Bhakar*. An account left behind by an unknown Marathi writer describes Maratha activities in northern India from 1753 onward. It also gives a detailed description of Bhau's battle plan.

58. Duff, *History of the Marathas*, ed. Guha, 1:408.

59. Duff, *History of the Marathas*, ed. Guha, 1:409.

60. The huzurats were also mounted on the finest horses available in India at the time from Arabia and Afghanistan. This is in marked contrast to the inferior local breeds used by the cavalry of the sirdars. Many of them were later run down and killed by pursuing Afghan cavalry after the battle, even though they had fled the field before the collapse of the Maratha center.

61. The alliance between Durrani and his Indian allies began to crumble almost immediately after the battle. The Indo-Afghans were horrified at the brutality of the Afghans toward the thousands of Indian camp followers. Shuja-ud-Daulah posted his own troops to guard the captives from the Afghans. All the Indo-Afghan chiefs were also appalled at the Afghans' desire to take the body of Vishwasrao back to Afghanistan and pleaded with the grand wazir for the return of his body to the Marathas so that he could be cremated according to Hindu custom. A similar appeal to spare the lives of Ibrahim Khan and Jankoji Sindhia was ignored, and both captives were killed. A few weeks after the battle Durrani soldiers began to demand payment from their Indian allies. Shuja-ud-Daulah, feeling threatened, removed himself from the Durrani camp in secrecy, and Ahmad Shah Durrani left India soon afterward. See Pundit, *An Account*, 40–52; Duff, *History of the Marathas*, ed. Guha, 1:408.

62. The word *sepoy* is derived from the Persian *sipah*, meaning "soldier."

4. Colonial Warfare in Bengal and Mysore

1. Lyall, *The Rise and Expansion*, 24.

2. Lyall, *The Rise and Expansion*, 24.

3. Roberts, *Historical Geography*, 37.

4. Roberts, *Historical Geography*, 38.

5. Vigie, *Dupleix*, 198–282. One of the English defenders of Madras who became a prisoner of the French was Robert Clive, a young copywriter in the service of the company. He had joined the company at the age of seventeen in 1748.

6. Vigie, *Dupleix*, 295–344. See also Culturu, *Dupleix*, 257–58.

7. Malleson, *Lord Clive*, 39–42.

8. Vigie, *Dupleix*, 448–79; Culturu, *Dupleix*, 355–59; and Vincent, "Dupleix."

9. Perrod, "La findu rêve."

10. Hill, *The Indian Record Series*, 1:xxxiii.

11. Hill, *The Indian Record Series*, 2:307; Broome, *History of the Rise*, 1:114.

12. Griffith, *The British Impact*, 72.

13. Malleson, *Lord Clive*, 76.

14. According to Broome, the total British casualties numbered seventy-two dead and wounded, including seven Europeans killed and thirteen wounded and sixteen sepoys killed and thirty-six wounded. *History of the Bengal Army*, 148–49. Hill gives a slightly different distribution of the casualties: four Europeans killed and fifteen wounded and fifteen sepoys killed and thirty-eight wounded. *The Indian Record Series*, 1:ccii.

15. Carnac, *The Presidential Armies*, 27.

16. *Imperial Gazetteer*, 4:326.

17. Seton, *The India Office*, 187.

18. Carnac, *The Presidential Armies*, 52.

19. Seton, *The India Office*, 187.

20. Orme, *A History of the Military Transactions*, 1:104.

21. Cadell, *History of the Bombay Army*, 49.

22. Walter, *India and Her Colonial Forces*, 83.

23. Broome, *History of the Bengal Army*, 92.

24. Derived from the English word "platoon," itself a corruption of the French word *peloton*. Cardew, *A Sketch*, 5.

25. "Return of the Mand Forces," November 1761, L/MIL/10/130, IOR.

26. Wilson, *History of the Madras Army*, 1:142.

27. Wilson, *History of the Madras Army*, 1:138–52.

28. Cotton, "The Life of General Avitable," 550–51.

29. Singh, *The Indian Army*, 8.

30. Sandhu, *The Indian Cavalry*, 31–32.

31. For a detailed study of the evolution of the Bengal army see Barat, *The Bengal Native Infantry*.

32. Grose, *Voyage to the East Indies*, 2:376; Dutta, *The Dutch in Bengal*, 38–48.

33. Often referred to as "Sombre" by the British, he had deserted from one of the company's European battalions to become a mercenary for hire. He earned his unfortunate nickname while in the service of Mir Kasim when he supervised the massacre of forty British prisoners at Patna in 1763. See Bidwell, *Swords for Hire*, 11–12.

34. For further details of the campaign against Mir Kasim see Verma, *Plassey to Buxar*; Malleson, *The Decisive Battles*, 18–35.

35. Carnac, in fact, faced a near-mutinous situation in both his sepoy and European units over the nonpayment of reward money and even over the issue of reinstalling Mir Jafar on the Bengal throne, which some European soldiers found most distasteful.

36. Details of the battle have been gleaned from Oldham, "The Battle of Buxar"; Malleson, *The Decisive Battles*, 126–63; Verma, *Plassey to Buxar*.

37. After the battle of Buxar Shuja did make strenuous attempts to revamp his army, especially his artillery and infantry. He hired a number of French, Armenian, and Abyssinian officers to train his men (mostly Rajput, Brahmin, and Sheikzada). He established a number of factories for making muskets and foundries for cannons. However, even with these improvements Shuja never again took to the field against the British. In November 1768 the latter, worried by Shuja's military improvements, imposed a new treaty on him, forcing him to limit his forces to 35,000 men with a maximum of only 10,000 sepoys trained and organized along European lines. See Barker to Council, 7 June 1768, Select Committee Proceedings, no. 14, 272–74, Foreign Department, NAI; Harper to Council, n.d., Select Committee Proceedings, no. 14, 613–16, Foreign Department, NAI; Srivastava, *Shuja-ud-Daulah*, 1945 ed., 2:84–85.

38. Major Munro's Evidence, 3 April 1767, AM no. 18,469, fol. 46.

39. Richard Smith, Commander in Chief (Company Forces Avadh), to Henry Verelst, President and Governor of Fort William and Select Committee, 6 February 1767, Bengal Secret Consultations, Fort William Consultations, 23 February 1768, P/A/8, IOR.

40. Shuja was particularly harsh on his commanders if they cheated their sepoys out of their pay, a common practice in many Indian armies at the time. See Henry Verelst, President and Governor, Fort William, to Select Committee, 6 February 1767, Bengal Secret Consultations, Fort William Consultations, 23 February 1768, P/A/8, IOR.

41. The word Telinga appears to have been taken from the Mysore army. Telingas were infantry recruits from the Telinga region of southern India. See Barnett, *North India between Empires*, 135.

42. Richard Smith, Commander in Chief, to Henry Verelst, President and Governor, Fort William, and to Select Committee, 6 February 1769, Bengal Secret Consultations, Fort William Consultations, 23 February 1768, P/A/8, IOR.

43. Col. Richard Smith to Select Committee, 3 November 1767, Bengal Secret Consultations, Fort William Consultations, 17 November 1767, P/A/7, IOR.

44. Alavi notes that the pre-Buxar Avadh army, composed mainly of gentlemen troopers (*sheikzadis*) known as *najibs*, resented the new and larger section of the peasant infantry force. This antagonism was returned by the peasant sepoys, who had the favor of Shuja. The sepoys were now in a position to curtail the power of the cavalry. Alavi, *The Sepoys and the Company*, 22, 24–25.

45. Mansa Ram later passed the title on to his son and successor, Balwant Singh. Mansa Ram then found favor with Shuja, and he replaced Rustam Ali as amil of Banaras. In 1773 his grandson Cheyt Singh obtained the first legal title of property from Warren Hastings. Under Balwant Singh, the Banaras zamindari conquered neighboring Brahmin and Rajput zamindari holdings in the region. See Alavi, *The Sepoys and the Company*, 26–27 n. 47.

46. Broughton, *Letters Written in a Maratha Camp*, 103.

47. Details of the Banaras army are from Fakir Khair-ud-Din Khan, *Tufha-i-Taza*, translated by F. Cruwen as *Balwantnamah* (Allahabad, 1875), 1–45, quoted in Alavi, *The Sepoys and the Company*, 27–30.

48. Bayly, *Rulers, Townsmen and Bazaars*, 18.

49. Alavi, *The Sepoys and the Company*, 31.

50. Alavi, *The Sepoys and the Company*, 32.

51. Alavi also notes that the recruiting of the army seems to have been yet another manifestation of the regime's increasing projection of itself as a Hindu raj (with new rights for Brahmins). This "Hinduization" of the Banaras zamindari came to a halt with the crushing of the rebellion in 1782. See Alavi, *The Sepoys and the Company*, 33–34.

52. The helpless nature of the nawab's position is starkly highlighted in the correspondence between himself and the British, Wellesley in particular. See Secret Department, August 1800, no. 107, 12 June 1800, nos. 34, 35, NAI; Bengal Secret Consultations, 12 June 1800, nos. 120, 122, NAI.

53. See Read, "Sketch of Revenue Management." See also Guha, *Pre-British State System*, 17–19.

54. Tellicherry to Bombay, Consultations, 11 March 1763, Range 341, 26:171, Bombay Public Consultations, IOR.

55. Hyder to Bombay, n.d., Consultations, 22 March 1763, Range 341, 26:202, Bombay Public Consultations, IOR.

56. Board minutes, Consultations, 22 March 1763, Range 341, 26:196–97, Bombay Public Consultations, IOR.

57. Ali, *British Relations*, 75–81.

58. Hyder's force, 23 July 1767, Orme Manuscripts, 33:64, IOR.

59. Madras to Bombay, Consultations, 5 February 1767, MMSP, Range 251, 57:91, IOR.

60. Cosby's journal, 26 September 1767, Orme Manuscripts, 215:42, IOR.

61. Board minutes, Consultations, 10 April 1768, MMSP, Range 251, 165:261, IOR.

62. Madras had a garrison of 400 Europeans, 2,000 sepoys, and some light artillery. The main British forces under Smith were only 10 miles away, hot on Hyder's heels and with Lang not far behind on the Arcot road. Hyder's men and horses were fatigued after their forced march, but the garrison seems to

have been unaware of Hyder's situation and was sufficiently nonplussed by his unexpected appearance to agree to talks on his terms. Smith to Orme, 26 June 1769, Orme Manuscripts, 10:164, IOR.

63. The French actually gave up Mahe to Col. James Braithwaite without firing a shot. Braithwaite to Madras, 19 March 1779, Consultations, 5 April 1779, MSCP, Range C, 66:46–49, IOR. Hyder was so angered by the French action that he ordered Pondicherry to be sacked.

64. Hughes's dispatches to England, Home Miscellaneous Series, 1780, 166: 413–14, IOR.

65. "First Report of the Committee of Secrecy," 1781, AM no. 13,638, pp. 49–59.

66. Baille to Madras, 6 September 1780, Consultations, 7 September 1780, MSCP, Range D, 1:1435, IOR.

67. Wilson, History of the Madras Army, 2:6.

68. Munro's minutes, Consultations, 9 October 1780, MSCP, Range D, 3:1790, IOR.

69. Munro, Narrative, 166–72.

70. This was probably the greatest error Hyder made in his campaigns against the British. Sir Eyre Coote noted, "I am almost confident had Hyder Ali followed up his success at that time to the gates of Madras, he would have been in possession of that most important fortress" (Secret Proceedings, 18 November 1780, pp. 2137–38, NAI).

71. Although Hastings had initially decided to send all available men and money immediately, there was some opposition from officials of the Bengal government who thought they were pouring scarce resources into a lost cause. After some debate it was decided to send immediately a small force of 330 Europeans, 200 artillery barrels, 6 guns, and 600 lascars (local gunners) by sea, while a force of 8 battalions of sepoys was ordered to march to Madras through Cuttack. Madras to Bengal, 14 September 1780, Consultations, 2 October 1780, Bengal Secret and Military Consultations, 1778–82, Range A, 56:241–45, IOR. Sir Edward Hughes recommended that Bengal lay aside all measures, including the war against the Marathas in aiding Madras. See Hughes to Bengal and Bengal to Madras, Consultations, 2 October 1780, Bengal Secret and Military Consultations, 1778–82, Range A, 56:249, 423, IOR.

72. Madras to Bengal, Consultations, 1 April 1781, MSCP, Range D, 6:746, IOR; also Madras to Bengal, Consultations, 20 September 1781, MSCP, Range D, 8:2293, IOR.

73. The French governor of Mauritius, François, vicomte de Souillac, had sent seven sails of the line and five frigates with soldiers under D'Ovres to study the situation in India. Unfortunately for Hyder, D'Ovres stuck to his orders literally and did not use his initiative to continue the blockade. Had he done

so Hyder and the French could have dealt another Yorktown-like defeat upon the British. D'Ovres's departure was naturally a source of great relief, for the British were sure that they were about to be starved into submission. Coote to Goddard, 1 March 1781, Consultations, 19 March 1781, MSCP, Range D, 5:565, IOR.

74. The battle, which took place on 1 July 1781, lasted from 8:00 AM to 4:00 PM Coote to Madras, 2 July 1781, Consultations, 5 July 1781, MSCP, Range D, 7:1498–1500, IOR; also Consultations, 11 July 1781, MSCP, Range D, 7:1605, IOR.

75. The Mysoreans won a reprieve when Tippu, who had been dispatched with 10,000 cavalry, a large number of infantry, 20 cannons, and 400 European troops under a Frenchman, De Lally, to Tanjore, managed to crush a British force of 1,600 men (100 Europeans) and 300 cavalry under Colonel Braithwaite at Annagudi. Coote to Madras, Consultations, 21 February 1782, MSCP, Range D, 11:513–14, IOR; see also Secret Proceedings, 11 March 1782, p. 983, NAI.

76. The last major confrontation of the war took place on 30 May 1782 at Arni, a major supply center of the Mysoreans. By threatening this depot Coote was able to provoke a direct confrontation with Hyder, which he won. But on 8 June Hyder retaliated by annihilating an elite unit of Coote's army known as the Grand Guard, killing some 166 men and taking 2 cannons. Coote to Madras, 13 June 1782, MSCP, Range D, 13:1820, IOR.

77. Board's secret letters, vol. 1, March 8, July 19, September 20, 1786, in Phillips, *The East India Company*, 66 n. 1.

78. Cornwallis to Foster, 23 October 1787, Secret Proceedings, 8 November 1787, NAI.

79. Cornwallis to Malet, 14 December 1787, Secret Proceedings, NAI.

80. Foreign Department Secret Proceedings, 7 July 1790, no. 3, NAI. The British also entered into treaties with the rajas of Coorg and Cochin and the various Malabar chieftains, all of whom renounced their loyalties to Tippu Sultan.

81. Secret and Political Proceedings, 13 October 1790, Consultation no. 9, NAI.

82. Cornwallis blamed this initial setback on the slowness of the allies in invading Mysore. Maratha cavalry in particular would have been invaluable in providing early warning of Tippu's movements. Cornwallis to Malet, 11 October 1790, Consultations, 13 October 1790, no. 18, NAI.

83. The fall of Bangalore came none too soon for the besieging British forces. Cornwallis wrote: "The army had sustained tremendous difficulty in laying siege to Bangalore" and added that "our distress for forage nearly occasioned a failure in the undertaking" (23 April 1791, 147B:1898, Military Consultations, TNA).

84. Cornwallis refused a Maratha offer to provision his army for an immediate renewal of the assault on Seringapatam because he would not place himself

in a "state of wretched dependence on the Maratha bazar [market]," where he would be "obliged to pay an immense price for a scanty subsistence" (17 June 1791, 149B:2986, Military Consultations, TNA).

85. Cornwallis had apparently ignored an earlier letter from a nervous Henry Dundas, president of the Board of Control in London, advising him to secure a treaty with Tippu as soon as possible even if it meant sacrificing all the gains of the war. Board's secret letter, I, 21 September 1791, quoted in Phillips, *The East India Company*, 68 n. 7.

86. Political Proceedings, 2 March 1792, Consultation no. 2, NAI.

87. At the signing ceremony Tippu is said to have told Haripant Phadke, the Maratha commander, "I am not at all your enemy. Your real enemy is the Englishman of whom you must beware" (Sardesai, *New History of the Marathas*, 3:192). According to information from Duff, the Marathas were already aware of the growing power of the British. Haripant, prior to joining the British, had met the nizam of Hyderabad in Pangal, where the two had agreed that while Tippu was to be "humbled," he was not to be destroyed. Duff, *History of the Marathas*, ed. Guha, 2:202.

88. The net revenue from the Malabar coast alone amounted to some 25 lakhs of rupees, which was instrumental in helping launch the rise to power of the Bombay Presidency, up until that time the weakest of the three presidencies. However, it must be noted that Tippu's revenue collection problems date back to before the treaty itself. Like his father before him, Tippu too dealt severely with corrupt revenue officers, but the inherent weakness of his patrimonial bureaucracy meant that significant reform was impossible. See Guha, *Pre-British State System*, 32. The *desathas*, or Maratha Brahmins, the traditional local elites, constantly found ways to thwart the centralizing efforts of Hyder and Tippu and even for a while the British who followed them. See Frykenberg, *Guntur District*, 231–36.

89. "Proceedings of a Jacobin Club at Seringapatam," European Manuscripts, D.99, pp. 19–24, IOR.

90. Martin, ed., *Despatches Minutes and Correspondence*, 1:54.

91. The nizam's agreement to sign the treaty, however, came about only after the British managed to disarm and disband (October 1798) the 11,000-man sepoy force established by the late General Raymond (its French officers were arrested). For details of the treaty negotiations with the nizam and the disbandment of the French corps see Secret Consultations, 23 August 1798, no. 67, 3 October 1798, no. 73, 30 October 1798, no. 74, 20 November 1798, no. 75, and 31 August 1800, no. 106, all in NAI.

92. Although the British were doubtful of the peshwa's ability to launch a Maratha offensive, they were hopeful that his reinstated minister of state, Nana Phadnavis, whom they highly respected, would prevail upon the "irresolute"

peshwa to cooperate effectively with the British against the peshwa. See Secret Consultations, 20 November 1798, nos. 31–33, NAI.

93. Wellesley to J. A. Kirkpatrick (acting resident at Hyderabad), 8 July 1798, Secret Consultations, 23 August 1798, no. 67, NAI; also Martin, ed., *Despatches Minutes and Correspondence*, 1:326.

94. Wellesley to Sir Hugh Christian, Secret Consultations, 23 November 1798, no. 32, NAI. See also Political Despatches to England, 4 September 1797, 4:141–42, NAI.

95. Political Despatches to England, 4 September 1797, 4:454, NAI.

96. Wellesley described the Madras army assembled in Vellore as "unquestionably the most completely equipped, the most amply and liberally supplied, the most perfect in point of discipline, and the most fortunate in the acknowledged experience and the abilities of its officers in every department, which ever took the field in India." The Bombay army, which took to the field under General Stuart, was declared to be "in an equally efficient state" (23 February 1799, 254A:3397ff., Military Consultations, TNA).

97. Tippu, apparently suspecting such treachery, had imprisoned many of these officers, but he later released them on guarantee of good conduct in future. Political Proceedings, 10 July 1797, Consultations, nos. 20, 24, NAI. Wellesley even suggested that attempts be made to incite the Muslim inhabitants of Mysore by distributing "those passages of the correspondence, and of the documents received from Constantinople, which expose the character of the French Republic and the outrages committed [Napoleon's invasion of Egypt] by the French against the acknowledged head of the Mahommedan Church" (22 February 1799, 254:3334, Madras Records, Military Consultations, TNA).

98. The terms of the treaty called upon Tippu to surrender half of his kingdom, pay a huge indemnity, and offer his sons and generals as hostages of the British. Harris to Tippu, 22 April 1799, Military Sundry Book, 109a:104–5, 111–12, Madras Records, Military Consultations, TNA. Tippu's letter to Harris on the 20th proposing an amicable settlement of the conflict was ignored. Military Sundry Book, 254:3383–97, Madras Records, Military Consultations, TNA.

99. An eyewitness account of the siege and fall of Seringapatam is available in the "Seedapore Letter" from Maj. Lachlam Macquarie of the Seventy-seventh Regiment serving in the Bombay army. Macquarie also kept a daily journal of the bombardment and assault of Seringapatam from 14 April 1799 to the final assault on 5 May 1799. As an officer on the general staff of Lieutenant General Stuart's Bombay army headquarters, he was privy to all of the British operational planning for the final Mysore campaign. See "Seedapore Letter" and "Seringapatam Journal," Mitchell Library, Sydney, Australia. A typed transcript of the journal is available in MS no. 814 (6), pp. 92–154, Miscellaneous Documents, Home Miscellaneous Series, IOR.

100. Fernandes, *The Tiger of Mysore*, 48.

101. Mohammed, *The History of Hyder Shah*, 157–58. The Orme Manuscripts give Hyder's strength as 12,800 cavalry, 18,000 infantry, and 210 Europeans with 49 guns. See Orme Manuscripts, 33:64, IOR.

102. Guha, *Pre-British State System*, 26–29.

103. Secret Consultations, 23 July 1799, vol. 57B, NAI. In addition, some of the junior officers of these departments also received smaller jagirs, or land grants.

104. Military Sundry Book, 101:93, Madras Records, Military Consultations, TNA.

105. Military Sundry Book, 102b:1796–97, 572, Madras Records, Military Consultations, TNA.

106. Zain-ul-Abidin Shusthari, "Fath-ul-Mujahidin," Royal Asiatic Society of Bengal, MSS f.60b, quoted in Hasan, *History of Tippu Sultan*, 351.

107. Military Sundry Book, 101:110, Madras Records, Military Consultations, TNA.

108. Military Sundry Book, 101:101, Madras Records, Military Consultations, TNA.

109. The *askar* was divided into *cutcheris* (brigades), *mokums* (regiments), *risalas* (squadrons), and *yaz* (troops). See Military Sundry Book, 94:101, Madras Records, Military Consultations, TNA.

110. Military Sundry Book, 101:111, 202–3, Madras Records, Military Consultations, TNA.

111. Dodwell, "Transportation," 266–72.

112. Madras to Court, 26 January 1782, Letter Received, vol. 10, par. 66, IOR (Government Records).

113. Macartney to Coote, 26 November 1781, Home Miscellaneous Series, 246:481, IOR (Government Records).

114. Gleig, *Thomas Munro*, 1:81–82.

115. Wylly, *Life of Lieutenant-General Sir Eyre Coote*, 204.

116. Smith to Madras, 2 December 1767, Consultations, 5 December 1767, MMSP, Range 251, 60:1351, IOR.

117. Owen, *A Selection*, 59–61.

118. Coote to Madras, 28 April 1781, Consultations, 6 May 1781, MSCP, Range D, 6:983, IOR.

119. Gleig, *Thomas Munro*, 1:30.

120. Coote to Macartney, 27 February 1782, Home Miscellaneous Series, 245:371, IOR. Hyder seized the bullocks despite the fact that his force of 200 cavalry was greatly outnumbered by Major Byrne's escort of 3,000 men. Coote to Madras, 25 February 1782, MSCP, Range A, 11:558, IOR.

5. Fauj-e-Hind, the Army of Hindustan

1. Joshi, ed., *Selections from the Peshwa Daftar*, letters 72, 74.

2. Joshi, ed., *Selections from the Peshwa Daftar*, letters 169–70, 181.

3. Mill, *The History of British India*, 3:566.

4. Deodhar, *Nana Phadnis*, 46.

5. Kantak, *The First Anglo-Maratha War*, 208–9.

6. Deodhar, *Nana Phadnis*, 108. In October 1781 Mahadji Sindhia had signed a separate peace treaty with the British in order to ensure that he had a free hand in northern India. Secret Consultations, 28 August 1787, no. A and 14 November 1783, no. 31, Foreign Department, NAI. His "advice" to Nana Phadnavis to accept the British offers for peace leading to the Treaty of Salbai was resented by Nana and all the other chieftains. The British, needing Mahadji Sindhia as an ally, were forced to accept his control of Delhi. Secret Proceedings, 28 December 1784, no. 9, Foreign Department, NAI.

7. Kantak, *The First Anglo-Maratha War*, 218. The chief culprit who caused all of this, Raghunathrao, was left free to continue his disastrous plotting.

8. He had managed to survive the debacle at Panipat with only a wound that left him with a noticeable limp.

9. Mahadji Sindhia was appointed *wakil-i-mutlaq*, or regent plenipotentiary, the highest post in the imperial government. Sen, *Anglo-Maratha Relations*, 26.

10. British attempts to gain Maratha support against Hyder Ali had begun in earnest as early as late 1781, when Charles Chapman, the British representative in Nagpur, sought Maratha aid from Mudhoji Bhonsle on the grounds that "an alliance of the Hindus with the English was more natural and more political than any other power, foreign or domestic in the Peninsula." See Chapman's letter to the governor general from Nagpur, 28 January 1782, Secret Proceedings, 18 March 1782, Foreign Department, NAI.

11. Although the British had treaty obligations to come to the aid of the nizam, they were unwilling to antagonize the Marathas; in fact, appeasement of the Marathas was a chief element of British diplomacy at this time. Political Consultation, 20 February 1795, no. 27, Foreign Department, NAI.

12. They included Tukoji Holkar (with his revamped European-style infantry brigade under Dudrennerc), Raghoji Bhonsle, Parashuram Bhau, and Daulatrao Sindhia (Mahadji's son), whose forces were led by Jivba Bakshi (a force of six battalions of infantry under Perron, who had replaced de Boigne).

13. Dighe, ed., *Poona Residency Correspondence*, 4:266–68.

14. Dighe, ed., *Poona Residency Correspondence*, 4:299.

15. For details of the battle and the treaty see Kulkarni, *Battle of Kharda*.

16. Secret Consultations, 20 November 1798, nos. 31–33, NAI.

17. Sardesai, *New History of the Marathas*, 3:373.

18. Sardesai, *New History of the Marathas*, 3:379. Wellesley had foreseen such a move as early as August 1800 and had already drawn up a draft treaty "admitting the *Peshwa* to the Company's avowed and public protection" (Secret Consultations, 1 May 1800, nos. 61, 62, 64, NAI).

19. Owen, *A Selection*, 233–40.

20. Owen, *A Selection*, 350. Some have suggested that the document was, in fact, a British forgery.

21. The sixth was actually part of Baille's ill-fated force, but de Boigne escaped this disaster because he was on detached duty escorting a supply column.

22. Bidwell, *Swords for Hire*, 27.

23. Dundas, *Principles of Military Movement*.

24. The *golandaz*, or gunners, were paid 8 rupees, while the kelasis got 4.5–8 rupees.

25. De Boigne recruited the bulk of his men from the Doab, a fertile region between the Yamuna and Ganges Rivers, Avadh, Rohilkhand, Rajput, and Rajputana.

26. Mahadji Sindhia was appointed regent plenipotentiary in December 1784. His appointment led to the British recalling their agent in Delhi, Maj. James Browne, who had served as the British representative there since 11 December 1783. Shah Alam II himself saw the British withdrawal as a slight to his authority. See Macpherson to Browne, 1 March 1785, Secret Consultations, 1 March 1785, no. 7, NAI; Browne to Macpherson, 19 March 1785, Secret Consultations, 9 April 1785, no. 4, NAI; Browne to Macpherson, 20 April 1785, Secret Consultations, 12 May 1785, no. 2, NAI.

27. Secret Consultations, 20 April 1781, no. 1, Foreign Department, NAI.

28. The square, each side of which measured about 60 yards, was comprised of roughly 320 men in three ranks of 106 to each face. Bidwell, *Swords for Hire*, 40.

29. The square's front was a mass of carcasses, as the Rajputs were subject to the full fury of case shot. See Bidwell, *Swords for Hire*, 40; Sarkar, *Sindhia as Regent*, 2:4–6; Sen, *Anglo-Maratha Relations*, 133–34.

30. Bidwell, *Swords for Hire*, 43–45.

31. Sarkar, *Fall of the Mughal Empire*, 3:273.

32. Secret Consultations, 3 October 1787, no. 14, Foreign Department, NAI.

33. Sarkar, *Fall of the Mughal Empire*, 3:298.

34. Ghulam Kadir was briefly under siege at Meerut, escaping from there on 17 December. He fled to Gahusgarh, where he was captured and taken to Mahadji Sindhia at Mathura on the 31st. He was finally executed on 3 March 1789, and his eyeballs, nose, and ears were sent to the emperor in Delhi. Sarkar, *Fall of the Mughal Empire*, 3:330.

35. The troopers were armed with compact matchlocks, troopers pistols, and swords. See Major Palmer (resident with Scindia) to Bengal Political Board,

6 January 1796, Boards Collection, 1796–97, extract, Bengal Political Consultations, 22 January 1796, F/4/9, IOR.

36. Duff, *History of the Marathas*, ed. Guha, 2:150; Bidwell, *Swords for Hire*, 54–58.

37. Smith, *A Sketch*, 64.

38. By this time the British resident in Delhi, William Palmer, was sending alarming notes detailing the rise of Mahadji Sindhia's regulars under de Boigne. See Palmer to Cornwallis, 30 April 1790, Political Consultations, 12 May 1790, no. 23, Foreign Department, NAI; see also Secret Proceedings, 9 September 1789, no. 4, Foreign Department, NAI.

39. Sarkar, *Sindhia as Regent*, 2:28; Sarkar, *Fall of the Mughal Empire*, 3:18.

40. Compton, *A Particular Account*, 53–60.

41. Sarkar, *Sindhia as Regent*, 2:42.

42. Quoted in Sarkar, *Fall of the Mughal Empire*, 4:35.

43. Ismail Baig escaped to Kanaud, where after a siege he surrendered to Perron on 15 April 1792. Palmer to Malet, 17 May 1792, Political Consultations, 27 June 1792, Foreign Department, NAI.

44. Mahadji Sindhia had arrived in Poona on 11 June 1792 and had been received with great honor by Nana Phadnavis. On the 22nd he invested the young peshwa with the title of wakil-i-mutlaq on behalf of the Mughal emperor, presenting him with the imperial *firman* and the *khilat*, or investiture dress. At the same time he paid great attention to the impressionable young peshwa, showering him with many gifts. Political Consultations, 3 August 1792, no. 5, Foreign Department, NAI.

45. Political Consultations, 24 May 1793, no. 53, Foreign Department, NAI.

46. Sarkar, *Fall of the Mughal Empire*, 4:94.

47. Sarkar, *Fall of the Mughal Empire*, 4:95.

48. He died in his camp in Wanvadi near Pune, suffering from an as yet undiagnosed illness on 12 February 1794 at the age of sixty-seven. Political Consultations, 7 April 1794, no. 6, Foreign Department, NAI.

49. By some accounts it amounted to more than 400,000 British pounds. See Holman, *Sikander Sahib*, 15. In Calcutta de Boigne was feted by the British, who considered him to be the greatest general "India ever produced" (Compton, *A Particular Account*, 105).

50. Central to Daulatrao's trouble was his inability to manage the subcaste rivalries that always simmered within the Maratha Brahmin community. Under Mahadji, a balance of sorts had been achieved between the Deshata Brahmins (Aba Chitnis, Krishnoba Chitnis, and Gopal Bhau), who were put in charge of civil administration, and the Shenvi Brahmins (Jivba Dada, Jagu Bapu, Lukhwa Dada, Baloba Tantya Pagnis, and Sadashiv Malhar), who were military commanders. Under Daulatrao, however, the Shenvis soon began to displace the

Deshatas from civilian posts too. When Daulatrao had a falling out with Lukhwa Dada, his northern viceroy, and other Shenvi ministers in his administration, he was forced to reinstate Aba Chitnis. The end result was that much of Maratha-administered Hindustan fell into disarray, with gross revenue mismanagement and embezzlement. Sen, *Anglo-Maratha Relations*, 190–91.

51. Duff, *History of the Marathas*, ed. Guha, 2:250–53.

52. George Thomas, an Irishman, joined the Royal Navy in 1780. He immediately deserted his ship when it docked in Madras in 1781. He quickly found employment in the forces of the southern *poligars*, or local warlords, and may even have served with Maratha raiders. In 1787 he joined Sumroo Begum (the widow of Walter Reinhardt) and her trained battalions in Delhi. In 1792 he joined the Maratha chief Appa Khandirao, and in 1798 he finally established his own principality in the desolate Hariyana region, which had been unclaimed by any power during this chaotic period. See Hennessey, *The Rajah from Tipperary*. George Thomas Memoirs, AM no. 13,580.

53. Holman, *Sikander Sahib*, 43–58.

54. Yaswantrao probably realized that the peshwa, who in the course of his alliance with Daulatrao Sindhia had put his brother Vithoji to death, would never voluntarily submit himself to the "protection" of the Holkars. Bengal Secret and Political Consultations, 3 June 1801, no. 49, IOR.

55. Total force available to Daulatrao Sindhia and the peshwa amounted to Dawe's four battalions and twenty guns along with the peshwa's force of 10,000 cavalry under Ambaji Anglia. Martin, ed., *Despatches Minutes and Correspondence*, 5:10.

56. Bengal Secret and Political Consultations, 21 February 1803, no. 56, IOR.

57. The advanced force under Gen. Arthur Wellesley had 8,930 men, and there were another 7,922 with Colonel Stevenson. In Gujrat there were 7,352 men, allowing for garrison duty. This left some 4,281 under Colonel Murray's command for field service available for Wellesley's use. An additional force of 3,595 men was left in the Deccan for the "protection" of Hyderabad and Pune, while a covering force of some 7,826 men under General Stuart established itself between the Kistna and Tungabhadra Rivers. To the north, in Hindustan proper, there was an army of 10,500 men under General Lake. There was another force of 3,500 men in Allahabad to act on the siege of Bundelkhand, and another 5,216 men were destined for the invasion of Raghoji Bhonsle's territories in Kuttack. Duff, *History of the Marathas*, ed. Guha, 2:273–78.

58. Smith, *A Sketch*, 37.

59. Duff, *History of the Marathas*, ed. Guha, 2:279.

60. One such officer was James Skinner, an Anglo-Indian who would later go on to establish one of the most senior regiments of the Indian army, the famed Skinner's Horse, which lives on to this day. See Holman, *Sikander Sahib*, 73–76.

61. Anthony Pohlman, formerly a Hanoverian, was a sergeant in the German regiment employed by the company. Bidwell, *Swords for Hire*, 235.

62. Duff, *History of the Marathas*, ed. Guha, 2:276–78; also Pitre, *The Second Anglo-Maratha War*.

63. The "rescue" of the aged emperor Shah Alam in Delhi from the clutches of the Marathas (Mahadji Sindhia and Perron) appears to have been a major goal of the British during the war. Wellesley and Lake were concerned that the Marathas might force the emperor to rally support against the British. Lord Lake to governor general, 8 August 1803, Secret Consultations, 2 March 1804, no. 53, NAI; also Lord Lake to governor general, 1 September 1803, Secret Consultations, 2 March 1804, no. 63, NAI.

64. Agra fell to Lake on 18 October without any bloodshed after its commander, George Hessing, and all of the European officers surrendered the fort to the British.

65. Duff, *History of the Marathas*, ed. Guha, 2:285–87.

66. Khanna, *Monson's Retreat*.

6. The Anglo-Sikh Wars and Pax Britannica

1. Sachdeva, *Polity and Economy*, 147.

2. Sachdeva, *Polity and Economy*, 151–52.

3. Secret and Separate Consultations, 17 October 1808, no. 13, Foreign Department, NAI. Although Yaswantrao Holkar fled to the Punjab in 1805 and begged for support from the Sikhs, Ranjit Singh wisely refused him aid.

4. Metcalfe informed Ranjit that the "friendship" that existed between him and the British had induced Lord Minto to depute him to Lahore. Metcalfe to Edmonstone (Secretary to the Government), 23 September 1808, Secret and Separate Consultations, 17 October 1808, no. 19, Foreign Department, NAI. The first formal appointment of a British political resident took place in 1764, when Samuel Middleton was appointed to the court of Murshidabad. Select Committee Proceedings, 1764, 19:645–46, NAI.

5. Metcalfe to Edmonstone, 12 January 1809, Secret Consultations, 13 March 1809, no. 45, Foreign Department, NAI.

6. Metcalfe to Edmonstone, 7 March 1809, Secret Consultations, 3 April 1809, no. 49, Foreign Department, NAI.

7. Bakshi, *British Diplomacy*, 34–35.

8. Amarnath, *Zafarnama-i-Ranjit Singh*, 28; also Secret and Separate Consultations, 11 July 1808, no. 12, Foreign Department, NAI.

9. These forces included Telingas, Poorbiyas, and Rohillas. Secret and Separate Consultations, 5 December 1808, no. 1, Foreign Department, NAI.

10. Secret and Separate Consultations, 5 December 1808, no. 1, Foreign Department, NAI.

11. Bajwa, *Military System*, 50; Kohli, *Catalogue*, 1:7–12, 2:13–65.

12. Kohli, *Catalogue*, 1:9; Bajwa, *Military System*, 51.

13. Both were officers in the Italian army of Joseph Bonaparte. Allard ended his career in the French army as a captain in the Cuirassiers and took part in the battle of Waterloo. Ventura saw extensive action in the Modenese contingent of Napoleon's army at Wagram and in Russia in 1812. He ended his career with the rank of colonel and took part in the battle of Waterloo. See Garrett and Grey, *European Adventurers*, 80–81, 93–94; see also Griffin, *Ranjit Singh*, 137–38.

14. Kohli, *Catalogue*, 1:16; Bajwa, *Military System*, 63.

15. See the report of Captain Matthews, who describes them as "tolerantly good" (Secret and Political Consultations, 25 May 1808, no. 12, also 11 July 1808, no. 14, Foreign Department, NAI).

16. Cotton, "The Life of General Avitable." Gen. Claude Auguste Court was a Napoleonic officer who had been educated at the Ecole Polytechnique in Paris. Gen. Paolo Bartholemeo Avitable was a Neapolitan artillery officer who had served under Murat in Italy. A third officer, Col. Alexander Gardner, an American mercenary (the only known American mercenary in India at that time), joined Ranjit's service in 1831.

17. According to one British report in 1822, "These officers [French] said that they possessed two books of instructions for the horse and foot and that in four years the sepoys would be perfect. The Maharaja [Ranjit] was pleased beyond measure" (Political Proceedings, 24 August 1822, Consultation no. 4, Foreign Department, NAI). See also the account left behind by Ranjit's biographer, Suri, *Umdat-ut-Tawarikh*, vol. 3, pt. 1, p. 298. A Persian translation of the French training manual – Munshi Har Bhagat Rai's *Zafarnama* – can be found in the Punjab Government Record Office in Patiala.

18. Kohli, *Catalogue*, 1:23; Bajwa, *Military System*, 64.

19. According to one British observer, Captain Burns, Ranjit's irregular cavalry strength, including the feudal forces, numbered 50,000 in 1832. See Secret Consultations, 21 May 1832, nos. 9–10, Foreign Department, NAI.

20. Hugel, *Travels*, 198.

21. Suri, *Umdat-ut-Tawarikh*, vol. 3, pt. 1, p. 1516; Bajwa, *Military System*, 73.

22. News of Ranjit Singh's court for 1825: diary of daily life and routine of Ranjit Singh for 1825, pp. 347, 486, 590, NAI.

23. Hugel, *Travels*, 400.

24. Hugel, *Travels*, 400.

25. See payrolls in Kohli, *Catalogue*, vol. 1; Bajwa, *Military System*, 71.

26. Kohli, *Catalogue*, 1:33.

27. "General officers have been selected from the sons of Sardars who have been carefully trained in the European system of military tactics" (Secret Pro-

ceedings, 4 April 1845, no. 12, Foreign Department, NAI). See also Secret Consultations, 20 December 1845, no. 113, Foreign Department, NAI.

28. The number varies according to different observers: 145,000 men with 70,000 regulars in Steinbach, *The Punjab*, 74; 150,000 men with 50,000 regulars in Orlich, *Travels in India*, 167; 118,000 men with 71,543 regulars in Griffin, *Ranjit Singh*, 143.

29. Foreign Miscellaneous Consultations, vol. 349, 22 January 1844, NAI; Secret Proceedings, 4 April 1845, no. 12, Foreign Department, NAI; Secret Consultations, 20 December 1845, no. 113, Foreign Department, NAI.

30. According to one British observer, Major Broadfoot, the frontier agent, Sikh officers did not take a very active role in these committees. See Major Broadfoot's report, 3 May 1841, Secret Consultations, 7 June 1841, nos. 64–65, Foreign Department, NAI.

31. The British saw a stable Punjab under Maharaja Ranjit Singh as a buffer between India and Afghanistan. However, official policy noted that if there was instability in the Punjab and there was a danger of the Muslims coming to power in the Punjab, then the British should step in. In Hardinge's own words, "The Government of Punjab must be Sikh or British." See Hardinge to Ripon, 8 January 1845, Ripon Papers, AM no. 40,871, fols. 27, 81–91.

32. Hardinge to Ripon, 3 December 1845, Ripon Papers, AM no. 40,874, fol. 273.

33. *Despatches and General Orders*; also Cook, *The Sikh Wars: The British Army*, 40–51.

34. The Sikhs always preferred the sword to the bayonet for close fighting. Sgt. Thomas Malcolm of the Tenth Foot recalled that during the battle of Multan on 12 October 1848 Sikh soldiers continued to fight with their swords even after being impaled on British bayonets. Caine, ed., *Barracks to Battlefields*, 28. The regular infantry sword carried by British troopers and officers was very flimsy in comparison to the Indian tulwar and often shattered under the impact of a collision with the latter. Furthermore, the light British swords were unable to penetrate the wadded clothing worn by Sikh soldiers. (British cavalry faced a similar problem in the Crimea when they tried to hack through the thick Russian greatcoats.) Indian *sowars*, or troopers, well aware of the inferiority of British swords, relied instead on pistols. On several occasions their British commanders confiscated these unofficial sidearms in an effort to get them to use their swords. Thackwell, *Narrative*, 29, 81, 92–93.

35. The British were bivouacked on the battlefield and were subjected to artillery fire and mines throughout the night, while the Sikhs tried to shore up their old positions. Hardinge to Ripon, 27 December 1845, Peel Papers, AM no. 40,466, fols. 341–42.

36. Hardinge to Ripon, 27 December 1845, Peel Papers, AM no. 40,466, fols. 323, 340; see also 22 December.

37. *Despatches and General Orders*, 27–37; Cook, *The Sikh Wars*, 52–69.

38. *Despatches and General Orders*, 81–87; Cook, *The Sikh Wars*, 72–83.

39. The information reached Gough through Lal Singh's agent, Shamsuddin.

40. *Despatches and General Orders*, 128–37; Cook, *The Sikh Wars*, 85–93.

41. For terms of the treaty see Aitchison, *A Collection*, vol. 7, pt. 2, pp. 161–62.

42. Hardinge felt that the annexation of the Punjab was not feasible at this time, since the Khalsa had shown itself to be a formidable force, and powerful garrisons were still present in Peshawar, Lahore, Multan, and Govindgarh near Amritsar. Hardinge to Hogg, 19 April 1846, Ripon Papers, AM no. 40,876, fol. 61.

43. Lahore, 14 and 15 February 1846, Secret Proceedings, 26 December 1846, p. 370, Foreign Department, NAI.

44. Mulraj was to hand over power on 19 April 1848. The same day his forces attacked two British officers who were present to oversee the handover. The unfortunate officers were subsequently killed on the 20th, by which time Mulraj was in open rebellion against the British. Dalhousie to Hobhouse, 2 May 1848, Broughton Papers, AM no. 36,476, fol. 56; also Dalhousie to Hobhouse, 4 May 1848, Broughton Papers, AM no. 36,476, fol. 68.

45. The order "threes about" was distinctly heard by men of the Fourteenth Dragoons. Thackwell, *Narrative*, 68.

46. Thackwell, *Narrative*, 165–74; Cook, *The Sikh Wars*, 163–78. The battle called into question Gough's ability as a commander. The governor general, Dalhousie, noted that Gough's confidence in himself was gone and that the army officers and men openly proclaimed that they had little confidence in him. Dalhoisie to Hobhouse, 7 February 1849, Broughton Papers, AM no. 36,475, fol. 379.

47. Thackwell, *Narrative*, 99–141, 182–208; Cook, *The Sikh Wars*, 181–92. Dalhousie described the battle as a "splendid victory and a comparatively bloodless one." Dalhousie to Hobhouse, 7 October 1848, Broughton Papers, AM no. 36,476, fol. 409; see also Dalhousie to Hobhouse, 21 February 1849, Broughton Papers, AM no. 36,476, sec. 6, no. 3, p. 659.

48. Dalhousie had decided as early as September 1848 that the Punjab must be annexed and that Sikh power must be destroyed: "The Government of India after anxious and grave deliberations have without hesitation resolved, that the Punjab can no longer be allowed to exist as a power and must be destroyed." Dalhousie to Hobhouse, 7 October 1848, Broughton Papers, AM no. 36,476, fol. 252. For terms of the annexation treaty see Nijar, *Anglo-Sikh Wars*, app. B, 120–23.

49. General Lake quoted in Pitre, *The Second Anglo-Maratha War*, 135. General Lake was also a veteran of the bloody battle of Lincelles in France in 1793.

50. At Aligarh, for example, the garrison refused British terms for an honorable surrender and fought to the last after imprisoning their last remaining European officer, Colonel Pedron.

51. See Ralston, *Importing the European Army*, chaps. 3–6.

52. James Tod describes the Maratha impositions on the Rajputs as draining the "very life-blood" of the Rajputs. See Tod, *Annals and Antiquities*, 1:516.

53. Political Consultations, 10 May 1793, no. 20, Foreign Department, NAI. One lakh equals 100,000 rupees, which in turn equaled 12,500 British pounds in 1800.

54. When Udaipur could not deliver on his demand for a sum of 40 lakhs of rupees, he stripped the palace and levied compulsory contributions on the city, thus collecting some 12 lakhs. He then took hostages from the royal family and the leading citizens as security for the remainder. Tod, *Annals and Antiquities*, 1:529–35.

55. Bengal Secret and Political Consultations, 21 February 1803, no. 80, IOR. Holkar's officers were particularly brutal in their sack of Poona and tortured to death many leading citizens in an effort to extract every last item of value.

56. Datta, *Siraj-ud-Daulah*, 45.

57. In the 1770s the nawab of Avadh had to reduce his military strength so that he could entrust the defense of his territories to the British by assigning part of his revenue to the company. See Marshall, "British Expansion," 41.

58. Statement of Supples to Madras, 26 February 1781, Bengal Select Committee Proceedings, Range A, 59:620, IOR.

59. Bengal to Coote, 7 January 1781, Consultations, 9 January 1781, Bengal Select Committee Proceedings, Range A, 59:28–29, IOR; Bengal to Madras, Consultations, 26 February 1781, Bengal Select Committee Proceedings, Range A, 59:628, IOR.

60. Coote to Madras, 16 March 1781, Consultations, 19 March 1781, MSCP, Range D, 5:602, IOR.

61. Mill, *History of British India*, 6:80.

62. Wink, *Land Sovereignty in India*, 306.

63. The East India Company spared no effort and money in order to recruit the best and the brightest from Britain to staff its civil service bureaucracy in India and its army officer corps. In the latter case it even went so far as to establish its own military academy in Addiscombe near Croydon to train its officer cadets. An often repeated sentiment of the period was that "in no service of the world are the pay and allowances [on] so liberal a scale as that of the E.I.C." (Marshall, "The Whites of British India," 41).

64. For a complete discussion of the patrimonial state and its many variants see Weber, *Economy and Society*.

65. The "military revolution" theory has generated one of the most intense and heated debates in early modern European and military history. It was first proposed by Michael Roberts in 1955 in his inaugural lecture at Queens University in Belfast. In recent times its most prominent espousal has come from Geoffrey Parker, *The Military Revolution*, particularly in regard to the relationship between the "revolution" and rise of the West. Since then many historians have challenged contentions made by Roberts, Parker, and other proponents of the military revolution theory, but most seem to agree that the era in question was a period of major military and political upheaval in the European continent. For a recent examination of the debate see Rogers, ed., *The Military Revolution Debate*.

66. Porter, *War and the Rise of the State*, 36, 67.

67. Alavi, *The Sepoys and the Company*, 4–5.

68. Rosen, *Societies and Military Power*.

69. Rosen, *Societies and Military Power*, 172–91, 194–96.

70. The site became so important that soldiers who were recruited from there became known as Baksariyas, a name that for most of the eighteenth century was identified with Hindustani matchlock men. See Kolff, *Naukar, Rajput, and Sepoy*, 169.

71. Kolff, *Naukar, Rajput, and Sepoy*, 176. Although the East India Company did away with the jobbers, it would continue to recruit from the northern Indian and primarily eastern military labor market right up until the rebellion of 1857.

72. Metcalf, *Land, Landlords, and the British Raj*, 379–80.

73. Alavi, *The Sepoys and the Company*, 36–39.

74. Recruits below 5 feet, 6 inches were considered unfit. Minutes of the Council in the Military Department, 8 August 1796, Bengal Military Consultations, Fort William Consultations, 8 August 1796, P/19/19, IOR.

75. The Treaty of Banaras, signed between Asaf-ud-Daulah and the company, not only forced the nawab to agree to a reduction in his army but also resulted in the appointment of British officers to his surviving regiments. In addition, a larger subsidy of Rs 31.2 million per annum was to be paid for the maintenance of the company's brigade in Avadh. See Barnett, *North India*, 144–45.

76. Brig. Gen. G. Stibbert to Warren Hastings, governor general, 10 February 1779, Military Department Proceedings, January–June 1779, 6 March 1779, NAI.

77. Kolff, *Naukar, Rajput, and Sepoy*, 160.

78. Quoted in *Parliamentary Papers*, 1859 VIII (354) 143–46, H.C. PP, cited in Barat, *The Bengal Native Infantry*, 120.

79. Longer, *Red Coats to Olive Green*, 29.

80. Uthoff, the assistant resident at Poona, noted the stark disparity in regu-

lar pay for soldiers in de Boigne's army and the rest of the Maratha armies. Foreign Department, Political Consultations, 13 November 1795, no. 5, NAI.

81. Barat, *The Bengal Native Infantry*, 140–43; Alavi, *The Sepoys and the Company*, 110–19.

82. As in Bengal the early armies of Bombay and Madras relied heavily on locally available recruits. In Bombay this meant a ragtag collection of Muslims, Topasses (Indian Christians), Rajputs (from the hinterland), Coffrees (Africans), and Indian Jews. In Madras, in addition to the Topasses and Coffrees, most of the recruits were Telingas. By comparison, Bengal sepoys were referred to as the "tallest, best-formed and of noblest presence." Toward the close of the nineteenth century the Bombay and Madras armies continued to have this mix of recruits: Marathas, "foreigners" from the west, including Punjabis, Baluchis, Jats, Rajputs, "low Hindu castes," Deccani Brahmins, Telingas, Parwaris, Christians, Jews, and others in the Bombay army, while Musalmans (Muslims), Telingas or Telegus, Tamils, and "other classes" that included Christian "low castes," Brahmins, Rajputs, Marathas, and Gurasians served in the Madras army. Most of these classes would be rejected as "nonmartial" following Lord Roberts's takeover, leading to the virtual disappearance of the Madras army. Longer, *Red Coats to Olive Green*, 12, 42, 53, 131.

83. Bengal sepoys would not strike the gong of his quarter-guard, and men called *gunta pandays* were actually maintained by the company to do this duty for them. Longer, *Red Coats to Olive Green*, 53.

84. Alavi, *The Sepoys and the Company*, 89–90.

85. Alavi, *The Sepoys and the Company*, 6, 8–9, 90–93.

86. See the chapters on ancient and medieval Indian warfare.

87. Moorcroft report, Military Department Proceedings, 15 October 1811, no. 80, fol. 287, NAI; R. Firth to Secretary of Board of Superintendence for the Improvement of the Breed of Cattle, 9 May 1808, fols. 540–41, NAI; W. Moorcroft to Secretary of Board, 13 February 1813, fol. 150, NAI.

88. MMSP, P/D/45, 26 January 1761, fol. 87, IOR.

89. MMPP, P/253/10, January 1793, fol. 608, IOR; MMPP, P/253/33, 4 October 1794, fol. 4109, IOR.

90. Military Department Proceedings, 13 February 1813, Moorcroft to Secretary of the Board, fols. 137–38, NAI.

91. Alder, "The Origins of the Pusa Experiment," 10–12.

92. Alder, "The Origins of the Pusa Experiment" for Bengal; Wilson, *History of the Madras Army*, 2:149; Mollo, *The Indian Army*, 16.

93. Foreign and Political Department, S, 2 February 1778, no. 21, NAI.

94. Orme Manuscripts, OV.108, fol. 89, IOR.

95. The Madras government had already concluded some decades earlier that it would have to forgo the overland trade routes and obtain horses via a sea

route. See E. Wyatt's report, Military Department Proceedings, 27 November 1813, no. 108, NAI; MMSP, P/252/18, 3 August 1787, fols. 407–9, IOR; MMSP, 14 October 1787, fol. 485, IOR; MMPP, 17 October 1787, fol. 536, IOR; MMPP, P/253/10, January 1793, fol. 565, IOR; MMPP, P/253/75, 10 January 1797, fol. 156, IOR.

7. The Army of the Raj

1. Strachan, *From Waterloo to Balaclava*, 26.

2. Strachan, *From Waterloo to Balaclava*, 68.

3. Strachan, *From Waterloo to Balaclava*, 125.

4. "Report of the Commissioners Appointed to Inquire into the Organization of the Indian Army" (Peel Commission), *Parliamentary Papers*, House of Commons, 1859, C.2515, v.

5. Military dispatch to India no. 213, 3 August 1876, quoted in Saxena, *The Military System of India*, 182–83.

6. Bond, "The Effect," 229–36; also "Cardwells' Army Reforms," 108–17.

7. Military dispatch to India no. 213, 3 August 1876, quoted in Saxena, *The Military System of India*, 183–84.

8. *Report of the Special Commission Appointed by His Excellency the Governor-General in Council to Enquire into the Organization and Expenditure of the Army in India* (Eden Commission) (Simla: Government of India, 1879), L/MIL/17/5/168, 5, IOR.

9. *Report of the Special Commission*, 17, 43, 71.

10. The 2.75-inch screw gun was venerated by the Indian army not least because of its portability, and it was even immortalized by Kipling in a poem. See Elliot, ed., *A Choice of Kipling's Verse*, 176–78.

11. See *Scheme for the Re-Distribution of the Army in India* (Calcutta: Government of India, 1904), L/MIL/17/5/1741, IOR; *Scheme for Re-Distribution of the Army in India and Preparation of the Army in India for War* (India Office, 1904), L/MIL/17/5/1742, IOR. Kitchener's emphasis on the North West Frontier was based largely on his concern over Russian influence and encroachment in Afghanistan. See "Note by Lord Kitchener: The Strength of the Army in India," 21 October 1907, L/MIL/17/5/1745, IOR.

12. The Meeting of the Army Council, no. 278, 21 June 1906, WOP 163/11, PRO.

13. See Barua, "Inventing Race."

14. See telegram no. 112 from Secretary of State for War Lord Kitchener to Field Marshal Sir John French, 27 August 1914, WOP 95/3911, PRO.

15. War Office to GHQ France, 29 August 1914, WOP 33/713, PRO; War Diary Lahore Division, WOP 95/3911, PRO.

16. See views of Haig's Chief of Intelligence, Brig. Gen. John Charteris, in *At GHQ*, 66.

17. Greenhut, "The Imperial Reserve," 69.

18. C.R.[?] to Lord Crewe, no. 266, 25, Commissions for Indians, Indianization, 1915–42, col. 430, L/MIL/7/19006, IOR.

19. MSS.Eur.F.111/442. 18, IOR.

20. Extract from War Cabinet Minutes no. 203, 2 August 1917, MSS.Eur.F.111/442, 42, IOR.

21. Telegram no. 828, Secretary of State to Viceroy, 5 April 1918, MSS.Eur.F.111/442, 47, IOR.

22. See *Progress in the Indianization of the Indian Army: Report of a Committee Appointed by His Excellency the Commander-in-Chief in India, June 1923* (Simla: Government of India, 1923) (Secret), L/MIL/17/5/1779, IOR.

23. Sinha and Chandra, *Valor and Wisdom*, 95–96, 130.

24. Manager of Publications, *Regulations Respecting Admission to the Indian Military Academy in Dehra Dun and for the First Appointments to His Majesty's Land Forces, 1931* (Delhi: Government of India Press, New Delhi, 1937), L/MIL/17/5/2284, 1–2, IOR.

25. The Jacob Committee reported a failure rate of 60 percent in the first four years of the Sandhurst program. This figure had improved considerably to 30 percent by the time of the Skeen Committee report. Nevertheless, it still remained high compared to the mere 3 percent failure rate for British cadets at Sandhurst. Jacob Committee Report, L/MIL/17/5/1779, 4, IOR; dispatch no. 38 to His Majesty's Secretary of State for India, 13 October 1927, Birkenhead Collection, MSS.Eur.D.703/38, 4, IOR; "Recommendation of the Government of India on the Report of the Indian Sandhurst Committee," n.d., L/MIL/17/5/1787, IOR.

26. They included eight courses for British cadets (fresh from the schools in Britain) taught between October 1941 and October 1943. Gen. Gul Hassan Khan (Pakistan army), who joined the Indian Military Academy in January 1941, recalls that during his first term the course proceeded at a leisurely pace, seemingly unaffected by the war. It was only after the first term that he and other cadets of his course were given a dose of concentrated training and passed out at the end of the year. See Khan, *Memoirs*, 9–10.

27. Sinha and Chandra, *Valor and Wisdom*, 155–59.

28. Sinha, *A Soldier Recalls*, 42.

29. Sinha, *A Soldier Recalls*, 158.

30. Denning, *The Future of the British Army*, 60–61.

31. "During most of the British rule strategic decisions were jointly made by India and Whitehall. The Indian Army had considerable autonomy in minor matters, but important decisions were made with the concurrence of the Viceroy and often referred to London for further consideration by the British government and the senior military [British] leadership" (Cohen, *The Indian Army*, 170–71).

32. *Report of the Army in India Committee, 1919–20* (Esher Committee), L/MIL/5/ 1762, pt. 4, p. 7, IOR.

33. *Legislative Assembly Debates*, vol. 1, no. 15, 1683–1762, in L/MIL/7/108222, IOR.

34. Chelmsford to Montagu, 12 February 1919, Montagu Collection, MSS.Eur. D.523, 8:26, IOR.

35. Rawlinson to Lord Derby, 30 March 1921, Derby Collection, MSS.Eur.D. 605/5, IOR.

36. Take, for example, a private letter to Sir Alexander Cobbe from the commander in chief, Sir Chetwoode, in which he noted that "a lot of nonsense was talked by Moonje, Gidney, etc., etc., but we got everything we wanted out of them without using the official majority at all." Extract from personal and private letter from Sir Philip Chetwoode to Alexander Cobbe, Simla, 21 August 1931, L/MIL/5/885, 97, IOR.

37. *Report of the Indian Retrenchment Committee, 1922–1923* (London: His Majesty's Stationery Office, 1923), in L/MIL/17/5/1780, IOR.

38. Report of the Indian Military Requirements Sub-Committee, 22 June 1922, CAB.16/38, vol. 1, paper 130-D, PRO.

39. *Tribunal on Certain Questions in Regard to Defense Expenditure in Dispute between the Government of India and the War Office and the Air Ministry* (Garran Tribunal), November 1932, L/MIL/17/5/1911, IOR.

40. Quoted in Bond, *British Military Policy*, 112.

41. Pownall was the director general of ordinance and intelligence.

42. "The Defence Problems of India and the Composition and Organization of the Army and the R.A.F. in India" (Pownall Committee), 12 May 1938, L/MIL/5/886, 331, IOR.

43. "The Defence Problems," 331.

44. "The Defence Problems," 393–95. At the same time the Pownall Committee was making its report, an unofficial Indian army committee led by Major General Auchinleck was reaching much the same conclusion and urging the government of India to set up local munition- and weapon-manufacturing facilities to modernize the army. See *Report of the Modernization Committee* (Auchinleck Committee) (Simla: Army HQ, October 1938), L/MIL/17/5/1801, IOR.

45. "Report of the Expert Committee on the Defence of India, 1938–39" (Chatfield Committee), L/MIL/5/886, 451, 459, 463, 477–78, IOR.

46. Defense requirements, 1938–39, Chatfield Committee, "Notes on the Report by Generals Muspratt and Auchinleck," WS 1934-L/WS/1/155, 15, IOR.

47. One British cavalry regiment and six British infantry battalions to return to England and three Indian cavalry regiments, four companies of Indian Sappers and Miners, and fourteen Indian infantry battalions to be disbanded.

48. "Notes on the Report by Generals Muspratt and Auchinleck," 7.

49. Plan for modernization of the army, 1939 (operations), General Staff India, ws 2099-L/ws/1/170, IOR.

50. Hart, *The Defence of Britain*, 305–6; see also Hart, *Memoirs*, 91–97.

51. This was after his 1927 tour of India. See Fuller, *On Future War*, 262.

52. Winton, *To Change an Army*, 124. See also Edwards, "Second (Military) Prize Winning Essay," 458–73.

53. Future military expenditure, August 1921, CAB.27 – Cabinet Committees, 27/164 GRC (D.D.)8, PRO.

54. Rawlinson to Derby, 25 November 1920, Derby Collection, MSS.Eur.D. 605/1, IOR.

55. Secretary of State to Viceroy, 18 January 1921, Chelmsford Collection, MSS.Eur.E.264, 14:50, IOR.

56. Viceroy to Secretary of State, 22 January 1921, Chelmsford Collection, MSS.Eur.E.264, 14:33, IOR.

57. Monthly returns: distribution of the army, WOP 73/115, PRO.

58. Letter from Secretary of State for War to Prime Minister, 1 November 1937, quoted in Minney, *The Private Papers*, 66.

59. Minney, *The Private Papers*, 66.

60. On 1 December 1937 Hore-Belisha wrote to Deverell asking him to step down. The latter concurred with the comment, "Time will show that your criticisms as far as I am concerned are unjust as they are cruel" (Minney, *The Private Papers*, 69, 72).

61. Hore-Belisha called for "the new army to be made more flexible." Among other things, he proposed the reduction of personnel by creating a greater number of "smaller"(!) divisions that would be easier to move and support. See Minney, *The Private Papers*, 92–94.

62. Ad-hoc Sub-Committees of the Committee for Imperial Defense, CAB.16/38, vol. 2, IMR/14, PRO.

63. Viceroy (Army Department) to Secretary of State, 21 July 1921, L/MIL/3/2513, 1631, IOR.

64. Since November 1921 a Committee for Imperial Defense subcommittee had been examining the Rawlinson proposals at a leisurely pace. See "The Proceedings of the Indian Military Requirements Sub-Committee," CAB.16/38, vol. 1, PRO. In explaining the British cabinet's rejection of the proposal, the secretary of state for India, Montagu, stated that the cabinet felt that further reduction of British troops in India was not possible in view of the political condition in India and the frontier situation. Secretary of State to Viceroy, 14 February 1922, L/MIL/3/2534 M.1348/1922, no. 1, IOR.

65. Maurice, *The Life of General Lord Rawlinson of Trent*, 313.

66. Maurice, *The Life of General Lord Rawlinson of Trent*, 109.

67. Jeffery, *The British Army*, 88.

68. Minutes and consultations of cabinet meetings and conferences of ministers, cabinet meeting, 25 August 1921, CAB.23/26/72(21), PRO.

69. The actual withdrawal began in December 1922. See CAB.23/32/68(22), app. 2, PRO.

70. Bond, *British Military Policy*, 106.

71. "Examination for the Admission to the Staff Colleges at Camberley and Quetta, 1936, 1937 (February–March)," War Office, London, His Majesty's Stationery Office, L/MIL/17/5/2281, 2–4, IOR.

72. Bond, *British Military Policy*, 106.

73. Winton, *To Change an Army*, 65.

74. Although mopping-up operations continued until the second half of 1922, the back of the rebellion had been broken by November 1921, thanks to Burnett-Stuart's mobile columns. See Mackinnon, "The Moplah Rebellion." In 1926 Burnett-Stuart became commander of the Third Division at Salisbury Plains and oversaw the development of the Experimental Armored Force from 1927 onward. See Bond, *British Military Policy*, 62, 65.

75. While at Quetta Montgomery met Auchinleck and Alexander; both were then brigade commanders. He is reported to have remarked that "the best man, was a chap called Auchinleck." Auchinleck had also served as chief instructor at Quetta from 1930 to 1932 and was three years older than Montgomery. See Hamilton, *Monty*, 248–49, 258.

76. One of the exceptions was Gen. Percy Hobart ("Hobo"), the first commander of the permanent tank brigade in 1933 who also served as instructor at Quetta, where he developed many of his radical and uncompromising views of armored warfare. See Macksey, *Armored Crusader*, 82–83.

77. Winton, *To Change an Army*, 85.

78. Winton, *To Change an Army*, 33–34.

79. Bond, *British Military Policy*, 67–68.

80. Bond, *British Military Policy*, 67.

81. Wavell, "The Army and the Prophets," 671.

82. Wavell also served as commander of the Second Aldershot Division from 1935 to 1937.

83. CGS Army HQ to all commands, 13 December 1938, WS 2047-L/WS/1/164, 94, IOR.

84. CGS Army HQ to all commands, 95.

85. Letter from Army HQ to Southern Command, 15 July 1939, WS 2047-L/WS/1/164, 56, IOR.

86. CGS Army HQ to all commands, 96–97.

87. Bond, *British Military Policy*, 123–24.

8. The Indian Army during the Second World War

1. *Gazette of India*, 3 September 1939.

2. "India and the War 1939–1945: The Facts," Information Department, India Office, 1 January 1946, L/MIL/17/5/4263, IOR.

3. Bharucha, *Official History*, 91–93; also Stevens, *Fourth Indian Division*, 16.

4. The headquarters of the Deccan District, which had proceeded to Egypt to form the headquarters of the Fourth Indian Division, was reconstituted, and these new brigades plus the Poona Horse were formed into the Fifth Indian Division. See General Staff India, *India's Part in the War 1940* (Simla: Government of India Press, 1940), L/MIL/5/4261, 5, IOR.

5. Individual battalion attacks like those by the 4/16th Rajputana Rifles during the first battle of Keren received the support of the entire divisional artillery – forty-four twenty-five-pounders, eight 6-inch howitzers, and four 3.7-inch howitzers. See Bisheswar Prasad, *Official History*, 68, 121.

6. Stevens, *Fourth Indian Division*, 46.

7. An Indian army circular issued in 1942 acknowledged that minefields and German 88 mm high velocity antitank guns posed a serious obstacle to tank-infantry cooperation. *War Information Circular no. 26A, General Staff* (New Delhi: Government of India Press, 1942), L/MIL/17/5/4265, IOR.

8. Bidwell, "The Development," 92.

9. Agar-Hamilton, *The Sidi Rezegh Battles*, 474–75.

10. These proposals were accepted by the War Office, and a circular was sent to all commands specifying the following composition for armored and infantry divisions. Infantry division: two infantry brigades, one tank brigade, plus supporting arms (the tank brigade was later replaced by an infantry brigade); armored division: one armored brigade, one lorried infantry brigade, plus supporting arms. See War Office letter to various commands and theaters, 20 May 1942, WS 12048-L/WS/616, 264, IOR.

11. "Proposals from the Commander-in-Chief Middle East – Extensive Reorganization of Armored Division in That Theater," WS 6385-L/WS/1/448, 281, IOR. Auchinleck also proposed giving brigades more supporting arms to make them a self-sufficient tactical unit – the so-called Brigade Group – capable of fighting independently of a division. This proposal was in part influenced by similar independent formations frequently utilized by the Afrika Korps. See Playfair, *The Mediterranean and the Middle East*, 3:213–15, 254, 286–87. However, this proposal was not so well received. The secretary to the India Office, Military Department, felt that independent brigade groups would not be an economic use of force and that if supporting arms were permanently decentralized to brigade groups they would be difficult to withdraw. See Maj. Gen. R. M. M.

Lockhart to Gen. S. W. Kirby, GHQ New Delhi, 9 April 1942, WS 6385-L/WS/448, 218–19, IOR.

12. Connell, *Auchinleck*, 684.

13. Hart, ed., *The Rommel Papers*, 248.

14. Agenda and minutes of commanders conference, meeting at GHQ BTE, 15 July 1942, WOP 201/2050, PRO.

15. Indeed, with the possible exception of the U.S. army, none of the combatants in the Second World War had the necessary resources to conduct large-scale mechanized operations.

16. Barnett, *The Desert Generals*, 229, 264.

17. Stevens, *Fourth Indian Division*, 191.

18. Bidwell, "The Development," 90.

19. Stevens, *Fourth Indian Division*, 191.

20. Tuker, *Approach to Battle*, 153.

21. Bailey, *Field Artillery and Firepower*, 185–86 n. 44.

22. Tuker, *Approach to Battle*, 224.

23. Tuker, *Approach to Battle*, 361–64.

24. English, *A Perspective on Infantry*, 175.

25. Juin, *Memoires*, 1:232.

26. The Indian army had considerable difficulty in trying to pry its divisions away from the Italian theater. In a letter to the Allied headquarters in Algiers, the commander in chief's office in New Delhi pointed out that the Indian government had never contracted "to keep three or any other number of Indian divisions in the Mediterranean theater – the fact that five Indian divisions are there is purely fortuitous." See telegram, Commander-in-Chief India to War Office and Armed Forces HQ Algiers, 13 June 1944, WS 5725-L/WS/1/431, 3–4, IOR. The Fourth Indian Division never got to Burma. It was transferred to Greece in September 1944 to try and put a damper on the budding civil war.

27. See annexure 9. *Report to the Combined Chiefs of Staff*, 265–72.

28. Slim, *Defeat into Victory*, 116–17.

29. Sri Nandan Prasad, *Official History*, 48.

30. Pemberton, *The Development*, 308–9.

31. Forward observers were then called visual command posts. See Pemberton, *The Development*, 341 n. 67.

32. Calvert, "Victory in Burma," 631.

33. For a detailed analysis of the Indian army's role in the evolution of British military strategy and doctrine from 1919 to 1945 see Barua, "Strategies and Doctrines."

34. For details of the experiences of Indian army officers in the Western Desert see Barua, *Gentlemen of the Raj*, chap. 6.

35. Prasad, *Campaign in the Eastern Theatre*, 167.

36. Sinha and Chandra, *Valor and Wisdom*, 150.

37. Evans, *Thimmaya of India*, 194–201.

38. Thorat, *From Reveille to Retreat*, 54.

39. GHQ India to BGS, India Office, 8 February 1945, WS 12048-L/WS/1/616, 3, IOR.

40. Sandhu, *The Indian Armour*, 212.

41. For details of the experiences of Indian army officers in the Burma theater see Barua, *Gentlemen of the Raj*, chap. 6.

42. Sinha, *A Soldier Recalls*, 67.

43. This corps headquarters was redesignated Headquarters Allied Forces Netherlands East Indies. It had three Indian divisions, two Dutch divisions, an independent armored brigade, and an independent parachute brigade.

44. Sinha, *A Soldier Recalls*, 68.

45. Wainwright, *Inheritance of Empire*, 68.

46. It was one of ten expert committees set up to cover every aspect of government.

47. Wainwright, *Inheritance of Empire*, 77.

9. Kashmir and the McMahon Line

1. Number 2 Troop and Number 5 Troop (Rifle) of the Seventh Cavalry under Lt. Noel David had orders to "take up position behind the tribals facing East, as though supporting them. On the word 'go' open fire on the enemy to destroy him in coordination with the assault by 1st Sikh and 1st Kumaon" (Proudfoot, *We Lead*, 108).

2. Sen, *Slender Was the Thread*, 93–99.

3. Praval, *Valour Triumphs*, 172.

4. Prasad, *History of the Operations*, 86.

5. Prasad, *History of the Operations*, 67, 85.

6. Prasad, *History of the Operations*, 113–18; Praval, *India's Paratroopers*, 145.

7. Prasad, *History of the Operations*, 120.

8. Prasad, *History of the Operations*, 134.

9. Praval, *The Indian Army*, 66–67.

10. New units, including the Seventy-seventh Brigade and the 163rd Brigade, were inducted or created from scratch to create these new divisions. (The Sri Division later became the Twenty-sixth Division, and the Jammu Division became the Nineteenth Division.)

11. Prasad, *History of the Operations*, 162; Praval, *The Indian Army*, 162.

12. Prasad, *History of the Operations*, 179. The first large-scale engagement between Pakistani regulars and Indian troops occurred on 10 May, when three companies of the Frontier Force Rifles joined raiders in an abortive attempt to

retake Jhangar. Rahman, *The Wardens of the Marches,* 50; see also Praval, *India's Paratroopers,* 156.

13. The Domel offensive was not altogether unsuccessful. On 27–28 June the 2/3 Gurkha Rifles, part of the 161st Brigade, attacked Pirkanthi, a hill dominating the approaches to Chakothi and Uri along the Srinagar-Domel road. While the headquarters platoon was used to feint a thrust from the west, A and B Companies struck from the east and seized a forward position called "Bushy Pimple." C and D Companies then followed through but were pinned short of their objective. However, renewed attacks by A Company through gaps that had opened in the Pakistani defenses succeeded, and by 5:30 AM on the 28th the position was in Indian hands. See Proudfoot, *Flash of the Khukri,* 44–45.

14. The commanding officer of the Second Bihar (the unit defending this position), Lieutenant Colonel Tur, was placed under arrest by Brig. Henderson Brooks and subsequently court-martialed for withdrawing without orders. See Prasad, *History of the Operations,* 213 n. 3. For details of the Pakistani attack see Riza, *Izzat-o-Iqbal,* 71.

15. Prasad, *History of the Operations,* 238–40.

16. Prasad, *History of the Operations,* 241–42.

17. The First Parachute Battalion (Kumaon) launched a night attack to surprise the enemy at Bhimbar Gali. See Praval, *Valour Triumphs,* 207–8.

18. Two squadrons of Central Indian Horse (Stuart tanks) provided close support. C Squadron provided flank cum decoy security for the 268th Brigade's attack on Pir Badesar on 14–15 October. In addition to preventing the enemy from reinforcing Pir Badesar, it protected the brigade's left flank by pushing into the Seri Valley. A Squadron, along with the regimental headquarters, provided fire support for the 1/4 Gurkhas and Fourth Madras (part of the Fifth Brigade) during their attacks on Point 5982 and Pir Kalewa on the night of 26 October. During this action the leading infantrymen indicated enemy locations by torchlight to the tanks. The latter used tracers to mark and then engage targets, some of which were at a distance of 3,280 yards, a remarkable feat for the 37 mm guns of the Stuarts. See Sandhu, *The Indian Armour,* 292.

19. Sandhu, *The Indian Armour,* 315.

20. Prasad, *History of the Operations,* 351.

21. Proudfoot, *Valour Enshrined,* 25.

22. Praval, *The Indian Army,* 84.

23. Praval, *The Indian Army,* 85; Prasad, *History of the Operations,* 358. Wireless intercepts of messages from Pakistan army headquarters reveal that they were disbelieving of the reports from their garrison in Zojila Pass that Indian tanks were attacking them. They asked for repeated conformation whether these were armored carriers and not tanks. See Proudfoot, *We Lead,* 121.

24. Praval, *The Indian Army,* 186; Prasad, *History of the Operations,* 364.

25. Hamid, *Disastrous Twilight*, 278.
26. Smith, *India's "Ad Hoc" Arsenal*, 70.
27. Smith, *India's "Ad Hoc" Arsenal*, 53; also Blackett, *Scientific Problems*.
28. Terhal, "Foreign Exchange Costs," table 1; also Kavic, *India's Quest for Security*, app. 1.
29. Smith, *India's "Ad Hoc" Arsenal*, 56–59.
30. *Aviation Week*, 23 July 1962: 24; *Flight International*, 2 July 1964: 17.
31. Achutan, *Soviet Arms Transfer Policy*, 34–35.
32. Achutan, *Soviet Arms Transfer Policy*, 59; Kavic, *India's Quest for Security*, 117.
33. Venkateswaran, *Defense Organisation in India*, 147–50.
34. A plan for a more drastic cut of a further 100,000 was dropped in 1951–52. See Venkateswaran, *Defense Organisation in India*, 84–85.
35. Quoted in Praval, *The Indian Army*, 203.
36. Palit, *War in the High Himalaya*, 56.
37. In this case the rationale seems to have been a misguided attempt at "friendly diplomacy" rather than economic considerations. Kavic, *India's Quest for Security*, 95.
38. Kavic, *India's Quest for Security*, 96.
39. Maxwell, *India's China War*, 189; Praval, *The Indian Army*, 222–23.
40. Kavic, *India's Quest for Security*, 159–60, 191.
41. Kavic, *India's Quest for Security*, 193.
42. Praval, *The Indian Army*, 230.
43. See Vertzberger, "India's Strategic Posture."
44. Vertzberger, "India's Strategic Posture," 245.
45. The North East Frontier Agency, or NEFA, was divided into four frontier divisions: Kameng, Siang, Lohit, and Tirap. The Chinese claimed all of them except for Tirap.
46. Maxwell, *India's China War*, 292.
47. Praval, *The Indian Army*, 254.
48. Praval, *The Indian Army*, 253.
49. Umrao Singh protested in writing after serious differences arose between him and Sen over the launching of Operations Eviction and Leghorn, part of the forward policy. See Maxwell, *India's China War*, 321; Praval, *The Indian Army*, 258.
50. On 8 October the army headquarters forwarded a report from the Indian consul general in Lhasa to Kaul informing him that the Chinese had concentrated a division group of artillery behind Thag La. See Maxwell, *India's China War*, 336.
51. Praval, *The Indian Army*, 272.
52. Kaul, *The Untold Story*, 386; Maxwell, *India's China War*, 355.
53. Kaul, *The Untold Story*, 390.

54. Dalvi, *Himalayan Blunder*, 327.

55. Saigal, *The Unfought War*, 79, 169–70. Saigal was the deputy assistant adjutant and quartermaster general of the Forty-eighth Brigade. See also Praval, *The Red Eagles*, 273–76.

56. Praval, *The Red Eagles*, 291.

57. Johri, *Chinese Invasion of* NEFA, 211.

58. Praval, *Valour Triumphs*, 242; Praval, *The Red Eagles*, 306.

59. Proudfoot, *Flash of the Khukri*, 98. The Fourth Sikh (Saragrahi Battalion) was also deployed on both sides of the Lohit River and suffered heavy casualties during the withdrawal. See Singh and Ahluwalia, *Saragrahi Battalion*, 175–83.

60. Praval, *Valour Triumphs*, 242.

61. Johri, *Chinese Invasion of* NEFA, 250–54.

62. The withdrawal came in the nick of time, but A Company of the Sixth Mahar had to provide machine-gun fire to cover the retreat of the Second J&K Rifles, the 2/8th Gurkhas, and the Second Madras. See Longer, *Forefront for Ever*, 109.

63. Maxwell, *India's China War*, 89.

64. Praval, *The Indian Army*, 240.

65. Praval, *The Indian Army*, 245.

66. This post had already been encircled by the Chinese and was being supplied by air.

67. Singh, *The Saga of Ladakh*, 62. In 1962 Gen. Jagjit Singh was the brigade major of the 114th Brigade.

68. Johri, *The Chinese Invasion of Ladakh*, 137–38. Praval says Daulet Singh visited Chushul on 9 October. See Praval, *The Indian Army*, 311.

69. Singh, *The Saga of Ladakh*, 66.

70. Johri, *The Chinese Invasion of Ladakh*, 158.

71. Praval, *The Indian Army*, 311.

72. Singh, *The Saga of Ladakh*, 72.

73. Johri, *The Chinese Invasion of Ladakh*, 162.

74. Singh, *The Saga of Ladakh*, 77, 80.

75. As in the NEFA the Chinese used 57 mm and 75 mm recoilless rifles to blast the Kumaoni bunkers. Their 132 mm rockets left craters 4 feet deep on the solid rock face. Praval, *Valour Triumphs*, 250–53.

76. Praval, *Valour Triumphs*, 86–95; Johri, *The Chinese Invasion of Ladakh*, 178–85.

77. Praval, *Valour Triumphs*, 96–101.

78. Praval, *Valour Triumphs*, 106–8.

79. In the aftermath of the debacle, the new chief of army staff, General Chaudhuri, appointed a commission to conduct a limited operations review into the Indian army collapse. The team was led by Lt. Gen. Thomas Bryan Henderson-Brooks and Brig. P. S. Bhagat. The 200-page report has not yet been

released to the public. However, a few researchers who have seen the report have commented on it extensively. One such individual is Neville Maxwell, who based much of his landmark 1970 book, *India's China War*, on the report. In a recent series of articles on the Web-based news magazine *Rediff on the Net* Maxwell claims that the army itself threw hurdles in the path of the commission. He notes that Chaudhuri greatly circumscribed the scope of the enquiry, especially by ruling that the functioning of army headquarters during the crisis lay outside the commission's purview. But Henderson-Brooks and Bhagat rejected this restriction and noted in their report that "it would have been convenient and logical to trace the events [beginning with] Army HQ, and then moving down to the commands for more detail . . . ending up with the field formations for the battle itself." However, Maxwell reserves his harshest criticism for the director of military operations, Brigadier Plait, one of the few senior officers involved in the planning of the forward policy who managed to retain his army career after the conflict. According to Maxwell the commission report made it clear that Plait played a very destructive role "throughout the Army High Command's politicization, and through inappropriate meddling in command decisions, even in bringing about the debacle in the north-east." Maxwell alleges that Plait recognized the enquiry as a grave threat to his career and did all he could to obstruct it. Maxwell notes that it was Plait who ruled that the commission should not have access to any documents generated by the civilian side so as to hide the civil-military nexus. Maxwell also characterizes Plait's 1991 autobiography as "self admiring" and "grossly misrepresentative." For the above-mentioned quotes and commentary see Maxwell, "How the East Was Lost."

80. The lack of air support was not a result of the Indian air force's unwillingness to act. Indeed, the chief of air staff, Air Marshal Aspy M. Engineer, was most anxious to provide close-air support, but he did not receive a request from the army. See Lal, *Some Problems of Defense*, 68. It is probable that the decision not to use the IAF in an offensive role was a political one.

81. Saigal, *The Unfought War*, 93.

10. The Second Indo-Pakistan War

1. Praval, *The Indian Army*, 326.

2. *Ministry of Defence Report*, 23.

3. The deal for Soviet armor predates the 1962 conflict. See Smith, *India's "Ad Hoc" Arsenal*, 181.

4. Stockholm International Peace Research Institute, *The Arms Trade*, 477.

5. Marwah, "India's Military Power," 124.

6. Thomas, *The Defence of India*, 106, 151.

7. Marwah, "India's Military Power," 129, table 4.2.

8. The massive increase in the size of the army was to be achieved in part by means of emergency commissions. See *Ministry of Defence Report*, 24.

9. International Institute for Strategic Studies, *The Military Balance 1965–1966*, section on India.

10. International Institute for Strategic Studies, *The Military Balance 1965–1966*, 34–36.

11. Singh, *1965 War*, 24–26.

12. Musa, *Jawan to General*, 137.

13. See Thomas, "Security Relationships," 699; and Cohen, "U.S. Weapons in South Asia," 50.

14. Pakistan and America signed the Mutual Defense Agreement in May 1954. This was followed by Pakistan joining SEATO and the Baghdad Pact (later called CENTO) in September 1955. America obtained an air base at Peshawar. Pakistan perceived its relationship with the United States as a security umbrella against India. Tahir-Kheli, *The United States and Pakistan*, 1–4.

15. Brines, *The Indo-Pakistani Conflict*, 288.

16. Musa, *Jawan to General*, 160.

17. Musa, *My Version*, 35–36.

18. Musa, *My Version*, 39.

19. Singh, *Behind the Scene*, 72.

20. Singh, *Behind the Scene*, 104–5. The loss of Chaamb in 1965 resulted in a spate of welcome debate on the conduct of the Indian army in this area prior to and during the battle. While Gen. Joginder Singh blames General Katoch, the commander of the Fifteenth Corps, for a lack of preparedness, Col. K. P. P. Nair, a GSO Grade I officer of the Tenth Indian Division at the time of the battle, is critical of Gen. Harbaksh Singh's (the general officer commanding, Western Command) handling of the battle and accuses him of making a scapegoat out of Maj. Gen. D. B. Chopra, the commander of the Tenth Division, and sacking him to cover for his own indecisiveness in dealing with the Pakistani attack. See Nair, "A Review."

21. Singh, *Behind the Scene*, 116; Musa, *My Version*, 39.

22. Singh, *Behind the Scene*, 116.

23. Praval, *The Indian Army*, 350–51.

24. Singh, *Behind the Scene*, 118; Musa, *My Version*, 40.

25. Singh, *Behind the Scene*, 119.

26. Singh, *Behind the Scene*, 92–93.

27. Singh, *Behind the Scene*, 132.

28. Praval, *The Indian Army*, 358.

29. The brigade's objective was to capture Bhasin on the west bank of the Ichogil and northwest of Dograi. The 1/3 Gurkhas and Third Garhwal Rifles

were ordered to capture the village before first light on the 8th. Unfortunately, there was a delay in relaying the order, and the assault was launched without artillery or tank support and with no previous reconnaissance. Not surprisingly, the attack failed in the face of heavy defensive fire from dug-in Pakistani tanks. It took two full days to regroup the scattered elements of the 1/3 Gurkhas after the abortive attack. See Proudfoot, Flash of the Khukri, 110–11.

30. The commander of the Sixteenth Punjab, Lieutenant Colonel Golewala, fell during the fighting. See Proudfoot, Flash of the Khukri, 393.

31. Singh and Ahluwalia, Saragrahi Battalion, 199–202.

32. Praval, The Red Eagles, 310–11. The Pakistani First Armored Division consisted of the Third Armored Brigade: Nineteenth Lancers (Patton tanks) and Second Mechanized Battalion (M-113 APCs); the Fourth Armored Brigade: Fourth Cavalry (Patton), Fifth Horse (Patton), and one mechanized battalion; the Fifth Armored Brigade: Twenty-fourth Cavalry (Patton), two mechanized battalions, and divisional reconnaissance – Twelfth Cavalry with M-24 Chaffees. This is a puzzling assignment, as the Fourth Mountain was the weakest of the three Indian divisions in terms of its antitank assets. Prior to its departure from its home base in Ambala, the division had been given a regiment of Sherman Mk 4 tanks (Deccan Horse), and its firepower was further augmented with the addition of the Fortieth Medium Artillery Regiment. The division also received four 106 mm recoilless rifles for each of its battalions, but this was still fewer than the six deployed in standard infantry divisions. The Fourth also had priority call on the services of the Second Armored Brigade, which was comprised of the Third Cavalry (Centurion tanks), Eighth Cavalry (AMX-13s), and Seventh Cavalry (Soviet PT-76 amphibious light tanks). See Sandhu, The Indian Armour, 312–42.

33. Musa, My Version, 54.

34. The Medium Field Regiment fired 3,000 rounds and badly damaged the bridge over the Ichogil. While the Fourth Indian Division regrouped, the Shermans of the Deccan Horse provided rearguard protection. See Praval, The Red Eagles, 321.

35. Musa, My Version, 56.

36. Praval, The Indian Army, 374–75.

37. Praval, The Indian Army, 376; Singh, Behind the Scene, 159.

38. Musa, My Version, 61.

39. Praval, The Red Eagles, 322.

40. Singh, Behind the Scene, 159.

41. Rahman, The Wardens of the Marches, 96–97. Also Musa, My Version, 57. The same day Maj. Gen. Nasir Ahmed had a close brush with death when his reconnaissance party of three Jeeps was ambushed by a light machine-gun team of the Fourth Indian Grenadiers on the Bhikwind road between Asal Uttar and

Chima. (Musa says this happened on the 9th, while Colonel Palsokar says the 10th.) His artillery commander, Brig. A. R. Shamin, was killed, and the body was recovered by the Grenadiers. According to Musa, this incident further disrupted Pakistani plans for an offensive. See Musa, *My Version*, 56; Palsokar, *The Grenadiers*, 334–35.

42. All told, in addition to the commanding officer, 4 officers, 4 JCOs, and 121 other ranks were captured. Singh and Ahluwalia, *Saragrahi Battalion*, 208.

43. Longer, *Forefront for Ever*, 150.

44. Praval, *Valour Triumphs*, 283–84.

45. Singh, *Behind the Scene*, 201–2.

46. The First Corps had under its command the First Armored Division under Maj. Gen. Rajinder Singh, the Sixth Mountain Division under Maj. Gen. S. K. Korla, the Fourteenth Infantry Division (a newly raised unit) under Maj. Gen. R. K. Ranjit Singh, and the Twenty-sixth Infantry Division under Maj. Gen. M. L. Thapan. See Praval, *The Indian Army*, 395.

47. Sandhu, *The Indian Armour*, 341.

48. Pakistan's Sixth Armored Division had been built up from the 100th Independent Armored Brigade. It included the Twentieth Lancer, the divisional recognizance unit with M-24 Chaffee light tanks, the Tenth Guide Cavalry armed with Pattons, the Eleventh Cavalry armed with a mix of Pattons and M-36B2 tank destroyers, and the Twenty-second Cavalry armed with Shermans. See Sandhu, *The Indian Armour*, 343. As in the case with India over the Chaamb battle, a considerable controversy has arisen in Pakistan over the deployment of its Sixth Armored Division. According to General Musa, this division was held back as general headquarters reserve until definite information on India's offensive had crystallized (*My Version*, 64). However, this has been hotly disputed by other Pakistani officers, including Col. S. G. Mehdi, the former colonel staff of the Fifteenth Pakistani Division, who states that the Sixth Armored Division had been sent on a wild goose chase for phantom Indian paratroopers on the Grand Trunk Road near Wazirabad. The division made it back to Sialkot in the nick of time on the night of 7–8 September to meet the Indian attack. See Col. S. G. Mehdi, "1965 War – A Betrayal of Pakistan's Fundamental Interests?" in Mehdi, *Mehdi Papers*, serial 1, 1:21–22.

49. Considerable confusion seems to have resulted in the Pakistani ranks as a result of the Indians advances. On 9 September the Ninth Battalion, the Frontier Force Rifles, took up defensive positions on the Phillora-Zafarwal road. On 14 September at 7:30 PM the battalion started to withdraw, but its units broke when they were ambushed at Phillora. See Rahman, *The Wardens of the Marches*, 79.

50. The Kumaon of the Sixty-ninth Mountain Brigade made its final approach to attack Pagowal just as dawn broke on the 13th. Despite intense shelling by

Pakistani artillery and 120 mm mortars, Pagowal was captured, and the trench lines behind it were brought under fire. See Praval, *Valour Triumphs*, 274–75.

51. According to Pakistani accounts, Buttur Dograndi fell at 4:00 PM on the 16th. See Rahman, *The Wardens of the Marches*, 82.

52. Praval, *The Indian Army*, 403; Singh, *Behind the Scene*, 219. The Sixth Maratha, part of the Thirty-fifth Brigade, was the only battalion from the Sixth Division to capture its objective: a position to the west of Chawinda. In the process it lost 40 killed, including its commanding officer, Lt. Col. Mathew Manohar, and 110 taken prisoner. See Proudfoot, *Valour Enshrined*, 99.

53. Lal, *My Years with the* IAF, 31–47; also Hussain and Quereshi, *History of the Pakistan Air-Force*, 10–15.

54. Hussain and Quereshi, *History of the Pakistan Air-Force*, 22–24.

55. Figures in Fricker, "Thirty Seconds over Sargodha," 16.

56. Singh, *Behind the Scene*, 117, 228.

57. Lal, *Some Problems of Defense*, 82.

58. Sinha, *Higher Defense Organisation*, 19.

59. For an account of the Pakistani claims see Fricker, *Battle for Pakistan*.

60. Fricker, *Battle for Pakistan*, 138.

61. *Newsweek*, 4 October 1965: 45.

11. The Third Indo-Pakistan War

1. Mellor, "The Indian Economy."

2. Thomas, *Indian Security Policy*, 184, table 5.5.

3. Interview with the general in Praval, *The Indian Army*, 432–33.

4. International Institute for Strategic Studies, *The Military Balance 1971–1972*, 46; "Quantity or Quality? The Indian Dilemma," *Air International* (October 1975): 174–75.

5. International Institute for Strategic Studies, *The Military Balance 1971–1972*, 50.

6. International Institute for Strategic Studies, *The Military Balance 1971–1972*, 46; Sandhu, *The Indian Armour*, 428–31.

7. International Institute for Strategic Studies, *The Military Balance 1971–1972*, 50; Saliq, *Witness to Surrender*, 126–27.

8. Saliq, *Witness to Surrender*, 124.

9. The division had two field artillery regiments and one reconnaissance and support battalion.

10. Two field artillery regiments, a reconnaissance and support battalion, and an armored regiment with M-24 Chaffee light tanks supported the division.

11. One field artillery regiment, two mortar batteries, and one troop of M-24 Chaffee light tanks supported the division.

12. All dispositions and reinforcement information from Saliq, *Witness to Surrender*, 124–27.

13. Saliq, *Witness to Surrender*, 123.

14. Singh, *The Liberation of Bangladesh*, 1:72–73. Sukhwant Singh was the deputy DMO at army headquarters in Delhi.

15. Singh, *The Liberation of Bangladesh*, 1:91–92; Praval, *The Indian Army*, 441.

16. Saliq, *Witness to Surrender*, 128.

17. It included the Fourth Mountain Division, Ninth Infantry Division, Fiftieth Parachute Brigade, Forty-fifth Cavalry Regiment (PT-76 amphibious light tanks), Sixty-third Cavalry's (T-55s) B Squadron, and Ninth Punjab Mechanized Battalion (SKOT APCs).

18. This force included the Twentieth Mountain Division, Sixth Mountain Division, Sixty-ninth Armored Regiment (PT-76), Sixty-third Cavalry (less B Squadron), and Fifth Maratha Light Infantry Mechanized (SKOT APCs).

19. Its strength included the Eighth, Twenty-third, and Fifty-seventh Mountain Divisions, two squadrons of PT-76 light tanks (from the Seventh and Sixty-third Cavalry), and one squadron of Ferret Scout cars (also from the Sixty-third). The Second and Thirty-third Corps had a medium regiment each of the Soviet-built 130 mm field guns, and the Thirty-third Corps also had the Seventy-first Mountain Brigade with D Squadron of the Sixty-ninth Armored Regiment (eight PT-76 tanks) and one battery from the corps's medium regiment. See Praval, *The Indian Army*, 440–41; Sandhu, *The Indian Armour*, 429.

20. Praval, *The Indian Army*, 444.

21. Praval, *The Indian Army*, 447.

22. Saliq, *Witness to Surrender*, 139–40.

23. Saliq, *Witness to Surrender*, 144.

24. Praval, *The Indian Army*, 449. Saliq says that the town was abandoned at 11:00 AM See *Witness to Surrender*, 145.

25. Praval, *The Red Eagles*, 390.

26. Praval, *The Red Eagles*, 392; Saliq, *Witness to Surrender*, 145.

27. The remnants of the shattered Pakistani units were redeployed in Faridpur. See Praval, *The Red Eagles*, 403; Saliq, *Witness to Surrender*, 147. The Thirty-eighth Pakistani Frontier Force Rifles withdrew across the Madhumati to Kamarkhali on the night of the 10th. They withdrew from there to Faridpur on the 15th after an arduous cross-country march with their wounded. See Rahman, *The Wardens of the Marches*, 149. Their retreat was no doubt hastened by the fact that on the 15th at 11:00 AM the Fifth Indian Maratha Light Infantry crossed the Madhumati to attack Kamarkhali. See Proudfoot, *Valour Enshrined*, 191.

28. Proudfoot, *Valour Enshrined*, 192–93.

29. Hayat had earlier asked for and had been refused permission by General Ansari to withdraw from Jessore at the start of hostilities. Ansari was sticking

to Niazi's directive that units not withdraw until they had suffered 75 percent casualties. See Saliq, *Witness to Surrender*, 140–42.

30. Saliq, *Witness to Surrender*, 143; Praval, *The Red Eagles*, 455.

31. In doing so Dalbir Singh probably avoided the debacle that was inflicted on Indian troops at Kushtia. See Singh, *The Liberation of Bangladesh*, 1:142. In the course of its advance to Khulna, the Ninth Indian Division found itself road-bound near Daulatpur some 8.5 miles from Khulna. Off-road access was blocked on the left by the Bhairab River and on the right by marshes. Initial attacks up the road by the Twenty-sixth and Eighth Madras failed. The Fourth Sikh, attacking with the support of divisional artillery, managed to subdue the 107th Pakistani Brigade's defenses at Siramani on the 15th and at Syamganj on the 16th, a day before the cease-fire. See Singh and Ahluwalia, *Saragrahi Battalion*, 235–38.

32. Saliq, *Witness to Surrender*, 149.

33. Praval, *The Indian Army*, 458.

34. Praval, *The Indian Army*, 458.

35. Saliq, *Witness to Surrender*, 153.

36. The 2/5 and 5/11 Gurkhas captured Pirganj, and the latter battalion also established a roadblock to cut Pirganj from the north. Sharma, *The Path of Glory*, 115–16.

37. Sharma, *The Path of Glory*, 155.

38. Hilli was captured by first light on the 12th by the Twenty-second Maratha Light Infantry after a bloody night attack, during which the Marathas lost twenty-three dead and fifty-nine wounded. See Proudfoot, *Valour Enshrined*, 210.

39. Bhaduria, a built-up area, was heavily defended by a network of bunkers manned by two companies of the Eighth Baluch, one company of the Thirteenth Frontier Force Rifles, a troop of tanks, two 75 mm guns, and a battery of 105 mm howitzers. In the course of the assault the Seventeenth Kumaon lost two officers, three JCOs, and fifty-two other ranks. The retreating Pakistanis left behind eighty-two of their own dead. See Praval, *Valour Triumphs*, 329–30.

40. The 5/11 Gurkhas succeeded in capturing the Mahastan bridge over the Kartaya River before Pakistani sappers could blow it up. See Sharma, *The Path of Glory*, 124.

41. Saliq himself was witness to these effective attacks. See Saliq, *Witness to Surrender*, 156.

42. Fighting in the closing stages of the war in this area was very intense, and the Indian progress slowed. The Seventh Maratha Light Infantry was unable to take the Kantanagar bridge some 5 miles from Pirganj. See Proudfoot, *Valour Enshrined*, 199. The Twelfth Rajputana Rifles fought a bloody action at the Ichamati-Kharkharia river crossings on the 15th against the Forty-eighth Punjab (Pakistan). See Sethna and Katju, *Traditions of a Regiment*, 89–90. The Twenty-

sixth Pakistani Frontier Force Rifles withdrew from Dinajpur to Saidpur only after blowing up all the rail and road bridges behind it. The unit surrendered at Saidpur on the 17th. See Rahman, *The Wardens of the Marches*, 144.

43. Its Twenty-seventh Brigade, led by Brigadier Saadullah, was directly responsible for the defense of the Bhairab bridge and was deployed on the Akhaura–Brahmanbaria–Bhairab Bazar axis (this was also the Fourteenth Division's headquarters). The ad hoc 202nd Brigade, under Brigadier Salimullah, was in Sylhet proper, and the 313th Brigade, under Brig. Iftikhar Rana, was stationed at Maulvi Bazar.

44. Rahman, *The Wardens of the Marches*, 161.

45. Saliq notes that Gangasagar fell on 1 December. See Saliq, *Witness to Surrender*, 156; Praval, *The Indian Army*, 469. The Twelfth Frontier Force Rifles, the unit defending Akhaura, withdrew its positions to the west side of the Titas bridge. See Rahman, *The Wardens of the Marches*, 115.

46. Singh, *The Liberation of Bangladesh*, 1:156.

47. Saliq, *Witness to Surrender*, 161–62.

48. Tactical headquarters of the Fourteenth Pakistani Division had already moved from Brahmanbaria to Bhairab Bazar on the 8th. See Saliq, *Witness to Surrender*, 163.

49. Saliq, *Witness to Surrender*, 163; Praval, *The Indian Army*, 471.

50. Singh, *The Liberation of Bangladesh*, 1:87–88.

51. Praval, *The Indian Army*, 464; Saliq, *Witness to Surrender*, 168.

52. Saliq, *Witness to Surrender.*

53. Saliq, *Witness to Surrender*, 170. Attiqur Rahman says that the Thirtieth Frontier Force Rifles had only two weakened companies at this time. See Rahman, *The Wardens of the Marches*, 147.

54. Saliq, *Witness to Surrender*, 166–67. The Tenth Mahar took Maulvi Bazar just as the 313th Pakistani Brigade was completing its chaotic withdrawal, leaving behind all of its heavy equipment. See Longer, *Forefront for Ever*, 185.

55. Longer, *Forefront for Ever*, 171.

56. The Kumaon took most of the bulge on the night of 16–17 November. The remainder was taken between the 25th and the 28th with the help of the Ninth Kumaon. See Praval, *Valour Triumphs*, 311–12.

57. Praval, *The Indian Army*, 464, 471.

58. Singh, *The Liberation of Bangladesh*, 1:89–90.

59. Saliq states that it was the Sixty-first Indian Brigade that was involved in this attack. See Saliq, *Witness to Surrender*, 172. The Third Kumaon was the first Indian unit to enter Main Bazar, which fell at 12:05 PM on the 4th. Six officers, including the commanding officer, and 202 other ranks of the Twenty-fifth Frontier Force Rifles surrendered to the 1/11 Gurkhas. The commanding officer of the Twenty-fifth Frontier Force Rifles remarked that it was the fire support

from the independent squadron of PT-76 tanks of the Seventh Indian Light Cavalry that was instrumental in forcing their capitulation. See Proudfoot, *We Lead*, 207–8; Rahman, *The Wardens of the Marches*, 136.

60. Praval, *The Indian Army*, 473. The 1/11 Gurkha Rifles captured Mudafarganj on the morning of the 5th. See Sharma, *The Path of Glory*, 108.

61. Saliq, *Witness to Surrender*, 179. On the 14th 14 officers, 27 JCOs, and 1,077 other ranks of the Fifteenth Baluch, Twenty-third Punjab, Twenty-fifth Frontier Force Rifles, Twenty-first Azad Kashmir Battalion, Fifty-third Field Regiment, and police units surrendered to C Company, Twelfth Kumaon, south of Chandina. See Praval, *Valour Triumphs*, 333.

62. On the 9th the Third Kumaon, supported by the First Squadron of the Seventh Cavalry, secured Chandpur. See Proudfoot, *We Lead*, 210. The Seventh Rajputana Rifles took part of the Lalmai Hill on the 10th. See Sethna and Katju, *Traditions of a Regiment*, 163.

63. "Kilo" Force, led by the Thirty-second Mahar Regiment, advanced some 46.5 miles into Chittagong sector. See Longer, *Forefront for Ever*, 185–87.

64. On the 14th a platoon was landed ashore by motor launch. See Sharma, *The Path of Glory*, 329–30.

65. Singh, *The Liberation of Bangladesh*, 1:183–86.

66. Saliq, *Witness to Surrender*, 181.

67. Proudfoot, *Valour Enshrined*, 175–78.

68. Praval, *The Indian Army*, 478–79.

69. The battalion was ordered in for the defense of the capital. See Saliq, *Witness to Surrender*, 188.

70. By first light on 11 December some 60 Pakistanis had been captured, and 234 dead and 20 wounded were found in front of and within the First Maratha Light Infantry's battalion area. The remnants of the garrison surrendered the next day: 3 officers, 10 JCOs, and 372 other ranks were taken prisoner in what turned out to be the bloodiest battle of the campaign. See Proudfoot, *Valour Enshrined*, 181–82.

71. Proudfoot, *Valour Enshrined*, 189.

72. This operation became the independent Indian army's first major paradrop operation. It was finally sanctioned because of the total air superiority enjoyed by the IAF over East Pakistan. Lieutenant Colonel Pannu's Second Battalion Parachute Regiment was supported by the Forty-ninth Parachute Field Artillery Regiment and other support units. It was comprised of 27 officers, 25 JCOs, and 734 other ranks. The operation was mounted from Kalaikunda airfield with twelve AN-12s, twenty Fairchild Packets, and two Caribous. The force dropped at 4:00 PM some 5 miles northeast of Tangail. The entire drop was completed in about fifty minutes. See Praval, *India's Paratroopers*, 291–93.

73. On 16 December at 10:45 AM the Second Parachute Battalion became the first Indian unit to enter Dacca. See Praval, *India's Paratroopers*, 298.

74. For this and Pakistani strengths and deployments see Sandhu, *The Indian Armour*, 424–26; Praval, *The Indian Army*, 491–94.

75. Sisson and Rose, *War and Secession*, 215. In 1972 the Soviets once again volunteered to act as a mediator. This time India – based on its Tashkent experience – politely declined the offer, preferring instead to negotiate with Pakistan on a bilateral basis, which enabled it to maintain control of the gains made in Kashmir in 1971.

76. Its strength included the Thirty-sixth, Thirty-ninth, and Fifty-fourth Infantry Divisions, the Second and Sixteenth Armored Brigades, and one artillery brigade.

77. They were supported by the Twentieth Lancers, one squadron of the Seventieth Armored Regiment (antitank missiles), and the No. 3 and No. 6 Independent Armored Squadrons. All data on Indian forces are from Sandhu, *The Indian Armour*, 430–31; Praval, *The Indian Army*, 491–92.

78. Singh, *India's Wars since Independence*, 13.

79. Singh, *India's Wars since Independence*, 10–12; Sandhu, *The Indian Armour*, 431.

80. Saeed, *The Battle of Chaamb*, 10–13.

81. Saeed, *The Battle of Chaamb*, 15.

82. Singh, *India's Wars since Independence*, 66–67.

83. Considerable confusion reigned on the Indian side. The Seventh Kumaon, based at Akhnur, was preparing to relieve the 3/4 Gurkhas when it was diverted on 4 December at 9:30 PM to hold the east bank of the Munawar Tawi and to deny the Mandiala crossing to the Pakistanis. See Praval, *Valour Triumphs*, 338.

84. Singh, *India's Wars since Independence*, 71. The Third Frontier Force Rifles entered Chaamb at 9:00 AM on 7 December. See Rahman, *The Wardens of the Marches*, 155.

85. Saeed, *The Battle of Chaamb*, 67–70.

86. These crossings were held by the Ninth Jat and Tenth Garhwal Rifles. See Saeed, *The Battle of Chaamb*, 78; Praval, *The Indian Army*, 498.

87. Praval, *The Indian Army*, 499; Sandhu, *The Indian Armour*, 488.

88. Saeed, *The Battle of Chaamb*, 74.

89. Praval, *The Indian Army*, 504; Singh, *India's Wars since Independence*, 78–86. The 7/11 Gurkhas, Eleventh Guards, Ninth Parachute, and 3/5 Gurkhas were involved in the attack. See Sharma, *The Path of Glory*, 138.

90. Praval, *The Indian Army*, 506; Singh, *India's Wars since Independence*, 90–92.

91. Singh, *India's Wars since Independence*, 96; Sandhu, *The Indian Armour*, 495.

92. Khan, *Pakistan's Crisis in Leadership*, 199–200.

93. Sandhu, *The Indian Armour*, 494; Singh, *India's Wars since Independence*, 94.

94. Saeed, *The Battle of Chaamb*, 201; Singh, *India's Wars since Independence*, 94.

95. Singh, *India's Wars since Independence*, 100.

96. Praval, *The Indian Army*, 508.

97. Praval, *The Indian Army*, 508.

98. Praval, *The Indian Army*, 509.

99. The Grenadiers stormed Chakra on the night of 10–11 December. See Palsokar, *The Grenadiers*, 394–97. The Sixth Kumaon's attack on Dehrla began early in the morning of the 10th with artillery cover from the Sixty-ninth Field Regiment. According to the battalion diary, "it had gone entirely according to the book," and Dehrla was taken by 5:30 AM See Praval, *Valour Triumphs*, 343.

100. Praval, *Valour Triumphs*, 511; Singh, *India's Wars since Independence*, 104. The Third Grenadiers captured Jarpal on the 16th. See Palsokar, *Grenadiers*, 388–97. On the night of 15 December the Eighteenth Mechanized (TOPAS APCs) Rajputana Rifles, part of the Sixteenth Armored Brigade, crossed the Basanthar minefields, captured Saraj-Chak, and flushed the enemy out of the Lalial forest. The battalion then provided security for the Seventeenth Horse by flushing enemy antitank positions out of the Supwal ditch. See Sethna and Katju, *Traditions of a Regiment*, 165.

101. Sandhu, *The Indian Armour*, 506–8.

102. The Thirty-fifth Pakistani Frontier Force Rifles launched a hurried attack against Jarpal on the 17th. Its sister battalion, the Twenty-ninth, stationed to the west of Jarpal, was unaware of the attack and did not provide any support. The attack failed, with the Thirty-fifth losing fifty-four killed and sixty-nine wounded, including the commanding officer, Lt. Col. Muhammad Akram Raja, who died leading the attack at 4:00 AM See Rahman, *The Wardens of the Marches*, 171–72. On the Indian side, the Third Grenadiers lost one officer (Maj. Hoshiar Singh), three JCOs, thirty-two other ranks killed, and three officers, three JCOs, and eighty-six other ranks wounded. See Palsokar, *Traditions of a Regiment*, 389–91.

103. Praval, *The Indian Army*, 514.

104. In addition to the Sixty-sixth Armored Regiment and the Third Cavalry, the integral armored support units of the two infantry divisions, the Eleventh Indian Corps also had the support of the Fourteenth Indian Armored Brigade (Eighteenth Cavalry T-54s, Sixty-second Cavalry T-55s, Sixty-fourth Cavalry T-54s, Seventieth Cavalry SS-11 antitank missiles, Seventy-first Armored Regiment T-55s, Ninety-second Independent Reconnaissance Squadron PT-76s, and 1/8th Gurkhas Mechanized). The main Indian strike force, made up of the First Armored Division – the First Armored Brigade with Second Lancers, Sixty-fifth, Sixty-seventh, and Sixty-eighth Cavalry (all Vijayanta), and Forty-third Lorried Brigade with three mechanized battalions (TOPAS APCs and the Ninety-third Independent Reconnaissance Regiment AMX-13s) – and the Fourteenth Indian

Infantry Division, concentrated in the Muktasar area in the second week of October, where it remained all through the war. See Praval, *The Indian Army*, 523.

105. The Mahar part of the Forty-eighth Infantry Brigade took the Shejra bulge (21 square miles) on the night of 5–6 December. See Longer, *Forefront for Ever*, 200.

106. Praval, *The Indian Army*, 524.

107. Khan, *Pakistan's Crisis in Leadership*, 209; Praval, *The Indian Army*, 525–26. The attack by the 105th Brigade was launched at 6:00 PM on 3 December and succeeded in surprising the Indians. By 7:00 PM the Sixth Frontier Force Rifles had taken Jhangar Post, the village of Nor Mohammad, and the Gurmukh bridge over the Sabuna tributary. See Rahman, *The Wardens of the Marches*, 177.

108. Praval, *The Indian Army*, 210.

109. The division had concentrated at Kishangarh on the night of 4–5 December for the forthcoming offensive when news came of the attack on Longenwalla. The division (including the Thirteenth Kumaon) diverted to Longenwalla to defend its divisional headquarters at Tanot.

110. Praval, *The Indian Army*, 532.

111. The Second Rajputana Rifles formed the reserve for the Eighty-fifth Brigade's attack on Parbat Ali. This battalion failed to establish a roadblock on the Umarkot-Naya-Chor road on 11 December. See Sethna and Katju, *Traditions of a Regiment*, 58.

112. Parbat Ali fell to the Second Mahar and Tenth Sikh after a bitter fight on the night and morning of 12–13 December. See Longer, *Forefront for Ever*, 194.

113. These attacks were launched by Lt. Col. Bhawani Singh's Tenth Para-commando Battalion between 5 and 17 December. See Praval, *India's Paratroopers*, 306–9.

114. By 1967 the PAF had three MiG-19 squadrons. See "Pakistan Air Force," 43.

115. The Canadian-built Luftwaffe Sabres were obtained from a Swiss Company. See Hunt, "Reflections," 203.

116. Fricker, "Post-Mortem," 229.

117. The SU-7s appear to have been purchased to offset the failed, locally developed HF-24 fighter-bomber project. See "Quantity or Quality?"

118. In Rajasthan fully operational combat air bases were established at Jodhpur, Barmer, and Jaisalmer. These air bases were established to offset the air-superiority advantage the Pakistanis had enjoyed there in 1965. See Lal, *My Years with the IAF*, 164.

119. Singh, *Aircraft of the Indian Air Force*, 143–44.

120. Lal, *My Years with the IAF*, 164–65.

121. Lal, *My Years with the IAF*, 174. According to Lt. Gen. S. K. Sinha the improved army-air coordination in 1971 had much to do with the compatible

personalities of the army, air, and naval chiefs (Gen. Sam Manekshaw, Air Chief Marshal P. C. Lal, and Adm. S. M. Nanda) and their ability to get along with the prime minister (Indira Gandhi), the defense minister (Jagjivan Ram), and the defense secretary (K. B. Lall). See Thomas, *Indian Security Policy*, 139.

122. Thomas, *Indian Security Policy*, 175–76.

123. Chopra, "Gnat," 75.

124. Chopra, "Journal of an Air War," 197.

125. Chopra, "Journal of an Air War," 180.

126. Fricker, "Post-Mortem," 228.

127. On 7 December the 110th Helicopter Unit moved 254 troops from Laila-shahar to the Sylhet sector under heavy ground fire. The next day it airlifted an additional 279 troops and 97 tons of equipment from Kulaura during a night mission. Between the 9th and the 10th the unit airlifted 584 troops, 125 tons of supplies, and 9 field guns to reinforce the buildup against the 313th Pakistani Brigade, which defended Sylhet. On the 11th the 110th Helicopter Unit moved 1,350 troops and 192 tons of equipment from Brahmanbaria to Narsingdi, including the lead battalion – the 4/5 Gurkhas – across the Meghna River to the southeast of Sylhet, forcing the much larger Pakistani defending forces to beat a hasty retreat into Sylhet to avoid being cut off from the rear. On the 14th the unit lifted 810 troops and 23 tons of equipment across the Meghna (from Daudkandi) to Baidya Bazar. The next day it flew 1,209 troops and 38 tons of equipment across the Meghna to strengthen the Baidya Bazar airhead.

128. Chopra, Green, and Swanborough, eds., *The Indian Air Force*, 52.

129. Chopra, "Journal of an Air War," 172.

130. Chopra, "Journal of an Air War," 177; Shaheen, "The PAF at War," 11.

131. Department of State, *Sitrep*, 9 December 1971, quoted in Sisson and Rose, *War and Secession*, 231 n. 37.

132. See Shaheen Foundation, *The Story of the Pakistan Air Force*, 443; Tanham and Agmon, *The Indian Air Force*, 40–41.

133. Kohli, *Sea Power*, 21–34, 133–34.

134. Thomas, *Indian Security Policy*, 153.

135. Thomas, *Indian Security Policy*, 192, table 5.9.

136. All data from the International Institute for Strategic Studies, *The Military Balance 1971–1972*.

137. Kaul, "The Indo-Pakistani War," 186, 188.

138. The first recruits for this camp were six East Pakistani submariners who had defected while undergoing training on the Daphne-class submarines in France. See Chopra, *India's Second Liberation*, 157.

139. Rai, *A Nation and Its Navy*, 55.

140. The Seahawks launched daytime strikes, while the Alizes launched nightly raids. See Chopra, "Journal of an Air War," 275–79.

141. For attacks on Karachi and the bombardment see Kohli, *We Dared*, 49–55, 59–64.

142. Rai, *A Nation and Its Navy*, 138–41.

143. It appears that while trying to evade the *Rajput* the *Ghazi* ran into one of its own mines that it had laid at the approaches to the Indian navy base at Vishakapatnam. See Krishnan, *No Way but Surrender*, 40–43; Goodman and Mazumdar, "East Meets West."

144. Aron, *Clausewitz*, 346, 352.

12. Insurgencies, Interventions, and High Altitude Warfare

1. Elements of the 181st, Seventeenth Rajput, Second Sikh, and 1/3rd Gurkhas were inducted between August and September 1953. See Thomas, "Forever in Operations," 180.

2. Praval, *The Indian Army*, 559. Palsokar says that Maj. Gen. R. K. Kochar was appointed general officer commanding, Naga Hills and Tuensang, in April 1956.

3. Anand, *Conflict in Nagaland*, 125, 560. In one particularly bloody engagement one JCO and thirty-two other ranks of the Ninth Punjab were ambushed on 1 April 1957, with only one soldier escaping. See Thomas, "Forever in Operations," 181.

4. Praval, *The Indian Army*, 561.

5. Goakhle, "Nagaland – India's Sixteenth State."

6. Thomas, "Forever in Operations," 182.

7. Nair, "Employment of Military Helicopters," 103.

8. Reddi, "The Forgotten Naga Insurgency," 42.

9. The divisional motto is "An eye for the insurgents and heart for the Naga." See Thomas, "Forever in Operations," 188.

10. Thomas, "Forever in Operations," 735.

11. Praval, *India's Paratroopers*, 273–76.

12. Kasturi, "The Indian Experience," 77.

13. The reasons for the migration are not hard to discern. According to the 1984 *World Bank Development Report*, Bangladesh has a population density of about 1,300 persons per square mile against India's 56, an annual population growth rate of 2.9 percent to India's 1.9 percent, and, more important, a per capita income of U.S. $140 compared to India's U.S. $260. See *The World Bank Development Report*, 218–54.

14. Handke, "The Conflict in India's Northeast," 432.

15. Mendiratta, "Insurgent Assam," 65.

16. Thomas, "IDR Comments," 5.

17. Sood, "Insurgencies in the North-East," 27.

18. Sood, "Insurgencies in the North-East," 27.

19. "Army Begins."

20. Singh, "Socio-Economic Bases."

21. For a full account of the battle of the Golden Temple and the ensuing troop mutinies see Tully and Jacob, *Amritsar*.

22. For further analysis of the mutinies see Barua, "Ethnic Conflict."

23. Joshi, "The Pakistan Connection."

24. Gupta, "Punjab"; "Punjab's Winter of Despair."

25. Awasthi, "Terrorism."

26. Ramakrishnan, "The Zero Story," 125.

27. The western army commander, Lt. Gen. B. C. Joshi, talking to reporters on the eve of his assumption of the COAS position, noted that the secret to the army's success in the Punjab was its "low profile" approach. See Sharma, "Joshi Lauds."

28. Swahney, "Plugging the Dyke," 101.

29. Press conference by Lt. Gen. B. K. N. Chibber, commander of the Eleventh Corps, in *Indian Express*, 5 June 1992.

30. Joshi, "Receding Terror," 62.

31. The noted Sikh journalist Kushwant Singh, a longtime critic of the Indian government's handling of the Punjab issue, published a two-part article in the *Times of India* that was highly critical of the insurgents. His views mirror the dramatically changing attitudes of average Sikhs to the Punjab problem. See Singh, "Punjab-Today – I" and "Punjab-Today – II."

32. De Silva, *Managing Ethnic Tensions*, 339.

33. For more information on the evolution of the Liberation Tigers of Tamil Eelam and other Tamil separatist groups see Oberst, "Sri Lanka's Tamil Tigers"; Austin and Gupta, *Lions and Tigers*.

34. For a detailed and highly negative analysis of the role played by Indian intelligence agencies in the Sri Lankan conflict see Gunaratna, *Indian Intervention*.

35. Gunaratna, *Indian Intervention*, 39.

36. At the same time it was combating the Liberation Tigers of Tamil Eelam and other Tamil militant groups, the Sri Lankan government was also engaged in a bloody campaign against the Janatha Vimukhti Perumana, a Marxist/nationalist movement led by Rohana Wijeweera.

37. Gunaratna, *Indian Intervention*, 197.

38. Sardeshpande, *Assignment Jaffna*, 12.

39. See the special report "Operation Pawan," 73.

40. "Operation Pawan," 74–75.

41. "Operation Pawan," 73–74.

42. Singh, "Peacekeepers in Sri Lanka," 30.

43. Singh, "Peacekeepers in Sri Lanka," 31.

44. Gunaratna, *Indian Intervention*, 247.

45. Banerjie, "Coming Home," 26.

46. "Operation Pawan," 75.

47. Singh, "Peacekeepers in Sri Lanka," 27.

48. They included the Fifty-seventh Mountain Division, which had moved from Mizoram to the Batticaloa sector, the Fourth Infantry Division, from Allahabad to the Vavuniya sector, the Fifty-fourth Air Assault Division, from Secunderabad to Jaffna, and the Thirty-sixth Infantry Division, from Sagar in Madhya Pradesh to the Trincomalee sector, for a total of almost fifteen brigades.

49. Banerjie, "Coming Home," 22.

50. Singh, "Peacekeepers in Sri Lanka," 32–33. The Mi-25 helicopter gunships were nicknamed "crocodiles" by the Liberation Tigers of Tamil Eelam and proved devastating in the battlefield support role. They were armed with 57 mm rockets, a 12.7 mm multibarreled heavy machine gun, and 1,100-pound bombs.

51. Joshi, "The Price of Peace," 17–21.

52. See, by special arrangement, "In Their Lair."

53. Sardeshpande, *Assignment Jaffna*, 64. Sardeshpande's book contains several useful after-action reports of battles between the Indian Peace-Keeping Force and the Liberation Tigers from October 1987 to May 1989 (93–137).

54. Subramaniam, "Sri Lanka," 102–5.

55. Bobb, "IMSF."

56. Gunaratna, *Indian Intervention*, 280–305.

57. Padmanabhan, "Tiger Talk."

58. Menon, "Sri Lanka," 64.

59. Sardeshpande, *Assignment Jaffna*, 64.

60. For more information on the events leading up to the violent insurgency movement in 1990 see Puri, *Kashmir*.

61. Wirsing report quoted in Wirsing, *India, Pakistan, and the Kashmir Dispute*, 119.

62. Gupta, "Kashmir."

63. Pachauri, "Jammu & Kashmir Border."

64. See Thomas, "IDR Comments."

65. Thomas, "IDR Comments," 5.

66. Indian army deployment in J&K, 1993, as per Pakistani military intelligence: Fifteenth Corps (HQ Srinagar; Kashmir and Ladakh subdivisions): Third Infantry Division, Leh (Ladakh); Eighth Mountain Division, Sharifabad (Kashmir); Nineteenth Infantry Division, Baramulla (Kashmir); Twenty-eighth Infantry Division, Kupwara (Kashmir). Sixteenth Corps (HQ Nagrota; Jammu subdivision and Punjab): Tenth Infantry Division, Akhnur (Jammu); Twenty-fifth Infantry Division, Rajouri (Jammu); Twenty-sixth Infantry Division, Jammu

(Jammu); Twenty-ninth Infantry Division, Mamun (Punjab and Jammu). All data from Wirsing, *India, Pakistan, and the Kashmir Dispute*, 146.

67. See Amnesty International, *India*.

68. The BSF and other paramilitary bodies deployed in the state such as the Central Reserve Police Force, the Indo Tibetan Border Police, and the Rashtriya Rifles have sole responsibility for cordon and search operations in Srinagar and primary responsibility for such operations in the rest of the state.

69. See Additional Director-General of BSF E. N. Rammohan's interview with Tony Davis in *Jane's Defence Weekly*, 22 October 1994: 32.

70. The unit was originally given the go-ahead by the government of Prime Minister V. P. Singh in 1990. See Bhattacharya, "The Rashtriya Rifles."

71. Subramanian, "CI Operations." An article in a British defense news journal in 2001 stated that Israeli counterterrorism experts were deeply involved in training their Indian counterparts in Kashmir. See Blanche, "Mutual Threat."

72. Shashikumar, "Life in the Bunker"; Swami, "Flashpoint Kashmir."

73. See the interview with Lt. Gen. Krishen Pal, "We Have Exercised Utmost Restraint."

74. The growing sophistication of the militants coincided with the arrival of Pakistan- and Afghanistan-based militants from the mid-1990s on. See Ramakrishnan, "A New F."

75. Vinayak, "Wireless Wars."

76. "Militancy in Jammu & Kashmir."

77. Shashikumar, "Civil Lines."

78. Wirsing, "The Siachen Glacier Dispute."

79. Chibber, "Siachen."

80. Chibber, "Siachen," 148–51.

81. Ali, *Fangs of Ice*, 50–52.

82. Bajwa, "Staring Death in the Face." According to Bajwa, the Fourth J&K Light Infantry lost forty-one men in taking Qaid Post.

83. Details of this battle have been taken from both Indian and Pakistani sources. See "Heroic Defence of Siachen"; Ali, *Fangs of Ice*, 76–84.

84. The Kumar supply base is the most distant location for the Indian-made 105 mm field gun, which was disassembled, airlifted, and reassembled there.

85. This panoramic description of life on the glacier for Indian troops has been taken from Sidhu, "Siachen." The photos taken by Pramod Pushkarna for this special feature are also noteworthy. For more spectacular pictures and details of the ongoing hardships of Indian and Pakistani troops in Siachen see Fedarko, "The Coldest War."

86. For this quote and further details on the Pakistani deployment against the Indians see Cécile, "Siachen."

87. Hasnain, "Pakistan."

88. The tapes are believed to have been made by the CIA and routed to the Indian government via RAW. The transcripts of the conversation can be found on the Indian army's Kargil website: http://vijayinkargil.org/features/features6 .html.

89. See Hasnain, "Pakistan." See also "How I Started a War."

90. See "Pakistani Army's Plan."

91. Vinayak, "Kargil Assault"; "Army Chief Flies to Kargil."

92. Kumar, "Intelligence Failure." Maps discovered on the body of Ali Mohammed Dar, a Hizb-ul-Mujahedeen commander killed in Srinagar by the Special Operations Group of the Jammu & Kashmir Police, and information from Azhar Shafi Mir, a Hizb-ul-Mujahedeen operative arrested by the BSF in the Poonch area and whom G-branch (the intelligence wing of the BSF) interrogated, revealed that Pakistan was planning an operation in the Dras-Kargil area to sabotage the Leh-Srinagar highway. Furthermore, in October 1998 intelligence branch operatives in Leh passed on reports of 350 irregulars being trained in two camps in the area of Olthingthang, Pakistan's forward headquarters in the Kargil area. The Leh reports specifically noted that the groups would infiltrate the Kargil area in April 1999. Soon thereafter another report from Leh warned that Pakistan was using remotely piloted vehicles to monitor the Leh-Kargil area. All of this information was sent to the Ministry of Defense in the third week of October 1998, but it received no reaction. Through the winter of 1998–99 the RAW's Aviation Research Center, based in Saraswa in western Uttar Pradesh state, carried out no surveillance flights along the Kargil line of control, nor did the IAF send out its high altitude recce patrols. The army too failed to begin wide-area surveillance operations with its Cheetah light helicopters until May 1999. As K. Subramanyam, director of the Joint Intelligence Committee from 1977 to 1979 pointed out, the intelligence failure in Kargil was not the lack of information but the failure to assess and interpret the available data. See "War in Kargil"; Swami, "The Bungle in Kargil"; and Joshi and Baweja, "Kargil War: Blasting Peace."

93. Joshi and Baweja, "Kargil War: Blasting Peace."

94. Kumar, "IAF Pounds Infiltrators."

95. Shashikumar and Pushkarna, "War in Kashmir."

96. Joshi and Baweja, "Kargil War: Blasting Peace."

97. Joshi and Chengappa, "Kargil War."

98. Sawant, "Job Done."

99. Swami, "A Long Haul Ahead"; Sawant, "Long, Hard Battle Ahead."

100. Vinayak, "Wangchuk's War."

101. Aneja, "Indian Troops." The Second Rajputana were led by Col. M. B. Ravindranath and suffered one officer, two JCOs, and seven soldiers killed in the attack. See Vinayak and Banerjee, "Taking Tololing."

102. Sawant, "Big Guns Boom." The 155 mm shells of the Bofors proved particularly effective against the Pakistani bunkers. Its high rate of fire, accuracy, and weight of shell meant that it was in constant demand. See Sawant, "Zero to Hero."

103. Shashikumar and Pushkarna, "Miles to Go."

104. The army suffered twenty-six dead, including three officers (Maj. P. Acharya, Lt. Vijayant Thapar, and Lt. N. Kenguruse), in this operation. At the end of this series of operations the army's total casualties stood at 201 dead (including 14 officers), 384 wounded (including 25 officers), and 9 missing (including 2 officers). See Sawant, "Army Peaks"; and "Army Regains Four More Heights."

105. "Key Positions in Dras, Batalik Regained."

106. Swami, "The Final Assault."

107. "21 Pak Army Regulars, Militants Killed."

108. The Kargil operations presented peculiar problems to the IAF's close air support pilots. Melting and shifting snow would change land contours constantly, cloud cover impeded laser targeting, and wind speeds in excess of 50 knots made high altitude bombing imprecise. Under these conditions the IAF found that laser-guided weaponry was not cost-effective, so according to Group Capt. S. P. S. Virk, chief engineering officer of the Gwalior-based Mirage 2000 squadron, "slight modifications were made to the iron bombs of World War II vintage, and the old bombs did the trick." A primary Pakistani fortification atop Tiger Hill was destroyed on 24 June after IAF Mirage 2000s managed to engage a target lock only after the cloud cover on the mountaintop blew away briefly. See "Kargil: A Saga."

109. The Grenadiers was subsequently awarded a "unit citation" by the army chief. See "Tiger Hill Falls"; "Major Success for Indian Troops"; Constable, "India Captures."

110. "Army Captures 3 Heights."

111. "Three More Heights Secured."

112. "Army Consolidating Gains in Batalik, Dras."

113. The figures were given by Air Marshal Patney, air officer commanding in chief, Western Air Command, on 12 July 1999. See "IAF to 'Wait and Watch.'"

114. Shaikh, "Cabinet Endorses."

115. Ved, "Kargil Operations"; and "Pak Forces Begin Pullout."

116. "Pak, India DGMOs Meet at Wagha."

117. The Indian army also revised its estimates of Pakistani casualties to 698 dead, including 41 officers. The Indian army claimed to have recovered a total of 249 bodies of Pakistani soldiers in the Dras, Mushkoh Valley, and Batalik sectors. Indian casualty figures rose to 410 killed and 593 wounded. The miss-

ing total fell to 4. See "Bodies of Pak Officers, Soldiers Identified"; "IAF Sorties Reveal Pullout"; and "Pakistani Withdrawal Almost Complete."

118. List of awards at http://www.PakDef.com/army/awards.html.

119. See, for example, the article by retired army chief Gen. Mirza Aslam Beg, "Retreat from Kargil."

120. The committee, headed by K. Subrahmanyam, a member of the National Security Advisory Board, has been criticized by the press for failing to meet "the minimum standards of what would constitute an impartial inquiry." See Swami, "The Kargil Conflict."

121. Letter no. 132/GSI/Pak/China, reproduced in Swami, "Warnings in Vain."

122. "Interview of the Week."

123. Joseph, "Army Draws Up Strategy."

13. The Evolution of a Regional Military Power

1. Thomas, "The Growth of Indian Military Power," 36.

2. International Institute for Strategic Studies, *Strategic Survey, 1993–1994,* 226.

3. "India Sets 5% Lower Budget."

4. Joshi, "The Resource Crunch."

5. India's gross national income in 1999 was $2.23 trillion compared to $8.8 trillion for the United States, $4.45 trillion for China, and $3.19 trillion for Japan. See "India Now 4th Largest."

6. Thomas, *Indian Security Policy,* 189.

7. Smith, *India's "Ad Hoc" Arsenal,* 115.

8. International Institute for Strategic Studies, *The Military Balance 1995–1996,* 153–54. A Finance Ministry report noted that imported defense equipment amounted to 9 percent of India's external debt in 1993. Of this amount, some 90 percent was owed to the Russians in unrequited rupee credits, with a dollar-denominated component of about $1 billion.

9. Military research and development increased by 12.9 percent to Rs 43.8 billion, while special projects such as the Arjun main battle tank and the integrated missile development program got Rs 329.2 billion. Allocation for defense factories stood unchanged, at Rs 15.65 billion. See Bedi, "Indian Budget," 12.

10. D'Souza, "Never Enough Courage."

11. "Govt Plans Supplementary Defense Budget."

12. "Defense Budget Must Be Increased"; see also Swamy, "India's Defense Needs"; "Defense Allocation Pegged at 41,000"; "Defense Outlays up by 14%."

13. Nadkarni, "How Can One Modernize."

14. "Rs. 8,000 Crore Defense Spending Hike Likely."

15. Joshi, "Tank Power."

16. Figures from the Stockholm International Peace Research Institute arms trade database in Smith, *India's "Ad Hoc" Arsenal*, 231–46.

17. Bobb, "The Bofors Blast."

18. "Army Seeks Ultimate Man-Machine Balance."

19. Bedi, "India Set to Test."

20. Bedi, "Arms Deals."

21. "India's Main Battle Tank."

22. "Army Seeks Ultimate Man-Machine Balance."

23. The spectacular success of the guided missile program is largely due to the efforts of Dr. Abdul Kalam, head of India's defense research program. For more information on Kalam and the guided missile program see Chengappa, "The Missile Man."

24. The deal to acquire the six s-300v systems came about after several rounds of "meticulous negotiations" between Indian Defense Secretary Ajit Kumar and Russian First Deputy Defense Minister Nikolai Mikhailov in June 1998. See "India Signs Missile Deal with Russia"; "Army Seeks Ultimate Man-Machine Balance."

25. Gupta, "Shooting Ahead"; Joshi, "The Missile Edge."

26. Mama, "Process," 963.

27. The army is said to have a requirement for seventy-five Prithvi Is. See "Army Seeks Ultimate Man-Machine Balance."

28. "Pinaka Was Tested in Kargil."

29. Gupta, "INSAS."

30. "India to Buy Anti-Mine Vehicles."

31. Mama, "AREN Network"; Gupta, "The New Thrust."

32. Existing local data area networks are in place at army headquarters, as are wide-area networks. See "Army Seeks Ultimate Man-Machine Balance."

33. "Army Networks for Future Combat."

34. "Army Networks for Future Combat."

35. According to Lt. Gen. Prakash Gokran, "The Corps of Signals is aware of the lurking danger to our automated information systems in the nuclear age and is busy creating firewalls against any attempt to go for the nation's electric jugular." See "Corps of Signals Gears Up."

36. Thomas, "The RAPID."

37. "Massive Restructuring of the Army's Infantry Division."

38. Mohan, "Fernandes."

39. Maharaj, "Indian Air Force," 46. The Litening pods were battle tested during the Kargil confrontation with Pakistan when they were mounted on Mirage 2000 fighters. See "Israeli Night Fighting Pods." A report in October 1999 stated that HAL, in cooperation with British Aerospace, was preparing to manufacture an upgraded version of the Jaguar. It is not known if these will be

attrition replacement aircraft or an entirely new production batch. See "HAL to Manufacture Upgraded Jaguars."

40. "India to Acquire N-Capable Mirage"; and "Indian Ties with France." The IAF's interest in the Mirage strike aircraft is curious given the tremendous strike potential of the Russian-built SU-30, which was inducted into service in 1998. The reports suggest that the purchase may be a "reward" to France for its noncondemnation of India's nuclear tests and for delaying the delivery of a batch of older Mirage-5 fighters to Pakistan during the Kargil conflict. India is also said to have concluded a deal to purchase ten additional Mirage 2000H fighters to replace four aircraft lost to attrition from the current IAF Mirage fleet.

41. Chopra, Green, and Swanborough, eds., The Indian Air Force, 54.

42. "IAF Team in Israel."

43. The deal was allowed to proceed by the new Israeli defense minister, Moshe Arens. The Israelis defended the deal by noting that the weapon system was "defensive in nature" and wholly developed in Israel with no U.S. technology. See "Israel Sold Electronic Warfare System."

44. Lake, "Mikoyan MiG-23/27 'Flogger.'"

45. Indian pilots became the first non-Soviet pilots to fly the MiG-29 when two IAF officers evaluated the aircraft during a twenty-five-flight program in 1984. More evaluation teams visited the Soviet Union during 1985, with the result that India became the first foreign country to order the MiG-29. Pilots and ground crew underwent training at Lugovaya and Frunze in Kazakhstan during October 1986 and were the first foreigners to convert to the aircraft. Deliveries were delayed until December 1986 due to India's insistence on being given the full standard aircraft. See Lake, "Mikoyan MiG-29 'Fulcrum.'"

46. HAL produced 580 of the 830 MiG-21s used by the IAF. See Steinemann, "India's Fabulous 'Fishbeds.'"

47. The aircraft will be equipped with new radar, avionics, and missiles. See "Indian MiG 21 Upgrade Plans."

48. All data from the SIPRI register are in Smith, India's "Ad Hoc" Arsenal, app. C.

49. "Decision on AJT Aircraft Soon"; "Kashmir Conflict Hastens India's Jet Trainer Decision."

50. Chengappa, "LCA Project."

51. Mukherjee, "Green Light."

52. Rai, "Wanted."

53. "India's LCA Set to Undergo."

54. Prasannan, "No Mirage This"; Chengappa, "Miles to Go."

55. "India Reveals Details"; and "Astra Missile."

56. "LCA and ALH Projects."

57. "Indian Ties with France."

58. "Offer to Help HAL."

59. Chengappa, "The Missile Man."

60. The HTV is a smaller, lower cost version of the hyperplane proposed by DRDO chief Dr. A. P. J. Abdul Kalam in 1995. See "Next Indian Satellite."

61. A defense committee of the cabinet approved the establishment of the ADGES Maintenance Command Establishment in September 1970. See *Report of the Controller*, 33.

62. Saradzhyan, "India to Buy $500 Million Missile Shield." The deal was part of a larger ten-billion-dollar arms package.

63. KALI had been in development since 1985 and was originally developed for industrial purposes. Ron noted that the 26-ton KALI was too heavy and bulky and needed "compacting." The system had already been used to test the vulnerability of the LCAs avionics and to enhance the electronic systems of Indian satellites and missiles to protect them from electromagnetic impulses generated by nuclear weapons. See "Delhi Is Finalizing Work."

64. "Russian-Indian SU-30MK Delivery Contract."

65. The government set aside Rs 26.5 billion in the FY 1996–97 budget for fifteen to twenty SU-30 fighter bombers. See Bedi, "Indian Budget."

66. *Vayu Aerospace Review* 1 (1994): 43.

67. The navy also utilized the Sea Eagle missiles in an IAF Jaguar squadron (only eight aircraft), which has a dedicated antiship mission.

68. All data are from the SIPRI register in Smith, *India's "Ad Hoc" Arsenal*, app. C.

69. Manoj Joshi notes that while the German Type-209 stresses comfort and automation, the Soviet Kilo is more crowded, with an "obvious accent on ruggedness and performance." See "Run Silent, Run Deep."

70. "India to Get Latest Submarine."

71. Feller, "Russia Starts Building"; "Navy to Acquire Three Russian Frigates"; Makarov, "New Sword."

72. The Alfa P-10 will become the standard cruise missile of the Indian navy, equipping its ships, submarines, and aircraft. The potent weapon will give the Indian navy a huge leap in antiship strike capability. See "New Russian Missiles."

73. "India to Produce Indigenous Nuclear Subs."

74. "Indian Nuclear Submarine"; also Sullivan, "Indian Nuclear Sub Plan Reported."

75. "Prithvi to Find Naval Platform."

76. Kumar, "Go Ahead."

77. "Prithvi to Find Naval Platform."

78. "Russia Sets Deadline." In August 1999 the government signed a contract to purchase four AEW versions of the Kamov-31 naval helicopter from Russia to

equip the *Gorshkov* and its indigenously built carrier. See "India Buys Four KA-31 Helicopters."

79. "Modification Package."

80. "INS *Delhi*: Battle Ready."

81. "Prime Minister Vajpayee Commissions INS *Mysore.*"

82. "Mazagon Dock to Build India's First Stealth Warship."

83. Dasgupta, "The Navy in Troubled Waters."

84. Mama, "INS *Khukri.*"

85. International Institute for Strategic Studies, *The Military Balance 1995–1996*, 158–59.

86. "New Navy Base in India."

87. Sharma, "For a Base at Karwar."

88. Immediately after independence it was decided to have combined initial training for officers of the army, navy, and air force at the National Defense Academy. The Joint Services Wing of the National Defense Academy was established in Dehra Dun in 1949. Until 1952, after schooling with the Joint Services Wing, the naval cadets went to HMS Britannia, the Royal Naval College in Dartmouth, England, for naval training. Thereafter, the naval cadets of the technical branches continued to go through RNC Dartmouth until 1955. In the meantime, the Joint Services Wing moved to the newly built National Defense Academy at Khadakvasla, Pune. The officer intake into the navy was solely through the NDA. Since this was considered to be inadequate, a temporary academy to train naval officers was set up at Cochin in 1971. This facility moved to larger facilities in Goa in 1986. The Goa facilities will serve the navy until the completion of the Ezhimala academy. See Ramunny, *Ezhimala*, 77–78.

89. "Work Begins on Vertically-Launched Trishul." The missiles will equip the Brahmaputra-class (the improved Godavari-class) frigates being built at the Garden Reach Yards in Calcutta.

90. Kapur, *India's Nuclear Option*, 194.

91. After the explosion the Ministry of Foreign Affairs received the now famous telegram that read: "Buddha is smiling." Prime Minister Indira Gandhi was present at the test. Smith, *India's "Ad Hoc" Arsenal*, 186.

92. In March 1996 Pakistan appeared to be preparing for its first nuclear test in the Chagai test area as a counter to the Indian moves. See "India and Pakistan in Dance of War."

93. "Agni-II Successfully Test-Fired."

94. Chengappa, "PSLV."

95. "India Building Missile."

96. Chengappa, "Worrying over Broken Arrows."

97. Diwanji, "It Will Be PM's Finger."

98. Diwanji, "It Will Be PM's Finger." The draft declaration of India's nuclear

doctrine drew an immediate attack from the G-8 members meeting in Washington DC. The group resolved to maintain sanctions imposed on India after the Phokran II blast. White House spokesperson James Rubin declared that the doctrine "is not in the security interests of India, the subcontinent, the United States or the world." See "N-Doctrine Invites G-8 Wrath"; Constable, "India Drafts Doctrine"; Bedi, "India Reveals Thinking"; Ramachandran, "Unclear Nuclear Identity"; and Kasturi, "From Technology Demonstration."

99. Sinha, "Evolution."

100. Venkateswaran, *Defense Organization in India*, 80–157; Thomas, *Indian Security Policy*, 120.

101. Quoted in Ramdas, "Navy, Nation."

102. Sinha, "Higher Defense Organization, Part II."

103. Sinha, "Evolution," 12.

104. Sinha, "Evolution."

105. Chari, "The Policy Process."

106. Joshi, "Directions."

107. Mehta, "An Emasculated Defense Planning Staff."

108. Joshi, "Directions," 88.

109. For a full examination of the ill-fated run of the DPS see Mehta, "An Emasculated Defense Planning Staff," 33–39.

110. The defense chiefs did not participate in this committee, which included the minister of internal security (then Arun Nehru); the defense minister (Arun Singh); the foreign minister; the defense secretary; the head of the Intelligence Organization, Research and Analysis Wing; and the IDSA's director, Mr. Subrahmaniam.

111. Sinha, "Evolution," 13–14. See also Vohra, "Establish NSC."

112. Joshi, "Directions," 88–89.

113. The task force included Jaswant Singh, deputy chairman of the Planning Commission, as a member and Jasjit Singh, director of the Institute of Defense Studies and Analysis, as its convener.

114. "Task Force Okays Formation."

115. "Task Force Okays Formation." See also Iype, "Pant's Task Force."

116. Sahay, "National Security Council."

117. "Government Should Improve NSC's Structure."

118. "Government Should Improve NSC's Structure."

119. Gupta, "The New Order."

120. Gupta, "The New Order." See also "Defence Intelligence Agency on Anvil"; Prasannan, "Systemic Pointers."

121. A press report in July 1998 indicated that Prime Minister Atal Behari Vajpayee had decided to induct a political appointee, former Defense Minister K. C. Pant, to the all-important post of national security advisor. See Iype, "Pant May

Head NSC." A February 1999 press report claimed that an interservice battle had broken out among the services over the proposed appointment of a chief of defense staff. The air force and navy were said to be fearful that the chief would always be selected from the army. See "Indian Service Chiefs Fall Out."

122. An article by M. D. Nalapat in the *Times of India* notes that the defense ministry bureaucracy also vets low level postings and promotions in the three services. As a result, Nalapat alleges that junior-level officers in the three services have less respect for their chiefs and have been encouraged to bypass the usual "service channels" and approach the bureaucrats and politicians directly. The cumulative effect has been to diminish the command and control system within the three services. Article quoted in Ramdas, "Navy, Nation."

123. "Please Don't Tell Us."

124. "Please Don't Tell Us."

125. For more information on the deterioration and the military's role in defense policy making see Kak, "Management" and "Directions."

126. Tanham, "Indian Strategic Thought."

127. Kautilya, the Brahman advisor to Emperor Chandragupta Maurya, used the mandala concept in his treatise on the art of government. See Shamasastry, *Kautilya's Arthashastra*, 22–24.

128. Tanham, "Indian Strategy in Flux?" 112–39.

129. Tanham, "Indian Strategy in Flux?" 136.

130. For a complete examination of the Tanham essays and the rejoinders to it see Bajpai and Mattoo, *Securing India*.

131. Mattoo, "*Raison d'etat*."

132. Bajpai, "State, Society, Strategy."

133. Sahni, "Just Another Big Country."

134. Tanham and the others do discuss military ability in terms of weapon systems potential and the finances of such acquisitions but are silent on doctrines of air, naval, and land warfare.

135. The army did in fact undertake limited offensive actions in all three wars, especially in 1971, when several corps seized East Pakistan in a swift fourteen-day campaign.

136. See Dutt, *Re-organization;* and Thapan, *Review*.

137. IDR Research Team, "Some Thoughts."

138. Dutt, "Wanted."

139. Kasturi, "Future Combat."

140. Kasturi, "Future Combat."

141. Prasannan, "War Games."

142. "AMC Prepares for N-Attack."

143. "AMC Prepares for N-Attack."

144. "AMC Prepares for N-Attack."

145. Joshi, "Atomic Age Warfare." General Sundarji died in February 1999 after a long and debilitating illness. See Kasturi, "Obituary."

146. "Army Chief Bemoans."

147. Kasturi, "Now Hyper War."

148. The military ties between India and Israel go back to the 1962 war with China when Israel supplied India with much-needed 81 mm and 120 mm mortars and pack howitzers. In the mid-1960s the chief of the Israeli army, Gen. David Shaltiel, visited India, and the two countries signed a secret pact for military intelligence exchanges and supply of military hardware to each other. In the 1967 Arab-Israeli war India reciprocated by supplying Israel with badly needed spares for its Mystère and Ouragon fighters and AMX-13 tanks. In the 1971 Indo-Pakistan war Israel delayed sending back until the end of hostilities some eighty Pakistani F-86 Sabre jets sent to it for maintenance and also warned India about the transfer of eleven Jordanian F-104 Starfighters to the PAF. Since then the relationship has remained mainly in the realm of intelligence cooperation. Israel has outfitted one of RAW's Boeing 707s with electronic intelligence-gathering equipment. The two countries have also been cooperating on nuclear and missile technology issues for the past two decades. See Joshi, "Military Diplomacy."

In 1998, at the height of the Kargil conflict, Israel speeded up military shipments to India while at the same time using its influence in Washington to ease some of the sanctions imposed on India by the United States following the Phokran II tests. In the words of a senior Israeli official in Prime Minister Ehud Barak's government, "From the moment we established diplomatic relations seven years ago, we found a common language. . . . The deep understanding between us enabled us to have a fluent and clear dialogue with them." See Ben, "Israel Speeds Arms Shipments."

In July 2001 India and Israel signed a landmark two-billion-dollar defense cooperation agreement. See Barzidai, "IAI, India Sign"; and O'Sullivan, "Israel, India Keen."

149. "Army Seeks Ultimate Man-Machine Balance."

150. "Army Seeks Ultimate Man-Machine Balance."

151. Lal, My Years with the IAF, 174.

152. Tanham and Agmon, The Indian Air Force, 25–26.

153. "Long Range Agni III on Anvil."

154. Gupta, "Key Cold War Concept."

155. Cherian, "War Games."

156. Cherian, "War Games."

157. Goldrick, No Easy Answers, 14–44.

158. Quoted in Goldrick, No Easy Answers, 16 n. 1.

159. Mookerjee and Singh, "Aircraft Carriers."

160. Mookerjee and Singh, "Aircraft Carriers."

161. Tellis, "India's Naval Expansion."

162. Thomas, "The Sources of Indian Naval Expansion"; and Tellis, "Securing the Barrack."

163. Tellis, "Securing the Barrack."

164. See Tanham, "India's Strategic Culture"; Thomas, "The Growth of Indian Military Power," 36; Gordon, "Domestic Foundations"; and Tellis, "Securing the Barracks."

165. Tellis, "Securing the Barracks," 9; Elkin, "New Delhi's Indian Ocean Policy."

166. Christie goes on to add that a further legacy of this colonial inheritance gained clearer expression in the emergence of the "Indira doctrine" from the late 1970s, whereby the late prime minister asserted the right to "intervene in the affairs of neighboring countries if internal disorder threatens Indian security interests." See Christie, India's Naval Strategy, 10.

167. Gordon argues that "although the navy is likely to emerge as a more modern and balanced force it will not be significantly larger by the year 2000 than it is today (1992)." See Gordon, "Domestic Foundations," 12. Quote from Christie, India's Naval Strategy, 11. In an earlier article Christie noted: "Realistically, the navy will struggle to maintain rather than expand its fleet of around 100 vessels over the next decade. It is less a question of a third, possibly CTOL carrier, and indigenous construction than how to maintain/replace the current two." See "India an 'Incomplete' Regional Power?" quoted in Christie, India's Naval Strategy, 11.

168. "Prithvi to Find Naval Platform."

169. Triamph-98 was the largest triservices amphibious exercise conducted since Trishakti, held some eleven years before.

170. Gupta, "India's Largest Amphibious Exercise."

171. Prasannan, "War Games." Bhagwat also noted that the navy had taken up the issue of restructuring the intelligence system, as it was not getting "actionable intelligence" from RAW or the Joint Intelligence Command.

172. Prasannan, "War Games." In the aftermath of the nuclear tests the three services and the navy in particular have declared that India's strategic frontier lies far beyond the physical land and maritime boundaries. The navy's move to create the Far Eastern Naval Command in the Andaman Islands is a recognition of India's strategic interests in this vital region. Admiral Bhagwat declared that "the FENC (Far Eastern Naval Command) has come into place because of India's growing geo-economic realities in the Andaman sea and in accordance with the Government's Look East Policy." See "India to Have New Naval Command."

173. Gupta, "Indian Navy Eyes South China Sea"; see also "India Challenges China." The exercise drew a swift protest from the Chinese government. See "China Objects to Indian Presence."

174. "Navy Set to Chart New Course."

BIBLIOGRAPHY

Unpublished Sources

Additional Manuscripts, British Museum, London
    Broughton Papers
    First Report of the Committee of Secrecy
    George Thomas Memoirs
    Major Munro's Evidence
    Peel Papers
    Ripon Papers
Bharat Ithihas Shamshodak Mandal, Poona
    Persian Manuscripts
India Office Records, British Library, London
    Bengal Military Consultations
        Fort William Consultations
    Bengal Political Consultations
    Bengal Secret and Military Consultations
    Bengal Secret and Political Consultations
    Bengal Secret Consultations
        Fort William Consultations
    Bengal Select Committee Proceedings
    Birkenhead Collection
    Bombay Public Consultations
    Chelmsford Collection
    Derby Collection
    Extract from War Cabinet Minutes
    Home Miscellaneous Series
        Diary of Major Lachlan Macquarie
    Madras Military and Political Proceedings
    Madras Military and Secret Proceedings
    Military Department Papers
    Military Select Committee Proceedings
    Montagu Collection
    Orme Manuscripts
    "Proceedings of a Jacobin Club in Seringapatam"
    War Staff Papers
National Archives of India, Delhi
    Bengal Secret Consultations

Foreign and Political Department
Foreign Department
  Political Consultations
  Political Proceedings
  Secret and Political Consultations
  Secret and Separate Consultations
  Secret Consultations
  Secret Proceedings
  Select Committee Proceedings
  Foreign Miscellaneous Consultations
  Military Department Proceedings
  Political Proceedings
  Secret and Political Proceedings
  Secret and Separate Consultations
  Secret Consultations
  Secret Department
  Secret Proceedings
  Select Committee Proceedings
Public Records Office, London
  Cabinet Office Papers
  Chatham Papers
  Cornwallis Papers
  War Office Papers
Tamil Nadu Archives, Madras
  Madras Records
  Military Consultations
  Military Sundry Book

Published Sources

Achutan, Nisha Sahai. *Soviet Arms Transfer Policy in South Asia since 1955–1981: The Politics of International Arms Transfers.* New Delhi: Lancer International, 1988.

Agar-Hamilton, J. A. I. *The Sidi Rezegh Battles.* Cape Town, South Africa: Oxford University Press, 1957.

Agarwal, Ashwini. *Rise and Fall of the Imperial Guptas.* Delhi: Motilal Banarasidas, 1989.

"Agni-II Successfully Test-Fired." *Rediff on the Net,* 11 April 1999. http://216.32 .165.70/news/1999/apr/11agni.htm.

Ahluwalia, H. S. *Saragrahi Battalion, Ashes to Glory: History of the 4th Battalion of the Sikh Regiment.* New Delhi: Lancer International, 1987.

Aitchison, C. U. *A Collection of the Treaties, Engagements and Sanads Relating to India and Neighbouring Countries.* Calcutta, 1892; reprint, Delhi: Mittal Publications, 1983.

Alam, Muzaffar. *The Crisis of Empire in Mughal North India: Avadh and the Punjab, 1707–48.* Delhi: Oxford University Press, 1986.

Alavi, Seema. *The Sepoys and the Company: Tradition and Transition in Northern India, 1770–1830.* Delhi: Oxford University Press, 1995.

Alder, G. J. "The Origins of the Pusa Experiment: The East India Company and Horse-Breeding in Bengal, 1793–1808." *Bengal Past and Present* 98, no. 1 (1979): 10–12.

Ali, B. Sheik. *British Relations with Haider Ali, 1760–1782.* Mysore: Rao and Raghavan, 1963.

Ali, M. Athar. *The Mughal Nobility under Aurungzeb.* New Delhi: Asia Publishing House, 1966.

Ali, Syed Ishfaq. *Fangs of Ice: The Story of Siachen.* Rawalpindi: Pak American Commercial, 1991.

Allami, Abul Fazal. *Ain-i-Akbari.* 3 vols. Vol. 1, trans. H. Blochman; vols. 2 and 3, trans. H. S. Jarrett. Calcutta: Baptist Mission Press, 1873.

Allan, John. *Catalogue of the Coins of the Gupta Dynasties and Sasanka, King of Gauda, in the British Museum.* London: British Museum, 1914.

Amarnath, Dewan. *Zafarnama-i-Ranjit Singh.* Ed. Sita Ram Kohli. Lahore: Superintendent of Government Printing, 1928.

Ambasthaya, B. P. *Decisive Battles of Sher Shah.* Patna: Janaki Prakashan, 1977.

"AMC Prepares for N-Attack." *Deccan Herald,* 30 December 1999. http://www .bharat-rakshak.com/LAND-FORCES/Army/News/98-Dec.html.

Amnesty International. *India: Torture and Deaths in Custody in J&K.* New York: Amnesty International U.S.A., 1995.

Anand, Vijay Kumar. *Conflict in Nagaland: A Study of Insurgency and Counter-Insurgency.* Delhi: Chankya Publications, 1980.

Aneja, Atul. "Indian Troops Capture Key Peak in Dras." *Hindu,* 14 June 1999. http://www.hinduonline.com/today/stories/01140002.htm.

Apte, B. K. "The Maratha Weapons of War." *Bulletin of the Deccan College Research Institute* 19, nos. 1–2 (1958): 106–24.

Apte, D. V., ed. *Selections from the Chandrachud Daftar.* Poona: Bharat Ithihas Shamshodak Mandal, 1920.

"Army Begins Operation Flush-out in Assam." *Hindustan Times,* 16 May 1999.

"Army Captures 3 Heights in Batalik Sector." *Deccan Herald,* 7 July 1999. http:// www.deccanherald.com/deccanherald/jul07/army.htm.

"Army Chief Bemoans Poor Defense Integration." *Deccan Herald,* 13 February 1999. http://www.bharat-rakshak.com/LAND-FORCES/Army/News/99-Feb .html.

"Army Chief Flies to Kargil." *Hindustan Times,* 23 May 1999. http://hindustan times.com/nonfram/240599/detFRO03.htm.

"Army Consolidating Gains in Batalik, Dras." *Deccan Herald*, 10 July 1999. http://www.deccanherald.com/jul11/prime.htm.

"Army Networks for Future Combat." *Indian Express*, 28 December 1998. http://www.bharat-rakshak.com/LAND-FORCES/Army/News/98-Dec.html.

"Army Regains Four More Heights." *Times of India*, 1 July 1999. wysiwyg://61/http://www.timesofindia.com/today/01home2.htm.

"Army Seeks Ultimate Man-Machine Balance." *Jane's Defence Weekly*, 5 May 1999. http://www.bharat-rakshak.com/Land-Forces/Army/News/99-May.html.

Aron, Raymond. *Clausewitz: Philosopher of War.* Trans. Christine Booker and Norman Stone. Englewood Cliffs NJ: Prentice-Hall, 1985.

"Astra Missile Steals the Show." *Economic Times*, 11 December 1998. http://www.bharat-rakshak.com/MISSILES/News/98-Dec.html.

Austin, Dennis, and Anirudha Gupta. *Lions and Tigers: The Crisis in Sri Lanka.* London: Center for Security and Conflict Studies, 1988.

Awasthi, Dilip. "Terrorism: Expanding Turf." *India Today*, 30 September 1991: 74–75.

Baden Powell, B. H. "Notes on the Origin of the Lunar and Solar Aryan Tribes and the Rajput Clans." *Journal of the Royal Asiatic Society of Great Britain and Ireland*, no. 31 (1899): 297–328.

Bailey, J. B. A. *Field Artillery and Firepower.* Oxford: Military Press, 1989.

Bajpai, Kanti P. "State, Society, Strategy." In Kanti P. Bajpai and Amitabh Mattoo, eds., *Securing India: Essays by George K. Tanham with Commentaries.* New Delhi: Manohar, 1996, 140–59.

Bajpai, Kanti P., and Amitabh Mattoo, eds. *Securing India: Essays by George K. Tanham with Commentaries.* New Delhi: Manohar, 1996.

Bajwa, Fauja Singh. *Military System of the Sikhs during the Period 1799–1849.* Delhi: Motilal Banarasidas, 1964.

Bajwa, Mehmud Bashir. "Staring Death in the Face." *Pakistan Army Journal* 32, no. 3 (September 1991): 75–86.

Bakshi, Nizam-ud-Din Ahmad. *Tabakat-i Akbari.* Trans. Sir H. M. Elliot, ed. John Dawson (Pakistani ed.). Reprint, Lahore: M. Masood, Sind Sagar Academy, 1975.

Bakshi, S. R. *British Diplomacy and Administration in India, 1807–13.* New Delhi: Munshiram Manoharlal, 1971.

Bana. *Harshacharita.* Trans. E. B. Cowell and F. W. Thomas. Oriental Translation Fund, new series, subseries 2, vols. 1–8. London: Royal Asiatic Society, 1897.

Bana-Bhatta. *Harsha-Charita*, with the commentary of Sankara. Ed. Kasinatha Pandurang Parab. Bombay: Nirnaya Sangara Press, 1925.

Banerjie, Indranil. "Coming Home." *Sunday* (Bombay), 14–20 May 1989: 20–28.

Barat, Amiya. *The Bengal Native Infantry: Its Organization and Discipline, 1796–1852.* Calcutta: K. L. Mukhopadhayay, 1962.

Bar-Kochva, Bezalel. *The Selucid Army: Organization and Tactics in the Great Campaigns.* Cambridge: Cambridge University Press, 1976.

Barnett, Corelli. *The Desert Generals.* Bloomington: Indiana University Press, 1960.

Barnett, Richard. *North India between Empires: Avadh, the Mughals and the British, 1720–1801.* Berkeley: University of California Press, 1980.

Barth, Auguste, and Abel Bregaigne. *Inscriptions sanscrites du Cambodge et Campa.* Paris, 1885.

Barua, Pradeep P. "Ethnic Conflict in the Military of Developing Nations: A Comparative Analysis of India and Nigeria." *Armed Forces and Society* 19, no. 1 (1992): 123–37.

———. *Gentlemen of the Raj: The Indian Army Officer Corps 1817–1949.* Westport CT: Praeger, 2003.

———. "Inventing Race: The British and India's Martial Races." *Historian* 58, no. 1 (1995): 107–16.

———. "Strategies and Doctrines of Imperial Defence: Britain and India, 1919–45." *Journal of Imperial and Commonwealth History* 25, no. 2 (May 1997): 240–66.

Barzidai, Ammon. "IAI, India Sign $2 Billion Cooperation Accord." *Ha'aretz,* 17 July 2001. http://www3.haaretz.co.il/eng/scripts/print.asp?id=124470.

Bayly, C. A. *Rulers, Townsmen and Bazaars: North Indian Society in the Age of British Expansion.* Cambridge: Cambridge University Press, 1983.

Bayly, Stephen. *Saints, Goddesses and Kings: Muslims and Christians in South Indian Society 1700–1900.* Cambridge: Cambridge University Press, 1989.

Barzidai, Ammon. "IAI, India Sign $2 Billion Cooperation Accord." *Ha'aretz,* 17 July 2001. http://www3.haaretz.co.il/eng/scripts/print.asp?id=124470.

Beal, Samuel, trans. *Buddhist Records of the Western World: Translated from the Chinese of Hiuen Tsiang ca.* A.D. *629.* London: Keegan Paul, Trench, Trubner and Co. Ltd., 1968.

———. *Si-Yu-Ki, Buddhist Records of the Western World.* Vol. 1. London: Trubner, 1884.

Bedi, Rahul. "Arms Deals in the Making." *Frontline,* 3–16 August 2002. http://www.hinduonnet.com/fline/fl1916/19160260.htm.

———. "Indian Budget Tempers Plans for Modernization." *Jane's Defence Weekly,* 24 April 1996: 12.

———. "India Reveals Thinking on Nuclear Strategy." *Jane's Defence Weekly,* 20 August 1999. wysiwyg://main100/http://jdw.janes.com/sample/jdw4172.html.

———. "India Set to Test Bofors Self-Propelled Howitzers." *Jane's Defence Weekly,* 29 October 1999. wysiwg://main.236/http://jdw.janes.com/sample/jdw4724.html.

Beg, Mirza Aslam. "Retreat from Kargil." *Frontier Post,* 7 July 1999. http://www.frontierpost.com.pk/art1july-07.htm.

Ben, Aluf. "Israel Speeds Arms Shipments to India." Ha'aretz, 12 August 1999. http://www3.haaretz.co.il/eng/htmls/ka3_9.htm.

Beteille, Andre. Caste, Class and Power: Changing Patterns of Stratification in a Tanjore Village. Berkeley: University of California Press, 1965.

Bhandarkar, D. R. "The Guhilots." Journal of the Asiatic Society of Bengal, no. 5 (1909): 167–87.

Bharucha, P. C. Official History of the Indian Armed Forces in the Second World War: The North African Campaign 1940–1943. New Delhi: Combined Inter-Services Historical Section India and Pakistan, 1956.

Bhattacharya, B. "The Rashtriya Rifles." Bharat Rakshak Monitor 3, no. 2 (September–October 2000). http://www.bharat-rakshak.com/MONITOR/ISSUE3-2/batt.html.

Bhattacharya, Sukumar. The Rajput States and the East India Company: From the Close of the 18th Century to 1820. New Delhi: Munshiram Manoharlal, 1972.

Bidwell, R. G. S. "The Development of British Field Artillery Tactics 1940–1942." Journal of Royal Artillery 94, no. 2 (September 1967): 83–93.

Bidwell, Shelford. Swords for Hire: European Mercenaries in Eighteenth Century India. London: John Murray, 1971.

Blackett, P. M. S. Scientific Problems of Defense in Relation to the Indian Armed Forces: A Report to the Honorable Defense Minister. New Delhi: Ministry of Defence, 10 September 1948.

Blake, Stephen P. "The Patrimonial-Bureaucratic Empire of the Mughals." In Herman Kulke, ed., The State in India, 1000–1700. Delhi: Oxford University Press, 1995, 280–99.

Blanche, Ed. "Mutual Threat of Islamic Militancy Allies Israel and India." Jane's Terrorism and Security Monitor, 14 August 2001. http://www.janes.com/security/international_security/news/jtsm/jtsm010814_1_.shtml.

Bobb, Dilip. "The Bofors Blast." India Today, 15 May 1987: 18.

———. "IMSF: The New Centurions." India Today, 30 April 1988: 156–57.

"Bodies of Oak Officers, Soldiers Identified." Deccan Herald, 16 July 1999. http://www.deccanherald.com/deccanherals/jul16/soldier.htm.

Bond, Brian. British Military Policy between the Two World Wars. Oxford: Clarendon Press, 1980.

———. "Cardwells' Army Reforms." Army (April 1962): 108–17.

———. "The Effect of the Cardwell Reforms." RUSI Journal (November 1960): 229–36.

Bosworth, A. B. Conquest and Empire: The Reign of Alexander the Great. Cambridge: Cambridge University Press, 1988.

Bosworth, Clifford Edmund. The Ghaznavids: Their Empire in Afghanistan and Eastern Iran 994–1040. Edinburgh: Edinburgh University Press, 1963.

Brines, Russell. The Indo-Pakistani Conflict. London: Pall Mall Press, 1968.

Broome, Arthur. *History of the Bengal Army*. London, 1850.

———. *History of the Rise and the Progress of the British Army* (the Bengal Army). Vol. 1. Calcutta: W. Thacker and Co., 1850.

Broughton, Thomas Duer. *Letters Written in a Maratha Camp during the Year 1809: Description of the Costume, Character, Manners, Domestic Habits and Religious Ceremonies of the Marathas*. London: John Murray, 1913.

Buhler, G. "The Madhuban Copper-Plate of Harsha, Dated Samvat 25." In James Burgess, E. Hultzch, and A. Fuhrer, eds., *Epigraphica Indica, a Collection of Inscriptions Supplementary to the Corpus Inscriptionum Indicarum of the Archeological Survey*. 15 vols. Calcutta: Superintendent of Government Printing, 1892, 1:72–73.

Burgess, James, E. Hultzch, and A. Fuhrer, eds. *Epigraphica Indica, a Collection of Inscriptions Supplementary to the Corpus Inscriptionum Indicarum of the Archeological Survey*. 15 vols. Calcutta: Superintendent of Government Printing, 1892.

Cadell, P. *History of the Bombay Army*. London: Longmans and Co., 1938.

Caine, Caesar, ed. *Barracks to Battlefields in India: The Experiences of a Soldier of the 10th Foot*. 1891; reprint, Patiala, Punjab: Languages Department Punjab, 1971.

Calvert, Michael. "Victory in Burma." In E. Bauer, *The History of World War II*. London: Orbis, 1979, 631.

Cardew, F. G. *A Sketch of the Services of the Bengal Native Army to the Year 1895*. Reprint, New Delhi: Today and Tomorrow's Printers and Publishers, 1971.

Careri, John Francis Gemelli. *A Voyage round the World: A Collection of Voyages*. In Awnsham Churchill and John Churchill, *Churchill's Voyages*. London: A. and J. Churchill, 1704.

Carnac, R. *The Presidential Armies of India*. London: W. H. Allen and Co., 1890.

Cécile, Jean-Jacques. "Siachen: The World's Highest Battlefield." RAIDS, no. 46 (September 1995): 32–38.

Chakravarti, R. "Horse Trade and Piracy at Tana in Maharashtra: Gleanings from Marco Polo." *Journal of the Economic and Social History of the Orient* 34, no. 2 (1991): 160–84.

Chari, P. R. "The Policy Process." In J. M. Roherty, ed., *Defense Policy Formulation: Towards a Comparative Analysis*. Durham NC: Carolina Academic Press, 1980, 143.

Charteris, John. *At GHQ*. London: Cassell and Co., Ltd., 1931.

Chengappa, Raj. "LCA Project: A Testing Time." *India Today*, 31 August 1988: 132–35.

———. "Miles to Go." *India Today*, 15 January 2000. http://www.india-today.com /itoday/20010115/defence.shtml.

———. "The Missile Man." *India Today*, 15 April 1994: 66–75.

———. "PSLV: Coming of Age." *India Today*, 7 June 1999. http://www.india-today.com/itoday/22061998/cover.html.

———. "Worrying over Broken Arrows." *India Today*, 13 July 1998. http://www
.india-today.com/3071998/defence.html.

Cherian, John. "War Games." *Frontline*, 2 January 1999. http://www.the-hindu
.com/fline/fl1601/16010260.htm.

Chibber, M. L. "Siachen: The Untold Story." *Indian Defence Review* (January 1990):
146–48.

"China Objects to Indian Presence in South China Sea." *Indian Express*, 14 October
2000. http://bharat-rakshak.com/NAVY/News/00-Oct.html.

Chopra, Pran. *India's Second Liberation*. New Delhi: Vikas Publishing House, 1973.

Chopra, Pushpinder S. "Gnat." *Air International* (August 1974): 75.

———. "Journal of an Air War." *Air Enthusiast* (April 1972): 197.

Chopra, Pushpinder S., William Green, and Gordon Swanborough, eds. *The
Indian Air Force and Its Air Craft, 1982*. London: Ducimus Books, 1982.

Christie, D. N. *India's Naval Strategy and the Role of the Andaman and Nicobar Islands*.
Canberra: Strategic and Defense Studies Center, Australian National University, 1995.

Cohen, Stephen P. *The Indian Army: Its Contribution to the Development of a Nation*.
Berkeley: University of California Press, 1971.

———. "U.S. Weapons in South Asia: A Policy Analysis." *Pacific Affairs* 49, no. 1
(Spring 1976): 50.

Compton, H. *A Particular Account of the European Military Adventurers of Hindustan
1784–1803*. London: T. Fisher Unwin, 1892.

Connell, John (pseud.). *Auchinleck*. London: Cassell, 1959.

Constable, Pamela. "India Captures Strategic Peak." *Washington Post Foreign
Service*, 5 July 1999: A15. http://search.washingtonpost.com/wp-srv/wplate/
1999–07/05/1021–070599-idx.htm.

———. "India Drafts Doctrine on Nuclear Arms." *Washington Post Foreign Service*,
18 August 1999: A1. http://www.washingtonpost.com/wp-srv/wplate/1998–
08/18/0811–081899-idx.html.

Cook, H. C. B. *The Sikh Wars*. Reprint, Delhi: Thompson Press, 1975.

Cook, Hugh. *The Sikh Wars: The British Army in the Punjab, 1845–1849*. London: Leo
Cooper, 1975.

Coomaraswamy, A. K. "Horseriding in the Rigveda and the Atharvaveda." *Journal
of the American Oriental Society* no. 62 (1942): 139–40.

"Corps of Signals Gears up to Face Nuclear Threat." *Rediff on the Net*, 14 February 1999. http://www.bharat-rakshak.com/LAND-FORCES/Army/News/99-
Feb.html.

Cotton, J. J. "The Life of General Avitable." *Calcutta Review*, no. 26 (October
1906): 531, 550–51.

Culturu, Prosper. *Dupleix*. Paris: Librairie Hachette et Cie, 1901.

Cunningham, Alexander. *The Ancient Geography of India*. Varanasi: Indological Book House, 1963.

———. *The Stupa of Bharut: A Buddhist Monument Ornamented with Numerous Sculptures Illustrative of Buddhist Legend and History in the Third Century* B.C. Varanasi: Indological Book House, 1962.

Dalvi, John. *Himalayan Blunder: The Curtain Raiser to the Sino-Indian War of 1962*. Bombay: Thacker, 1968.

Dasgupta, Sunil. "The Navy in Troubled Waters." *India Today*, 30 April 1994: 131.

Datta, Kalinkar. *Siraj-ud-Daulah*. Calcutta: Orient Longman, 1971.

Day, Upendra Nath. *The Government of the Sultanate*. New Delhi: M. L. Gupta and Kumar Brothers, 1972.

"Decision on AJT Aircraft Soon." *Hindustan Times*, 22 December 1998. http://www .bharat-rakshak.com/IAF/News/98-Dec.html.

"Defence Intelligence Agency on Anvil." *Hindu*, 19 October 2000. wysiwyg://10/ http://www/the-hindu.com/stories/01190008.htm

"Defense Allocation Pegged at 41,000." *Times of India*, 2 June 1998. http://www .timesofindia.com/today/02home5.htm.

"Defense Budget Must Be Increased Says Panel." *Rediff on the Net*, 9 July 1998. http://www/rediff.com/news/1998/09def.htm.

"Defense Outlays up by 14%." *Indian Express*, 2 June 1998. http://www.express india.com/ie/daily/19980602/15350684.html.

Delbruck, Hans. *Antiquity*. Vol. 1 of *History of the Art of War*. Translated from the German by Walter J. Renfroe Jr. Westport CT: Greenwood, 1975.

"Delhi Is Finalizing Work on 'Soft-Kill' Weapon System." *Jane's Defence Weekly*, 1 September 1999. http://www.bharat-rakshak.com/IAF/News/99-Sept.html.

Denning, B. C. *The Future of the British Army*. London: Witherby, 1928.

Deodhar, Y. N. *Nana Phadnis and the External Affairs of the Maratha Empire*. Bombay: Popular Book Depot, 1962.

De Silva, K. M. *Managing Ethnic Tensions, Sri Lanka 1980–1985*. New York: New York University Press, 1986.

Despatches and General Orders Announcing the Victories Achieved by the Army of the Sutlej over the Sikh Army at Moodkee, Ferozshah, Aliwal and Sobraon. Reprint, Patiala, Punjab: Languages Department, Punjab, 1970.

Devahuti, D. *Harsha: A Political Study*. Oxford: Oxford University Press, 1970.

Dighe, V. G., ed. *Poona Residency Correspondence*. Vol. 4. Bombay: Government of Bombay Press, 1937.

Dirks, Nicholas. "Political Authority and Structural Change in Early South Indian History." *Indian Economic and Social History Review* 13, no. 2 (1976): 125–57.

Dirom, Alexander. *A Narrative of the Campaign in India*. London: G. Nicol, 1794.

Diwanji, Ambersih K. "It Will Be PM's Finger on India's Nuclear Trigger." *Rediff on the Net*, 17 August 1999. http://216.32.165.70/news/1999/aug/17akd.htm.

Dodwell, H. "Transportation and the Second Mysore War." *Journal of the Society for Army Historical Research* 3 (October 1924): 266–72.

D'Souza, Dillip. "Never Enough Courage." *Rediff on the Net*, 3 June 1998. http://www/rediff.com/news/1998/03dilip.htm.

Duff, James Grant. *A History of the Marathas.* 3 vols. Calcutta: R. Cambray and Co., 1912.

———. *History of the Marathas.* Ed. J. P. Guha. 2 vols. New Delhi: Associated Publishing House, 1971.

Dundas, David. *Principles of Military Movement.* London: T. Cadell, 1788.

Dutt, J. K. "Wanted: A Doctrine for Armour." *Journal of the United Services Institute of India* (October–December 1977): 45–52.

Dutt, Som. *Re-organization of the Infantry Division.* Seminar no. 1. New Delhi: United Services Institute of India, 1973.

Dutta, K. K. *The Dutch in Bengal and Bihar 1740–1825.* Delhi: Motilal Banarasidas, 1968.

Edwards, J. Keith. "Second (Military) Prize Winning Essay for 1927." *Journal of the Royal United Services Institute*, no. 73 (August 1928): 458–73.

Eisenstadt, S. N., and Harriet Hartman. "Historical Experience, Cultural Tradition, State Formation and Political Dynamics in India and Europe." In Martin Doornbos and Sudipta Kaviraj, eds., *Dynamics of State Formation: India and Europe Compared.* New Delhi: Sage Publications, 1997, 39.

Elkin, Jerold, and Andrew Ritezel. "New Delhi's Indian Ocean Policy." *Naval War College Review* 40, no. 4 (1987): 51–63.

Elliot, H. M. *The History of India as Told by Its Own Historians.* 15 vols. Ed. John Dawson. New York: AMS Press, 1966.

Elliot, T. S., ed. *A Choice of Kipling's Verse.* London: Faber and Faber, 1951.

English, John A. *A Perspective on Infantry.* New York: Praeger, 1981.

English Records on Shivaji. Poona: Shivacharita Karyalaya, 1931.

Evans, Humphrey. *Thimmaya of India: A Soldier's Life.* New York: Harcourt Brace and Co., 1960.

Fedarko, Kevin. "The Coldest War." *Outside* 28, no. 2 (February 2003): 39–59, 98–99.

Feller, Gordon. "Russia Starts Building India's Three Krivak Class Destroyers." *Defence Systems Daily*, 22 March 1999. http://defence-data.com/current/page4009.htm.

Fernandes, Praxy. *The Tiger of Mysore: A Biography of Haider Ali and Tipu Sultan.* Reprint, New Delhi: Viking Books, 1991.

Ferrill, Arthur. *The Origins of War: From the Stone Age to Alexander the Great.* New York: Thames and Hudson, 1986.

Feuerstein, Georg, Subash Kak, and David Frawley. *In Search of the Cradle of Civilization: New Light on Ancient India.* Wheaton IL: Quest Books, 2001.

Firishtah, Muhammad Kasim. *History of the Rise of Mahomedan Power in India till the Year A.D. 1612.* Translated from the original Persian of Mahomed Kasim Ferishta by John Briggs. Reprint, Calcutta: R. Cambray and Co., 1908.

Fleet, John F., ed. *Corpus Inscriptionum Indicarum.* Vol. 3, *Inscriptions of the Early Gupta Kings and Their Successors.* Calcutta: Superintendent of Government Printing, 1888.

Forrest, George William. *Selections from the Letters, Despatches and Other State Papers Preserved in the Bombay Secretariat.* Maratha Series, vol. 1. Bombay: Government Central Press, 1885.

Foss, Virginia. *The Forts of India.* London: Collins, 1986.

Fox, Richard G. *Kin, Clan, Raja and Rule: State-Hinterland Relations in Preindustrial India.* Berkeley: University of California Press, 1971.

Fricker, John. *Battle for Pakistan: The Air War of 1965.* London: Ian Allan Ltd., 1979.

———. "Post-Mortem of an Air War." *Air Enthusiast* (May 1972): 228–29.

———. "Thirty Seconds over Sargodha." *Air Enthusiast* (June 1971): 16.

Frykenberg, R. E. *Guntur District, 1788–1848: A History of Local Influence and Central Authority in South India.* Oxford: Oxford University Press, 1965.

Fuller, J. F. C. *The Generalship of Alexander the Great.* London: Eyre and Spottiswoode, 1958; reprint, New York: Da Capo, 1989.

———. *On Future War.* London: Sifton Praed and Co., 1928.

Furber, Holden. *Henry Dundas: The First Viscount Melville 1742–1811.* London: Oxford University Press, 1931.

Garrett, H. L. O., and C. Grey. *European Adventurers of Northern India, 1785–1849.* Lahore: Superintendent of Government Printing, 1929.

Ghauri, Ifthikar Ahmad. *War of Succession between the Sons of Shah Jahan.* Lahore: Publishers United Ltd., 1964.

Ghazi, Zahiru'd-din Muhammad Babaur Padshah. *Babur-Nama.* Trans. Annette Susannah Beveridge. 2 vols. New Delhi: Oriental Books Reprint Corp., 1970.

Ghosh, A., ed. *An Encyclopedia of Indian Archeology.* 2 vols. Vol. 2, *A Gazetteer of Explored and Excavated Sites in India.* Delhi: Munshiram Manoharlal Publishers, 1989.

Gleig, G. R. *Thomas Munro, Bart and K.C.B.* 3 vols. London: Henry Colburn and Richard Bentley, 1830.

Goakhle, B. G. "Nagaland, India's Sixteenth State." *Asian Survey* 1, no. 3 (May 1961): 36–40.

Goldrick, James. *No Easy Answers: The Development of the Navies of India, Pakistan, Bangladesh and Sri Lanka 1945–1996.* New Delhi: Lancer Publications, 1997.

Goodman, Syd, and Mrutyunjoy Mazumdar. "East Meets West." *Warships Interna-*

tional *Fleet Review* (May 1999). http://www.bharat-rakshak.com/NAVY/Article 10.html.

Gordon, D. H. "The Early Use of Metals in India and Pakistan." *Journal of the Royal Anthropological Institute* 80 (1952): 55ff.

———. *The Prehistoric Background of Indian Culture.* Bombay: Bhulabhai Memorial Institute, 1958.

Gordon, Sandy. "Domestic Foundations of India's Security Policy." In Ross Babbage and Sandy Gordon, eds., *India's Strategic Future: Regional State or Global Power?* London: Macmillan, 1992.

Gordon, Stewart. *Marathas, Marauders and State Formation in Eighteenth-Century India.* Delhi: Oxford University Press, 1994.

———. *The Marathas 1600–1818. The New Cambridge History of India,* Gordon Johnson, gen. ed. Cambridge: Cambridge University Press, 1993.

"Government Should Improve NSC's Structure Says Subrahmanyam." *Rediff on the Net,* 20 November 1998. http://rediff.com/news/1998/nov/20nsc.htm.

"Govt Plans Supplementary Defense Budget to Address Security Concerns." *Rediff on the Net,* 14 July 1997. http://www/rediff.com/news/jul/14defen.htm.

Greenhut, Jeffrey. "The Imperial Reserve: The Indian Corps on the Western Front 1914–1915." *Journal of Imperial and Commonwealth History* 12, no. 1 (October 1983): 66, 69.

Griffin, L. P. *Ranjit Singh.* Oxford: Clarendon Press, 1911.

Griffith, Percival. *The British Impact on India.* Hamden CT: Archon Books, 1965.

Griffiths, R. T. H., trans. *The Hymns of the Rigveda,* with a popular commentary and emendations. 2 vols. Benares: E. J. Lazarus, 1896–97.

Grose, John Henry. *Voyage to the East Indies: The Viceroyalties of the Deccan and Bengal.* 2 vols. London: S. Hooper and A. Morley, 1757–66.

Guha, Nikhiles. *Pre-British State System in South India, Mysore, 1761–1799.* Calcutta: Ratna Prakashan, 1985.

Gulati, Y. B. *History of the Regiment of Artillery: Indian Army.* London: Leo Cooper, 1972.

Gunaratna, Rohan. *Indian Intervention in Sri Lanka: The Role of India's Intelligence Agencies.* Columbo: South Asia Network on Conflict Research, 1993.

Gupta, B. L. "Horse Trade in North India: Some Reflections on Socio-Economic Life." *Journal of Ancient Indian History* 14 (1983–84): 188–91.

Gupta, Hari Ram. *Marathas and Panipat.* Chandigarh: Punjab University, 1961.

Gupta, Shekar. "INSAS: Packing More Punch." *India Today,* 15 September 1988: 149–50.

———. "Kashmir: Lives on the Line." *India Today,* 15 August 1990: 36–39.

———. "The New Thrust." *India Today,* 15 November 1985: 59–61.

———. "Punjab: The Rule of the Gun." *India Today,* 15 January 1991: 24–34.

———. "Shooting Ahead: Prithvi's Flight Trial Successful." *India Today*, 31 March 1988: 170–71.

Gupta, Shishir. "Indian Navy Eyes South China Sea." *Hindustan Times*, 25 April 2000. http://www.hindustantimes.com/nonfram/250400/detNAT02.htm.

———. "India's Largest Amphibious Exercise Conducted on the Western Coast." *Hindustan Times*, 18 November 1998. http://www.hindustantimes.com/ht/nonfram/181198/detnato6.htm.

———. "Key Cold War Concept Is New Defense Doctrine." *Hindustan Times*, 29 April 1999. http://www.hindustantimes.com/nonfrm/290499/detNATO.htm.

———. "The New Order: Intelligence Revamp." *India Today*, 4 June 2001. wysi wyg://27/http://www.india-today.com/itoday/20020604/defence.shtml.

Habibullah, A. B. M. *The Foundation of Muslim Rule in India: A History of the Establishment and Progress of the Turkish Sultanate of Delhi, 1206–90 A.D.* Allahabad: Central Book Depot, 1961.

Hallissey, Robert C. *The Rajput Rebellion against Aurungzeb: A Study of the Mughal Empire in Seventeenth-Century India.* Columbia: University of Missouri Press, 1977.

"HAL to Manufacture Upgraded Jaguars." *Deccan Herald*, 18 October 1999. http://www.bharat-rakshak.com/IAF/News.99-Oct.html.

Hamid, Shahid. *Disastrous Twilight: A Personal Record of the Partition of India.* London: Leo Cooper, 1986.

Hamilton, Nigel. *Monty: The Making of a General, 1887–1942.* New York: McGraw-Hill, 1981.

Hamilton, Walter. *Geographical, Historical and Statistical Description of Hindustan and the Adjacent Countries.* 2 vols. London: John Murray, 1820.

Handke, Werner. "The Conflict in India's Northeast." *Aussen Politik* 31, no. 4 (1980): 432.

Hanson, Victor Davis. *Carnage and Culture: Landmark Battles in the Rise of Western Culture.* New York: Random House, 2001.

———. *The Western Way of War: Infantry Battle in Classical Greece.* New York: Oxford University Press, 1989.

Hardy, P. "Decline of the Mughal Empire: Commentary and Critique." *Journal of Asian Studies* 35 (1976): 261.

Hart, B. H. Liddell. *The Defence of Britain.* London: Faber, 1939.

———. *Memoirs.* London: Cassell, 1959.

———, ed. *The Rommel Papers.* London: Collins, 1953.

Hasan, Mohibbul. *History of Tipu Sultan.* Calcutta: World Press, 1971.

Hasnain, Ghulam. "Pakistan: Under Cover of Night." *Times.com Asia*, 12 July 1999. http://pathfinder.com/time/asia/magazine/1999/990712/loc1.html.

Heathcote, T. A. *The Military in British India: The Development of British Land Forces in South Asia 1600–1947.* Manchester: Manchester University Press, 1995.

Hennessey, Maurice. *The Rajah from Tipperary.* London: Sidgwick and Jackson, 1971.

"Heroic Defence of Siachen." *Times of India* (Bombay), 6 March 1988: 7.

Hill, S. C. *The Indian Record Series, Bengal in 1756–7.* 3 vols. London: John Murray, 1895–1905.

Holman, Dennis. *Sikander Sahib: The Life of Colonel James Skinner, 1778–1841.* London: Heinemann, 1961.

Hopkins, E. W. *The Social and Military Position of the Ruling Caste in India, as Represented in the Sanskrit Epics.* Varanasi: Bharat Bharati, 1972.

"How I Started a War: A Pakistani Soldier's Account of the Kashmir Battle." *Time,* 12 July 1999: 40.

Hugel, Charles. *Travels in Kashmir and the Punjab: Containing a Particular Account of the Government and Character of the Sikhs, from the Journal of Baron Charles Hugel.* Trans. T. B. Jervis. London: J. Peterham, 1845.

Hultzch, E., ed. *South Indian Inscriptions.* Vol. 2, *Tamil Inscriptions of Rajaraja, Rajendra-Chola and Others in the Rajeshwara Temple at Tanjavur.* Madras: Superintendent of Government Printing, 1891.

Hunt, David. "Reflections of the Canadair Sabre." *Air Enthusiast* (April 1972): 203.

Hussain, Syed Shabir, and M. Tariq Quereshi. *History of the Pakistan Air-Force, 1947–1982.* Karachi: PAF Press, 1982.

"IAF Sorties Reveal Pullout of Pakistani Forces." *Deccan Herald,* 16 July 1999. http://www.deccanherald.com/deccanherals/jul16/soldier.htm.

"IAF Team in Israel Sent Packing after N-Tests." *Deccan Chronicle,* 7 December 1998. http://www.bharat-rakshak.com/IAF/News/98-Dec.html.

"IAF to 'Wait and Watch.' To Continue Reconnaissance Missions." *Indian Express,* 12 July 1999. http://www.expressindia.com/news/1931999.htm.

IDR Research Team. "Some Thoughts on the Evolution of Infantry Organization and Tactics." *Indian Defence Review* (July 1991): 47–56.

Imperial Gazetteer of India. 25 vols. Oxford, 1907.

Inden, Ronald. *Imagining India.* Oxford: Blackwell, 1990.

"India and Pakistan in Dance of War." *Jane's Defence Weekly,* 3 April 1996: 18.

"India Building Missile with 5000 Km Range." *Deccan Herald,* 24 October 1999. http://bharat-rakshak.com/MISSILES/News/99-Oct.html.

"India Buys Four KA-31 Helicopters from Russia." *Jane's Defence Weekly,* 25 August 1999. http://www.bharat-rakshak.com/NAVY/News/99-Oct.html.

"India Challenges China in South China Sea." *Defence Systems Daily,* 26 April 2000. http://defence-data.com/current/page7039.htm.

Indian Antiquary. Bombay: Archeological Survey of India, 1907.

"Indian MiG 21 Upgrade Plans." *Air Forces Monthly* (February 1999): 17.

"Indian Nuclear Submarine to Be Ready by 2006." *Deccan Chronicle*, 23 July 1999. http://www.bharat-rakshak.com/NAVY/News/99-July.html.

"India Now 4th Largest in Purchasing Power Parity." *Economic Times*, 30 April 2001. wysiwg://14/http://www.economictimes.com/today/30lead02.htm.

"Indian Service Chiefs Fall out over Supremo." *Jane's Defence Weekly*, 3 February 1999. http://www.bharat-rakshak.com/LAND-FORCES/Army/News/99-Feb.html.

"Indian Ties with France Will Soar with Mirage Buy." *Jane's Defence Weekly*, 1 September 1999. http://www.bharat-rakshak.com/IAF/News/99-Sept.html.

"India Reveals Details of BVR Missile." *Jane's Defense Weekly*, 16 December 1998. http://www.bharat-rakshak.com/MISSILES/News/98-Dec.html.

"India Sets 5% Lower Budget." *Jane's Defence Weekly*, 21 March 1992: 462.

"India Signs Missile Deal with Russia." *Indian Express*, 19 June 1998.

"India's LCA Set to Undergo Dynamic Testing." *Jane's Defence Weekly*, 16 December 1998. http://www.bharat-rakshak.com/IAF/News/98-Dec.html.

"India's Main Battle Tank." *Indian Defence Review* (January 1990): 184–87.

"India to Acquire N-Capable Mirage." *Deccan Chronicle*, 28 August 1999. http://www.bharat-rakshak.com/IAF/News/99-Aug.html.

"India to Buy Anti-Mine Vehicles from South Africa." *Deccan Herald*, 1 August 1998. http://www.bharat-rakshak.com/ARMY/News/98-Aug.html.

"India to Get Latest Submarine from Russia." *Hindu*, 16 January 1999. http://www.webpage.com/hindu/daily/980116/03/03/03160005.htm.

"India to Have New Naval Command." *Deccan Herald*, 29 July 1999. http://www.bharat-rakshak.com/NAVY/News/98-July.html.

"India to Produce Indigenous Nuclear Subs." *Deccan Herald*, 27 July 1999. http://www.bharat-rakshak.com/NAVY/News/99-July.html.

"INS Delhi: Battle Ready." *India Today*, 22 September 1997: 29–33.

International Institute for Strategic Studies. *The Military Balance 1965–1966.* London: Institute for Strategic Studies, 1966.

———. *The Military Balance 1971–1972.* London: Institute for Strategic Studies, 1972.

———. *The Military Balance 1995–1996.* London: Oxford University Press, 1995.

———. *Strategic Survey, 1993–1994.* London: Brassey's, 1993.

"Interview of the Week: Major General V. S. Budhwar." *India Today*, 20 September 1999. wysiwyg://53/http://www.india-today.com/itoday/19990920/defence.html.

"In Their Lair." Photo spread, *Frontline*, 1–14 April 1989: 107–9.

Irvine, William. *The Army of the Indian Moghuls: Its Organization and Administration.* New Delhi: Eurasia Publishing House, 1962.

"Israeli Night Fighting Pods for IAF." *Hindu*, 13 October 1999. http://www
.bharat-rakshak.com/IAF/News.99-Oct.html.

"Israel Sold Electronic Warfare System to India." *Indian Express*, 28 April 1999.
Agence France Presse. http://www.indian-express.com/ie/daily/1990428/ige280
73.html.

Iype, George. "Pant May Head NSC." *Rediff on the Net*, 1 July 1998. http://www
.rediff.com/news/1998/jul/01pant.htm.

———. "Pant's Task Force Recommends NSC Be Set up on Priority Basis." *Rediff
on the Net*, 26 June 1998. http://www.rediff.com/news/1998/jun/26nsc.htm.

Jabar, Ahmad bin Yahya bin (better known as Al-Biladhuri). *Kitab Futuh al-Buldan*.
Ed. Francis Clark Murgotten. 2 vols. Vol. 1, ed. Phillip Khuri Hitti. Columbia:
Columbia College, 1916.

Jalal, Ayesha. "India's Partition and the Defence of Pakistan: An Historical Perspective." *Journal of Imperial and Commonwealth History* 15 no. 3 (1987): 290–310.

Jeffery, Keith. *The British Army and the Crisis of Empire 1918–1922*. Manchester:
Manchester University Press, 1984.

Jha, D. N. *Economy and Society in Early India: Issues and Paradigms*. New Delhi:
Munshiram Manoharlal, 1993.

Johri, Sita Ram. *The Chinese Invasion of Ladakh*. Lucknow: Himalaya Publications,
1969.

———. *Chinese Invasion of* NEFA. Lucknow: Himalaya Publications, 1968.

Joseph, Josy. "Army Draws up Strategy to Secure Kashmir." *Rediff on the Net*, 31
August 1999. wysiwg://176/http://216.32.165.70/news/1999/aug/31josy.htm.

Joshi, Manoj. "Atomic Age Warfare." *India Today*, 20 July 1998. http://www.india-
today.com/itoday/20071998/defence.html.

———. "Directions in India's Defense and Security Policies." In Ross Babbage
and Sandy Gordon, eds., *India's Strategic Future: Regional State or Global Power?*
London: Macmillan, 1992, 87.

———. "Military Diplomacy." *India Today*, 6 April 1998. http://www.india-today
.com/itoday/06041998/defence.html.

———. "The Missile Edge." *Frontline*, 12–15 April 1988: 35–39.

———. "The Pakistan Connection." *Frontline*, 28 May–10 June 1988: 13–15.

———. "The Price of Peace." *Frontline*, 18–31 March 1989: 17–21.

———. "Receding Terror." *Frontline*, 23 April 1993: 62.

———. "The Resource Crunch." *Frontline*, 20 August–2 September 1988: 88–93.

———. "Run Silent, Run Deep." *Frontline*, 12–25 December 1987: 4–9.

———. "Tank Power." *Frontline*, 6–19 February 1987: 58–69.

Joshi, Manoj, and Harjinder Baweja. "Kargil War: Blasting Peace." *India Today*,
7 June 1999. http://www.india-today.com/itoday/07061999/cover.html.

———. "Kargil War: Intelligence Failure." *India Today*, 14 June 1999. http://www
.india-today.com/itoday/07061999/cover.html.

Joshi, Manoj, and Raj Chengappa. "Kargil War: The Marathon War." *India Today*, 21 June 1999. http://www.india-today.com/itoday/21061999/cover.html.

Joshi, P. M., ed. *Selections from the Peshwa Daftar*. New series no. 3, *Revival of Maratha Power 1761–1772*. Bombay: Government Central Press, 1962.

Juin, Alphonse. *Memoires*. Vol. 1. Paris: Fayard, 1959.

Kadam, V. S. *Maratha Confederacy: A Study in Its Origins and Development*. Delhi: Munshiram Manoharlal, 1993.

Kak, Kapil. "Directions of Higher Defense." *Strategic Analysis* 22, no. 4 (July 1998): 501–13.

―――. "Management of India's Security and Higher Defense – I." *Strategic Analysis* 22, no. 3 (June 1998): 327–37.

Kangle, R. P. *The Kautilya Arthashastra*. 3 vols. Bombay: University of Bombay Press, 1972.

Kantak, M. R. *The First Anglo-Maratha War 1774–1783: A Military Study of Major Battles*. Bombay: Popular Prakashan, 1993.

Kapur, A. *India's Nuclear Option: Atomic Diplomacy and Decision Making*. New York: Praeger, 1976.

"Kargil: A Saga of Odds and Ingenuity." *Indian Express*, 6 October 1999. http://www.bharat-rakshak.com/IAF/News/99-oct.html.

"Kashmir Conflict Hastens India's Jet Trainer Decision." *Jane's Defence Weekly*, 11 August 1999. http://www.bharat-rakshak.com/IAF/News/99-Aug.html.

Kasturi, Bhashyam. "From Technology Demonstration to Assured Retaliation: The Making of Indian Nuclear Doctrine." *Strategic Analysis* 22, no. 10 (January 1999): 1467–81.

―――. "Future Combat." *India Today*, 21 December 1998. http://www.india-today.com/itoday/21121998/defence.html.

―――. "The Indian Experience in the Use of Military Helicopters." *Indian Defence Review* 10, no. 3 (July–September 1995): 77.

―――. "Now Hyper War." *India Today*, 10 May 1999. http://www.india-today.com/itoday/10051999/defence.html.

―――. "Obituary: Warrior as Scholar." *India Today*, 22 February 1999. http://india-today.com/itoday/22021999/obit.html.

Kaul, B. M. *The Untold Story*. Bombay: Allied Publishers, 1967.

Kaul, Ravi. "The Indo-Pakistani War and the Changing Balance of Power in the Indian Ocean." *USNI Proceedings* (May 1973): 186–88.

Kavic, Lorne J. *India's Quest for Security: Defense Policies 1947–1965*. Berkeley: University of California Press, 1967.

Kazim, Mirza Muhammad. *Alamgirnama*. Bibliotheca Indica Series. Calcutta: Asiatic Society of Bengal, 1868.

Keegan, John. *The Face of Battle*. London: Jonathan Cape Ltd., 1976.

―――. *A History of Warfare*. New York: Vintage Books, 1993.

Kenoyer, Jonathan Mark. *Ancient Cities of the Indus Valley Civilization*. Karachi: Oxford University Press, 2000.

————. "The Indus Valley Tradition of Pakistan and Western India." *Journal of World Prehistory* 5, no. 4 (1991): 331–85.

"Key Positions in Dras, Batalik Regained." *Times of India*, 2 July 1999. wysig://48/ http://www.timesofindia.com/today/02home2.htm.

Khafikhan, Muhammad Hashim. *Muntakhabulluhab*. Bibliotheca Indica Series. Calcutta: Asiatic Society of Bengal, 1868.

Khan, Fazal Muqeem. *Pakistan's Crisis in Leadership*. Lahore: National Book Foundation, 1973.

Khan, Gul Hassan. *Memoirs*. Karachi: Oxford University Press, 1993.

Khan, Iqtidar Alam. "Origin and Development of Gunpowder Technology in India: A.D. 1250–1500." *Indian Historical Review* 4, no. 1 (July 1977): 26–27.

Khan, Muhammad Hashim Khafi. *Muntakhab-ul-Lubub*. Ed. Maulvi Kabir al-Din Ahmad and Ghulam Qadir. 2 vols. Calcutta: Royal Asiatic Society of Bengal, 1869.

Khan, Saqi Mustaid Khan. *Ma'asir-i-Alamgiri*. Ed. Agha Ahmad Ali. Calcutta: Royal Asiatic Society of Bengal, 1870–73.

————. *Masire Alamgiri*. Trans. Sir Jadunath Sarkar. Calcutta: M. C. Sarkar and Sons, 1947.

Khanna, D. D. *Monson's Retreat*. Allahabad: University of Allahabad, 1981.

Khobrekar, V. G., ed. *Tarikh-i-Dilkasha*. Bombay: Department of Archives, Maharashtra, 1972.

Kohli, S. N. *Sea Power and the Indian Ocean*. New Delhi: Tata McGraw-Hill, 1978.

————. *We Dared: Maritime Operations in the 1971 War*. New Delhi: Lancer International, 1989.

Kohli, Sita Ram. *Catalogue of the Khalsa Darbar Records*. 2 vols. Lahore: Superintendent of Government Printing, 1919.

Kolff, Dirk H. A. *Naukar, Rajput, and Sepoy: The Ethnohistory of the Military Labour Market in Hindustan, 1450–1850*. Cambridge: Cambridge University Press, 1990.

Krishnan, N. *No Way but Surrender*. Delhi: Vikas Publishing House, 1980.

Kulkarni, G. T. *Battle of Kharda: Challenges and Responses*. Pune: Deccan College, 1980.

Kulke, Herman. "The Early Imperial Kingdom: A Processual Model of Integrative State Formation in Early Medieval India." In Herman Kulke, ed., *The State in India 1000–1700*. Delhi: Oxford University Press, 1995, 232–62.

Kumar, Dinesh. "Go Ahead for Home-made Aircraft Carrier." *Times of India*, 18 June 1999. http://www.bharat-rakshak.com/NAVY/News/99-June.html.

————. "IAF Pounds Infiltrators." *Times of India*, 27 May 1999. http://www.timesofindia.com/today/127home1.htm.

———. "Intelligence Failure at Kargil." *Times of India*, 25 May 1999. http://www
.timesofindia.com/today/25home3.htm.

Lake, John. "Mikoyan MiG-29 'Fulcrum.'" *World Air Power Journal* 4 (Winter
1990–91): 44–91.

———. "Mikoyan MiG-23/27 'Flogger.'" *World Air Power Journal* 8 (Spring 1992):
81–82.

Lal, P. C. *My Years with the* IAF. New Delhi: Lancer International, 1986.

———. *Some Problems of Defense*. New Delhi: United Services Institution of India,
1977.

"LCA and ALH Projects Severely Hit by Sanctions." *Deccan Herald*, 13 July 1998.
http://www.bharat-rakshak.com/IAF/info/IAF News.html.

Longer, V. *Red Coats to Olive Green: A History of the Indian Army, 1600–1974*. Bombay:
Allied Publishers, 1974.

———. *Forefront for Ever: The History of the Mahar Regiment*. Saugor: Mahar Regimental Center, 1981.

"Long Range Agni III on Anvil." *Times of India*, 7 May 1999. http://www.bharat-
rakshak.com/MISSILES/News/99-May.html.

Lyall, A. C. "The Rajput States of India." *Asiatic Studies*, no. 1 (1875): 203–64.

Lyall, Alfred. *The Rise and Expansion of British Dominion in India*. London: John
Murray, 1929.

Lynn, John A. *Battle: A History of Combat and Culture*. Boulder CO: Westview Press,
2003.

MacKay, E. J. H. *Further Excavations at Mohenjodaro. Being an Official Account of the Archeological Excavations at Mohenjodaro Carried out by the Government of India between
1927 and 1931; with Chapters by A. S. Hemmy; B. S. Guha; P. C. Basu etc.* 2 vols.
Delhi: Manager of Publications, 1938.

Mackinnon, A. C. B. "The Moplah Rebellion 1921–1922." *Army Quarterly*, no. 8
(1924): 260–77.

Macksey, Kenneth. *Armored Crusader: Major General Percy Hobart*. London: Hutchin-
son, 1967.

Maharaj, Sanjay Badri. "Indian Air Force." *Air Forces Monthly* (August 1999): 46.

Maisey, F. C. *Sanchi and Its Remains*. London: Kegan Paul, Trench, Trubner and
Co., 1892.

"Major Success for Indian Troops as Tiger Hill Falls." *Deccan Herald*, 5 July 1999.
http://www.deccanherald.com/deccanherald/jul05/lead.htm.

Majumdar, R. C. *Ancient Indian Civilization in South East Asia*. Baroda: University of
Baroda Press, 1963.

———. *The Classical Accounts of India: Being a Compilation of the English Translations
of the Accounts Left by Herodotus, Megasthenes, Arrian, Strabo, Quintius, Diodorus,
Silucus, Justin, Plutarch, Frontinus, Nearchus, Apollonius, Pliny, Ptolemy, Aelaian and
Others.* Calcutta: Firma K. L. Mukhopadhyay, 1960.

———, ed. *History and Culture of the Indian Peoples*. 11 vols. Bombay: Bharatiya Vidya Bhavan, 1970–77.

Makarov, Yuri. "New Sword for the Indian Navy." *Military Parade* (July 2000). http://www.milparade.com/2000/40/05_01.shtml.

Malleson, G. B. *Lord Clive*. London: W. H. Allen and Co., 1882.

———. *The Decisive Battles of India*. Reprint, New Delhi: Sagar Publications, 1969.

Mama, Hormuz P. "AREN Network for the Indian Army." *International Defense Review* 21, no. 3 (March 1988): 259.

———. "INS *Khukri*: A Powerful New Class of Corvette." *International Defense Review*, no. 12 (1989): 1685–86.

———. "Progress on India's New Tactical Missiles." *International Defense Review* 22, no. 7 (July 1989): 960–67.

Mandelbaum, D. G. *Society in India*. 2 vols. Berkeley: University of California Press, 1970.

Manucci, Nicola. *Storia De Mogor 1653–1708*. 4 vols. Trans. and ed. William Irvine. London: John Murray, 1907 (Royal Asiatic Society).

Marshall, John. *A Guide to Sanchi*. Delhi: Government of India, 1955.

Marshall, P. J. "British Expansion in India in the Eighteenth Century: A Historical Revision." In P. J. Marshall, *Trade and Conquest: Studies on the Rise of British Dominance in India*. Aldershot, Hampshire: Variorum Collected Studies Series, 1993, 41.

———. "The Whites of British India, 1780–1830: A Failed Colonial Society?" *International History Review* 12 (1990): 41.

Martin, R. M., ed. *Despatches Minutes and Correspondence of the Marquis of Wellesley*. 5 vols. London: John Murray, 1836–37.

Marwah, Onkar. "India's Military Power and Policy." In Onkar Marwah and Jonathan D. Pollack, eds., *Military Power and Policy in Asian States: China, India, Japan*. Boulder CO: Westview Press, 1980.

"Massive Restructuring of the Army's Infantry Division." *Rediff on the Net*. http://www.rediff.com/news/Oct/23infan.htm.

Mattoo, Amitabh. "*Raison d'etat* or Military Adhocism." In Kanti P. Bajpai and Amitabh Mattoo, eds., *Securing India: Essays by George K. Tanham with Commentaries*. New Delhi: Manohar, 1996, 201–11.

Maurice, Frederick. *The Life of General Lord Rawlinson of Trent*. London: Casell, 1928.

Maxwell, Neville. "How the East Was Lost." *Rediff on the Net*, 24 May 2001, "Part I: The Genesis of the Sino-Indian War." wysiwyg://3/http://www.rediff.com/news/2001/may/24spec.htm.

———. *India's China War*. New York: Pantheon Books, 1970.

"Mazagon Dock to Build India's First Stealth Warship." *Rediff on the Net*, 12 July 2001. http://cgi.rediff.com/cgi-programs/print/printpage.cgi.

McCrindle, J. W. *The Invasion of India by Alexander the Great as Described by Arrian, Q. Curtius, Diodorus, Plutarch and Justin.* 1896; reprint, New York: Barnes and Noble, 1969.

McIntosh, Jane R. *A Peaceful Realm: The Rise and Fall of the Indus Civilization.* Boulder CO: Westview Press, 2002.

McNeill, William H. *The Pursuit of Power: Technology, Armed Force, and Society since AD 1000.* Chicago: University of Chicago Press, 1982.

Mehdi, S. G. *Mehdi Papers.* Karachi: Mehdi Foundation, 1985.

Mehta, Ashok. "An Emasculated Defense Planning Staff." *Indian Defense Review* 11, no. 1 (January–March 1996): 34.

Mellor, J. W. "The Indian Economy: Objectives, Performance and Prospects." In J. W. Mellor, ed., *India: A Rising Middle Power.* Delhi: Select Book Service Syndicate, 1981, 100–103.

Mendiratta, D. R. "Insurgent Assam." *Indian Defence Review* 10, no. 3 (July–September 1995): 65.

Menon, Ramesh. "Sri Lanka: Return of the Tigers." *India Today,* 15 April 1990: 64.

Metcalf, Thomas R. *Land, Landlords, and the British Raj: Northern India in the Nineteenth Century.* Berkeley: University of California Press, 1979.

"Militancy in Jammu & Kashmir Reduced to a Trickle." *Deccan Herald,* 29 December 1998. http://bharat-rakshak.com/LAND-FORCES/Army/News/98-Dec.html.

Mill, James. *The History of British India,* with notes and continuation by H. H. Wilson, ed. London: Baldwin, Craddock and Jay, 1840–48.

————. *History of British India.* Ed. H. H. Wilson. Vols. 1–6. London: J. Madden, 1840–48.

Ministry of Defence Report, 1963–1964. New Delhi: Government of India Press, 1964.

Minney, R. J. *The Private Papers of Hore-Belisha.* London: Collins, 1960.

Miscellaneous Inscriptions from the Tamil Country. Pt. 1: *Inscriptions at Ukkal, Melpadi, Karuvur, Manirrangalam and Tirruvalam.* Madras: Superintendent of Government Printing, 1899.

"Modification Package for Aircraft Carrier *Gorshkov* Finalized." *Hindustan Times,* 26 October 1999. http://www.bharat-rakshak.com/NAVY/News/99-Oct.html.

Mohammed, Gholam. *The History of Haider Shah, Alias Hyder Ali Khan Bahadur, and Son Tipoo Sultan, by M.M.D.L.T. General in the Army of the Mughal Empire, Revised and Corrected by His Highness Prince Gholam Mohammed the Only Surviving Son of Tipoo Sultan.* 1855; reprint, Delhi: Cosmo Publications, 1976.

Mohan, C. Raja. "Fernandes Unveils 'Limited War' Doctrine." *Hindu,* 25 January 2000. wysiwyg://11/http://www.the-hindu.com/stories/01250001.htm.

Mollo, B. *The Indian Army.* London: Poole, 1981.

Mookerjee, Subimal, and Jasjit Singh. "Aircraft Carriers for the Indian Navy: The Case for and Against." *Vayu* 6 (1995): 19–28.

Mukherjee, S. J. "Green Light for Indian LCA." *Jane's Defence Weekly*, 16 March 1985: 437.

Munro, Innes. *Narrative of the Military Operations on the Coromandel Coast from 1780 to 1784*. London: T. Bensley, 1789.

Musa, Mohammad. *Jawan to General: Reflections of a Pakistani Soldier.* Karachi: East and West Publishing, 1984.

———. *My Version: India-Pakistan War, 1965.* Lahore: Wajidalis, 1983.

Nadkarni, J. G. "How Can One Modernize the Indian Army on Rs 2,000 Crore?" *Rediff on the Net*, 23 March 1999. http://www.216.32.165.70/news/1999/mar/23nad.htm.

Nadkarni, Rajaram Venkatesh. *The Rise and Fall of the Maratha Empire.* Bombay: Popular Prakashan, 1966.

Nair, K. P. P. "A Review of the 1965 Chaamb Battle." *Indian Defence Review* 8, no. 3 (July 1993): 94–104.

Nair, V. K. "Employment of Military Helicopters: Part II: The Indian Experience and Compulsions." *Indian Defence Review* (January 1992): 103–17.

Narayan, B. K. *General J. N. Chaudhuri: An Autobiography*, as narrated to B. K. Narayan. New Delhi: Shipra Publications, 1994.

Nathan, Mirza. *Baharistan-i-Ghyabi: A History of the Mughal Wars in Assam, Cooch Behar, Bengal, Bihar and Orissa during the Reigns of Jahangir and Shah Jahan.* Trans. M. I. Borah. 2 vols. Gauhati, Assam: Department of Historical Records and Antiquarian Studies, 1936.

"Navy Set to Chart New Course." *Hindustan Times*, 20 July 2000. http://bharat-rakshak.com/NAVY/News/00-Oct.html.

"Navy to Acquire Three Russian Frigates." *Rediff on the Net*, 24 June 1998. http://www.rediff.com/news/1998/jun/24ins.htm.

Nazim, Muhammad. *The Life and Times of Sultan Mahmud of Ghazna.* Cambridge: Cambridge University Press, 1931.

"N-Doctrine Invites G-8 Wrath, Sanctions to Stay." *Times of India*, 20 August 1999. wysiwyg://360/http://www.timesofindia.com/200899/20home.htm.

"New Navy Base in India." *Jane's Defence Weekly*, 15 November 1986.

"New Russian Missiles to Arm Navy." *Indian Express*, 3 October 1999. http://www.bharat-rakshak.com/NAVY/News/99-Oct.html.

"Next Indian Satellite Will Have Surveillance Capability." *Deccan Herald*, 2 August 1999. http://www.bharat-rakshak.com/SPACE/News/99-Aug.html.

Nijar, Bakshish Singh. *Anglo-Sikh Wars (1845–1849).* New Delhi: KB Publications, 1976.

Oberst, Robert C. "Sri Lanka's Tamil Tigers." *Conflict* 8 (1988): 185–202.

"Offer to Help HAL in Avionics Software." *Deccan Herald*, 12 December 1999. http://www.bharat-rakshak.com/IAF/News/99-Dec.html.

Oldham, Charles. "The Battle of Buxar." *Journal of the Bihar and Orissa Research Society* 12, no. 1 (March 1926): 1–38.

"Operation Pawan: In a Rush to Vanquish." *India Today*, 31 January 1988: 73.

Orlich, L. V. *Travels in India Including the Sind and the Punjab*. London: Longman, 1845.

Orme, Robert. *A History of the Military Transactions of the British Nation in Indostan.* 3 vols. Madras: Atheaneum Press, 1861.

O'Sullivan, Arieh. "Israel, India Keen on Joint Arms Effort." *Jerusalem Post*, 20 July 2001. wysiwg://25/http://cgis.jpost.cpm/cgi-bi./Editions/200/07/News .30845.html.

Owen, S. J. *A Selection of the Despatches Relating to India of the Duke of Wellington*. Oxford: Clarendon Press, 1877, 1880.

Pachauri, Pankaj. "Jammu and Kashmir Border: On Battle Stations." *India Today*, 30 June 1990: 36–38.

Padmanabhan, Mukund. "Tiger Talk." *Sunday* (Bombay), 14–20 May 1989: 29–30.

"Pak Forces Begin Pullout." *Deccan Herald*, 12 July 1999. http://www.deccanherald .com/deccanherald/jul12/lead.htm.

"Pak, India DGMOs Meet at Wagha." *Frontier Post*, 12 July 1999. http://frontierpost .com.pk/top1.html.

"Pakistan Air Force Built around MiG-19." *Aviation Week and Space Technology*, 2 December 1968: 43.

"Pakistani Army's Plan for the Kargil Intrusions." http://vijayinkargil.org/ features/features6.html.

"Pakistani Withdrawal Almost Complete." *Deccan Herald*, 17 July 1999. http:// www.deccanherald.com/deccanherald/jul16/soldier.htm.

Palakapaya. *Hastayayur-Veda*. Anandasram Sanskrit Series no. 26. Poona: Anandasrama Press, 1894.

Palit, D. K. *War in the High Himalaya: The Indian Army in Crisis, 1962*. New York: St. Martin's Press, 1991.

Palsokar, R. D. *The Grenadiers: A Tradition of Valour*. Jabalpur: Commandant, the Grenadiers Regimental Center, 1980.

Pant, G. N. *Studies in Indian Weapons and Warfare*. New Delhi: Army Educational Stores, 1970.

Parasnis, D. B., ed. *Peshwa Daftaratil Nivadak Kagadpatra, Fouj Saranjam Sambandhi Mahiti*. Bombay: Nirnayasagar, 1917.

Parker, Geoffrey. *The Military Revolution: Military Innovation and the Rise of the West, 1500–1660*. Cambridge: Cambridge University Press, 1988.

Pearson, M. N. "Shivaji and the Decline of the Mughal Empire." *Journal of Asian Studies* 35, no. 2 (1976): 221–35.

Pelliot, P. "Le Fou-nan." *Bulletin de l'Ecole Française d'Extreme-Orient* (1903): 269.

Pemberton, A. L. *The Development of Artillery Tactics and Equipment.* London: War Office, 1950.

Perrin, Bernadotte, trans. *Plutarch's Lives.* 2 vols., 1914–26, ed. T. E. Page and W. H. D. Rousse. New York: Macmillan, 1912–.

Perrod, Pierre-Antoine. "La findu rêve d'empire." In Rose Vincent, ed., *Pondicherry, 1624–1761: L'échec d'un rêve d'empire.* Paris: Les Editions Auttrement, 1993, 221–33.

Phillips, C. H. *The East India Company 1784–1834.* Manchester: Manchester University Press, 1940.

"Pinaka Was Tested in Kargil." *Press Trust of India,* 22 August 1999. http://www .bharat-rakshak.com/LAND-FORCES/Army/News/99-Aug.html.

Pitre, K. G. *The Second Anglo-Maratha War 1802–1805.* Pune: Dastane Ramchandra and Co., 1990.

Playfair, I. S. O. *The Mediterranean and the Middle East.* 6 vols. London: Her Majesty's Stationery Office, 1954–88.

" 'Please Don't Tell Us How to Fight,' the Army Says." *Indian Express,* 5 June 1998. http://www.bharat-rakshak.com/ARMY/News/98-June.html.

Porter, Bruce. *War and the Rise of the State: The Military Foundations of Modern Politics.* New York: Free Press, 1994.

Prasad, Bisheswar. *Campaign in the Eastern Theatre: The Retreat from Burma 1941–1942.* New Delhi: Combined Inter-Services Historical Section, India and Pakistan, Orient Longmans, 1959.

———. *Official History of the Indian Armed Forces in the Second World War 1939–1945.* New Delhi: Combined Inter-Services Historical Section, India and Pakistan, 1956.

Prasad, Sri Nandan. *History of the Operations in Jammu and Kashmir.* New Delhi: History Division, Ministry of Defence, Government of India; Distributed by Controller of Publications, Government of India, 1987.

———. *Official History of the Indian Armed Forces in the Second World War: Campaign in the Eastern Theater, the Reconquest of Burma.* New Delhi: Combined Inter-Services Historical Section, India and Pakistan, Orient Longmans, 1959.

Prasannan, R. "No Mirage This." *Week,* 14 January 2000. http://www.the-week .com/21jan14/events.htm.

———. "Systemic Pointers: Kargil Report." *Week,* 12 March 2000. http://www .the-week.com/20mar12/events9.htm.

———. "War Games." *Week,* 13 December 1998. http://www.bharat-rakshak .com/LAND-FORCES/Army/Articles.html.

Praval, K. C. *The Indian Army after Independence*. New Delhi: Lancer International, 1987.

———. *India's Paratroopers: A History of the Parachute Regiment of India*. Faridabad, Haryana: Thompson Press, 1974.

———. *The Red Eagles: A History of the Fourth Division of India*. New Delhi: Vision Books, 1982.

———. *Valour Triumphs: A History of the Kumaon Regiment*. Faridabad, Haryana: Thompson Press, 1976.

"Prime Minister Vajpayee Commissions INS Mysore." *Deccan Herald*, 3 June 1999. http://bharat-rakshak.com/NAVY/News/99-June.html.

"Prithvi to Find Naval Platform on Republic Day." *Rediff on the Net*, 1 December 1998. http://www.rediff.com/news/1998/dec/01navy.htm.

Proudfoot, C. L. *Flash of the Khukri: History of the 3rd Gorkha Rifles, 1947–1980*. New Delhi: Vision Books, 1984.

———. *Valour Enshrined: A History of the M.L.I.* Vol. 2. Belgaum: MLI Regimental Centre, 1980.

———. *We Lead: 7th Light Cavalry 1784–1990*. New Delhi: Lancer International, 1991.

Pundit, Casi Raja. *An Account of the Battle of Panipat*. Ed. H. G. Rawlinson. London: Oxford University Press, 1926.

"Punjab's Winter of Despair." *Frontline*, 8–21 December 1990: 5.

Puri, Balraj. *Kashmir: Towards Insurgency*. New Delhi: Orient Longmans, 1993.

"Quantity or Quality? The Indian Dilemma." *Air International* (October 1975): 175–85.

Rahaya, Gloria Goodwin. "India: Caste, Kinship and Dominance Reconsidered." *Annual Review of Anthropology* 17 (1988): 497–552.

Rahman, M. Attiqur. *The Wardens of the Marches: A History of the Piffers, 1947–1971*. Lahore: Wajidalis, 1980.

Rai, Ranjit. *A Nation and Its Navy at War*. Delhi: Lancer International, 1987.

Rai, Saritha. "Wanted: A Foreign Match." *India Today*, 31 January 1994: 66–69.

Ralston, David B. *Importing the European Army: The Introduction of European Military Techniques into the Extra-European World 1600–1914*. Chicago: University of Chicago Press, 1990.

Ramachandran, R. "Unclear Nuclear Identity." *Frontline*, 28 August–10 September 1999. http://www.the-hindu.com/fline/fl1618/16180160.htm.

Ramakrishnan, Venkitesh. "A New Front in the Proxy War." *Frontline*, 20 June–3 July 1998. http://www.the-hindu.com/fline/fl1513/15130180.htm.

———. "The Zero Story: Fear Keeps the Voters Away." *Frontline*, 29 February–13 March 1992: 125.

Ramdas, L. "Navy, Nation and National Security." *Frontline*, 16–29 January 1999. http://www.the-hindu.com/fline/fl1602/16020170.htm.

Ramunny, Murkot. *Ezhimala: The Abode of the Naval Academy*. New Delhi: Northern Book Center, 1993.

Rao, P. Setu Madhav. "Maratha-Nizam Relations." *Journal of the University of Bombay* 28, pt. 4 (January 1958): 1–25.

Rao, V. Narayan, and S. Subrahmanyam. *Symbols of Substance: Court and State in Nayace Period Tamilnadu*. Delhi: Oxford University Press, 1992.

Read, Alexander. "Sketch of Revenue Management in Countries North of the Kaveri under the Gentu, the Moorish and the Hon'ble Company's Government." 15 November 1792, in *Baramahal Records*, sec. 1, Management. Madras: Government of Madras, 1907, 140 (Records of Fort St. George).

Reddi, G. B. "The Forgotten Naga Insurgency." *Indian Defence Review* 10, no. 1 (January–March 1995): 42.

Renfrew, Colin. *Archaeology and Language: The Puzzle of the Indo-European Origins*. Cambridge: Cambridge University Press, 1982.

———. "Archaeology and Linguistics: Some Preliminary Issues." In T. L. Markey and J. A. C. Sreppin, eds., *When Worlds Collide: Indo-Europeans and Pre-Indo-Europeans*. Ann Arbor MI: Karoma Publishers, 1990, 15–24.

Report of the Controller and Auditor General of India for the Year Ended March 1992, No. 9 of 1993 (CAG Report). New Delhi: Government of India, 1993.

Report to the Combined Chiefs of Staff by the Supreme Commander South East Asia 1943–1945, Vice-Admiral the Earl Mountbatten of Burma. London: His Majesty's Stationery Office, 1951.

Richards, J. F. "The Imperial Crisis in the Deccan." *Journal of Asian Studies* 35 (1976): 237–56.

Riza, Shaukat. *Izzat-o-Iqbal: History of the Pakistan Artillery*. Nowshera: School of Artillery for MGA, Artillery Directorate, GHQ, Rawalpindi, 1980.

Roberts, P. E. *Historical Geography of British India*. Reprint, Delhi: Amol Publications, 1985.

Rogers, Clifford J., ed. *The Military Revolution Debate: Readings on the Military Transformation of Early Modern Europe*. Boulder CO: Westview Press, 1995.

Rosen, Stephen Peter. *Societies and Military Power: India and Its Armies*. Ithaca NY: Cornell University Press, 1996.

Roux, Jean-Paul. *Histoire des grands Moghuls: Babur*. Paris: Fayard, 1986.

Roy, Atul Chandra. *A History of the Mughal Navy and Naval Warfare*. Calcutta: World Press, 1972.

Roy, S. B. *Date of the Mahabharata Battle*. Gurgaon, Haryana: Academic Press, 1976.

Roychaudhuri, Hemchandra. *Political History of Ancient India*. Calcutta: University of Calcutta, 1923.

"Rs. 8,000 Crore Defense Spending Hike Likely." *Times of India*, 21 October 1999. http://www.bharat-rakshak.com/LAND-FORCES/Army/News/99-oct.html.

"Russian-Indian SU-30MK Delivery Contract under Realization." *Military Parade*,

Russian/CIS Aerospace and Arms Market #18.1998. http://www/milparade
.ru/market/9/01_01.htm.

"Russia Sets Deadline for Purchase of Aircraft Carrier." *Hindustan Times*, 6 May
1999. http://www.bharat-rakshak.com/NAVY/News/99-May.html.

Saberwal, Satish. "A Juncture of Traditions." In Martin Doornbos and Sudipta
Kaviraj, eds., *Dynamics of State Formation: India and Europe Compared*. Delhi: Sage
Publications, 1997, 84.

Sachdeva, Veena. *Polity and Economy of the Punjab during the Late Eighteenth Century*.
Delhi: Manohar, 1993.

Saeed, Ahmad. *The Battle of Chaamb, 1971*. Rawalpindi: Army Education Press,
1973.

Sahay, Tara Shankar. "National Security Council Set Up." *Rediff on the Net*,
19 November 1999. http://216.32.165.70/news/1998/nov/19nsc.htm.

Sahni, Varun. "Just Another Big Country." In Kanti P. Bajpai and Amitabh Mattoo, eds., *Securing India: Essays by George K. Tanham with Commentaries*. New Delhi:
Manohar, 1996, 160–73.

Saigal, J. R. *The Unfought War of 1962: The Debacle in* NEFA. Bombay: Allied Publishing, 1979.

Saliq, Siddiq. *Witness to Surrender*. Karachi: Oxford University Press, 1977.

Sandhu, Gurcharan Singh. *The Indian Armour: History of the Indian Armoured Corps
1941–1971*. New Delhi: Vision Books, 1987.

———. *The Indian Cavalry*. New Delhi: Vision Books, 1981.

Sane, K. N., ed. *Bhau Sahebanchi Bhakar*. Poona: Arya Bhooshan Press, 1932.

Saradzhyan, Simon. "India to Buy $500 Million Missile Shield." *Moscow Times*,
7 June 2001. wysiwg://13/http://www.themoscowtimes.com/stories/2001/06/
07/04/.html.

Sardesai, G. S. *Main Currents in Maratha History*. Bombay: Phoenix Publications,
1949.

———. *New History of the Marathas*. Vol. 1, *Shivaji and His Line, 1600–1707*. Bombay:
Phoenix Publications, 1946.

———. *New History of the Marathas*. Vol. 2, *Expansion of Maratha Power, 1707–72*.
Bombay: Phoenix Publications, 1948.

———. *New History of the Marathas*. Vol. 3. Bombay: Phoenix Publications, 1948.

———, ed. *Selections from the Peshwa Daftar*. 45 vols. Bombay: Government Press,
1934–40.

Sardeshpande, S. C. *Assignment Jaffna*. New Delhi: Lancer Publishers, 1992.

Sarkar, Jadunath. "Assam and the Ahoms in 1660 A.D." *Journal of the Bihar and
Orissa Research Society* 1, no. 2 (1915): 179–95.

———. "The Conquest of Chatagaon, 1666." *Journal of the Asiatic Society of Bengal*
3 (1907): 405–17.

————. "Shaista Khan in Bengal, 1664–66." *Journal of the Asiatic Society of Bengal* 2, no. 6 (June 1906): 257–67.

Sarkar, Jadunath, and Raghuvir Sinha. "Shivaji's Visits to Aurungzeb at Agra." In Indian History Congress, Research Series no. 1, *Rajisthan Records*. Calcutta, 1963, 22.

Sarkar, Jagdish Narayan. "An Early Supporter of Shivaji." *Indian Historical Quarterly* 7 (1931): 362–64.

————. "Events Leading up to the Battle of Panipat, 1761." *Indian Historical Quarterly* 11, no. 3 (September 1935): 547–58.

————. *Fall of the Mughal Empire*. 4 vols. Calcutta: M. C. Sarkar and Sons, 1932.

————. *The Life of Mir Jumla: The General of Aurungzeb*. New Delhi: Rajesh Publishing, 1979.

————. *The Military Despatches of a Seventeenth Century General, Being an English Translation of the "Haft Anjuman" of Munshi Udairaj Alias Taleyar Khan*. Benares Ms. 53b–93b. Calcutta: Scientific Book Agency, 1969.

————. "Panipat: 1761." *Indian Historical Quarterly* 10, no. 2 (June 1934): 258–73.

————. *Sindhia as Regent of Delhi*. Persian Records of Maratha History. Bombay: Central Government Press, 1953.

————. *Shivaji*. 6th ed. Calcutta: M. C. Sarkar and Sons, 1961.

————. *Shivaji and His Times*. Calcutta: M. C. Sarkar and Sons, 1920.

————. "Some Little Known Facts Regarding Ram Singh's Assam Campaign and Career Thereafter." In J. B. Bhattacharjee, ed., *Studies in the History of North-East India*. Shillong: North Eastern Hill University Publication, 1996, 58–59.

Sastri, K. A. Nilakanta. *The Cholas*. University of Madras Historical Series no. 9. Madras: University of Madras, 1955.

Sastri, T. Ganapati, ed. *Nitisara Kamandaka*. Trivandrum Sanskrit Series no. 14. Trivandrum: Travancore Government Press, 1912.

Sawant, Gaurav C. "Army Peaks at Dras to Reach LoC." *Indian Express*, 1 July 1999. http://www.expressindia.com/ie/daily/19990701/ige01065.html.

————. "Big Guns Boom All Night, Key Post Taken." *Indian Express*, 14 June 1999. http://www.indian-express.com/ie/daily/19990614/ige14005.html.

————. "Job Done, Elite Troops Savor Common Joys." *Indian Express*, 27 June 1999. http://www.expressindia.com/ie/daily/19990627/ige27002.html.

————. "Long, Hard Battle Ahead for the Army." *Indian Express*, 22 June 1999. http://www.indianexpress.com/ie/daily/19990622/ige22050.html.

————. "Zero to Hero – Bofors Gun Comes a Long Way." *Indian Express*, 16 June 1999. http://www.indian-express.com/ie/daily/19990616/ige16054.html.

Saxena, K. M. L. *The Military System of India 1850–1900*. New Delhi: Sterling Publishers, 1974.

Schoff, W. H. "The Eastern Iron Trade of the Roman Empire." *Journal of the American Oriental Society*, no. 35 (1915): 224–39.

———, trans. *The Periplus of the Erythraean Sea*. London: Longman, Green, 1912.

Selincourt, Aubrey de. *The Life of Alexander the Great*. Harmondsworth: Penguin Books, 1958.

Sen, L. P. *Slender Was the Thread*. Bombay: Orient Longmans, 1969.

Sen, Sailendra Nath. *Anglo-Maratha Relations, 1785–96*. Delhi: Macmillan, 1974.

Sen, Surendra Nath. *Administrative System of the Marathas*. Calcutta: University of Calcutta Press, 1925.

———, ed. *Indian Travels of Thevenot and Careri*. Delhi: National Archives of India, 1949.

———. *The Military System of the Marathas*. Reprint, Calcutta: K. P. Bagchi and Co., 1979.

———. *Siva Chatrapati*. Calcutta: University of Calcutta, 1920.

Sethna, A. M., and Valmiki Katju. *Traditions of a Regiment: Story of the Rajputana Rifles*. New Delhi: Lancer Publications, 1983.

Seton, Malcolm. *The India Office*. London: G. P. Putnam and Sons, 1926.

Shaheen. "The PAF at War." *Journal of the Pakistan Air Force* (May–August 1972): 11.

Shaheen Foundation. *The Story of the Pakistan Air Force: A Saga of Courage and Honour*. Islamabad: Shaheen Foundation, 1988.

Shaikh, Shakil. "Cabinet Endorses PM's Initiative on Kashmir." *News International*, 11 July 1999. http://www.jang.com.pk/thenews/jul99-daily/11-07-99/main/main1.htm.

Shamasastry, R., trans. *Kautilya's Arthashastra*. Mysore: Mysore Printing and Publishing House, 1967.

———. *Kautilyas Arthashastra*. Mysore: Printed at the Wesleyan Mission, 1929.

Sharma, G. N. *Social Life in Medieval Rajasthan*. Agra: Agarwala Publishers, 1962.

Sharma, Gautam. *The Path of Glory: Exploits of 11 Gorkha Rifles*. New Delhi: Allied Publishers, 1988.

Sharma, Ravi. "For a Base at Karwar." *Frontline*, 11 September 1998. http://www.the-hindu.com/fline/fl1518/15180680.htm.

Sharma, Vivek. "Joshi Lauds Army's Role in the Punjab." *Tribune*, 11 April 1993.

Shashikumar, V. K. "Civil Lines: The Army's Psy-Ops Win over Villages in Baramulla." *Week*, 23 May 1999. http://www.the-week.com/99may23/events1.htm.

———. "Life in the Bunker." *Week*, 23 August 1998. http://www.bharat-rakshak.com/LAND-FORCES/Army/Article2.html.

———. "Miles to Go." *Week*, 11 July 1999. http://www.the-week.com/99jul11/cover.htm.

Shashikumar, V. K., and Vijaya Pushkarna. "War in Kashmir." *Week*, 6 June 1999. http://www.the-week.com/99Jun06/cover.htm.

Shaw, S. "The Origins of Ottoman Military Reform: The Nizam-i Cedid Army of Sultan Selim III." *Journal of Modern History*, no. 3 (September 1965): 291–95.

Shejwalkar, T. S. *Panipat 1761*. Poona: Deccan College, 1946.

Shivkalin Putrusar Sangarha. 3 vols. Poona: Bharat Itihas Samshodak Mandal, n.d.

Shyam, Radhey. *Life and Times of Malik Ambar*. Delhi: Munshiram Manoharlal, 1968.

Sidhu, W. P. S. "Siachen: The Forgotten War." *India Today*, 31 May 1992: 58–71.

Singh, Bhupinder. *1965 War: Role of Tanks in the Indo-Pakistan War*. Patiala, Punjab: BC Publishers, 1982.

Singh, Ganda. *Ahmad Shah Durrani, Father of Modern Afghanistan*. Bombay: Asia Publishing House, 1959.

Singh, Gopal. "Socio-Economic Bases of the Punjab Movement." In Abida Sammiuddin, ed., *The Punjab Crisis: Challenges and Responses*. Delhi: Mittal Publications, 1985, 75–89.

Singh, Jagjit. *The Saga of Ladakh: Heroic Battles of Rezang La and Gurung Hill 1961–62*. Delhi: Vanity Books, 1983.

Singh, Joginder. *Behind the Scene: An Analysis of India's Military Operations, 1947–1971*. New Delhi: Lancer International, 1993.

Singh, Kanwaljit, and H. S. Ahluwalia. *Saragrahi Battalion, Ashes to Glory: History of the 4th Battalion the Sikh Regiment, XXXVI*. New Delhi: Lancer International, 1987.

Singh, Kushwant. "Punjab-Today – I." *Times of India* (Delhi), 27 October 1992.

———. "Punjab-Today – II." *Times of India* (Delhi), 28 October 1992.

Singh, Madan Paul. *The Indian Army under the East India Company*. New Delhi: Sterling Publishers, 1976.

Singh, Mohan. *A Soldier's Contribution to Indian Independence*. New Delhi: Army Education Stores, Radiant Publishers, 1974.

Singh, Pushpinder. *Aircraft of the Indian Air Force, 1933–74*. New Delhi: English Book Store, 1974.

———. "Peacekeepers in Sri Lanka." *World Air Power Journal* 4 (Winter 1990–91): 26–33.

Singh, Sarva Daman. *Ancient Indian Warfare with Special Reference to the Vedic Period*. Leiden, The Netherlands: E. J. Brill, 1965.

Singh, Sukhwant. *India's Wars since Independence: Defence of the Western Border*. Vol. 2. Delhi: Vikas Publishing House, 1981.

———. *The Liberation of Bangladesh*. Vol. 1. New Delhi: Vikas Publishing House, 1980.

Sinha, B. P. N., and Sunil Chandra. *Valor and Wisdom: Genesis and Growth of the Indian Military Academy*. New Delhi: Oxford and IBH Publishing, 1992.

Sinha, S. K. "Evolution of the Present Higher Defense Organization, Part I."

Journal of the United Service Institution of India 121, no. 503 (January–March 1991): 10.

———. Higher Defense Organisation in India. New Delhi: United Services Institution of India, 1980.

———. "Higher Defense Organization, Part II." Journal of the United Service Institution of India 121, no. 504 (April–June 1991): 143.

———. A Soldier Recalls. New Delhi: Lancer International, 1992.

Sircar, D. C. The Bharata War and Puranic Genealogies. Calcutta: University of Calcutta, 1969.

Sisson, Richard, and Leo E. Rose. War and Secession: Pakistan, India and the Creation of Bangladesh. Berkeley: University of California Press, 1990.

Slim, William. Defeat into Victory. New York: David McKay and Co., 1961.

Smith, Chris. India's "Ad Hoc" Arsenal: Direction and Drift in Defence Policy? New York: Oxford University Press, for SIPRI, 1994.

Smith, Louis Ferdinand. A Sketch of the Rise, Progress and Termination of the Regular Corps Formed and Commanded by Europeans in the Service of the Native Princes of India. Calcutta, 1805.

Sood, V. K. "Insurgencies in the North-East: Has the Army Delivered?" Indian Defence Review (October 1992): 23–28.

South Indian Inscriptions. Vols. 1–13. Madras: Superintendent of Government Printing, 1890–1953.

Spellman, John W. Political Theory of Ancient India: A Study of Kingship from Earliest Times to A.D. 300. London: Oxford University Press, 1964.

Srivastava, A. L. Shuja-ud-Daulah. Calcutta: S. N. Sarkar, the Midland Press, 1939.

———. Shuja-ud-Daulah. Vol. 2. Lahore: Minerva, 1945.

Stein, Aurel. Archeological Reconnaissances in North Western India and South Eastern Iran. London, 1937.

———. An Archeological Tour in Gedrosia. Memoirs of the Archeological Survey of India, no. 43. Calcutta: Government of India, Central Publication Branch, 1931.

———. An Archeological Tour in Waziristan and North Baluchistan. Memoirs of the Archeological Survey of India. Calcutta: Government of India, Central Publication Branch, 1929.

Stein, Burton. Peasant State and Society in Medieval South India. New Delhi: Oxford University Press, 1980.

———. "The Segmentary State Revisited." In Herman Kulke, ed., The State in India 1000–1700. Delhi: Oxford University Press, 1995, 137–47.

Steinbach, Henry. The Punjab. London: Smith and Elder, 1845.

Steinemann, Peter. "India's Fabulous 'Fishbeds.'" World Air Power Journal 9 (Summer 1992): 100–107.

Stevens, G. R. Fourth Indian Division. Toronto: Mclaren and Son, n.d.

Stockholm International Peace Research Institute. *The Arms Trade with the Third World*. Stockholm: Almqvist & Wiksell, 1971.

Strachan, Hew. *From Waterloo to Balaclava: Tactics, Technology, and the British Army, 1815–1854*. Cambridge: Cambridge University Press, 1985.

Subramaniam, T. S. "Sri Lanka: Unsung Heroes." *Frontline*, 15–28 April 1989: 102–5.

Subramanian, L. N. "CI operations in Jammu and Kashmir." *Bharat Rakshak Monitor* 3, no. 2 (September–October 2000). http://www.bharat-rakshak.com/MONITOR/ISSUE3-2/Ins.html.

Suchaus, Edward C. *Alberuni's India*. 2 vols. Lahore: Ferozsons Ltd., 1962.

Sullivan, Kevin. "Indian Nuclear Sub Plan Reported." *Washington Post Foreign Service*, 27 June 1998: A20. http://www.washingtonpost.com/wp-srv/wplate/1998-06/27/105-062798-idx-html.

Suri, Lala Sohan Lal. *Umdat-ut-Tawarikh*. Daftar 3, 4 parts. Lahore: Publisher varies, 1885–.

Swahney, Praveen. "Plugging the Dyke: Operation Rakshak in Punjab." *Indian Defence Review* (April 1992): 101.

Swami, Praveen. "The Bungle in Kargil." *Frontline*, 19 June–2 July 1999. http://www.the-hindu.com/fline/fl1613/16130040.htm.

———. "The Final Assault, and the Withdrawal." *Frontline*, 17–30 July 1999. http://www.the-hindu.com/fline/fl1615/16150040.htm.

———. "Flashpoint Kashmir." *Frontline*, 15 August 1998. http://www.the-hindu.com/fline/fl1517/15170040.htm.

———. "The Kargil Conflict: A Probe and Its Prospects." *Frontline*, 14–27 August 1999. http://www.the-hindu.com/fline/fl1617/1617030.htm.

———. "A Long Haul Ahead." *Frontline*, 19 June–2 July 1999. http://www.the-hindu.com/fline/fl1613/16130100.

———. "Warnings in Vain." *Frontline*, 11–24 September 1999. http://www.the-hindu.com/fline/fl1619/16190430.htm.

Swamy, Subramanian. "India's Defense Needs." *Hindustan Times*, 1 July 1998. http://www.hindustantimes.com/ht/nonfram/010798/detopio1.htm.

Tahir-Kheli, Shirin. *The United States and Pakistan*. New York: Praeger, 1982.

Tanham, George K. "Indian Strategic Thought: An Interpretative Essay." In Kanti P. Bajpai and Amitabh Mattoo, eds., *Securing India: Essays by George K. Tanham with Commentaries*. New Delhi: Manohar, 1996, 28–111.

———. "Indian Strategy in Flux?" In Kanti P. Bajpai and Amitabh Mattoo, eds., *Securing India: Essays by George K. Tanham with Commentaries*. New Delhi: Manohar, 1996, 112–39.

———. "India's Strategic Culture." *Washington Quarterly* (Winter 1992): 130.

Tanham, George K., and Marcy Agmon. *The Indian Air Force: Trends and Prospects*. RAND study for the USAF, 1994.

Tarn, W. W. "Two Notes on Selucid History." *Journal of Hellenic Studies*, no. 60 (1940): 76–77.

"Task Force Okays Formation of the National Security Council." *Times of India*, 27 June 1998. http://www.bharat-rakshak.com/ARMY/News/98-June.html.

Tellis, Ashley. "India's Naval Expansion: Reflections on History and Strategy." *Comparative Strategy* 6, no. 2 (1987): 193.

———. "Securing the Barrack: The Logic Structure and Objectives of Indian Naval Expansion." In Robert H. Bruce, ed., *The Modern Indian Navy and the Indian Ocean*. Perth, Australia: Curtin University, 1989, 5–50.

Terhal. "Foreign Exchange Costs of the Indian Military, 1950–1972." *Journal of Peace Research* 19, no. 3 (1982): table 1.

Thackwell, Joseph. *Narrative of the Second Sikh War*. Reprint, Patiala, Punjab: Languages Department Punjab, 1970.

Thapan, M. L. *Review of the Organizational Pattern of the Indian Army*. Seminar no. 7. New Delhi: United Services Institute of India, 1976.

Thapar, Romilla. *Early India: From the Origins to* A.D. *1300*. Berkeley: University of California Press, 2002.

———. *From Lineage to State*. Bombay: Oxford University Press, 1984.

———. *Interpreting Early India*. New Delhi: Oxford University Press, 1993.

———. *The Mauryas Revisited*. Calcutta: K. P. Bagchi and Co., 1987.

Thomas, Matthew. Book review of *Forever in Operations: A History of 8 Mountain Division* by R. D. Palsokar. *Defence Today* 1, no. 1 (August 1993): 179–88.

———. "IDR Comments." *Indian Defence Review* (July 1990): 5–7.

———. "The RAPID: An Appraisal of India's New-Look Infantry Division for Warfare in the Plains." *Indian Defence Review* (January 1989): 92–101.

Thomas, Raju C. *The Defence of India: A Budgetary Perspective of Strategy and Politics*. Delhi: Macmillan, 1978.

———. "The Growth of Indian Military Power: From Sufficient Defence to Nuclear Deterrence." In Ross Babbage and Sandy Gordon, eds., *India's Strategic Future: Regional State or Global Power?* London: Macmillan, 1992, 36.

———. *Indian Security Policy*. Princeton NJ: Princeton University Press, 1986.

———. "Security Relationships in Southern Asia: Differences in Indian and American Perspectives." *Asian Survey* 21, no. 7 (July 1981): 699.

———. "The Sources of Indian Naval Expansion." In Robert H. Bruce, ed., *The Modern Indian Navy and the Indian Ocean*. Perth, Australia: Curtin University, 1989, 95–108.

Thorat, S. P. P. *From Reveille to Retreat*. New Delhi: Allied Publishers, 1986.

"Three More Heights Secured." *Hindustan Times*, 9 July 1999. http:/www.hindustantimes.com/nonfram/090799/detFRO03.htm.

"Tiger Hill Falls, 10 Pak Soldiers Killed." *Hindustan Times*, 4 July 1999. http://www.hindustantimes.com/nonfram/050799/detFRO01.htm.

Tod, James. *Annals and Antiquities of Rajasthan* Ed. W. Crooke. 3 vols. London: Humphrey Milford, 1920.

Tone, William Henry. *Illustrations of Some Institutions of the Maratha People.* Calcutta: Oriental Press, 1818.

Trautmann, Thomas R. *Kautilya and the Arthashastra.* Leiden: E. J. Brill, 1971.

Trench, Charles Chevenix. *The Indian Army and the King's Enemies.* London: Thames and Hudson, 1988.

Tripathi, R. S. *History of Kanauj to the Moslem Conquest.* Delhi: Motilal Banarasidas, 1964.

Tuker, Francis. *Approach to Battle.* London: Cassell, 1963.

Tully, Mark, and Satish Jacob. *Amritsar: Mrs. Gandhi's Last Battle.* London: Jonathan Cape, 1985.

"21 Pak Army Regulars, Militants Killed." *Deccan Herald,* 4 July 1999. http://www.deccanherald.com/deccanherald/jul04/lead.htm.

Vad, G. S. *Selections from the Satara Raja's and Peshwa's Diaries.* Vols. 1, 3, and 9. Poona: DVT Society, 1907.

Van Leur, J. C. *Indonesian Trade and Society.* The Hague: W. van Hoeve, 1955.

Vats, Madho Sarup. *Excavations at Harappa. Being an Account of Archeological Excavations at Harappa Carried out between the Years 1920–21 and 1933–34, etc.* 2 vols. Delhi: Manager of Publications, 1940.

Ved, Mahendra. "Kargil Operations May End Soon: Brajesh Mishra." *Times of India,* 12 July 1999. http://www.timesofindia.com/today/12home2.htm.

Venkateswaran, A. L. *Defense Organisation in India.* New Delhi: Publications Division, Ministry of Information and Broadcasting, Government of India, 1967.

Verma, D. C. *Plassey to Buxar: A Military Study.* New Delhi: KB Publications, 1976.

Verma, S. D. *To Serve with Honour: My Memoirs.* Kasauli: By the author, 1988.

Vertzberger, Y. "India's Strategic Posture and the Border Defeat of 1962: A Case Study of Miscalculation." *Strategic Studies* 5, no. 3 (September 1982): 370–92.

Vigie, Marc. *Dupleix.* Paris: Librairie Arthème Fayard, 1993.

Vinayak, Ramesh. "Kargil Assault: Nasty Surprise." *India Today,* 31 May 1999. http://india-today.com/itoday/31051999/kargil.htm.

——. "Wangchuk's War." *India Today,* 21 June 1999. http://www.india-today/itoday/21061999/cover4.html.

——. "Wireless Wars." *India Today,* 14 September 1998. http://www.india-today.com/itoday/14091998/war.html.

Vinayak, Ramesh, and Dillip Banerjee. "Taking Tololing." *India Today,* 5 July 1999. http://www.india-today.com/05071999/cover2.html.

Vincent, Rose. "Dupleix: une ambitieuse politique." In Rose Vincent, ed., *Pondicherry, 1624–1761: L'échec d'un rêve d'empire.* Paris: Les Editions Auttrement, 1993, 121–44.

Vohra, A. M. "Establish NSC and Restructure MOD." *Journal of the United Service Institution of India* 121, no. 508 (April–June 1992): 155.

Wainwright, A. Martin. *Inheritance of Empire: Britain, India and the Balance of Power in Asia.* Westport CT: Praeger, 1994.

Wakaskar, V. S., ed. *Sabhasad Bakhar.* Poona: Venus Prakashan, 1962.

Wallbank, T. W. *A Short History of India and Pakistan.* New York: Scott, Foresman and Co., 1958.

Walter, Richard. *India and Her Colonial Forces.* London, 1850.

"War in Kargil." *Frontline,* 5–18 June 1999. http://www.the-hindu.com/fline/fl1612/16120040.htm.

Watter, Thomas. *On Yuan Chwang's Travels in India.* Edited after his death by T. W. Rhys Davids and S. W. Bushnell. 2 vols. London: Royal Asiatic Society, 1904.

Wavell, A. P. "The Army and the Prophets." *Journal of the Royal Services Institute,* no. 75 (November 1930): 671.

Weber, Max. *Economy and Society: An Outline of Interpretative Sociology.* Ed. Guenther Roth and Claus Wittich. New York: Bedminister Press, 1968.

"We Have Exercised Utmost Restraint." *Frontline,* 15 August 1998. http://www.the-hindu.com/fline/fl1517/15170090.htm.

Wheeler, Mortimer. *Early India and Pakistan to Ashoka.* New York: Frederick A. Praeger, 1959.

———. "Harappa, 1946: The Defenses and Cemetery R37." In *Ancient India,* no. 3, Bulletin of the Archeological Society of India. New Delhi, 1947, 59.

———. *The Indus Valley Civilization.* Supplementary vol., *Cambridge History of India.* Cambridge: Cambridge University Press, 1960.

Wheeler, R. E. M. *Rome beyond the Imperial Frontiers.* London: Bell, 1954.

Wilson, W. J. *History of the Madras Army from 1746 to 1826.* 4 vols. Madras: Government Press, 1882–88.

Wink, Andre. *Land Sovereignty in India: Agrarian Society and Politics under the Eighteenth-Century Maratha Swarajya.* New York: Cambridge University Press, 1986.

Winternitz, Moriz. *A History of Indian Literature.* Trans. S. Ketkar and H. Kohn. Calcutta: University of Calcutta, 1959.

Winton, Harold R. *To Change an Army: General Sir John Burnett-Stuart and British Armored Doctrine, 1927–1938.* Lawrence: University Press of Kansas, 1988.

Wirsing, Robert G. *India, Pakistan, and the Kashmir Dispute: On Regional Conflict and Its Resolution.* New York: St. Martin's Press, 1994.

———. "The Siachen Glacier Dispute: Can Diplomacy Untangle It?" *Indian Defence Review* (July 1991): 95–107.

"Work Begins on Vertically-Launched Trishul." *Hindustan Times,* 17 July 1998. http://bharat-rakshak.com/NAVY/News/98-July.html.

The World Bank Development Report. Washington DC, 1984.

Wylly, H. C. *Life of Lieutenant-General Sir Eyre Coote.* Oxford: Clarendon Press, 1922.

Zaman, M. K. *Mughal Artillery.* Delhi: Idrah-i-Adabiyat-i, 1983.

INDEX

The Grand Illusion
The Prussianization of the Chilean Army
William F. Sater and Holger H. Herwig

The Paraguayan War: Volume 1, Causes and Early Conduct
Thomas L. Whigham

The Challenge of Change
Military Institutions and New Realities, 1918–1941
Edited by Harold R. Winton and David R. Mets